THE CHICANO HERITAGE

This is a volume in the Arno Press collection

THE CHICANO HERITAGE

Advisory Editor
Carlos E. Cortés

Editorial Board
Rodolfo Acuña
Juan Gómez-Quiñones
George F. Rivera, Jr.

*See last pages of this volume
for a complete list of titles.*

THE UNITED STATES CONQUEST OF CALIFORNIA

*With an Introduction
by Carlos E. Cortés*

ARNO PRESS
A New York Times Company
New York — 1976

Editorial Supervision: LESLIE PARR

Reprint Edition 1976 by Arno Press Inc.

Copyright © 1976 by Arno Press Inc.

California in 1846 and Notes of a Military
 Reconnoissance were reprinted from copies
 in the State Historical Society of Wisconsin
 Library.

A Doctor Comes to California was reprinted
 from a copy in the Princeton University
 Library.

THE CHICANO HERITAGE
ISBN for complete set: 0-405-09480-9
See last pages of this volume for titles.

Manufactured in the United States of America

Library of Congress Cataloging in Publication Data
Main entry under title:

The United States conquest of California.

(The Chicano heritage)
CONTENTS: Lewis, O., ed. California in 1846.--
Emory, W. H. Notes of a military reconnoissance.--
Griffin, J. S. A doctor comes to California.
 1. California--History--1846-1850--Sources.
I. Lewis, Oscar, 1893-   California in 1846. 1934.
II. Emory, William Hemsley, 1811-1887. Notes of a
military reconnoissance. 1848. III. Griffin,
John Strother, 1816-1898. A doctor comes to California. 1943. IV. Series.
F864.U62   979.4'03   76-7303
ISBN 0-405-09542-2

THE UNITED STATES CONQUEST OF CALIFORNIA

Introduction

In 1846, as part of the United States-Mexican War, U. S. troops invaded and occupied Mexican California. Despite military resistance by poorly-armed Mexican volunteers, this occupation ultimately led to the annexation of California into the United States under the 1848 Treaty of Guadalupe Hidalgo. The primary documents in this anthology provide perspectives on this dramatic event, which is still the subject of historical controversy.

The first selection, *California in 1846,* is a collection of eye-witness descriptions of late Mexican California and the U. S. conquest era. These include an 1846 invasion-eve report to the U. S. government by Thomas O. Larkin, U. S. Consul at Monterey, and a series of 1846 and 1847 letters from participants in and observers of the conquest. In addition, the book includes a number of copies of important documents of the era.

The other two selections in the anthology are the two known complete diaries of the march of General Stephen Watts Kearny's Army of the West from Santa Fe, New Mexico, and its invasion of California. The first diary, by Lieutenant William H. Emory, an Army Engineer, not only covers the army's military encounters with the Mexican forces, but also includes a broad discussion of the people and geography of California, Arizona, and New Mexico. The second diary, by Dr. John S. Griffin, Assistant Surgeon of the Army of the West, gives a particularly good description of the Mexican victory over Kearny's troops at the Battle of San Pascual in southern California.

The prevalence of Anglo-American accounts of the U. S. invasion of California has created problems for historical analysis. Nevertheless, the Anglo-American descriptions contained in this anthology, when used with care and an awareness of the perspectives involved, are still a vital source for studying this controversial event.

CARLOS E. CORTÉS
Professor of History
Chairman, Chicano Studies
University of California, Riverside
June, 1976

CONTENTS

Lewis, Oscar, editor
CALIFORNIA IN 1846: Described in Letters from Thomas O. Larkin, "The Farthest West," E. M. Kern, and "Justice."
San Francisco, 1934

Emory, W. H.
NOTES OF A MILITARY RECONNOISSANCE, From Fort Leavenworth in Missouri, to San Diego, in California, Including Part of the Arkansas, Del Norte, and Gila Rivers. (U. S. House of Representatives Executive Document No. 41, Thirtieth Congress, First Session), Washington, D. C., 1848

Griffin, John Strother
A DOCTOR COMES TO CALIFORNIA: The Diary of John S. Griffin, Assistant Surgeon with Kearny's Dragoons, 1846-1847. With an Introduction and Notes by George Walcott Ames, Jr. and a Foreword by George D. Lyman. San Francisco, 1943

CALIFORNIA

IN

1846

CALIFORNIA

IN

1846

DESCRIBED IN LETTERS FROM THOMAS O. LARKIN, "THE
FARTHEST WEST," E. M. KERN, AND "JUSTICE."
NOTES AND INTRODUCTION
by *Oscar Lewis*

---★★★★---

San Francisco : *The Grabhorn Press*
1934

COPYRIGHT 1934, BY THE GRABHORN PRESS

CONTENTS

INTRODUCTION *page* vii

CALIFORNIA IN 1846   I

Larkin's report on conditions in California on the eve of the Conquest was prepared for the State Department for the purpose of supplying information that might be useful in furthering plans then being laid at Washington for the acquisition of the territory by the United States. The report was published in *The Pacific Monthly* of December 1863.

LETTERS FROM "THE FARTHEST WEST"   17, 31, 37

This contemporary account of events in California during June 1846 appeared in three issues (October 15, November 16, and December 1, 1846) of *The Friend*, a missionary paper published in Honolulu. In the issue of October 15, appeared the following editorial note: "The long letter from California occupying so much of our columns of to-day, is the first of a series that was written for one of the leading newspapers in New York . . . The contents . . . will doubtless be perused with some interest, inasmuch as they are described by an eye witness. The rapid changes and revolutions which California has undergone during the last few months impart interest to every item of intelligence from that quarter." The identity of the writer of the letters is not known.

LETTER OF E. M. KERN   44

Written from "Fort Sacramento" on July 27, 1846, this is one of the few letters extant giving the contemporary views of a participant in the early stages of the Conquest. Its writer, E.M.Kern (after whom the Kern River was named) was an officer of Frémont's exploring party; to him fell the task of guarding the prisoners, including General Vallejo, taken during the capture of Sonoma. The Kern Letter is printed, by permission, from the original in the Henry E. Huntington Library and Art Gallery.

LETTER FROM "JUSTICE"   52

When it was first printed in the *Missouri Republican* for June 14, 1847, this letter was prefixed by the following note: "Letter from California. – A very concise, and apparently impartial narrative of affairs in California, developing some very extraordinary facts, will be found in our columns to-day. It was received by the last arrival from Santa Fé." The authorship of the letter has been attributed to Lieutenant Colonel Cooke, who arrived in California, in command of the Mormon Battalion, early in '47.

BIOGRAPHICAL SKETCHES   61

ILLUSTRATIONS

COMMODORE STOCKTON *frontispiece*
From an engraving in "The Annals of San Francisco," New York, 1855.

MONTEREY *facing page* 1
California's first capital as it appeared at the time of the Conquest.

SAN FRANCISCO IN 1846 17

CASTRO'S PROCLAMATION 20
A copy, bearing the signature of Governor Pio Pico, of General Castro's Proclamation charging Frémont with having disregarded orders to leave the territory, and calling on the Californians to repel the invader. Size of the original, 12 by 20½ inches. A translation appears on page 49.

"THE CALIFORNIAN" OF SEPTEMBER 5, 1846 32
Facsimile of Vol. I, No. 4 of California's first newspaper, containing an installment of Walter Colton's account of the Bear Flag Revolt. This copy is signed by William B. Ide, whose "Sonoma Proclamation" is there reproduced.

SUTTER'S FORT 37
John A. Sutter's establishment at New Helvetia.

FIRST PAGE OF E. M. KERN LETTER 44
A facsimile of page one of a three-page letter written by E. M. Kern from "Fort Sacramento" (Sutter's Fort), where he was in charge of the prisoners taken in the capture of Sonoma. From the original in the Henry E. Huntington Library and Art Gallery.

PAROLE OF M. G. VALLEJO 48
Facsimile of the parole granted General Vallejo and his brother - in - law, Julio Carrillo (and signed by them), upon their release from custody at Sutter's Fort. The document, in the handwriting of E. M. Kern, bears Sutter's signature as witness.

LETTER OF STOCKTON 54
Commodore Stockton's order to Captain Mervine of the "Savannah," directing that he proceed to the relief of Lieutenant Gillespie's forces, who were besieged at Los Angeles by the Californians. Dated, "Harbour of San Francisco, October 2nd, 1846."

JOHN C. FRÉMONT 61
From a lithograph probably issued during Frémont's campaign for the Presidency in 1856.

NOTE: *Unless otherwise stated, the originals of the documents reproduced in this book are owned by Edwin Grabhorn.*

Introduction

BY OSCAR LEWIS

THE *purpose of this book is to picture, from a somewhat unusual viewpoint, the swiftly changing series of happenings in California during the most eventful year in its history. The attempt has been made to tell the story of* 1846 *in the words, not of later historians, but of eye-witnesses and participants, written on the spot and while the events they describe were still very fresh in memory. This method of presenting history — that is, in the first-hand accounts of observers — has of course some disadvantages. So many things happened in California in* 1846, *and happened so quickly, that no collection of contemporary narratives can be expected to give a complete and unified picture of the whole scene. In historical writing, perspective and balance can be obtained, if they are to be obtained at all, only long after the event; after the evidence has been assembled and weighed, conflicting claims sifted, and the complete story, stripped of its non-essentials, its fictions and prejudices, put into logical order.*

Introduction

The following pages present no such judicious, compact and neatly arranged narrative of events in California in 1846; the latter is available in formal histories of the period. What the reader will find here is the story of California's loss by Mexico and of her conquest by the forces of the United States, written by men on the spot, and often with the impact of these events, the turmoil and excitement, reflected in their words. While these narratives are not themselves history, they are material of which history is made, and they bear closely upon events as important as any in the annals of the state.

In stating that 1846 was the most eventful year in California's history, one does not disregard the momentous happenings of two years later. The discovery of gold focused the world's attention on California and set in motion the tide of immigration that was to populate and transform it. The spectacular features of the '48 – '49 period have tended to overshadow the no less dramatic and far-reaching events of '46. Consider the change brought about in the territory during that one crowded year: In January, California was a Mexican colony, a remote, pastoral semi-wilderness that had undergone no very material changes either political or economic for generations. Before the year ended the colony had been shaken by a long series of sensations: Frémont's defy of Castro, the arrival of Gillespie, Merritt's capture of the horses from Arce, Sonoma and the Bear Flag; then, in rapid succession, the occupation of Monterey, San Francisco, Sonoma and the southern towns by American forces, the recapture of Los Angeles by the Californ-

Introduction

ians, Dominguez, Natividad and, as the year closed, Kearny's defeat at San Pasqual in the most sanguinary battle ever fought on California soil.

The events that reached their climax in '46 were, of course, the result of influences that had been long at work. Mexico's hold on the colony had from year to year been growing more tenuous. When, early in '46, Thomas O. Larkin wrote that "the pear is near ripe for falling" he was expressing an opinion shared by every well-informed man in the territory; the only question was into whose lap the prize would drop. Three nations, France, Great Britain and the United States had been secretly contending for it, the latter more industriously than the others. In this contest, the United States had two weighty advantages: Larkin, its resourceful consul at Monterey, and the preponderance of its citizens among the foreigners in the territory.

With the details of this situation in California at the beginning of '46 it is unnecessary to dwell here, for the subject is treated in Larkin's admirable account which begins on page 1. Nor is this the place to enter into a discussion of those three highly controversial aspects of the Conquest; the motives and propriety of Frémont's actions prior to the declaration of war with Mexico; the ethics of the Bear Flag Revolt; and the Kearny-Stockton-Frémont quarrel that was actively brewing as the year closed. On these points opinions have differed and will continue to do so; it is sufficient for readers of the following pages to recognize that some of these accounts are biased, some are based on incomplete know-

Introduction

ledge, and that all have the defects — and the advantages — of having been written by men who were on the spot at the time, who wrote of what they saw with their own eyes and heard — whether true or not — with their own ears.

A word should be added concerning the "editing" of the material here printed. Because much of it was written hurriedly, under the stress of the events described, and in some cases just as hurriedly put into print, errors were both frequent and inevitable. Only in instances where these mistakes tend to render passages unintelligible have they been corrected, for it is felt that such slips were in large part due to the unusual circumstances under which the narratives were written, and that they should, therefore, be retained. Hence, the reader will observe such misspellings as Merrit for Merritt, Micheltoreno for Micheltorena, Vallego for Vallejo, and others equally easy to recognize.

MONTEREY — CAPITAL OF CALIFORNIA
from a lithographic illustration in Revere's "Tour of Duty in California," 1849

A REPORT TO THE U. S. GOVERNMENT

reprinted from "The Pacific Monthly," December, 1863.

CALIFORNIA IN

1846

AND ITS RESOURCES AS THEN KNOWN

BY THOMAS O. LARKIN

IN THE YEAR 1825, the Missions might be considered at the height of their prosperity. At that time, they counted from 2,000 to 3,000 Indians, and from 60,000 to 100,000 head of black cattle; an equal number of sheep, and such immense herds of horses that large numbers were killed in order to avoid the destruction of pasturage. Before the year 1822, the only trade of the Missions was with vessels from San Blas and Callao, to purchase tallow. In the year 1822, an English house established in Lima, through their agent (W. E. P. Hartnell, in Monterey), made a contract with a greater part of the Missions, to receive all the hides at one dollar a piece, and tallow and grease at three dollars an arroba (of 25 lbs.), that they could produce. In the same year, an American ship arrived from Boston and prepared the way for the future trade, which, since that day, has been carried on almost exclusively by the New Englanders.

California and its Resources

The present export (1846) amounts to about 85,000 hides, 60,000 arrobas of tallow, 10,000 fanegas of wheat, 1,000,000 feet of lumber, some staves and shingles, soap to the value of $10,000, beaver and otter skins worth $20,000, 1100 barrels of aguadiente and wine, and 200 ounces of gold worth $17 per ounce. The Missions are now almost entirely destroyed. Some that had formerly from 2,000 to 3,000 Indians, have now not above 100; others none. But few Missions have any cattle. About the year 1835, a law was made to take away the management of the temporalities of the Missions from the priests and give it to the secular administrator, who, in a very short time, managed to completely ruin the establishments, without, in general, benefiting themselves — even taking the tiles off the roofs of the houses. The land has, in a great degree, been divided out among private individuals. Although the Mission cattle have disappeared, there are as many, if not more, hides shipped from California at this period as there were when the Missions were in their prosperity, arising from the increase of private farms.

Exclusive of countless wild Indians and some neophytes, California has perhaps some 15,000 inhabitants, descendants of Spanish or Mexican fathers, mostly from native mothers. The baptized Indians now released by the demolishing of the Missions, are engaged by the inhabitants as servants, while many of the inhabitants are hired by each other to do the more superior work of the farms. The Indians who were taught by the Spanish padres the different mechanical arts are now dead, and no more of their

by Thomas O. Larkin

tribe will ever take their place. Foreigners are now doing all the work of this class in California. The farms now occupied are owned by Mexicans, Californians, and naturalized foreigners, who become so by signing a simple memorial (some even by proxy), stating that such was their wish; when a letter of citizenship was immediately filled up for the petitioner, without any form, oath or ceremony on his part. The farms are given to any petitioner (who is a citizen) from one to eleven square leagues, as he may ask for it, with no expense. The land joining the seacoast is principally taken up: also that immediately on the bay of San Francisco, and a few on the river Sacramento, but none on the San Joaquin river. Taking the whole extent of the country, but a small portion of it is divided into ranchos having owners. A part of the Mission lands still belongs to the government, and all other unclaimed lands. Some few farms are being vacated by the Californians, for fear of further depredation by the wild Indians, who yearly steal thousands of horses even out of the enclosed yards near their dwelling houses. They are now (almost every week) committing depredations of this kind. The whites but seldom follow them to regain their property. The Indians are losing all fear of the inhabitants, and with their arrows have shot several of them during the years 1845 and 1846.

There are from one thousand to twelve hundred foreigners (including their families) in California, a majority of them residing on the bay of San Francisco and on the Sacramento river. One-third of the men are citizens of this country.

California and its Resources

Many of them never expect to speak the prevailing language of the country, so that at this early period a knowledge of the English language is, to a merchant, of more importance than the Spanish. In the year 1832, there were in the whole department some two hundred or three hundred foreigners. There are now some eight or ten who have resided here twenty-five years. They were sailors, now farmers, entrapped from their vessels by the former Spanish government.

The first arrival of American settlers on the Sacramento river has been since 1840. Three-fourths of the full number of foreigners in this country are Americans. Of the remaining fourth, the subjects of Great Britain predominate, and of this fourth a majority are in expectation of being under the government of the United States. Probably all are willing, in preference to remaining as they now are. For the last five years, the largest portion of the immigrants have arrived at New Helvetia (Captain Sutter's establishment) excepting a few of them from Oregon. They leave Independence, Missouri, which is the starting point, every April or May, arriving on the Pacific in September or October. Soon after their arrival at New Helvetia, they scatter over the river Sacramento, and the bay of San Francisco, asking for farms from the government or settling on private grants, by the owners' consent. Some have arrived at the pueblo de los Angeles, via Santa Fé, some of whom had married at the latter place. A few arrived by water from Valparaiso, Callao and the Sandwich Islands. A person traveling from San Diego to San Francisco or Bodega, can stop at

by Thomas O. Larkin

a foreigner's farm house almost every four hours, and travel without any knowledge of the Spanish language.

Among the emigrants from Independence, there are several German families, who have resided in the United States and are attached to her institutions. The majority of immigrants are from the Western States (farmers, mechanics and laborers). Others are young men from New England or the Middle States, who left home seeking a fortune in the Western States, thence here. The immigration in 1845 amounted to from four hundred to five hundred. From the U. S. newspaper reports, from one thousand to two thousand are expected to arrive this August to October.

Immigrants leaving Independence for the Pacific should furnish themselves (if a family of five or six persons) with one good wagon, four or five yoke of oxen, three or four cows, three horses, and to each person two hundred and fifty pounds of flour, one hundred and fifty pounds of bacon, thirty pounds of coffee, fifty pounds of sugar, twenty pounds of rice, two good blankets, and a few cooking utensils. Every male person over fourteen years of age should have one good rifle, ten pounds of powder, thirty pounds of lead, two thousand percussion caps and a good horse. On arriving on the banks of the Sacramento and finding a convenient piece of land that the immigrant can occupy, he should begin sowing wheat from December to February; beans, peas and corn in April or May; and should also procure himself cows two years old, worth from four to five dollars; young bulls at two or three dollars; thirty or forty mares at five or six dollars; a stallion

California and its Resources

at fifteen or twenty dollars, and a few sheep at two dollars each. One hundred cows will produce from seventy to ninety calves between the 2d and 12th months. From $1,000 to $1,500 in cash will start an enterprising man in breeding animals for a California farm.

For a few years the settler may find purchasers for produce among the immigrants and throughout the country. In time he will find a market in the Sandwich Islands, Northwest Coast, San Blas, Mazatlan, and elsewhere. Wheat produces from forty to fifty fold under the most imperfect cultivation. The Spanish padres for many years obtained one hundred fold at some of the Missions: one hundred and eighty fold was once gathered near the Mission of San José. Wild oats and mustard cover the country: the former from three to four feet high; the latter so high and compact that it is almost impossible for a traveler to find his horses when they stray among it. Rye and buckwheat have not been proved. Hemp was raised by the former padres. Cotton has been proved to advantage, but no quantity has been planted. Every kind of vegetable yet planted has produced well. Apples, pears, quinces and peaches are common all over California. In parts of the country there are limes, oranges, almonds, figs and walnuts. Plums and cherries have not been introduced. Grapes of the very best quality, and in the greatest abundance, are in different sections of the country. Latitude south of thirty-nine degrees produces the best. With imperfect means good wine could be produced and distilled. The climate of California is surpassed by no other. The

by Thomas O. Larkin

lowest rate of the thermometer in the shade at Monterey in 1845, was forty-four degrees, the highest eighty-six degrees. From sixty to seventy degrees are the common rates throughout the year.

When General Micheltorena met the Californians near the town of the Angels, there were six hundred men in the field, one-fifth being foreigners. Many of the latter joined Micheltorena at the suggestion of Captain Sutter, under the General's promise of land. (General M. gave to Captain Sutter a public document, granting him power to grant land to those who took up arms at that time.) They soon left him in disgust. At present General [José] Castro and Governor Pio Pico are opposed to each other; Castro at the north and Pico at the south. In a popular cause, the two could bring into the field from eight hundred to one thousand men, who would continue under arms a month, and some of them longer, whether paid or not. Could these two officers be on terms of friendship, they could bring [defy?] this number of Mexican troops introduced into California. Should the Mexicans be too numerous, the Californians would remain quiet two years, by which time the new comers, from a dislike to the people, from mutual enmity and disgust with the service, from want of pay, provisions and clothing, would be glad of any occasion to return to Mexico. Pico or Castro could at present collect some three or four hundred of their countrymen to join the Mexican army in expelling the immigration. Should the army not arrive until the immigrants had possession two or three years, the Californians would see the advantage of their neighbors, and would not be brought out against them. By a law of September, 1845, President Herrera allowed the Governor of California two-thirds of the duties [collected at Monterey]; by Paredes' law of January, 1846, General Castro was to have the whole. This adds more fuel to the enmity existing between the two (Castro and Pico).

A continual dread exists here from the apprehension of some commanders arriving from Mexico with troops to take the command from the present chieftains. The arrival of this class of people, their fears of expulsion from the coast, and in sending commissioners to Mexico to explain their views and define their position, leaves the country in a continued state of disturbance, and always in debt.

Those only who live by absence of law, flourish under the present aspect of things and affairs. It would be a sound policy to pension some of those high in office and influence, or give them a sinecure. They would thus gently and quietly carry many of their countrymen along with them, as they might (on viewing a prospect of change from the present state to another), excite the people and array themselves against a new government, when the whole succession would, for an equivalent, be amicably settled.

Many foreigners now hold land under the expectation of the United States' flag being hoisted. This idea already enhances the value of land. No one league has yet brought $1,000. On the Sacramento, four-fifths of the farms unoccupied, would not bring $200 per league. An unoccupied piece of land (of average quality,

by Thomas O. Larkin

without any horses or cattle on it, sixty miles above New Helvetia, of four leagues on the river by two back — twelve miles by six — or 46,000 acres), sold this year under $1,000, by a Californian to an English purchaser living in Monterey.

Some of the Californians are quietly waiting the result; some are indifferent on the subject, and others against it. In two years after the safe and sure possession by the United States, giving the inhabitants an opportunity of knowing their own safety of person and property, the extreme cheapness of goods to counterbalance the extravagant prices now paid, an increased and constant market for their produce, and circulation of gold and silver to supply their wants and sales, they would object to their returning to their present state. The deplorable state they are now in, arising from the robbery of their horses, and so forth, will hasten the result. They are convinced that a proper administration of affairs would put down the Indians, and there are sufficient Californians to drive them out, but the energetic aid of government is required, which they cannot obtain from the Mexican authorities.

At the present period, Señores Castro, Vallejo, Alvarado, Pico and Carrillo are the men of most note and standing. The cause of dispute between Pico and Castro is on account of the inhabitants of Monterey and the pueblo de los Angeles wishing to have their respective towns the capital, and each aiming for the custom house to be in their vicinity, making two parties in California, and until the Governor and General reside in the same town, it will continue so.

California and its Resources

But a few years must pass (even under the present routine), before the capital and port of entry must be in some part of the bay of San Francisco.

With a better state of affairs and an industrious race of inhabitants, Upper California could supply all the Polynesian Islands, San Blas, Mazatlan, Acapulco and the Northwest Coast, with wheat, beans, peas, flour, fat, tallow, butter, cheese, pork, bacon, salmon, horses, mules, spars, boards, shingles, staves and vessels; and with sufficient capital and laborers will have, from her own mines, gold, silver, lead, sulphur, coal and slate, and has perhaps the largest quicksilver mines in the world, actually having mountains with veins extending for leagues, of the very best of ore, producing over twenty per cent. of pure quicksilver, with but very little expense for outfits. The magnificent waters of San Francisco could this day harbor all the vessels afloat in the world. Many whale ships already visit it for supplies, and more would do so, were it not for the vacillating laws, and desertion of the men from their vessels, favored by those on shore. And the Anglo-Saxon race would soon send their exports over the whole Pacific ocean. It must and will be the medium stopping-place from New Orleans and New York to the China ports, now open to all the world.

The present inhabitants of California are naturally very hospitable, and have good natural abilities. They have no establishments of education, beyond common day-schools for the first rudiments of learning. There are many foreigners of different

by Thomas O. Larkin

nations married in this country, of wealth, information and influence. There are many others, natives and foreigners, now dormant, who would bring themselves forward in a time of great change, and would occupy a conspicuous situation. On the other hand, some now eminently known would retire before those less passive or sedentary.

The regular Boston traders generally have two vessels on the coast at a time. After collecting in company for periods varying from twelve to eighteen months, one of them returns home, leaving the other until a fresh ship supplies her place, or relieves her; by this means constantly keeping the work of collecting going on. Their hide-houses are in San Diego, to which place each vessel proceeds two or three times during the year, to land such hides and tallow as they may have collected from nine or ten ports between San Francisco and San Diego, the customer being expected to pay a part of his debt every time the vessel anchors.

There are no Mexican vessels in California owned by Mexicans or Californians. They belong to foreigners naturalized in the country. The laws of Mexico are but little [known], and observed only when they are for the interest of this country. Not much regard is paid to the tariff. The Collector of Monterey imposes such duties as he considers requisite at the time. Although against the laws of Mexico, the governor and generals of California, since their independence, have allowed the coasting-trade from San Diego to San Francisco, to all foreign vessels which have paid their duties in Monterey.

California and its Resources

In 1844 or 1845, General Micheltorena levied a tax of $50 per month on foreign vessels. For this license of coasting, $5,000 was collected. On March 28th, 1846, Governor Pico annulled this law. He was promised by President Santa Ana, in addition to the receipt of duties in Monterey, $8,000 per month to support his army. During his command of 1842, '43 and '44, he issued drafts upon the custom-house of Mazatlan for about $150,000, a part of which was paid by the collector, the balance protested by contrary orders from the capital.

The whole revenue of California is derived from the custom-house in Monterey, which for the last seven years has averaged $86,000 per year (in 1845, $138,000). The bishop [there was but one in 1846] and padres, throughout the country, claim from the farmers one tenth of the increase of their stock, of which tenth not one quarter is collected; many farmers never having paid it a single year. On two or three occasions, the commandante-general (when a native) has received the amount collected.

The payment of duties received at the custom-house are made in about ninety, one hundred and thirty, and one hundred and eighty days. The supercargoes in general agree upon the second payment, payable in cash, and bullock hides at two dollars apiece: cash, should the vessel pay less than $6,000; from $6,000 to $12,000, two thirds cash and one third hides; from $12,000 to $18,000, half cash; over $18,000, one third cash, two thirds hides.

On the collector's arranging the amount, the mode of payment, and taking two securities, he retains sufficient for the salaries of

by Thomas O. Larkin

his officers, and passes the remainder to the treasurer. They both then draw in sums of from $4,000 to $5,000 on the supercargo or agent, payable at the specified time; some orders for cash, some for hides; the creditors and officers receiving a draft on the *pro rata* system, as far as the duties of the vessel thus entering may suffice.

By the laws of Mexico, two thirds of the revenue of this cusomhouse should be paid over to the commandante-general for the military chest, the other third to the civil list. As the governor chooses to live only in his native town, four hundred miles from Monterey, the general allows but a small proportion of the funds to reach there. Although they are responsible to the supreme government for these funds, but very imperfect accounts ever go to Mexico; perhaps from the present authorities none whatever. Should the minister in Mexico draw on this treasurer for any sum, large or small, it would not be paid or noticed. Not a *real* [12½ cents] is ever sent to Mexico, nor does the supreme government ever make requisitions on this department for funds to be sent to the general treasurer.

The supercargo or agent has a store fitted up on board ship with shelves, show-cases, drawers and scales, selling from one pound of tea, &c., to a box or bag, and from a yard of silk or calico to a bale.

From Boston, cargoes consist of groceries, furniture, dry goods, crockery, hardware, &c., from which cargo the holder of the draft can choose the amount drawn for in his favor, or a part

California and its Resources

of it, taking the supercargo's due bill for the balance, both drafts and due bills being negotiable. They are sometimes cashed at a discount of two per cent. a month. In many cases the supercargo has debts against the holder of the draft, which is always accepted as payment for his or any other demand.

The duties of the principal vessels amount to from $5,000 to $25,000. They also pay one real for each large bale for storage in the custom-house, half of that sum for wharfage, and have the use of the custom-house and warehouses for storage and sales until the arrival of the next vessel which may require the buildings. The tonnage duties are one dollar and fifty cents per ton to all foreign vessels and Mexican vessels from foreign ports. There are no other port charges, no wharfage, pilotage or light-house fees, nor any health or quarantine regulations. There is no one article of goods prohibited by the custom-house of this country, no prohibitions or restrictions of any class, nor bounties, or navigation acts, no draw-backs on shipping or their cargoes, no board of trade, or other establishments relative to commerce in California.

Coins, currencies, weights and measures of England and the United States are of common use here.

By long custom, whale ships are allowed to enter the ports of Monterey and San Francisco, by paying from ten to twenty dollars port charges, and a certain percentage on such goods as they may barter for supply.

The imports from San Blas, Mazatlan and Acapulco consist of rice, sugar, panoche, nux vomica, saddlery, silk and cotton re-

by Thomas O. Larkin

bozas (a scarf), cotton and woolen serapes, shoes, and some English, American and German goods.

Imports from the United States and elsewhere are domestics in very large quantities – shoes, hats, furniture, and farming utensils, chiefly of New England manufacture, groceries, China goods, iron, hard, and crockery ware – which are sold to the merchants and rancheros (farmers), on the coast, on a credit of from one to two years, payable in hides, tallow, dried beef, fat, lumber, soap, etc., etc.

The vessel obtains a coasting license to trade and collect produce until she is filled, which occupies from twelve to twenty-four months, the vessel's consort the next year taking the balance of the cargo and debt for collection.

The Boston vessels return to that port with from 20,000 to 40,000 bullock hides, the owner expecting one hide to each dollar invested in cargo, disbursements, wages and value of vessel. The tallow is exchanged for hides with vessels bound to Callao.

In former years considerable fur was exported (prime sea otter skins for the Canton market, being worth here as high as forty dollars each). There is now some fur and gold shipped.

Within a few years there will be gold, lead, and a large quantity of quicksilver exported. There are now shingles, lumber, spars and horses shipped to the Sandwich Islands: beef, fat, wheat and beans to the Russian settlements on the northwest coast, in exchange for drafts on St. Petersburg.

From 1836 to 1845, about $25,000 of the duties have been ex-

California and its Resources

pended in building custom-house, houses for legislature, alcalde and civil offices and a wharf. During the time, several bloodless revolutions have taken place, and almost every Mexican commander and his troops have been expelled.

SAN FRANCISCO IN 1846
from a lithographic illustration in Colton's "Deck and Port," 1850

THE FIRST LETTER

of "The Farthest West" printed in "The Friend," Oct. 15, 1846.

CALIFORNIA IN 1846

Yerba Buena, *San Francisco Bay,*

June 10th, 1846

DEAR SIR: There are strange things in this world, happening every day, but none to me more so than that I should find myself in California, and writing a letter to be taken to you by the first overland express; and certainly the longest ever attempted in America. A friend has kindly volunteered to put this into the hands of the gallant Capt. Frémont, who is now encamped on the Sacramento, and about to proceed direct to the U. S. after arduous, and dangerous journeys across the great desert, from the salt lake to the California mountains, his extensive explorations in *California* and northward as far as "Klamet Lake;" from whence he has just now returned to the valley of the Sacramento and from whence he proceeds to the States, though by what route it is hard to say, as I believe the gallant Captain

Letters from "The Farthest West"

rarely or never travels where any one has gone before. I have heard many interesting details of his present trip to the shores of the Pacific, but there is no one who can tell his story so well as himself, and it would be useless for me to attempt it. There have been, however, certain transactions taking place concerning him and his command, while he was here in the early spring, of which I may write, and as the Californians have sent their account of them to Mexico, you have undoubtedly had a version of them in the U. S. If their account of the matter should be in keeping with their acts towards him, there will certainly be much to correct.

I have seen it stated in U. S. papers, that Capt. Frémont was to proceed to California by way of the "Youta" or "Great Salt Lake," and thence to strike out in a new and untravelled route, which he said had never been travelled before. He did come that way, and when he reached the California mountains, divided his command into two parties, a part going round the south end and up the great "Tulare" valley, while he proceeded to pass the mountains and explore its passes. I have heard it said that a gig can travel that route from the U. S. (via Fort Hall), but whether this is on the authority of Capt. Frémont or the emigrants, I am not informed, however I have seen in Monterey, the waggons that have travelled from the U. S. across this range of mountains, the people who came in them and the cattle that drew them and all in good condition; indeed none the worse for wear. One of the company told me the pass, in September, '45, was very easy of travel – not the least difficulty. It is the same pass first attempted by Dr. Town-

Yerba Buena, June 10, 1846

send and party, late in the season of '44. They were the first to attempt it, but not arriving there till December, they found the snow on the mountains ten feet deep, they suffered exceedingly, especially the ladies of the party — and finally were compelled to build log houses near the summit and store their loads, themselves crossing on horses with their provisions packed. Most of the company got over the summit notwithstanding the snow, and all their property was found safe in the spring; but the Doctor and others who "cached" on the east side of the summit lost all, the snow left the east side first. The Indians followed up their trail, and stripped their houses. When the party returned in June, '45, they found the Indians had been about 6 to 8 days before them. The loss was a very serious one.

To return from this digression. Capt. Frémont having united his command about eighty miles from this place, proceeded to the valley of San Juan to recruit his animals, before he could travel to Oregon. He had an interview with the Commandant General, Castro, and told him he desired to remain in the country till the spring in the north, and to recruit in the valley; that he was on a purely scientific exploration; merely armed for *defence* against hostile Indians; and prepared to pay cash for all his wants. His camp soon became a valuable mart for the farmers, who were delighted to find a party in the country who paid *dollars* for all they required. Capt. Frémont paid a visit to the Consul at Monterey, Mr. Larkin, and returned to his camp. All seemed well. In a few days he received an insulting note from Castro, tel-

Letters from "The Farthest West"

ling him to "leave the country at once, or he would drive him out." Now that was a threat easily made, but not so easily accomplished. Some Californians who visited Capt. Frémont's camp told Castro that it would require 1000 men (Californians), to *drive* out such men as Frémont commanded, though but 60. The Captain was certainly surprised at such a change of conduct, but he prepared for defence, taking a commanding position on the summit of San Juan where he could see the whole country for twenty miles round. Castro by dint of impressing, coaxing and whipping! got together about 200 men, with some cannon. With this force he posted himself at the Mission of San Juan, while Frémont was daily out scouring the country in hopes of having an interview and asking the meaning of all this. In four days Capt. Frémont found that Castro was not coming to him, so he quietly descended from his mountain camp, crossed the plain of San Juan to the Tulare valley, and thence to the banks of the Sacramento, where he again encamped free from all annoyance from this redoubtable hero, who contented himself with issuing a proclamation declaring that, Capt. Frémont at the "head of robbers" had been driven from the country by the chivalric sons of California and then to cap the climax of this farce he chartered a ship at the expense of six thousand dollars to carry a commissioner to Mexico with this highly important news. Castro has since said that after he had seen Frémont and given him permission to stay in the country (only asked out of courtesy) he received an order from Mexico not to permit him to enter and if he did to drive

El Ciudadano José Castro Teniente Coronel de Caballería del Egército Megicano y Comandante General Interino del Departamento de las Californias.

Comprovincianos: Una porción de bandoleros que sin respetar las leyes, ni autoridades del Departamento, osadamente se han introducido en el pais acaudillados por el Capitan del Egército de los Estados Unidos D. N. C. Fremont, han desoídos las órdenes de esta Comandancia General y Prefectura del Segundo Distrito, en las que le previene a dicho oficial que inmediatamente emprendiera su marcha fuera de los límites de nuestro territorio, y sin contestar otras notas por escrito, y solo de palabra, mandó decir el expresado Capitan, que en la Sierra del Gabilan estaba preparado para resistir a las fuerzas que las autoridades osasen atacarlo, las providencias consiguientes de esta Comandancia General y la Prefectura, poniendo en acción todos los elementos posibles, dieron por resultado a la vista de doscientos patriotas, que abandonó el campo que ocupaba dejando en el alguna ropa y otros utiles de guerra, y según informan los esploradores tomó el rumbo de los Tulares. Compatriotas la acción de haber enarbolado en la Serranía el Pabellon Americano los insultos y amenazas proferidas contra las autoridades del pais, son dignos de la execración y odio de los Megicanos, preparaos pues para hacer la defensa de nuestra independencia, para que unidos repelamos con mano fuerte el atrevimiento de hombres ingratos que recibiendo todos los testimonios de una verdadera hospitalidad en nuestro pais, corresponden con tanta ingratitud a los bienes que se adquieren por nuestra cordialidad y condescendencia. Cuartel General de San Juan Bautista 13 de Marzo de 1846.— José Castro.

Es copia

Yerba Buena, June 10, 1846

him out. It is also said, and this I believe, that Castro has received a severe reprimand from Don Pio-pico, the governor, resident at the *Pueblo de los Angeles,* on account of his conduct. It is certain that for some cause Castro is much enraged against the governor and has been stirring up trouble but his conduct meets with such universal contempt from all classes, that he cannot raise over forty men now, when a few months since he was almost supreme. He was the prime mover of the infamous arrest of the Foreigners in 1841 and sending them to Mexico; for which, by the bye, our citizens have not yet the least redress: a day of reckoning I trust is not far off. A large band of Americans would have been in Frémont's camp to reinforce him on the first move of Castro with a sign of attacking him. Castro was closely watched by them but knowing that Capt. Frémont was not in the country on any hostile expedition they did not wish to show front until it became necessary to aid him as it would embroil them with the authorities after he should leave; although they were on the alert, they felt certain "Castro" dared not approach his camp. I do not think he was more than five miles off Frémont's Camp at any time. I am informed that Capt. Frémont's men were highly exasperated and excited, that it required all the Captain's coolness and decision to keep his men from attacking Castro. Indeed I believe they would have done some hostile or retaliatory act had they seen his proclamation before they left the Valley of "San Juan." Capt. Frémont has in his party (or had) nine "Delawares" (he has since lost one) who have said they will yet take a big "scalp" off Castro's head.

Letters from "The Farthest West"

Capt. Frémont having recruited on the "Sacramento" proceeded north on his way toward the Walla-Walla in Oregon (at least I suppose from the route he took) when he was overtaken at the north "Klamet" lake by an express from the U. S. via Mexico which caused him to return to the Sacramento Valley and prepare (as I understand he now is preparing) for his return to the U. S. He is now one year out having left the U. S. in June last. The gentleman who came from the U. S. with the express to Capt. Frémont is now at the "Yerba-Buena" whence I write; and as I have listened to his description of his journey in pursuit of the Captain and the stirring incidents attending it, I will proceed to give you them in detail.

He left "Sutter's Fort" on the Sacramento, hoping to find Frémont at his Camp 20 miles north, on the bank of the same river, but when he got that far the Capt. had been gone eight days – go after him he must at all hazards. He accordingly organized a small party, only six in all, with a good guide, who had previously been of Frémont's Company, (in 1844). They proceeded on, doing their utmost to gain on him, but the Captain as usual must go where no one ever did before; he turned east over the snow covered mountains, passing up the Sacramento which here passes through the mountain rising, I believe, in Pitt's lake. Their route led them into the snow, and they encamped on the summit ridge, with the tall shaft of St. Joseph (*rising from the top of the range covered with perpetual snow to its base*) called a "Snowy Bute," as a near companion for the night. They got over the mountains and pro-

Yerba Buena, June 10, 1846

ceeded north between Pitt and Klamet lakes. They now entered the Oregon Territory. From the appearance of the Camps Capt. Frémont had left on his "trail" he was still six days ahead, their provisions were gone, they were living on *horse meat*, and that would soon be gone, or they must kill those they rode and go on foot. The guide now proposed to push ahead, and thought he could overtake the Captain in two days, and in *three* they could return and meet their starving companions. He took one man and went on, knowing the Indians to be bad, and treacherous, he kept a bright lookout, and yet he narrowly escaped after being chased by a large party for *fifteen miles*, fortunately their shouting was not heard by a party fishing on Klamet lake (he was riding up the west bank) or he must have been cut off; he got by safe, and as he hoped, by hard riding and without food, he reached Capt. Frémont the night of the second day. The Captain at once (early the next morning) took a few picked men and set out on his "trail" to meet the little party in his rear. They met on the 2d day or 4th after the guide left. The party of four not having made much progress in consequence of their inability to cross the outlet of "Klamet" lake until a band of Indians, with a chief at their head came to them with canoes and ferried them across. They were well armed, but appeared perfectly friendly, giving them *Salmon* to eat. They had been without food for thirty-six hours. They now pushed on with high spirits, and before night joyfully met Captain Frémont, who came up to them just after they had encamped for the night. A night which will long be remembered by them

Letters from "The Farthest West"

all; on account of the horrors of a night attack, and the loss of three brave fellows, who died by their sides. But I must give you particulars. Capt. Frémont with the bearer of his dispatches, sat talking to a late hour, near midnight, when they lay down to sleep, their men (thirteen) around their horses. They were soon awakened by a scuffle and saw the two "Delawares" of their captain engaged in close fight with a body of Indians. One of the Delawares instantly shot away the handle of the attacking chief's tomahawk, the other snapped his rifle at the breast of the chief, it missed fire and the brave Delaware at once fell, with three arrows in his breast, mortally wounded. The Chief soon fell under a shower of bullets from the whole camp, yet he had time to throw from his bow no less than *eleven arrows*. The chief had three balls in his body when he fell. The whole camp was up, and the party of attacking Indians fled with the fall of their chief, they could not pursue them in the dark, but proceeded to examine their camp when to their horror they found that the savage foe had stolen upon their camp so quietly as to kill two men (Canadian French) with their tomahawks and arrows without waking them from sleep; and it was not till the resistance they met with from the brave "Delawares" that the camp was aware of their presence. The next day Capt. Frémont buried the brave dead, and rejoined his camp, when preparations were at once made to punish the "tribe" from whence came this savage attack. He proceeded round the north end of the lake (north Klamet) and approached their lodges on the fourth day, when his whole command attacked

Yerba Buena, June 10, 1846

stores of provision, the produce of their spring salmon fishery, and in fair fight killed twenty or more men who made all the resistance they could; but the commander escaped without the loss of a man. They found in the lodges some articles which the Indians had hastily picked up when they killed the two Frenchmen.

It is to be hoped that this salutary lesson will teach these savages that they cannot attack with impunity, parties of travellers through the country however small they may appear.

I understand Capt. Frémont has been attacked by Indians no less than ten times since he left the U. S.; of course he must repel them, and then punish them for the security of less formidable parties of travellers. I believe he has not lost a man in battle until this night attack although he has been previously attacked in a similar way. With regard to *California*, I am of opinion from what I have seen of it that it does not present such flattering prospects to emigrants from the U. S. as certain persons have led them to believe, most are very much disappointed in the country *not in its climate or soil*, although a large proportion of it is only suitable I think for grazing cattle and sheep, the same use to which the Roman Catholic Mission applied it; (these missions are now all in ruins) but because *they cannot get a good title to land not even by purchase*. California is under Mexican authority although only nominal – none but Californians are permitted to hold office – or such men being foreigners by birth who have become Californians by marrying California women. The California Gov. no longer gives grants of land, and many of the titles now held would

Letters from "The Farthest West"

be lost under a strictly legal Government. Nearly all the land not in actual possession of "Wild Indians," of the great valley of "Tulare" is held by a few men who own immense tracts, some 10, 20, and 40 leagues; some have large herds of cattle (10,000 head), others none on these vast tracts. Most of these landed proprietors were originally the "administrators of the missions" in 1830, when the Gov. of Mexico took the titles from the church; a few only have titles by purchase. Capt. Sutter on the Sacramento, obtained a grant of eleven leagues from the Governor. Since that he bought out the Russian Fur Co., to pay them in wheat. In his extensive projects, he has employed men and paid them high wages in cattle, until he has reduced his stock to less than two hundred head. He has an immense crop of wheat growing finely, but the probability is, he cannot reap it, as the Indians show a disposition against doing any work for him this year, and it is even asserted that "Castro" is inciting them to destroy the crops of all the foreigners. All the foreigners have left "Sutter's Fort" and gone to work for themselves, taking his cattle to pay the amounts due them. He has fifteen hundred acres of wheat growing at this time. There is no doubt but Sutter has greatly aided the emigrants on their coming into the country. All the expenses of living in California are enormous. Every thing except fresh beef and horses, costs four times what it would in the States; this bears hard on the emigrants who expend nearly their all to get here; in consequence of this many have turned northward into Oregon where our government gives them land and produce is not so high, and their

Yerba Buena, June 10, 1846

cattle and horses are worth much more than here. California may be said to be entirely without schools, though there is one at Monterey.

A large emigration is looked for here this fall, if so, California cannot long remain under the Mexican flag, and even now the legislature of the department is about to assemble (June 15), and the general opinion is that the country will declare itself independent of Mexico. There is no accountability for anything, the military power, contemptible as it is (less than 100 men actually under arms), look with contempt on the civil authority – while Castro, the military chief, absorbs the entire revenue of the country, which for 1844 and '45 was about $200,000, collected entirely from the importations, principally Boston ships, engaged in the "hide trade." The duties collected on importations for the last ten years, have averaged $85,000 annually; last year $135,000, but not over $60,000, if that, can be collected this year.

The debts of California (public) are about $150,000, the most of which are acknowledged claims for military services.

There is but one or two vessels under the Mexican flag trading on the coast. The American ships are the Barnstable and Moscow (arrived this season), from Boston – cargoes costing at home $25,000 each – the Tasso, Sterling and Vandalia, also all of Boston, collecting hides to proceed home in February next. The three will take about 100,000 hides, the probable amount of this year's "Matanza" killing. The Vandalia's cargo cost, in Boston, $37,000; paid duties, $27,000; sold for $134,000, to be paid in hides at $2

Letters from "The Farthest West"

each. In paying the duties they only pay one-fourth cash, the balance in goods, at from three to four hundred per cent on cost in Boston. I believe the voyages of these ships average from home thirty months. I am told the owners expect one hide for every dollar expended in cost of cargo, ship, wages and expenses of the voyage. This is the cause of the high prices in California – they sell the cargo on credit and collect the proceeds as fast as they can. If cargo is not all sold, the ship which comes out to relieve takes balance and debts, and goes on with the trade. The ships are both wholesalers and retailers, selling from twelve and one-half cents value to the whole cargo, as they can find safe purchasers. This is done under a general coasting license. The cargoes from Boston consist of a general collection of Yankee notions, American manufactures, of the lowest prices at home. American prints are retailed at 75 cents per yard; common cottons, 50 cents; tickings, $1; Lowell broadcloth, such as I can buy at home for $2 to $2.50 the yard, $12; coffee, 30 cents the lb., on board; sugar, 25; brown sugar, at the stores on shore, is worth even more, and coffee 37 1-2 cents the lb., even when sold for cash; American flour, $18 the bbl.; country flour, $16. Indeed, all the necessaries of life are four, six and eight hundred per cent above prices in New York. Shot retails for 37 1-2 cents per lb.; powder, $3. Emigrants should think of these things.

There is little specie in circulation – hides are to California what "shin plasters" were in New York in '37, only they have a real value. In trade they are worth $2 each. The killing of one

Yerba Buena, June 10, 1846

thousand head of cattle by a farmer produces him about $8000 in goods at the prices above named.

California will soon be another "El Dorado" in her mineral wealth. Mines of gold, silver, copper, lead, sulphur and quicksilver ore being found in all directions. But there is no capital nor people as yet to work them. Two quicksilver mines of rich ore, yielding 30 per centum of pure quicksilver, are now in operation, one on the north, the other on the south side of San Francisco Bay. Already 2000 pounds of quicksilver have been taken from the latter. They are considered about equal in richness of ore and facilities for working and exportation. I wish I could send you a specimen of the ore, but that is impossible. Americans have interests in both these mines. No less than seventy announcements of mines have been made to the Alcalde of San Jose within the last five months. Pure lead is found; also pure sulphur – at least I never saw better from any laboratory at home than has been taken out of the mine at Sonoma. To the southward, back of the Pueblo de los Angeles, there is a gold "placer" or washing, which is said to be eighteen leagues square. This cannot be held as a mine by the laws. Any one can go there and wash the sand for gold. I am told that the most lazy Indian can get his twelve reals ($1.50) per day with ease. Many thousand dollars have been sent in dust already to the United States. I have only time to refer to these things now; before I leave the country, I hope to collate many facts regarding the mineral resources of California, for the information of our countrymen. The evidences now are that

Letters from "The Farthest West"

there is a vast field for mining operations about to open here.

The Hudson's Bay Company have sold out their establishment at this place, and are now embarking their people and effects on board the "Vancouver," bound to Columbia River. Messrs. Howard and Mellish, of Boston, supercargoes of ships on the coast here, bought the lands and buildings. Mr. Leidesdorff, the efficient Vice-Consul of the United States, has just put up extensive buildings at an expense of $15,000. He has a valuable contract for supplying the Russian Fur Company with beef, flour, and other provisions.

There is some trade between San Francisco and the Sandwich Islands. I am convinced the trade between the Columbia River and the Islands has been over-estimated at home, from what I see in the papers from the Islands, and I think some of our merchants who have sent out their ships under the expectation of high freights, will find a very small *maogiu* on the return. There is no port in the whole world so difficult and dangerous to enter as the Columbia. The Hudson's Bay Co.'s vessels, with the best of pilots and captains, long familiar with the river, are detained on an average six weeks to get in and out. That bar will need buoys, beacons and steam, to make it safe or even passable for commercial purposes.

Yours truly,
THE FARTHEST WEST.

THE SECOND LETTER

of "The Farthest West" printed in "The Friend," Nov., 16, 1846.

CALIFORNIA IN 1846

YERBA BUENA, *San Francisco Bay,*

June 24th, 1846

WHEN I took my pen in hand to give you a line a few days since, I neither expected to have the opportunity to repeat it so soon, nor any thing of special interest to add, if I had; but the last ten days has been prolific of striving events in *California*, and as I cannot yet see *"the beginning of the end,"* I may well begin at the beginning, and you shall have the end when I do see it.

The American Emigrants in California are in arms, attempting to revolutionize the country. The first movement took place on the 13th inst., when a party of 12 men from Sacramento River, surprised a body of fifteen men who were driving 150 horses from the North side of the Bay to the Camp of the Military Commandant of California, (Col. Don Jose Castro) at Santa Clara, sixty miles

Letters from "The Farthest West"

South of this place, and on the Southern arm of San Francisco Bay. The captors took the horses, but let the prisoners go free, and told them if they did not like the surprise, they could take their arms and have a fair field fight for it; this, they declined doing; they were then told "go to the camp of General Castro, and tell him that we have seen the proclamation of the Californians, threatening to destroy or drive out every foreigner in California – that the war has begun and we hope he will come on." They then retired up the Sacramento to *Sutter's Fort* – took possession of it, he (Sutter), found them with what force he had. On the 15th they had increased to 40 men; when 34 well mounted, pushed down the North side of the Bay, and at day-light, on the 15th, surprised the military post of "*Sonoma*," where they took 18 prisoners, 8 pieces of cannon, 250 stand of arms and 250 horses; of the latter, they only selected fifty for their own use. Among the prisoners (indeed with the arms they were the main object of the expedition), they took Colonel Don Guadalupe Vallego, with his brother, Capt. Vallego, and Lt. Col. Prudon. The Colonel was the Military Commandant of the Northern frontier of California; he has not been averse to the settlers; but, on the contrary, kind, and has many friends among them. These officers were at once escorted to Sutter's Fort, leaving a garrison of 25 men in *Sonoma*, from whence we now have a flaming *Proclamation*, signed by *William B. Ide, Commander-in-Chief, by the will of the people!* – I have no doubt but the prisoners will receive kind treatment. Before Gen. Vallego was taken from Sonoma, he requested a friend

[*William B. Ide's copy of the fourth issue of the* Californian]

Yerba Buena, June 24, 1846

to proceed to the U. S. Ship Portsmouth, at anchor in the Bay, to tell her commander, Capt. Montgomery, what had happened to him, and as he could not see any *head* to the attacking party, he hoped his friend, Capt. Montgomery, would send an officer there to (Sonoma) to use his influence with the garrison to treat the people well, whom he had so suddenly been compelled to leave, as he thought, in the hands of the lawless set. This messenger had scarcely reached the ship-of-war, before there arrived another from *General Ide*, setting forth the change which had taken place in the political condition of Sonoma and the Sacramento Valley; he bore assurances to all in the country, that all private property should be respected – that they had taken up arms in self defence, having been threatened with *extermination* if they did not leave at once. (See Ide's proclamation.) Ide's messenger stated that no violence had been committed, nor would be, and that all was quiet at Sonoma and in the surrounding country. He hoped an officer would be sent, that he might see that such was the case. As this seemed the desire, now, of both parties, an officer was dispatched, taking with him both messengers; he was at Sonoma on the 17th, and found all quiet, although the ladies of Col. Vallego's party thought there was some danger, inasmuch as they could not distinguish between the chief and his men in dress (they were all dressed in Buck-skin hunting shirts) and they did not like the *flag* they had hoisted. What was it? you may ask – a *white field* with a *red border*, a *large star* and a Grisly Bear. The star being the "*Union*," with the Bear on his haunches, going at it! –

Letters from "The Farthest West"

such is the flag of *Young California!* Madam Vallego, looking at it, said it was not a flag for *Christians to hoist*; if they would only haul it down and hoist the American Flag, and the Lieut. of the ship stay there, she should feel perfectly safe; but that could not be; so taking with him a copy of the last proclamation for his Commander, and seeing there was no occasion for his services as a *mediator*, he returned to the ship. At his request, however, the Commander of the garrison permitted a courier to proceed to the camp, at Sutter's, with an open letter from Mrs. Vallego to her husband. There could be no doubt, on hearing of these events, that *Castro* would charge upon *"Frémont,"* with being the leader of this revolution; and were not to be long in doubt, even if we had any, for on the 17th, he stated in official letters, that *Frémont had captured "Sonoma,"* and issued a *"proclamation"* on the same day, commencing as follows:

The General-in-Chief to the people of California; –

"FELLOW CITIZENS, – *The base policy of the Agents of the U.S. in California* have already organized a body of adventurers, who boldly commence its invasion, surprising the military post of Sonoma, &c., &c., (naming the prisoners).

Fellow Countrymen, the defence of our liberty – the true religion which our fathers professed, and our independence, oblige us to sacrifice ourselves before losing these inestimable gifts – turn and behold these families and innocent children, whose fathers have been dragged from them, and prisoners with our en-

Yerba Buena, June 24, 1846

emies, call us to their aid, &c. Divine Providence will direct us on the road to glory, and this little garrison of Santa Clara, with your chief, will be the first to sacrifice themselves for your good and liberty.

(Signed) JOSE CASTRO.

Head Quarters, Santa Clara,
June 17th, 1846."

As the garrison of Santa Clara was only composed of 25 men, I am truly astonished that the Revolutionists did not surprise it and Sonoma at the same time. They could have done so with impunity; as it is, Castro will give them trouble, if the Californians rally to his standard, and I understand they are doing so; it is also said that the Revolutionists have, today, 150 men, Castro about the same number. We have just learned that a body of 40 to 50 have passed from Santa Clara to the *Narrows of the Bay* (going down on the last side of the Santa Clara *arm* of the Bay), last night, and that Castro comes here to-day, on his way over, to unite his forces for an attack on Sonoma; as at present advised, I cannot predict the result, but I am confident, if the Revolutionists whip Castro on his first attack, it is all up with California as a *Department of Mexico*. Whether Mexico be at war with the U. S. or not, if this Revolution keep on foot till the arrival of the emigration, this fall (say September), California will be independent of Mexico, as she should be. It is only surprising that the public men now at her head, do not make her so themselves. At the same time I

Letters from "The Farthest West"

should say, what is truly the fact, that in *all but the name*, she is now independent – *neither have the least benefit from the connection.*

Yours truly,

FARTHEST WEST.

P.S. A boat from the bay states that last evening, the band mentioned above, as on their way to Sonoma, were crossing the narrows, within fifteen miles of Sonoma. I presume, therefore, we shall soon hear of a fight.

SUTTER'S FORT — NEW HELVETIA
from a lithographic illustration in Revere's "Tour of Duty in California," 1849

THE THIRD LETTER
of "The Farthest West" printed in "The Friend," Dec. 1, 1846.

CALIFORNIA IN 1846

YERBA BUENA, *San Francisco Bay,*
June 26th, 1846

T*HE first bloodshed in battle in California flowed yesterday on the plains of Sonoma.* – (Heretofore all the revolutions have been bloodless, so far as I can learn, except perhaps an occasional assassination 'a la Espanole.') News has this moment reached this point, that the party mentioned in the postscript No. 2, as having crossed the "narrows" on the evening of the 23d, were met yesterday by 20 men of the revolutionary party, and defeated. "The Californians," says the letter bringing the news, "were 77, the twenty Americans attacked them, killed *two* and wounded *two,* when the whole body retreated, leaving the 20 masters of the field." This comes from the Californian side, who add that the report is the Sonoma party also lost two. This brings the certain intelligence that the little band of braves at Sonoma are

Letters from "The Farthest West"

not to be caught napping at any rate, and the inference of this little fight is, that they have now sufficient force to destroy the party which have crossed over before Castro can reinforce them, since they could have a scout of 20 out of camp. If the revolutionists have fifty men at Sonoma, or had them yesterday, that party of Californians will be destroyed. You must not consider this little battle a trifle, when you realize where it has been fought; for as I said above, I am not aware of there ever having been a life lost in battle in California. All the Mexican Generals, — which the Californians have with the aid of foreigners, from time to time driven out, even to the *soi disant* "Thunderbolt," Micheltoreno — have been expelled the country without the loss of a man on either side.—Micheltoreno capitulated in April, 1845, near the lower Pueblo. He had 250 men all told, — the Californians about the same number, being the entire force of the country, including over two hundred Mexican soldiers who left with him after his capitulation. The foreigners engaged on both sides, agreed mutually not to fight each other, as it was a Mexican and Californian quarrel — a family affair — to let them settle it among themselves. They looked on; Micheltoreno opened his cannon, and Castro his; they fired at each other for two days, within short cannon range. At the end of the second day, Micheltoreno capitulated. The total loss on both sides was *six horses killed* and two men injured but not by shot. It is also said that when Micheltoreno capitulated, the "missing list" was very large. Therefore it is now considered that Castro can scarce bring over two hun-

Yerba Buena, June 26, 1846

dred men into the field, and if this advanced party are whipped, it will then be impossible to get his men to stand at all. — While enjoying a social game of whist last evening at the Consul's a Russian gentleman remarked, that from a long residence in the country, he was satisfied the Californians would run as soon as the first man fell. The news to-day would seem to show that he held a correct opinion. I am fully satisfied that the Americans have only to make their force up to two hundred fighting men and their long rifles will sweep all California of anything that will willingly oppose them. In these remarks I do not choose to give my opinion of the justice of their cause, but simply to remark what is apparent to every eye-witness.

I have mentioned particularly the Americans, as engaged in this revolution. There are some Europeans among them, but they claim to be American citizens.

You are aware that in all Mexican revolutions, the "Pronunciados" always exhibit their "plano" on the base of the new system which they intend to erect in the place of the old. This "plano," Capt. Vallego was very anxious to have exhibited to him when he was taken prisoner by Ide and his party, but they had none! He then said to them, "You say you are Americans, — show me your authority from the Government of the U.S." "We have none," they replied; "our authority is our own will, our arms shall execute it." I thought to have sent you Ide's proclamation, but as it can be much condensed, I only give the main points. It is addressed to all Californians, and especially the citizens in and

Letters from "The Farthest West"

about Sonoma, desiring them "to continue their usual avocations without any fear of molestation." It declares that personal and private property of all kinds shall be respected, and no one shall be molested in any way who does not oppose them in arms. He then declares his "object to be to defend himself and companions in arms, who have taken up arms in self defence; that they were invited into the country with a promise of land on which to settle themselves and families; and instead of being permitted to have land, or purchase it of their friends, they had been threatened with extermination if all foreigners did not leave the country, leaving behind them their arms, their property and their beasts of burden." That thus without the means of defence, they were to be driven into the wilderness inhabited by savage Indians to certain destruction. That in coming to the country they were promised a Republican Government, in which they could participate, instead of which they were ruled by a military despotism; and that the chief officer of this despotism had thus threatened them if they did not leave. To overturn this despotism, to destroy a Government which has seized upon the property of the missions for its individual aggrandizement, and to erect a republican Government, with liberty of speech and the press, – toleration for all religions, – to put down the enormous exactions enforced upon the people, and to encourage industry, commerce and mechanic arts"—he declared to be "the settled determination of the brave men who are now in arms;" and then with strong appeals to their "love of liberty and hatred of tyranny," he invites

Yerba Buena, June 26, 1846

them to join their standard at Sonoma, signing himself, "Wm. B. Ide, Commander-in-Chief by the voice of the people." Some may ask is all this true? Have they been thus threatened? I think not to the extent complained of; certainly not in the official manner he declares it. In April last, the Sub-Prefect of this place and district, issued an order to all the judges of towns, that they could not permit any unnaturalized person to become possessed of "bienes raias, o dicha clase de propriedes" (landed property or of that character), as the right only belonged to native or naturalized citizens, and to inform all persons who had or should make such acquisitions, that they were null and void. The U. S. Consul was requested to translate it and send it into the valley of the Sacramento. A foment has been brewing ever since, and lately the topic has become current that Castro had excited the Indians against the foreigners generally, and made them promises of valuable presents if they would burn the crops and destroy the people. In consequence of this belief, they have attacked the Indians three times in the valley, and killed nearly two hundred in the three fights. And now they assert that the Indians confess that they agreed to do this, and were to be rewarded for it. The Indians are inveterate horse stealers, and during six days in May, while I was making an excursion of three hundred miles on horseback, they stole over *four hundred horses* from the farms I visited, or the immediate neighborhood, until the distressed farmers thought they should lose every horse in their "Caballadas." The foreigners invariably pursue the Indians and retake the

Letters from "The Farthest West"

horses, but the lethargic Californian reports "los maldites Indios" to Alcalde, and the Priest, if there is one near, and quietly submits to his loss.

But to return to the revolution and its merits; the truth is just here: the emigrants came into the country after innumerable labor and toil on their journey, in which they have spent all they had (and many of them have sold pretty places to visit this "Eldorado") to get here. They see abundance of wild and good land, inhabited by a few naked, thieving, most miserable Indians, and they think it no wrong to put this land to a better use; and then if the Californian Government are so blind as not to see that every sturdy farmer with his wife and children is a blessing to this vast country, lying waste for the want of physical power, and in place of aiding, annoy them, and threaten them with extermination,— they need not be astonished if having arms in their hands, they rise upon them and compel them to yield up their authority to a race which will carry liberty and toleration—industry and commerce — schools and literature, wherever it goes. California has been in possession of the Catholic (Roman) mission, for over half a century. All it had accomplished was the building of huge mission establishments of sun dried brick, by Indian labor, in payment of which the Indians were regaled with the service of mass, and a bullock now and then, while thousands on thousands roved the plains, of no value but its hide, which was worth in trade one dollar. The Priests lived in luxury, with fine meats, fruits and wines; the Indians served them. In 1830, the Mexican Government took

Yerba Buena, June 26, 1846

the power from the Priests and gave the missions into the hands of "Administrators." These now robbed the Government, the Priests and the Indians, until the missions are in ruins, scarce a Priest in the country; and the Indians have returned to their native plains and hills, vastly worse for all they learned, since they have wants they cannot now satisfy, and are partially unfitted for savage life. They bear no comparison with the tall manly figures on our western frontier. They look a broken down, naked, starved and miserable race, and have no resources but to prey upon the white man's property or serve him as his slave.

Yours truly,

THE FARTHEST WEST.

P.S. SUTTER'S FORT, June 29, 1846. — To-day leaves not a doubt of the entire success of the revolutionists. The advance of the emigration from Oregon arrived last night, and proceeded at once to the camp at Sonoma. One hundred more will be in in a few days. The foreigners are flocking from all points to Sonoma, and this place. I shall probably be at some of the most interesting points during the progress of events, and shall continue to "jot down." I find here that Sutter is making a superb crop of wheat, — about 300 Indians actually cutting and storing it at this moment, under the directions of their chiefs, who bring them in for that purpose. As I have an object on hand for to-day and a few days to come, which will keep me in the saddle, I cannot expect to add to this. But if I mistake not, my next will give you some interesting details of passing events. T. F. W.

LETTER OF E. M. KERN

from the original in the Huntington Library and Art Gallery.

CALIFORNIA IN 1846

U. S. Fort SACRAMENTO
July 27th, 1846

DICK — By the favor of Com. Sloat, I am enabled to send you a few lines of the doings in this newly acquired Terr. of the U.S. Little did I think when sitting at home in our office in F St. that I would ever raise to be a Mil. character, a real Commandante of a Fort. With power to do as I pleased and shoot people if they do not obey me, & all that sort of thing. "But there is a tide in the affairs of men which taken at the turn may lead to glory." Any how, strange as you may think it, here I am, vested with the aforesaid authority and surrounded by a Garrison of runaway seamen and Indians (I would not march through Coventry with them!), and the most ungodly hord of the largest & hardest to catch—highest jumping—& hard biting, putting-your-finger-on-and-not-to-[be]-found fleas that have ever worried

U.S. Fort Sacramento July 2/ 1846

Dick.

By the favor of Com. Sloat, I am enabled to send you a few lines of the doings in this newly acquired Ter. of the U.S. Little did I think when sitting at home in our office in I St. that I would soon raise to be a Mil. Character a rale commandante of a Fort. With power to do as I pleased & shoot people if they did not obey me, & all that sort of thing. "But there is a tide in the affairs of men which taken at the two may lead to —— ." Any how, strange as you may think it here I am, vested with the aforesaid authority and surrounded by a Garrison of Run away Midshipmen & Indians (I would not march through the country with them) & the most ungodly hord of the largest & hardest to catch highest jumping - & hard biting putting your finger on - and not to found fleas that have ever worried man since the days of Adam. They are a staple production of the country. Before entering upon my blood & thunder narrative of the Wars I will give you a sketch of some of the People concerned therein.

6ft 6in brother to Senator Simple Jones where from the W. My last was from Klee C. From that place we had taken up our line of march for home & had got as far as the head of Klamath Lake when an express arrived for our immediate return to the tune of naked rlizzars. We last 3 of our men they were murdered in bed - We revenged ourselves vi the Indians by killing & burning wherever an opportunity offered. Lieut Gillespie the courier had been followed some days by the Nasty Inds. When a party sent from our camp to meet him. On the night they camped

U.S. Fort Sacramento, July 27, 1846

man since the days of Adam. They are a staple production of the country.

Before entering upon my blood & thunder narrative of the Wars, I will give you a sketch of some of the People concerned. [SKETCH: *below the figure of Semple, the following*; A long 6 ft. 8 in. brother to Senator Semple some where from the W.]

My last was from Deer C. From that place we had taken up our line of March for home & had got as far as the head of Klamath Lake when an express arrived for our immediate return to the land of naked Diggers. We lost 3 of our men – they were murdered in bed. We revenged ourselves on the Indians by killing and burning whenever an opportunity offered. Lieut. Gillespie, the courier, had been followed some days by the Shasta Inds: a party was sent from our Camp to meet him. On the night they came up with them was the intended time of attack. It came, and lost us 3 of our best men. It was but an exchange – 3 for 4. Had the Lieut. missed us that night it is more than likely 'ere this reaches you I should have been at home.

What we were to return to Cal. for no one knows (but to return was sure of creating a row with the yellow bellies), we had been ordered out on March last, and abused by a Proclamation (a copy inclosed) and left the country without a fight. It [the return] appeared equivalent to a declaration of war. When fairly down in the Valley, couriers were running here and yon & nobody knew what for. At last word was sent to José Castro that we had returned. Then came a rumor that he was marching against us with

Letter of E. M. Kern

a force of 300 men. Then the Foreigners living around the upper part of the Country, about 20 or 25, were called into camp – as a Proclamation had been issued stating that all foreigners, Americans in particular, should leave the country at once, leaving their property to be disposed of as Govt. should think fit or abide by the consequence. Indians were bribed to burn the crops as soon as they should be ripe enough, thereby cutting off all supplies for the Emigrants when they should arrive this fall. A gun had been given to an Indian to shoot Capt. J. A. Sutter, owner of this fort, and all such unmanly things that none but a cowardly Spaniard would think of.

Now to the commencement of hostilities. Having collected what forces could be raised in the upper country [we] moved from the Buttes towards the fort. The Spaniards were reported to be on the W. side of the Sacramento R. We supposed they would move upwards & sweep the country down, attacking us in the rear, defeat (of course easily) & have possession of the whole upper country. But there was no army following – it turned out to be a corporal with 12 men driving a band of horses for the use of Castro. Here was an opening to commence business, & Merrit, a R. Mountain man at the head of 12 men started and returned with the whole Cavillarda. Not a blow struck. He sent word to Castro that he was there, [that] he took the horses, and that if he (C.) wanted them, to come and get them if he was a man.

The next move was the attack and taking of Sonoma, a bold and beautifully managed affair. Our information [was] that this

U.S. Fort Sacramento, July 27, 1846

post was garrisoned with about 80 or 100 men & about 200 Indians. We had every reason to suppose that they were on the alert, as the business had commenced. Merrit started with 25 men to the place, his forces increasing to 45 all told when he arrived there. The charge was made but there was no resistance, simply because there was no one to resist. A garrison was stationed under the command of one Ide, a Mormon, while our party returned bringing with them as proof of Victory, Gen. M. G. Vallejo, Col. S. Vallejo, Col. Victor Prud'homme, a Frenchman, & J. P. Lease, an American. They had made no resistance, but when the head is cut off the legs can't go. I have them at present under my charge. The next move of the insurgents (for they had it all to themselves, our camp laying by as mere spectators) was the issue of a proclamation from Headquarters at Sonoma signed by said Ide, calling on the people who loved their liberty to fly to arms &c., &c. This produced a counter one from Castro calling everybody thieves &c. in the country & ordering the people to arm themselves in defence of their fire sides, which were about to be invaded by a Party of Barbarians, & that he particularly believed himself the chosen of God to avenge their wrongs. A movement was made a few days after the taking of S. by the Spaniards to regain so desirable a position & arms contained therein. Supposing the garrison to consist of but 15 men, a force of 70 were crossed below under the command of Joaquin la Torrers [Joaquin de la Torre]. They had come upon 3 of the boys unawares & taken them prisoners. When they were met by 15 of the garrison whom

Letter of E. M. Kern

they surrounded, and the boys let loose on them, killing an ensign and wounding 2 more, one mortally. A retreat was the consequence, leaving their prisoners behind them.

You may judge of their valor from this act. The next thing was catching a couple of Americans who were riding peaceably along the road. After detaining them for an hour or 2 they tied them to trees and there butchered them in cold blood, cutting to pieces with their swords, &c., proceedings that would disgrace even a Pi-Eute. But such is their nature – beat them and they will love you, treat them well and they'll kill you. I should never allow myself to be taken by them alive. This produced an order from our side to take no more prisoners. Capt. F. now marched to the assistance of the garrison. Martial law [was] proclaimed throughout the country. Our next attack was on San Raphael, but like Sonoma there was no one to fight, so of course it was taken. Two spies were killed on the road and no questions asked. Frémont is now camped at Monterey with a force of 200 men. Castro has gone down the country with an equal force; desperation may drive a fight out of him, he knowing in the field he will receive no mercy. At present he is encamped at the Rincoon [Rincon] on the coast, the strongest position in California. Bounded by bluffs on three sides and the ocean on the other, it is impassable. Ten men would be good against 1000. [It is] on the highway with no other road to pass to the lower settlements. Here and here only he may be brought to a stand.(?)

On the 7th of July Com. J. D. Sloat took possession of Monte-

Fort Sacramento
New Helvetia
August 2nd 1846

This is to certify that having been made a Prisoner by the residents of California in arms asserting their Independence of California, I, in consideration of being set at Liberty, hereby most solemnly pledge my sacred word of honor, not to take up arms against the United States of North America or the Residents of California. That I will not furnish supplies, carry communications or in any way assist any person or persons who may be opposed to the United States of North America or the above named residents of California; Or leave my proper district without permission from the Commander at Yerba Buena, understanding distinctly that if this pledge is not faithfully performed my life is forfeited wherever I may be found.

And hereunto I affix my hand and seal.

Witness
J A Sutter

{seal} M G Vallejo

{seal} Julio Carrillo

U.S. Fort Sacramento, July 27, 1846

rey, and the U. S. flag is now flying at the principal places in the upper country. To take or kill Castro will close the affair. Com. Stockton has relieved Sloat in command of the Pacific Squadron. This is about all that has occurred in the way of war. Had the revolutionists been left to themselves, a few weeks would have settled the business by their defeating themselves. [There were] a few honest & well disposed persons among them who truly intended the movement for the best, but the majority [were] moved by nothing but the chance of plunder. Without the slightest principles of honor to guide them, they must have defeated the cause.

Here is Castro's Proclamation:

The citizen José Castro, Lieut. Col. of the Mexican Army and Commander in Chief of the Department of California.

Fellow Citizens: A band of robbers commanded by a Captain of the U. S. Army, J. C. Frémont, have without respect to the laws and authority of the Department, daringly introduced themselves into the country and disobeyed both the orders of your Commander-in-Chief and of the Prefect of the District by which he was required to march forthwith, out of the limits of our Territory, and without answering their letters he remains encamped at the farm "Natividad" from which he sallies forth committing depredation, and making scandalous skirmishes.

In the name of our native country I invite you to place yourselves under my immediate orders at headquarters, where we will prepare to lance the ulcer which (should it not be done) would de-

Letter of E. M. Kern

stroy our liberties and independence, for which you ought to sacrifice yourselves as will your friend and fellow-citizen.

Headquarters at "San Juan"   JOSÉ CASTRO
8 March 1846

As pretty a piece of bombast as was ever written. We have had two other Proclamations from the same Gent. and of the same nature. As for his valor, it is like Hudibras' wit, "he's devilish shy of using it," &c. If he could only be caught in his Holyday garb, we might get a fight out of him. Matters turning out as they have, it will be almost impossible for us to reach home this winter, as it will be so late before we get through business here that the snows will have set in & though we could cross the Cal. Mts. the R. Mts. will be unpassable—we would have to winter somewhere. I am in hopes of getting a furlough when I am relieved and may have a chance of seeing something more of the settlements. I am so far away from any place at this fort that it is only now & then when an express comes that I am enabled [to] know what is going on at all.

There is a large emigration expected this fall from the states, led by Hastings, author of the Emigrant's Guide &c., as big an ass as any. There is a party of Mormons reported to be on their way here from N.Y. by the way of the Islands. The lord knows where they will settle, as there are so many rumors of their doings that the people are opposed to their entrance. A kind of Catholic religion is the religion of the country – among the Foreigners there is no particular one. What a field this country will be for those

U. S. Fort Sacramento, July 27, 1846

miserable pests the missionaries, here they can find the untutored child of the forest in a perfect state of nature – women preachers could do a better business than the men. This is a damned unhealthy neighborhood—& as I'm Dr. I made a mush of one cub, & liked to have fixed off one of the prisoners. That would have been a bad job, as people would have said he had been poisoned – it might have happened for aught I know.

I hope you are still engaged at the Institute and are in a thriving condition. But like the old lady who fancied herself an hourglass, I must stop, being run out. Somebody turn me up.

Remember me to all,

E. M. KERN

LETTER OF "JUSTICE"
from "The Missouri Republican" of June 14, 1847.

CALIFORNIA IN 1846-47

SAN DIEGO, UPPER CALIFORNIA
February, 1847

ABOUT ten months ago, the people of California who had long suffered the want of the protection of a regular government, and utterly disgusted with their neglect and treatment by the remote parent State, Mexico, entertained in their assembly the subject of declaring their severance from Mexico, and applying to some powerful nation for protection. It is well known that the majority not only favored the proposition, but an application for a political connexion with the United States. The most influential and best informed of the citizens, with one voice express the conviction that then, or after the war, the presence in the territory of a single individual of high standing and character, and commissioned by our government, would have insured a peaceful and honorable annexation, highly satisfactory to the mass of the people.

San Diego, February, 1847

About this time, Lieutenant Gillespie, of the marine corps, arrived in Monterey, and set off in haste to follow Captain Frémont, whom he overtook far on his way to the United States. The captain returned with him.

Immediately after and before the declaration of war was known, if made, a revolution was commenced under a flag with the device of a bear, and acts of war were committed upon a portion of the people. They were not acknowledged by the naval authorities, but supplies were furnished to Captain Frémont. A revolution even thus commenced with the assistance of the naval forces, was apparently successful in the course of the summer. An express was sent about the 1st of September to Washington, by the Rio Gila and New Mexico, announcing the peaceable possession of the territory by the United States.

On the 30th of June, 1846, Brigadier General S. W. Kearny (on that very day promoted by selection from the whole army) marched with an army from Fort Leavenworth. He was clothed with the most ample powers to revolutionize or subdue, and to govern, New Mexico first, and then California. The first task being most successfully accomplished, he marched from Santa Fé, on the 25th of September, in command of the 1st dragoons, the advance of his forces, for California, to fulfil the second of the high but laborious commissions of his government.

Before he left the Rio Grande, the messengers of peace from California were met by him. The general then reduced his force to the mere escort of a squadron of 100 men, and pursued his

Letter of "Justice"

course. After a march of a thousand miles over mountains of rocks, barren prairies, and deserts, without water, he arrived with his men only half mounted, and on broken down mules, at the first rancho, sixty miles from San Diego.

Then the following course and condition of affairs were soon learned. The Californians proper, who are a proud race, disgusted with the conduct of the revolution and the government which had been established, and suffering outrages from its irregular military hirelings, had risen in arms. They had re-taken all the towns south of Monterey; Lieutenant Gillespie having surrendered the capital, the Pueblo de los Angeles. An attack on it from its seaport, San Pedro, under the orders of Commodore Stockton, had signally failed. San Diego, commanded from the sea, was now in our possession, but blockaded by land. Commodore Stockton (styling himself Governor) was there with the Congress and Portsmouth, and perhaps other ships of war. Lieutenant Colonel Frémont had retired two months before to the upper country, to raise an irregular force, and was reported on his return with 400 men and some Indians. The Californians, individually, the most formidable horsemen in America, were under arms to the number of 800, and carried on a guerrilla warfare. About 100 of them were posted at San Pasqual, on the best road from General Kearny's position to San Diego.

Before learning this last item, the general succeeded in giving information of his approach at San Diego, and Captain Gillespie, an officer of the navy, and a small party of mounted volunteers

U.S. Frigate Congress
Harbor of San Francisco
Oct. br 2nd 1846

Sir
  You will proceed in the Savannah to San Pedro as soon as possible, for the purpose of assisting to put down an insurrection which I am informed has broken out amongst the natives.
  Captain Gillespie with fifty mounted Riflemen were left at the City of the Angels, when I came from there; and fifty men in the neighbourhood.
  I cannot of course say more to you at this time than thus to state the general object of your expedition to be for the relief of our fellow Citizens, at the South; and to put down and punish the insurrectionists.
  Your prudence is relied upon, that you will not unnecessarily expose your ship or men to hazard.
  But if it is necessary to hazard both; you will be prompt to do your duty.
  The Chief of the Wallowwallows, is daily expected here to see me. It wont do for me or the Portsmouth to leave now.
  The Chief must be impressed strongly with our force. But I'll be after you as soon as possible.

     Faithfully
     Ob't &c. Serv't
     R. F. Stockton
     Commodore &c.

San Diego, February, 1847

joined him on his march on the 5th of December; that evening he learned of the force at San Pasqual, ten or twelve miles distant; he attempted to surprise them at daybreak the next morning. The night was uncomfortably cold and rainy; the enemy had received information of the approach of foes, they knew not whom, and were found fully prepared at dawn of day. They were impetuously charged and driven from their ground, more than half of the squadron being mounted on worthless mules; they were pursued rashly and too far by the others, despite the general's effort to stop it. The enemy then, in daylight rallied, surrounded and attacked, with every advantage, the foremost pursuers, 38 in number, all of whom but one were killed or wounded. Then the dragoons met with the irreparable loss of these fine officers and some of the best non-commissioned officers and men. The general himself received two severe wounds. The remnant of this heroic band, with bleeding wounds, succeeded in rallying on a mountain howitzer which then approached, and the enemy again retired. They encamped on the ground. The next day, reduced by twenty killed, and encumbered with seventeen wounded, having marched about ten miles, they were threatened with attack on the plain by the enemy in increased numbers. The dragoons charged them, and drove them from a rocky hill which they themselves took possession of; that night a messenger, with written information on their situation, succeeded in passing the enemy's videttes, and carrying it to Commodore Stockton, about 25 miles off San Diego. He sent a written refusal by three men who

Letter of "Justice"

were captured. The general and his party remained besieged on the hill for three days; fortunately, water was obtained by digging at its foot, and they subsisted on mule flesh.

The most intelligent persons in San Diego believed them lost; there was time for an overwhelming force to arrive from the Pueblo; large re-inforcements were on their way.

After two days, on the third night, Lieutenant Beal, of the navy, who would not believe that succor could be refused, succeeded in making his way to San Diego. The next night 150 men were sent; they arrived at the close of the fourth night thus passed on the hill, and just as the general, determined to cut his way through the enemy at all hazards, had burned all his baggage.

Arrived in San Diego, General Kearny exhibited to Commodore Stockton his commission and powers to command, and govern in the territory; but badly wounded, and with the command of so slight a military force, he with proper delicacy refrained, for the present, to exert his authority, and so he expressed himself. In about two weeks, having recovered his strength, and anxious for the public service and the safety of Lieutenant Colonel Frémont, he spoke and wrote to Commodore Stockton, urging that a force should be marched for the Pueblo for his support, or at least to make a demonstration in his favor. This was roughly refused for two days, and Frémont was denounced by Commodore Stockton. He was induced finally to change his mind, and on the 29th of December, General Kearny marched in command of about 700 dismounted dragoons, marines and sailors. Commo-

San Diego, February, 1847

dore Stockton had by this time, however, refused to submit to the authority of the government, and to General Kearny's commission and powers from the President of the United States! He refused to surrender his assumed authority as governor and commander-in-chief of all the forces. Only anxious for the service of his country, General Kearny submitted to serve her as best he could. Commodore Stockton accompanied the march.

On the route some citizens who had been neutral arrived in camp, commissioned by the Californians to ascertain what terms would be granted to them. Commodore Stockton, in reply, offered such as are generally considered not only extraordinary, but insulting.

On the 8th of January — the memorable and glorious anniversary — about mid-day, the enemy made his appearance on the opposite side of the San Gabriel river. He was about five hundred strong in cavalry, and formidable in artillery, which included some 9-pounders. Commodore Stockton rode up to General Kearny and proposed that the army should go into camp. General Kearny positively refused, and, under the cover of his artillery fire, crossed the river in the presence of the enemy, and by a general charge, which he headed in person, drove him from the field.

The next day, the 9th, there was another engagement, principally of artillery, in which the Californians were driven from a strong position, and at night the army encamped on the river of the Pueblo, in the suburbs of the capital. That night it was evacuated by the enemy, and taken possession of next morning by our

Letter of "Justice"

troops. Then General Kearny urged that a force might be given him to go to the assistance of Lieutenant Colonel Frémont, whom it was reported and believed the enemy had gone to attack. It was refused.

Meanwhile the enemy, insultingly rejected by Commodore Stockton, sought terms of capitulation from Lieutenant Colonel Frémont. This officer, knowing that General Kearny and Commodore Stockton were within five miles, made with them articles of capitulation and peace, which he signed as "military commandant of California."

On hearing this, Commodore Stockton was indignant, and used threatening language. As a counter action, Frémont threatened to report to General Kearny.

Lieutenant Colonel Frémont visited General Kearny, and asked him if he would make him governor. The general, not then acquainted with some occurrences, gave him reason to expect the appointment in a month or two, when affairs should be so settled as to admit the control of a civil government.

Lieutenant Colonel Frémont then went to Commodore Stockton, and he made him governor on the spot.

General Kearny, about this time, had sent Lieutenant Colonel Frémont a copy of his powers, which gave him the command of troops "raised in California," together with an order. Lieutenant Colonel Frémont refused to obey the order, with the excuse, in substance, that he could not obey him, before his difficulty as to command should be settled with Commodore Stockton.

San Diego, February, 1847

General Kearny, finding himself "one too many" at the Pueblo, then immediately marched back with his handful of dismounted dragoons to San Diego, where he arrived on the 23rd of January.

On the 20th, Lieutenant Colonel Cooke arrived there with his battalion of infantry volunteers, with which he brought wagons through from Santa Fé. The general, leaving him in command of all the troops, set sail on the 30th for Monterey and San Francisco.

Information has since been received of the arrival at Monterey of Commodore Shubrick, commander-in-chief of the naval forces in the Pacific, in the ship Independence, and also, of the storeship Lexington, with the company of artillery.

The permanency of the late suspension of arms has generally been doubted, but now the dawn of a better state of affairs may be perceived.

One more incident, which was overlooked. Commodore Stockton issued a flaming order, as commander-in-chief of the battles of San Gabriel and the Plains of Mesa; in them he had no command or control.

On the impulse he wrote, as he said, dispatches, in which he praised General Kearny and Captain Turner (1st dragoons), who commanded a third of the troops. Afterwards he said he had no idea of "trumping up" his enemies, and that he would send after the dispatches and alter them. Lieutenant Gray, of the navy, had been sent to bear dispatches by Panama; he was overtaken and stopped at San Diego, and then again sent forward. On learning these facts, General Kearny sent Lieutenant Emory, topogra-

Letter of "Justice"

phical engineer, to accompany Lieutenant Gray to Washington.

The officers of the navy, with one exception, and those of the army, have been on excellent terms.

The government has no money and no rations in this country. The troops live exclusively on fresh beef.

I have given a hasty sketch of prominent transactions and facts in this country. I have neither time nor inclination to comment upon them. I have not been an actor in any of the scenes, and this is written without the knowledge or even suspicion of any of those actors.

JUSTICE.

JOHN C. FRÉMONT
from a lithograph issued about 1856 by Bufford's Print Publishing House, Boston

BIOGRAPHICAL SKETCHES

OF

Important Figures

IN THE AMERICAN CONQUEST

OF CALIFORNIA

This list consists of brief biographical sketches of those men, both Californians and Americans, who played conspicuous parts in the events described in this book. The sketches of Pio Pico, Castro, Vallejo, and Sutter are reprinted from a list of "The Prominent Men of California in 1846," written by Thomas O. Larkin, U. S. Consul at Monterey, for Secretary of State James Buchanan; they were first published in The Pacific Monthly, *August, 1863.*

GOVERNOR PIO PICO; ranchero, aged forty-five years [1846]; born in California; married; a man of wealth, good local information, of good influence, standing and popularity; always engaged in the politics of his country; many years in office. From the oldest member of the legislature became governor, now confirmed by the supreme government. A well-meaning person of quiet disposition, not anxious for salary; owes his influence more to his office than to actual abilities.

JOSÉ CASTRO; born in California; aged thirty-six years [1846]; of a medium family; from his youth up been in public life; rising from a subordinate position to lieutenant-colonel by appointment of the President; having driven Micheltorena from California, he became acting commandante general, now tacitly acknowledged as such by Mexico; a partisan officer, not much talent or general information; of much influence among many, and among all the lower classes; respected by many of his countrymen; feared by others; of quick, inventive, intriguing mind; able to endure much fatigue in a campaign or foraging party; could collect and keep together more of his countrymen in an opposing state than any other Californian; has a strong and decided dislike to having Mexican rulers or soldiers in his country; of little property; fond of fame; not avaricious nor particular in appropriating public funds; generous and willing to oblige, but it is hard to understand him.

MARIANO G. VALLEJO; born in Monterey; aged thirty-six years [1846]; named a cadet when fifteen or sixteen years of age; holds the commission of lieutenant-colonel, which he received from Bustamente; his father a Spanish sergeant, equal in power to a cap-

Biographical Sketches

tain of the present day; a man of very large property; married; very studious for a Californian; of much knowledge and general information; anxious to improve himself and country; in 1837 assisted Castro and Alvarado in expelling the Mexicans; from that time has gradually retired from active military life, although he has always some command at his place of residence; has been formal, stiff, pompous and exacting towards his countrymen and foreigners of the lower and middle class; within a year has become pleasant and condescending; anxious for popularity and the good-will of others; in Sonoma, he has immense tracts of land, herds of cattle and horses, and extensive houses; is hospitable to those who are highly respectable or recommended to him; ostentatious and, for a Californian, a close observer of every passing event; as a private person has but little regard for Mexico – as an officer, more; is confident that Mexico will not assist or protect California, and that his own countrymen have not the capacities; has given much work and employment to American immigrants, always speaking in their favor; he has no wish for government pay (it owes him $20,000 or $30,000); speaks English indifferently; would always prefer rank, perhaps office, after affairs are well settled; has much influence all over the country; has his part of California the most free from robbery or insubordination, with more safety of life and property, than any other town in California.

JOHN A. SUTTER; born in Switzerland; aged forty-four years [1846]; many years captain in Charles the Tenth's Swiss Guard; a resident of California six or eight years; now a citizen; General Micheltorena appointed him alcalde and commandante of the Sacramento settlement; continues to hold the same by the tacit consent of both Californians and foreigners; of good information and improving talents; holds large tracts of lands; cattle on the decrease from overrating his means of paying laborers; his establishment consists of farmers, blacksmiths, carpenters, shoemakers, saddlers, hatters, tanners, coopers, weavers, and gunsmith shops, which is now beyond his means of keeping up; but he anticipates better times under a new government; it is of the utmost importance to the immigrants on their first arrival in California, and he is willing to assist them. In 1844, he mustered over one hundred armed men (foreigners) to assist Micheltorena; has influence over a great part of the people of the Sacramento; active, enterprising, well-informed, but too sanguine; lives but in expectation of this country's belonging to the United States; a capable man for many different offices; now much borne down with debt from the loss of two or three harvests by dry weather, and from too largely extending his business. Captain Sutter has a quadrangular fort of one hundred and sixty yards long, and one hundred yards wide, built entirely of adobes, and protected by bastions having some fourteen or fifteen cannon mounted. This square encloses all the houses and workshops of himself and people, with large gates which, when closed, render it impenetrable to Indians, or any common force. He has some armed Indians, with a large stock of arms and ammunition. This establishment, the first on the Sacramento, was begun in 1839, and fortified against the Indians. It would now be used against others who might attempt to attack it. General Castro sometimes talks of building another fort on the Sacramento, but has no funds, and but little energy to do so. Captain Sutter owes the Russian American Company on the northwest coast $30,000. The Mexican Government has proposed as-

Biographical Sketches

suming this and other debts, and taking Captain Sutter's establishment. In 1845, when the U. S. consul conversed with the Russian Governor, he was convinced that Captain Sutter was the best and surest debtor, and objected to any arrangement that the Mexican Government would make; and Sutter would not vacate the place for any sum that could be obtained.

THOMAS O. LARKIN, born in Massachusetts, 1802; arrived at Monterey in '32, set up as merchant there the following year; by '46, due to shrewdness, industry and more than average ability, he had become both prosperous and influential. Although he retained his American citizenship and served, from '44, as U.S. consul, he maintained close relations, business and personal, with local officials. Believing that the territory would eventually be annexed to the United States and, from '45 onward, working toward that end under secret instructions from Washington, Larkin did much to further the plan, discharging his difficult task with tact and good sense. His hopes for a peaceable transfer blasted by the Bear Flag Revolt, he continued to render able services by cooperating with the American forces. His official duties ending with the signing of the peace treaty, he lived for a time in New York, returning to California in '53 to manage his extensive properties. He died at San Francisco in 1858.

JOHN C. FRÉMONT, a native of Georgia, as lieutenant of topographical engineers led, '42 – '45, several exploring and mapping expeditions to the West; first visited California in '44. In '41, married a daughter of Thomas H. Benton. His reasons for disregarding Castro's orders to leave California in '46, and his subsequent actions before and during the Conquest have long been subjects of debate. Gave tacit support to Bear Flag exploit, later organized and led the California Battalion of volunteers and, becoming involved in a quarrel with General Kearny, was finally arrested by the latter, tried by court-martial, and convicted. Pardoned by President Polk, he resigned from the army, returned to California in '49, served briefly as U. S. senator and, in '56, ran for President, being defeated by Buchanan. Later engaged in business, with varying fortunes; held minor public offices. Died, 1890. Age in 1846, thirty-three years.

ARCHIBALD H. GILLESPIE, born in Pennsylvania; as lieutenant of marines carried, in '45 – '46, secret dispatches from Washington to Larkin and Frémont. Reached Monterey in April '46, after Frémont had left the territory; overtook the latter in southern Oregon and returned with him to the Sacramento Valley. Participated in subsequent events, became adjutant of Frémont's California Battalion; commanded garrison at Los Angeles which, October '46, was driven out by revolt of Californians; led re-enforcements to Kearny in December; wounded at San Pasqual; took part in recapture of Los Angeles; received second wound at San Gabriel, January '47; went East with Stockton's party later that year. Returned to California in '48 and died at San Francisco in '73. In '46, was thirty-three years of age.

WILLIAM B. IDE, born in Massachusetts, 1786; reached California with Grigsby-Ide party, 1845; settled in northern Sacramento Valley. Participated in capture of Sonoma, where he was chosen leader of Bear Flag party and, June 15, issued a Proclamation detailing the grievances of the settlers and announcing the establishment of a "Republican Government." Later served as private in Frémont's California Battalion; held office un-

Biographical Sketches

der Governor Mason and, after varied experiences in the mines, acquired and settled on a large ranch near Red Bluff. There, after holding a variety of county offices, he died, December 1852.

STEPHEN W. KEARNY, army officer, born in New Jersey; at outbreak of Mexican War was made brigadier general, commanded expedition to conquer and occupy New Mexico and California. Left most of his force at Santa Fé and, after difficult march across the desert, reached California in December '46; engaged Californians at San Pasqual, suffering severe defeat. Wounded, he and his diminished force reached San Diego and, early in '47, joined Stockton in an expedition to recapture Los Angeles. Assumed rank of military governor March 1, '47, served until June 1; then returned East over central route. During major part of stay in California was involved in controversy with Stockton and Frémont over question of authority; on his return preferred charges of mutiny against Frémont, which were sustained by court-martial. Died in 1848.

ROBERT FIELD STOCKTON, commodore, U. S. Navy; born in New Jersey; reached Monterey on the *Congress*, July, '46. Succeeded Sloat in command of the Pacific Squadron and, as military governor – July '46 – January '47 – directed operations against the Californians, working in close cooperation with Frémont. Blunt and decisive by nature, his lack of tact in dealing with the Californians prolonged their resistance; engaged him in controversy with Kearny over military governorship. Returned East in '47; resigned from Navy two years later; served one term, '51 – '52, as senator from New Jersey and, in '56, narrowly missed nomination for Presidency. Died, 1886.

550 COPIES PRINTED AT THE GRABHORN PRESS
IN SEPTEMBER, 1934

THIRTIETH CONGRESS—FIRST SESSION.

Ex. Doc. No. 41.

NOTES OF A MILITARY RECONNOISSANCE,

FROM

FORT LEAVENWORTH, IN MISSOURI,

TO

SAN DIEGO, IN CALIFORNIA,

INCLUDING PART OF THE

ARKANSAS, DEL NORTE, AND GILA RIVERS.

BY LIEUT. COL. W. H. EMORY.
MADE IN 1846-7, WITH THE ADVANCED GUARD OF THE "ARMY OF THE WEST."

FEBRUARY 9, 1848.—Ordered to be printed.
FEBRUARY 17, 1848.—*Ordered*, That 10,000 extra copies of each of the Reports of Lieutenant Emory, Captain Cooke, and Lieutenant Abert, be printed for the use of the House; and that of said number, 250 copies be furnished for the use of Lieutenant Emory, Captain Cooke, and Lieutenant Abert, respectively.

WASHINGTON:
WENDELL AND VAN BENTHUYSEN, PRINTERS.
::::::::::
1848.

LETTER

FROM

THE SECRETARY OF WAR,

TRANSMITTING

A communication from the Colonel of the corps of Topographical Engineers, enclosing copies of the reports of Lieutenant Emory, of portions of the report of Captain Cook, of the report of Lieutenant Abert, and of the journal kept by Captain Johnston, in compliance with a resolution of the House of Representatives of the 17th January, 1848.

WAR DEPARTMENT,
Washington, February 9, 1848.

SIR: In compliance with a resolution of the House of Representatives of the 17th ultimo, I have the honor to transmit herewith a communication of the colonel of the corps of topographical engineers, enclosing copies of "the report and map of Lieutenant Emory, of the topographical engineers, of the route of the army under General Kearny, from the Missouri river to the Pacific ocean, with such parts of the report of Captain Cook as related to his deviation from such route, and the reports and map of Lieutenant Abert, of the same corps, of his examinations in the province of New Mexico." I also transmit herewith a copy of the "journal of the expedition, kept by Captain Abraham R. Johnston."

These, with the documents communicated on the 24th ultimo, comprise all those required by the resolution above referred to.

Very respectfully, your obedient servant,
W. L. MARCY,
Secretary of War.

Hon. ROBERT C. WINTHROP,
Speaker of the House of Representatives.

NOTES

OF

A MILITARY RECONNOISSANCE,

FROM

FORT LEAVENWORTH, IN MISSOURI, TO SAN DIEGO, IN CALIFORNIA,

INCLUDING

PART OF THE ARKANSAS, DEL NORTE, AND GILA RIVERS.

INSTRUCTIONS, AND EXPLANATORY REMARKS.

WASHINGTON, *September* 1, 1847.
To Col. J. J. ABERT,
  Chief of the Corps of Topographical Engineers:
SIR: The following order was received by me June 5th, 1846:

> BUREAU OF TOPOGRAPHICAL ENGINEERS,
> *Washington, June* 5, 1846.
>
> SIR: You will repair, without delay, to Fort Leavenworth, and report yourself and party to Colonel Kearny, 1st dragoons, as field and topographical engineers of his command. In addition to yourself, the party will consist of—
>
> First Lieutenant Warner, now at Washington;
> Second Lieutenant Abert, do.
> Second Lieutenant Peck.
>
> Lieutenant Peck is at West Point, but he has been ordered to repair to St. Louis, and report to you at that place. Should Colonel Kearny be at St. Louis, which you will ascertain on passing through that place, you will report to him at St. Louis.
>
> Although ordered to report as field and topographical engineers, under the regulations, you will not consider these in the light of exclusive duties, but will perform any military duty which shall be assigned to you by Colonel Kearny in accordance with your rank.
>
> Should Colonel Kearny have moved on the prairies with his command, you will make every effort to overtake him.
>
> Respectfully, sir, your obedient servant,
>   J. J. ABERT,
>   *Colonel Topographical Engineers.*
>
> To Lieut. W. H. EMORY, *Top. Eng.*

Anticipating that the route of Colonel Kearny's command would be through unexplored regions, your suggestions required, that in all cases where it did not interfere with other and more immediate military demands of the service, the attention of myself, and the officers assigned to duty with me, should be employed in collecting data which would give the government some idea of the regions traversed.

The column commanded by Colonel Kearny, to which we were attached, styled "The Army of the West," to march from Fort Leavenworth, was destined to strike a blow at the northern provinces of Mexico, more especially New Mexico and California.

It was supposed we would barely reach Fort Leavenworth in time to join the army, and but twenty-four hours were allowed us in Washington to collect the instruments and other conveniences for such an expedition. This was quite sufficient for all the objects appertaining directly to our military wants, but insufficient for the organization and outfit of a party intended for exploration. In submitting the following notes, they should be received as observations made at intervals snatched from other duties, and with an expedition whose movements were directed by other considerations than those which would influence the views and conveniences of an explorer.

We left Washington on the 6th of June, unable to procure a pocket chronometer, or telescope of power sufficient to observe eclipses; but through your intercession, and by the kindness of the Chief of Hydrography, U. S. N., we were provided with two excellent box chronometers, No. 783 and No. 2,075, by Parkinson and Frodsham, and we received from the bureau two of Gambey's 8½-inch sextants.

Crossing the Alleghanies the stage capsized with us, and placed the chronometers in great danger, but the prudence of Mr. Bestor, who carried them in a basket on his arm, saved them from destruction. Their rates were changed very materially by the accident, but subsequent observations showed no other injury had been incurred.

Elaborate observations for time and rate were made at St. Louis; from which place, being tolerably well established in geographical position, it was intended to carry the longitude by chronometer, but, on reaching Fort Leavenworth, the chronometers were again found to have changed their rates materially, owing to the peculiarly unsteady and jarring motion of the steamer upon which we ascended.

The meridian of Fort Leavenworth, as determined by Mr. Nicollet, is therefore taken as that to which all the determinations of longitude as far as Bent's fort, by the chronometer, are referred, and any change which subsequent observations may make in the longitude of Fort Leavenworth, will be common to them. The travelling rates of chronometer 783 were, as the observations will show, very uniform, and longitudes deduced from it, compared with direct measurements of lunar distances made at various points, give satisfactory comparisons as far as camp 70, October 9th, on the Rio del Norte. At this point we left the wagons, thence crossing the mountains to the Gila river, some irregularity in the rates is discoverable, until we reach camp 83, October 26th, on the Gila river.

From that point (camp 83) to San Diego, on the Pacific, the rates were very uniform. Assuming Captain Belcher's determination of that point, $7h.\ 48m.\ 44s.$, west from Greenwich, and carrying my longitudes back, they compare well with the longitudes derived from the direct measurements of lunar distances made at different points on the route.

The longitude between the camps of October 9th and October 26th, are derived from direct measurements, and from lunar distances.

Of the latitudes.

The latitudes were determined by measuring with one of the Gambey sextants the double altitudes of stars near the meridian, and at all important points by observations on north and south stars as nearly as they could be obtained of equal altitudes. At these last points, where the observations are multiplied, their places may be depended upon to the nearest five seconds.

Of local time.

The local time was, in all cases, determined by altitudes of the heavenly bodies on different sides of the meridian.

The astronomical observations,   in number, were computed, in the first place, by myself and Mr. Bestor, and subsequently by Professor J. C. Hubbard. The results, as given in the appendix, are the final computations of Professor Hubbard, whose well-earned reputation as a computer entitles his work to entire confidence. These observations establish the geographical position of 52 points, extending from Fort Leavenworth to the Pacific, most of which lie in regions before undetermined.

Heights above the sea.

At Fort Leavenworth, through the liberality of the medical department, I was furnished with a syphon barometer, by Bunten, No. 515, the comparison of which, with the standard at Paris, is given in the subjoined note.

Observatoire.—Comparaison du baromètre à Syphon, No. 515 de Bunten, avec le baromètre de l'observatoire.
Paris, le.................................... 1843

Le baromètre No. 515, donne des hauteurs plus grandes que celles qui sont indiquées par le baromètre de l'observatoire, la différence est de 0.45 centièmes de millimètre.

Baromètre, { No. 515 .... 759.19
           { Observatoire 758.74

Différence........................ +0.45

Baromètre de.

	L'observatoire.		No. 515.	
12.9	758.20	+0.40	758.60	12.5
12.0	761.50	+0.50	762.00	11.8
11.3	762.14	+0.56	762.70	11.0
10.3	758.06	+0.44	758.50	10.0
8.7	753.80	+0.35	756.15	8.8
		2.25		
		+0.45		

Paris, le 3 Fevrier, 1843.

GORYOZ.

The discussion of the data upon which the heights indicated by the barometer have been founded, would, if pursued, occupy some space; for the present, it will be sufficient to say that the basis of comparison, as far as Santa Fé, is a series of observations made at Fort Leavenworth, with the same instrument, running through two years; and the height of the hospital at Fort Leavenworth above the sea assumed at 912 feet.

From Santa Fé, down the Del Norte, and thence west as far as camp 83, of October 26th, the basis of comparison is the series of observations, running through two months, at Santa Fe.

From the camp of October 26th, on the Gila, the basis of comparison is the mean of the observations made at San Diego, on the Pacific, near the level of the sea. The barometer was left on the Pacific, under the charge of Lieutenant Warner, topographical engineers; and the further observations made with it on that coast will afford, at some future time, data upon which to reconsider the results now given, particularly those in the last section. In the absence of corresponding observations, the object has been, to get a column of reference, progressing west, with the places observed at.

The formula used is that of Altman's. The heights deduced are marked on the map; but they should be considered, at best, but as near approximations to the truth.

The time of day at which the observations were made is not that which experience has shown to be best; but, the halts being beyond my control, I was compelled to yield to circumstances.

As far as Santa Fé, I received the assistance of Lieutenants J. W. Abert and G. W. Peck, of the corps of topographical engineers; both of whom had but too recently returned from an exploring expedition in less favored climates, and fell ill—the first at Bent's fort, and the last at Santa Fé.

From Santa Fé to the Pacific, I was aided by First Lieutenant W. H. Warner, of the topographical engineers, and Mr. Norman Bestor; all of whom deserve notice for the zeal and industry with which they performed their duty. Whilst with me, Lieutenant Peck made the topographical sketches; after he left, they were made by Lieutenant Warner.

I would here gladly avail myself of the opportunity of thanking Colonel Robert Campbell and Dr. Engelmann,* of St. Louis, for the disinterested and efficient aid they rendered us in St. Louis in our hurried preparations.for a long and tedious journey. The advice given us by Colonel Campbell, a gentleman of great experience in prairie life, was felt beneficially to the last of the journey.

The country between Fort Leavenworth and Santa Fé, traversed by the army of the west, may be divided into three great divisions, distinct in character, climate, and products, viz: from Fort Leavenworth to Pawnee fork, from Pawnee fork to Bent's Fort, and from Bent's Fort to Santa Fé.

The two first divisions have been so often traversed, that I have omitted my diary embracing them, contenting myself with a few general remarks; but the scientific, and especially astronomical observations referring to them, are as full as in regard to the other regions.

---

*An interesting account of the cacti observed on the route, furnished by Dr. Englemann, will be found in Appendix No. 2, continued.

For the information of detachments moving on that route, a table of distances has been prepared; which, with the map, (though on rather too small a scale for military purposes,) may enable movements to be made without other guides.

Between Fort Leavenworth and Pawnee fork, the country is a high, rolling prairie, traversed by many streams, the largest of which is the Kansas, or "Kaw;" and all but this river may be forded, except during freshets.

The beds of the streams are generally deeply indented in the soil, and their banks almost vertical, developing, where the streams make their incisions in the earth, strata of fossiliferous limestone, of various shades of brown, filled with the remains of crinoidea.

On a branch of the Wah-Karrussi, where the Oregon trail strikes it, a seam of bituminous coal crops out. This is worked by the Indians, one of whom we met driving an ox-cart loaded with coal, to Westport. For the most part, the soil is a sandy loam, covered with rich vegetable deposite; the whole based upon a stratum of clay and limestone.

Trees are to be seen only along the margins of the streams, and the general appearance of the country is that of vast, rolling fields, enclosed with colossal hedges. The growth along these streams, as they approach the eastern part of the section under consideration, consists of ash, burr oak, black walnut, chesnut oak, black oak, long-leaved willow, sycamore, buck-eye, American elm, pig-nut hickory, hack-berry, and sumach; towards the west, as you approach the 99th meridian of longitude, the growth along the streams becomes almost exclusively cotton-wood. Council Grove creek forms an exception to this, as most of the trees enumerated above flourish in its vicinity, and render it, for that reason, a well-known halting-place for caravans, for the repairs of wagons, and the acquisition of spare axles.

On the uplands the grass is luxuriant, and occasionally is found the wild tea, (amorpha canescens,) and pilot weed, (silphium lacinatum;) the low grounds abound in prickly rush, narrow leafed asclepias, white flowering indigo, flowering rush, spotted tulip, bedstraw, wild burgamot, spider wort, pink spider wort, pomme blanche, (psoralea esculenta,) scarlet malva, pilot weed, hazel, button bush, wild strawberry, cat-tail, and arrow rush.

As you draw near the meridian of Pawnee Fork, 99° west of Greenwich, the country changes, almost imperceptibly, until it merges into the arid, barren wastes described under that section. The transition is marked by the occurrence of cacti and other spinose plants, the first of which we saw in longitude 98°.

Near the same meridian the buffalo grass* was seen in small quantities, and, about noon, our party was cheered for the first time by the sight of a small "band" of buffalo, two of which we killed, at the expense of a couple of fine horses, which never recovered from the chase. Horses occasionally fed on grain become very weak feeding on grass alone, and should never in that condition be subjected to quick work. A violation of this precept

---

* For a description of this famous grass, see Appendix No. 2.

has cost many volunteers their horses, and entailed trouble without end on many inexperinced travellers "westward bound." The next day immense herds of the buffalo were seen.

We were now on ground (see map of July 10th) which is traversed by the nomadic tribes of Pawnees, Sioux, Osages, and occasionally the Comanches. Their range is seldom farther east than Council Grove. The country thence, to the western borders of Missouri, is in the hands of Indians owing allegiance to, and receiving stipends from the United States; they live in log-houses, cultivate the soil, rear cattle, and pursue some of the arts of peace. They form the connecting link between the savage of the plains and the white man of the States.

The latitude of our camp, a few thousand feet southeast of where the road crosses the Pawnee Fork, is 38° 10' 10"; and the longitude, by chronometer, is 98° 55' 22". The height above the sea, indicated approximately by the barometer, is 1,932 feet; the point, as will be seen on the map, is but a short distance from the junction of the Pawnee Fork and the Arkansas river.

The section of country embraced between this point and Bent's Fort is totally different in character from that just described, but the change is gradual, and may be anticipated from what has been said in referrence to the appearance of the country so far east as the 98th degree, or even the 97th meridian.

The position of our camp near Bent's Fort, determined by 29 altitudes of polaris and 35 circum-meridian altitudes of alpha aquilæ, is 38° 02' 53," and the longitude, by the measurement of distances between ☾ and the * alpha aquilæ and the * spica virginis, is 103° 01', agreeing within 34s. with the chronometric determination of the same point.—(See Appendix.)

Our route from Pawnee Fork to this point, was along the Arkansas river. The approximate height of Bent's Fort above the sea is 3,958 feet, and the height where we first struck the river, at the bend, is 1,658 feet, the distance between these two points being 311 miles, the fall of the river is about seven feet and four-tenths per mile. Its bed is of sand, sometimes of rounded pebbles of the primitive rock. It is seldom more than 150 yards wide, and, but for the quicksands, is every where fordable. The bottom land, a few feet above the level of the water, varies in width from half a mile to two miles, and is generally covered with good nutritious grass. Beyond this the ground rises by gentle slopes into a wilderness of sand hills on the south and into prairie on the north. There are one or two exceptions; for instance, at the great bend, the sand hills from the south impinge abruptly on the course of the river; at Pawnee rock, a long swell in the ground terminates in an abrupt hill of highly ferruginous sand stone; and ten miles above Choteau's island, the hills along the river are vertical, as if the river had cut a passage through them; and as you approach Bent's Fort, the hills generally roll in more boldly on the river, and the bottoms become narrower, and the grass more precious.

At these places the geological formation can be seen distinctly. On the lower part of the river it is a conglomerate of pebbles, sometimes shells cemented by lime and clay overlaying a stratum of soft sand stone, which, in turn, over lays a blue shale, and sometimes the richest description of marl.

Higher up the river, we find the same formation, but in addition argillaceous lime stone, containing amonites and other impressions of shells in great variety, and in more than one instance distinct impressions of oyster shells. The dip in both cases about 6°, and a little north of east.

The soil of the plains is a granitic sand, intermixed with the exuviæ of animals and vegetable matter, supporting a scanty vegetation. The eye wanders in vain over these immense wastes in search of trees. Not one is to be seen. The principal growth is the buffalo grass, cacti in endless variety, though diminutive, yucca angustifolia, (soap plant,) the Darlingtonia brachyloba, schrankia uncinata, prairie gourd (cucurbita aurantia,) and very rarely that wonderful plant, the Ipomea leptophylla, called by the hunter man root, from the similarity of its root in size and shape to the body of a man. It is esculent, and serves to sustain human life in some of the many vicissitudes of hunger and privation to which men who roam the prairies, as an occupation, are subjected.

July 24—Near the dry mouth of the Big Sandy creek, the yucca angustifolia, palmillo of the Spaniards, or soap plant, first made its appearance, and marked a new change in the soil and vegetation of the prairies.

The narrow strip which I have described as the bottom land of the Arkansas, varying from half a mile to two or three miles wide, contains a luxuriant growth of grasses, which, by the judicious selection and distribution of the camps, sustained all the animals of the army of the west whilst on the river. The only tree of any magnitude found on its course is the cotton-wood, (populus canadensis,) and it frequently happens that not one of these is seen in a whole day's journey, and the buffalo dung and wild sage constitute the only fuel to be procured. About 35 miles before reaching Bent's Fort is found what is called the "big timber." Here the valley of the river widens, and the banks on either side fall towards it in gentle slopes. The "big timber" is a thinly scattered growth of large cotton woods not more than three quarters of a mile wide, and three or four miles long. It is here the Chyennes, Arapahoes, and the Kioways sometimes winter, to avail themselves of the scanty supply of wood for fuel, and to let their animals browse on the twigs and bark of the cotton-wood. The buffaloes are sometimes driven by the severity of the winter, which is here intense for the latitude, to the same place to feed upon the cotton-wood. To this point, which has been indicated to the government as a suitable one for a military post, Mr. Bent thinks of moving his establishment.

In addition to the grasses and cotton-wood mentioned, we find in the bottoms wild plum, wild cherry, willow, (salix longifolia,) summer grape, (vitis æstivalis,) cat-tail, (typha latifolia,) scouring rush, (equisetum hyemale,) a powerful diuretic upon horses, commelina angustifolia, Mexican poppy, (argemone Mexicana,) monarda fistulosa, coreopsis tinctoria, psoralea esculenta, cassia chamæcrista, several varieties of solidego, œnothera, and helianthus; among which was the common sunflower.

The animals of this section of the country are the buffalo, deer, antelope, elk, marmot, wolf, agama cornuta, &c.; but, for a more specific knowledge of the natural history and herbarium of the region from Fort Leavenworth to Bent's Fort, reference is made to the interesting notes of one of my assistants, Lieutenant Abert, in appendix No. 6.

Except the buffalo, game is very scarce, and cannot be depended upon to support a party of men, however small their number. The buffalo, where they range, may be relied upon to support a column of many thousand men; but their range is very uncertain. This year it was westward, between the 98th degree and the 101st meridian of longitude.

For an account of the country from Bent's Fort to the Pacific, I submit my notes, in which I have set down what passed under my own observation.

The accompanying map is also limited chiefly to the route followed, based upon the data exhibited in the appendices, and numbered from 3 to 5.

For a more specific knowledge of the plants peculiar to the country traversed than will be found in the journal, I refer to the catalogue prepared by that eminent botanist, Dr. John Torrey, to whom all the plants and drawings were submitted—forming appendix No. 2. The specimens brought home to aid me in elucidating the geology of the route, were submitted to Professor John Frazer, of the Pennsylvania University, to whose learning and knowledge I am under great obligation.

The military force under Colonel Kearny, destined for the conquest of New Mexico and the countries beyond, consisted of two batteries of artillery, (6-pounders,) under the command of Major Clark, three squadrons of the first dragoons, under Major Sumner, the first regiment of Missouri cavalry, under Colonel Doniphan, and two companies of infantry, under Captain Agney. This force was detached in different columns from Fort Leavenworth, and were concentrated with admirable order and precision on the 1st of August, at a camp nine miles below Bent's Fort.

And here I would take occasion to speak of the excellent understanding which prevailed throughout between regulars and volunteers, and the cheerfulness with which they came to each others assistance whenever the privations and hardships of the march called for the interchange of kindly offices among them. The volunteers, though but recently accustomed to the ease and comforts of smiling homes, bore up against fatigue, hunger, and the vicissitudes of a long and tedious march, through unexplored regions, with a zeal, courage, and devotion that would have graced time-worn veterans, and reflect the highest credit on their conduct as soldiers. There was a noble emulation in the conduct of regulars and volunteers, which, in no small degree, benefitted the service; while, at the same time, it promoted that cordiality in their interests which will make their future meetings, in the more peaceful walks of life, a gladsome event to both.

NOTES.

August 2, 1846.—I looked in the direction of Bent's Fort, and saw a huge United States flag flowing to the breeze, and straining every fibre of an ash pole planted over the centre of a gate. The mystery was soon revealed by a column of dust to the east, advancing with about the velocity of a fast walking horse—it was "the Army of the West." I ordered my horses to be hitched up, and, as the column passed, took my place with the staff.

A little below the fort, the river was forded without difficulty, being paved with well attritioned pebbles of the primitive rock, and not more than knee deep.

We advanced five miles along the river, where its bed slides over a black carbonaceous shale, which has been mistaken for coal, and induced some persons to dig for it.

Here we turned to the left, and pursued our course over an arid elevated plain for twenty miles, without water. When we reached the Timpas, we found the water in puddles, and the grass bad.

Colonel Doniphan was ordered to pursue the Arkansas to near the mouth of the Timpas, and rejoin the army by following the bed of that stream.

Near where we left the Arkansas, we found on the side of the slope several singular demi-spheroids, about the size of an umbrella, coated with carbonate of lime, in pyramidal crystals, which, at a distance, resembled the bubbles of a huge boiling caldron.

Along the Arkansas the principal growth consists of very coarse grass, and a few cotton-woods, willows, and euphorbia marginata. The plains are covered with very short grass, sesleria dactyloides, now burnt to cinder; artemisia, in abundance; Fremontia vermicularis; yucca angustifolia, palmillo, of the Spaniards; verbena; eurotia lanata, and a few menzelia nuda.

The only animals seen were one black-tailed rabbit and an antelope; both of which were killed.

Our march was 26 miles, that of the army 37; the last 20 miles without water.

The artillery arrived about 11, p. m.; both men and horses were parched with thirst. The teamsters, who had to encounter the dust, suffered very much. When water was near, they sprang from their seats and ran for it like mad men. Two horses sank under this day's march.

Our ascent was considerable to-day. The height, indicated by the barometer, being 4,523 feet above the level of the sea.

August 3.—We ascended the Timpas six and three-quarter miles, and halted for the day near running water; the grass was all burned dry, and not a green sprig to be seen. Three buttes were passed of singular appearance; some idea of which will be given by the sketch. They were composed of lime-stone, and were garnished at their bases with nodules of carbonate of lime, like those described yesterday. A part of our road was on the dry bed of a river, paved with argillaceous lime-stone, containing, now and then, the impression of oyster shells very distinctly. The valley in which we are now encamped presents the appearance of a crater, being surrounded with buttes capped with stunted cedar, (juniperus Virginianus.) The stratification, however, appears regular, and to correspond on different sides of the valley.

The growth of to-day was similar to that found on the plains yesterday, to which may be added an evergreen and a magnificent cactus three feet high, with round limbs shaped like a rope, three and a half inches in diameter, branching at right angles. It is said the Mexicans make hedges of it.

Colonel Doniphan's regiment passed our camp about 4, p. m.

The water was in pools, charged with vegetable matter and salt.

The formation of the adjacent hills was distinct; first, a stratum of lime-stone, ten feet thick, then hard sand-stone, with amonites and a variety of other shells, &c., overlaying blue marl. From the sides of the hills protruded geodes, with crystallized lime-stone, and the ground was everywhere strewed with detached pieces of ferruginous sand-stone. On these hills we found cedar growing, very stunted; Missouri flax; several varieties of wild currants; a very stunted growth of plums; moss and cacti in great variety, but diminutive.

The latitude of this camp, by nine observations on Polaris, out of the meridian, is 37° 44' 56".

The longitude derived from the chronometer, by an estimate of the local time derived from eight measurements of the double altitude of arcturus on the west, and seven of alpha aquilæ in the east, is 6h. 54m. 06.7s.

The barometer reading indicates a height above the sea of 4,761 feet.

August 4.—The road wound through the valley of the Timpas. The soil, being impregnated with lime, rendered the dust, which rose in dense columns, distressing.

Dwarfed cedar skirted the road on each side. The strata of hills on either side of the valley were the same as described yesterday; but the ferruginous nodules and blocks of sand-stone were more frequent.

Thirteen miles' march brought us to the crossing of the Timpas. The only water we found there was in a hole 40 feet in diameter, into which the men rushed with great eagerness, disturbing the vegetable deposit formed on its surface, and thereby rendering it unfit for use. Nine miles farther on we came to "the hole in the rock"—a large hole filled with stagnant, though drinkable, water.

We saw at times, during the day, a few antelopes, rabbits, wild horses, two jack daws, (magpie,) meadow larks, king birds, and bob o'lincolns.

The pasture was so bad that Colonel Kearny determined to march to the "hole in the prairie," the neighborhood of which, though said to be destitute of water, affords some dry grass.

We passed a dead horse belonging to the infantry, black, with crows, and a wolf in their midst, quietly feeding on the carcase. This gave us unpleasant forebodings for our noble, but now attenuated, horses.

We reached the "hole in the prairie" at 10, p. m., the distance being 14½ miles, and found grass, as we expected: we were agreeably surprised to find water also. The night was delicious, and all slept in the open air. The infantry were encamped here.

The total distance to-day was 36 miles. The horses were now falling away in an alarming manner, but the mules seem to require the stimulus of distention, and nothing else: this the dry grass affords.

On the march, about sunset, the Wattahyah (twin hills) rose suddenly to view, south 75° west; and then Pike's peak, 20 or 30 degrees farther to north. At the same time the dim outline of the great spine of the Rocky mountain chain began to show itself. We were now crossing the dividing line between the waters of the Timpas and those of the Purgatory, or Los Animos, of the Spaniards.

The vegetation was the same as that of yesterday, as far as we could judge from its burned and parched condition; to which may be added a plant described by Dr. Torrey, as physalis perbalis, and one eriogonum tomentosum.

Height of this camp 5,560 feet.

August 5.—To-day we descended eleven and a half miles, and reached the valley of the Purgatory, called, by the mountain men, Picatoire, a corruption of Purgatoire, a swift-running stream, a few yards in width, but no grass of any amount at the crossing. The blighted trunks of large cotton-wood and locust trees were seen for many miles along its course, but the cause of decay was not apparent.

The growth of the bottom, which is very narrow, was black locust, the everlasting cotton-wood, willow, wild currants, hops, plum and grape, artemisia, clematis Virginiana, salix, in many varieties; and a species of angelica, but no fruit was on the bushes. Beyond this stream five and a half miles, we encamped on the bed of a tributary to the Purgatory, which comes down from the north side of the Raton, or Mouse, which is the name given to a chain of ragged looking mountains that strikes the course of the Purgatory nearly at right angles, and separates the waters of the Arkansas from those of the Canadian. The banks of the Purgatory, where this stream debouches, begin to assume something of a mountain aspect, different from scenery in the States. The hills are bare of vegetation, except a few stunted cedars; and the valley is said to be, occasionally, the resort of grizzly bear, turkeys, deer, antelope, &c.

Passing the rear wagons of the infantry, we found their horses almost worn out, and the train followed by wolves.

Captain Cook, of the 1st dragoons, was sent ahead the day before yesterday, to sound Armijo. Mr. Liffendorfer, a trader, married to a Santa Fé lady, was sent in the direction of Taos, with two Pueblo Indians, to feel the pulse of the Pueblos and the Mexican people, and, probably, to buy wheat if any could be purchased, and to distribute the proclamations of the colonel commanding.

Yesterday Wm. Bent, and six others, forming a spy-guard, were sent forward to reconnoitre the mountain passes. In this company was Mr. F. P. Blair, jr., who had been in this country some months, for the benefit of his health.

Measured 13 double altitudes of polaris, in the north, for latitude, and 7 of alpha aquilæ, in the east, for local time, and the resulting latitude is $37°\ 12'\ 10''$, and longitude $6h.\ 56m.\ 48s$. The height indicated by the barometer is 5,896 feet.

August 6.—Colonel Kearny left Colonel Doniphan's regiment and Major Clarke's artillery at our old camp-ground of last night, and scattered Sumner's dragoons three or four miles up the creek, to pass the day in renovating the animals by nips at the little bunches of grass spread at intervals in the valley. This being done, we commenced the ascent of the Raton, and, after marching 17 miles, halted with the infantry and general staff, within a half-mile of the summit of the pass. Strong parties were sent forward to repair the road, which winds through a picturesque valley, with the Raton towering to the left. Pine trees (pinus rigida) here obtain a respectable size, and lined the valley through the whole day's march. A few oaks, (quercus olivaformis,) big enough for axles, were found near the halting-place of to-night. When we first left the camp this morning, we saw several clumps of the pinon, (pinus monophyllus.) It bears a resinous nut, eaten by Mexicans and Indians. We found also the lamita in great abundance. It resembles the wild currant, and is, probably, one of its varieties; grows to the height of several feet, and bears a red berry, which is gathered, dried, pounded, and then mixed with sugar and water, making a very pleasant drink, resembling currant cordial. We were unfortunate in not being able to get either the fruit or flower. Neither this plant, the pinon, nor any of the plum trees, nor grape vines, had any fruit on them; which is attributable to the excessive drought. The stream, which was last year a rushing torrent, is this year dry, and in pools.

The view from our camp is inexpressibly beautiful, and reminds persons of the landscapes of Palestine. Without attempting a description, I refer to the sketch.

The rocks of the mountain were chiefly a light sandstone—in strata, not far from horizontal; and the road was covered with many fragments of volcanic rocks, of purplish brown color, porous, and melting over a slow fire.

The road is well located. The general appearance is something like the pass at the summit of the Boston and Albany railroad, but the scenery bolder, and less adorned with vegetation.

An express returned from the spy-guard, which reported all clear in front. Captain Cook and Mr. Liffendorfer have only reached the Canadian river. It was reported to me that, at Captain Sumner's camp, about 7 miles above where we encamped last night, and 12 miles from the summit, an immense field of coal crops out; the seam being 30 feet deep. To-night our animals were refreshed with good grass and water.

Nine observations on polaris give, for the latitude of the place, 37° 00' 21".

Seven on arcturus, in the west, and 7 on alpha aquilæ, in the east, give the chronometric longitude $6h. 57m. 01.35s.$

Height above the sea, 7,169 feet.

August 7, camp 36.—We recommenced the ascent of the Raton, which we reached with ease, with our wagons, in about two miles. The height of this point above the sea, as indicated by the barometer, is 7,500 feet. From the summit we had a beautiful view of Pike's peak, the Wattahyah, and the chain of mountains running south from the Wattahyah. Several large white masses were discernible near the summits of the range, which we at first took for snow, but which, on examination with the telescope, were found to consist of white limestone, or granular quartz, of which we afterwards saw so much in this country. As we drew near, the view was no less imposing. To the east rose the Raton, which appeared still as high as from the camp, 1,500 feet below. On the top of the Raton the geological formation is very singular, presenting the appearance of a succession of castles. As a day would be required to visit it, I was obliged to forego that pleasure, and examine it merely with the glass. The mountain appears to be formed chiefly of sandstone, disposed in strata of various shades of color, dipping gently to the east, until you reach near the summit, where the castellated appearance commences, the sides become perpendicular, and the seams vertical. The valley is strewed with pebbles and fragments of trap rock, and the fusible rock described yesterday, cellular lava, and some pumice.

For two days our way was strewed with flowers; exhilarated by the ascent, the green foliage of the trees in striking contrast with the deserts we had left behind, they were the most agreeable days of the journey. Among the flowers and shrubbery was the campanula rotundifolia, (hare bell,) sida coccinea, galium triflorum, the snowberry, eriogonum, geranium Frémontii, clematis virpuenna, ranunculus aquatilis, euphorbia marginata, linum perenne, malva pedata, lippia cuneifolia, and many pretty varieties of convolvulus.

There is said to be a lake, about ten miles to the east of the summit, where immense hordes of deer, antelope, and buffalo congregate, but may be doubted.

The descent is much more rapid than the ascent, and, for the first few miles, through a valley of good burned grass and stagnant water, containing many beautiful flowers. But frequently you come to a place where the stream (a branch of the Canadian) has worked itself through the mountains, and the road has to ascend and then descend a sharp spur. Here the difficulties commence; and the road, for three or four miles, is just passable for a wagon; many of the train were broken in the passage. A few thousand dollars judiciously expended here, would be an immense saving to the government if the Santa Fé country is to be permanently occupied, and Bent's Fort road adopted. A few miles from the summit we reached a wide valley where the mountains open out, and the inhospitable looking hills recede to a respectable distance to the right and left. Sixteen miles from camp 36 brought us to the main branch of the Canadian, a slow running stream, discharging a volume of water the thickness of a man's waist. We found here Bent's camp. I dismounted under the shade of a cotton-wood, near an ant-hill, and saw something black which had been thrown out by the busy little insects; and, on examination, found it to be bituminous coal, lumps of which were afterwards found thickly scattered over the plain. After crossing the river, and proceeding about a mile and a quarter, I found the party from which I had become separated encamped on the river, with a plentiful supply of grass, wood, and water; and here we saw, for the first time, a few sprigs of the famous grama, Atheropogon oligostaclyum.

The growth on to-day's march was piñon in small quantities, scrub oak, scrub pine, a few lamita bushes, and, on the Canadian, a few cotton-wood trees; except at the camp, there was little or no grass. The evening threatened rain, but the clouds passed away, and we had a good night for observations. We have had no rain since we left Cow creeks, thirty days ago.

We are now in what may be called the paradise of that part of the country between Bent's Fort and San Miguel; and yet he who leaves the edge of the Canadian or its tributaries must make a good day's march to find wood, water, or grass.

There may be mineral wealth in these mountains, but its discovery must be left to some explorer not attached to the staff of an army making forced marches into an enemy's country.

To-day commenced our half-rations of bread; though not suffering for meat, we are anxious to seize on Santa Fé and its stock of provisions as soon as possible.

August 8.—We remained in camp all day to allow Colonel Doniphan's regiment and the artillery to come up. During the day, we had gusts of wind, and clouds discharging rain to the west. Captain Sumner drilled his three squadrons of dragoons, and made quite an imposing show.

The latitude of the camp is 36° 47' 34"; the longitude 6h. 56m. 59.7s.

On the 7th, I measured 8 altitudes of arcturus in the west, and 8 of alpha aquilæ in the east; and, on the 8th, 10 of arcturus and 8 of alpha aquilæ—showing the rate of chronometer 783 to be losing 3s. per day.

The height determined approximately, is 6,112 feet above the sea.

August 9.—We broke up camp at 2½ o'clock, and marched with the colonel's staff and the first dragoons 10½ miles, and encamped under the mountains on the western side of the Canadian, on the banks of a small stream, a tributary of the Canadian. The grass was short, but good; the water in small quantities, and in puddles. Here we found a trap-dyke—course north 83 west—which shows itself also on the Canadian, about four miles distant in the same course.

At the distance of six miles from last night's camp, the road forks—one fork running near the mountains to the west, but nearly parallel to the old road, and never distant more than four miles, and almost all the time in sight of it. The army was divided—the artillery, infantry, and wagon train ordered to take the lower, and the Missouri volunteers and first dragoons the upper road. The valley here opens out into an extensive plain, slightly rolling, flanked on each side by ranges of perpendicular hills covered with stunted cedar and the piñon. In this extensive valley or plain may be traced by the eye, from any of the neighboring heights, the valleys of the Canadian and its tributaries, the Vermejo, the Poni, the Little Cimarron, the Rayada, and the Ocaté. We saw troops of antelopes, horses, deer, &c.; also cacti in great abundance, and in every variety; also a plant which Dr. De Camp pointed out as being highly balsamic; and having collected quantities of it during his campaign to the Rocky mountains, and tested its efficacy as a substitute for balsam cop.

To-night we observed a great number of insects, the first remarked since leaving the Arkansas. Birds were equally rare, with the exception of the cow-bunting, which has been seen in great numbers on the whole route, and in a state so tame as to often alight on our horses. The horned frog (agama cornuta) also abounds here, as well as on the route westward from Chouteau's island.

August 10.—Colonel Kearny was dissatisfied with the upper road, and determined to strike for the old road. We did so after reaching the Vermejo, $9\frac{1}{2}$ miles in a diagonal line, and rejoined it at the crossing of the Little Cimarron, where we found the infantry encamped—total distance $20\frac{1}{2}$ miles. The grass good, and water plenty, though not flowing. Another trap-dyke, parallel nearly to the last, and three mile distant, presented its wall-like front. It was strewed with fragments of fernigenous sand-stone and crystalized carbonate of lime.

A Mexican came into camp from Bent's Fort, and reported Lieutenant Abert much better. Colonel Kearny allowed him to pass to Taos, which place (60 miles distant by a bridle path) he expected to reach to-night. The colonel sent by him copies of his proclamation.

Five Mexicans were captured by Bent's spy company; they were sent out to reconnoitre our forces, with orders to detain all persons passing *out* of New Mexico. They were mounted on diminutive asses, and presented a ludicrous contrast by side of the big men and horses of the first dragoons. Fitzpatrick, our guide, who seldom laughs, became almost convulsed whenever he turned his well practised eye in their direction.

Mr. Towle, an American citizen, came to head-quarters at the Vermejo, and reported himself just escaped from Taos. He brought the intelligence that, yesterday, the proclamation of Governor Armijo reached there, calling the citizens to arms, and placing the whole country under martial law; that Armijo has assembled all the Pueblo Indians, numbering about 2,000, and all the citizens capable of bearing arms; that 300 Mexican dragoons arrived in Santa Fé the day Armijo's proclamation was issued, and that 1,200 more were hourly expected; that the Mexicans to a man were anxious for a fight, but that half the Pueblo Indians were indifferent on the subject, but would be made to fight.

A succession of thunder storms passed yesterday to the north and west, but did not reach us. The ground indicates recent rain, as also does the grass, which looks as in the spring, just sprouting. The hills to the left, as near as I can judge, the same as in the Raton, were of different colored sand stone, regularly stratified, and dipping gently to the east, topped by a mural precipice of green stone. The growth on the mountains, piñon and cedar. On the plains, which are covered with scoriæ, scarcely a tree is to be seen.

We encamped on the little Cimarron, and observed at night for latitude and time. 7 altitudes of polaris give for the latitude 36° 27′ 50″; 7 on arcturus in the west, and the same number on alpha aquilæ in the east give the meridian by chronomoter differences 6h. 58m. 39s. Approximate height 6,027 feet.

The plants of to-day, in addition to many of plants heretofore mentioned, were the Erysinum Arkansanum, lippa cuneifolia, myosotis glomerata, so frequently found on the plains, lytherus linearis, hypercium ellipticium, several verbenas, and several new varieties of oxybaphus, wild sage, and on the streams a few cottonwood and willows.

August 11.—We made a long march to-day with the advanced guard and the 1st dragoons, to the Ocaté, 31⅔ miles. The road approaches the Ocaté, at the foot of a high bluff to the north, where the river runs through a cañon, making it inaccessible to animals. We ascend the river for four or five miles, to where the road crosses; there we left the road, and at that point, the river being dry, continued to ascend it a mile, and found good grass, and, occasionally, running water. The scenery to-day was very pretty, sometimes approaching to the grand; the road passed through a succession of valleys, and crossed numerous "divides" of the Rayada and Ocaté. The Rayada is a limpid running stream, ten miles from the little Cimarron, the first of the kind noted, though we have been traversing the bases of many mountains for days past. The pasture, however, is not good. At points two and four miles farther, at the foot of the mountains, there are springs and good grass. At the last point we overtook the infantry, where they halted. About five miles before reaching the Ocaté, the road descends into a valley, overhung by confused and rugged cliffs, which give promise of grass and water, but, on going down, we found that this beautiful valley had no outlet, but terminated in a salt lake. The lake is now dry, and its bed is white with a thin saline encrustation. Here the road is indistinct, and takes a sudden turn to the left.

At this moment we discovered coming towards us, at full speed, Bent's spy-guard. All thought they had met the enemy; I was ordered to ride forward to meet them, followed by Mr. Fitzpatrick and two dragoons. It proved to be a false alarm; they had missed their road, and were galloping back to regain it.

The hills are composed principally of basalt and a porous volcanic stone, very hard, with metallic fracture and lustre, traversed by dykes of trap. The lava is underlayed by sand stone. From the uniform height of these hills, one would think they originally formed the table land, and that the valleys had been formed by some denuding process, and their limits determined by the alternate existence or non-existence of the hard crust of volcanic rocks.

Matters are now becoming very interesting. Six or eight Mexicans were captured last night, and on their persons was found the proclamation of the Prefect of Toas, based upon that of Armijo, calling the citizens to arms, to repel the " Americans, who were coming to invade their soil and destroy their *property and liberties;*" ordering an enrolment of all citizens over 15 and under 50. It is decidedly less bombastic than any Mexican paper I have yet seen. Colonel Kearny assembled these prisoners, altogether some ten or twelve, made a speech to them, and ordered that, when the rear guard of the army should have passed, they should be released. These men were not deficient in form or stature; their faces expressed good nature, bordering on idiocy ; they were mounted on little donkies and jennies, guided by clubs instead of bridles.

Two more Mexicans, of a better class, were captured to-night, or rather they came into camp. Their story was, that they had come out by order of the alcalde of the Moro town to look out for their standing enemies, the Eutaws, who were reported in the neighborhood. That they had heard of our advance some time since, but believed us to be at the Rayada, 22 miles back; but seeing our wagons, and having faith in the Americanos, they rode without hesitation into our camp. When they said they had faith in us, the colonel ordered them to shake hands with him. They were ordered to be detained for a day or two, for it was quite evident to all they were spies, who had come too suddenly into the little ravine in which we were encamped.

They appeared well pleased, and one of them, after proceeding a few steps with the guard, turned back and presented the colonel with a fresh cream cheese.

The grass was interspersed with a great variety of new and beautiful flowers—the œnothera; Stanley pinnatifida; anemone Pennsylvania; eriogonum tomentosum; erysinum, Arkansanum, &c. &c. The hills were sparsely covered with cedar and piñon. Antelopes and horned frogs in abundance, but no other animals were seen.

Height of this camp 6,946 feet.

August 12.—The elder Mexican was discharged, giving him two proclamations; one for the alcalde, another for the people of his town. A message was sent to the alcalde to meet us at the crossing of the Moro, with several of his chief men. The other Mexican was retained as a guide. About 12 o'clock the advance was sounded, and the colonel, with Sumner's command, marched 20 miles, and halted in a beautiful valley of fine grass and pools of cool water, where the wild liquorice (glycyrrhiza lepidota) grew plentifully. The stream, where flowing, is a tributary of the Moro.

From the drift wood, &c., found in its wide, well-grassed bed, I infer it is subject to great freshets. In crossing from the Ocaté to the valley of the Moro, the mountains become more rolling; and as we approached the Moro, the valley opened out, and the whole country became more tame in its appearance.

Ten miles up the Moro is the Moro town, containing, we were informed, 200 houses.

It is off the lower road; but a tolerable wagon road leads to the village from our camp of last night.

The plains were strewed with fragments of brick-dust colored lava, scoriæ and slag; the hills, to the left, capped with white granular quartz. The plains are almost destitute of vegetation; the hills bear a stunted growth of piñon and red cedar. Rains have fallen here recently, and the grass in the bottoms is good. The grama is now found constantly. We saw to-day some ground squirrels, with stripes on their sides: in their habits, resembling the common prairie dog. A flight of birds was seen to the south, but too distant to distinguish. We were attracted to the left by an object which was supposed to be an Indian, but, on coming up to it, it was discovered to be a sand-stone block standing on end and topped by another shorter block. A mountain man, versed in these signs, said it was in commemoration of a talk and friendly smoke between some two or three tribes of Indians.

The latitude of the place, from 7 observations on polaris, is 35° 54' 21", and the longitude, deduced from the local time by 7 altitudes of alpha lyræ in the west, and 11 of ☉ in the east, was 6h. 59m. 49s.

The height above the sea 6,670 feet.

August 13.—At 12 o'clock, as the rear column came in sight, the call of "boots and saddles" was sounded, and in 20 minutes we were off. We had not advanced more than one mile when Bent, of the spy-guard, came up with four prisoners. They represented themselves to be an ensign and three privates of the Mexican army, sent forward to reconnoitre and ascertain our force. They said 600 men were at the Vegas to give us battle. They told many different stories; and finally delivered up a paper, being an order from a Captain Gonzales to the ensign, to go forward on the Bent's Fort road to ascertain our position and numbers. They were corss-examined by the colonel, and detained.

As soon as we commenced the descent into the valley of the Moro creek, some one reported a company of Mexicans at the crossing; Colonel Kearny ordered me to go forward with twelve of the Laclède rangers, and reconnoitre the party, and if they attempted to run, to pursue and capture as many as we could. As Lieutenant Elliot and myself approached this company, they appeared to be motionless, and on coming up, we found them to consist of nothing but the pine stakes of a corrál. The dragoons were sadly disappointed; they evidently expected either a fight or a chase. Six miles brought us to the first settlement we had yet seen in 775 miles. The first object I saw was a pretty Mexican woman, with clean white stockings, who very cordially shook hands with us and asked for tobacco. In the next house lived Mr. Boney, an American, who has been some time in this country, and is the owner of a large number of horses and cattle, which he manages to keep in defiance of wolves, Indians, and Mexicans. He is a perfect specimen of a generous open-hearted adventurer, and in appearance what, I have pictured to myself, Daniel Boone, of Kentucky, must have been in his day. He drove his herd of cattle into camp and picked out the largest and fattest, which he presented to the army.

Two miles below, at the junction of the Moro and Sapillo, is another American, Mr. Wells, of North Carolina; he has been here but six months, and barring his broad-brimmed sombrero, might have been taken for a sergeant of dragoons, with his blue pantaloons with broad gold-colored stripes on the sides, and his jacket trimmed with lace. I bought butter from him at four bits the pound.

We halted at the Sapillo, distance nine and a half miles from our last night's encampment, in a tremendous shower of rain; the grass was indifferent, being clipped short by the cattle from the rancheria. Wood and water plenty.

At this place a Mr. Spry came into camp, on foot, and with scarcely any clothing. He had escaped from Santa Fé on the night previous, at Mr. H——'s request, to inform Colonel Kearny that Armijo's forces were assembling; that he might expect vigorous resistance, and that a place called the Cañon, 15 miles from Santa Fé, was being fortified; and to advise the Colonel to go round it.

The cañon is a narrow defile, easily defended, and of which we have heard a great deal. War now seems "inevitable;" and the advantages of ground and numbers will, no doubt, enable the Mexicans to make the fight interesting. The grass was miserable, and the camp ground inundated by the shower of to-day,—which was quite a rarity.

Barometric height 6,395 feet.

August 14.—The order of march to-day was that which could easily be converted into the order of battle. After proceeding a few miles we met a queer cavalcade, which we supposed at first to be the looked for alcalde from Moro town, but it proved to be a messenger from Armijo; a lieutenant, accompanied by a sergeant and two privates, of Mexican lancers. The men were good looking enough, and evidently dressed in their best bib and tucker. The creases in their pantaloons were quite distinct, but their horses were mean in the extreme, and the contempt with which our dragoons were filled was quite apparent. The messenger was the bearer of a letter from Armijo. It was a sensible, straightforward missive, and if written by an American or Englishman, would have meant this: "You have notified me that you intend to take possession of the country I govern. The people of the country have risen, en masse, in my defence. If you take the country, it will be because you prove the strongest in battle. I suggest to you to stop at the Sapillo, and I will march to the Vegas. We will meet and negotiate on the plains between them."

The artillery were detained some time in passing the Sapillo. This kept us exposed to the sun on the plains for four hours, but it gave the colonel time to reflect on the message with which he should dismiss the lancers; as there was some apprehension that Captain Cook was detained, their discharge became matter for reflection. Sixteen miles brought us in sight of the Vegas, a village on the stream of the same name.

A halt was made at this point, and the colonel called up the lieutenant and lancers and said to them, "The road to Santa Fé is now as free to you as to myself. Say to General Armijo, I shall soon meet him, and I hope it will be as friends."

At parting, the lieutenant embraced the colonel, Captain Turner, and myself, who happened to be standing near.

The country to-day was rolling, almost mountainous, and covered in places with scoriæ. Grass began to show itself, and was interspersed with malva pedata, lippia cunefolia, and several new species of geraniacæ, bartonia, and convolvulus. The soil was good enough apparently, but vegetation was stunted from the want of rain. As we emerged from the hills into the valley of the Vegas, our eyes were greeted for the first time with waving corn. The stream was flooded, and the little drains by which the fields were irrigated, full to the brim. The dry soil seemed to drink it in with the avidity of our thirsty horses. The village, at a short distance, looked like an extensive brick-kiln. On approaching, its outline presented a square with some arrangements for defence. Into this square the inhabitants are sometimes compelled to retreat, with all their stock, to avoid the attacks of the Eutaws and Navahoes, who pounce upon them and carry off their women, children, and cattle. Only a few days since, they made a descent on the town and carried off 120 sheep and other stock. As Captain Cook passed through the town some ten days' since, a murder had just been committed on these helpless people. Our camp extended for a mile down the valley; on one side was the stream, on the other the cornfields, with no fence or hedge interposing. What a tantalizing prospect for our hungry and jaded nags; the water was free, but a chain of sentinels was posted to protect the corn, and strict orders given that it should not be disturbed.

Captain Turner was sent to the village to inform the alcalde that the colonel wished to see him and the head men of the town. In a short time down came the alcalde and two captains of militia, with numerous servants, prancing and careering their little nags into camp.

Observations.—9 altitudes of polaris in the north, 7 of arcturus in the east, and 7 of alpha aquilæ in the east.

Latitude 35° 35′ 05″.
Longitude 7h. 00m. 46s.
Height, by the barometer, 6,418 feet.

August 15.—12 o'clock last night information was received that

600 men had collected at the pass which debouches into the Vegas, two miles distant, and were to oppose our march. In the morning, orders were given to prepare to meet the enemy. At 7, the army moved, and just as we made the road leading through the town, Major Swords, of the quartermaster's department, Lieutenant Gilmer, of the engineers, and Captain Weightman joined us, from Fort Leavenworth, and presented Colonel Kearny with his commission as brigadier general in the army of the United States. They had heard we were to have a battle, and rode sixty miles during the night to be in it.

At eight, precisely, the general was in the public square, where he was met by the alcalde and people; many of whom were mounted, for these people seem to live on horseback.

The general pointed to the top of one of their houses, which are built of one story, and suggested to the alcalde that if he would go to that place he and his staff would follow, and from that point, where all could hear and see, he would speak to them; which he did, as follows:

"Mr. Alcalde and people of New Mexico: I have come amongst you by the orders of my government, to take possession of your country, and extend over it the laws of the United States. We consider it, and have done so for some time, a part of the territory of the United States. We come amongst you as friends—not as enemies; as protectors—not as conquerors. We come among you for your benefit—not for your injury.

"Henceforth I absolve you from all allegiance to the Mexican government, and from all obedience to General Armijo. He is no longer your governor; [great sensation.] I am your governor. I shall not expect you to take up arms and follow me, to fight your own people who may oppose me; but I now tell you, that those who remain peaceably at home, attending to their crops and their herds, shall be protected by me in their property, their persons, and their religion; and not a pepper, nor an onion, shall be disturbed or taken by my troops without pay, or by the consent of the owner. But listen! he who promises to be quiet, and is found in arms against me, I will hang.

"From the Mexican government you have never received protection. The Apaches and the Navajhoes come down from the mountains and carry off your sheep, and even your women, whenever they please. My government will correct all this. It will keep off the Indians, protect you in your persons and property; and, I repeat again, will protect you in your religion. I know you are all great Catholics; that some of your priests have told you all sorts of stories—that we should ill-treat your women, and brand them on the cheek as you do your mules on the hip. It is all false. My government respects your religion as much as the Protestant religion, and allows each man to worship his Creator as his heart tells him is best. Its laws protect the Catholic as well as the Protestant; the weak as well as the strong; the poor as well as the rich. I am not a Catholic myself—I was not brought up in that faith; but at least one-third of my army are Catholics, and I respect a good Catholic as much as a good Protestant.

"There goes my army—you see but a small portion of it; there are many more behind—resistance is useless.

"Mr. alcalde, and you two captains of militia, the laws of my country require that all men who hold office under it shall take the oath of allegiance. I do not wish for the present, until affairs become more settled, to disturb your form of government. If you are prepared to take oaths of allegiance, I shall continue you in office and support your authority."

This was a bitter pill; but it was swallowed by the discontented captain, with downcast eyes. The general remarked to him, in hearing of all the people: "Captain, look me in the face while you repeat the oath of office." The hint was understood; the oath taken, and the alcalde and the two captains pronounced to be continued in office. The citizens were enjoined to obey the alcalde, &c. &c. The people grinned, and exchanged looks of satisfaction; but seemed not to have the boldness to express what they evidently felt—that their burdens, if not relieved, were at least shifted to some ungalled part of the body.

We descended by the same ricketty ladder by which we had climbed to the tops of the houses, mounted our horses, and rode briskly forward to encounter our 600 Mexicans in the gorge of the mountains, two miles distant.

The sun shone with dazzling brightness; the guidons and colors of each squadron, regiment, and battalion were for the first time unfurled. The drooping horses seemed to take courage from the gay array. The trumpeters sounded "to horse," with spirit, and the hills multiplied and re-echoed the call. All wore the aspect of a gala day; and, as we approached the gorge, where we expected to meet the enemy, we broke into a brisk trot, then into a full gallop, preceded by a squadron of horse. The gorge was passed, but no person seen.

One by one the guidons were furled; the men looked disappointed, and a few minutes found us dragging our slow lengths along with the usual indifference in regard to every subject except that of overcoming space.

Two miles further brought us to another pass as formidable as the first, and all the intermediate country was broken and covered with a dense growth of pine, piñon, and cedar. Here the mountains of red sand-stone, disposed in horizontal strata, begin to rise to the height of a thousand feet above the road. Nine miles more brought us to Tacoloté.

Here we met the alcalde and the people in the cool and spacious residence of the former, where the drama above described was again enacted. This time it was graced by the presence of the women with their bare ankles, round plump arms, and slippered feet.

We marched ten miles farther, to the Vernal springs, and halted at the upper spring, and observed for time and latitude about 500 feet south of the upper spring.

Observed 9 altitudes of polaris, 7 of alpha aquilæ, and 7 of arcturús. Latitude 35° 23′ 19″; longitude 7h. 01m. 23s.

Height indicated by the barometer 6,299 feet.

August 16.—We marched to San Miguel, where General Kearny assembled the people and harangued them much in the same manner as at the Vegas.

Reports now reached us at every step that the people were rising, and that Armijo was collecting a formidable force to oppose our march at the celebrated pass of the Cañon, 15 miles from Santa Fé. About the middle of the day's march the two Pueblo Indians, previously sent in to sound the chief men of that formidable tribe, were seen in the distance, at full speed, with arms and legs both thumping into the sides of their mules at every stride. Something was now surely in the wind. The smaller and foremost of the two dashed up to the general, his face radiant with joy, and exclaimed, "they are in the Cañon, my brave, pluck up your courage and push them out." As soon as his extravagant delight at the prospect of a fight, and the pleasure of communicating the news, had subsided, he gave a pretty accurate idea of Armijo's force and position.

The road passed over to-day was good, but the face of the country exceedingly rugged, broken, and covered with piñon and cedar. To the left, one or two miles distant, towers a wall, nearly perpendicular, 2,000 feet high, apparently level on the top, and showing, as near as I could judge from the road, an immense stratum of red sand-stone.

We turned from the road to the creek, where there were a few rancherias, to encamp; at which place we passed an uncomfortable night, the water being hard to reach, and the grass very bad.

Barometric height 6,346 feet.

August 17.—The picket guard, stationed on the road, captured the son of Saliza, who, it is said, is to play an important part in the defence of this country, and the same who behaved so brutally to the Texan prisoners. The son was at San Miguel yesterday, and heard from a concealed place all that passed. It is supposed, at this time, he was examining the position, strength, &c., of our army, to report to his father.

A rumor has reached camp that the 2,000 Mexicans assembled in the Cañon to oppose us, have quarrelled among themselves; that Armijo, taking advantage of the dissensions, fled with his dragoons and artillery to the south. He has long been suspected of wishing an excuse to fly. It is well known he has been averse to a battle, but some of his people threatened his life if he refused to fight. He has been, for some days, more in fear of his own people than of the American army. He has seen what they are blind to: the hopelessness of resistance.

As we approached the ruins of the ancient town of Pecos, a large fat fellow, mounted on a mule, came towards us at full speed, and extending his hand to the general, congratulated him on the arrival of himself and army. He said, with a roar of laughter, Armijo and his troops have gone to hell, "and the Cañon is all clear." This was the alcalde of the settlement, two miles up the Pecos from the ruins, where we encamped, 15¾ miles from our last camp, and two miles from the road.

Pecos, once a fortified town, is built on a promontory or rock, somewhat in the shape of a foot. Here burned, until within seven years, the eternal fires of Montezuma, and the remains of the architecture exhibit, in a prominent manner, the engraftment of the Catholic church upon the ancient religion of the country. At one end of the short spur forming the terminus of the promontory, are the remains of the estuffa, with all its parts distinct; at the other are the remains of the Catholic church, both showing the distinctive marks and emblems of the two religions. The fires from the estuffa burned and sent their incense through the same altars from which was preached the doctrine of Christ. Two religions so utterly different in theory, were here, as in all Mexico, blended in harmonious practice until about a century since, when the town was sacked by a band of Indians.

Amidst the havoc of plunder of the city, the faithful Indian managed to keep his fire burning in the estuffa; and it was continued till a few years since—the tribe became almost extinct. Their devotions rapidly diminished their numbers, until they became so few as to be unable to keep their immense estuffa (forty feet in diameter) replenished, when they abandoned the place and joined a tribe of the original race over the mountains, about sixty miles south. There, it is said, to this day they keep up their fire, which has never yet been extinguished. The labor, watchfulness, and exposure to heat consequent on this practice of their faith, is fast reducing this remnant of the Montezuma race; and a few years will, in all probability, see the last of this interesting people. The accompanying sketches will give a much more accurate representation of these ruins than any written descriptions. The remains of the modern church, with its crosses, its cells, its dark mysterious corners and niches, differ but little from those of the present day in New Mexico. The architecture of the Indian portion of the ruins presents peculiarities worthy of notice.

Both are constructed of the same materials: the walls of sun-dried brick, the rafters of well-hewn timber, which could never have been hewn by the miserable little axes now used by the Mexicans, which resemble, in shape and size, the wedges used by our farmers for splitting rails. The cornices and drops of the architrave in the modern church, are elaborately carved with a knife.

To-night we found excellent grass on the Rio Pecos, abreast of the ruins where the modern village of Pecos is situated, with a very inconsiderable population.

August 18. —We were this morning 29 miles from Santa Fé. Reliable information, from several sources, had reached camp yesterday and the day before, that dissensions had arisen in Armijo's camp, which had dispersed his army, and that he had fled to the south, carrying all his artillery and 100 dragoons with him. Not a hostile rifle or arrow was now between the army and Santa Fé, the capital of New Mexico, and the general determined to make the march in one day, and raise the United States flag over the palace before sundown. New horses or mules were ordered for the artillery, and every thing was braced up for a forced march. The

RUINS OF PECOS - CATHOLIC CHURCH

RUINS OF PECOS – AZTEK CHURCH

distance was not great, but the road bad, and the horses on their last legs.

A small detachment was sent forward at day-break, and at six the army followed. Four or five miles from old Pecos the road leads into a cañon, with hills on each side from 1,000 to 2,000 feet above the road, in all cases within cannon shot, and in many within point blank musket shot; and this continues to a point but 12 or 15 miles from Santa Fé.

The scenery is wild; the geological formation much the same as before described, until you begin to descend towards the Del Norte, when granitic rocks and sands are seen in great abundance on the road as far as Santa Fé. Cedar, piñon, and a large growth of long-leafed pine are densely crowded wherever the rock affords a crevice, until within six or eight miles of the town. Fifteen miles from Santa Fé we reached the position deserted by Armijo. The topographical sketch, by Lieutenant Peck, will give some idea of it. It is a gateway which, in the hands of a skilful engineer and one hundred resolute men, would have been perfectly impregnable.

Had the position been defended with any resolution, the general would have been obliged to turn it by a road which branches to the south, six miles from Pecos, by the way of Galisteo.

Armijo's arrangements for defence were very stupid. His abattis was placed behind the gorge some 100 yards, by which he evidently intended that the gorge should be passed before his fire was opened. This done, and his batteries would have been carried without difficulty.

Before reaching the cañon the noon halt was made in a valley covered with some gama, and the native potato in full bloom. The fruit was not quite as large as a wren's egg. As we approached the town, a few straggling Americans came out, all looking anxiously for the general, who, with his staff, was clad so plainly, that they passed without recognizing us. Another officer and myself were sent down to explore the by-road by which Armijo fled. On our return to the main road, we saw two Mexicans; one the acting secretary of state, in search of the general. They had passed him without knowing him. When we pointed in the direction of the general, they broke into a full run; their hands and feet keeping time to the pace of their nags. We followed in a sharp trot; and, as we thought, at a respectable distance. Our astonishment was great to find, as they wound through the ravine, through the open well-grown pine forest, that they did not gain on us perceptibly. "Certainly they are in a full run, and as certainly are we only in a trot," we both exclaimed. I thought we were under some optical delusion, and turned to my servant to see the pace at which he was going. "Ah!" said he, "those Mexican horses make a mighty great doing to no purpose." That was a fact; with their large cruel bits, they harrass their horses into a motion which enables them to gallop very long without losing sight of the starting place.

The acting secretary brought a letter from Vigil, the lieutenant governor, informing the general of Armijo's flight, and of his readiness to receive him in Santa Fé, and extend to him the hopitalities of the city. He was quite a youth, and dressed in the fashion of the Americans. Here, all persons from the United States are called Americans, and the name is extended to no other race on the continent. To-day's march was very tedious and vexatious; wishing to enter Santa Fé in an imposing form, frequent halts were made to allow the artillery to come up. Their horses almost gave out, and during the day mule after mule was placed before the guns, until scarcely one of them was spared.

The head of the column arrived in sight of the town about three o'clock; it was six before the rear came up. Vigil and twenty or thirty of the people of the town received us at the palace and asked us to partake of some wine and brandy of domestic manufacture. It was from the Passo del Norte; we were too thirsty to judge of its merits, any thing liquid and cool was palatable. During the repast, and as the sun was sitting, the United States flag was hoisted over the palace, and a salute of thirteen guns fired from the artillery planted on the eminence overlooking the town.

The ceremony ended, we were invited to supper at Captain ———'s, a Mexican gentleman, formerly in the army. The supper was served very much after the manner of a French dinner, one dish succeeding another in endless variety. A bottle of good wine from the Passo del Norte, and a loaf of bread was placed at each plate. We had been since five in the morning without eating, and inexhaustible as were the dishes was our appetite.

August 19.—I received an order to make a reconnoissance of the town and select the site for a fort, in co-operation with Lieutenant Gilmer, of the engineers. This occupied me diligently on the 19th and 20th, and on the 21st the general was furnished with the map, a copy of which is sent to the Adjutant General and another to the Bureau of Topographical Engineers.

The site selected and marked on the map is within 600 yards of the heart of the town, and is from 60 to 100 feet above it. The contour of the ground is unfavorable for the trace of a regular work, but being the only point which commands the entire town, and which is itself commanded by no other, we did not hesitate to recommend it. The recommendation was approved. On the 22d we submitted a complete plan of the work, which was also approved. It is computed for a garrison of 280 men.

On the 23d, the work was commenced with a small force; on the 27th, 100 laborers were set to work on it, detailed from the army; and, on the 31st, 20 Mexican masons were added.

As it was determined to send an express to the States on the 25th, I commenced to project and plot my map of the route of the Army of the West, that the government might have at once the benefit of my labors. It was rather a bold undertaking to compress, in a few days, the work of months. My astronomical observations were brought up from day to day as we advanced on the march, without which the understanding would have been impracticable. We all worked day and night, and, with the assistance of several gentlemen of the volunteers, I succeeded in accomplishing the work; not, however, in a very satisfactory manner.

Events now begin to crowd on each other in quick succession, but my duties keep me so constantly occupied in my office and in the field, that I cannot chronicle them in regular order or enter much upon details. On the morning of the 19th, the general assembled all the people in the plaza and addressed them at some length.

The next day, the chiefs and head men of the Pueblo Indians came to give in their adhesion and express their great satisfaction at our arrival. This large and formidable tribe are amongst the best and most peaceable citizens of New Mexico. They, early after the Spanish conquest, embraced the forms of religion, and the manners and customs of their then more civilized masters, the Spaniards. Their interview was long and interesting. They narrated, what is a tradition with them, that the white man would come from the far east and release them from the bonds and shackles which the Spaniards had imposed, not in the name, but in a worse form than slavery.

They and the numerous half-breeds are our fast friends now and forever. Three hundred years of oppression and injustice have failed to extinguish in this race the recollection that they were once the peaceable and inoffensive masters of the country.

A message was received the same night from Armijo, asking on what terms he would be received; but this proved to be only a ruse on his part to gain time in his flight to the south. Accounts go to show that his force at the Cañon was 4,000 men, tolerably armed, and six pieces of artillery. Had he been possessed of the slightest qualifications for a general, he might have given us infinite trouble. A priest arrived last night, the 29th, and brought the intelligence that at the moment of Armijo's flight, Ugarté, a colonel in the regular service, was on his march, at this side of the Passo del Norte, with 500 men to support him. That, had he continued, he would have been enabled to rouse the whole southern district, which is by far the wealthiest and most populous of the whole country.

In the course of the week, various deputations have come in from Taos, giving in their allegiance and asking protection from the Indians. That portion of the country seems the best disposed towards the United States. A Taos man may be distinguished at once by the cordiality of his salutation.*

A band of Navajoes, naked, thin, and savage looking fellows, dropped in and took up their quarters with Mr. Robideaux, our interpreter, just opposite my quarters. They ate, drank, and slept all the time, noticing nothing but a little cinnamon-colored naked brat that was playing in the court, which they gazed at with the eyes of gastronome's; and Mr. Fitzpatrick told me these people sometimes eat their own offspring, and consider it a great delicacy.

Various rumors have reached us from the south that troops are moving on Santa Fé, and that the people are rising, &c. To quiet

---

* Since this was written, the massacre of the excellent Governor Bent has taken place in Taos. It proves the profound duplicity of this race.

them, an expedition of 150 miles down the river has been determined on, to start on the 1st September.

August 30.—To-day we went to church in great state. The governor's seat, a large, well stuffed chair, covered with crimson, was occupied by the commanding officer. The church was crowded with an attentive audience of men and women, but not a word was uttered from the pulpit by the priest, who kept his back to the congregation the whole time, repeating prayers and incantations. The band, the identical one used at the fandango, and strumming the same tunes, played without intermission. Except the governor's seat and one row of benches, there were no seats in the church. Each woman dropped on her knees on the bare floor as she entered, and only exchanged this position for a seat on the ground at long intervals, announced by the tinkle of a small bell.

The interior of the church was decorated with some fifty crosses, a great number of the most miserable paintings and wax figures, and looking glasses trimmed with pieces of tinsel.

The priest, a very grave, respectable looking person, of fair complexion, commenced the service by sprinkling holy water over the congregation; when abreast of any high official person he extended his silver water spout and gave him a handful.

When a favorite air was struck up, the young women, whom we recognised as having figured at the fandango, counted their beads, tossed their heads, and crossed themselves to the time of the music.

All appeared to have just left their work to come to church. There was no fine dressing nor personal display that will not be seen on week days. Indeed, on returning from church, we found all the stores open, and the market women selling their melons and plums as usual.

The fruits of this place, musk melon, apple, and plum, are very indifferent, and would scarcely be eaten in the States. I must except, in condemning their fruit, the apricot and grapes, which grow in perfection. On leaving the narrow valley of the Santa Fé, which varies from a thousand feet to a mile or two in width, the country presents nothing but barren hills, utterly incapable, both from soil and climate, of producing anything useful.

The valley is entirely cultivated by irrigation, and is *now*, as will be seen on the sketch, covered with corn. Five miles below the town, the stream disappears in the granitic sands.

The population of Santa Fé is from two to four thousand, and the inhabitants are, it is said, the poorest people of any town in the province. The houses are of mud bricks, in the Spanish style, generally of one story, and built on a square. The interior of the square is an open court, and the principal rooms open into it. They are forbidding in appearance from the outside, but nothing can exceed the comfort and convenience of the interior. The thick walls make them cool in summer and warm in winter.

The better class of people are provided with excellent beds, but the lower class sleep on untanned skins. The women here, as in many other parts of the world, appear to be much before the men in refinement, intelligence, and knowledge of the useful arts. The higher class dress like the American women, except, instead of the bonnet, they wear a scarf over the head. This they wear, asleep or awake, in the house or abroad.

The dress of the lower class of women is a simple petticoat, with arms and shoulders bare, except what may chance to be covered by the reboso.

The men who have means to do so, dress after our fashion; but by far the greater number, when they dress at all, wear leather breeches, tight round the hips and open from the knee down; shirt and blanket take the place of our coat and vest.

The city is dependant on the distant hills for wood, and at all hours of the day may be seen jackasses passing laden with wood, which is sold at two bits (twenty-five cents) the load. T ese are the most diminutive animals, and usually mounted from behind, after tne fashion of leap-frog. The jackass is the only animal that can be subsisted in this barren neighborhood without great expense; our horses are all sent to a distance of twelve, fifteen, and thirty miles for grass.

Grain was very high when we first entered the town, selling freely at five and six dollars the fanegas, (one hundred and forty pounds.) As our wagons draw near, and the crops of wheat are being gathered, the price is falling gradually to four dollars the fanegas.

Milk at six cents per pint, eggs three cents a piece, sugar thirty-five cents per pound, and coffee seventy-five cents. The sugar used in the country is principally made from the cornstalk.

A great reduction must take place now in the price of dry goods and groceries, twenty per cent. at least, for this was about the rate of duty charged by Armijo, which is now, of course, taken off.

He collected fifty or sixty thousand dollars annually, principally, indeed, entirely, on goods imported overland from the United States. His charge was $500 the wagon load, without regard to the contents of the wagon or value of the goods, and hence the duty was very unjust and unequal.

Mr. Alvarez informed me that the importations from the United States varied very much, but that he thought they would average about half a million of dollars yearly, and no more. Most of the wagons go on to Chihuahua without breaking their loads.

New Mexico contains, according to the last census, made a few years since, 100,000 inhabitants. It is divided into three departments—the northern, middle, and southeastern. These are again sub-divided into counties, and the counties into townships. The lower or southern division is incomparably the richest, containing 48,000 inhabitants, many of whom are wealthy and in possession of farms, stock, and gold dust.

New Mexico, although its soil is barren, and its resources limited, unless the gold mines should, as is probable, be more extensively developed hereafter, and the culture of the grape enlarged, is, from its position, in a commercial and military aspect, an all-important military possession for the United States. The road from Santa Fé to Fort Leavenworth presents few obstacles for a railway, and, if it continues as good to the Pacific, will be one of the routes to be considered, over which the United States will pass immense quantities of merchandise into what may become, in time, the rich and populous States of Sonora, Durango, and Southern California.

As a military position, it is important and necessary. The mountain fastnesses have long been the retreating places of the warlike parties of Indians and robbers, who sally out to intercept our caravans moving over the different lines of travel to the Pacific.

The latitude of Santa Fé, determined by 52 circum-meridian altitudes of alpha aquilæ, 23 of beta aquarii, and 36 altitudes of polaris out of the meridian, is N. 35° 44′ 06″. The longitude, by the measurement of 8 distances between the ✱ alpha aquilæ and the ☾, and 8 between ✱ antares and the ☾, is respectively 7h. 04m. 14s.7 and 7h. 04m. 22s.4. The mean of which is 7h. 04m. 18s. and the longitude brought by the chronometer from the meridian of Fort Leavenworth is 7h. 04m. 05s.5.—(See Appendix No. 4.)

The place of observation was the court near the northeast corner of the public square. The latitude may be considered fixed; but satisfactory as the longitude may appear, I should, nevertheless, have greatly multiplied the number of lunar distances, had I not been in daily expectation of receiving a transit instrument, with which a set of observations on moon culminating stars could have been made at this important geographical point.

The mean of all the barometric readings at Santa Fé indicates, as the height of this point above the sea, 6,846 feet, and the neighboring peaks to the north are many thousand feet higher.

August 31.—Lieutenant Warner arrived to-day, but cannot yet be relieved from ordnance duty. To-morrow an expedition goes to Taos, but, as Mr. Peck is sick, I have no officer to send with it. To-day apparently well authenticated accounts have arrived that Armijo met Ugarté, about 150 miles below, coming up with a force of 500 regulars and some pieces of artillery; that he turned back, and is now marching towards us with a large force, rallying the people as he passes, and that numbers are joining him from the upper towns. In consequence of these reports, the general has strengthened the force with which he is to march the day after to-morrow to meet him.

September 2.—We marched out of Santa Fé at 9 o'clock, a. m., taking no one of my party except Mr. Bestor, and leaving Lieutenant Peck, who is still an invalid, to assist Lieutenant Gilmer. We descended the valley of the Santa Fé river, nearly west, for five miles, when we left the river and struck across a dry arid plain intersected by arroyos, (dry beds of streams,) in a southwesterly course. Twenty-three miles brought us to the Galisteo creek, which, at that time, was barely running. The bed of the creek is sand and pebbles of the primitive rock, and lies between steep clay and lime-stone, traversed occasionally by trap dykes, which in one place are so regular as to resemble a wall pierced with windows. From this place to its mouth there is scarcely the sign of vegetation. At the dry mouth of the Galisteo, and directly on the Del Norte, is the town of Santo Domingo. Before reaching Galisteo creek, but after leaving Santa Fé some miles, a few sprigs of grama tempted us to halt and bait our nags; but the principal growth on the plains was ephedra, Frémontia vermicularis, diotis lanata, (Romeria of the Spaniards,) hendecandia Texana. There was also picked up in to-day's journey a verbena pinnatifida, sphaeralcea stellata, a cleome integrifolia, (a handsome purple flowered herb,) several aster and a species of dicteria, which Dr. Torrey thinks new.

September 3.—This has been a great day. An invitation was received, some days since, from the Pueblo Indians to visit their town of Santo Domingo. From height to height, as we advanced, we saw horsemen disappearing at full speed. As we arrived abreast of the town we were shown by a guide, posted there for the purpose, the road to Santo Domingo. The chief part of the command and the wagon train were sent along the highway; the general with his staff and Captain Burgwyn's squadron of dragoons, wended his way along the bridle path nearly due west to the town. We had not proceeded far, before we met ten or fifteen sachemic looking old Indians, well mounted, and two of them carrying gold-headed canes with tassels, the emblems of office in New Mexico.

Salutations over, we jogged along, and, in the course of conversation, the alcalde, a grave and majestic old Indian, said, as if casually, "We shall meet some Indians presently, mounted and dressed for war, but they are the young men of my town, friends come to receive you, and I wish you to caution your men not to fire upon them when they ride towards them."

When within a few miles of the town, we saw a cloud of dust rapidly advancing, and soon the air was rent with a terrible yell, resembling the Florida war-whoop. The first object that caught my eye through the column of dust, was a fierce pair of buffalo horns, overlapped with long shaggy hair. As they approached, the sturdy form of a naked Indian revealed itself beneath the horns, with shield and lance, dashing at full speed, on a white horse, which, like his own body, was painted all the colors of the rainbow; and then, one by one, his followers came on, painted to the eyes, their own heads and their horses covered with all the strange equipments that the brute creation could afford in the way of horns, skulls, tails, feathers, and claws.

As they passed us, one rank on each side, they fired a volley under our horses' bellies from the right and from the left. Our well-trained dragoons sat motionless on their horses, which went along without pricking an ear or showing any sign of excitement.

Arrived in the rear, the Indians circled round, dropped into a walk on our flanks until their horses recovered breath, when off they went at full speed, passing to our front, and when there, the opposite files met, and each man selected his adversary and kept up a running fight, with muskets, lances, and bows and arrows. Sometimes a fellow would stoop almost to the earth to shoot under his horses' belly, at full speed, or to shield himself from an impending blow. So they continued to pass and repass us all the way to the steep cliff which overhangs the town. There they filed on each side of the road, which descends through a deep cañon, and halted on the peaks of the cliffs. Their motionless forms projected against the clear blue sky above, formed studies for an artist. In the cañon we were joined by the priest, a fat old white man. We were escorted first to the padre's, of course; for here, as every where, these men are the most intelligent, and the best to do in the world, and when the good people wish to put their best foot foremost, the padre's wines, beds, and couches have to suffer. The entrance to the portal was lined with the women of the village, all dressed alike, and ranged in treble files; they looked fat and stupid.

We were shown into his reverence's parlor, tapestried with curtains stamped with the likenesses of all the Presidents of the United States up to this time. The cushions were of spotless damask, and the couch covered with a white Navajoe blanket worked in richly colored flowers.

The air was redolent with the perfume of grapes and melons, and every crack of door and windows glistening with the bright eyes and arms of the women of the capilla. The old priest was busily talking in the corner, and little did he know the game of sighs and signs carried on between the young fellows and the fair inmates of his house. We had our gayest array of young men out to-day, and the women seemed to me to drop their usual subdued look and timid wave of the eye-lash for good hearty twinkles and signs of unaffected and cordial welcome—signs supplying the place of conversation, as neither party could speak the language of the other. This little exchange of the artillery of eyes was amusing enough, but I was very glad to see the padre move towards the table, and remove the pure white napkins from the grapes, melons, and wine. We were as thirsty as heat and dust could make us, and we relished the wine highly, whatever its quality. The sponge cake was irreproachable, and would have done honor to our best northern housekeepers. Indeed, wherever we have been feasted, the sponge cake has been in profusion, and of the best kind. After the repast, the general went forward on the portal and delivered a speech to the assembled people of the town, which was first interpreted into Spanish, and then into Pueblo.

It is impossible to arrive at the precise population of the town, but I should judge it to be about six hundred, and the quantity of ground under tillage for their support about five hundred acres.

The valley of the Del Norte is here quite narrow, and the soil sandy. The river itself was viewed by me, for the first time, with a strange interest. The hardships, trials, and perseverance of the gallant Pike, and the adventures of the pious and brave soldiers of the cross, Rivèra and La Ford, came forcibly to my mind; as I kneeled down to drink of its waters my thoughts were of them. Leaving Santo Domingo, we struck the highway in about four miles, and two more brought us to the pretty village of San Felippe, overhung by a steep craggy precipice, upon the summit of which are the ruins of a Roman Catholic church, presenting in the landscape sketch the appearance of the pictures we see of the castles on the Rhine.

SAN FELIPPE, NEW MEXICO.

Between San Felippe and the Angosturas, six miles below, the valley of the river is very narrow, affording no interval for agriculture. On the west side, the banks are steep walls, crowned by seams of basalt forming the table lands. The east is composed of rolling sand hills, rising gradually to the base of the mountains, and covered with large round pebbles. I must except from this the poverty-stricken little town of Algodones, which has some ground round it in cultivation.

The observations for the determination of this camp, about one mile below the town of San Felippe, were made on my return, (September 10th,) and will be found under that date in Appendix No. 5. The height indicated by the barometer of this, the first camp on the Rio del Norte, is 5,000 feet above the level of the sea.

September 4.—Below the Angosturas, the valley of the river opens into a plain, varying from two to six miles in width, generally sufficiently low and level to admit the water of the river to be carried over it for the purposes of irrigation; but the soil is very sandy, and better adapted to Indian corn than wheat. Of this last we saw but few stubbles, the ground being chiefly planted with corn. The vegetation is much the same as that described after leaving Santa Fé, with the addition of quite a number of compositæ; among which was a species of linosyris, artemesia filifolia, aster, helicladus, &c.

News now began to arrive which left but little doubt that the reports which caused our movement down the river were exaggerated, if not wholly without foundation. People had passed down the river, as was reported, but in no great numbers. A messenger came in from the alcalde of Tomé with an official note, stating that Armijo had left with him one hundred mules, pressed into service to meet us at the cañon, and that Armijo had also notified him that one hundred more would be left at the Passo del Norte. These belonged to citizens of New Mexico, and had been taken from them without their consent. It was his practice, in peace or in war, to seize the person or property of any who fell under his displeasure.

The town of Bernallilo is small, but one of the best built in the territory. We were here invited to the house of a wealthy man, to take some refreshment. We were led into an oblong room, furnished like that of every Mexican in comfortable circumstances. A banquette runs around the room, leaving only a space for the couch. It is covered with cushions, carpets, and pillows; upon which the visiter sits or reclines. The dirt floor is usually covered a third or a half with common looking carpet. On the uncovered part is the table, freighted with grapes, sponge-cake, and the wine of the country. The walls are hung with miserable pictures of the saints, crosses innumerable, and Yankee mirrors without number. These last are suspended entirely out of reach; and if one wishes to shave or adjust his toilet, he must do so without the aid of a mirror, be there ever so many in the chamber.

We passed on to the house of our host's wealthy son, where we were invited to dine. Here we found another refreshment table;

and, after waiting some hours, dinner was announced. It was a queer jumble of refinement and barbarism; the first predominating in every thing, except in the mode of serving, which was chiefly performed by the master, his Mexican guests, and a few female serfs.

The plates, forks, and spoons were of solid New Mexican silver, clumsily worked in the country. The middle of the table was strewed with the finest white bread, cut in pieces, and within the reach of every cover. At close intervals were glass decanters, of Pittsburg manufacture, filled with wine made on the plantation. The dishes were served separately. The first was soup maigre; then followed roast chicken, stuffed with onions; then mutton, boiled with onions; then followed various other dishes, all dressed with the everlasting onion; and the whole terminated by chilé, the glory of New Mexico, and then frigolé.

Chilé the Mexicans consider the chef-d'œuvre of the cuisine, and seem really to revel in it; but the first mouthful brought the tears trickling down my cheeks, very much to the amusement of the spectators with their leather-lined throats. It was red pepper, stuffed with minced meat.

From Bernallilo the valley opens, but narrows again at Zandia, an Indian town on a sand-bank at the base of a high mountain of the same name, said to contain the precious metals.

They were treading wheat here, which is done by making a circular corral on a level ground of clay; upon this floor they scatter the wheat, turn in a dozen or more mules, and one or two Indians, who, with whoops, yells, and blows, keep the affrighted brutes constantly in motion. To separate the wheat from the chaff, both Indians and Mexicans use a simple hand-barrow, with a bottom of raw bull's hide perforated with holes. I should suppose it must take an hour to winnow a bushel.

After dining sumptuously at Sandival's, we went to our camp in the Allemada. Here the valley is wide and well cultivated. The people of the surrounding country flocked in with grapes, melons, and eggs. Swarms of wild geese and sand cranes passed over camp. They frequent the river and are undisturbed, save when some American levels his rifle.

By observation, the latitude of this camp is 35° 11' 50", and the longitude 106° 45' 00" west of Greenwich.

September 6.—We encamped last night on very indifferent grass. Breakfasted with Don José Charvis, at Perdilla. When sitting, our chins just reached the table. There were five or six courses, ending with coffee. Before breakfast, we were summoned to mass in Don José's private chapel, where the eccentric person we met at yesterday's dinner officiated. Priest, fop, courtier, and poet were curiously combined in one person. Proud of his pure white hand, he flourished it incessantly, sometimes running his fingers through his hair, in imitation of some pretty coquette, and ever and anon glancing in one of the many looking-glasses with which the church was decorated. After mass, to our surprise, he delivered an eloquent discourse, eulogising the grandeur, magnanimity, power, and justice of the United States.

Attending mass before breakfast proved anything but an appetizer. The church was crowded with women of all conditions, and the horrid reboso, which the poor use for shawls, bonnet, handkerchief, and spit-box, sent out an odor which the incense from the altar failed to stifle.

One fact struck me as singular in all the houses that we visited, the ladies never made their appearance; and it was always by the merest accident that we caught a glimpse of one of the family.

At Isoletta, I became tired of the show, and, seeing my servant talking at the door of one of his acquaintances, I took the liberty of asking permission to take a quiet siesta; but this was out of the question. The good woman overwhelmed me with a thousand questions about the United States, which could only be stopped by questioning her in return. She denounced Armijo; said, with a true Castilian flash of the eye, "I do not see how any man wearing those things," pointing to my shoulder straps, "could run away as he did. He had a good army to back him, and could have driven you all back."

The valley suddenly contracts below Perdilla, between Isoletta and Peralta. On the east side of the river there is deep sand, and the country is perfectly barren.

I observed to-night, for time and latitude at my camp, about 500 feet northwest of Senora Charvis's private chapel, thirteen altitudes of polaris give for the latitude of this place, 34° 50′ 57″; and twelve of corona borealis, and nine of alpha pegasi, give the chronometric longitude $7h.\ 07m.\ 8s.4$.

September 7.—The early part of last evening was most beautifully bright and serene; the air was of the most delightful temperature, varied occasionally by a gentle breeze from the south, wafting along the perfume of the vineyards. I made some observations for time and latitude; the last unsatisfactorily, owing to the brightness of the moon dimming the southern stars. About 11 o'clock, the whole character of the night was changed by an east wind that came rustling down from the mountains, driving the sand before it. Nearly the whole distance travelled in the last three days has been over drifting sand, with only occasional patches of firm soil.

After rising early to attend to some business, I walked over the town of Peralta, which is interspersed with cotton wood, growing in nearly the regular order of an apple orchard. I then repaired to head-quarters, at the palace of Mr. Hortera, a spacious one story edifice, five hundred feet front.

We marched and encamped near Tomé. It was the eve of the fête of Tomé in honor of the Virgin Mary, and people from all parts of the country were flocking in crowds to the town. The primitive wagons of the country were used by the women as coaches. These wagons were heavy boxes mounted on wheels cut from large cotton wood; over the top of the box was spread a blanket, and inside were huddled, in a dense crowd, the women, children, pigs, lambs, and "every thing that is his." The man of the family usually seated himself on the tongue of the wagon, his time divided between belaboring his beasts and scratching his head. In one of these a violin was being played, and the women who were sitting on their feet, made the most of the music by brandishing their bare arms and moving their heads to the cadence. At night there was a theatrical representation in the public square. The piece dramatized was from the Old Testament.

During the day I had been puzzled by seeing at regular intervals on the wall surrounding the capilla, and on the turrets of the capilla itself, (which be it remembered is of mud,) piles of dry wood. The mystery was now to be cleared up. At a given signal all were lighted, and simultaneously a flight of rockets took place from every door and window of the chapel, fire-works of all kinds, from the blazing rocket to children's whirligigs, were now displayed in succession. The pyrotechny was the handicraft of the priests. I must say the whole affair did honor to the church, and displayed considerable chemical knowledge. Most of the spectators were on mules, each with his woman in front, and it was considered a great feat to explode a rocket under a mule's belly without previous intimation to the rider.

September 8.—Long shall I remember the fête of Tomé, a scene at once so novel and so striking. To-day, my duties called me off early in the morning.

I had to examine guides in reference to the route to California, and engage such as I might think fit for the trip.

My last interview of this kind to-day was in a species of public building, or guard-house, where a number of Mexicans had collected with arms. Several written tablets hung round the walls, but they were perfectly illegible. Our business was cut short by the sound of passing music. A strange sight presented itself. In a sedan chair, borne by four men, was seated a wax figure nearly as large as life, extravagantly dressed; following immediately were three or four priests, with long tallow candles, a full yard in length. Some American officers followed, each holding a candle. Unfortunately I emerged just as this group was passing; there was no escape, and the moment I joined a grave Mexican (apparently a man in authority,) thrust a candle into my hand. I thought of my coat, my only coat, the coat which was on my back, and which must take me to California, and back again into the interior of Mexico! Suddenly there was a halt without any word of command, and in the confusion we jostled against each other and distributed the tallow in great profusion.

It was thought proper that the officers should show every respect to the religious observances of the country, consequently they did not decline participation in these ceremonies.

The procession ended at the church. After the services there were concluded we repaired to the house of the padre, where we found a collation.

We had proposed attending a theatrical representation going on in the open air, but a heavy squall of wind and a few drops of rain put a stop to this amusement, and all retired to dress for the fandango, which is the name given to all collections of people where there is music and dancing.

A cotillion was attempted in honor of the Americans present, but this cold and formal dance soon gave way to the more joyous dances of the country, the Coona, the Bolero, and the Italiana. Every variety of figure was introduced, but the waltz was the basis of all, except the Bolero, which, as danced here, resembles our negro jig.

At the dance we found a very plain, but very intelligent woman, the sister of Armijo, who said he would return as soon as he settled his affairs in Chihuahua.

September 11.—Returned to Santa Fé.

September 15.—Sent Lieutenant Warner, with a party consisting of Lieutenant Peck and three men, to determine the latitude of Taos and the topography of the road.

From the 15th to 25th September I was busily engaged in fitting out for California.

Lieutenant Abert, who was left dangerously ill at Bent's Fort, had not arrived on the 25th, but accounts reached me that he was convalescent, and on his way to Santa Fé, where he might shortly be expected. Lieutenant Peck was also an invalid, and neither being able to accompany us to California, I left, by the general's direction, the subjoined order for them to make a map of New Mexico, based upon the astronomical points and measurements determined by myself, and to furnish from the best statistical sources, an account of the population and resources, military and civil, of the province.

SANTA FE, *September* 14, 1846.

SIR : I am charged by the general commanding to inform you that you will remain for the present in the territory of New Mexico, and should your health, or that of Lieutenant Peck, be sufficiently restored to return to duty, that you will continue the survey of this territory commenced by myself, and follow it to completion, provided it does not interfere with other military duties which may be required of you by the officer left in command of the territory.

With the limited number of instruments that can be placed in your hands, it is not expected that you will conduct the survey on strict geodetic principles, yet it is believed that sufficient precision can be attained to answer all the requirements of the military and civil service.

The country from Taos to Fra Cristobal contains nearly all the ground that is under cultivation, and nearly all that is worth cultivating; and for this whole distance it is open and bounded by high and conspicuous peaks, affording great facilities for conducting your operations.

I have established the astronomical positions of six points in this territory, viz: camp 42, at Vegas; camp 43, Vernal springs, Santa Fé; camp 55, 1¼ miles south of the church of San Felippe; camp

49, at the Alameda; camp 51, at Peralta, at the mill, and I shall establish two more, one at Taos, and the other at Secoro.

These points are quite sufficient, and will be the base of your operations; and upon them you will form a trigonometric canevas. For this purpose the rule requiring every angle of the series to be greater than 30°, may be wholly disregarded. And after having determined by triangulation the position of any three conspicuous peaks, the position of any other points, which are in view of the three first named, may be determined by the problem of three points, as is practised in hydrographic surveys. Many such points will present themselves.

The canevas completed, the course of the Del Norte, that of its tributaries to the base of the mountains or beyond the settlements; the width of the valleys; the quantity of land under cultivation; the position of the towns, churches, hills, and all other topographical features of the country, can be determined with the Schmalkalde's compasses.

If your force is sufficient, the operation described in this last paragraph may be carried on simultaneously with the triangulation. You are aware that I have no theodolite at my disposal, the triangulation must, therefore, be made with the sextant.

The population, number of cattle, horses, and sheep, and the quantity of grain and other agricultural products, the facilities and best localities for water power to propel machinery, and also, the mineral resources of the country, it is very desirable to know. You will, therefore, give particular attention to acquiring all the information on these subjects which the present statistical knowledge in the country will afford.

A requisition for five thousand dollars will be made on the Bureau of Topographical Engineers for the survey, to be placed to your credit with Mr. Robert Campbell of St. Louis, upon whom, I should think, you might safely draw, without waiting to hear from Washington.

I made a requisition on the bureau, dated June 18, 1846, for a transit instrument, and also for an instrument to obtain the magnetic dip and declination. Should these arrive, you will unpack them, mount the instruments near the place where I observed in Santa Fé, and commence a series of observations for longitude by moon culminating stars, and for the magnetic dip and declination.

The series for longitude will be continued for at least three lunations, and, should an opportunity present itself, I wish the observations and results to be communicated to me in California.

I am, very respectfully, your obedient servant,
W. H. EMORY,
First Lieut. Corps Top. Engineers.

Lieutenant J. W. ABERT, or, in his absence,
Lieutenant W. G. PECK.

General orders were issued designating the force to march on California. It consisted of three hundred United States 1st dragoons, under Major Sumner, who were to be followed by the battalion of Mormons, five hundred in number, commanded by Captain Cook.

Colonel Doniphan's regiment was to remain in New Mexico until relieved by Colonel Price's regiment, which was daily expected to reach there from the United States, when Colonel Doniphan's regiment was directed to effect a junction with General Wool at Chihuahua.

Major Clarke's two batteries of artillery were divided—one company, Captain Fisher's, to be left in New Mexico; the other, Captain Weightman's, to accompany Colonel Doniphan. The battalion of foot, under Captain Agney, was directed to remain in Santa Fé.

Thus was the army of the west divided into three columns, to operate in regions remote from each other, and never to unite again in one body.

September 25.—I received notice that the general was to march at 2, p. m., for California. His force consisted of three hundred dragoons, to be followed by a battalion of Mormons on foot that had not yet arrived in Santa Fé.

My requisition for twelve pack-saddles and eight mules not being filled, I determined to delay starting for an hour or two, and did not reach my camp, sixteen miles distant, till long after dark. I found my tent pitched, my supper smoking, and corn secured for my mules; this was gratifying, and I congratulated myself on the reorganization of my party, at least so far as the *personel* was concerned, for I had never found my camp so well attended to.

The day was excessively hot, the night very cold, the thermometer 32 degrees.

Memorandum.—My party is now organized as follows:

Lieutenant Warner, topographical engineers, &c.
J. M. Stanly, draughtsman.
Norman Bestor, assistant.

Men.

James Early, driver to instrument wagon;
W. H. Peterson, in charge of horizon box and cantina for sextants;
Baptiste Perrot, driver of transportation wagon;
Maurice Longdeau, in charge of spare mules;
François de Von Cœur, in charge of spare mules;
Frank Ménard, assistant teamster;
James Riley, assistant to Bestor;
Dabney Eustis, assistant to Stanly,
and the private servants of Lieutenant Warner and myself.

Our road is over the ground heretofore travelled and chronicled as far as Tomé.

As an evidence of the ignorance of the people here respecting the topography of the country, and also the ignorance of foreigners who have lived fifteen or twenty years in Santa Fé, no one could tell me where the Rio Santa Fé debouched into the Rio Grande.

I may here remark, that every night I furnished the distances travelled over to General Kearny at headquarters, and very often (whenever required) the latitude of the camp. In many cases these and the distances have been published; I shall, therefore, not repeat them. The latitudes in some cases have been incorrectly reported, and in others recomputed, and are therefore now given as final results.

September 26, 27, 28, 29, and 30.—We marched over the same ground already travelled over and described, between the 2d and 7th of September.

Below Zandia we were attracted by a great noise. It proceeded from a neighboring rancheria, where we saw eight or ten naked fellows hammering away in a trough full of cornstalks, as I had never seen Mexicans exert themselves before. The perspiration from their bodies was rolling off into the trough in profusion, and mingling with the crushed cane. This was then taken out, boiled, and transferred to a press, as primitive in construction as any thing from the hands of Father Abraham.

The hopper was the trunk of a scooped cotton wood tree, into this was inserted a billet of wood, upon which the lever rested about midway. Men, women, and children were mounted on each end; all see-sawing in the highest glee. I suggested, as an improvement, that one end of the lever be confined, and the whole of the living weight be transferred to the other end. "No! No!" said the head man, "if I do that, the fun of see-sawing will be over, and I can't get any body to work." The man was a disciple of Charles Fourier, and desired "to make labor attractive."

The morning of the 29th opened with a grand trade in mules and horses. A few days' experience was quite enough to warn us that our outfit would not answer, and the general directed that all the poor mules and horses should be exchanged for fat ones. The scene reminded one more of a horse market than a regular camp. The more liberal were our offers for the animals, the more exorbitant became the demands of the Mexicans.

At Albuquerque I was directed to call and see Madame Armijo, and ask her for the map of New Mexico, belonging to her husband, which she had in her possession. I found her ladyship sitting on an ottoman smoking, after the fashion of her countrywomen, within reach of a small silver vase filled with coal. She said she had searched for the map without success; if not in Santa Fé, her husband must have taken it with him to Chihuahua.

We crossed the Rio Grande del Norte at Albuquerque, its width was about twenty-five yards, and its deepest part just up to the hubs of the wheels. It is low at present, but at no time, we learned, is its rise excessive—scarcely exceeding one or two feet.

We encamped a little more than half way between Albuquerque and Pardillas, on a sandy plain, destitute of wood, and with little grass.

A NEW MEXICAN INDIAN WOMAN.
C. B. Graham, Lith.

We saw myriads of sand crane, geese, and brant.

September 30.—Feeling no desire to go over the same ground twice, I struck off on the table lands to the west, and found them a succession of rolling sand hills, with obione canescens, franseria acanthocarpa, yerba del sapa of the Mexicans, and occasionally, at very long intervals, with scrub cedar, about as high as the boot-top.

I saw here the hiding places of the Navajoes, who, when few in numbers, wait for the night to descend upon the valley and carry off the fruit, sheep, women, and children of the Mexicans. When in numbers, they come in day-time and levy their dues. Their retreats and caverns are at a distance to the west, in high and inaccessible mountains, where troops of the United States will find great difficulty in overtaking and subduing them, but where the Mexicans have never thought of penetrating. The Navajoes may be termed the lords of New Mexico. Few in number, disdaining the cultivation of the soil, and even the rearing of cattle, they draw all their supplies from the valley of the Del Norte.

As we marched down the river to meet Ugarté and Armijo, the Navajoes attacked the settlements three miles in our rear, killed one man, crippled another, and carried off a large supply of sheep and cattle. To-day we have a report, which appears well authenticated, that the Mexicans taking courage at the expectations of protection from the United States, had the temerity to resist a levy, and the consequence was, the loss of six men killed and two wounded.

They are prudent in their depredations, never taking so much from one man as to ruin him. Armijo never permitted the inhabitants to war upon these thieves. The power he had of letting these people loose on the New Mexicans was the great secret of his arbitrary sway over a people who hated and despised him. Any offender against Armijo was pretty sure to have a visit from the Navajoes.

I stopped at the little town of Isoletta, to visit my friend, the alcalde, who has the reputation, Indian though he be, of being the most honest man and best maker of brandy in the territory. Mr. Stanly accompanied me, for the purpose of sketching one of the women as a specimen of the race. I told the alcalde our object, and soon a very beautiful woman made her appearance, perfectly conscious of the purpose for which her presence was desired. Her first position was exquisitely graceful, but the light did not suit, and when Stanly changed her position, the charm of her attitude was gone.

We came down from the table lands through a ravine, where the lava, in a seam of about six feet, overlaid soft sand-stone. At the point of junction, the sand was but slightly colored. The lava was cellular, and the holes so large that the hawks were building nests in them.

At this ravine the Navajoes descended when they made their last attack; at the same moment the volunteers were ascending the other slope of the hill, on their way to garrison Cibolletta.

The camp of this date (September 30) is near the camp of September 6; and my observations this evening verified, in a very satisfactory manner, the travelling rate assumed for the chronometer 783. The longitude of camp of September 7, given by chronometer, is 7h. 07m. 00s.5; that of this present camp, which is one mile west of it, is 7h. 8m. 00s. Here, in addition to my usual observations for time and latitude, I took a set of lunar distances, with east and west stars.—(See Appendix.)

Above this camp, there is on the river a considerable growth of cotton-wood; among which are found some "signs" of beaver. The plains and river bottoms were covered with much the same growth as that heretofore noted; to which may be added an erythera, a handsome little gentian-like plant, with deep rose-colored flowers, and a solanum, a kind of wild potato, with narrow leaves, which Dr. Torrey says is different from any in the United States.

October 1.—To-day, for the first time for six days, I was able to rise from my bed without assistance. The air was elastic, and fragrant with the perfumes of the wild sage from the adjacent hills. Every thing was, in truth, couleur de rose; for the sun beamed out bright and red, infusing the same tint over the landscape, till near meridian. I crossed to Tomé, in search of some non-complying guides. We recrossed at Tomé, and measured the section of the river. Accordingly, we found the Rio Grande del Norte, many hundred miles from its source,

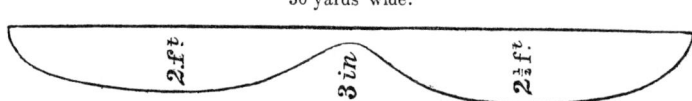

This section is about the same as at San Felippe and Santo Domingo. If to it we add the section of a stream of water carried off by two large zequias, each nine feet by two, we shall have an estimate of the volume of water discharged by this famous river, for 150 miles, through the most populous and fertile part of its valley.

Below Tomé, for a few miles, the valley widens, the soil improves, and the cultivation is superior to any other part, particularly that of the rancherias around the pleasant little village of Belen.

October 2.—This morning we passed the pretty church in the village of Sabinal, after which the settlements became very few and far between. We encamped opposite La Lloya, at the bend of the river Del Norte, where the low sand hills on either side seem to unite and shut up the valley.

We received a message from the major domo of the neighboring rancheria, cautioning us to we watchful of our animals, that forty of the Navajoes had passed the river last night. The incursions of these Indians have prevented the settlement and cultivation of this part of the country.

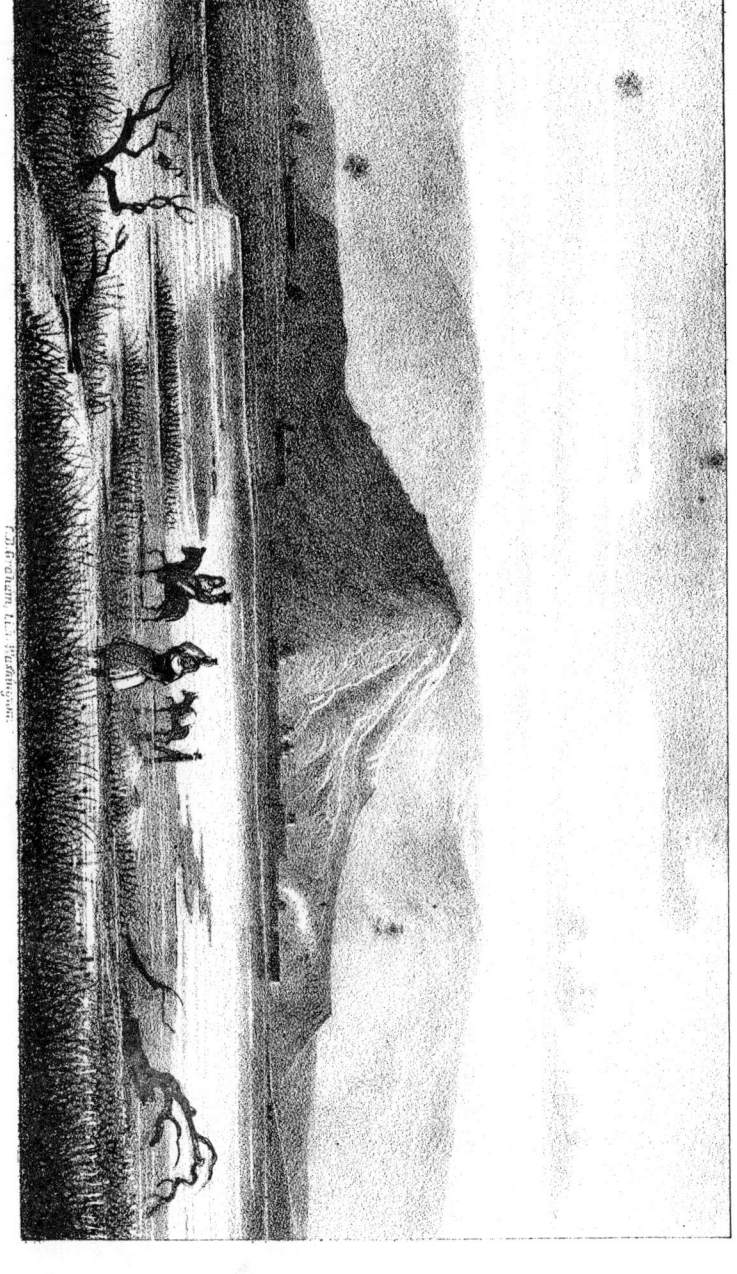

VALENCIA, NEW MEXICO

The sand bank, at the foot of which we are encamped, is filled with serpentine, harder than that which is dug in such quantities from the site of Fort Marcy, near Santa Fé.

Now and then we came to spots from which the waters were prevented from escaping by the sand, and had evaporated, leaving saline incrustations; about these we found growing abundantly atriplex and salicornia.

We found to-day lycium in great abundance, senecis longilobus, martynia proboscidea, (*cuckold's horns*,) and a small shrub with flower like convolvulus.

October 3.—The wagons from the rear not being up, we laid by all day, in hourly expectation of their arrival and an order to march. An express from Colonel Price came up, informing us of his arrival in Santa Fé.

About 12 o'clock in the day, a Mexican came into camp, with his horse foaming, to say that the Navajoes had made an attack on the town of Pulvidera. One company of dragoons was immediately despatched to the place, about twelve miles distant.

This camp was one of the prettiest of the whole march, on the curve of the river, fringed with large cottonwoods growing at intervals. The air was mild and balsamic, the moon shone brightly, and all was as still as death, except when a flock of geese or sandcranes were disturbed in their repose. Several large cat fish and soft-shell turtle were caught, and we saw blue-winged ducks, plovers, doves, and a few meadow larks.

No fact proves the indolence and incapacity of the Mexican for sport or for war more glaringly, than that these immense flights of sand-cranes and geese are found quietly feeding within gunshot distance of their houses and largest towns. Going into Albuquerque, I started a hungry-looking wolf in a water melon patch, close under the walls of the town.

October 4.—The wagons mounted the sand hills with great difficulty. The river inpinges so close on the hills as to make it necessary, on the western side, to mount the table lands. These plains, reaching to the base of the mountains, are of the same character as heretofore mentioned, of rolling sand hills, covered with obione, canescens, prosopis glandulosa, (romeria,) riddellia tagetina, paga-paga —an abundant shrubby plant, belonging to the family of the amaranths, but a genus not yet described—a new dieteria, a new fallugia, baileya multiradiata, abronia mellifera, and a few patches of grama. This last is the only nutriment the plains afford for horses and cattle; but mules and asses, when hard pressed, will eat the trato and the romeria. The chamisa grows to a considerable height, and the stalk is sometimes two or three inches in diameter; a fire can be made of it sufficient to boil a kettle or roast an egg. To-day I eat, for the first time, the fruit of the prickly pear, the "yerba de la vivera," of the Mexicans; as I was thirsty, it tasted truly delicious, having the flavor of a lemon with crushed sugar.

Below La Joya two sand hill spurs, overlaid with fragments of lava and trap, project from the east and west, closing the valley, just leaving sufficient space for the river to pass between. The river winds below in a beautiful semicircle, bending to the west. On either side is excellent grass, apparently untouched, and shaded by large cottonwoods. To the west, the hills of Pulvidera form an amphitheatre. The whole picture, the loveliest I have seen in New Mexico, loses nothing by being projected, from where we stood, against the red walls of the Sierra Grande, which extend from Zandia southward, dividing the waters of the Puerco, of the east, from those of the Rio Grande.

I longed to cross these mountains and explore the haunts of the Apaches, and the hiding place of the Camanches, and look up a nearer route home by the way of the Red river, which the hunters and voyageurs all believe to exist. But onward for California was the word, and he who deviated from the trail of the army must expect a long journey for his jaded beast and several days' separation from his baggage. We were not on an exploring expedition; war was the object; yet we had now marched one thousand miles without fleshing a sabre.

Arrived at the town of Pulvidera, which we found, as its name implies, covered with dust, we received full accounts of the attack made on the town by the Apaches the day before. The dragoons arrived too late to render assistance.

About one hundred Indians, well mounted, charged upon the town and drove off all the horses and cattle of the place. The terrified inhabitants fled to their mud houses, which they barricaded. The people of Lamitas, a town two miles below, came to the rescue, and seized upon the pass between the Sierra Pulvidera and the Sierra Secoro. The Indians seeing their retreat with the cattle and goats cut off, fell to work like savages as they were, killing as many of these as they could, and scampered off over the mountains and cliffs with the horses and mules, which they could more easily secure.

This same band entered the settlements some miles above when we were marching on Santa Fé, and when Armijo had called all the men of the country to its defence. In this foray, besides horses, they carried off fifteen or sixteen of the prettiest women.

Women, when captured, are taken as wives by those who capture them, but they are treated by the Indian wives of the capturers as slaves, and made to carry wood and water; if they chance to be pretty, or receive too much attention from their lords and masters, they are, in the absence of the latter, unmercifully beaten and otherwise maltreated. The most unfortunate thing which can befal a captive woman is to be claimed by two persons. In this case, she is either shot or delivered up for indiscriminate violence.

These banditti will not long revel in scenes of plunder and violence. Yesterday Colonel Doniphan's regiment was directed to march into their country and destroy it. One of their principal settlements, and farming establishments, is said to be nearly due west from here, about two days' march; the road leading through the formidable pass above noted.

Yesterday and to-day we came across some unoccupied strips of ground. Their number yesterday was greater than to-day; for, since we passed Pulvidera, the sand-hills encroach on the river and leave the valley scarcely a mile wide. The cottonwood, however, is getting more plentiful, and we have not been obliged to use the "bors de vache" in cooking for some days.

To-night I measured two sets, or 18 lunar distances, east and west ɑ, 12 altitudes of polaris, 10 of andromedæ, and 8 of alpha lyræ. The resulting latitude 34° 07′ 39″.
Longitude 7h. 07m. 54s.

October 5.—Camp near Secoro.—Last night a Mexican came into camp, and said we should now leave the river and strike for the Gila, nearly due west. He was one of the men engaged by me as guide while on the first trip to Tomé. We accordingly moved only six miles to-day, and encamped a little north of Secoro, preparatory to taking the hills to-morrow. The prospect is forbidding; from the Sierra Lescadron, opposite the amphitheatre, as far south as the eye can reach on the western side of the river, is a chain of precipitous basaltic mountains, traversed by dykes of trap. Through these we are to pass.

I rode to the base of the Sierra Secoro, overhanging the town of that name, and about three miles distant from the river. It is a confused mass of volcanic rocks, traversed by walls of a reddish colored basalt and seams of porphyritic lava and metamorphic sand stone. In one or two places, where the water had washed away the soil near the base, I found specimens of galena and copper ore very pure; but of the extent of these beds I can form no opinion, nor can I say positively they were not erratic. The ore in this mountain is said at one time to have been worked for gold, but the difficulty of getting quicksilver induced the operator to move to a mine on the opposite side of the river, near Manzanas, where, it is said, quicksilver is to be found; but the specimens from that place, of what the inhabitants exhibited as rock containing quicksilver, on analysis, was found to contain none. Should the command halt to-morrow to prepare for the mountains, I shall be enabled to give the place a more thorough examination.

To the east, close to the banks of the river, still runs the Sierra Grande, which commences at Zandia with such towering heights, but here tapers down to moderate sized hills. The formation is apparently of different colored sand stone, and wherever the stratification shows itself, dipping about 25 degrees to the south and east; but in some places it is horizontal, and in others showing great disturbance. With the glass may be seen walls of light-colored stone, basalt or trap, running off for miles in a straight line nearly north and south. The town of Secoro, containing about one hundred inhabitants, is prettily situated in the valley of the river which is here almost circular, and about three or five miles in diameter. The church, as usual, forms the salient point, which meets the eye at a great distance.

The growth on the sand plains to-day was chiefly iodeodonda*

---

* Since writing the above, the following extract of a note from Dr. Torrey was received in reference to this plant, which is so remarkable, and extends over so great a surface.

"The *iodeodonda* I find described in a late work by Moricand, entitled '*Plantes nouvelles ou rares d'Amerique.*' It is described by him as a new genus, under the name larrea. It is well figured in his 48th plate as *Larrea Mexicana.* In its affinities it is allied to *guiacum.*"

and a little stunted acacia. The iodeodonda is a new plant, very offensive to the smell, and, when crushed, resembling kreosote. Its usual growth is the height of a man on horseback, and is the only bush which mules will not eat when excessively hungry; besides this were varieties of ephedra, erythercea, helianthus petiolaris, and two well known and widely diffused grasses, the reed grass, and a short salty grass, uniola distichophylla.

October 6.—It was determined to follow the river still farther down before turning west. Great difficulty was experienced in getting teams to assist us. The Mexicans we had engaged, as if by universal agreement, refused to go farther, alleging fear of the Apaches; but the truth was they expected to extort money. In Armijo's day, when a thing was wanted for government, it was taken. Our treatment turned their heads, and, like liberated slaves, there was no limit to their expectations and exactions. We used every means to bring these people to reason, but finding them intractable, and that the progress of the army was arrested, the quartermaster, Major Swords, seized what wagons and animals were needed, and paid a liberal price for them. To our surprise they were perfectly enchanted at the whole business; first at being paid at all, but principally at being relieved from the responsibility of deciding for themselves what they would take for the chattels. A likely boy who had been engaged to go to California as arriero, was to-day claimed by his creditor or master. He owed the man sixty dollars, and was by the law of the country paying this debt by serving at two dollars per month; out of this he was to feed and clothe himself, his master being sutler. It was plain he could not pay his debt in his lifetime. When such debtors get old and unfit for labor, it is the custom to manumit them with great pomp and ceremony. This makes the beggars of the country. The poor debtors thus enthralled for life for a debt of sixty dollars are called peons, and constitute, as a class, the cheapest laborers in the world. The price of the labor for life of a man was, in the case we have stated, sixty dollars, without any expense of rearing and maintenance in infancy or old age, the wages covering only a sum barely sufficient for the most scanty supply of food and clothing.

I saw some objects perched on the hills to the west, which were at first mistaken for large cedars, but dwindled by distance to a shrub. Chaboneau (one of our guides) exclaimed "Indians! There are the Apaches." His more practised eye detected human figures in my shrubbery. They came in and held a council, swore eternal friendship, as usual, no doubt with the mental reservation to rob the first American or Mexican they should meet unprotected.

The women of this tribe rode à la Duchesse de Berri, and one of them had an infant, about two months old, swung in a wicker basket at her back. Their features were flat, and much more negrolike than those of our frontier Indians; a few Delawares in camp presented a strong contrast, in personal appearance and intelligence, with the smirking, deceitful looking Apache. Some of them had fire arms, but the greater part were armed with lance and bow. They were generally small legged, big bellied, and broad shouldered.

Came into camp late, and found Carson with an express from California, bearing intelligence that that country had surrendered without a blow, and that the American flag floated in every port.

October 7.—Camp 68.—Two Mexicans deserted from my party last night, frightened by the accounts of the hardships of the trip brought by Carson and his party. Yesterday's news caused some changes in our camp; one hundred dragoons, officered by Captain Moore and Lieutenants Hammond and Davidson, with General Kearny's personal staff, Major Swords, Captain Johnson, Captain Turner, adjutant general to the army of the west, Messrs. Carson and Robideaux, my own party, organized as before mentioned, and a few hunters of tried experience, formed the party for California. Major Sumner, with the dragoons, was ordered to retrace his steps. Many friends here parted that were never to meet again, some fell in California, some in New Mexico, and some at Cerro Gordo.

Arrived in camp late, after a most fatiguing day, watching and directing the road for my overloaded and badly horsed wagon. I sat up until very late, making astronomical observations.

About two miles below the camp of last night, we passed the last settlement, and in about four miles left the beaten road, which crosses the east side of the river, and thenceforth a new road was to be explored. The land passed over to-day, although unsettled, is incomparably the best in New Mexico; the valley is broader, the soil firmer, and the growth of timber, along the river, larger and more dense.

The ruins of one or two deserted modern towns, probably Valverde, and remains of ditching, for irrigation, were passed to-day. The frequent incursions of the Indians are said to cause the desertion of this part of the valley.

As we approached our camp, the lofty range of mountains sweeping to the northwest, around the head of the Gila, became unmasked, at the same moment that the Puerco range showed themselves on the eastern side of the river Del Norte, stretching boldly and far away to the south. This last ridge of mountains is to the east, and altogether distinct from that commencing at Zandia, and tapering off to the south close to the river.

I have heretofore revelled in the perfect stillness and quietude of the air and scenery of New Mexico; yesterday and to-day have been exceptions, for the wind has been very high from the south, and the dust overwhelming.

Computed to-day the height of the Secoro mountain to be 2,700 feet above the level of the plain. Several officers guessed at the height of the mountain, and the mean of all the guesses was 1,200 feet, and the distance of the peak only two and a half miles, while it was, in fact, upwards of four miles. He who attempts to reckon the height and distance of hills in this pure, dry atmosphere, after coming from ours, will always fall as much short of the mark.*

One or two large white cedars were seen to-day, and, in addition

---

* Attention is asked to my meteorological record in the Appendix. A wonderful difference between the thermometer and wet bulb will there be seen, showing the dryness of the atmosphere.

to the usual plants, was that rare one cevallia sinuata, gauva parviflora, œnothera sinuata, and a species of wild liquorice, but with a root not sweet, like the European kind.

The latitude of this camp by 10 altitudes of polaris, 33° 41′ 19″. Longitude of this camp, 18 observations, east and west stars, 7h. 08m. 57s.

October 8.—*Camp* 69.—The valley of the Del Norte, as we advance, loses what little capacity for agriculture it possessed. The river commences to gather its feeble force into the smallest compass to work its way around the western base of Fra Cristobal mountain. The Chihuahua road runs on the eastern side, and that part of it is the dreaded jornado of the traders, where they must go most seasons of the year ninety miles without water.

Our road over hill and dale led us through a great variety of vegetation, all totally different from that of the United States. To-day's observations of the plants may be taken as a fair specimen of the southern part of New Mexico. First, there were cacti in endless variety and of gigantic size, our new and disagreable friend, the larrea Mexicana, Fremontia vermicularis, obione canescens, tessaria borealis, diotis lanata, franseria acanthocarpa, several varieties of mezquite, and among the plants peculiar to the ground passed over, were several compositæ, a species of malva convolvulus, an unknown shrub found in the beds of all deserted rivers; larger grama, as food for horses, nearly equal to oats, and dalea formosa, a much branced shrub, three feet high, with beatiful purple flowers. The infinite variety of cacti could not be brought home for analysis, and this department of the Flora must be left to the enterprise of some traveller, with greater means of transportation than we possessed. A great many were sketched, but not with sufficient precision to classify them.

The table lands, reaching to the base of the mountains to the west, are of sand and large, round pebbles, terminating in steep hills from a quarter to a half mile from the river, capped with seams of basalt. Some curious specimens of soft sand stone were seen to day, of all shapes and forms, from a batch of rolls to a boned turkey.

October 9.—The country becomes broken, and the valley narrows into a cañon which sweeps at the base of Fra Cristobal mountain, making it necessary to rise to the table lands on the west side, which we found traversed by deep arroyos, crowned on their summits by basalt, underlayed by sand stone.

I shot two or three quails, (*ortix squamosa?*) differing from ours in their plumage, but entirely similar to them in their habits. We also killed a hawk resembling, in all respects, our sparrow-hawk, except in the plumage, which, like the quail, was that of the landscape, lead colored.

Game in New Mexico is almost extinct, if it ever existed to any extent. To-day we saw a few black tailed rabbits, and last night Stanly killed a common Virginia deer.

Three distinct ranges of mountains, on the west side of the river, are in view to-day, running apparently northwest, and nearly parallel to each other. The lesser range commences at Secoro; the

THE LAST DAY WITH THE WAGONS

next at Fra Cristobal mountain, and the last at a point farther west, yet to be determined. The ravines between are broad, and show the beds of dry streams, which would probably be found watered when near their sources. A butte was seen in the distance, close to the river, and surrounded by trees, which was at first taken for an adobe house, but the near approach showed it a conglomerate cemented by lime, which had been left standing when the surrounding earths were washed away. At its base I found some rare specimens of olivine set in lava. The road was unbroken, obstructed by bushes, and so bad that the wagons made only 11½ miles, and the teams came into camp "*blown*" and staggering after their day's work. Expecting nothing better ahead, it was determined to leave the wagons and send back for pack-saddles. My own pack-saddles having been brought along, I had time to observe the rates of my chronometers and make other preparations necessary for so important a change in our mode of proceeding.

October 10th, 11th, and 12th were passed in camp waiting for the pack-saddles.

We are now 203 miles from Santa Fé, measured along the river; 16 circum-meridian altitudes of beta aquarii, and 17 altitudes of polaris give me for the latitude of the place 33° 20' 02", and the longitude, by the chronometer, 7h. 08m. 57s. We must soon leave the river. A cross section of it at this point is 118 feet wide, with a mean depth of 14 inches, flowing over large round pebbles, making it, at this point, unsuitable fo navigation with any kind of boats.

The height of our first camp on the Del Norte, one mile north of San Felippe, indicated by the barometer, was 5,000 feet, showing we had descended, from Santa Fé, 1,800 feet.

Here the height is 4,241 feet, showing an average fall in the Del Norte, from the camp near San Felippe to this place, of four feet and a half per mile. The greater part of the way the fall is uniform and unobstructed by rapids, and the river flows, for the most part, over a bed of sand, without any sensible increase or diminution in its volume of water. Sometimes its tranquil course is rippled by large angular fragments of basalt, trapp, lava, and amygdaloid, which everywhere strew the table lands of New Mexico.

Our present camp is in a valley 70 or 100 acres in extent, well grassed and wooded, and apparently untrodden by the foot of man; for here we saw, for the first time in New Mexico, any considerable "signs" of game in the tracks of the bear, the deer, and the beaver. We flushed several bevies of the blue quail, saw a flock of wild geese, summer duck, the avocet, and crows.

Above and below us is a cañon, and on the eastern side of the river the Fra Cristobal shoots up to a great height. We saw on its sides, reaching nearly to the top, large black objects which we could not distinguish with our indifferent glasses, but which must be either shrubbery or rocks.

For the last night or two it has been unusually cold, the thermometer ranging from 25° to 32° Fahrenheit, but during the day it mounts up to 75° and 80°.

October 13.—Moved one mile to get better grass. Just as we had pitched our new camp Lieutenant Ingalls came up with a mail, and gave the pleasant information that the saddles were only about six hours behind.

October 14.—We parted with our wagons, which were sent back under charge of Lieutenant Ingalls, and, in doing so, every man seemed to be greatly relieved. With me it was far otherwise. My chronometers and barometer, which before rode so safely, were now in constant danger. The trip of a mule might destroy the whole. The chronometers, too, were of the largest size, unsuited to carry time on foot or horseback. All my endeavors, in the 24 hours allowed me in Washington to procure a pocket chronometer, had failed. I saw then, what I now feel, the superiority of pocket over large chronometers for expeditions on foot or horseback. The viameter for measuring distances, heretofore attached to the wheel of the instrument wagon, was now attached to the wheel of one of the small mountain howitzers.

The valley narrows into a cañon at Bush peak, and opens again a mile or so wide, where we encamped for the night. Growth of to-day much the same as yesterday.

Bush peak is, on its river face, a steep escarpment of basalt, and abreast of it, on the west side of the river, we saw many chips of metalliferous limestone. To-day, met a solitary Mexican mounted on a mule, driving before him a horse, with his back literally skinned with the saddle. He was beating the poor beast over the galled place. The Mexicans generally treat their horses and mules in a barbarous manner, riding and packing them when their backs are running with sores.

October 15.—After travelling three and a half miles, we turned off from the Del Norte and took final leave of it at a pretty little grove, where we found two Mexicans returning from a trading expedition to the Apaches. They were attending a poor worn out jennet, (that had been maltreated and overtasked,) in the hope that a few days' rest would enable it to take their lazy bodies to the settlements.

At this point, several intelligent guides were detached to look up a road further south, by which Captain Cook, who is to follow us with the Mormons, may turn the mountains with his wagons.*

After mounting to the table land, some 200 feet above the valley, it is very level, except where the table land is indented by the streams from the mountains, most of which are now dry. We passed two in succession, both deep and wide enough to contain all the water of the Mississippi, and presenting the appearance of the deserted beds of once large and turbulent rivers. The beds were paved with large round pebbles, mostly of the red feldspathic granite.

On the table land the winter grama (a more delicate grass than summer grama) was in great abundance, but now dry and sun burnt. The other growth noticed to-day consisted of malva, senecio longilobus, small mezquite, fraxinus, (ash,) different from any in the United States; castilleja and datura.

---

* The route followed by Colonel Cooke will be found traced on the map.

Far off to the south, between the peaks of two high mountains, stretched the table land contiguous to the valley of the Del Norte. For the first time since leaving the Arkansas the mirage was seen, and gave the wide opening the appearance of a sheet of water disturbed by the wind. Two distant peaks looming up looked, for all the world, like a fore and-aft-schooner. As I was observing this my mule came to a halt at the edge of a steep precipice. Below were green trees and luxuriant foliage, the sure indication of water. The stream was clear, limpid, and cool, the first, but one, I had seen since crossing the Alleghanies, where water could be drunk without imbibing a due proportion of mud and sand. Its name, Paloma, (Pigeon creek.)

In the valley grows cotton wood, a new variety of evergreen oak, with leaves like the holly, a new variety of ash, and a new kind of black walnut, with fruit about half the size of ours. The oak was covered with round red balls, the size and color of apricots—the effects of disease or the sting of an insect.

Four miles further brought us to another creek of clear water, running sluggishly, and like the last the size of a man's waist. In its valley were many large trees, uprooted, presenting the appearance of new ground.

On the plains and in the dry valleys were many rare specimens of chalcedony. The only living thing seen was a small rattlesnake, the first since we left Vegas, of the size and mark of the small prairie snake, but of reddish hue, like that of the ground it inhabited.

Observed to-night for latitude and longitude; our height was (approximately) 4,810 feet above the sea.

October 16.—We commenced the approach to the Mimbres mountains over a beautiful rolling country, traversed by small streams of pure water, fringed with a stunted growth of walnut, live oak and ash. The soil in the valleys and to the hill tops of the best quality, covered with a luxuriant growth of grama, a species of entriana differing from the large grama. Nothing but rain is required to make this part of the country inhabitable. There were several new and beautiful varieties of cactus and the entamario (tessaica borealis) diotis lanata in great luxuriance; one a miniature tree, with the stalk six inches in diameter, a new species of dieteria like an aster, with fine purple-flowers; aster hebecladus and three-leaved barberry (berberis trifoliolata.)

This must one day become a great grazing country, particularly for sheep. The pure dry air is eminently adapted to them, and they are said to be in all New Mexico very prolific, an ewe seldom failing to drop two lambs.

October 17.—We ascended from the stream, on which we were encamped, by a narrow valley for $2\frac{1}{2}$ hours before reaching the summit between it and the Mimbres, which was so indistinct that I passed it several miles before discovering it. We descended in an arroyo towards the Rio Mimbres, very narrow, and full of shattered pitch stone; the sides and bank covered with a thick growth of stunted live oak. In full view, nearly the whole time of our descent, was a mountain of peculiar symmetry, resembling the segment of a spheroid. I named it "the Dome". Our road led along its base to the north; another path leading to Janos, a frontier town in Sonora, passes down the Mimbres on the south side. The Mimbres was traversed only a mile; for that distance its valley was truly beautiful, about one mile wide of rich fertile soil, densely covered with cotton wood, walnut, ash, &c. It it is a rapid, dashing stream, about fifteen feet wide and three deep, affording sufficient water to irrigate its beautiful valley. It is filled with trout. At this place we found numberless Indian lodges, which had the appearance of not having been occupied for some time. We turned westward and ascended all the way to our camp.

The mountains appeared to be formed chiefly of a reddish amygdaloid and a brown altered sandstone, with chaledonic coating. In places, immense piles of conglomerate protruded; disposed in regular strata, dipping to the south at an angle of 45°. There was also one pile of volcanic glass brittle, in strata about a half an inch thick, dipping 45° to the south. The character of the country and its growth to-day are very similar to those of yesterday; several new plants and shrubs, amongst which was the cercocarpus parvifolius, a curious rosaceous shrub, "with a spiral, feathery tail, projecting from each calyx when the plant is in seed." The spiral tailed or barbed seed-vessels fall when ripe, and, impelled by the wind, work into the ground by a gyratory motion. The cedar seen to-day was also very peculiar; in leaf resembling the common cedar of the States, but the body like the pine, except that its bark was much rougher. (For the rest of to-day's growth, see catalogue of plants for this date.)

At night, 12 circum-meridian altitudes of beta aquarii, and seven altitudes of Polaris, give for the latitude of the camp 42° 11'.

October 18.—A succession of hills and valleys covered with cedar, live oak and some long leafed pine. We passed at the foot of a formidable bluff of trapp, running northwest and southeast, which I named Ben Moore, after my personal friend, the gallant Captain Moore, of the 1st dragoons. In many places the path was strewed with huge fragments of this hard rock, making it difficult for the mules to get along. Turning the north end of Ben Moore bluff, we began to drop into the valley of what is supposed an arm of the Mimbres, where there are some deserted copper mines. They are said to be very rich, both in copper and gold, and the specimens obtained sustain this assertion. We learned that those who worked them made their fortunes; but the Apaches did not like their proximity, and one day turned out and destroyed the mining town, driving off the inhabitants. There are the remains of some twenty or thirty adobe houses, and ten or fifteen shafts sinking into the earth. The entire surface of the hill into which they are sunk is covered with iron pyrites and the red oxide of copper.

Many veins of native copper were found, but the principal ore is the sulphuret. One or two specimens of ammoniate of silver were also obtained.

Mr. McKnight, one of the earliest adventurers in New Mexico,

VALLEY OF THE MIMBRES

C.B.Graham, Lith.

VIEW OF THE COPPER MINE.

was the principal operator in these mines, and is said to have amassed an immense fortune. On his first arrival in the country he was suspected to be an agent of the United States, and thrown into prison in Sonora, where he was kept in irons for eleven years. He is said to have stated that the gold found in the ore of these mines paid all the expenses of mining, and the transportation of the ore to the city of Mexico, where it was reduced.

We were disappointed in not meeting the Apaches yesterday and to-day. This afternoon three men came in dressed very much like the Mexicans, mounted on horses. They held a talk, but I do not know the purport. This afternoon I found the famous mezcal, (an agave,) about three feet in diameter, broad leaves, armed with teeth like a shark; the leaves arranged in concentric circles, and terminating in the middle of the plant in a perfect cone. Of this the Apaches make molasses, and cook it with horse meat.

We also found to-day the dasylirion graminifolium, a plant with a long, narrow leaf, with sharp teeth on the margin, with a stalk eighteen feet high. According to Doctor Torrey, it has lately been "described by Zuccarini," who says "four species of this genus are now known, all of them Mexican or Texan."

The elevation of this camp was 6,167 feet.

October 19.—I tried last night to get observations for latitude, &c.; but the early part was cloudy, and we fell asleep and did not wake till broad daylight. In the afternoon there was a thunder-storm to the west, which swept around towards the north, where it thundered and lightened till nearly 9 o'clock. The country passed over in the first part of to-day was beautiful in the extreme; a succession of high, rolling hills, with mountains in the distance. The soil rich, and waving with grama. The latter part was more barren, and covered with artemisias.

The spring of San Lucia, $13\frac{1}{2}$ miles from the copper mines, very large and impregnated with sulphur, is in a beautiful valley, surrounded, at the distance of ten or fifteen miles, with high mountains. This was the place appointed for meeting the Apaches, at 11, a. m.; but arriving at 12, and not finding them as we expected, and the grass all eaten up, we moved on to Night creek, making 30 miles. We halted at night on unknown ground, by the side of a creek, so miry that the mules, some of which had not drunk since morning, refused to approach it. It was dark; many of the men mistook the trail and got on the wrong side of the treacherous creek. The mules begun to bray for water, and the men to call out for their messmates; all were in confusion. My thoughts of last night came vividly to my mind, as I heard the voice of my chronometer man on the other side, asking to be shown the way across. I sent him word to retrace his steps two or three miles.

The assembly call was sounded, which seemed to settle all things; and, as far as the clouds would allow me, I obtained observations. This is only the second time since leaving the 100th degree of longitude that I have been interrupted by clouds in my observations. Nothing has been heretofore more rare than to see the heavens overcast.

An Apache has just come in, and says the people who agreed to meet us at the spring yesterday are coming on with some mules to trade.

Three miles from the camp of last night we had reached the "divide," and from that point the descent was regular and continuous to Night creek. The ravines on either side of the "divide" are covered with fragments of blue limestone and rich specimens of the magnetic oxides of iron.

October 20.—My curiosity was excited to see by daylight how my camp was disposed and what sort of place we were in. It was quite certain the broad, level valley we had been traveling the last few miles was narrowing rapidly, by the intrusion of high precipices; and the proximity of great mountains in confused masses indicated some remarkable change in the face of the country. We were, in truth, but a few miles from the Gila, which I was no less desirous of seeing than the Del Norte.

The general sent word to the Apaches he would not start till 9 or 10. This gave them time to come in, headed by their chief, Red Sleeve. They swore eternal friendship to the whites, and everlasting hatred to the Mexicans. The Indians said that one, two or three white men might now pass in safety through their country; that if they were hungry, they would feed them; or, if on foot, mount them. The road was open to the American now and forever. Carson, with a twinkle of his keen hazel eye, observed to me, "I would not trust one of them."

The whole camp was now busily engaged in attempting to trade. The Indians had mules, ropes, whips and mezcal. We wished to get a refit in all save the mezcal, offering to give in exchange red shirts, blankets, knives, needles, thread, handkerchiefs, &c., &c.; but these people had such extravagant notions of our wealth, it was impossible to make any progress. At length the call of "boots and saddles" sounded. The order, quickness and quietude of our movements seemed to impress them. One of the chiefs, after eyeing the general with great apparent admiration, broke out in a vehement manner: "You have taken New Mexico, and will soon take California; go, then, and take Chihuahua, Durango and Sonora. We will help you. You fight for land; we care nothing for land; we fight for the laws of Montezuma and for food. The Mexicans are rascals; we hate and will kill them all." There burst out the smothered fire of three hundred years! Finding we were more indifferent than they supposed to trade, and that the column was in motion, they became at once eager for traffic.

They had seen some trumpery about my camp which pleased them, and many of them collected there. My packs were made. One of my gentlest mules at that moment took fright, and went off like a rocket on the back trail, scattering to the right and left all who opposed him. A large, elegant looking woman, mounted a straddle, more valiant than the rest, faced the brute and charged upon him at full speed. This turned his course back to the camp; and I rewarded her by half a dozen biscuit, and through her intervention, succeeded in trading two broken down mules for two

MOUTH OF NIGHT CREEK.

good ones, giving two yards of scarlet cloth in the bargain. By this time a large number of Indians had collected about us, all differently dressed, and some in the most fantastical style. The Mexican dress and saddles predominated, showing where they had chiefly made up their wardrobe. One had a jacket made of a Henry Clay flag, which aroused unpleasant sensations, for the acquisition, no doubt, cost one of our countrymen his life. Several wore beautiful helmets, decked with black feathers, which, with the short shirt, waist belt, bare legs and buskins gave them the look of pictures of antique Grecian warriors. Most were furnished with the Mexican cartridge box, which consists of a strap round the waist, with cylinders inserted for the cartridges.

These men have no fixed homes. Their houses are of twigs, made easily, and deserted with indifference. They hover around the beautiful hills that overhang the Del Norte between the 31st and 32d parallels of latitude, and look down upon the States of Chihuahua and Sonora; and woe to the luckless company that ventures out unguarded by a strong force. Their hills are covered with luxuriant grama, which enables them to keep their horses in fine order, so that they can always pursue with rapidity and retreat with safety. The light and graceful manner in which they mounted and dismounted, always upon the right side, was the admiration of all. The children are on horseback from infancy. There was amongst them a poor deformed woman, with legs and arms no longer than an infant's. I could not learn her history, but she had a melancholy cast of countenance. She was well mounted, and the gallant manner in which some of the plumed Apaches waited on her, for she was perfectly helpless when dismounted, made it hard for me to believe the tales of blood and vice told of these people. She asked for water, and one or two were at her side; one handed it to her in a tin wash basin, which, from its size, was the favorite drinking cup.

We wended our way through the narrow valley of Night creek. On each side were huge stone buttes shooting up into the skies.

At one place we were compelled to mount one of these spurs almost perpendicular. This gave us an opportunity of seeing what a mule could do. My conclusion was, from what I saw, that they could climb nearly as steep a wall as a cat. A pack slipped from a mule, and, though not shaped favorably for the purpose, rolled entirely to the base of the hill, over which the mules had climbed.

A good road was subsequently found turning the spur and following the creek, until it debouched into the Gila, which was only a mile distant.

Some hundred yards before reaching this river the roar of its waters made us understand that we were to see something different from the Del Norte. Its section, where we struck it, (see the map,) 4,347 feet above the sea, was 50 feet wide and an average of two feet deep. Clear and swift, it came bouncing from the great mountains which appeared to the north about 60 miles distant. We crossed the river, its large round pebbles and swift current causing the mules to tread wearily.

We followed its course, and encamped under a high range of symmetrically formed hills overhanging the river. Our camp resembled very much the centre of a yard of huge stacks.

We heard the fish playing in the water, and soon those who were disengaged were after them. At first it was supposed they were the mountain trout, but, being comparatively fresh from the hills of Maine, I soon saw the difference. The shape, general appearance, and the color are the same; at a little distance, you will imagine the fish covered with delicate scales, but on a closer examination you will find that they are only the impression of scales. The meat is soft, something between the trout and the cat-fish, but more like the latter. They are in great abundance.

We saw here also, in great numbers, the blue quail. The bottom of the river is narrow, covered with large round pebbles. The growth of trees and weeds was very luxuriant; the trees chiefly cotton-wood, a new sycamore, mezquite, pala, (the tallow tree of our hunters,) a few cedars, and one or two larch. There were some grape and hop vines.

16 circum-meridian observations beta aquarii, and 9 of polaris, give the latitude of this camp 32° 50′ 08″. Its approximate longitude is 108° 45′ 00″.

October 21.—After going a few miles, crossing and recrossing the river a dozen times, it was necessary to leave its bed to avoid a cañon. This led us over a very broken country, traversed by huge dykes of trap and walls of basalt. The ground was literally covered with the angular fragments of these hard rocks.

From one of these peaks we had an extended view of the country in all directions. The mountains run from northwest to southeast, and rise abruptly from the plains in long narrow ridges, resembling trap dykes on a great scale. These chains seem to terminate at a certain distance to the south, leaving a level road, from the Del Norte about the 32d parallel of latitude, westward to the Gila. These observations, though not conclusive, agree with the reports of the guides, who say Colonel Cooke will have no difficulty with his wagons.

The mountains were of volcanic rock of various colors, feldspathic granite, and red sand stone, with a dip to the northwest, huge hills of a conglomerate of angular and rounded fragments of quartz, basalt, and trap cemented by a substance that agrees well with the description I have read of the puzzolana of Rome.

The earth in the river bed, where it was not paved with the fragments of rocks, was loose, resembling volcanic dust, making it unsafe to ride out of the beaten track. A mule would sometimes sink to his knee; but the soil was easily packed, and three or four mules in advance made a good firm trail.

This was a hard day on the animals, the steep ascents and descents shifting the packs, and cutting them dreadfully.

The howitzers did not reach camp at all.

A few pounds of powder would blast the projections of rock from the cañon, and make it passable for packs, and possibly for wagons also. The route upon which the wagons are to follow is,

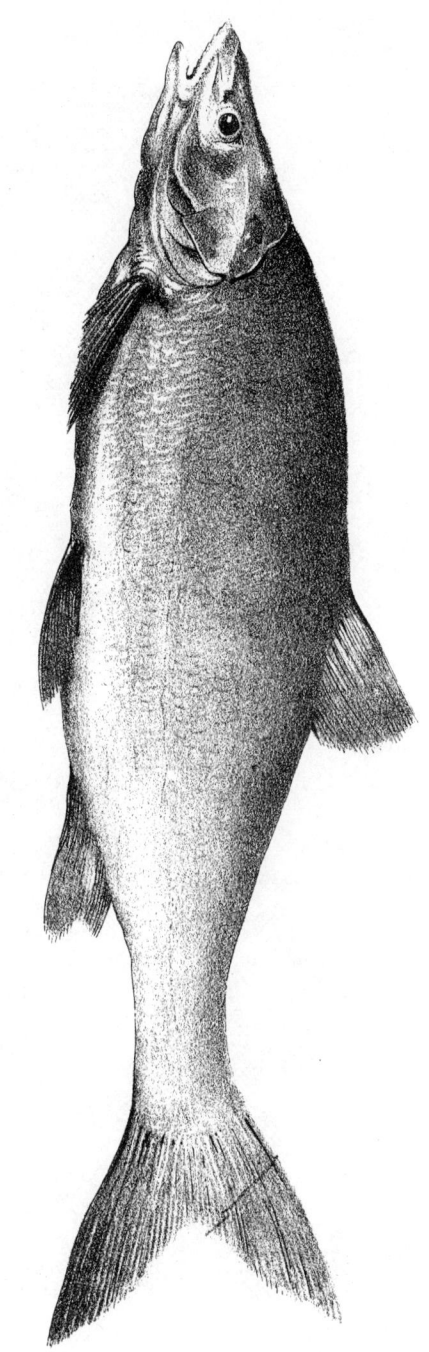

GILA TROUT

C.E. Graham, Lith.

HYEROGLIPHICS

however, to the south of this. Under this date, in the catalogue of plants will be found many differing from those heretofore observed; amongst them the zanschneria Californica, also a new shrub with an edible nut, a grass allied to the grama, Adam's needle, artemisia cana, and many varieties of mezquite.

October 22.—The howitzers came up about nine o'clock, having, in the previous day's work, their shafts broken, and, indeed, everything that was possible to break about them. We again left the river to avoid a cañon, which I examined in several places, and saw no obstacles to a good road. The cañon was formed by a seam of basalt, overlaying limestone and sand-stone in regular strata. Through these the river cuts its way.

Many deep arroyos have paid tribute to the Gila, but in none have we yet found water. Following the bed of one of these, to examine the eccentric geological formation it displayed, I found unknown characters written on a rock, copies of which were made, but their antiquity is questionable.

We were now fast approaching the ground where rumor and the maps of the day place the ruins of the so called Aztec towns. This gave the characters alluded to additional interest; they were indented on a calcareous sandstone rock, chrome colored on the outside, presenting a perfectly white fracture. This made them very conspicuous, and easily seen from a distance. The coloring matter of the external face of the rock may proceed from water, as there was above the characters a distinct water-line, and every appearance that this gorge had more than once been the scene of overflows and devastation.

We encamped on a bluff high above the river, in view of a rock which we named, from its general appearance, Steeple rock.

Latitude of our camp to-night, by 17 circum-meridian altitudes of beta aquarii, 32° 38′ 13″. Longitude 109° 07′ 30″.

October 23.—Last night the heavens became overcast, the air damp, and we expected for the first time since leaving Santa Fé, (a month to-morrow,) to have a sprinkle of rain; but, at 9 this morning, the clouds had all been chased away, and the sun careered up in undisputed possession of all above the horizon. The atmosphere resumed its dryness and elasticity, and at night the stars looked brighter, and the depth of the spaces between greater, than ever.

The changes of temperature are very great, owing to the distance from the influence of large masses of water, and, if they were accompanied by corresponding changes in humidity, they would be insupportable. Last night we went to bed with the thermometer at 70° Fahrenheit, and awakened this morning shivering, the thermometer marking 25°; yet, notwithstanding, our blankets were as dry as though we had slept in a house.

The table land, 150 feet above the river, was covered so thick with large paving pebbles, as to make it difficult to get a smooth place to lie upon.

The growth of to-day and yesterday, on the hills and in the valleys, very much resembles that on the Del Norte, the only exceptions being a few new and beautiful varieties of the cactus. After leaving our last night's camp, for a mile, the general appearance, width of the valley, and soil, much resemble the most fertile parts of that river. This, so far, has decidedly the best soil, and the fall of the river being greater, makes it more easy to irrigate.

To-day we passed one of the long sought ruins. I examined it minutely, and the only evidences of handicraft remaining, were immense quantities of broken pottery, extending for two miles along the river. There were a great many stones, rounded by attrition of the water, scattered about; and, if they had not occasionally been disposed in lines forming rectangles with each other, the supposition would be, that they had been deposited there by natural causes.

October 24.—To-day we laid by to recruit. Although the moon was not in a favorable position, I availed myself of the opportunity to get a few lunar distances. 18 circum-meridian altitude of beta aquarii, and 12 altitudes of polaris, give for the latitude of the place 32° 44′ 52″, and 8 distances between ⊄ and Fomalhaut give for the longitude 109° 22′ 00″. We feasted to-day on the blue quail and teal, and at night Stanly came in with a goose. "Signs" of beaver and deer were very distinct; these, with the wolf, constitute the only animals yet traced on the river.

October 25.—The general character of the country is much the same as before represented; but towards camp, it broke into irregular and fantastic looking mountains. A rose-colored tint was imparted to the whole landscape, by the predominance of red feldspar. The road became broken and difficult as it wound its way around two short cañons.

We were now in the regions made famous in olden times by the fables of Friar Marcos, and eagerly did we ascend every mound, expecting to see in the distance what I fear is but the fabulous " Casa Montezuma." Once, as we turned a sharp hill, the bold outline of a castle presented itself, with the tops of the walls horizontal, the corners vertical, and apparently one front bastioned. My companion agreed with me that we at last beheld this famed building; on we spurred our unwilling brutes; restless for the show, I drew out my telescope, when to my disappointment a clay butte, with regular horizontal seams, stood in the place of our castle; but to the naked eye the delusion was complete. It is not impossible that this very butte, which stands on an imposing height in the centre of a vast amphitheatre of turreted hills, has been taken by the trappers, willing to see, and more especially to report marvellous things, for the " Casa Montezuma." The Indians here do not know the name Aztec. Montezuma is the outward point in their chronology; and as he is supposed to have lived and reigned for all time preceding his disappearance, so do they speak of every event preceding the Spanish conquest as of the days of Montezuma.

The name, at this moment, is as familiar to every Indian, Puebla, Apache, and Navajoe, as that of our Saviour or Washington is to us. In the person of Montezuma, they unite both qualities of divinity and patriot.

We passed to-day the ruins of two more villages similar to those of yesterday. The foundation of the largest house seen yesterday was 60 by 20 feet; to-day, 40 by 30. About none did we find any vestiges of the mechanical arts, except the pottery; the stone forming the supposed foundation was round and unhewn, and some cedar logs were also found about the houses, much decayed, bearing no mark of an edged tool. Except these ruins, of which not one stone remained upon another, no marks of human hands or footstep have been visible for many days, until to-day we came upon a place where there had been an extensive fire. Following the course of this fire, as it bared the ground of the shrubbery, and exposed the soil, &c., to view, I found what was to us a very great vegetable curiosity, a cactus, 18 inches high, and 18 inches in its greatest diameter, containing 20 vertical volutes, armed with strong spines. When the traveller is parched with thirst, one of these, split open, will give sufficient liquid to afford relief. Several of these cacti were found nearly torn from the earth, and lying in the dry bed of a stream.

These and the mezquite, acacia, prosopis odorata, and prosopis glandulosa, now form the principal growth. Under the name mezquite, the voyageur comprises all the acacia and prosopis family.

Last night, about nine o'clock, I heard the yell of a wolf, resembling that of a four months' old pup. In a few minutes there was a noise like distant thunder. "Stampede!" shouted a fellow, and in an instant every man was amongst the mules. With one rush they had broken every rope; and this morning, when we started, one of our mules was missing, which gave us infinite annoyance. Our party is so economically provided that we could not afford to lose even a mule, and I left four men to look it up, who did not rejoin us till night.

A question arose involving a serious point of mountain law, which differs somewhat from prairie law. One of my party captured a beautiful dun colored mule, which was claimed by another party; the one claiming the prize for having first seen the animal and then catching it with the lazo. The other pleaded ownership of the rope, used as a lazo, as its title. It was settled to the satisfaction of the first.

The mule was one which Carson had left on his way out, and on being asked why he did not claim it, he said it was too young to be useful in packing, and as we now had plenty of beef, it would not be required for food, and he did not care about it.

October 26.—Soon after leaving camp, the banks of the river became gullied on each side by deep and impassable arroyos. This drove us insensibly to the mountains, until at length we found ourselves some thousand feet above the river, and it was not until we had made sixteen miles that we again descended to it. This distance occupied eight and a half hours of incessant toil to the men, and misery to our best mules. Some did not reach camp at all, and when the day dawned one or two, who had lost their way, were seen on the side of the mountain, within a few steps of a high precipice, from which it required some skill to extricate them. The men named this pass "the Devil's turnpike," and I see no reason to change it. The whole way was a succession of steep ascents and descents, paved with sharp, angular fragments of basalt and trap. The metallic clink of spurs, and the rattling of the mule shoes, the high black peaks, the deep dark ravines, and the unearthly looking cactus, which stuck out from the rocks like the ears of Mephistopheles, all favored the idea that we were now treading on the verge of the regions below. Occasionally a mule gave up the ghost, and was left as a propitiatory tribute to the place. This day's journey cost us some twelve or fifteen mules; one of mine fell headlong down a precipice, and, to the surprise of all, survived the fall.

The barometric height was taken several times to-day. Long and anxious was my study of these mountains, to ascertain something of their general direction and form. Those on the north side swept in something like a regular curve from our camp of last night to the mouth of the San Carlos, deeply indented in two places by the ingress into the Gila of the Prierte (Black) and Azul (Blue) rivers. Those on the south, where we passed, were a confused mass of basalt and trap, and I could give no direction to the axis of maximum elevation. They seemed to drift off to the southeast. Wherever the eye wandered, huge mountains were seen of black, volcanic appearance, of very compact argillaceous limestone, tinged at times with scarlet from the quantities of red feldspar. Through these the Gila (now swift) has cut its narrow way with infinite labor, assisted by the influx of the Prierte, the Azul and San Carlos rivers. As the story goes, the Prierte flows down from the mountains, freighted with gold. Its sands are said to be full of this precious metal. A few adventurers, who ascended this river hunting beaver, washed the sands at night when they halted, and were richly rewarded for their trouble. Tempted by their success, they made a second trip, and were attacked and most of them killed by the Indians. My authority for this statement is Londeau, who, though an illiterate man, is truthful.

October 27.—After yesterday's work we were obliged to lay by to-day. The howitzers came up late in the afternoon. They are small, mounted on wheels ten feet in circumference, which stand apart about three feet, and with the assistance of men on foot, are able to go in almost any place a mule can go.

I strolled a mile or two up the San Carlos, and found the whole distance, it has its way in a narrow cañon, worn from the solid basalt. On either side, in the limestone under the basalt were immense cavities, which must have been at times the abodes of Indians and the dens of beasts. The remains of fire and the bones of animals attested this. Near its mouth we found the foundation of a rectangular house, and on a mound adjacent that of a circular building, a few feet in diameter. The ruin was probably that of a shepherd's house, with a circular building adjoining as a look-out, as there was no ground in the neighborhood which was suited for irrigation. Both these ruins were of round unhewn stones, and the first was surrounded by pieces of broken pottery. Digging a few feet brought us to a solid mass which was most likely a dirt floor, such as is now used by the Spaniards.

In my walk I encountered a settlement of tarantulas; as I approached, four or five rushed to the front of their little caves in an attitude of defence. I threw a pebble at them, and it would be hard to imagine, concentrated in so small a space, so much expression of defiance, rage, and ability to do mischief, as the tarantula presents.

Our camp was near an old Apache camp. The carcasses of cattle in every direction betokened it to have been the scene of a festival after one of their forays into the Spanish territory.

The Gila at this place is much swollen by the affluence of the three streams just mentioned, and its cross section here is about 70 feet by 4. The waters change their color, and are slightly tainted with salt; indeed, just below our camp there came from the side of an impending mountain, a spring so highly charged with salt as to be altogether unpalatable. Several exquisite ferns were plucked at the spring, and a new green barked acacia, covering the plains above the river bed, but vegetation generally was very scarce; this is the first camp since leaving the Del Norte, in which we have not had good grass.

At 8*h*. 40*m*., a meteor of surpassing splendor started under constellation lyra, about 20 degrees above the horizon, and went off towards the south, projected against a black cloud.

The clouds interfered with my observations; but such as they were, 12 altitudes of polaris, 9 of alpha andromedæ, and 9 of alpha lyræ, and 16 distances between the ☽ and alpha pegasi, gave the latitude of the camp 32° 53′ 16″, and the longitude 109° 31′ 34″.

October 28.—One or two miles' ride, and we were clear of the Black mountains, and again in *t*he valley of the Gila, which widened out gradually to the base of Mount Graham, abreast of which we encamped. Almost for the whole distance, twenty miles, were found at intervals the remains of houses like those before described. Just before reaching the base of Mount Graham, a wide valley, smooth and level, comes in from the south-east. Up this valley are trails leading to San Bernadino, Fronteras and Tucsoon. Here also the trail by the Ojo Cavallo comes in turning the southern abutments of the Black mountains, along which Capt. Cook is to come with his wagons.

At the junction of this valley with the Gila are the ruins of a large settlement. I found traces of a circular wall 270 feet in circumference. Here also was one circular enclosure of 400 yards. This must have been for defence. In one segment was a triangular shaped indenture, which we supposed to be a well. Large mezquite now grow in it, attesting its antiquity. Most of the houses are rectangular, varying from 20 to 100 feet front; many were of the form of the present Spanish houses, thus:

Red cedar posts were found in many places, which seemed to detract from their antiquity, but for the peculiarity of this climate, where vegetable matter seems never to decay. In vain did we search for some remnant which would enable us to connect the inhabitants of these long deserted buildings with other races. No mark of an edge tool could be found, and no remnant of any household or family utensils, except the fragments of pottery which were every where strewed on the plain, and the rude corn grinder still used by the Indians. So great was the quantity of this pottery, and the extent of ground covered by it, that I have formed the idea it must have been used for pipes to convey water. There were about the ruins quantities of the fragments of agate and obsidian, the stone described by Prescott as that used by the Aztecs to cut out the hearts of their victims. This valley was evidently once the abode of busy, hard-working, people. Who were they? And where have they gone? Tradition among the Indians and Spaniards does not reach them.

I do not think it improbable that these ruins may be those of comparatively modern Indians,* for Venegas says: "The father Jacob Sedelmayer, in October, 1744, set out from his mission, (Tubutuma,) and, after travelling 80 leagues, reached the Gila, where he found six thousand Papagos, and near the same number of Pimos and Coco Maricopas;" and the map which he gives of this country, although very incorrect, represents many Indian settlements and missions on this river. His observations, however, were confined to that part of the Gila river near its mouth.

Great quantities of green-barked acacia on the table lands, and also the chamiza, wild sage and mezquite; close to the river, cotton wood and willow. We found, too, amongst many other plants, the eriodictyon Californicum, several new grasses, and a sedge, very few of which have been seen on our journey.

We saw the trail of cannon up the valley very distinct; that of an expedition from Sonora against the Indians, which was made a few years since, without achieving any results.

Wherever the river made incisions, was discoverable a metamorphic, close grained, laminated sandstone, and in many places were seen buttes of vitrified quartz, (semi-opal.)

October 29.—The dust was knee deep in the rear of our trail; the soil appeared good, but, for whole acres, not the sign of vegetation was to be seen. Grass was at long intervals, and, when found, burned to cinder. A subterraneous stream flowed at the foot of Mount Graham, and fringed its base with evergreen. Every where there were marks of flowing water, yet vegetation was so scarce and crisp that it would be difficult to imagine a drop of water had fallen since last winter. The whole plain, from 3 to 6 miles wide, is within the level of the waters of the Gila, and might easily be irrigated, as it no doubt was by the former tenants of these ruined houses.

---

* Since these notes were written, a very interesting letter was received from the venerable Mr. Gallatin connected with the history of these ruins. The letter, with my reply, will be found in the Appendix.

The crimson tinted Sierra Carlos skirted the river on the north side the whole day, and its changing profiles formed subjects of study and amusement. Sometimes we could trace a Gothic steeple; then a horse; now an old woman's face; and, again, a veritable steamboat; but this required the assistance of a light smoky cloud, drifting to the east, over what represented the chimney stack. Wherever the river abraded its banks, was seen, in horizontal strata, a yellowish argillaceous limestone.

October 30.—Mount Turnbull, terminating in a sharp cone, had been in view down the valley of the river for three days. To-day about three o'clock, p. m., we turned its base forming the northern terminus of the same chain, in which is Mt. Graham.

Half a mile from our camp of last night was another very large ruin which appeared, as well as I could judge, (my view being obstructed by the thick growth of mezquite,) to have been the abode of five or ten thousand souls. The outline of the buildings and the pottery presented no essential difference from those already described. But about eleven miles from the camp, on a knoll, overlooked in a measure by a tongue of land, I found the trace of a solitary house, somewhat resembling that of a field work *en cremallière*. The enclosure was complete, and the faces varied from ten to thirty feet. The accompanying cut will give a more accurate idea than words.

Clouds had been seen hovering over the head of Mount Turnbull; and as we passed, the beds of the arroyos leading from it were found to be damp, showing the marks of recent running water.

Last evening about dusk, one of my men discovered a drove of wild hogs, and this morning we started on their trail, but horse flesh had now become so precious that we could not afford to follow any distance from our direction, and although anxious to get a genuine specimen of this animal, we gave up the chase and dropped in the rear of the column. The average weight of these animals is about 100 pounds, and their color invariably light pepper and salt. Their flesh is said to be palatable, if the musk which lies near the back part of the spine is carefully removed.

Many "fresh signs" of Indians were seen, but, as on previous days, we could not catch a glimpse of them. They carefully avoided us. This evening, however, as Robideaux unarmed was riding in advance, he emerged suddenly from a cavity in the ground, thickly masqued by mezquite. He had discovered two Indians on horseback within twenty yards of him. The interview was awkward to both parties, but Robideaux was soon relieved by the arrival of the head of our column. The Indians were thrown into the greatest consternation; they were tolerably mounted, but escape was hopeless. Two more miserable looking objects I never beheld; their legs, (unlike the Apaches we left behind) were large and muscular, but their faces and bodies (for they were naked,) were one mass of wrinkles, almost approaching to scales. They were armed with bows and arrows, and one with a quiver of fresh cut reeds. Neither could speak Spanish, and the communication was by signs. They were directed to go with us to camp, where they would receive food and clothing; but they resolutely refused, evidently thinking certain death awaited them, and that it would be preferable to meet it then than suffer suspense. The chief person talked all the time in a tongue resembling more the bark of a mastiff, than the words of a human being. Our anxiety to communicate to the tribe our friendly feeling, and more especially our desire to purchase mules, was very great; but they were firm in their purpose not to follow, and much to their surprise, (they seemed incapable of expressing joy,) we left them and their horses untouched.

They were supposed by some to be the Cayotes, a branch of the Apaches, but Londeau thought they belonged to the tribe of Tremblers, who acquired their name from their emotions at meeting the whites.

Observed to-night 12 altitudes of polaris for latitude, and measured 9 lunar distances for longitude.

Lat. 33° 12' 10". Long. 110° 20' 46".

October 31.—To-day we were doomed to another sad disappointment. Reaching the San Francisco about noon, we unsaddled to refresh our horses and allow time to look up a trail by which we could pass the formidable range of mountains through which the Gila cut its way, making a deep cañon impassable for the howitzers. A yell on the top of a distant hill announced the presence of three well mounted Indians, and persons were sent out to bring them in. Our mules were now fast failing, and the road before us unknown. These Indians, if willing, could supply us with mules and show us the road. Our anxiety to see the result of the interview was, consequently, very great. It was amusing, and at the same time very provoking. They would allow but one of our party to approach. Long was the talk by signs and gestures; at length they consented to come into camp, and moved forward about a hundred yards, when a new apprehension seemed to seize them, and they stopped. They said, as well as could be understood, that the two old men we met yesterday had informed their chief of our presence, and wish to obtain mules; that he was on his way with some, and had sent *them* ahead to sound a parley. They were better looking, and infinitely better conditioned, than those we met yesterday, resembling strongly the Apaches of the copper mines, and like them decked in the plundered garb of the Mexicans.

The day passed, but no Indians came; treacherous themselves, they expect treachery in others. At everlasting war with the rest of mankind, they kill at sight all who fall in their power. The conduct of the Mexicans to them is equally bad, for they decoy and kill the Apaches whenever they can. The former Governor of Sonora employed a bold and intrepid Irishman, named Kirker, to hunt the Apaches He had in his employment whites and Delaware Indians, and was allowed, besides a per diem, $100 per scalp, and $25 for a prisoner. A story is also told of one Johnson, an Englishman, an Apache trader, who, allured by the reward, induced a number of these people to come to his camp, and placed a barrel of flour for them to help themselves; when the crowd was thickest of men, women, and children, he fired a six pounder amongst them from a concealed place and killed great numbers.

13 circum-meridian altitudes of beta aquarii, and 10 altitudes of polaris give the latitude of this camp 33° 14' 29''. The longitude by 12 lunar distances E. and W. is 110° 30' 24''.

November 1.—No alternative seemed to offer but to pursue Carson's old trail sixty miles over a rough country, without water, and two, if not three days' journey. Under this, in their shattered condition, our mules must sink. We followed the Gila river six or seven miles, when it became necessary to leave it, how long was uncertain. Giving our animals a bite of the luxurious grama on the river banks, we filled every vessel capable of holding water, and commenced the jornada. The ascent was very rapid, the hills steep, and the footing insecure. After travelling five or six miles, ascending all the way, we found trails from various directions converging in front of us, evidently leading to a village or a spring; it proved to be the last. The spring consisted of a few deep holes, filled with delicious water, overgrown with cotton wood; and, although the grass was not good, we determined to halt for the night, as the howitzers were not yet up, and it was doubtful when we should meet with water again. I took advantage of the early halt to ascend, with the barometer, a very high peak overhanging the camp, which I took to be the loftiest in the Piñon Lano range on the north side of the Gila.

Its approximate height was only 5,724 feet above the sea. The view was very extensive; rugged mountains bounded the entire horizon. Very far to the northeast was a chain of mountains covered with snow, but I could not decide whether it was the range on the east side of the Del Norte or the Sierras Mimbres. Near the top of this peak the mezcal grew in abundance, and with the stalk of one 25 feet long we erected a flag-staff. Here too we found huge masses of the conglomerate before described, apparently as if it had been arrested in rolling from an impending height, but there was no point higher than this for many miles, and the intervening ravines were deep. Lower down we found a large mass of many thousand tons of the finer conglomerate, the shape of a truncated pyramid standing on its smallest base. It appeared so nicely balanced, a feather might have overthrown it. A well levelled seat of large slabs of red ferruginous sand-stone altered by heat indicated we were not on untrodden ground. It was the watch-tower of the Apache; from it he could track the valley of the Gila beyond the base of Mount Graham.

At the point where we left the Gila, there stands a cactus six feet in circumference, and so high I could not reach half way to the top of it, with the point of my sabre by many feet; and a short distance up the ravine is a grove of these or pitahaya, much larger than the one I measured, and with large branches. These plants bear a saccharine fruit much prized by the Indians and Mexicans. "They are without leaves, the fruit growing to the boughs. The fruit resembles the burr of a chesnut and is full of prickles, but the pulp resembles that of the fig, only more soft and luscious." In some it is white, in some red, and in others yellow, but always of exquisite taste.

A new shrub bearing a delicious nutritious nut and in sufficient abundance to form an article of food for the Apaches. Mezcal and the fruit of the agave Americana, and for the first time arctostaphylos pungens. Two or three new shrubs and flowers.

The formation near the mouth of the San Francisco is diluvion, overlaying a coarse grained highly calcareous sand-stone and limestone. The mountains were chiefly of granite with red feldspar, and near our camp was discernible a stratum of very compact argillaceous lime-stone, dipping nearly vertically to the west.

November 2.—The call to water sounded long before day-light, and we ate breakfast by the light of the moon; the thermometer at 25°. As day dawned we looked anxiously for the howitzers, which were beginning to impede our progress very much. My camp was pitched on the opposite side of a ravine some distance apart from the main camp, the horses were grazing on the hill side still beyond and out of sight. We were quietly waiting for further orders, when our two Mexican herdsmen came running into camp much alarmed and without their arms, exclaiming: "The Indians are driving off the mules. "To arms" was shouted, and before I could loosen a pistol from the holster my little party were in full run to the scene of alarm, each with his rifle. On turning the hill we found the horses tranquilly grazing, but the hill overlooking them was lined with horsemen. As we advanced, one of the number hailed us in Spanish, saying he wished to have "a talk."

They were Apaches, and it had been for some time our earnest desire to trade with them, and hitherto we had been unsuccessful. "One of you put down your rifle and come to us," said the Spanish-tongued Indian. Londeau, my employé before-mentioned, immediately complied, I followed; but before reaching half-way up the steep hill, the Indian espied in my jacket the handle of a large horse pistol. He told me I must put down my pistol before he would meet me. I threw it aside and proceeded to the top of the hill, where, although he was mounted and surrounded by six or eight of his own men armed with rifles and arrows, he received me

CERUS GIGANTEUS.
Engleman, Appendix N° 2 Continued.

MOUNT GRAHAM

with great agitation. The talk was long and tedious. I exhausted every argument to induce him to come into camp. His principal fear seemed to be the howitzers, which recalled at once to my mind the story I had heard of the massacre by Johnson. At last a bold young fellow tired of the parley threw down his rifle, and with a step that Forrest in Metamora might have envied, strode off towards camp, piloted by Carson. We were about to follow when the chief informed us it would be more agreeable to him if we remained until his warrior returned.

The ice was now broken, most of them seeing that their comrade encountered no danger, followed one by one. They said they belonged to the tribe of Piñon Lanos; that "they were simple in head, but true of heart." Presents were distributed; they promised a guide to pilot us over the mountain, five miles distant, to a spring with plenty of good grass, where they engaged to meet us next day with 100 mules.

The mezcal flourishes here; and at intervals of a half a mile or so we found several artificial craters, into which the Indians throw this fruit, with heated stones, to remove the sharp thorns and reduce it to its saccharine state.

Observed last night for latitude and time, and our position is in latitude 33° 14′ 54″, longitude 110° 45′ 06″. Our camp was on the the head of a creek which, after running in a faint stream one hundred yards, disappeared below the surface of the earth. On its margin grew a species of ash unknown in the United States, and the California plane tree, which is also distinct in species from our sycamore.

November 3.—Our expectations were again disappointed, the Indians came, but only seven mules were the result of the days' labor, not a tenth of the number absolutely required.

Our visitors to-day presented the same motley group we have always found the Apaches. Amongst them was a middle-aged woman, whose garrulity and interference in every trade was the annoyance of Major Swords, who had charge of the trading, but the amusement of the by-standers.

She had on a gauze-like dress, trimmed with the richest and most costly Brussels lace, pillaged no doubt from some fandango-going belle of Sonora; she straddled a fine grey horse, and whenever her blanket dropped from her shoulders, her tawny form could be seen through the transparent gauze. After she had sold her mule, she was anxious to sell her horse, and careered about to show his qualities. At one time she charged at full speed up a steep hill. In this, the fastenings of her dress broke, and her bare back was exposed to the crowd, who ungallantly raised a shout of laughter. Nothing daunted, she wheeled short round with surprising dexterity, and seeing the mischief done, coolly slipped the dress from her arms and tucked it between her seat and the saddle. In this state of nudity she rode through camp, from fire to fire, until, at last, attaining the object of her ambition, a soldier's red flannel shirt, she made her adieu in that new costume.

A boy about 12 years of age, of uncommon beauty, was among

our visiters. Happy, cheerful, and contented, he was consulted in every trade, and seemed an idol with the Apaches. It required little penetration to trace his origin from the same land as the gauze of the old woman. We tried to purchase him, but he said it was *long, long,* since he was captured, and that he had no desire to leave his master who, he was certain, would not sell him for any money. All attempts were vain, and the lad seemed gratified both at the offer to purchase, and the refusal to sell. Here we found the mountains chiefly of red ferruginous sandstone, altered by heat.

November 4.—Six miles from our camp of last night we reached a summit, and then commenced descending again rapidly towards the Gila, along a deeply cañoned valley, the sands of which were black with particles of oxide and peroxide of iron. Near the summit, the hills on each side were of old red sandstone, with strata sloping to the southwest at an agle of 25°, and under this were strata of black slate and compact limestone, and then granite.

In the ravines we found, at places, a luxuriant growth of sycamore, ash, cedar, pine, nut-wood, mezcal, and some walnut, the edible nut again, Adam's needle, small evergreen oak and cottonwood, and a gourd the cucumis perennis.

There was every indication of water, but none was procured on the surface; it could, no doubt, have been found by digging, but the Gila was only twenty miles distant.

The last six or eight miles of our route was down the dry bed of a stream, in a course east of south, and our day's journey did not gain much in the direction of California. It was necessary to ascend the river a mile in search of grass, and then we got but an indifferent supply. Except in the two camps nearest to Mount Turnbull, and the one at the San Carlos, we have never before, since leaving Santa Fé, had occasion to complain of the want of grass.

We encamped in a grove of cacti of all kinds; amongst them the huge pitahaya, one of which was fifty feet high.

Geological formation on this slope of the Piñon Lano Mountains: 1st. Conglomerate of sandstone and pebbles; then, red sandstone in layers a foot thick; then, granite very coarse. The depth of the two first was many hundred feet, and in some places its stratification much deranged. Many large masses of sandstone, with thin seams of vitrified quartz.

In the dry creek down which we travelled, we saw a cave of green sandstone, in which a fire had been built; for what purpose I cannot conjecture, as it was too small to admit a man.

The Apaches gave us to understand that a marauding party of their people were in Sonora. The broad fresh trail of cattle and horses leading up the arroyo, induces the belief that they have returned—successful, of course.

Last night was mild, the thermometer at 63° Fahrenheit; and, what was very unusual here, the heavens were overcast, which prevented my getting the rate of the chronometers.

Although we have had no rain except at Mount Graham, where

A TRIBUTARY OF THE GILA

we had a shower which scarcely sufficed to lay the dust, yet the whole face of the country bears marks of rains, and running water met with in no other part of our journey. The absence of vegetation will, in some measure, account for the deep incisions made by running water in the earth.

November 5.—The howitzers did not reach camp last night, yet, the grass was so bad, and our beds, on the round pebbles everywhere covering the surface of the ground, so uncomfortable, it was determined to move camp.

The Gila now presents an inhospitable look; the mountains of trap, granite, and red sandstone, in irregular and confused strata, but generally dipping sharply to the south, cluster close together; and one ignorant of the ground could not tell from what direction the river came, or in what direction it flowed onwards to its mouth. The valley, not more than 300 feet from base to base of these perpendicular mountains, is deep, and well grown with willow, cottonwood, and mezquite.

At several places, perpendicular walls of trap dyke projected from the opposite side of the river, giving the idea that the river waters had once been dammed up, and then liberated by the blow of a giant; for the barrier was shattered—not worn away. In the course of six miles we had crossed and re-crossed the river twice as many times, when we left it by turning abruptly up a dry ravine to the south. This we followed for three miles, and crossed a ridge at the base of Saddle-Back mountain, (so named from its resemblance to the outline of a saddle,) and descended by another dry creek to the San Pedro, running nearly north.

The valley of this river is quite wide, and is covered with a dense growth of mezquite, (acacia prosopis,) cotton wood, and willow, through which it is hard to move without being unhorsed. The whole appearance gave great promise, but a near approach exhibited the San Pedro, an insignificant stream a few yards wide, and only a foot deep.

For six miles we followed the Gila. The pitahaya and every other variety of cactus flourished in great luxuriance. The pitahaya, tall, erect, and columnar in its appearance, grew in every crevice from the base to the top of the mountains, and in one place I saw it growing nearly to its full dimensions from a crevice not much broader than the back of my sabre. These extraordinary looking plants seem to seek the wildest and most unfrequented places.

The range of mountains traversed to-day is the same we have been in for some days, and is a continuation of that of Mount Graham, which turns sharply westward from Turnbull's peak, carrying with it the Gila.

Saddle-Back is an isolated peak of red sandstone that has every appearance of having once formed the table land, and being harder than the surrounding surface, having withstood the abrasion of water.

The uplands covered as usual with mezquite, chimáza, ephydræ, the shrub with the edible nut, and cactus, of this a new and beautiful variety. In the cañon we heard in advance of us the crack of a rifle; on coming up we found that old Francisco, one of the guides, had killed a calf, left there, doubtless, by the Apaches.

The dry creek by which we crossed to the San Pedro river was the great highway leading from the mountain fastnesses into the plains of Santa Cruz, Santa Anna, and Tucsoon, frontier towns of Sonora. Along this valley was distinctly marked the same fresh trail, noted yesterday, of horses, cattle and mules.

The bed of this creek was deeply cut, and turned at sharp angles, forming a zigzag like the bayoux laid by sappers in approaching a fortress, each turn of which (and they were innumerable) formed a strong defensive position. The Apache once in possession of them is secure from pursuit or invasion from the Mexican.

Since the 1st November, we have been traversing, with incredible labor and great expenditure of mule power, the stronghold of these mountain robbers, having no other object in view than making our distance westward; yet here we are at this camp, only five seconds of time west of camp 89, at Disappointment creek, and one minute and four seconds west of our camp at the mouth of the San Francisco.

Nature has done her utmost to favor a condition of things which has enabled a savage and uncivilized tribe, armed with the bow and lance, to hold as tributary powers three fertile and once flourishing states, Chihuahua, Sonora, and Durango, peopled by a Christian race, countrymen of the immortal Cortez. These states were at one time flourishing, but such has been the devastation and alarm spread by these children of the mountains, that they are now losing population, commerce and manufactures at a rate which, if not soon arrested, must leave them uninhabited.

November 6.—For the double purpose of allowing the howitzers to come up, and to recruit our mules, it is decided this shall be a day of rest. The grama is good, but sparsely scattered over the hills, and it is necessary to loosen every animal and let them graze at will.

We are yet 500 miles from the nearest settlement, and no one surveying our cavalry at this moment would form notions favorable to the success of the expedition.

Except a few saddle mules, the private property of officers, which have been allowed to run loose, every animal in camp is covered with patches, scars, and sores, made by the packs in the unequal motion caused by the ascent and descent of steep hills.

The failure of the Apaches to bring in their mules, was a serious disappointment, and entirely justifies the name given to the creek, where they agreed to meet us. Besides, being the only means of transportation, they are, in extremity, to serve us as food, and the poor suffering creatures before us, give no very agreeable impression of the soup which their meat will furnish. However grave the subject may appear, it is the common source of merriment. All seem to anticipate it as a matter of course, and the constant recurrence of the mind to the idea, will no doubt accustom us to it, and make mule as acceptable as other soup.

VEGITATION ON THE GILA

In the sandy arroyos where our fires burn, that look as if they had been formed but a year or two since, was broken pottery, and the remains of a large building, similar in form, substance, and apparent antiquity to those so often described. Strolling over the hills alone, in pursuit of seed and geological specimens, my thoughts went back to the States, and when I turned from my momentary aberrations, I was struck most forcibly with the fact that not one object in the whole view, animal, vegetable, or mineral, had any thing in common with the products of any State in the Union, with the single exception of the cotton wood, which is found in the western States, and seems to grow wherever water flows from the vertebral range of mountains of North America; this tree we found growing near the summit of the Piñon Lano range of mountains, indeed, always where a ravine had its origin.

In one view could be seen clustered, the larrea Mexicana, the cactus, (king) cactus, (chandelier) green wood acacia, chamiza, prosopis odorata, and a new variety of sedge, and then large open spaces of bare gravel.

The only animals seen were lizards, scorpions, and tarantulas.

I made elaborate observations for time and latitude, and for longitude by measurement of lunar distances. Anxious to observe eclipses of Jupiter's satellites, I determined once more to try the small telescope with which the satellites of Jupiter could just be discerned. I strained my eyes for two nights in succession to see if I could discover the moment of immersion and emersion of I and III satellites of Jupiter, which were visible from our camp. My efforts were fruitless, and the result to myself is a distressing nervous affection of the eye, which may injure the correctness of my other observations of this night.

The resulting latitude of the place is 32° 57′ 43″.
longitude   "   "   7h. 23m. 19s.
Rate of chronometer 2075, losing 12″ 7s. per day.
The height by barometer 2115 feet above the sea.
The latitude was deduced from 13 circum-meridian altitudes of beta aquarii, and 12 altitudes of polaris. The longitude from 8 distances between alpha arietis and the ☽, 9 of regulus and the ☽, and 5 of aldebaran and the ☽.

November 7.—About two miles from our camp the San Pedro joins the Gila just as the latter leaps from the mouth of the cañon. The place of meeting is a bottom three miles wide, seeming a continuation of that of the Gila.

It is principally of deep dust and sand, overgrown with cotton wood, mezquite, chamiza, willow, and the black willow. In places there are long sweeps of large paving pebbles, filled up with drift wood, giving the appearance of having been overflowed by an impetuous torrent. The hills on both sides of the river, still high, but now farther off, and covered to the top with soil producing the mezquite and pitahaya, as the day advanced, began to draw in closer, and before it closed, had again contracted the valley to a space little more than sufficient for the river to pass; and at halt, after making seventeen miles, we found ourselves encompassed by hills much diminished in height, but not in abruptness. The road, except the deep dust which occasionally gave way and lowered a mule to his knee, was good, that is, there were no hills to scale. The river was crossed and re-crossed four times. At 12 and 14 miles there were good patches of grama, burned quite yellow, but for most of the way, and at our camp, there was little or no grass, and our mules were turned loose to pick what they could of rushes and willow along the margin of the stream.

Wherever the formation was exposed along the river, it was a conglomerate of sandstone, lime and pebbles, with deep caverns.

Nearly opposite our camp of this date, and about one-third the distance up the hill, there crops out ore of copper and iron, easily worked, the carbonate of lime and calcareous spar. A continuation of the vein of ore was found on the side where we encamped, and a large knoll strewed with what the Spaniards call guia, the English of which is "guide to gold."

The night has set in dark and stormy; the wind blows in gusts from the southwest, and the rain falling in good earnest, mingled with the rustling noise of the Gila, which has now become swift and impetuous, produces on us, who have so long been accustomed to a tranquil atmosphere, quite the impress of a tempest. We have been so long without rain as to cease to expect or make provision against it, and the consequence is the greatest difficulty in getting the men to provide coverings for the destructible portion of our rations.

Three Indians hailed us just before making camp, and after much parley were brought in. They feasted heartily, and promised to bring in mules. At first they denied having any; but after their appetites were satisfied, their hearts opened, and they sent the youngest of their party to their town, which was at the head of the dry creek of our camp, of the night before last. The fellow went on his way, as directed, till he met the howitzers, which so filled him with surprise and consternation that he forgot his mission, and followed the guns to camp in mute wonder. These people are of the Piñon Lano (piñon wood) tribe, and we had been told by the Pinoleros (pinole eaters) that the chief of this band had mules.

Flights of geese and myriads of the blue quail, and a flock of turkies, from which we got one.

The river bed, at the junction of the San Pedro, was seamed with tracks of deer and turkey; some signs of beaver and one trail of wild hogs.

Our camp was on a flat, sandy plain, of small extent, at the mouth of a dry creek, with deep washed banks, giving the appearance of containing at times a rapid and powerful stream, although no water was visible in the bed. At the junction, a clear, pure stream flowed from under the sand. From the many indications of gold and copper ore at this place, I have named it Mineral creek; and, I doubt not, a few years will see flat-boats descending the river from this point to its mouth, freighted with its precious ores.

CHAIN OF NATURAL SPIRES ON THE GILA

There was a great deal of pottery about our camp, and just above us were the supposed remains of a large Indian settlement, differing very slightly from those already described.

November 8.—The whole day's journey was through a cañon, and the river was crossed twelve or fifteen times. The sand was deep, and occasionally the trail much obstructed by pebbles of paving-stone. The willow grew so densely in many places as to stop our progress, and oblige us to look for spots less thickly overgrown, through which we could break.

The precipices on each side were steep; the rock was mostly granite and a compact sandy limestone, with occasional seams of basalt and trap; and towards the end of the day, calcareous sand stone, and a conglomerate of sandstone, feldspar, fragments of basalt, pebbles, &c. The stratification was very confused and irregular, sometimes perfectly vertical but mostly dipping to the southwest, at an angle of 30°. Vast boulders of pure quartz; the river, in places, was paved with them.

About two miles from camp, our course was traversed by a seam of yellowish colored igneous rock, shooting up into irregular spires and turrets, one or two thousand feet in height. It ran at right angles to the river, and extended to the north, and to the south, in a chain of mountains as far as the eye could reach. One of these towers was capped with a substance, many hundred feet thick, disposed in horizontal strata of different colors, from deep red to light yellow. Partially disintegrated, and laying at the foot of the chain of spires, was a yellowish calcareous sandstone, altered by fire, in large amorphous masses.

For a better description of this landscape, see the sketch by Mr. Stanly.

To the west, about a mile below us, and running parallel to the first, is another similar seam, cut through by the Gila, at a great butte, shaped like a house. The top of this butte appears to have once formed the table land, and is still covered with vegetation. Through both these barriers the river has been conducted by some other means than attrition. Where it passes the first, it presents the appearance of a vast wall torn down by blows of a trip hammer. Under to-day's date, in appendix No. 2, will be found many interesting plants, but the principal growth was as usual, Pitahaya, acacia, prosopis, Fremontia, and obione canescens.

The latitude of this camp, which is within a mile of the spot where we take a final leave of the mountains, is, by the mean of the observations on north and south stars, polaris and beta aquarii, 33° 05′ 40″; its longitude, derived by measurement and also by the chronometric difference of meridian between this and the camp of November 5th, is 111° 13′ 10″ west of Greenwich, and the height of the river at this point above the sea, as indicated by the barometer, 1,751 feet.

At night, for the first time since leaving Pawnee Fork, I was interrupted for a moment in my observations, by moisture collecting on the glass of my horizon shade, showing a degree of humidity in the atmosphere not before existing. In the States there is scarcely a night where the moisture will not collect on the glass exposed to the air, sufficient in two or three minutes to prevent the perfect transmission of light.

November 9.—The effect of last night's dampness was felt in the morning, for, although the thermometer was only 37°, the cold was more sensible than in the dry regions at 25°.

We started in advance of the command to explore the lower belt of mountains by which we were encompassed. The first thing we noticed in the gorge was a promontory of pitch-stone, against which the river impinged with fearful force, for it was now descending at a rapid rate. Mounting to the top of the rock, on a beautiful table, we found sunk six or eight perfectly symmetrical and well-turned holes, about ten inches deep and six or eight wide at top; near one, in a remote place, was a pitch-stone well turned and fashioned like a pestle. These could be nothing else than the corn-mills of long extinct races. Above this bed of pitch-stone, a butte of calcareous sand-stone shot up to a great height, in the seams of which were imbedded beautiful crystals of quartz. Turning the sharp angle of the promontory, we discovered a high perpendicular cliff of calcareous spar and baked argillaceous rock, against which the river also abutted, seamed so as to represent distinctly the flames of a volcano. A sketch was made of it, and is presented with these notes. On the side of the river opposite the igneous rocks, the butte rose in perpendicular and confused masses.

This chain continued, not parallel, as I supposed, to the first described barrier, but circled round to the east, and united with it. It also united on the north side, forming a basin three or four miles in diameter, in which we encamped last night. Except a few tufts of larrea Mexicana, these hills were bare of vegetation. Away off to the south, and bordering on the banks of the river, covering the surface of the ground for one or two feet, was an incrustation of black cellular lava or basalt, like that seen about the Raton. Nothing more was wanted to give the idea of an immense extinct volcano. Through the centre of the crater the Gila now pursues its rapid course.

The Gila at this point, released from its mountain barrier, flows off quietly at the rate of three miles an hour into a wide plain, which extends south almost as far as the eye can reach. Upon this plain mezquite, chamiza, the green acacia, prosopis, artemisia, obione canescens, and petahaya, were the only vegetation. In one spot only we found a few bunches of grass; more than four-fifths of the plain were destitute of vegetation; the soil, a light brown loose sandy earth, I supposed contained something deleterious to vegetation*

---

* A specimen of this soil was submitted to Professor Fraser, who says: "It is a light brown, loose sandy earth containing scarcely anything soluble in water, the solution giving only faint indications of common salt and carbonate of lime. A very small portion of iron pyrites is also contained in it, but I imagine its want of fertility may more properly be attributed to its deficiency in organic matters."

We made our noon halt at the grass patch. At this place were the remains of an immense Indian settlement; pottery was everywhere to be found, but the remains of the foundations of the houses were imbedded in dust. The outlines of the acequias, by which they irrigated the soil, were sometimes quite distinct.

The soil was moist, and wherever the foot pressed the ground the salts of the earth effloresced, and gave it the appearance of being covered with frost. In this way the numberless tracks of horses and other animals, which had at times traversed the plains, were indelible, and could be traced for great distances, by the eye, in long white seams.

We found fresh trails of horses, which might be those of General Castro, or the Indians. When leaving California, Castro's determination, as we learn from Carson, was to go to Sonora, beat up recruits, and return. Our route might easily be reached, for we are now marching along a road everywhere accessible, and within three days' march of the settlements of Sonora and the fort at Tucsoon, said to be regularly garrisoned by Mexican soldiers.

We passed the deserted lodges of Indians, and, at one place remote from the lodges, we saw thirteen poles set up in a sort of incantation formula; twelve on the circumference of a circle, twenty feet in diameter, and one in the centre. Radii were drawn on the ground from the centre pole to each one in the periphery of the circle. It was the figuring of some medicine man of the Apaches or Pimos, we could not tell which, for it was on neutral ground about the dividing line of the possessions claimed by each.

After leaving the mountains all seemed for a moment to consider the difficulties of our journey at an end. The mules went off at a frolicsome pace, those which were loose contending with each other for precedence in the trail. The howitzers, which had nearly every part of their running gear broken and replaced, were, perhaps, the only things that were benefitted by the change from the mountains to the plains. These were under the charge of Lieutenant Davidson, whose post has been ho sinecure. In overcoming one set of difficulties we were now to encounter another. In leaving the mountains we were informed that we bade adieu to grass, and our mules must henceforth subsist on willow, cotton wood, and the long green ephedra.

November 10.—The valley on the southern side of the Gila still grows wider. Away off in that direction, the peaks of the Sonora mountains just peep above the horizon. On the north side of the river, and a few miles from it, runs a low chain of serrated hills. Near our encampment, a corresponding range draws in from the southeast, giving the river a bend to the north. At the base of this chain is a long meadow, reaching for many miles south, in which the Pimos graze their cattle; and along the whole day's march were remains of zequias, pottery, and other evidences of a once densely populated country. About the time of the noon halt, a large pile, which seemed the work of human hands, was seen to the left. It was the remains of a three-story mud house, 60 feet square, pierced for doors and windows. The walls were four feet thick, and formed by layers of mud, two feet thick. Stanly made an elaborate sketch of every part; for it was, no doubt, built by the same race that had once so thickly peopled this territory, and left behind the ruins.

We made a long and careful search for some specimens of household furniture, or implement of art, but nothing was found except the corngrinder, always met with among the ruins and on the plains. The marine shell, cut into various ornaments, was also found here, which showed that these people either came from the sea coast or trafficked there. No traces of hewn timber were discovered; on the contrary, the sleepers of the ground floor were round and unhewn. They were burnt out of their seats in the wall to the depth of six inches. The whole interior of the house had been burnt out, and the walls much defaced. What was left bore marks of having been glazed, and on the wall in the north room of the second story were traced the following hieroglyphics.

Where we encamped, eight or nine miles from the Pimos village, we met a Maricopo Indian, looking for his cattle. The frank, confident manner in which he approached us was in strange contrast with that of the suspicious Apache. Soon six or eight of the Pimos came in at full speed. Their object was, to ascertain who we were, and what we wanted. They told us the fresh trail we aw up the river was that of their people, sent to watch the movements of their enemies, the Apaches. Being young, they became much alarmed on seeing us, and returned to the town, giving the alarm that a large body of Apaches were approaching.

Their joy was unaffected at seeing we were Americans, and not Apaches. The chief of the guard at once despatched news to his chief, of the result of his reconnoissance. The town was nine miles distant, yet, in three hours, our camp was filled with Pimos loaded with corn, beans, honey, and zandias (water melons.) A brisk trade was at once opened. This was my *observing* night; but the crowd of Indians was great, and the passing and repassing, at full speed so continuous, that I got an indifferent set of observations.

The camp of my party was pitched on the side nearest the town, and we saw the first of these people and their mode of approach. It was perfectly frank and unsuspicious. Many would leave their packs in our camp and be absent for hours, theft seeming to be unknown among them. With the mounted guard, which first visited us, was a man on foot, and he appeared to keep pace with the fleetest horse. He was a little out of breath when he reached us, but soon recovering, told us he was the interpreter to Juan Antonio Llunas, chief of the Pimos.

We were taking some refreshments at the time, and invited him to taste of them. The effect was electric; it made his bright, intelligent eye flash, and loosened his tongue. I asked him, among other things, the origin of the ruins of which we had seen so many; he said, all he knew, was a tradition amongst them, that in bygone days, a woman of surpassing beauty resided in a green spot in the mountains near the place where we were encamped. All the men admired, and paid court to her. She received the tributes of their devotion, grain, skins, &c., but gave no love or other favor in return.

ACOMA No. 3.

THE INTERPRETER OF THE PIMOS.
BY BIRTH A COCO MARICOPAS.

C. B. Graham, Lith.

Her virtue, and her determination to remain unmarried were equally firm. There came a drought which threatened the world with famine. In their distress, people applied to her, and she gave corn from her stock, and the supply seemed to be endless. Her goodness was unbounded. One day, as she was lying asleep with her body exposed, a drop of rain fell on her stomach, which produced conception. A son was the issue, who was the founder of a new race which built all these houses.

I told the interpreter repeatedly, he must go and report to the general, but his answer was, "let me wait till I blow a little." The attraction was the aquardente. At length he was prevailed on to go to head-quarters, leaving at our camp his bows and arrows and other matters, saying he would return and pass the night with us.

November 11.—Leaving the column, a few of us struck to the north side of the river, guided by my loqacious friend, the interpreter, to visit the ruins of another Casa Montezuma. In the course of the ride, I asked him if he believed the fable he had related to me last night, which assigned an origin to these buildings. "No," said he, "but most of the Pimos do. We know, in truth, nothing of their origin. It is all enveloped in mystery."

The casa was in complete ruins, one pile of broken pottery and foundation stone of the black basalt, making a mound about ten feet above the ground. The outline of the ground plan was distinct enough.

We found the description of pottery the same as ever; and, among the ruins, the same sea shell; one worked into ornaments; also a large bead, an inch and a quarter in length, of bluish marble, exquisitely turned.

We secured to-day our long sought bird, the inhabitant of the mezquite, indigo blue plumage, with top knot and long tail. Its wings, when spread, showing a white ellipse.

Turning from the ruins towards the Pimos village, we urged our guide to go fast, as we wished to see as much of his people as the day would permit. He was on foot, but led at a pace which kept our mules in a trot.

We came in at the back of the settlement of Pimos Indians, and found our troops encamped in a corn field, from which the grain had been gathered. We were at once impressed with the beauty, order, and disposition of the arrangements for irrigating and draining the land. Corn, wheat, and cotton are the crops of this peaceful and intelligent race of people. All the crops have been gathered in, and the stubbles show they have been luxuriant. The cotton has been picked, and stacked for drying on the tops of sheds. The fields are sub-divided, by ridges of earth, into rectangles of about 200 × 100 feet for the convenience of irrigating. The fences are of sticks, wattled with willow and mezquite, and, in this particular, set an example of economy in agriculture worthy to be followed by the Mexicans, who never use fences at all. The houses of the people are mere sheds, thatched with willow and corn stalks.

With the exception of the chief, Antonio Llunas, who was clad in cast off Mexican toggery, the dress of the men consisted of a cotton serape of domestic manufacture, and a breech cloth. Their hair was very long, and clubbed up. The women wore nothing but the serape pinned about the loins, after the fashion of Persico's Indian woman on the east side of the Capitol, though not quite so low.

The camp was soon filled with men, women, and children, each with a basket of corn, frijolés, or meal, for traffic. Many had jars of the molasses expressed from the fruit of the pitahaya. Beads, red cloth, white domestic, and blankets, were the articles demanded in exchange. Major Swords, who had charge of the trading duty, pitched a temporary awning, under which to conduct the business, which had scarcely commenced before this place formed a perfect menagerie, into which crowded, with eager eyes, Pimos, Maricopas, Mexicans, French, Dutch, English, and Americans. As I passed on to take a peep at the scene, naked arms, hands, and legs protruded from the awning. Inside there was no room for bodies, but many heads had clustered into a very small space, filled with different tongues and nations. The trade went merrily on, and the conclusion of each bargain was announced by a grunt and a joke, sometimes at the expense of the quartermaster, but oftener at that of the Pimos.

November 12.—We procured a sufficiency of corn, wheat, and beans from the Pimos, but only two or three bullocks, and neither horses nor mules. They have but few cattle, which are used in tillage, and apparently all steers, procured from the Mexicans. Their horses and mules were not plenty, and those they possessed were prized extravagantly high. One dashing young fellow, with ivory teeth and flowing hair, was seen coming into our camp at full speed, on a wild unruly horse, that flew from side to side as he approached, alarmed at the novel apparition of our people. The Maricopa, for he was of that tribe, was without saddle or stirrups, and balanced himself to the right and left with such ease and grace as to appear part of his horse. He succeeded in bringing his fiery nag into the heart of the camp. He was immediately offered a very advantageous trade by some young officer. He stretched himself on his horse's neck, caressed it tenderly, at the same time shutting his eyes, meaning thereby that no offer could tempt him to part with his charger.

The general gave a letter to Governor Llunas, stating he was a good man, and directing all United States troops that might pass in his rear, to respect his excellency, his people, and their property. Several broken down mules were left with him to recruit, for the benefit of Cook's battalion as it passed along.

To us it was a rare sight to be thrown in the midst of a large nation of what is termed wild Indians, surpassing many of the christian nations in agriculture, little behind them in the useful arts, and immeasurably before them in honesty and virtue. During the whole of yesterday, our camp was full of men, women, and

JUAN ANTONIO — POMO HEAD CHIEF

C.B. Graham, Lith.

children, who sauntered amongst our packs, unwatched, and not a single instance of theft was reported.

I rode leisurely in the rear, through the thatched huts of the Pimos; each abode consists of a dome-shaped wicker-work, about six feet high, and from twenty to fifty feet in diameter, thatched with straw or cornstalks. In front is usually a large arbor, on top of which is piled the cotton in the pod, for drying.

In the houses were stowed watermelons, pumpkins, beans, corn, and wheat, the three last articles generally in large baskets; sometimes the corn was in baskets covered with earth, and placed on the tops of the domes. A few chickens and dogs were seen, but no other domestic animals, except horses, mules, and oxen. Their implements of husbandry were the axe (of steel,) wooden hoes, shovels, and harrows. The soil is so easily pulverized as to make the plough unnecessary.

Several acquaintances, formed in our camp yesterday, were recognized, and they received me cordially, made signs to dismount, and when I did so, offered watermelons and pinole. Pinole is the heart of Indian corn, baked, ground up, and mixed with sugar. When dissolved in water, it affords a delicious beverage, it quenches thirst, and is very nutritious. Their molasses, put up in large jars, hermetically sealed, of which they had quantities, is expressed from the fruit of the pitahaya.

A woman was seated on the ground under the shade of one of the cotton sheds. Her left leg was tucked under her seat and her foot turned sole upwards; between her big toe and the next, was a spindle about 18 inches long, with a single fly of four or six inches. Ever and anon she gave it a twist in a dexterous manner, and at its end was drawn a coarse cotton thread. This was their spinning jenny. Led on by this primitive display, I asked for their loom by pointing to the thread and then to the blanket girded about the woman's loins. A fellow stretched in the dust sunning himself, rose up leisurely and untied a bundle which I had supposed to be a bow and arrow. This little package, with four stakes in the ground, was the loom. He stretched his cloth and commenced the process of weaving.

We travelled $15\frac{1}{2}$ miles and encamped on the dividing ground between the Pimos and Maricopas. For the whole distance, we passed through cultivated grounds, over a luxuriantly rich soil. The plain appeared to extend in every direction 15 or 20 miles, except in one place about five miles before reaching camp, where a low chain of hills comes in from the southeast, and terminates some miles from the river. The bed of the Gila, opposite the village, is said to be dry; the whole water being drawn off by the zequias of the Pimos for irrigation; but their ditches are larger than is necessary for this purpose, and the water which is not used returns to the bed of the river with little apparent diminution in its volume.

Looking from our camp north, 30 west, you see a great plain with mountains rising in the distance on each side. This prospect had induced some travellers to venture from here in a direct line to

Monterey in California, but there is neither grass nor water on that passage, and thirst and distress overcame, undoubtedly, those who attempted it.

In almost an opposite direction north, 50 east, there is a gap in the mountains through which the Salt river flows to meet the Gila, making with it an acute angle, at a point ten or fifteen miles distant from our camp, bearing northwest. A little north of east, another gap, twenty or thirty miles distant, shows where the Rio San Francisco flows into the Salt river. From the best information I can collect, the San Francisco comes in from the north; its valley is narrow and much cañoned; good grass abounds all the way. Le Vonoceur, one of my party, came down that river in 1844 with a trapping party of forty-eight men. He states that they were much annoyed the whole way by the Apache Indians, a great many of whom reside on that river. Every night they were fired upon, and an attempt made to stampede their mules. Many traps were stolen, and one of their party, an old man, who had been in the mountains forty-five years, was killed by the Indians in this expedition.

Near the junction of the Gila and Salt rivers, there is a chain of low serrated hills coming in from both sides, contracting the valley considerably. Around the South Spur the Gila turns, making its course in a more southerly direction. To the east, except where the spurs already mentioned protrude, the plain extends as far as the eye can reach. A great deal of the land is cultivated, but there is still a vast portion within the level of the Gila that is yet to be put under tillage. The population of the Pimos and Maricopas together is estimated variously at from three to ten thousand. The first is evidently too low.

This peaceful and industrious race are in possession of a beautiful and fertile basin. Living remote from the civilized world, they are seldom visited by whites, and then only by those in distress, to whom they generously furnish horses and food. Aguardiente (brandy) is known among their chief men only, and the abuse of this, and the vices which it entails, are yet unknown.

They are without other religion than a belief in one great and over-ruling spirit.

Their peaceful disposition is not the result of incapacity for war, for they are at all times enabled to meet and vanquish the Apaches in battle, and when we passed, they had just returned from an expedition in the Apache country to revenge some thefts and other outrages, with eleven scalps and thirteen prisoners. The prisoners are sold as slaves to the Mexicans.

The Maricopas occupy that part of the basin lying between camp 97 and the mouth of the Salt river, and all that has been said of the Pimos, is applicable to them. They live in cordial amity, and their habits, agriculture, religion, and manufactures, are the same. In stature, they are taller; their noses are more aquiline, and they have a much readier manner of speaking and acting. I noticed that most of the interpreters of the Pimos were of this tribe, and also the men we met with in the spy guard.

PIMOS & COCO MARICOPAS INDIANS

Though fewer in number, they appear to be superior in intelligence and personal appearance.

Don Jose Messio is their governor, and, like the governor of the Pimos, holds his office by the appointment of the Mexican governor of California. The people have no choice in the selection. Both these Indians are respectable looking old men, and seem to be really worthy of the trust reposed in them.

We had not been long in camp before a dense column of dust down the river announced the approach of the Maricopas, some on foot, but mostly on horseback. They came into camp at full speed, unarmed, and in the most confident manner, bringing water melons, meal, pinole, and salt, for trade. The salt is taken from the plains; wherever there are bottoms which have no natural drainage, the salt effloresces and is skimmed from the surface of the earth. It was brought to us, both in the crystallized form, and in the form when first collected, mixed with earth.

My camp was selected on the side towards the village, and the constant galloping of horses rendered it difficult for me to take satisfactory observations, which I was desirous of doing, as it is an important station. When I placed my horizon on the ground, I found that the galloping of a horse five hundred yards off affected the mercury, and prevented a perfectly reflected image of the stars, and it was in vain to hope for these restless Maricopas to keep quiet. News got about of my dealings with the stars, and my camp was crowded the whole time.

The latitude of this camp by such observations as the Maricopas would allow me to make, was 33° 09′ 28″, and the longitude 112° 07′ 13″.

November 13 and 14.—With the morning came the Maricopas women, dressed like the Pimos. They are somewhat taller, and one peculiarity struck me forcibly, that while the men had aquiline noses, those of the women were *retroussés*. Finding the trade in meal had ceased, they collected in squads about the different fires, and made the air ring with their jokes and merry peals of laughter. Mr. Bestor's spectacles were a great source of merriment. Some of them formed the idea that with their aid, he could see through their cotton blankets. They would shrink and hide behind each other at his approach. At length, I placed the spectacles on the nose of an old woman, who became acquainted with their use and explained it to the others.

We were notified that a long journey was to be made without finding water, (to cut off an elbow in the river,) and the demand for gourds was much greater than the supply. One large gourd cost me four strings of glass beads, which was thought a high price. The interpreter who guided us to the Casa Montezuma, on the north side of the Gila, said that on the Salt river, about a day's journey and a half, there was one of those buildings standing, complete in all respects except the floors and roof. He said it was very large, with beautiful glazed walls; that the footsteps of the men employed in building the house could yet be seen in the adobe, and that the impression was that of a naked foot. Whenever a rain comes, the

Indians resort to these old houses to look for trinkets of shells, and a peculiar green stone which I think is nothing more than verde antique.

At 12 o'clock, after giving our horses a last watering, we started off in a southwestern direction to turn the southern foot of the range of hills pointing to the Salt river. Five miles brought us into a grove of the pitahaya, which had yielded a plentiful supply of fruit to the Indians. Our way was over a plain of granitic sand, ascending gradually and almost imperceptibly. After leaving the pitahaya, there was no growth except the larrea Mexicana, and occasionally, at long intervals, an acacia or inga.

We travelled till long after dark, and dropped down in a dust hole near two large green-barked acacias. There was not a sprig of grass or a drop of water, and during the whole night the mules kept up a piteous cry for both.

There was nothing but the offensive larrea, which even mules will not touch, when so hungry as to eat with avidity the dry twigs of all other shrubs and trees. As soon as the moon rose, at 3, a. m., the bugle sounded to horse, and we were up and pursuing our way. A little after sunrise, we had passed the summit and were descending towards the Gila. This summit was formed by a range of granite hills running southeast, and standing in pinnacles.

As the sun mounted, the mirage only seen once before since leaving the plains of the Arkansas, now began to distort the distant mountains, which everywhere bounded the horizon, into many fantastic shapes. The morning was sharp and bracing, and I was excessively hungry, having given my breakfast, consisting of two biscuits, to my still more hungry mule. I was describing to Mr. Warner how much more pleasant it would be to be jogging into Washington after a fox hunt, with the prospect of a hot breakfast, when up rose to our astonished view, on the north side of the Gila, a perfect representation of the capitol, with dome, wings, and portico, all complete. It remained for full twenty minutes with its proportions and outline perfect, when it dwindled down into a distant butte.

We went on briskly to the Gila, whose course, marked by the green cotton wood, could be easily traced. It looked much nearer than it really was. We reached it after making forty miles from our camp of yesterday.

Our poor brutes were so hungry they would drink no water, but fell to work on the young willows and cane. After letting them bite a few minutes, we moved down the river five miles farther, to a large and luxuriant patch of paspalum grass, shaded by the acacia and prosopis.

My eyes becoming sore with dust, I took a large object for my southern star to-night, the planet saturn. 16 circum-meridian altitudes of saturn and 9 altitudes of polaris give the latitude of the camp 35° 59′ 22″, and the longitude given by the chronometer is 112° 50′ 01″.

November 15.—In the morning the general found the mules so much worsted by the 45 miles journey without food or water, that

HYEROGLIPHICS.

he determined to remain for the day. Most of the mules belonging to my party have travelled 1800 miles, almost continuously. Two or three times they have all appeared on the eve of death; but a mule's vitality seems to recuperate, when life seems to be almost extinct, so I am in hopes the day's rest will revive them sufficiently to enable them to undertake what will be the most distressing part of the journey. From information collected from the Indians and others, it appears that we shall meet with no more grass from this spot to the settlements, estimated 300 miles distant.

This has been a gloomy day in the dragoon camp. The jornada cost them six or eight mules, and those which have survived give little promise of future service. The howitzers make severe draughts on them. Yesterday, within five miles of the river, Lieutenant Davidson was obliged to hitch his private mules to them. An order has been given to-day to dismount one-half the command and reserve the animals for packing.

From all accounts there is no difficulty in following the route of the river from camp 97 to this place, and the journey is but a trifle longer; I would, therefore, recommend parties in our rear to get a Coco Maricopa guide and keep the river.

Remains of an old zequia, and the plains covered with broken pottery. About us there are signs of modern Indian tenements, and the zequia may possibly have been the work of their hands. We know the Maricopas have moved gradually from the gulf of California to their present location in juxta position with the Pimos. Carson found them, so late as the year 1826, at the mouth of the Gila; and Dr. Anderson, who passed from Sonora to California in 1828, found them, as near as we could reckon from his notes, about the place we are now encamped in. The shells found to-day were, in my opinion, evidently brought by the Maricopas from the sea. They differ from those we found among the ruins.

Observed for time to-night and obtained the rates of my chronometers; that of chronometer No. 783, 12s. per day, showing a very satisfactory consistency in rate since leaving the mountains.

November 16.—The valley on the south side continues wide, and shows continuously the marks of former cultivation. On the north side the hills run close to the river.

After making ten miles we came to a dry creek, coming from a plain reaching far to the south, and then we mounted the table lands to avoid a bend in the river, made by a low chain of black hills coming in from the southeast. The table land was strewed with fragments of black basalt, interspersed with agate, chalcedony, vitrified quartz, and carbonate of lime. About the summit was a mound of granite boulders, blackened by augite, and covered with unknown characters; the work of human hands. These have been copied. On the ground near by were also traces of some of the figures showing some of the hieroglyphics, at least, to have been the work of modern Indians. Others were of undoubted antiquity, and the signs and symbols intended doubtless, to commemorate some great event. One stone bore on it what might be taken, with a little stretch of the imagination, to be a mastadon, a horse, a dog, and a man. Their heads are turned to the east, and this may commemorate the passage of the Aborigines of the Gila on their way south.

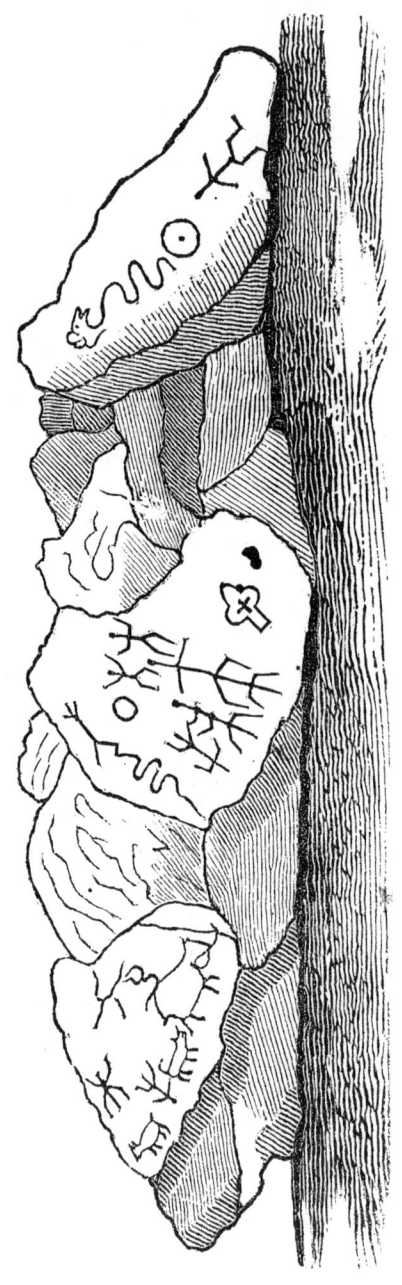

Many of the modern symbols are in imitation of the antique, and, doubtless, the medicine men of the present day resort to this mound to invoke their unseen spirits, and work the miracles which enable them to hold their sway amongst their credulous race. There are many more weird and mysterious looking places than this to be found along the banks of the Gila, and the first attraction to the modern Indian was, without doubt, the strange characters he saw inscribed.

Some of the boulders appear to have been written and re-written upon so often it was impossible to get a distinct outline of any of the characters.

We descended into the broad valley of the Gila, skirted on the south side of the table land, black with basalt pebbles, resting on a stratum of the carbonate of lime upon which the river impinged at every flood, and widened its valley.

The hills on the north side were of red and grey rocks, probably granite, irregular in form, varying from 500 to 1,000 feet. Finding no grass, we loosened our mules among the willows and cane.

November 17.—The route to-day was over a country much the same as that described yesterday. Wherever we mounted to the table lands to cut off a bend in the river, found them dreary beyond description, covered with blocks of basalt, with a few intervals of dwarf growth of larrea. Now and then a single acacia raised its solitary form and displayed its verdure in the black expanse. We crossed the dry beds of two creeks with sandy bottoms. Under the crust of basalt are usually sand-stone and a conglomerate of pebbles, sand-stone, and lime. This last is easily undermined by the river, and the basalt or lava then caves in.

The bottoms of the river are wide, rich, and thickly overgrown with willow and a tall aromatic weed, and alive with flights of white brant, (wing tipped with black,) geese, and ducks, with many signs of deer and beaver.

At night I heard the song of the sailors calling the depth of the water, and presently, Williams, Lieutenant Warner's servant, who had been missing all day, came out of the river with the hind quarters of a large buck, perfectly intoxicated with his unexpected success. Twelve miles back, he let his mule loose, went in pursuit of deer, and killed a buck. After lugging the whole of it for two miles, he lightened his load by leaving one-half.

We encamped down in one of the deserted beds of the Gila, where the ground was cracked and drawn into blisters. The night was cold, the thermometer at 6, a. m., 20°.

Latitude of the camp 32° 55′ 52″. Longitude of the camp 113° 25′ 25″.

November 18.—High wind from the northwest all day, showing that there was still a barrier of snow-clad mountains between ourselves and Monterey, which we must turn or scale.

Carson pointed to a flat rock covered with fur, and told that he had slaughtered a fat mule there. The names of several Americans were inscribed on the same rock.

After travelling some ten or twelve miles through the valley, we mounted to the table land, and at 12½ o'clock stopped to graze our horses at a little patch of dried spear grass. Leaving this, the ground, as far as the eye could reach, was strewed with the black, shining, well rounded pebbles. The larrea even was scarcely seen, and dreariness seemed to mantle the earth. The arroyo by which we descended to the river was cut from a bed of reddish pebbles 20 or 30 feet deep, and as we neared the river they were soldered together in a conglomerate of which lime was the cement.

We saw to-day on the rocks, other rude carvings of the Indians, but their modern date was apparent.

To-day there was a dead calm, about meridian intensely hot, and the dust rose in volumes as our party advanced.

We found the river spread over a greater surface, about 100 yards wide, and flowing gently along over a sandy bottom, the banks fringed with cane, willow, and myrtle.

Last night I took an involuntary plunge into it, for my mule sunk in a quick sand, while I was searching for a place to cross my party. To-night I took a swim, but found the waters disagreeably cold.

The chain of broken hills still continued on the north side, and when near our camp of this date, circled in an amphitheatre, with its arch to the north. The basaltic columns, rising into the shape of spires, domes, and towers, gave it the apperance, as we approached, of a vast city on the hills. The distance of the crown of this amphitheatre, determined by angulation, is —— miles, and Francisco informs me, that against its north base the Colorado strikes. So at this point, which is about six miles below our camp of this date, the Gila and Colorado must be near together. The hills and mountains appeared entirely destitute of vegetation, and on the plains could be seen, only at long intervals, a few stunted tufts of larrea Mexicana, and wild wormwood, artemisia cana.

November 19.—The table lands were the same as those described yesterday, but the valley widens gradually, and for most of the way is six or eight miles wide, and the soil excellent. Some remains of former settlements in broken pottery, corn grinders, &c.; but much fewer in number than above. Nine miles from camp a spur of mountains of an altered silicious sand-stone came in from the southeast, sharp as the edge of a case knife, and shooting into pinnacles. At their base we passed for half a mile over the sharp edges of a red altered sandstone, dipping southwest about 80°, indeed nearly vertical.

On this spur was killed a mountain sheep, one of a large flock, from which we named it Goat's spur. We encamped on an island where the valley is contracted by sand buttes in what had been very recently the bed of the river. It was overgrown with willow, cane, Gila grass, flag grass, &c. The pools in the old bed of the river were full of ducks, and all night the swan, brant, and geese, were passing, but they were as shy as if they had received their tuition on the Chesapeake bay, where they are continually chased by sportsmen. The whole island was tremulous

HEAD OF THE MOUNTAIN GOAT.

C. B. Graham, Lith.

with the motion of the mules grazing, and my observations were, therefore, not very satisfactory.

11 circum-meridian altitudes of procyon, and 12 altitudes of polaris, give the latitude of the camp, 32° 43′ 38″.

November 20.—The table lands were of sand, and the bottom of the river constantly received deposites from them, which changed its bed frequently, as might be seen from the different growths of cotton wood marking the old land. Our road, about five miles from last night's camp, was traversed by a spur of coarse grained granite underlaid by old red sandstone dipping some 80° to the south and west. The direction of the spur was nearly parallel to those before noted, northwest and southeast, which is the direction of the axis of the maximum elevation of most of the mountains traversing the course of the Gila.

Our camp was pitched on a little patch of grass two miles from the river, night came on before the horses reached it, and they were without water for twenty-four hours; there was a pond near the camp, but so salt that the horses could not drink it.

At noon, the thermometer was 74°, at 6, p. m., 52°, and at 6 o'clock the next morning, 19°, which has been about the average range of temperature for the last two weeks.

November 21.—To-day we marched only eight and a half miles, and halted for a patch of grama, which was an agreeable and beneficial change to our mules, that had been living on cane and willow for some days past.

The plains are now almost entirely of sand, and composed of sandy and calcareous loam with iron pyrites and common salt, covered sparsely with chamiza, larrea Mexicana, and a shrubby species of sage, (salvia.)

I observed at night for latitude and time, and there being two occultations of Jupiter's satellites, I was tempted to observe them with our inferior telescope, which only gave us another proof of its uselessness for the purpose.

November 22.—Mr. Warner and I started before the advance sounded, and climbed the sharp spur of a continuous comb of mountains coming from the southeast, to try if we could see the Colorado of the west. The mountains rose abruptly from the plains as they mostly do in this region, resembling in appearance large dykes terminating at top in a sharp ridge which a man could, at any part, straddle. They were of hard granite, pepper and salt colored, traversed by seams of white quartz. This spur gives the river Gila quite a bend to the north, and from that point to its mouth, which we reached at night, the river is straight in its general direction; but its course is crooked and dotted with sandbars, by incursions from the sandhills which now flank both its sides. The sand is brought down by the winds from the valley of the Colorado. Its volume seemed, I think, a little diminished, probably absorbed by the sand.

The day was warm, the dust oppressive, and the march, twenty-two miles, very long for our jaded and ill-fed brutes. The general's horse gave out, and he was obliged to mount his mule.

Most of the men were on foot, and a small party, composed chiefly of the general and staff, were a long way ahead of the straggling column, when, as we approached the end of our day's journey, every man was straightened in his saddle by our suddenly falling on a camp which, from the trail, we estimated at 1,000 men, who must have left that morning. Speculation was rife, but we all soon settled down to the opinion that it was General Castro and his troops; that he had succeeded in recruiting an army in Sonora, and was now on his return to California. Carson expressed the belief that he must be only ten miles below, at the crossing. Our force consisted only of 110 men. The general decided we were too few to be attacked, and must be the aggressive party, and if Castro's camp could be found, that he would attack it the moment night set in, and beat them before it was light enough to discover our force.

The position of our camp was decided, as usual, with reference to the grass. The lives of our animals were nearly as important as our own. It was pitched to-day in a little hollow encircled by a chain of sand hills, overgrown with mezquite.

The sergeant of the general's guard was behind, his mule having broken down, and when he came in reported having seen two Indians about five miles back. For a short time we supposed this immense trail was a band of Indians returning from a successful marauding expedition in Sonora or California; but this conjecture was soon dispelled by the appearance of a mounted Mexican on a sand butte overlooking our camp, who, after taking a deliberate survey, disappeared. The camp was arranged immediately for defence, and a cordon of sentinels stationed on the sand hills.

The two howitzers did not arrive till nine o'clock, and the officer in charge, Lieutenant Hammond, reported he had seen large fires to the right, apparently five miles distant, on the opposite side of the Gila.

The general said it was necessary for him to know who occupied the camp, its force, character, and destination.

He ordered me to take my party and fifteen dragoons, for the purpose of reconnoitering. After beating about in the mezquite for some time, we struck a slough of the Gila, where grew some tall willows. Up one of these I sent a dragoon, who saw no fire, but whose ears were gladdened by the neighing of horses. He slipped down the tree much faster than he climbed it, quite enchanted with the hope of exchanging his weary mule for a charger. Instead of reporting what he had seen, he exclaimed, "Yes, sir, there are enough for us all." "Did you see the fires?" "No! but they are all on horses; I heard them neighing, and they cover much ground." He pointed in the direction, and after proceeding a short distance, we all heard distinctly the noise of the horses, indicating a large number.

Silence was enjoined, and we proceeded stealthily along for some time, when a bright fire blazed before us. I halted the guard, and with two dragoons, Londeau and Martinez, proceeded unobserved until within a few feet of the fire. Before it stood an armed Mex-

JUNCTION OF THE GILA & COLORADO RIVERS

ican. I sent Londeau and Martinez with orders to assume the occupation of trappers, and ascertain whom, and what, the man guarded. The conference was short; other Mexicans advanced, and I sent in man for man. It was not Castro, as we expected, but a party of Mexicans with 500 horses from California, on their way to Sonora for the benefit of Castro.

I took the four principal men to the general, and left a guard to watch the camp and see that no attempt was made to escape. The men were examined separately, and each gave a different account of the ownership and destination of the horses.

The chief of the party, a tall, venerable looking man, represented himself to be a poor employé of several rich men engaged in supplying the Sonora market with horses. We subsequently learned that he was no less a personage than Jose Maria Leguna, a colonel in the Mexican service.

November 23.—We did not move camp to-day, in order to make a refit from last night's capture, and give our mules an opportunity to pick what little grass they could before taking the desert of 90 miles, which lies on the other side of the Colorado, and between us and water.

Warner, Stanley, and myself, saddled up to visit the junction of the Gila and Colorado, which we found due north from our camp, and about a mile and a half distant. The day was stormy, the wind blowing fiercely from the north. We mounted a butte of feldspathic granite, and, looking 25° east of north, the course of the Colorado was tracked by clouds of flying sand. The Gila comes into it nearly at right angles, and the point of junction, strangely chosen, is the hard butte through which, with their united forces they cut a cañon, and then flow off due magnetic west, in a direction of the resultant due to the relative strength of the rivers.

The walls of the cañon are vertical, and about 50 feet high, and 1,000 feet long. Almost before entering the cañon, in descending the Gila, its sea-green waters are lost in the chrome colored hue of the Colorado. For a distance of three or four miles below the junction, the river is perfectly straight, and about 600 feet wide; and up, at least, to this point, there is little doubt that the Colorado is always navigable for steamboats. Above, the Colorado is full of shifting sandbars, but is, no doubt, to a great extent susceptible of navigation.

The Gila, at certain stages, might be navigated up to the Pimos village, and possibly with small boats at all stages of water.

Near the junction, on the north side, are the remains of an old Spanish church, built near the beginning of the 17th century, by the renowned missionary, Father Kino. This mission was eventually sacked by the Indians, and the inhabitants all murdered or driven off. It will probably yet be the seat of a city of wealth and importance, most of the mineral and fur regions of a vast extent of country being drained by the two rivers. The stone butte through which they have cut their passage is not more than a mile in length. The Gila once flowed to the south, and the Colorado to the north of this butte, and the point of junction was below. What freak of nature united their efforts in forcing the butte, is difficult to say. During freshets, it is probable the rivers now discharge their surplus waters through these old channels. Francisco informs me that the Colorado, seven days' travel up from the butte, continues pretty much as we saw it.

There a cañon is reached impassable for horses or canoes. The country between is settled by the Coyotaros, or wolf-eaters, *cochineans*, (dirty fellows,) Los Tontears, or fools, and the Garroteros, or club Indians. These cultivate melons, beans, and maize.

On our return we met a Mexican, well mounted and muffled in his blanket. I asked him where he was going; he said, to hunt horses. As he passed, I observed in each of his holsters the neck of a bottle, and on his croup a fresh made sack, with other evidences of a preparation for a journey. Much against his taste, I invited him to follow me to camp; several times he begged me to et him go for a moment, that he would soon return. His anxiety to be released increased my determination not to comply with his request. I took him to General Kearny and explained to him the suspicious circumstances under which I had taken him, and that his capture would prove of some importance. He was immediately searched, and in his wallet was found the mail from California, which was of course opened.

Among the letters was one addressed to General Jose Castro, at Alta, one to Antonio Castro, and others to men of note in Sonora. All suspected of relating to public affairs were read, and we ascertained from them that a counter revolution had taken place in California, that the Americans were expelled from Santa Barbara, Puebla de los Angeles, and other places, and that Robideaux, the brother of our interpreter, who had been appointed alcalde by the Americans, was a prisoner in jail. They all spoke exultingly of having thrown off "the detestable Anglo-Yankee yoke," and congratulated themselves that the tri-color once more floated in California.

Captain Flores was named as the general and governor, pro tem., and the enthusiasm of the people described as overflowing in the cause of emancipation from the Yankee yoke. One letter gave a minute and detailed account of a victory stated to have been obtained over the Americans. It stated that 450 men landed at San Pedro, and were met, defeated, and driven back to the fort at San Pedro. This last was attributed by us to Mexican braggadocio, as it is usual with them to represent their defeats as victories; but that there was a disturbance of a serious kind in the province, we could not doubt, from the uniformity of the accounts on that head. We also learned that the horses captured were in part for General Castro. Nothing more was wanting to legitimize our capture, and Captain Moore was directed to remount his men.

The letters contained precise information, but being dated so far back as the 15th October, left us in great doubt as to the real state of affairs in California, and the Mexicans played their parts so dexterously, it was not in our power to extract the truth from them.

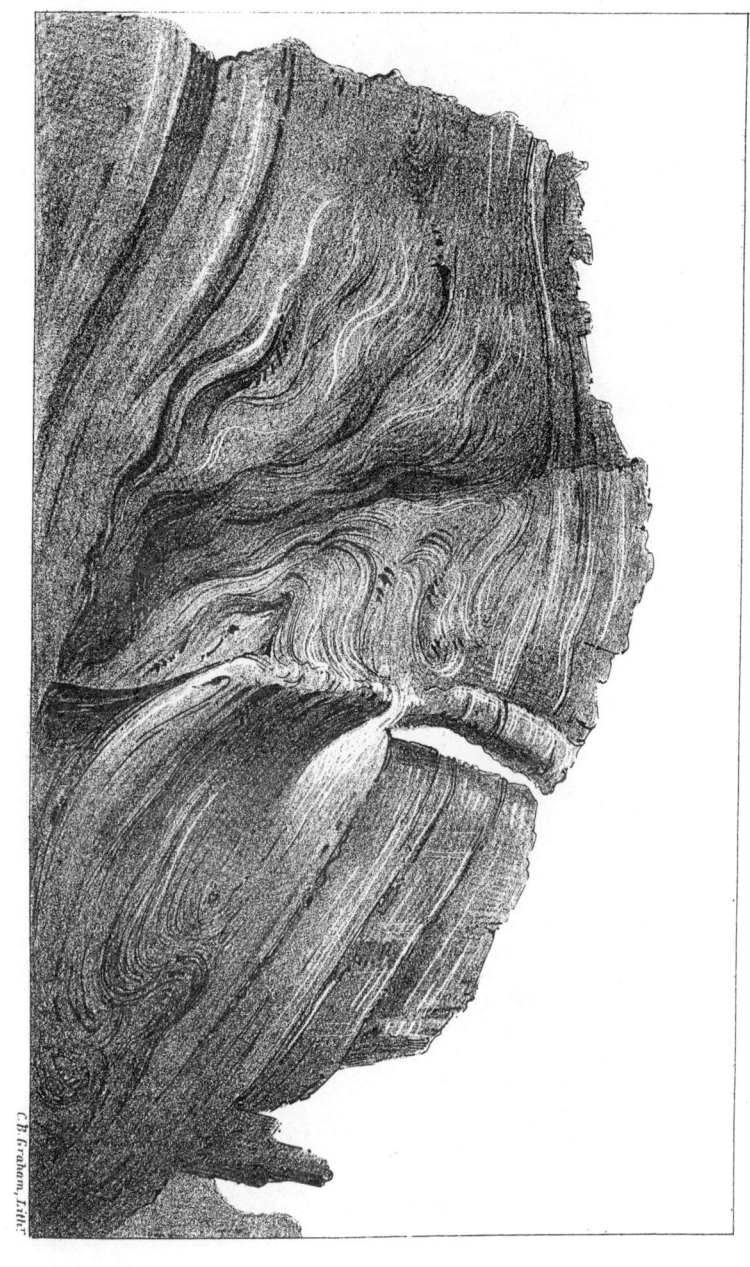

THE FIRE PLACE ROCK

C.B.Graham, Lith.

VIEW ON THE GILA.

C. B. Graham, Lith.

One of the party, who had received some little favor from Carson in California, was well plied with brandy, but all that could be extorted from him was the advice that we should not think of going to the Puebla with our small force, counsel that our friend soon learned we had not the slightest intention of following.

The position of our camp, about one mile and a half south of the junction of the Colorado and Gila rivers, determined by 12 circum-meridian altitudes of sirius, 6 of saturn, and 12 altitudes of polaris, is latitude 32° 42′ 09″. The longitude by one set of lunar distances, E. and W., 114° 37′ 09″, which agrees with the chronometric determination of the same place, determined by assuming the longitude of San Diego to be 117° 11′.

The clouds, together with my military duties, interfered with taking a more elaborate set of lunar distances. An inspection of the individual observations for latitude will show that the latitude of the camp may be relied on, but I regret it was not in my powe to measure the exact distance of our camp from the mouth of the Gila.

At night, passing my arm over the surface of the fur robe in which I was enveloped, electric sparks were discharged in such quantities as to make a very luminous appearance, and a noise like the rattle of a snake.

November 24.—We visited the camp of our Mexican friends, whom the general determined to release, and found there was a woman with the party in the agonies of childbirth. She was at once furnished from our stores with all the comforts we possessed. This poor creature had been dragged along, in her delicate situation, over a fearful desert.

The captured horses were all wild and but little adapted for immediate service, but there was rare sport in catching them, and we saw for the first time the lazo thrown with inimitable skill. It is a saying in Chihuahua that " a Californian can throw the lazo as well with his foot as a Mexican can with his hand," and the scene before us gave us an idea of its truth. There was a wild stallion of great beauty which defied the fleetest horse and the most expert rider. At length a boy of fourteen, a Californian, whose graceful riding was the constant subject of admiration, piqued by repeated failures, mounted a fresh horse, and, followed by an Indian, launched fiercely at the stallion.

His lareat darted from his hand with the force and precision of a rifle ball, and rested on the neck of the fugitive; the Indian, at the same moment, made a successful throw, but the stallion was too stout for both, and dashed off at full speed, with both ropes fly-in the air like wings. The perfect representation of Pegasus, he took a sweep, and followed by his pursuers, came thundering down the dry bed of the river. The lazos were now trailing on the ground, and the gallant young Spaniard, taking advantage of the circumstance, stooped from his flying horse and caught one in his hand. It was the work of a moment to make it fast to the pommel of his saddle, and by a short turn of his own horse, he threw the stallion a complete somerset, and the game was secure.

We traveled over a sandy plain a few miles, and descended into the wide bed of the Colorado, overgrown thickly with mezquite, willow, and cotton wood; after making about ten miles, we encamped abreast of the ford on a plateau covered with young willows, of which our horses were to lay in a sufficient supply to last them over the desert. Since writing the above, we have found a good patch of grass, and our people have been ordered to cut a ration for each mule to carry along.

The night was excessively cold and damp, and in the morning our blankets were covered with a little dew. For the first time, the bugle calls were distinctly reverberated, showing the atmospheric change as we approach the coast, and descend into the neighborhood of the sea level. In New Mexico, even when surrounded by hills and perpendicular walls, the report of fire arms, and the sound of the bugle, were unattended by any distinct echo. The reports were sharp and unpleasant, not rounded, as here, by the reverberation.

The country, from the Arkansas to this point, more than 1,200 miles, in its adaptation to agriculture, has peculiarities which must forever stamp itself upon the population which inhabits it. All of North Mexico, embracing New Mexico, Chihuahua, Sonora, and the Californias, as far north as the Sacramento, are, as far as the best information goes, the same in the physical character of its surface, and differ but little in climate or products.

In no part of this vast tract can the rains from Heaven be relied upon, to any extent, for the cultivation of the soil. The earth is destitute of trees, and in great part also of any vegetation whatever.

A few feeble streams flow in different directions from the great mountains, which in many places traverse this region. These streams are separated, sometimes by plains, and sometimes by mountains, without water and without vegetation, and may be called deserts, so far as they perform any useful part in the sustenance of animal life.

The cultivation of the earth is therefore confined to those narrow strips of land which are within the level of the waters of the streams, and wherever practised in a community with any success, or to any extent, involves a degree of subordination, and absolute obedience to a chief, repugnant to the habits of our people.

The chief who directs the time and the quantity of the precious irrigating water must be implicitly obeyed by the whole community. A departure from his orders, by the waste of water, or unjust distribution of it, or neglect to make the proper embankments, may endanger the means of subsistence of many people. He must therefore be armed with power to punish promptly and immediately.

The profits of labor are too inadequate for the existence of negro slavery. Slavery, as practised by the Mexicans, under the form of peonage, which enables their master to get the services of the adult while in the prime of life, without the obligation of rearing him in infancy, supporting him in old age, or maintaining his family, affords no data for estimating the profits of slave labor, as it exists in the United States.

No one who has ever visited this country, and who is acquainted with the character and value of slave labor in the United States, would ever think of bringing his own slaves here with any view to profit, much less wou'd he purchase slaves for such a purpose. Their labor here, if they could be retained as slaves, among peons, nearly of their own color, would never repay the cost of transportation, much less the additional purchase money.

I made many inquiries as to the character of the vast region of country embraced in the triangle, formed by the Colorado of the west, the Del Norte, and the Gila; and the information collected, will, at some future time, be thrown into notes for the benefit of future explorers, but are not given in this work, as I profess to write only of what I saw.

From all that I learn, the country does not differ, materially, in its physical character from New Mexico, except, perhaps, being less denuded of soil and vegetation. The sources of the Salinas, the San Francisco, Azul, San Carlos, and Prierte, tributaries of the Gila, take their rise in it. About their head waters, and occasionally along their courses, are presented sections of land capable of irrigation.

The whole extent, except on the margin of streams, is said to be destitute of forest trees. The Apaches, a very numerous race, and the Navajoes, are the chief occupants, but there are many minor bands, who, unlike the Apaches and Navajoes, are not nomadic, but have fixed habitations. Amongst the most remarkable of these are the Soones, most of whom are said to be Albinos. The latter cultivate the soil, and live in peace with their more numerous and savage neighbors.

Departing from the ford of the Colorado in the direction of Sonora, there is a fearful desert to encounter. Alta, a small town, with a Mexican garrison, is the nearest settlement.

All accounts concur in representing the journey as one of extreme hardship, and even peril. The distance is not exactly known, but it is variously represented at from four to seven day's journey. Persons bound for Sonora from California, who do not mind a circuitous route, should ascend the Gila as far as the Pimos village, and thence penetrate the province by way of Tucsoon.

November 25.—At the ford, the Colorado is 1,500 feet wide, and flows at the rate of a mile and a half per hour. Its greatest depth in the channel, at the ford where we crossed, is four feet. The banks are low, not more than four feet high, and, judging from indications, sometimes, though not frequently, overflowed. Its general appearance at this point is much like that of the Arkansas, with its turbid waters and many shifting sand islands.

The ford is entered at the lower extremity of the plateau upon which we encamped, and leads down the river, crossing three sand islands, which we sketched, but as they are constantly shifting, will perhaps afford no guide to the traveller, and may even lead him into error. They are therefore not furnished. The ford is narrow and circuitous, and a few feet to the right or left sets a horse afloat. This happened to my own horse.

Report makes the distance of the mouth of the Colorado, from the crossing, eighty miles, but unless the river is very crooked, this cannot be; Lieut. Hardy, of the royal navy, determined the mouth to be in latitude 31° 51' north, and longitude 114° 1'.

The growth on the river bottom is cotton wood, willow of different kinds, equisetum hyemale, (scouring rush,) and a nutritious grass in small quantities.

After crossing, we ascended the river three quarters of a mile, where we encountered an immense sand drift, and from that point until we halted, the great highway between Sonora and California lies along the foot of this drift, which is continually but slowly encroaching down the valley. Prosopis glandulosa, wild sage, and ephedra compose the growth; the first is luxuriant.

We halted at a dry arroyo, a few feet to the left of the road, leading into the Colorado, where there was a hole five or six feet deep, which by deepening furnished sufficient water for the men.

We are yet, by the indication of the barometer, but 20 or 30 feet above the river, and where the sands from the desert to the north have not encroached, the soil appears good. There are remains of zequias about five miles back, and where we halted, the remains of Indian settlements, but it is probable the water has been cut off by the drift, and cannot now be brought from the river above.

I made observations at night for time and latitude, and found the position of the place to be north latitude 32° 40' 22", and longitude 114° 56' 28", west of Greenwich.

We tied our animals to the mezquite trees, (prosopis glandulosa,) and remarking on the way that they showed an inclination to eat the bean of this plant, we sent the men to collect them; the few gathered were eaten with avidity.

November 26.—The dawn of day found every man on horseback, and a bunch of grass from the Colorada tied benind him on the cantle of his saddle. After getting well under way, the keen air at 26° Fahrenheit made it most comfortable to walk. We traveled four miles along the sand butte, in the same direction as yesterday, about south 75° west, (magnetic,) we mounted the buttes and found, after a short distance, a firmer footing covered with fragments of lava, rounded by water, and many agates. We were now fairly on the desert.

Our course now inclined a few degrees more to the north, and at 10, a. m., we found a large patch of grama, where we halted for an hour, and then pursued our way over the plains covered with fragments of lava, traversed at intervals by sand buttes, until 4 p. m., when, after travelling 24 miles, we reached the Alamo or cotton wood. At this point, the captured Spaniards informed us, that failing to find water, they had gone a league to the west, in pursuit of their horses, where they found a running stream. We accordingly sent parties to search, but neither the water nor their trail could be found.

Neither was there any cotton wood at the Alamo, as its name would signify; but Francisco said that it was nevertheless the place, the tree having probably been covered by the encroachments of the sand, which here terminates in a bluff 40 feet high, making the arc of a great circle convexing to the north.

Descending this bluff, we found in what had been the channel of a stream, now overgrown with a few ill-conditioned mezquite, a large hole where persons had evidently dug for water. It was necessary to halt to rest our animals, and the time was occupied in deepening this hole, which after a long struggle, showed signs of water. An old champagne basket, used by one of the officers as a pannier, was lowered in the hole, to prevent the crumbling of the sand. After many efforts to keep out the caving sand, a basket-work of willow twigs effected the object, and much to the joy of all, the basket, which was now 15 or 20 feet below the surface, filled with water. The order was now given for each mess to draw a camp-kettle of water, and Captain Turner was placed in charge of the spring, to see fair distribution.

When the messes were supplied, the firmness of the banks gave hopes that the animals might be watered, and each party was notified to have their animals in waiting; the important business of watering then commenced, upon the success of which depended the possibility of their advancing with us a foot further.

Two buckets for each animal were allowed. At 10, a. m., when my turn came, Captain Moore had succeeded, by great exertions, in opening another well, and the one already opened began to flow more freely, in consequence of which, we could afford to give each animal as much as he could drink. The poor brutes, none of which had tasted water in forty-eight hours, and some not for the last sixty, clustered round the well and scrambled for precedence.

At 12 o'clock I had watered all my animals, thirty-seven in number, and turned over the well to Captain Moore.

The animals still had an aching void to fill, and all night was heard the munching of sticks, and their piteous cries for more congenial food.

November 27 and 28.—To-day we started a few minutes after sunrise. Our course was a winding one, to avoid the sand-drifts. The Mexicans had informed us that the waters of the salt lake, some thirty or forty miles distant, were too salt to use, but other information led us to think the intelligence was wrong. We accordingly tried to reach it; about 3, p. m., we disengaged ourselves from the sand and went due (magnetic) west, over an immense level of clay detritus, hard and smooth as a bowling green.

The desert was almost destitute of vegetation, now and then an ephedra, œnothera, or bunches of aristida were seen, and occasionally the level was covered with a growth of obione canescens, and a low bush with small oval plaited leaves, unknown.

The heavy sand had proved too much for many horses and some mules, and all the efforts of their drivers could bring them no farther than the middle of this dreary desert. About 8 o'clock, as we approached the lake, the stench of dead animals confirmed the reports of the Mexicans, and put to flight all hopes of our being able to use the water.

The basin of the lake, as well as I could judge at night, is about three-quarters of a mile long and half a mile wide. The water had receded to a pool, diminished to one half its size, and the approach to it was through a thick soapy quagmire. It was wholly unfit for man or brute, and we studiously kept the latter from it, thinking that the use of it would but aggravate their thirst.

One or two of the men came in late and, rushing to the lake, threw themselves down and took many swallows before discovering their mistake; but the effect was not injurious except that it increased their thirst.

At the point where we left the sand, sketches were taken of the objects by which our pilot wended his way; these may serve to guide future travellers. From this point the traveller may go directly to the gap exhibited in the sketch, nearly magnetic west, through which the trail passes.

A few mezquite trees and a chenopodiaceous shrub bordered the lake, and on these our mules munched till they had sufficiently refreshed themselves, when the call to saddle was sounded, and we groped silently our way in the dark. The stoutest animals now began to stagger, and when day dawned, scarcely a man was seen mounted.

With the sun rose a heavy fog from the southwest, no doubt from the gulf, and sweeping towards us, enveloped us for two or three hours, wetting our blankets and giving relief to the animals. Before it had dispersed we came to a patch of sun-burned grass.

When the fog had entirely dispersed we found ourselves entering a gap in the mountains, which had been before us for four days. The plain was crossed, but we had not yet found water. The first valley we reached was dry, and it was not till 12 o'clock, m., that we struck the Cariso (cane) creek, within half a mile of one of its sources, and although so close to the source, the sands had already absorbed much of its water, and left but little running. A mile or two below, the creek entirely disappears.

We halted, having made fifty-four miles in the two days, at the source, a magnificent spring, twenty or thirty feet in diameter, highly impregnated with sulphur, and medicinal in its properties. No vessel could be procured to bring home some of the water for analysis, but I scraped a handful of the salt which had effloresced to the surface of the adjacent ground, and Professor Frazer finds it to contain sulphate of lime, magnesia, and chloride of sodium.

The spring consisted of a series of smaller springs or veins, varying in temperature from 68° to 75°. This variation, however, may have been owing to the different exposures of the fountains in which the thermometer was immersed. The growth was cane, rush, and a coarse grass, such as is found on the marshes near the sea shore.

The desert over which we had passed, ninety miles from water to water, is an immense triangular plain, bounded on one side by the Colorado, on the west by the Cordilleras of California, the coast chain of mountains which now encircles us, extending from the Sacramento river to the southern extremity of Lower California, and on the northeast by a chain of mountains, a continuation of the same spur noted on the 22d as running southeast and northwest. It is chiefly covered with floating sand, the surface of which in various places, is white with diminutive spinelas, and every where over the whole surface is found the large and soft muscle shell.

I have noted the only two patches of grass found during the "jornada." There were scattered, at wide intervals, the palafoxia linearis, atriplex, encelia farinosa, daleas, euphorbias, and a simsia, described by Dr. Torrey as a new species without rays.

The southern termination of this desert is bounded by the Tecaté chain of mountains and the Colorado; but its northern and eastern boundaries are undefined, and I should suppose from the accounts of trappers, and others, who have attempted the passage from California to the Gila by a more northern route, that it extends many days' travel beyond the chain of barren mountains which bound the horizon in that direction.

The portal to the mountains through which we passed, was formed by immense buttes of yellow clay and sand, with large flakes of mica and seams of gypsum. Nothing could be more forlorn and desolate in appearance. The gypsum had given some consistency to the sand buttes which were washed into fantastic figures. One ridge formed apparently a complete circle, giving it the appearance of a crater; and although some miles to the left, I should have gone to visit it, supposing it to be a crater, but my mule was sinking with thirst, and water was yet at some distance. Many animals were left on the road to die of thirst and hunger, in spite of the generous efforts of the men to bring them to the spring. More than one was brought up, by one man tugging at the halter and another pushing up the brute, by placing his shoulder against its buttocks. Our most serious loss, perhaps, was that of one or two fat mares and colts brought with us for food; for before leaving camp, Major Swords found in a concealed place one of the best pack mules slaughtered, and the choice bits cut from his shoulders and flanks, stealthily done by some mess less provident than others.

I observed at night for time and latitude; for longitude by measuring 18 distances between the ☾ and aldebaran, and the ☾ and fomalhaut.

Latitude 32° 52' 33". Longitude 116° 06' 09".

November 29.—The grass at the spring was anything but desirable for our horses, and there was scarcely a ration left for the men. This last consideration would not prevent our giving the horses a day's rest wherever grass could be found. We followed the dry sandy bed of the Cariso nearly all day, at a snail's pace, and at length reached the "little pools" where the grass was luxuriant but very salt. The water strongly resembled that at the head of the Cariso creek, and the earth, which was very tremulous for many acres about the pools, was covered with salt.

This valley is at no point more than half a mile wide, and on each side are mountains of grey granite and pure quartz, rising from 1,000 to 3,000 feet above it.

A few miles from the spring called **Ojo Grande**, at the head of the creek, several scattered objects were seen projected against the cliffs, hailed by the Florida campaigners, some of whom were along, as old friends. They were cabbage trees, and marked the locale of a spring and a small patch of grass. We found also to-day, in full bloom, the bronnia spinosa, a rare and beautiful plant; the plantago, new to our flora; a new species of eriogonum, very remarkable for its extremely numerous long hair-like fruit stalks and minute flowers.

We rode for miles through thickets of the centennial plant, agave Americana, and found one in full bloom. The sharp thorns terminating every leaf of this plant, were a great annoyance to our dismounted and wearied men whose legs were now almost bare. A number of these plants were cut by the soldiers, and the body of them used as food. The day was intensely hot, and the sand deep; the animals, inflated with water and rushes, gave way by scores; and, although we advanced only sixteen miles, many did not arrive at camp until 10 o'clock at night. It was a feast day for the wolves, which followed in packs close on our track, seizing our deserted brutes and making the air resound with their howls as they battled for the carcasses.

The water comes to the surface in pools at this place. It is a valley surrounded by high bleak mountains destitute of vegetation. The mountains are of a micaceous granite seamed with volcanic matter. The grass, which is coarse, extends for a mile or two along the valley.

A heavy cloud overhung the mountains to the west, and the wind blew a hurricane from that quarter; yet our zenith was never obscured, except for a minute at a time by a fleeting cloud detached from the great bank. A horse was killed for food, which was eaten with great appetite, and all of it consumed.

November 30.—Notwithstanding the water was saltish and in pools, and the grass unfavorable to the horses, yet we were compelled to avail ourselves of it for a day to recruit. The day and night were very unpleasant, from the high wind which came over the snow-clad mountains to the west. The ground, too, was tremulous, and my observations for time, by which I hoped to obtain the rate of my chronometers, were not such as I could desire.

December 1.—We ascended the valley, now destitute of both grass and water, to its termination, and then descended to the deserted Indian village of San Felippe. The mountains on either side are lofty, I suppose from 3,000 to 5,000 feet high, and those to the west encrusted on the top with snow and icicles. Our camp was in a long field of grass, three or four miles in extent, through which a warm stream flowed and drained through a cañon to the north, abreast of the village. We went to the barren hills and collected the dry sage and scrub mezquite, with which we made a feeble fire. The larrea Mexicana grew here also, but it is unfit for fuel.

About nine miles from the camp, we passed the summit which is said to divide the waters flowing into the Colorado from those flowing into the Pacific, but I think it is a mistake. The pass is much below the peaks on either side, and the height gives no indication of the elevation of the range, and, indeed, the barometric reading was but an indifferent index of the height of the pass, as the day was stormy. We are still to look for the glowing pictures drawn of California. As yet, barrenness and desolation hold their reign. We longed to stumble upon the rancherias, with their flocks of fat sheep and cattle. Meat of horses, may be very palatable when fat, but ours are poor and tough, and it is hard to satisfy the cravings of hunger with such indifferent food.

Early in the day's march, we met two Indians, a man and woman; they could give us no information of what was passing on the western side of the mountains They continued on with the utmost indifference, exhibiting no signs of fear or astonishment at this sudden apparition of ragged blue-coats. They had fine athletic figures, but were prematurely wrinkled from poverty and exposure to cold.

December 2 and 3.—We commenced to ascend another "divide," and as we approached the summit the narrow valley leading to it was covered with timber and long grass. On both sides, the evergreen oak grew luxuriantly, and, for the first time since leaving the states, we saw what would even there be called large trees. Emerging from these, we saw in the distance the beautiful valley of the Aqua Caliente, waving with yellow grass, where we expected to find the rancheria owned by an American named Warner.

As we passed, crows and wolves were seen in numbers.

Leaving the valley, we ascended the hills to the north covered with mezquite, estafiat, &c. Our progress was slow and painful; we thought Warner's rancheria never would open on our eager sight, when suddenly it burst upon our view at the foot of the hill. We were mistaken for Indians, and soon were seen horsemen at full speed leading off cattle and horses to the mountains. We quickened our pace to arrest this proceeding. The rancheria was in charge of a young fellow from New Hampshire, named Marshall. We ascertained from him, that his employer was a prisoner to the Americans in San Diego, that the Mexicans were still in possession of the whole of the country except that port, San Francisco, and Monterey; that we were near the heart of the enemy's stronghold, whence he drew his supplies of men, cattle and horses, and that we were now in possession of the great pass to Senora, by which he expected to retreat, if defeated, to send his prisoners if successful, and to communicate with Mexico.

To appease hunger, however, was the first consideration. Seven of my men eat, at one single meal, a fat full grown sheep. Our camp was pitched on the road to the Pueblo, leading a little north of west. To the south, down the valley of the Aqua Caliente, lay the road to San Diego. Above us was Mr. Warner's backwoods, American looking house, built of adobe and covered with a thatched roof. Around, were the thatched huts of the more than half naked Indians, who are held in a sort of serfdom by the master of the rancheria. I visited one or two of these huts, and found the inmates living in great poverty. The thermometer was at 30°, they had no fires, and no coverings but sheepskins. They told me, that when they were under the charge of the missions they were all comfortable and happy, but since the good priests had been removed, and the missions placed in the hands of the people of the country, they had been ill treated. This change took place in 1836, and many of the missions passed into the hands of men and their connexions, who had effected the change.

Near the house is the source of the Aqua Caliente, a magnificent hot spring, of the temperature of 137° Fahrenheit, discharging from the fissure of a granite rock a large volume of water, which, for a long distance down, charges the air with the fumes of sulphuretted hydrogen. Above it, and draining down the same valley, is a cold spring of the temperature of 45°, and without the aid of any mechanical instrument, the cold and warm water may be commingled to suit the temperature of the bather.

The Indians have made pools for bathing. They huddle around the basin of the spring to catch the genial warmth of its vapors, and in cold nights immerse themselves in the pools to keep warm. A day will come, no doubt, when the invalid and pleasure seeking portion of the white race, will assemble here to drink and bathe in these waters, ramble over the hills which surround it on all sides, and sit under the shade of the great live oaks that grow in the valley.

Our information in reference to the state of affairs in California was yet very imperfect and unsatisfactory. Marshall spoke of a Mr. Stokes, an Englishman, who lived fifteen miles distant, on the road to San Diego. The general at once despatched Marshall to him, and in three hours he appeared in our camp, presenting a very singular and striking appearance. His dress was a black velvet English hunting coat, a pair of black velvet trowsers, cut off at the knee and open on the outside to the hip, beneath which were drawers of spotless white; his leggins were of black buck-skin, and his heels armed with spurs six inches long. Above the whole bloomed the broad merry face of Mr. Stokes, the Englishman. He was very frank, proclaimed himself a neutral, but gave us all the information he possessed; which was, that Commodore Stockton was in possession of San Diego, and that all the country between that place and Santa Barbara was in possession of the "country people." He confirmed all that Marshall had said, and stated he was going to San Diego the next morning. The general gave him a letter for that place.

I made observations at night for time and latitude, but the flying clouds, and the trembling ground on which we were encamped, made it a delicate operation.

Information was received on the 2d, that fifteen miles distant, on the road to the Pueblo, a band of horses and mules were catched, belonging to General Flores and others. Tired as our people were, nightfall found twenty-five of them in the saddle, with fresh horses, under the command of Lieut. Davidson, accompanied by Carson, on their way in pursuit of the cache. Davidson was successful, and returned with the horses on the 3d, about meridian; but the animals, like those we captured at the mouth of the Gila, were mostly unbroken, and not of much service.

My observations give for the latitude of our camp of this date, which was on the meadow to the south of the rancheria, 33° 16' 57".

We remained in camp on the 3d to rest.

December 4.—The morning was murky, and we did not start till 9 o'clock, about which time it commenced to rain heavily, and the rain lasted all day. Our route was chiefly through narrow valleys overtopped by high hills of some fertility, covered with oaks. We were now in the region of rains, and the vegetation, though not luxuriant, was very much changed, but it was too late in the fall to get the flowers or fruits to determine the plants.

Our camp was pitched, after marching $13\frac{1}{2}$ miles, in the valley of the Rio Isabel, near the rancheria of Mr. Stokes, formerly the mission of Saint Isabel.

Mr. S. had gone, but he left his keys with a man whom the Spaniards called Signor Beel, with directions to entertain us. The Signor was a deserter from an English merchant-man, and had lived in the neighboring mountains some ten years; during this time he had acquired a little property, and some knowledge of Spanish, but the sailor was visible in all his acts. Before night Mr. Beel had made good use of his keys, and shone in his true colors as sailor Bill.

We were drenched to the skin, and looked forward with some pleasure to the idea of once more entering a house, with a blazing fire and plenty to eat and drink. In the last two items we were entirely satisfied, but sadly disappointed in finding no fire, the only chimney about the rancheria being in the kitchen.

The dragoons took the dinner intended for the officers, and we were obliged to stand, cracking our heels in the cold damp chapel, now converted into a hall, for two hours, before the Signor, or rather Sailor Bill, could cook another dinner.

The appearance of desolation which the rancheria presents is little calculated to impress us with favorable notions of the agricultural resources of this part of California. The land in the narrow valleys is good, but surrounded every where by high barren mountains, and where the land is good, the seasons are too dry for men to attempt cultivation without facilities for irrigation.

December 5.—A cold rainy day, and the naked Indians of the rancheria gathered around our fires. We marched from the rancheria of San Isabel to that of Santa Maria. On the way we met Capt. Gillespie, Lieut. Beale, and Midshipman Duncan of the navy, with a party of thirty-five men, sent from San Diego with a despatch to Gen. Kearny. We arrived at the rancheria after dark, where we heard that the enemy was in force nine miles distant, and not finding any grass about the rancheria, we pushed on and encamped in a cañon two miles below. It was long after night when we halted, and though there may have been plenty of grass, we could not find it. Besides the rain, a heavy fog obscured the landscape, and little could be seen of the country during the day's journeying; what we did see, however, did not impress us favorably as to its fertility.

Although this was the rainy season, no flowing streams were crossed after leaving the San Isabel, and the ground was destitute of grass. Our camp was in a valley, overgrown with large oak trees and other shrubbery; but it was too dark to distinguish their character.

A party under Lieut. Hammond was sent to reconnoitre the enemy, reported to be near at hand. By some accident the party was discovered, and the enemy placed on the qui vive. We were now on the main road to San Diego, all the "by-ways" being in our rear, and it was therefore deemed necessary to attack the enemy, and force a passage. About 2 o'clock, a. m., the call to horse was sounded.

December 6.—We marched nine miles before day-break over a hilly country, leaving our packs to come on in the rear. The general invited Mr. Warner and myself to ride with him, and taking four of my party, I left Messrs. Bestor and Stanly with the rest, six in number, to take care of the baggage, and look after the instruments and notes.

When within a mile of the enemy, whose force was not known to us, his fires shone brightly. The general and his party were in advance, preceded only by the advanced guard of twelve men under Captain Johnston. He ordered a trot, then a charge, and soon we found ourselves engaged in a hand to hand conflict with a largely superior force.

For an account of this engagement, reference may be made to the official report of the general, which has been published. The subjoined topographical sketch will show the first and second position of the enemy, and his final rout. As day dawned, the smoke cleared away, and we commenced collecting our dead and wounded. We found 18 of our officers and men were killed on the field, and 13 wounded.

Amongst the killed were Captains Moore and Johnston, and Lieutenant Hammond of the 1st dragoons.

The general, Capt. Gillespie, Capt. Gibson, Lieut. Warner, and Mr. Robideau badly wounded.

A large body of horsemen were seen in our rear, and fears were entertained lest Major Swords and the baggage should fall into their hands. The general directed me to take a party of men and go back for Major Swords and his party. We met at the foot of the first hill, a mile in rear of the enemy's first position. Returning, I scoured the village to look for the dead and wounded. The first object which met my eye was the manly figure of Capt Johnston. He was perfectly lifeless, a ball having passed directly through the centre of his head.

The work of plundering the dead had already commenced; his watch was gone, nothing being left of it but a fragment of the gold chain by which it was suspended from his neck. By my directions Sergeant Falls and four men took charge of the body and carried it into camp. Captain Johnston and one dragoon were the only

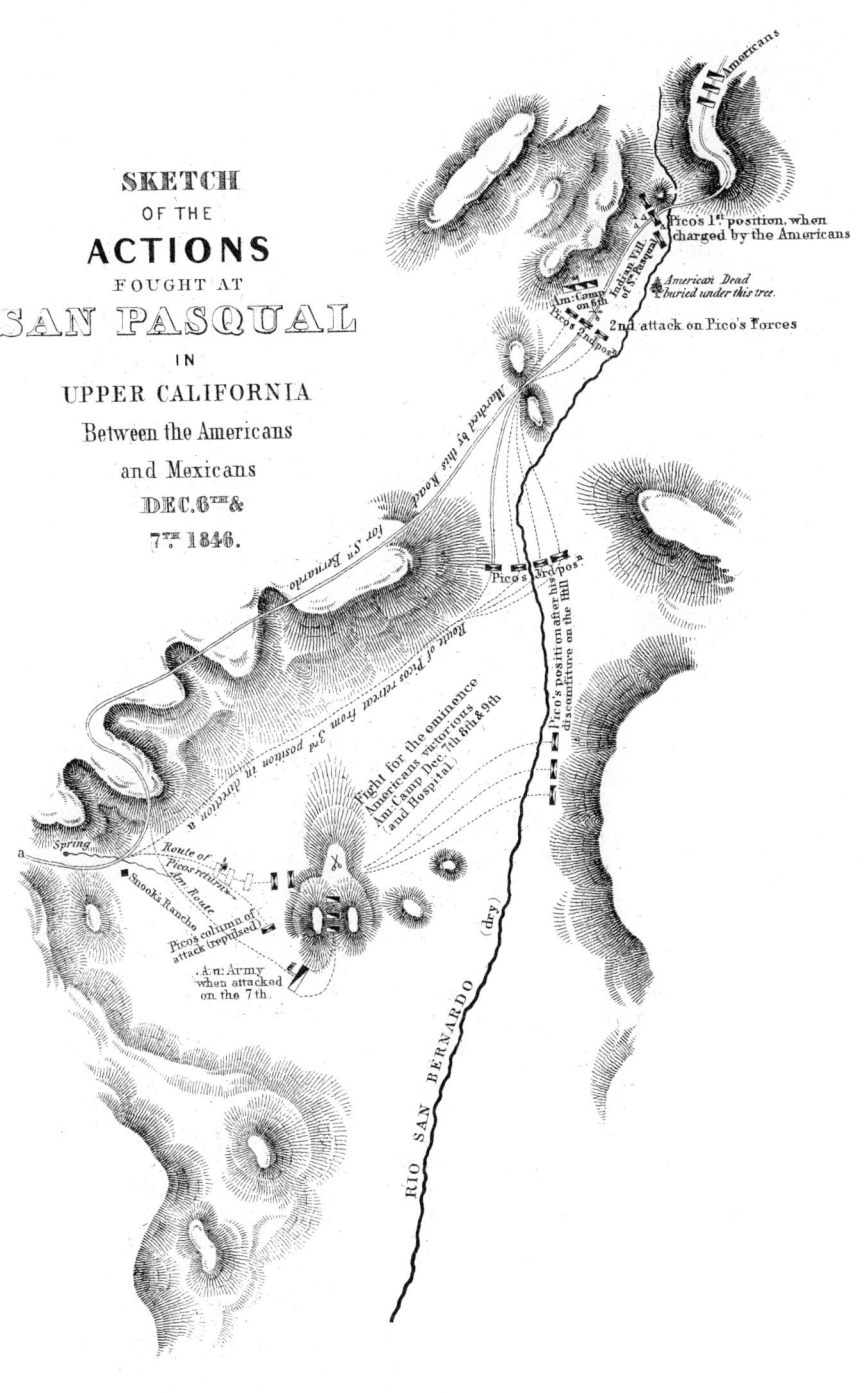

persons either killed or wounded on our side in the fight by firearms.

Information was received that the dead, no matter where buried, would be dug up to rob the bodies of their clothes, and orders were given to pack them on mules, with the intention of carrying them to San Diego, but it was found that there were not a sufficient number of strong animals left to convey both the dead and the wounded, and directions were given therefore to inter them at night as secretly as possible.

When night closed in, the bodies of the dead were buried under a willow to the east of our camp, with no other accompaniment than the howling of myriads of wolves attracted by the smell. Thus were put to rest together, and forever, a band of brave and heroic men. The long march of 2,000 miles had brought our little command, both officers and men, to know each other well. Community of hardships, dangers, and privations, had produced relations of mutual regard which caused their loss to sink deeply in our memories.

The general's wounds were so serious, that during the day Captain Turner assumed command and directed operations. There was but one surgeon in our party, Dr. Griffin, and notwithstanding his great skill and assiduty, he did not finish dressing the wounded till late in the afternoon, nor were the ambulances for their transportation completed. This, with the desire to bury our dead under cover of night, caused the forward movement to be postponed till morning.

Our provisions were exhausted, our horses dead, our mules on their last legs, and our men, now reduced to one third of their number, were ragged, worn down by fatigue, and emaciated. The officers of Captain Gillespie's party said there were wheel carriages at San Diego, 39 miles distant, and it was determined to send there for the means of conveying our wounded. Early in the day, Godey, with a few picked men, was on his way by a circuitous route to that place.

Our position was defensible, but the ground, covered with rocks and cacti, made it difficult to get a smooth place to rest, even for the wounded. The night was cold and damp, and notwithstanding our excessive fatigues of the day and night previous, sleep was impossible.

December 7.—Day dawned on the most tattered and ill-fed detachment of men that ever the United States mustered under her colors. The enemy's pickets and a portion of his force were seen in front. The sick, by the indefatigable exertions of Dr. Griffin, were doing well, and the general enabled to mount his horse. The order to march was given, and we moved off to offer the enemy battle, accompanied by our wounded, and the whole of our packs. The ambulances grated on the ground, and the sufferings of the wounded were very distressing. We had made for them the most comfortable conveyance we could, and such as it was, we were indebted principally to the ingenuity of the three remaining mountain men of the party, Peterson, Londeau, and Perrot. The fourth, the brave François Ménard, had lost his life in the fight of the day before. The general resumed the command, placing Captain Turner, of the dragoons, in command of the remnant of dragoons, which were consolidated into one company.

Arranging our wounded and the packs in the centre, we marched towards San Diego in the direction of the San Barnardo rancheria, taking the right hand road over the hills, and leaving the river San Barnardo to the left. The enemy retired as we advanced. When we arrived at the rancheria of San Barnardo, we watered our horses and killed chickens for the sick. The rancheria was the property of Mr. Snooks, an Englishman; it was deserted except by a few Indians.

Finding no grass about the rancheria, we moved on towards the bed of the river, driving many cattle before us. We had scarcely left the house and proceeded more than a mile, when a cloud of cavalry debouched from the hills in our rear, and a portion of them dashed at full speed to occupy a hill by which we must pass, while the remainder threatened our rear. Thirty or forty of them got possession of the hill, and it was necessary to drive them from it. This was accomplished by a small party of six or eight, upon whom the Californians discharged their fire; and strange to say, not one of our men fell. The capture of the hill was then but the work of a moment, and when we reached the crest, the Californians had mounted their horses and were in full flight. We did not lose a man in the skirmish, but, they had several badly wounded. By this movement we lost our cattle, and were convinced that if we attempted any further progress with the ambulances we must lose our sick and our packs. It was impossible to move in the open field with these incumbrances, a ainst an enemy more than twice our numbers, and all superbly mounted. The general, therefore, determined to halt, for the night to have the wounds of the sick redressed, and then to cut our way to San Diego.

December 8.—We bored holes for water, and killed the fattest of our mules for meat. In the morning a flag of truce was sent into our camp, informing us that Andreas Pico, the commander of the Mexican forces, had just captured four Americans, and wished to exchange them for a like number of Californians We had but one to exchange, and with this fellow I was sent to meet Andreas Pico, whom I found to be a gentlemanly looking, and rather handsome man.

The conversation was short; for I saw the man he wished to exchange was Burgess, one of those sent on the morning of the 6th to San Diego, and we were very anxious to know the result of his mission. Taking rather a contemptuous leave of his late captors, he informed us of the safe arrival of himself and Godey at San Diego. He also stated that when captured, his party, consisting of himself and two others, on their return from San Diego, had previously "cached" their letters under a tree, which he pointed out; but on subsequent examination, we found the letters had been abstracted.

Our wounded were still in no condition to move; to have attempted to transport them would have required one half of our fighting force, and it was decided most expedient to wait until they could be carried on horseback. At night, Lieutenant Beale, of the navy, Mr. Carson, and an Indian, volunteered to go to San Diego, 29 miles distant—an expedition of some peril, as the enemy now occupied all the passes to that town.

The observations made to-night give, for the latitude of this camp, 33° 03′ 42″, and the longitude 117° 03′ 29″.

Don Antonio Robideaux, a thin man of fifty-five years, slept next to me. The loss of blood from his wounds, added to the coldness of the night, 28° Fahrenheit, made me think he would never see daylight, but I was mistaken. He woke me to ask if I did not smell coffee, and expressed the belief that a cup of that beverage would save his life, and that nothing else would. Not knowing there had been any coffee in camp for many days, I supposed a dream had carried him back to the cafés of St. Louis and New Orleans, and it was with some surprise I found my cook heating a cup of coffee over a small fire made of wild sage. One of the most agreeable little offices performed in my life, and I believe in the cook's, to whom the coffee belonged, was, to pour this precious draught into the waning body of our friend Robideaux. His warmth returned, and with it hopes of life. In gratitude he gave me, what was then a great rarity, the half of a cake made of brown flour, almost black with dirt, and which had, for greater security, been hidden in the clothes of his Mexican servant, a man who scorned ablutions. I eat more than half without inspection, when, on breaking a piece, the bodies of several of the most loathesome insects were exposed to my view. My hunger, however, overcame my fastidiousness, and the morceau did not appear particularly disgusting till after our arrival at San Diego, when several hearty meals had taken off the keenness of my appetite, and suffered my taste to be more delicate.

Last night the brave Sergeant Cox died of his wounds, and was buried to-day deep in the ground, and covered with heavy stones, to prevent the wolves from tearing him up. This was a gallant fellow, who had, just before leaving Fort Leavenworth, married a pretty wife.

December 10.—The enemy attacked our camp, driving before them a band of wild horses, with which they hoped to produce a stampede. Our men behaved with admirable coolness, turning off the wild animals dexterously. Two or three of the fattest were killed in the charge, and formed, in the shape of a gravy-soup, an agreeable substitute for the poor steaks of our worn down brutes, on which we had been feeding for a number of days.

Doctor Griffin gave the welcome information that all the sick, but two, were able to get in the saddle, and orders were given to march the next morning.

There was little expectation that Carson and Lieutenant Beale would succeed in reaching San Diego; the hiding place pointed out by Burgess was examined, and the letters from San Diego were not found.

We were all reposing quietly, but not sleeping, waiting for the break of day, when we were to go down and give the enemy another defeat. One of the men, in the part of the camp assigned to my defence, reported that he heard a man speaking in English. In a few minutes we heard the tramp of a column, followed by the hail of the sentinel. It was a detachment of 100 tars and 80 marines under Lieutenant Gray, sent to meet us by Commodore Stockton, from whom we learned that Lieutenant Beale, Carson, and the Indian, had arrived safely in San Diego. The detachment left San Diego on the night of the 9th, cached themselves during the day of the 10th, and joined us on the night of that day. These gallant fellows busied themselves till day distributing their provisions and clothes to our naked and hungry people.

December 11.—The junction of our forces was a complete surprise to the enemy, and when the sun rose, but a small squadron of horse was to be seen at Stokes's rancheria. They had fled precipitately, leaving most of the cattle behind them, for which we had been contending for the last three days. None of our men were mounted—theirs were all mounted; and why they should have left their stock is inconceivable. It was certainly not incompatible with their safety to have carried them all away. The only way of accounting for it, is, by supposing our night attack had filled them with the unnecessary fear of being surprised. We drove the cattle before us.

Our march was in close order, over a road leading through a rolling country of light black soil, destitute of trees, and without water, covered with oats indigenuous to the soil, now fallen to decay. The grass in protected places was sprouting, but not in sufficient quantity to afford grazing to our stock. After marching twelve miles we arrived at the rancheria of Signor Alvarado, a person who was in the fight against us. The women and children had fled to the mountains, leaving plenty of turkies, chickens, goats and sheep behind; also two casks of wine, the produce of the country. The havoc committed on the comestibles was immense; the sheep not killed were driven by us into San Diego. The owner had taken the oath of allegiance to the United States and broken it.

The·navy took a prisoner at this house as they marched to meet us. He gave us much information, and was then liberated. He stated that Pico's force consisted of 160 men, 100 of which were drawn from the Pueblo, and the balance from the surrounding country. We subsequently received authentic accounts that his number was 180 men engaged in the fight, and that 100 additional men were sent him from the Pueblo, who reached his camp on the 7th.

There was a fine spring at this rancheria, and another two miles below it.

On the hill, before reaching the rancheria, the Pacific opened for the first time to our view, the sight producing strange but agreeable emotions. One of the mountain men who had never seen the ocean before, opened his arms and exclaimed: "Lord! there is a great prairie without a tree."

December 12.—We followed the Solidad through a deep fertile valley in the shape of a cross. Here we ascended to the left a steep hill to the table lands, which, keeping for a few miles, we descended into a waterless valley, leading into False bay at a point distant two or three miles from San Diego. At this place we were in view of the fort overlooking the town of San Diego and the barren waste which surrounds it.

The town consists of a few adobe houses, two or three of which only have plank floors. It is situated at the foot of a high hill on a sand flat, two miles wide, reaching from the head of San Diego bay to False bay. A high promontory of nearly the same width, runs into the sea four or five miles and is connected by the flat with the main land. The road to the hide houses leads eastward of this promontory, and abreast of them the frigate Congress and the sloop Portsmouth are at anchor. The hide houses are a collection of store houses where the hides of cattle are packed before being shipped; this article forming the only trade of the little town.

The bay is a narrow arm of the sea indenting the land some four or five miles, easily defended, and having twenty feet of water at the lowest tide. The rise is said to be five feet, making the greatest water twenty-five feet.

Standing on the hill which overlooks the town, and looking to the northeast, I saw the mission of San Diego, a fine large building now deserted. The Rio San Diego runs under ground in a direct course from the mission to the town, and sweeping around the hill, discharges itself into the bay. Its original debouche was into False bay, where, meeting the waters rolling in from the seaward, a bar was formed by the deposite of sand, making the entrance of False bay impracticable.

Well grounded fears are entertained that the immense quantity of sand discharged by this river will materially injure, if it does not destroy the harbor of San Diego; but this evil could be arrested at a slight cost, compared with the objects to be obtained. At present San Diego is, all things considered, perhaps one of the best harbors on the coast from Callao to Puget's Sound, with a single exception, that of San Francisco. In the opinion of some intelligent navy officers, it is preferable even to this. The harbor of San Francisco has more water, but that of San Diego has a more uniform climate, better anchorage, and perfect security from winds in any direction. However, the commercial metropolis must be at San Francisco, owing to the greater extent and superiority of the country adjacent, watered by the rivers Sacramento and San Joachim, unless indeed it should be made the terminus of a railroad leading by the route of the Gila to the Del Norte, and thence to the Mississippi and the Atlantic?

The rain fell in torrents as we entered the town, and it was my singular fate here, as in Santa Fé, to be quartered in the calaboose, a miserable hut, of one room, some 40 + 30 feet square. A huge old gun was mounted in this hovel, looking through an embrasure to the westward. In this building I was told that I could stow my party and my instruments safely.

We preferred the open air and the muddy plaza, saturated with all sorts of filth, to this wretched hole; but having no alternative, our chronometers and instruments were stowed in it and guarded by the indefatigable Mr. Bestor. I went off to accept from the hospitality of a friend the first bed I had seen in many months. About midnight there was one of those false alarms which ever and anon disturbed this goodly town. Four burly fellows rushed to man this gun, but they found themselves unexpectedly opposed by Mr. Bestor and two or three of my party. But for this timely resistance, my whole little stock of chronometers, barometer, &c., would have been totally destroyed. In the morning, through the kind exertions of my friend, Captain Gillespie, I was enabled to get a house with two rooms, the only unoccupied quarters in the town. Foreseeing employment of a different nature, my little party occupied themselves busily in collecting and bringing up the notes of our field-work.

On the 28th December I received notification from General Kearny to leave my party in San Diego and report to him for duty, as the acting adjutant general of the forces; Captain Turner, his adjutant general, having been assigned by him to the command of the remnant of the company of the 1st dragoons.

Mr. Warner was still too unwell, from the wounds received at San Pasqual, to accompany us, or to commence the survey of San Diego bay. Wishing to have a secure place to deposite my instruments, notes, &c., I applied to Captain Dupont to give them a place on board the Cyane. He granted this request, and kindly insisted that Mr. Bestor and Mr. Stanly should also go on board, where they could pursue their work unmolested.

I should be very ungrateful if I did not here make my acknowledgments to Captain Dupont, and all the officers of the navy with whom we were thrown in contact, for the uniform kindness and the generous hospitality with which they always supplied our personal wants, and the promptness with which they rendered assistance in any public enterprise.

My work as topographical engineer may be considered to end at this place; and that portion of the map embraced between San Diego and the Pueblo or Ciudad de los Angeles is compiled from existing maps, with slight alterations made by myself from a view of the ground, without the aid of instruments.

The coast is taken from old Spanish charts, published in Madrid in 1825, kindly furnished me by Captain Wilkes. The harbor of San Diego has been surveyed by Captain, Sir Edward Belcher, of the royal navy, whose determination of the longitude of the spit to the south of Punta Loma, published in his "voyage round the world," has been adopted, in the absence of time or instruments to enable me to make the requisite observations.

The longitude of the same point by Malispina 117° 17′, and the chronometric longitude brought by myself from my last station over the mountains, where lunar distances were observed, 117° 14′; but I have not hesitated to take the results of Sir Edward Belcher, although I have had no opportunity of seeing his observations.

Malispina's observations were made long since, and the results from the chronometers brought overland by me are liable to objections: first, from the imperfection in the determination of my intermediate stations by lunar distances, and, next, from the disturbances to which the chronometers were subjected in the battle of the 6th December, and the skirmish of the 7th, but more particularly the last, where a sudden charge was made in an open plain on our baggage by the enemy's cavalry.

The harbor was originally explored by Sebastian Vizcaino in 1603, but no settlement was made at San Diego until 1769.

Vessels may ride at anchor in the harbor, perfectly land-locked, but in very heavy southerly gales some inconvenience may be felt by those not provided with good ground tackle, from the immense volumes of kelp driven into the harbor.

The kelp (fucus gigantens) occupies a space in front of the harbor some miles in length and half a mile wide. At a distance, I took the kelp for a low island, but was informed of my error by Captain Schenck, who told me vessels were forced through it in a stiff breeze.

On the morning of the 29th December we marched out of San Diego with the following force:

	Capt.	Lieut.	Sergt.	Corpl.	Bug.	Privates.
Dragoons	1	1	2	4	2	47
Sailors acting artillery	1	1	2	4	–	39
Sailors and marines acting infantry	8	10	17	17	–	345
Volunteers	3	3	6	–	–	48

Three employés of the topographical engineers, three medical officers, and twenty-five men, Indians, and Californians; the whole divided into four divisions or battalions, commanded respectively by Captain Turner, Lieutenant Renshaw, Lieutenant Zielin, and Captain Gillespie.

Six pieces of artillery, of various calibre, got up with great exertion, under the orders of Commodore Stockton, by Lieutenant Tilghman of the navy, acting as captain of artillery.

A wagon train, consisting of one four-wheel carriage and ten ox carts, under the charge of Lieutenant Minor of the navy. The wagons were heavily laden, and our progress was slow in the extreme. We did not reach the Solidad, the first watering place, till 8 o'clock at night.

I was ordered to ride forward and lay out a defensive camp, hoping to give confidence to the sailors, many of whom were now, for the first time, transferred to a new element.

We soon found their habits of discipline aboard ship made the transition easy, and I speedily arrived at the conclusion that Jack, properly handled, made a very good infantry soldier.

The plan of the camp being approved, I was directed to make it the habitual order of encamping wherever the configuration of the ground would admit. The plan was the natural one to protect ourselves from the night attacks of the enemy, who were all mounted. The mode in which they designed to make their night attacks was to drive into our camp a manada of wild mares, and then take advantage of the confusion they might create to deliver a charge.

December 30.—We encamped at the rancheria of Alvéar.

December 31.—We encamped at the San Barnardo, having gone in three days only 30 miles. The ground passed over was the same as that described in the last two days of our march into San Diego.

January 1.—To-day we obtained some fresh oxen and a few fresh horses, which enabled us to do better and to make 17 miles before sunset. Our road to-day diverged from that heretofore described, and laid over a rolling country, destitute of water and trees. Cattle were seen, in small numbers, covering the plains in all directions, proving to us that the enemy had found it impracticable to fulfil their boast, that we should not get a hoof from the day we left San Diego.

We pitched our camp at the Indian settlement of Buena Vista, passing by the way a deserted rancheria, where there was a puddle of stagnant water, the only water on the route.

January 2.—Six and a half miles march brought us to the deserted mission of San Luis Rey. The keys of this mission were in charge of the alcalde of the Indian village, a mile distant. He was at the door to receive us and deliver up possession.

There we halted for the day to let the sailors, who suffered dreadfully from sore feet, recruit a little.

This building is one which, for magnitude, convenience, and durability of architecture, would do honor to any country.

The walls are of adobe, and the roofs of well made tile. It was built about sixty years since by the Indians of the country, under the guidance of a zealous priest. At that time the Indians were very numerous, and under the absolute sway of the missionaries. These missionaries at one time bid fair to christianize the Indians of California. Under grants from the Mexican government, they collected them into missions, built immense houses, and commenced successfully to till the soil by the hands of the Indians for the benefit of the Indians.

The habits of the priests, and the avarice of the military rulers of the territory, however, soon converted these missions into instruments of oppression and slavery of the Indian race.

The revolution of 1836 saw the downfall of the priests, and most of these missions passed by fraud into the hands of private individuals, and with them the Indians were transferred as serfs of the land.

This race, which, in our country, has never been reduced to slavery, is in that degraded condition throughout California, and do the only labor performed in the country. Nothing can exceed their present degraded condition.

For negligence or refusal to work, the lash is freely applied, and in many instances life has been taken by the Californians without being held accountable by the laws of the land.

This mission of San Luis Rey was, until the invasion of California by the Americans, in 1846, considered as public property. Just before that event took place, a sale was made of it for a small consideration, by the Mexican authorities to some of their own people, who felt their power passing away, and wished to turn an *honest penny* whilst there was power left; but this sale was undoubtedly fraudulent, and will, I trust, not be acknowledged by the American government. Many other missions have been transferred in the same way; and the new government of California must be very pure in its administration to avoid the temptations which these fictitious sales, made by the retiring Mexican authorities, offer for accumulating large fortunes at the expense of the government.

The lands belonging to this mission are extensive, well watered, and very fertile. It is said, and I believe it probable from appearances, that wheat will grow in the valleys adjacent, without irrigation.

January 3.—After marching a few miles the wide Pacific opened to our view. We passed the St. Marguerita rancheria, once a dependency of San Luis Rey, now in the possession of the Pico family. We encamped near Flores, a deserted mission. Just below it, and near the ocean, is an Indian village. Cattle were seen in great numbers to-day, and several well broken pairs of oxen were picked up on the way.

Distance 10.5 miles.

January 4.—After leaving Flores a few miles, the high broken ground projects close in upon the sea, leaving but a narrow, uneven banquette, along which the road wends through a growth of chapparal.

Here we met three persons, bearing a flag of truce; one an Englishman, named Workman, another Fluge, a German, the third a Californian.

They brought a letter from Flores, who signed himself governor and captain general of the department of California, proposing to suspend hostilities in California, and leave the battle to be fought elsewhere between the United States and Mexico, upon which was to depend the fate of California. There was a great deal of other matter in the letter, useless to repeat. The commission returned with a peremptory refusal of the proposition of the governor and captain general Flores.

After going nine miles from Flores, the high land impinges so close on the sea that the road lies along the sea beach for a distance of eight miles. Fortunately for us the tide was out, and we had the advantage of a hard, smooth road. Notwithstanding this, our column stretched out a great distance, and we were compelled to make frequent halts for the rear to come up.

This pass presents a formidable military obstacle, and, in the hands of an intrepid and skilful enemy, we could have been severely checked, if not beaten back from it; but we passed unmolested, and encamped late at night on an open plain at the mouth of the stream leading from the mission of San Juan de Capristano, and about two miles from the mission.

It was so dark I could not see to lay off the lines of the camp accurately, and I was glad, in the morning, that an early start gave no time for criticism. Distance 18.8 miles.

January 5.—The mission of San Juan has passed into the hands of the Pico family. The cathedral was once a fine strong building, with an arched cupola; only one-half of the building, capped by a segment of the cupola, is now standing, the other part having been thrown down by an earthquake in the year 1822, killing some thirty or forty persons who had fled to it for refuge.

Attracted by a house having a brush-fence round the door, as if to keep out intruders, I was told there were four men within, in the agonies of death, from wounds received at the battle of San Pasqual.

We moved to the Alisos (Sycamore) rancheria, where we found a spring of good water, but nothing to eat. Through the kindness of Mr. Foster, an Englishman, we received here a supply of fresh horses.

The road was principally through the valley of the stream watering the mission. On each side were beautiful rounded hills, covered with a delicate tinge of green from the grass, which was now sprouting freely near the sea-coast.

Up to this point, except a small patch at Flores, I had not seen the mark of a plough or any other instrument of husbandry. The rancherias were entirely supported by rearing cattle and horses. Distance 11.1 miles.

January 6.—To-day we made a long march of 19 miles to the upper Santa Anna, a town situated on the river of the same name. We were now near the enemy, and the town gave evidence of it. Not a soul was to be seen; the few persons remaining in it were old women, who, on our approach, had bolted their doors. The leaders of the Californians, as a means of inciting their people to arms, made them believe we would plunder their houses and violate their women.

Taking advantage of a deep ditch for one face of the camp, it was laid off in a very defensible position between the town and the river, expecting the men would have an undisturbed night's rest, to be in the morning ready for the fight, which might now be expected daily. In this hope we were mistaken. The wind blew a hurricane, (something very unusual in this part of California,) and the atmosphere was filled with particles of fine dust, so that one could not see and but with difficulty breathe.

January 7.—The wind continued to blow violently, which the enemy should have taken advantage of to attack us. Our weapons were chiefly fire-arms; his, the lance; and I was quite certain that in such a gale of wind as then blew, the difficulty of loading our arms would have proved a serious matter.

The Santa Anna is a fine, dashing stream, knee-deep, and about 100 yards wide, flowing over a sandy bed. In its valley are many valuable vineyards and corn fields. It is capable of affording water to a great many more. On its banks are considerable tracts

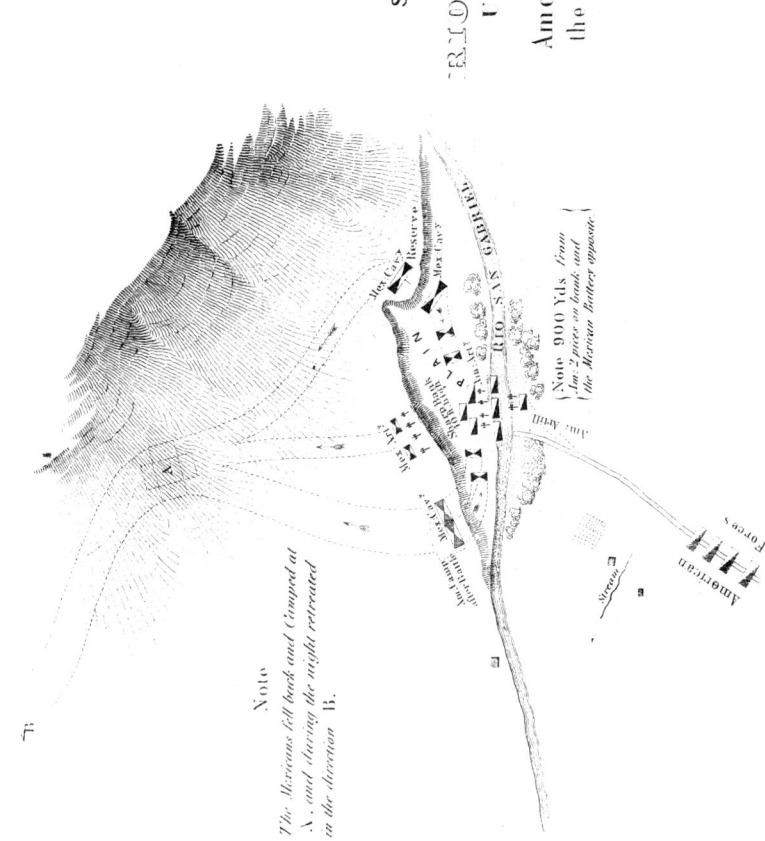

of uncultivated land within the level of irrigation. We now began to think there would be more formidable and united resistance by the enemy, but he failed to show himself; and such was the unanimity of the men, women and children, in support of the war, that not a particle of information could be obtained in reference to his force or position.

After travelling ten miles we came to the Coyotes, a rancheria owned by a rich widow lady, who had just married a handsome young fellow, who might well pass for her son. These people we found at home, and we learned from them that the enemy intended to give us battle the next day. Indeed, as we approached the rancheria, several horsemen drew off, reconnoitring us so closely as to make it doubtful if they were not some of our own vaqueros.

January 8.—We passed over a country destitute of wood and water, undulating and gently dipping towards the ocean, which was in view. About two o'clock we came in sight of the San Gabriel river. Small squads of horsemen began to show themselves on either flank, and it became quite apparent the enemy intended to dispute the passage of the river.

Our progress was necessarily very slow, our oxen being poor, and our wagons (the ox-carts of the country) with wheels only about two feet in diameter.

The enemy did not yet discover his order of battle, and we moved to the river in our habitual order of march, when near the enemy, viz: the 2d division in front, and the 1st and third on the right and left flanks respectively; the guard and a company of volunteer carbiniers in the rear; our cattle and the wagon train in the centre, making for them, what the sailors wittily termed, a Yankee corral. The artillery were distributed on the four angles of the rectangle.

This order of march was adopted from the character of the enemy's force, all of which was mounted; and in a measure from our own being men unaccustomed to field evolutions, it was necessary to keep them habitually in the order to resist cavalry attacks when in view of the enemy. We had no cavalry, and the object of the enemy was to deprive us of our cattle by sudden charges.

The river was about 100 yards wide, knee-deep, and flowing over quick-sand. Either side was fringed with a thick undergrowth. The approach on our side was level; that on the enemy's was favorable to him. A bank, fifty feet high, ranged parallel with the river, at point blank cannon distance, upon which he posted his artillery.

As we neared the thicket, we received the scattering fire of the enemy's sharp shooters. At the same moment, we saw him place four pieces of artillery on the hill, so as to command the passage. A squadron of 250 cavalry just showed their heads above the hill, to the right of the battery, and the same number were seen to occupy a position on the left.

The 2d battalion was ordered to deploy as skirmishers, and cross the river. As the line was about the middle of the river, the enemy opened his battery, and made the water fly with grape and round shot. Our artillery was now ordered to cross—it was unlimbered, pulled over by the men, and placed in counter battery on the enemy's side of the river. Our people, very brisk in firing, made the fire of the enemy wild and uncertain. Under this cover, the wagons and cattle were forced with great labor across the river, the bottom of which was quick sand.

Whilst this was going on, our rear was attacked by a very bold charge, and repulsed.

On the right bank of the river there was a natural banquette, breast high. Under this the line was deployed. To this accident of the ground is to be attributed the little loss we sustained from the enemy's artillery, which showered grape and round shot over our heads. In an hour and twenty minutes our baggage train had all crossed, the artillery of the enemy was silenced, and a charge made on the hill.

Half way between the hill and the river, the enemy made a furious charge on our left flank. At the same moment, our right was threatened. The 1st and 2d battalions were thrown into squares, and after firing one or two rounds, drove off the enemy. The right wing was ordered to form a square, but seeing the enemy hesitate, the order was countermanded; the 1st battalion, which formed the right, was directed to rush for the hill, supposing that would be the contested point, but great was our surprise to find it abandoned.

The enemy pitched his camp on the hills in view, but when morning came, he was gone. We had no means of pursuit, and scarcely the power of locomotion, such was the wretched condition of our wagon train. The latter it was still deemed necessary to drag along for the purpose of feeding the garrison, intended to be left in the Ciudad de los Angeles, the report being that the enemy intended, if we reached that town, to burn and destroy every article of food. Distance 9.3 miles.

January 9.—The grass was very short and young, and our cattle were not much recruited by the night's rest; we commenced our march leisurely, at 9 o'clock, over the "Mesa," a wide plain between the Rio San Gabriel and the Rio San Fernando.

Scattering horsemen, and small reconnoitring parties, hung on our flanks. After marching five or six miles, we saw the enemy's line on our right, above the crest made by a deep indentation in the plain.

Here Flores addressed his men, and called on them to make one more charge; expressed his confidence in their ability to break our line; said that "yesterday he had been deceived in supposing that he was fighting soldiers."

We inclined a little to the left to avoid giving Flores the advantage of the ground to post his artillery; in other respects we continued our march on the Pueblo as if he were not in view.

When we were abreast of him, he opened his artillery at a long distance, and we continued our march without halting, except for a moment, to put a wounded man in the cart, and once to exchange a wounded mule, hitched to one of the guns.

As we advanced, Flores deployed his force, making a horse shoe in our front, and opened his nine-pounders on our right flank, and two smaller pieces on our front. The shot from the nine-pounders

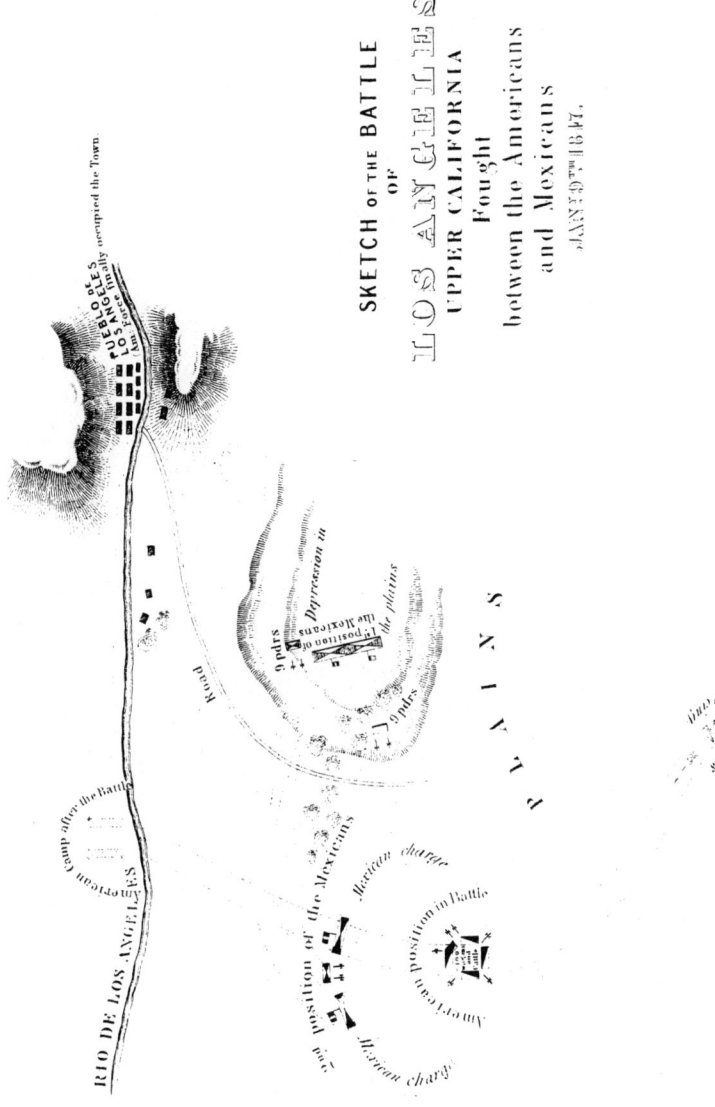

on our flank was so annoying that we halted to silence them. In about fifteen minutes this was done, and the order "forward" again given, when the enemy came down on our left flank in a scattering sort of charge, and notwithstanding the efforts of our officers to make their men hold their fire, they, as is usually the case under similar circumstances, delivered it whilst the Californians were yet about a hundred yards distant. This fire knocked many out of their saddles, and checked them. A round of grape was then fired upon them, and they scattered. A charge was made simultaneously with this on our rear, with about the same success. We all considered this as the beginning of the fight, but it was the end of it. The Californians, the most expert horsemen in the world, stripped the dead horses on the field, without dismounting, and carried off most of their saddles, bridles, and all their dead and wounded on horseback to the hills to the right.

It was now about three o'clock, and the town, known to contain great quantities of wine and aguardiente, was four miles distant. From previous experience of the difficulty of controlling men when entering towns, it was determined to cross the river San Fernando, halt there for the night, and enter the town in the morning with the whole day before us. The distance to-day, 6.2 miles.

After we had pitched our camp, the enemy came down from the hills, and 400 horsemen, with the four pieces of artillery, drew off towards the town, in order and regularity, whilst about sixty made a movement down the river, on our rear and left flank. This led us to suppose they were not yet whipped, as we thought, and that we should have a night attack.

January 10.—Just as we had raised our camp, a flag of truce, borne by Mr. Selis a Castilian, Mr. Workman an Englishman, and Alvarado the owner of the rancheria at the Alisos, was brought into camp. They proposed, on behalf of the Californians, to surrender their dear City of the Angels, provided we would respect property and persons. This was agreed to; but not altogether trusting to the honesty of General Flores, who had once broken his parole, we moved into the town in the same order we should have done if expecting an attack.

It was a wise precaution, for the streets were full of desperate and drunken fellows, who brandished their arms and saluted us with every term of reproach. The crest, overlooking the town, in rifle range, was covered with horsemen, engaged in the same hospitable manner. One of them had on a dragoon's coat, stolen from the dead body of one our soldiers after we had buried him at San Pasqual.

Our men marched steadily on, until crossing the ravine leading into the public square, when a fight took place amongst the Californians on the hill; one became disarmed, and to avoid death rolled down the hill towards us, his adversary pursuing and lancing him in the most cold-blooded manner. The man tumbling down the hill was supposed to be one of our vaqueros, and the cry of "rescue him" was raised. The crew of the Cyane, nearest the scene, at once, and without any orders, halted and gave the man that was lancing him a volley, strange to say he did not fall. Almost at the same instant, but a little before it, the Californians from the hill did fire on the vaqueros. The rifles were then ordered to clear the hill, which a single fire effected, killing two of the enemy. We were now in possession of the town; great silence and mystery was observed by the Californians in regard to Flores; but we were given to understand that he had gone to fight the force from the north, drive them back, and then starve us out of the town. Towards the close of the day we learned very certainly that Flores, with 150 men, chiefly Sonorians, and desperadoes of the country, had fled to Sonora, taking with him four or five hundred of the best horses and mules in the country, the property of his own friends. The silence of the Californians was now changed into deep and bitter curses upon Flores.

Some slight disorder took place among our men at night, from the facility of getting wine, but the vigilance of the officers soon suppressed it.

January 11.—It rained in torrents all day. I was ordered to select a site, and place a fort, capable of containing a hundred men; with this in view, a rapid reconnoissance of the town was made, and the plan of a fort sketched, so placed as to enable a small garrison to command the town and the principal avenues to it. The plan was approved. Many men came in during the day and surrendered themselves.

January 12.—I laid off the work, and, before night, broke the first ground. The population of the town, and its dependencies, is about 3,000; that of the town itself, about 1,500. It is the centre of wealth and population of the Mexico Californian people, and has heretofore been the seat of government. Close under the base of the mountains, commanding the passes to Sonora, cut off from the north by the pass at San Barbara, it is the centre of the military power of the Californians. Here all the revolutions have had their origin, and it is the point upon which any Mexican force from Sonora would be directed. It was therefore desirable to establish a fort, which, in case of trouble, should enable a small garrison to hold out till aid might come from San Diego, San Francisco, or Monterey, places which are destined to become centres of American settlements.*

January 13.—It rained steadily all day, and nothing was done on the work; at night I worked on the details of the fort.

Thursday 14.—We drank to-day the wine of the country, manufactured by Don Luis Vigne, a Frenchman. It was truly delicious, resembling more the best description of Hock than any other wine.

Many bottles were drunk, leaving no headache or acidity on the stomach. We obtained, from the same gentleman, a profusion of grapes and luscious pears, the latter resembling in color and taste the Bergamot pear, but different in shape, being longer and larger.

---

* Subsequently to my leaving the Ciudad de los Angeles, the entire plan of the fort was changed, and I am not the projector of the work finally adopted for the defence of that town.

January 15.—The details to work on the fort were by companies. I sent to Captain Tilghman, who commanded on the hill, to detach one of the companies under his command to commence the work. He furnished, on the 16th, a company of artillery (seamen from the Congress,) for the day's work, which they performed bravely, and gave me great hopes of success.

January 18, 19, *and* 20.—I received special orders which separated me from the command, and the party of topographical engineers that had been so long under my orders.

The battles of the 6th December, and the 8th and 9th January, had forever broken the Mexican authority in California, and they were daily coming in, in large parties, to sue for peace, and every move indicated a sincere desire on the part of the more respectable portion of the Californians to yield without further struggle to the United States authorities; yet small parties of the more desperate and revengeful hung about the mountains and roads; refusing or hesitating to yield obedience to their leaders, who now, with great unanimity, determined to lay down their arms. General Flores, with a small force, was known to have taken the road to Sonora, and it was believed he was on his way to that province, never to return to California.

Leaving General Kearny at San Juan de Capristano, on his return to San Diego, I took three men and pushed on for the latter place. Halting late in the evening at the deserted Indian rancheria of Santa Margarita, we broke open one of the Indian huts, and got some corn and pumpkins for our animals. When night came on, the number of insects about the hut, and the intolerable noise made by the wolves, kept us from sleep. The moon shone brightly, and about ten at night we saddled up to pursue our journey.

In this determination we were confirmed by the unexplained movement of several small parties of mounted Californians that reconnoitred our camp; a circumstance which afforded additional proof that some of the Californians were yet in arms, and led us very reasonably to the conclusion that our only safety was in changing our camp. We reached the mission of San Luis Rey, and found not a human being stirring The immense pile of building, illuminated by the pale cold rays of the moon, stood out in bold relief on the dim horizon; a monument of the zeal of the indefatigable priests, by whom it was built. Now untenanted and deserted, it offered no resting place for the weary and hungry, and we rode on, determined to halt at the first place where grass should be in abundance.

The road here divides into two branches; one leads to the west, by the rancheria of San Barnardo, the other directly to San Diego, over the high lands, running nearly parallel to the sea coast. The first is that by which we had marched on the Pueblo de los Angeles, fearing that the hills on the sea coast road would embarrass the movement of our artillery and ox carts.

Without a guide, we had great difficulty in striking at night the trail leading over the mountains; but consulting the stars for our course, and relying upon the sagacity of my three men, who had passed most of their days in traversing untrodden regions, we jogged along, shivering with the cold air of the elevated hills.

About twelve, we came to a large patch of luxuriant grass, wet with dew. Upon this we loosened our animals and attempted to get a little sleep, but, in the absence of blankets or fire, the cold deprived us of repose, and the dawn of day found us again in our saddles.

The only habitation on the road from San Luis Rey to San Diego is a hut about half way, where there is a good spring. Its occupants had just returned from the wars, quite as hungry as we were. They had preceded us not more than twenty minutes, yet they had a fat bullock killed, and choice bits of his flesh roasting before the fire. We outnumbered the party, and consequently received their hospitality, which was extended to us with a good deal of bonhommie.

They conversed freely of the battles fought but a few days before, acknowledged their participation in them, and expressed themselves satisfied of the uselessness of farther resistance without aid from Mexico.

The fresh meat of a bullock is all that is required by the Californian for breakfast, dinner, and supper.

Bread, tea, and coffee are rarely, if ever, used, and even when within their reach, looked upon with indifference.

We very soon fell into their habits, and it is probable the troops in California, at this time, would not consider it an excessive hardship to make a campaign with no other stores in the commissariat than a plentiful supply of fresh beef. The white teeth of the Californians, and the blood tingling in the cheeks of their olive colored faces would seem to prove this beef to be a very healthy diet.

The advantages in the movement of troops that are contented with this kind of subsistence is very great, enabling them to move without wagons, and with no other care for the morrow than herding the animals intended for food.

Our host was so well pleased with the manner in which we acquitted ourselves at his rude repast, that forgetting old animosities, he saddled up his jaded horse, and piloted us for five or six miles, until we reached the broad trail, leading to the Solidad.

About midday we reached San Diego, and next morning taking leave of my men and the animals that had done us such good service, I embarked on board the prize brig Malek Adhel, commanded by Lieutenant Schenck, of the navy, and prepared to take my leave of Upper or Alta California. Before doing so, however, I may venture upon a few general remarks, based upon personal observations, upon the topography, climate, and products of that portion of the country not covered by my survey, or that of others. These observations were made after I had become separated from my assistants and instruments, my mind being engrossed with other subjects. The information contained in them is, therefore, less precise than that contained in other portions of my journal.

The region, extending from the head of the Gulf of California to the parallel of the Pueblo, or Ciudad de los Angeles, is the only portion not heretofore covered by my own notes and journal, or by the notes and journals of other scientific expeditions fitted out by the United States.

The journals and published accounts of these several expeditions combined, will give definite ideas of all those portions of California susceptible of cultivation or settlement. From this remark is to be excepted the vast basin watered by the Colorado, and the country lying between that river and the range of Cordilleras, represented as running east of the Tulare lakes, and south of the parallel of 36°, and the country between the Colorado and Gila rivers.

Of these regions nothing is known except from the reports of trappers, and the speculations of geologists. As far as these accounts go, all concur in representing it as a waste of sand and rock, unadorned with vegetation, poorly watered, and unfit, it is believed, for any of the useful purposes of life. A glance at the map will show what an immense area is embraced in these boundaries; and, notwithstanding the oral accounts in regard to it, it is difficult to bring the mind to the belief in the existence of such a sea of waste and desert; when every other grand division of the earth presents some prominent feature in the economy of nature, administering to the wants of man. Possibly this unexplored region may be filled with valuable minerals.

I have alluded, elsewhere, to the population of this country, the savage character of which is another obstacle to its exploration, and has tended to veil in mystery its true character and resources.

Alta California, between the 31st and 34th parallels of latitude, presents to the eastern man, accustomed to navigable rivers and broad estuaries of the ocean, topographical features of a very unusual character.

Two chains of mountains traverse the country in a direction nearly parallel to the sea coast, slightly converging towards each other, and finally uniting near the parallel of 32°. Here they form the promontory of Lower California, extending its entire length, and terminating abruptly in the ocean, at Cape San Lucas.

The first chain (that nearest the coast) may be considered a steppe of the second or interior range of mountains. It impinges on the coast at three different points, Santa Barbara, San Juan de Capristano, and between San Luis Rey and San Diego—at the first two places with so much boldness as to make it necessary to conduct the road along the margin of the sea, between the lines of high and low water mark, so that both Santa Barbara and San Juan present points worthy of consideration to the military commandant charged with the defence of that country.

Between the first and second ranges of mountains there is a valley, traversed by a good road, leading directly from the great desert to the Pueblo de los Angeles, and a defending force would meet its adversary to the greatest advantage at Cariso Creek, the termination of the "jornada" across the desert. The description and locality of Cariso Creek has already been given.

The second or principal range of mountains lies at no great distance from the first, and the valley between offers some arable land. The distance between the first range and the sea coast varies from

1 to 20 or 30 miles. The surface covered with vegetation, though small, is difficult to estimate; and perhaps it is unimportant that an estimate should be made, since the productiveness of these regions depends on other considerations than smoothness of surface, and character of soil. The rains cannot be relied upon, and the tiller of the earth depends upon irrigation from the mountain streams for his crops. The extent of ground, capable of tillage, is thus reduced to very narrow limits, easy of computation. A knowledge of the water courses, their fall, volume and extent, and the quantity of lands on their margin, within the level of these waters, are the data upon which the computation must be based.

Taking this as a guide, an inspection of the accompanying map will give a general idea of the extent of arable ground, sufficiently correct for all practical purposes; but, in candor it should be said, that many streams laid down in it disappear in the sand, while the rocky cliffs, forming the banks of others, render irrigation impracticable. The scale upon which the map is projected is too small to represent these accidents of the ground.

Where irrigation can be had in this country, the produce of the soil is abundant beyond description. All the grains and fruits of the temperate zones, and many of those of the tropical, flourish luxuriantly.

Descending from the heights of San Barnardo to the Pacific, one meets every degree of temperature. Near the coast, the winds prevailing from the southwest in winter, and from the northwest in summer, produce a great uniformity of temperature, and the climate is perhaps unsurpassed in salubrity. With the exception of a very few cases of ague and fever of a mild type, sickness is unknown.

The season of the year at which we visited the country was unfavorable to obtaining a knowledge of its botany. The vegetation, mostly deciduous, had gone to decay, and no flowers nor seeds were collected. The country generally, is entirely destitute of trees. Along the principal range of mountains are a few live oaks, sycamore, and pine; now and then, but very rarely, the sycamore and cotton wood occur in the champaign country, immediately on the margins of the streams.

Wild oats every where cover the surface of the hills, and these, with the wild mustard and carrots, furnish good pasturage to the immense herds of cattle, which form the staple of California.

Of the many fruits capable of being produced with success, by culture and irrigation, the grape is perhaps that which is brought nearest to perfection.

Men experienced in growing it, and Europeans, pronounce the soil and climate of this portion of California, unequalled for the quality of the grape and the wine expressed from it.

We sailed from San Diego on the 25th of January, and coasted along the rocky and barren shores of Lower California. The information in reference to this country, which it was in my power to obtain, is not so precise as that which might be derived from an actual survey, and I have therefore embodied it in the appendix.

I have the honor to be, very respectfully, yours,

W. H. EMORY.

APPENDIX No. 1.

NEW YORK, *October* 1, 1847.

DEAR SIR: I return you my thanks for the very interesting information contained in your letter of the 20th of September.*

It unfortunately happens that I cannot wait for the arrival of your papers, or for the publication of the map of the War Department. My essay makes part of the second volume of the transactions of the New York Ethnological Society. The work is now in the press, completed with the exception of my essay; and the printer presses me for it. The map, which will accompany it, is principally intended to show the original abodes of the Indian tribes. It will be presented as a sketch, without pretensions to accurate correctness. But there is a consideration, which makes me anxious to obtain every possible information respecting the Rio Gila, and especially its upper waters.

You may not be aware that a work has lately been recovered and published, which contains a full and authentic account of an expedition in the year 1540–1542, by order of the viceroy Mindoça, and under the conduct of Vasquez Coronado. It consisted of 350 Spaniards and 800 Indians. Setting off from Culiacan, they reached the sources of the Rio Gila, passed across the mountains to the Rio del Norte, wintered twice in the province now called New Mexico, explored it through its whole length, from north to south, and afterwards, taking a northeast course, crossed the mountains, reached the buffalo plains, through which they wandered a considerable distance eastwardly, and as far north as the 40th degree of latitude. Finding no gold, they returned to Mexico. The Spaniards did not re-enter the country till the year 1581; and the conquest of New Mexico was not completed till about the year 1595.

The veracity of the narrator, Castenador, who was a volunteer in the expedition, and who wrote the account twenty years after, is fully established by a variety of circumstances, too multiplied to be inserted here. It is sufficient to say, that the Indians of the Rio Gila, and of the upper valley of the Rio del Norte, were an agricultural people, cultivating maize, beans, pumpkins, and cotton; depending exclusively on agriculture for their subsistence, dwelling in villages built of mud, (tochis,) mixed with certain balls of hardened matter, and well cemented together. The houses were generally four stories high, with no opening on the first floor, accessible only by moveable ladders, with top terraces, and an under ground apartment occupied exclusively by the men, and used as *estufas;*

---

* This letter gives a general outline of the route, and twenty words of the Coco Maricopas language, and a few of the Pinos.

in short, similar in every respect to the existing pueblos of New Mexico, and to the ruins of the Casas Grandes described, as I think, erroneously to the Aztecs.

With respect to New Mexico, one principal want is that of vocabularies, which would at once settle the question of identity with any of the Mexican nations. The same difficulty exists with respect to all the tribes of the country drained by the great Rio Colorado of the west. But there is an additional embarrassment respecting the actual situation of what were called the seven villages of Cibala; of which we can only say, that they were situated in a narrow valley six leagues long, and on the very sources of some one branch of the Rio Gila.

The phenomenon of this insulated semi-civilized population, is in itself remarkable, and difficult to be explained; and the discovery of the precise spot, where the seven Cibala villages were situated, is especially desirable. With this object in view, I beg leave to submit to you the following queries.

1st. On leaving the copper mines, on the 18th of October, and after having crossed the Sierra Mimbres, you reached the main branch of the river Gila on the 20th; now what I wish to know, is, from what quarter did that main branch come, or in other words, if you had ascended that main branch, what was its apparent course? What was the distance from the western foot of the Sierra Mimbres to that main branch where you struck it? Did you, along that distance, cross any tributary streams of the Rio Gila, and from what quarter did they come?

2d. Can you furnish me with the approximate latitude of some of the principal points observed when descending the river; principally the junction of the Salmas, the village of the Pimos Indians, any other spot where evident traces of ruins were discovered, and the mouth of the river Gila. From what quarter did the river Salmas come? Did you carry time with you, so as to obtain the relative longitude of some points? The most important would be the spot where you left the Rio del Norte, that where you struck the main branch of the Gila, the mouth of the Salmas, the Pimos village, and the mouth of the Rio Gila. If you had no other means, still your travelled distance may give a rough approximation.

It seems to me that the easiest way to answer these two queries, would be a rough approximate sketch of the country traversed by you. I will take special care not to commit you in any way. I am no plagiarist, and I must in general terms acknowledge that I am indebted to you for some important information; but I will at the same time refer to your intended complete report and map, which will give that precise information which was not within my reach.

3d. You did not visit the mouth of the great Rio Colorado: but General Kearny states in his letter that the mouth of the Gila was in about latitude 32°; that he crossed the Colorado ten miles below, and marched near it for thirty miles, when he left it, (turning off eastwardly across the desert,) without having reached its mouth. Now the generality of our maps place the mouth of the Colorado

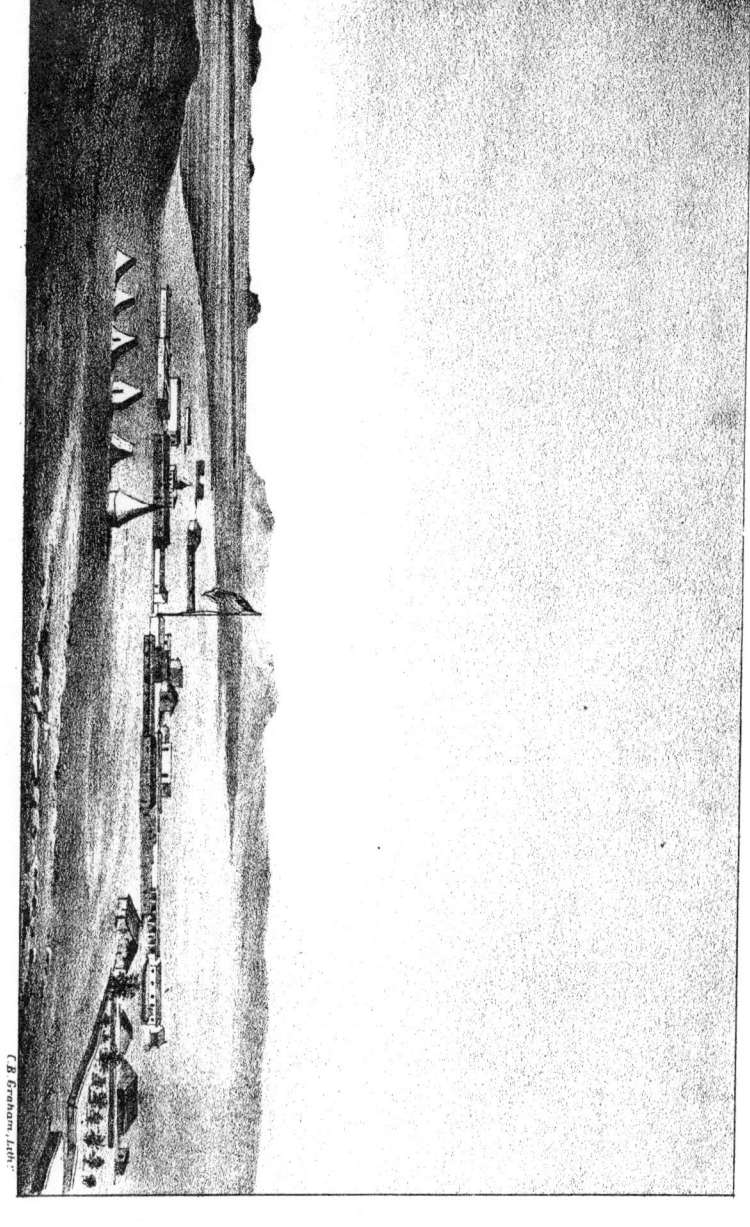
SAN DIEGO FROM THE OLD FORT

in latitude 32°, and it is clear from what precedes, that it must be nearly one degree further south. Do you think that I may in my sketch set it down at about latitude 31°?

4th. The cultivation of cotton is one of great general importance. As now informed, I believe that, independent of varieties, there are but two distinct species: the black seed, which is the native American, and found as such no where else, and the green seed, which adheres to the staple, of Asiatic origin, thence brought to the Levant and the Mediterranean, and imported into North America, of which it was not a native. I cannot obtain in this city a copy of Bomplant's great botanical work, which would have thrown much light on the subject. I wish now to know, whether you took any notice of the cotton cultivated by the Pimos, and what species it was? I presume that it was not a native of that region, and that the seed must have been imported from Mexico.

I now proceed to that which relates to the Indians, who are the principal objects of my researches.

1st. I have compared your vocabulary of the Coco Maricopas with those of the four Mexican languages in my possession, and of thirty-two well ascertained families of Indians, living within the United States or further north, and have found no resemblance with either. It is to me a quite new language, but there is a remarkable word. *Apache* is the word for *man;* and judging by analogy from several other Indian languages, they should be Apaches or belonging to that family. Thus, for instance, amongst the Algonquin tribes, the names assumed by two of them, Illinois and Linno Linap, are evidently derived from Linno, a man. However this may be, I wish to have some further information respecting that tribe; to know, with as much precision as you can, the quarter whence they came; their present location in reference to the Pimos, and particularly whether and what they do cultivate; also, whether they are wilder than the Pimos, and whether on good terms with them.

2d. You say that the accounts, by report, of the Indians to the mouth of the Gila are conflicting and of an indefinite character. This observation applies to every information derived from other sources. We have as yet only vague rumors. Yet I wish to collect all these, as far as possible. A few legitimate inferences may, perhaps, be drawn by comparing them together; but it is principally for the purpose of enabling me to point out the most important objects of inquiry that I wish to be thus informed. You will, therefore, oblige me by communicating such rough notes as you may have taken on that subject, and also what were the abodes and occupations of the few scattered Indians whom you met on your journey.

(a.) Have you, by any direct observation, ascertained within 30' the positive longitude, in reference to Greenwich, of any point on the Rio del Norte or vicinity which may serve as a starting point?

There must be some kind of a dividing ridge which separates the waters of the river Gila from the waters that empty into the gulf of California. From what you say of Colonel Cooke's route, I would infer that he left the Rio Norte a short distance above El

Passo, and that he must have traveled south of that ridge, in an almost due west course to the Rio Colorado.

I use the word "Sierra Madre" in the sense attached to it by the Mexicans, viz: that ridge which separates the waters that fall into the Atlantic from the rivers which empty into the Pacific ocean, without any regard to its elevation.

I pray you to accept the assurances of my distinguished consideration and personal regard.

Your most obedient and faithful servant,
ALBERT GALLATIN.

To Lieutenant W. H. EMORY,
U. S. Topographical Engineers, Washington.

WASHINGTON, *October* 8, 1847.

DEAR SIR: In answer to your letter of the 1st instant, I have the pleasure to send you, with the permission of the chief of my department, a table of twenty-three geographical positions determined by myself, which you are at liberty to use; and, should you think the information of sufficient importance, I should feel much flattered that you should, as you propose, communicate them to the Ethnological Society of New York for publication.

No astronomical observations that I am aware of have ever before been made on the same grounds, if we except the observations of Dr. Coulter at the mouth of the Gila, which have never yet been published.

You will see that the position of the Gila is very much changed, as well as that of Santa Fé, in New Mexico.

The observations were made with an $8\frac{1}{2}$ inch sextant, constructed by the celebrated Gambey, of Paris. In most cases, the determinations of the places in latitude are the mean of the results obtained by many observations on north and south stars, of nearly equal altitudes, by which the errors of eccentricity, &c., in the instrument were avoided.

The longitudes are derived from a combination of the results from the chronometers, and measurement of distances between the moon and stars, nearly equi-distant on either side of it.

The chronometers used were two very good box chronometers, by Parkinson & Frodsham, (Nos. 783 and 2,075.)

The observations themselves, including those between Santa Fé and Fort Leavenworth, (our point of departure,) in number 2,500 or 3,000, were all computed in the field, and are now undergoing verification by Professor Hubbard, a very accurate young computer, attached to the observatory at Washington.

The computations for all the points embraced in the table sent you, have been verified.

The objects of our expedition being purely military, the subjects of interest to scientific men were only pursued so far as they were incidental to the expedition, and did not interfere with its great object. The instruments with which I was furnished were not those, perhaps, which I would have selected; at the same time there was nothing for me to regret, except the absence of a good portable telescope, with which occultations of the fixed stars by the moon, and the immersion of Jupiter's satellites, could have been observed, and a few pocket chronometers.

We left Washington on twenty-four hours' notice, and time was not allowed to procure either the telescope or pocket chronometers.

1st. We struck the Gila, as the table will show, in latitude 32° 44′ 52″ and longitude 108° 45′ west from Greenwich; thence its course is very nearly west. As well as we could judge from the course of the mountains, its course from that point to its source was not very far from northeast or southwest.

No tributaries to the Gila were crossed before reaching it, except one named by me Night creek, a very insignificant stream. The Sierra Mimbres, 6,000 feet above the sea at the highest point where we crossed it, falls gradually and almost imperceptibly to the Gila.

2d. Your second interrogatory is answered principally by the table of geographical positions.

The Rio Salinas comes in from the *northeast*, a little west and north of camp 97, of November 12. (See table.) This camp, the astronomical position of which is given in the table, is about midway between the villages of the Pimos and Coco Marricopas Indians.

3d. The table will show you that the junction of the Gila and Colorado is on the parallel of 32° 43′ or 4′; and, in the absence of more specific information, I would advise you to place the mouth of the Colorado on the parallel of 31° 51′, which is the latitude given it by Lieutenant Hardy, of the royal navy, whose little book of travels in Mexico you have no doubt seen.

4th. Specimens of the seed of the cotton grown by the Pimos were obtained, but they have not yet reached me. Overcoming space was the great object we had in view when we passed the Pimos, and our investigations and collections were necessarily hasty and superficial. We passed with them only the part of a day, whereas, if exploration alone had been the object of our party, I should have considered a week as little enough to have devoted to this interesting people. When I left California, it was as a special envoy to the government, and on so short a notice that many of my collections and notes were left behind, with my assistants. Among the things so left, were the seed of the cotton.

Most of the plants collected, however, were brought home. These will show a very complete history of the botany of the country. They are in the hands of Doctor Torrey, who is preparing an elaborate catalogue and drawings of those plants, heretofore unknown. This catalogue I should be very glad to place at the disposal of your society.

The Coco Marricopas Indians come from the west. So late as 1826, Mr. Kit Carson, one of our guides, met these people at the mouth of the Colorado. Subsequently to that period, they were visited by Dr. Anderson (whom we met in Santa Fé) at a point about half way between their present village and the mouth of the Gila river.

They are taller and more athletic than the Pimos, and what struck me as very remarkable, the men had generally aquiline noses, whilst those of the women were retroussérs.

They occupy thatched cottages, thirty or forty feet in diameter, made of the twigs of cotton wood trees, interwoven with the straw of wheat, corn stalks and cane.

Cotton, wheat, maize, beans, pumpkins and water melons are the chief agricultural products of these people. Their fields are laid off in squares, and watered, by the Zequias, from the Gila river. Their implements of husbandry are the wooden plough, the harrow and the cast-steel axe, (procured probably from Sonora.) They have but few cattle, and not many horses. I observed, domesticated amongst them, ducks, chickens and pigs. They had many ornaments of sea-shells, showing, in my opinion, their recent migration from the gulf. From the character given of them by Carson, when he saw them in 1826, although they were then an agricultural people, I should think they had learned much by their proximity to their neighbors, the Pimos, whom they acknowledge as politically their superiors, and with whom they live on terms of intimate and cordial friendship.

The Marricopas impressed me as a more sprightly race than the Pimos; the interpreters of the Pimos were all natives of the Marricopas band.

The dress of both nations or bands was the same. That of the men a breech cloth and a cotton serape of domestic manufacture; that of the women the same kind of serape pinned around the waist and falling below the knees, leaving the breast and arms bare.

Both nations cherished an aversion to war, and a profound attachment to all the peaceful pursuits of life. This predilection arose from no incapacity for war, for they were at all times able and willing to keep the Apaches, whose hands are raised against all other people, at a respectful distance, and prevent depredations by those mountain robbers, who hold Chihuahua, Sonora, and a part of Durango in a condition approaching almost to tributary provinces.

They have a high regard for morality, and punish transgressions more by public opinion than by fines or corporeal punishments. Polygamy is unknown amongst them, and the crime of adultery, punished with such fearful penalties amongst Indian nations generally, is here almost unknown, and is punished by the contempt of the relatives and associates of the guilty parties.

The Indians we met between the Del Norte and the Pimos settlement were mostly wild Indians of the great Apache nation, which inhabits all the country north and south of the Gila, and both sides of the Del Norte, about the parallel of the Jornada and Dead Man's lakes.

They have no fixed habits, and the only vestiges of their abodes which we saw were temporary sheds, a few feet high, made of the twigs of trees. They live principally by plundering the Mexicans of New Mexico, Chihuahua, Sonora, and Durango.

No vocabulary of their language was procured. I am inclined to think they extend up to the head waters of the Gila.

Beyond them to the north is the warlike nation of the Navajoes, who, Mr. Fitzpatrick thinks, are allied to the Crow Indians.

Near the head waters of the Salinas, which runs in a course, it is said, nearly northeast and southwest, is a band of Indians called the Soones, who, in manners, habits, and pursuits, are said to resemble the Pimos, except that they live in houses scooped from the solid rock. Many of them are Albinos, which may be the consequence of their cavernous dwellings. Surrounded by the warlike Navajoe, and the thieving Apache, they nevertheless till their soil in peace and security.

Coming farther east, we reach the San José, a tributary to the Puerco, which is a tributary to the Rio del Norte from the *west*, not the Rio Puerco represented on the map to flow into the Del Norte south of El Passo.

Here is an Indian race living in four story houses, built upon rocky promontories inaccessible to a savage foe, cultivating the soil and answering the description of the seven cities of Vasquez Coronado, except in their present insignificance in size and population, and the fact that the towns, though near each other, are not in "a (continuous) valley six leagues long," but on different branches of the same stream. The names of these towns are Cibolleta, Moquino, Pojuato, Covero, Acona, Laguna, Poblacon; the last a ruin.

I did not visit these towns in person; but I hope to get a minute description from one who did, and, should I succeed, it will be sent to you.

The work you mention, of Castenada, has never been seen by me. My own impression, and it is so stated in my journal, is that the many ruins we saw on the Gila might well be attributed to Indians of the races we saw in New Mexico, and on the Gila itself. I mean by the last, the Pimos, who might easily have lost the art of building adobe or mud houses. In all respects, except their dwellings, they appeared to be of the same race as the builders of the numberless houses now level with the ground on the Gila river.

The implement for grinding corn, and the broken pottery, were the only vestiges of the mechanical arts which we saw amongst the ruins, with the exception of a few ornaments, principally immense well turned beads, the size of a hen's egg.

The same corn grinder and pottery are now in use among the Pimos. The corn grinder is merely a large stone, well worn, slightly concave, and another of different shape, convex, intended to fit the first and crush the corn between by the pressure of the hand.

The ruins on the Gila were first seen at camp 81, the position of which is shown in the table, from thence to the Pimos' village. Wherever the mountains did not impinge too close on the river and shut out the valley, they were seen in great abundance, enough, I should think, to indicate a former population of at least one hundred thousand; and in one place, between camps 91 and 97, there is a long wide valley, twenty miles in length, much of which is covered with the ruins of buildings and broken pottery.

These ruins are uniformly of the same kind; not one stone now remains on the top of the other; and they are only discoverable by the broken pottery around them, and stone laid in regular order, showing the trace of the foundation of a house.

Most of these outlines are rectangular, and vary from 40 × 50 to 200 and 400 feet front. The stone are unhewn, and are most of an amygdaloid, rounded by attrition.

Now of the tributaries which come into the Gila from the north, there are several besides the Salinas, which, at their mouths, are insignificant in size and can be stepped across; but in this whole region no legitimate inference can be drawn of the size of a river, throughout its course, from that at any one point.

It may be large near its source, and after traversing deserts of sand, through arid regions, unwatered by rains, become very small, and even disappear altogether.

Therefore, except the Salinas, of which we have oral accounts, nothing is known or can be inferred of the magnitude of these tributaries from their appearance at the junction. These tributaries come in near camp 81, where the mountains are so precipitous and bold no conjecture can be formed of their course.

The Salinas must have been the branch by which the expedition of Coronado ascended and crossed into New Mexico. Its general direction is not far from a line drawn from its mouth to Santa Fé, and nearly in this line are the seven towns mentioned as being on the head waters of the San José. Indiàns now pass from the Pimos village to New Mexico on this route.

I omitted to mention in its proper place, that we were informed by an intelligent Marricopas Indian that, about fifty miles from the mouth of the Salinas, was now standing, in a perfect state of preservation, the walls of a large three story building of mud, with its interior sides glazed and finely polished, and about it was to be seen many traces of large acequias, and broken pottery in great abundance.

There is another tribe of Indians called the Moquis, who, like the Pimos and Soones, cultivate the soil and live in peace with their neighbors; but the exact locality of this tribe I do not know, beyond the fact that it is on or near the head waters of some of the tributaries of the Gila.

I am, with great respect, your obedient servant,

W. H. EMORY.

APPENDIX No. 2.

COLLEGE OF PHYSICIANS AND SURGEONS,
New York, February 10, 1848.

MY DEAR SIR: I have examined the interesting collection of plants which you kindly placed at my disposal, and herewith send you a list of them, as complete as my numerous engagements permit me to make at present. The route which you passed over is exceedingly rich in botanical treasures, as is evident from the number of new species and genera which you were enabled to make under great disadvantages, and in an expedition which was almost wholly military in its character. Most of the new plants which you found are only indicated, or, at most, very briefly described in the following list. A more full account of them will be given hereafter.

I am, my dear sir, very respectfully, yours,

JOHN TORREY.

To Lieutenant Colonel W. H. EMORY.

JULY 22, 1847.

MY DEAR SIR: I give you the following written sketch of the route, not being able, as you request, to get a trace made from my map.

From the 27th June to July 11th, we were traversing the country between Fort Leavenworth and the bend of the Arkansas, a rich rolling prairie embraced between the 39th and 38th parallels of latitude, and the 94th and 98th meridians of longitude.

From July 11th to July 13th, followed the Arkansas to Pawnee fork, in longitude about 99. At this point the fertile soil ceases, except on the immediate margin of the streams.

From the 14th July to August 1st, we were in the valley of the Arkansas, occasionally crossing the spurs of low hills which interrupt the direct course of the Arkansas. This part lies in latitude 38°, and between longitude 99° and 103° 1'.

From the 1st August to the 8th, crossing the plain in a southerly direction and mounting the Raton mountain, about 7,000 feet above the sea, between latitudes 38 and 36.

From the 8th August to the 14th, in the valleys of the tributaries to the Canadian, and crossing the extensive plains between these valleys.

From the 14th August to the 18th, ascending the great ridge between the head of the Canadian and the waters of the Del Norte, halting at Santa Fé, in latitude 35° 41', on a tributary of the Del Norte, about 15 miles distant from the Del Norte, and about 1,500 feet above that river and 6,850 above the sea.

From August 18th up to the 14th October, all the collections were made in New Mexico, in the valley of the Del Norte, or on the table lands adjacent, and between Santa Fé and the 33d parallel of latitude; (230 miles below Santa Fé.)

From the 14th October to the 19th, we were crossing the great dividing ridge between the waters of the Del Norte and the waters of the Gila, nearly on the 33d parallel of north latitude, and between the 107th and 109th meridians of longitude, measured from Greenwich. The greatest height of this dividing ridge along our trail was about 6,000 feet above the sea.

From the 19th of October to the 22d November, we were following the course of the Gila river, occasionally forced into the mountains to avoid the cañons. This route is never far from the 33d parallel of latitude, and is embraced between the 109° and 114° 30' meridians of longitude, falling, during that distance, very uniformly from about 5,000 feet to near the level of the sea.

From the 22d November to the 24th, we were on the Colorado of the west, traversing a low sandy bottom.

From the 24th November to the 28th we were crossing the great desert of drifting sand in a course little north of west.

On the 28th November, we encamped at the Cariso (Reed) creek or spring, the waters of which, when first exposed, are warm, and emit the smell of sulphuretted hydrogen.

From the 28th November we commenced to ascend the Cordilleras of California, (the continuation of which forms the peninsula of Lower California,) and reached the highest point of the route December 5th, 3,000 feet above the sea, and as many below the overhanging peaks. From that point we descended to San Diego, a seaport on the level of the sea, in latitude 32° 45' and longitude 117° 11' west of Greenwich. This point we reached December 12.

With great respect, very truly yours,

W. H. EMORY.

Professor TORREY, *Princeton.*

RANUNCULACEÆ.

Ranunculus aquaticus, *Linn.* Plains of the Arkansas.

Clematis Virginiana, *Linn.* Raton mountain. An undetermined species of this genus was found in fruit November 10th on the Gila. The plumose tails of the carpels are nearly three inches long.

BERBERIDACEÆ.

Berberis pinnata, *Lagasca.* Highlands bordering the Gila. This appears to be a common species in the southern part of Upper California, and in Northern Mexico.

CRUCIFERÆ.

Lepidium ruderale, *Linn.* Valley of the Arkansas.
Erysimum Arkansanum, *Nutt.* Tributaries of the Canadian.

CAPPARIDACEÆ.

Polanisia graveolens, *Raf.* In flower and fruit September 26—October 3, valley of the Del Norte. The plant is taller, and the flowers are considerably larger than in the form that is common in the northern United States.

Cleome integrifolia, *Nutt.* This beautiful species is abundant on both sides of the mountains, from the plains of Oregon, and the upper waters of the Platte, to latitude 33° north.

VIOLACEÆ.

Viola cucullata, *Linn.* Pawnee fork of the Arkansas.

PORTULACACEÆ.

Portulaca oleracea, *Linn.* On the Arkansas. Perhaps introduced.

Sesuvium portulacastrum, *Linn.* In flower and fruit, November 17. Saline soils along the Gila. Leaves spatulate. Flowers nearly sesule, stamens numerous. Styles 3.

GERANIACEÆ.

Geranium Frémontii, *Torr. in Frém. 2d Rep.* On the Raton.

TYGOPHYLLACEÆ.

Kallstræmia maxima, *Torr. and Gr.* Tribulus maximus, *Linn.* Tributaries of the Canadian.

Larrea Mexicana, *Moricand, l. c. t.* 48. "*Creosote plant.*" *Iodeodondo* of the New Mexicans. Used externally for rheumatism. A shrub from three to six feet high. Abundant from the upper waters of the Arkansas, and valley of the Del Norte, to the great sandy deserts of California. It likewise occurs in the northern parts of Mexico. The plant abounds in a strong smelling resinous matter. No animal seems to feed on it, and it is useless for fuel, as it can scarcely be made to burn.

ANACARDIACEÆ.

Rhus glabra, *Linn.* From the upper part of the Arkansas to longitude 107°.

R. laurina, *Nutt.* A large shrub. Mountains of California towards the sea coast.

R. trilobata, *Nutt.* On the Gila. A shrub 18 inches high, found late in the autumn, with staminate aments nearly matured for the following spring. The whole plant is clothed with a dense velvety pubescence. It is, perhaps, a distinct species from *R. trilobata.*

MALVACEÆ.

Malva Munroana, *Dougl.* High sandy plains, and in the valley of the Gila. Flowers bright rose color.

M. pedata, *Torr. and Gr.* Upper part of the Arkansas.

Sphæralcea stellata, *Torr. and Gr.* Near Santa Fé, &c. Highlands between the del Norte and the Gila.

Sida coccinea, *DC.* On the Raton mountain. Several other undetermined Malvaceæ occur in the collection.

SAPINDACEÆ.

Sapindus marginatus, (*soap berry.*) Valley of the Gila.

RHAMNACEÆ.

Ceanothus ovalis, β., *Torr. and Gr.* On the Arkansas. A small scrubby species of this genus was found on the Cordilleras of California, towards San Diego. It has thorny branches, small ovate coriaceous, smooth entire leaves, which are supported on short petioles. The branches are glabrous and glaucous. There were neither flowers nor fruit on the specimen.

C. ovalis, *var.* intermedias, *Torr. and Gr.* On the Arkansas.

LEGUMINOSÆ.

Sesbania macrocarpa, *Muhl.* On the Gila. In fruit November 20.

Glycyrrhiza lepidota, *Nutt.* Near Santa Fé. Not found in flowers.

Psoralea esculenta, *Pursh.* (Pomme de Prairie.) On the Arkansas.

P. floribunda, *Nutt.* With the preceding.

Amorpha fruticosa, *Linn.* On the Gila. The specimens were without flower and fruit, and we therefore cannot be certain of the species.

Dalea formosa, *Torr. in Ann., lyc., N. York,* 2. *p.* 178. This beautiful species was first detected by Dr. James in Long's first expedition. It is a shrub about three feet high, with numerous crooked branches, and purplish flowers. Near Santa Fé, and valley of the Del Norte.

D. alopecuroides, *Willd.* With the preceding.

D. laxiflora, *Pursh.* Valley of the Arkansas.

Besides these daleæ, there were two other species, both shrubby, in the collection; but I have not ascertained whether they may not be already described. One of them is densely branched; the leaflets are in six to seven pairs, broadly obovate connate about

3 lines long, glabrous above, very villous, and furnished with large dark colored glands toward the margin underneath; they are obscurely toothed. The flowers are in short dense spikes; calyx with plumose subulate-setaceous teeth, which are as long as the tube. This species was found on the Gila river. It is very near D. ramosissima, Benth. in Bot. Sulph., p. 11 , t. 10.

The other species is canescently tomentose, and diffusely branched. The leaflets are narrowly oblong, in three to four pairs, which are distant. On both sides they are sparingly furnished with small red glands, which are nearly concealed in the down. The flowers are in short loose spikes, small, purple. Calyx-teeth subulate, shorter than the tube, plumose, Found on the great desert west of the Colorado.

Petalostemon gracile, β. oligophyllum. Stem erect; leaflets in 2—3, linear, slightly dotted underneath; calyx glabrous, longer than the subulate bracts, the teeth very short, ovate; petals oblong. Valley of the Del Norte.

Prosopis glandulosa, *Torr. in Ann., Lyc. N. York*, 2. p. 192, t. 2. (mezquite.) Abundant in the valleys of all the rivers, from Santa Fé, west. The trunk of this tree is sometimes 14 inches in diameter. The pods are long, flat, and filled with a sweetish pulph. They are excellent food for horses, and are sometimes used by men in times of scarcity.

P. (Strombocarpa) Emoryi, *n. sp.* Branches glabrous; spines in pairs, slender, short, straight, pinnæ a single pair; leaflets about 4 pairs, oblong, somewhat coriaceous; the under surface, and the petioles somewhat pubescent; legume spirally twisted into a compact cylinder. Found in fruit only; on the Gila river. This species is nearly allied to the P. odorata of Frémont's 2d report, but differs in its shorter, broader, and less numerous leaflets.

Schrankia uncinata, *Willd.* On the Arkansas, where it is called *sensitive vine.*

Darlingtonia brachyloba, *DC.* With the preceding.

Several other mimoseæ are in the collection, but the specimens are mostly without leaves and flowers.

Cassia chamæcrista, *Linn.* On the Arkansas.

ROSACEÆ.

Cerasus ilicifolius, *Nutt.* Mountains of California. The kernel of the fruit has a strong flavor of bitter almonds.

Geum Virginianum, *Linn.* On the Arkansas.

Fallugia paradoxa, *Endl. gen.* 6385, *Sieversia paradoxa, Don. in Linn., trans.* 14, *p.* 576, *t.* 22. A remarkable rosaceous shrub, with white flowers, and very long slender plumose tails to the carpels. It differs, in some respects, from Endlicher's character of the genus; but I have not had an opportunity of comparing it with Don's description and figure. It was found in various parts of the valley of the Del Norte. Can it be *Geum dryadoides, DC.?*

Cercocarpus parvifolius, *Nutt, Torr. and Gr., fl.* 2, *p.* 427. A shrub about 12 feet high, with numerous straight branches springing from near the ground. The carpels, with their long plumose spirally contorted *awns*, bore into the earth, after they have fallen. The action of the wind communicates to them a twisting motion, and retrorse pubescence retains them in the soil.

Spiraea Californica, *n. sp.* Shrubby; leaves ovate, lanceolate, undivided, nearly glabrous, glandularly serrate, conspicuously petiolate; flowers in compound corymbs, perfect, calyx segments broad, about as long as the tube; disk coherent with the tube of the calyx; stamens numerous; carpels 5, distinct, 2-valved; seeds 2, ascending, the testa expanded at the superior extremity into a membranaceous wing. Grows on high mountains near the Gila. This species is remarkable for its ascending winged seeds and coriaceous leaves. It can scarcely be referred to any of the sections into which the genus spiraea is at present divided.

Andenostoma fasciculata, *Hook and Arn.* Abundant in the Cordilleras of California. A shrub about five feet high.

A. sparsifolia, *n. sp.* Leaves scattered, linear subulate, dotted with glands. Cordilleras of California. A tree 30 feet high, with very numerous slender branches. Leaves nearly half an inch long, scarcely half a line wide, somewhat triangular, apparently evergreen. Flowers in small terminal paniculate spikes. Pedicels short, with numerous minute scarious bracts at the base. Calyx turbinate, campanulate, 10-striate, 5-toothed; the teeth ovate, obtuse, conspicuously imbricated. Stamens about 10; the filaments inserted into a crenulate glandular ring at the summit of the calyx tube. Ovary obovate, compressed, with 2 collateral suspended ovules. Very different in appearance from *A. fasciculata*, and destitute of the fleshy glands, with which the throat of the calyx-tube is furnished in that species.

Photinia arbutifolia, *Linn.* Cordilleras of California. A shrub 4-5 feet high.

LYTHRACEÆ.

Lythrum alatum, *Pursh.* On the Arkansas.

ONAGRACEÆ.

Zanschneria Californica, *Presl.* Valley of the Gila. A shrub with bright crimson flowers, resembling those of a fuchsia.

Œnothera albicaulis, *Nutt.* Valley of the Del Norte.

Œ. pinnatifida, *Nutt.* Tributaries of the Canadian river.

Œ. biennis, *Linn.* Valley of the Del Norte.

Several other undetermined species of Œnothera exist in the collection.

Gaura coccinea, *Nutt.* Tributaries of the Canadian.

G. parviflora, *Dougl.* Valley of the Del Norte.

LOASACEÆ.

Mentzelia pumila, *Nutt.* Stem whitish, slender, branching, and a little roughened above, smoothish and somewhat shining below;

leaves pinnatifid, or sinuate toothed; flowers (small) 2-3 together, pedicellate; petals 10, lanceolate; stamens very numerous; the outer filaments dilated; capsule turbinate, cylindrical; seeds numerous, winged. Valley of the Del Norte. Plant about a foot high. Flowers less than an inch in diameter. Capsule three-fourths of an inch long, 3 valved at the summit.

Cevallia sinuata, *Lagasca*. This interesting plant, which has been admirably illustrated by Fenzl, occurs in many parts of the valley of the Del Norte, from Santa Fé to Saltillo.

CUCURBITACEÆ.

Cucumis perennis, *James, Torr. and Gr.* On the Gila river, abundant. We are yet uncertain of the genus of this plant, which seems to be common in various parts of Mexico, particularly in arid sandy wastes. No specimens of the fruit have yet been sent to us. There are three other undetermined Cucurbitaceæ in the collection, distinct from any described in the Flora of North America.

CACTACEÆ.

Several interesting plants of this family were noticed by Colonel Emory, but they cannot be satisfactorily described from dried specimens. They are probably included among the numerous new species of Mexican cactaceæ soon to be described by Dr. Englemann.

CORNACEÆ.

Cornus paniculata, *l'Her.* On the Arkansas.

CAPRIFOLIACEÆ.

Symphoricarpus racemosus, *Linn.* (Snow berry.) On the Arkansas.

COMPOSITAE.

Vernonia fasciculata, *Michx.* Bent's Fort.
Liatris punctata, *Hook.* Rayada Creek.
Corethrogyne tomentella, *Torr. and Gr. fl. N. Am.* 2, p. 99. Very abundant on the Cordilleras of the Pacific, and called by the natives *estafiat*. It is a celebrated remedy for cholera, as noticed by Colonel Emory in his notes.

Dieteria incana, *Torr. and Gr.? Diplopappus incanus, Lindl.?* On the Gila. Differs from Douglass's Californian plant in its slender stem, and nearly glabrous, spinulose dentate leaves.

D. Coronopifolia, *Nutt.* Valley of the Del Norte, and the head waters of the Canadian.

D. asteroides, *n. sp.* Minutely scabrous, pubescent, stem paniculately branched above; leaves oblong-cuneate, somewhat rigid, sharply and rather coarsely toothed, involucre hemispherical, scales linear, in several series, with rather short herbaceous squarrose tips; rays 30 or more, violet; achenia, sparingly pubescent. Pappus of the ray much shorter than that of the disk. Elevated land between the Del Norte and the waters of the Gila. A well marked species, with leaves broader than in any other plant of the genus.

Aster hebecladus, *DC*. Valley of the Del Norte, and desert between the Colorado and Cordilleras of California.

A. (tripolium.) A branching species with the stems pubescent above, and middle sized flowers with purple rays. It seems to be undescribed. Valley of the Del Norte.

Solidago elongata, *Nutt*. Valley of the Gila.

Linosyris graveolens, *Torr. and Gr*. Chrysocoma dracunculoides, *Pursh*. A shrub about two feet high, and bright yellow heads of flowers. Abundant on the highlands between the Del Norte and the Gila.

Aplopapus spinulosus, *DC*. On Ocaté creek, &c., called *Pinette* by the natives.

A. Menziesii, *Torr. and Gr*. β. dentatus, leaves coriaceous, strongly dentate or pinnatifid, toothed, glutinous. Abundant in the great desert between the Colorado and the Cordilleras of California. Another form of this species was found near St. Diego, with the stem and their leaves clothed with a copius loose pubescence, and the serratures of the leaves few and small.

Grindelia. An apparently new species of this genus was found in ascending the Cordilleras of California, but the flowers had fallen from the heads, and one specimen is therefore scarcely sufficient for determination. The stem is very smooth and whitish; the leaves are oblong, clasping at the base, spinulose, serrate and glabrous, and the scales of the involucre are very acute, but scarcely recurved.

Chrysopsis canescens, *Torr. and Gr*. Near Ocaté creek: C. echioides, *Benth. in Bot. Sulph. p*. 25. Valley of the Gila.

Perityle, *Benth. in Bot. Sulph*. A new species of this genus (*P. Emoryi*, nob.) was found in ascending the Cordilleras of California. It differs from P. Californica of Bentham in its smaller and much more deeply lobed leaves, narrower achenia which are very hairy on the margins, and in other characters.

Baccharis Douglasii, *DC*. Valley of the Gila. Besides this there are three other species of Baccharis in the collection, none of which are described in the Flora of North America, but we cannot yet pronounce them new.

Tessaria borealis, *DC*. An aromatic shrub about three feet high, growing in all the deserted beds of the Gila, and in the valley of the Del Norte; usually with the Frémontia, both of which are abundant in those regions.

Hymenoclèa, *Torr. and Gr*. ined. This remarkable new genus is allied to ambrosia and xanthium. Another species of it (*H. Salsola*) was found in Frémont's second expedition, which, with the characters of the genus to which it belongs, will be published in another work. This species, from the scales of the involucre being in a single wheel, we propose to call *H. monogyra, Torr. and Gr.* It was found in various parts of the valley of the Gila.

Franseria Hookeriana. *Nutt.* (Yerba del Sapo.)

Ambrosia acanthocarpa, *Hooker.* Very abundant from Santa Fé to the 33d parallel of latitude.

Another species of this genus, and apparently an undescribed one, exists in the collection. It is suffretescent hoary, with the leaves bipinnatifidly, divided into very small obtuse segments. The flowers are wanting.

Ambrosia artemisiæfolia, *Linn.* Banks of the Gila.

DICORIS, *Torr. and Gr.* Another new genus, allied to Iva, of which a full description and figure will hereafter be given. It was found in the valley of the Gila, and in the desert of drifting sands west of the Colorado. (5 to 6 inches long, and 4 to 5 wide.)

Wyethia ovata, *n. sp., Torr. and Gr., ined*: Stem very stout, leaves orbicular, ovate, entire; somewhat coriaceous, pubescent, (as are also the petioles and branches,) scales of the involucre lanceolate, pappus of 3 to 4 acute rigid teeth, one of which is longer than the others. Abundant on the western side of the Cordilleras of California.

Silphium laciniatum, *Linn.* (Pilot weed.) On the Arkansas and its tributaries.

Another Silphium, with large ovate undivided leaves, was found on Cariso creek.

Englemannia pinnatifida, *Torr. and Gr. fl. N. Am.* 2, *p.* 283. Tributaries of the Canadian.

Lepachys columnaris, *Torr. and Gr.* Rudbeckia columnaris. *Pursh.* The rays vary from being wholly yellow to entirely purplish brown. From the head waters of the Canadian to Santa Fé.

Encelia farinosa, *Gray, ined.* An aromatic shrubby plant; exuding a yellowish resin from the braches. The leaves are ovate, softly pubescent, and hoary on both sides, with 3 to 5 prominent reticulated nerves underneath.

Helianthus patiolaris, *Nutt.* Upper part of the Arkansas, and valley of the Del Norte.

H. lenticularis, *Dougl.* With the preceding.

Coreopsis palmata, *Nutt.* Turkey Creek.

Simsia. A rayless, and probably new species of this genus, was found in the bed of the Agua Caliente, November 28th. It is a branching shrub, and the slender bark of the irregular twigs is covered with a whitish, very scabrous pubescence. The leaves are scarcely an inch long, ovate, entire obtuse, with short petioles, and scabrous on both sides. Chaff of the receptacle, embracing the obovate achenium, the margin of which is furnished with long silky hairs.

Wulfia.? Specimens of a plant with the floral characters of this genus, but with different foliage, were found in abundance on the higher grounds bordering the valley of the Gila. It also resembles Leighia, but is destitute of a pappus. Some of the genera, to which the plant is allied, will need revision before its place can be satisfactorily determined.

Ximenesia, *n. sp.?* Valley of the Del Norte, and along the Gila, September and October. This needs comparison with some of the Mexican species. It very nearly resembles *X. encelioides Cavan.*

Riddellia tagetina, *Nutt. Torr. and Gr. fl., N. Amer.* 2, *p.* 362. Valley of the Del Norte, about two hundred miles below Santa Fé. A beautiful plant with persistent flowers, first detected by Mr. Nuttall towards the sources of the Platte.

BAILEYA, *n. gen. Harv. and Gr., ined.* Two other species of this unpublished genus, dedicated to that profound observer of nature, Professor Bailey of West Point, exist among the California plants collected by Coulter, and will soon be described by Mr. Harvey and Dr. Gray. This is distinguished from the others by its numerous ray-flowers, and is the *B. multiradiata, Harv. and Gr.* The whole plant is clothed with a woolly pubescence, and varies from a few inches to a foot or more in height. The leaves are somewhat pinnatately cut into several narrow segments. The heads are on long naked peduncles, and when the rays are fully expanded are more than an inch and a half in diameter. The rays are 40 or 50 in number, in two or more series, obovate cuneate, of a bright orange yellow, and 7-nerved, carolla of the disk, flowers with five short segments which are glandularly pubescent, with intra-marginal nerves. Branches of the style short, somewhat dilated and truncate at the extremity. Very abundant along the Del Norte, and in the dividing region between the waters of the Del Norte and those of the Gila. Flowers from October 4th to November.

Gaillardia amblyodon, *Gay.* On the upper part of the Arkansas. This species has been beautifully figured by Dr. Gray in *Mem. Amer. acad.* (*n. ser.*) *t.* 4.

G. pulchella, *Foug.* Valley of the Del Norte.

Palafoxia linearis, *Lag.* New Mexico.

Hymenoxys odorata, *DC.* Great desert west of the Colorado.

Artemisia filifolia, *Torr. in Ann. lyc. N. York,* 2, *p.* 211. Valley of the Del Norte, and along the Gila; abundant.

A. dracunculoides, *Pursh.* Table lands of the Del Norte and Gila. A very common species of wormwood, often called *sage* by the hunters.

A. cana, *Pursh.* On the Raton Mountains.

Senecio longilobus, *Benth. in fl. Hartweg.* A bushy species about three feet high, growing abundantly in the region between the waters of the Del Norte and the Gila.

TETRADYMIA? (sub-genus Polydymia.) Heads about 16-flowered; the flowers all tabular and perfect. Involucre of 15 to 16 oblong obtuse coriaceo-chartaceous scales which are slightly concave but not carinate. Receptacle naked. Corolla with a rather slender tube; the lobes short, ovate, erect, furnished with long villous hairs externally. Anthers included. Branches of the style tipped with a very short obtuse pubescent cone. Achenia oblong-turbinate, villous with short hairs. Pappus of numerous, somewhat rigid, denticulate bristles. A suffrutescent prostrate much branched plant, canescently and densely tomentose; the leaves broadly obovate, toothed, narrowed into a petiole. Heads on short peduncles, terminating the somewhat corymbose branches.

T. (Polydymia) ramosissima, *n. sp.* Hills bordering the Gila. Stem spreading, with very numerous matted branches. Leaves about three-fourths of an inch in length, the lamina broader than long, with 5-7 indistinct rounded teeth, abruptly narrowed into a longish petiole. Heads about one-third of an inch in diameter, ovate. Involucral scales in several series, the exterior ones shorter than the interior. Hairs of the achenium smooth, slightly bifid at the summit. Pappus longer than the achenium. This plant is clearly allied to Tetradymia, but differs in the many flowered heads; numerous scales of the involucre; slightly cleft corolla tube, and in several other characters, so that it should perhaps form the type of a distinct genus.

Cirsium undulatum, *Spreng.* The locality of this plant is not recorded, but it was probably found on the upper part of the Arkansas.

Stephanomeria paniculata, *Nutt.* Ascending the Cordilleras of California.

Mulgedium pulchellum, *Nutt.* Pawnee Fork of the Arkansas.

ERICACEÆ.

Arctostaphylos pungens, *Kunth.?* Valley of the Gila and San Diego. Flowers in January.

A. tomentosa, *Dougl.?* A shrub 4 to 5 feet high. Cordilleras of California. This may be a smooth variety of Douglass plant. The leaves are orbicular-ovate, obtuse or truncate at the base, glabrous on both sides, with the petiole one-third the length of the lamina. It was not found in flower.

PLANTAGINACEÆ.

Plantago, *n. sp.?* Allied to *P. gnaphaloides*, *Nutt.* Great desert west of the Colorado, near the Cordilleras of California. The whole plant is clothed with a loose white tomentum, which is partly deciduous with age. The leaves are linear lanceolate, entire, and taper to a long narrow base. The peduncles are 5 to 6 inches long, and bear a close cylindrical spike, which is less than an inch in length. Sepals ovate, membranaceous, marked with a strong mid-rib, which is villous externally. Segments of the corolla ovate. Capsule 2 seeded.

PEDALIACEÆ.

Martynia proboscidea, *Linn.?* Abundant in the valley of the Del Norte. We have only the leaves and a drawing of the fruit. It is possibly *M. altheæfolia. Benth. in bot. Sulph.*

SCROPHULARIACEÆ.

Maurandia antirrhina, *Lindl.* On the San Francisco, a tributary of the Gila. A slender trailing plant, with beautiful purplish flowers.

Castilleja linearifolia, *Benth.* Valley of the Gila, and the region between that river and the waters of the Gila.

Penstemon Torreyi, *Benth.* Region between the Del Norte and the Gila.

Three or four other species of Pentstemon exist in the collection, but the specimens are incomplete, and have not yet been studied.

VERBENACEÆ.

Verbena bipinnatifida, *Nutt.* Valley of the Del Norte.

Lippia cuneifolia, *Steud.* Verbena cuneifolia, *Torr.* In Long's Rocky Mountain plants. Upper part of the Arkansas, and along the tributaries of the Canadian.

LABIATÆ.

Salvia carduacea, *Benth.* Western slope of the Cordilleras of California.

Another species of this genus was found with the preceding, but not in flower, It is entirely clothed with dense soft canescent pubescence. It is shrubby, with long stout branches springing from near the root. The leaves are oblong, coriaceous, entire, and two inches or more in length.

Several other undetermined labiatæ were found in the valley of the Del Norte and on the Gila.

BORAGINACEÆ.

Myosotis glomerata, *Nutt.* Tributaries of the Canadian.

Euploca grandiflora, *n. sp.* Hirsute, with rough appressed hairs. Leaves oblong-lanceolate, on short petioles. Flowers in leafy clusters. Calyx five-paired to the base, with linear lanceolate segments. Corolla white; (the expanded limb nearly three-fourths of an inch in diameter, obscurely 5-lobed, plaited; tube slender, somewhat ventricose below the middle; the throat naked. Stamens inserted toward the base of the corolla tube; the filaments short; anthers oblong-linear. Ovary 4-celled, style filiform, persistent, arising from the summit of the ovary; stigma capitate, with a tuft of stiff hairs at the extremity. Fruit 4-celled, 2-lobed, finally separating into indehiscent carpels; embryo curved, terete, surrounded with very thin albumen; radicle superior. On the Del Norte below Santa Fé. This plant is clearly a congener of *euploca convolvulaceæ* of Nuttall. It is nearly related to Tourneforbia.

HYDROLEACEÆ.

Eriodictyon, *Benth. in bot Sulph.*, p. 35. *Chois in DC*, *prod.* 10, *p*. 183. A well characterized Californian genus, containing three described species, one of which is the *Wigandia Californica*, *Hook and Arn*, which was found in rocky places near the mouth of San Carlos, on the Gila, and on the Cordilleras of California. The leaves are coriaceous, varying in form from narrowly linear to lanceolate, and from being perfectly entire to strongly dentate. The upper surface (as well as the branches,) is covered with a copious adhesive varnish, while the under-side is whitish tomentose, with strongly marked reticulated veins.

POLEMONIACEÆ.

Phlox, *n. sp.* This likewise occurs in Texas, and will be described by Dr. Gray. It was found in various places on the tributaries of the Canadian.

Gilia pulchella, *Dougl*. Ocaté creek, and other tributaries of the Canadian.

G. longifolia, *Benth*. Ipomœa longifolia, *Torr*. In Long's Rocky mountain plants. Valley of the Del Norte.

Fouquieria spinosa. (*Bronnia spinosa*, *Kunth. nov. gen.* 6, *p*. 84, *t*. 528.) *Benth. in bot. Sulph. p.* 16. Ascending the Cordilleras of California. A highly ornamental shrub, shooting up long smooth simple stems, to the height of from 12 to 25 feet, with a panicle of scarlet flowers at the summit. It differs slightly from the figure and description of Kunth, but seems to be the same plant. The leaves are obovate-oblong, glabrous and membranaceous, growin fascicles in the axils of the spines. The spines are from a half an inch to near an inch in length, slender, more or less spreading, or even somewhat recurved. At the base of each is a longitudinal protuberance which extends along the stem until it reaches the spine, which is on a line with it below. The panicle is usually contracted and elongated, but sometimes short, and almost corymbose. The flowers are on short pedicels which are furnished with deciduous bracts. Sepals 5, nearly orbicular, concave, strongly imbricated, persistent, about one fourth the length of the corolla. Corolla about three-fourths of an inch long; the tube cylindrical, and often curved; limb 5-cleft, with ovate rather acute segments. Stamens 13 to 16 exserted, hypogynous; the filaments thickened and somewhat coherent at the base; anthers linear oblong, mucronate. Ovary 3-celled, with about 6 ascending anatropous ovules in each cell, style 3, parted below the middle. Capsule oblong, acute, obtuse, triangular, coriaceous and glabrous, 3-valved, loculicidal, straight, or little curved, one-celled by the separation of the valves from the triangular axis. Seeds 3 to 6, white, ovate, pellate, much compressed, with a broad winged margin, which is an expansion of the testa, and which finally is resolved into numerous fine hairs. These are beautiful objects under the microscore. They are spiral vessels consisting of an extremely delicate sheath, containing the loosely coiled thread which frequently ramifies with anastomosing branches. The whole testa is formed of these singular vessels. Embryo nearly as large as the seed; cotyledons foliaceous; radicle pointing downward. There can be little doubt of the propriety of uniting Bronnia and Fouquieria. Each genus was founded on a single species, and both plants seem to be very little known to European botanists. Of the former the flowers are imperfectly described, and of the latter, the fruit is unknown. Our plant partakes of the characters of both genera. In the ovary the placentæ meet in the axis, but only slightly cohere; finally they unite, but in fruit the valves of the capsule separate from the axis, to which the seeds remain attached. As to the affinities of Fouquieria, I am inclined to adopt the opinion of Lindley, that it is very near Polemoniaceæ, and particularly to Cantua. It differs, however, in its distinct imbricated sepals, (which are exactly those of convolvulus,) more numerous and hypogynous stamens; and very sparing albumen, as well as in habit. It is certainly very unlike Frankeniaceæ, to which it is appended by Endlicher. Kunth placed it among genera allied to Portulacaceæ.

CONVOLVULACEÆ.

Ipomœa leptophylla, *Torr. in Frém. 1st report, p.* 94. Upper part of the Arkansas and head waters of the Canadian. The stems are often erect, about two feet high, and of a bushy appearance. From the appearance of the specimens, I should suppose the plant were a perennial, but according to Dr. James it is an annual.

One or two other Convolvulaceæ were in the collection, but I have not determined them to my satisfaction.

SOLANACEÆ.

Nycterium lobatum. Between Fort Leavenworth and the head of the Arkansas.

Datura metel, *Willd.?* Valley of the Gila. It grows from four to five feet high, with spreading branches. Perhaps introduced.

Solanum triflorum, *Nutt.* Upper part of the Arkansas, and on the tributaries of the Arkansas.

Another species of Solanum was found on the Del Norte below Santa Fé. The whole plant is clothed with a dense yellowish white pubescence. The stems are rough, with minute slender prickles. Leaves linear-oblong, entire, rather obtuse, prickly along the midrib. Flowers, two or three together at the summit of the branches, white.? stamens 5; anthers equal.

GENTIANACEÆ.

Eustoma Russelianum, *Don.* Near the bank of the San Pedro. A showy plant.

Erythræa Beyrichii, *Torr. and Gr. E. tricantha B. Griseb.* Valley of the Del Norte, and along the Gila.

OLEACEÆ.

Fraxinus velutina, *n. sp.* Branches, petioles, and under surface of the leaves, clothed with a dense soft pubescence. Leaflets 3 to 5, rhombic ovate, cuneate at the base, coarsely serrate or toothed, sparingly pubescent above. Fruit narrowly oblanceolate, nearly entire at the apex, about three-fourths of an inch long. A small tree, usually from 15 to 20 feet high. Grows in the region between the waters of the Del Norte and the Gila; also on the Mimbres, a tributary of the latter river.

NYCTAGINACEÆ.

Abronia mellifera, *Hook.* Valley of the Del Norte.

A. (*Tripterocalyx*) micranthum, *Torr. in Frém.* 1st report, p. 96. Valley of the Del Norte.

This differs in some respects from Frémont's plant. The peduncles are elongated, and the fruit is more than an inch long, with very broad wings. The structure of the seed is precisely the same as in that plant, the inner cotyledon of the conduplicate embryo being abortive. It is wanting also in A. mellifera. In several species of this genus, if not in all of them, the filaments adhere throughout nearly their whole length to the tube of the perianth. The lobes of the perianth are dilated, and deeply emarginate, but appear ovate in the bud, from the lobules being conduplicate.

CHENOPODIACEÆ.

Sarcobatus vermiculatus, *S. Maximilioni, Nees in Prince Maxim. trav., Engl. ed., p.* 518. *Frémontia vermicularis, Torr. in Frém.* 1st report, p. 95; and 2d report, p. 317. *Batis vermicularis, Hook, fl. Bor. Am.* 2, p. 188. Abundant on the Del Norte, and upper part of the valley of the Gila.

This is the *pulpy thorn* of Lewis and Clark. It has a very extensive range in the desert regions on both sides of the monntains. Since my notices of this plant were published in Frémont's reports, I have ascertained that Nees' description of his genus, Sarcobatus, dates a little anterior to mine, so that his name must be adopted.

Obione argentea, *Moq. Atriplex argentea, Nutt.* Abundant in sandy saline places on the Del Norte.

O. polycarpa, *n. sp.* Valley of the Gila.

Eurotia lanata, *Moq.* Valley of the Del Norte. A shrubby Salicornia, an Atriplex, and a species of Sueda, were found in saline soils along the Gila.

AMARANTHACEÆ.

Amaranthus hybridus, *Var.?* Glabu. Stem and leaves nearly smooth, flowers (purplish) crowded in a dense compound terminal spike; bracts somewhat awned, shorter than the flowers; utricle opening transversely. On the Del Norte, below Santa Fé.

POLYGONACEÆ.

Eriogonum trichopes, *n. sp.* Stem scape-like, verticillately and divaricately much branched, glabrous; peduncles capillary; involucre minute, few flowered, glabrous, 4-toothed; the teeth nearly equal, obtuse, erect; sepals ovate, acute, nearly equal, very hairy. Eastern slope of the Cordilleras of California. Our specimens of this remarkable species are imperfect, the leaves being wanting. They probably grow in a radical cluster. The flowering stems are a foot or more high, with the primary and secondary branches verticillate; the branchlets are bi-trichotomous, and the ultimate divisions or peduncles somewhat secund. Involucre scarcely half a line in length, 5—6 flowered, and only 4-toothed. The flowers are nearly twice as large as the involucres, sepals concave, erect spreading. Stamens scarcely exserted.

E. tomentosum, *Michx.* Abundant in the region between the valley of the Del Norte and the waters of the Gila; the most western station hitherto found of this species, which is almost the only eriogonum known east of the Mississippi.

E. Aberteanum, *n. sp.* Annual? Canescently tomentose; stem dichotomous above; leaves oblong-lanceolate, attenuated to a petiole at the base; involucres solitary, somewhat racemose on the branches, pedunculate, many flowered, campanulate, deeply 5—8=parted; exterior sepals nearly orbicular, deeply cordate at the base; inner sepals narrow, carinate below, contracted above, somewhat dilated and emarginate at the summit; stamens much shorter than the sepals. Very common in the region between the Del Norte and the Gila. Also found by Lieutenant Abert on the upper waters of the Arkansas. Just as I was sending these notes to the press, I received a visit from Mr. Nuttall, who informed me that a species allied to this was found by Mr. Gambel, in his late journey to California. He thinks its characters differ so much from all the eriogona hitherto described, that he has constituted of it a new genus under the name of EUCYCLA. A full account of Mr. Gambel's plants, by Mr. Nuttall, will soon be published in the journal of the academy of Philadelphia. Our plant is about a foot high, with loosely paniculate branches.

The heads and flowers are nearly as large as those of *E. tomentosum.* The sepals are yellowish, tinged with rose, the three inner ones differ widely from the others; they are carinate and glandular on the back below the middle, and closely embrace the pistil, the angles of which correspond with the keels of the sepals.

Imperfect specimens of several other eriogona occur in the collection.

SAURURACEÆ.

Anemopsis Californica, *Nutt. Hook. in bot. Beechey's voy.,* p. 390, *t.* 92. Valley of the Gila.

EUPHORBIACEÆ.

Eremocarpus setigerus, *Benth. in bot. of Sulph.*, p. 53, t. 26. Plains of San Diego, California.

Hendecandra Texensis, *Klotzsch.* '*H. multiflora, Torr. in Frém.* 1st report. Croton muricatum, *Nutt.* Valley of the Del Norte.

Another species of this genus, allied to *H. procumbens*, was found on the Cordilleras of Mexico, but the materials are scarcely sufficient for determining it satisfactorily.

Stillengia spinulosa, *n. sp.* Suffruticose? leaves rhombic-ovate, rigid, narrowed at the base, prominently 3-nerved, mucronately acuminate, dentate-spinulose on the margin; spikes axillary and terminal; sterile flowers sepile; bracts acuminate, with a stipitate gland on each side at the base. Abundant in the desert west of the Colorado. Stem (apparently) about a span high, with spreading branches. Leaves an inch or more in length, sessile, neatly margined, with spreading spinulose teeth, glabrous on both sides. Spikes numerous; with solitary fertile flowers at the base. Sterile flowers about as long as the scale. Perianth hemispherical, irregularly lobed and undulated. Stamens 2. Fertile flowers imperfect in our specimens. Fruit glabrous.

Euphorbia hernianoides, *Nutt.* Banks of the Gila. A pubescent variety of this species was found in the desert west of the Colorado.

CUPULIFERÆ.

Quercus Emoryi, *n. sp.* Leaves coriaceous, oblong, on very short petioles, remotely and repandly toothed, the serratures mucronate, smooth on both sides; fruit pedunculate, solitary and in pairs, gland ovoid-oblong, mucronate; cup hemispherical, the scales appressed. Common in the elevated country between the Del Norte and the Gila. This small leaved oak resembles *Q. agrifolia* and *Q. undulata*, (*Torr. in Ann. lyc. N. York* 2, p. 248, t. 4,) but is quite distinct from both.

SALICACEÆ.

Salix. Several narrow leaved willows were found along the Gila, and in the region west of the Colorado, but being without fructification they cannot be determined. One of them is used as food for cattle when there is no grass.

PLATANACEÆ.

Platanus Mexicanus, Moricand pl. *nouv. ou rars d'Amer.* t. 26. *P. Californicas, Benth. bot. Sulph.*, p. 54. *P. racemosus, Nutt.?* Valley of the Gila.

CONIFERÆ.

Ephedra occidentalis, *Willd.*? From the region between the Del Norte and the Gila, and the hills bordering the latter river to the desert west of the Colorado. A shrub 3—4 feet high, with numerous slender branches; its appearance being that of Scotch broom. (Spartium scoparium.) The sheaths are very long, 3-parted, with subulate-acuminate segments. This can hardly be the *E. Americana* of Quito, which is described as having 2-parted sheaths. The specimens are without either flowers or fruit. If the species should prove to be new, it may be called E. trifurcus. There seems to be still another species growing on the table lands of New Mexico, differing from the preceding in its very short sheaths.

Juniperus. Two undetermined species were found in crossing the country from the Del Norte to the Gila. Both of them have the general character of *J. Virginiana.* One is a large tree, with acerose leaves, and a bark like that of a pinus; the other has short closely appressed leaves and berries larger than a buck shot.

AMARYLLIDACEÆ.

Agave Americana, *Linn.* Found in descending the western slope of the Cordilleras of California. This is the *maguey* of the Mexicans. It shoots up a flowering stalk 10 or 15 feet high. The juice of the plant affords an intoxicating drink called *pulque.*

Another species of agave, or a very remarkable variety of the preceding was found in New Mexico, west of the Del Norte. It differs from *A. Americana* in its much shorter and broader leaves, which are furnished with smaller marginal spines.

LILIACEÆ.

Yucca. The leaves only, of what appear to be four species of this genus, occur in the collection, but we cannot identify them for want of the inflorescence.

ORCHIDACEÆ.

Spiranthes cernua, *Rich.* Low grounds in the valley of the Del Norte.

CYPERACEÆ.

Eleocharis quadrangulata, *R. Brown.* Valley of the Gila.
Cyperus Michauxianus, *Schultes.* Valley of the Gila.

GRAMINEÆ.

Chloris alba, *Presl.* Spikes umbellate-fasciculate, numerous, (8—12,) the peduncle inclosed in a broad compressed sheath; spikelets 2-flowered; upper glume nearly as long as the flowers,

2-toothed, with a short awn between the teeth; lower palea of the perfect flower obscurely 3-nerved, gibbous in the middle, the margin ciliate, with long hairs towards the summit; awn three times as long as the palea; neuter flower broad and truncate, inclosing a short aristiform rudiment; the awn twice as long as the palea. Bed of the Gila. Very near *C. barbata*, which differs in the entire glumes, which are only mucronate (not awned) in the entire straight lower palea of the perfect flower, and in the third or aristiform flower, being much exserted.

Boutelona racemosa, *Lagasca.?* Culm erect, simple; spikes numerous (20—40) reflexed, 3-flowered, lower glume linear-nebulate; upper one linear-lanceolate, scabrous, entire, nearly as long as the spikelets; lower palea of the perfect flower unequally tricuspidate, pubescent, abortive flower reduced to a slender awn, which is nearly as long as the perfect flower, furnished at the base, with 2 short and inconspicuous bristles. Valley of the Gila, rare. This plant agrees pretty well with Kunth's description of *B.* (*Eutriana*,) *racemosa*, except in the pubescent lower palea, and the minute bristles at the base of the neuter flower. Whether it be the plant of Lagasca or not is very difficult to determine from his brief character. It certainly is very different from *B. racemosa* of the United States, which has a large 3-awned neuter flower, and if distinct from Lagasca's, must receive another name. That of *B. curtipendula* would be appropriate.

Chondrosium eriopodum, *n. sp.* Culm simple, pubescent below; spikes 4—6, racemose appressed; spikes on short woolly peduncles, spikelets 2-flowered; flowers distichous; glumes very unequal, glabrous, linear-lanceolate, mucronate, entire; lower palea of the perfect flower glabrous, bifid at the apex, with a short bristle between the teeth; neuter flower pedicellate, with 3 slender awns. This is one of the species of "Grama" so useful as a fodder-grass in New Mexico. It is abundant along the Del Norte, and in the region between that river and the waters of the Gila. The culm is slender, a foot or more in height. Leaves are very narrow, 2—3 inches long, with glabrous sheaths; sessile almost wanting. Spikes about three-fourths of an inch long.

Chondrosium fœneum, *n. sp.* Leaves glabrous; spikes 2—3, oblong, folcate, spreading; rachis nearly half the length of the spikes; upper glume nearly as long as the perfect flower, with two rows of piliferous glands on the back; lower palea deeply 3-cleft, the segments lanceolate and mucronate, hairy on the margin; neuter flower of two truncate emarginate valves, with a 2-valved rudiment of a third flower, and 3 short stout awns. Uplands bordering the valley of the Del Norte. This is another of the grasses called *Grama* in New Mexico, and is the best kind, being almost as good fodder as oats. It is nearly allied to *Atheropogon* (*Chondrosium*,) *oligostachyum* of Nuttall.

Chondrosium polystachyum, *Benth. bot. Sulph. p.* 56. Uplands bordering the Gila. The smallest kind of "*Grama*" found on the journey. It is about 6 inches high, very slender. The spikes are narrowly linear, and almost half an inch long, erect, on short brownish peduncles. The other characters agree minutely with Mr. Bentham's admirable detailed description in the work quoted above.

Leptochloa filiformis, *Roem and Schults.* Valley of the Gila. Scarcely distinct from *L. mucronata* of the United States.

Sesleria? dactyloides, *Nutt.* Upper part of the Arkansas. This is the celebrated "*Buffalo* grass," so called because it constitutes the chief fodder of the wild buffalo, during the season that it flourishes. I have retained this plant, for the present, where it was placed by Mr. Nuttall, who noticed its anomalous characters. It differs from sesleria, and indeed from the Torbe *Festucaceæ*, in its habit, which is that of chondrosium. The stem throws off suckers which root at the joints, from whence leaves and culms of a few inches in height are thrown up. The spikes are two or three in number, on short spreading peduncles, They are oblong, about half an inch in length, and obtuse; bearing from 6 to 8 spikelets, which are unilateral, and form a double row on the rachis. The spikelets are usually 2-flowered, but I have occasionally found them with 3 flowers, and even the rudiment of a fourth. The glumes are very unequal, oblong-ovate; coriaceo-membranaceous, carinate and one-nerved, the upper one slightly mucronate. Palea oblong-lanceolate, and somewhat keeled, membranaceous, nearly equal, but longer than the glumes, entire glabrous, except on the keel; the lower 3-nerved, the upper bi-carinate. Anthers large, linear, fulvous. In all the specimens of this collection, as well as in those in my herbarium from numerous other localities, there are no fertile flowers, and only in a few instances rudimentary styles, so that the plant seems to be diœcious or polygamous by abortion.

Arundo Phragmites, *Linn.* Valley of the Del Norte, and along the Gila.

Andropogon argèntens, *DC.*, *Kunth. enum. t, p.* 500. Valley of the Gila. A handsome species, with the spikes in a terminal panicle, which has a white appearance from the abundant silky hairs of the flowers.

A. macronrus, *Michx.* With the preceding.

Besides these grasses, there were a few others, mostly collected in the valley of the Gila, but which I have not determined, as the specimens are not so complete as could be desired. Among them are a *glyceria*, two *agrostides*, five species of *pamcuin* and a *poa*, (*eragrostis*,) with large elongated spikelets. In some parts of the valley of the Del Norte, *sorghum vulgare* is cultivated, and was found partly naturalized.

EQUISETACEÆ.

Equisetum hyemale, *Linn.* Lower part of the Colorado.

FILICES.

Adiantum tenerum, *Swartz.* Valley of the Gila. This species is widely spread over the southern part of North America, and yet has not hitherto obtained a place in our Flora. We have it from Alabama, Florida, Texas, and various parts of California.

Lycopodium. A small species allied to *L. rupestre*, was found in descending the Gila. It differs in its incurved leaves, which are mucronate, but without a bristle at the tip. No fructification exists in the specimen.

St. Louis, *February* 13, 1848.

My Dear Sir: Your letter, together with the package containing the drawings of a number of most interesting cactaceæ, arrived safely here about two weeks ago.

O the occasion of my report on the botany of Dr. Wislizenus's voyage, I have made a careful investigation of the cactaceæ, of which he brought home with him more than 20 species, and have been enabled to elucidate several points which had been unknown, or obscure before; no doubt because in the hot-houses of European gardens, these curious plants, though they thrive pretty well, rarely produce flowers and fruit; so that from 800 species of cactaceæ at present cultivated in Europe, perhaps not one fourth is known as to its flower, and a much smaller proportion in fruit.

I am now able to distinguish all the different genera of cactaceæ by their seed, and sometimes even the different sections of one genus.

The small black shining seed sent me, belongs to a true *cereus*, probably the plant which you mention under the name of pitahaya, the larger opaque black seed is that of an *echinocactus*, and the largest white seed is the seed of an opuntia of the section *cylindraceæ*.

I have ventured to describe some of your species from the drawing; my descriptions, however, and the names given by me, must remain doubtful till we are able to obtain some more data to characterize the species. I have written it more for your information than for publication, but if you choose to append it to your published report, I have no objection to it, but must request you to make such corrections or alterations as your notes or your recollection of the plants will enable you to do; for example, as to size, as in some of the drawings no size is mentioned,* in which case I have assumed them to represent the natural size. I have, for convenience sake, numbered the different figures, and shall now proceed to copy for you the descriptions and remarks following my numbers.

1. Mammilaria, October 18, 1846.

Proliferous in the highest degree, forming hemispherical masses often of a diameter of 3½ feet; which are composed of 100—200 different heads or stems. Single heads conical, apparently about 4 or 5 inches high, and 2½—3 inches in diameter; color, bluish green; spines white or reddish.

---

* Where the size is not mentioned, the original drawings are the size of nature. W. H. E.

This species appears to be allied to *M. vivipara*, but is distinguished by the conical heads, and the hemispherical tufts, while *M. vivipara* has hemispherical or even depressed heads, and forms flat and spreading masses.

It may be an undescribed species, in which case the name of *M. aggregata* appears to be most appropriate.

2. *Mammilaria*, October 26, 1846. Rare.

Apparently a *mammilaria*, though the habit of the plant is more that of an *echinocereus*, but all *echinocerei* have the bunches of spines disposed in vertical ridges, which is not the case in the figure in question. Stems irregularly cylindrical, with divers contractions and swelling, about 4—6 inches high, and $1\frac{1}{4}$ to $1\frac{3}{4}$ inches in diameter, many (in the fig. 8) from one base.

The name of *M. fasciculata* would indicate the peculiarity of this species.

3. *Mammilaria*, "November 4th, 1846, abundant."

Several (fig. 3.) oval stems from one base, $1\frac{1}{2}$—$2\frac{1}{2}$ inches high, and $1\frac{1}{4}$ inch in diameter; tubercles in about 13 rows; spines whitish, short; 1 small obovate red berry toward the apex not more than $1\frac{1}{2}$ line long.

If the figure is correct, this species ought to be distinguished by the name of *M. microcarpa*, as I know of no other mammilaria with such a small fruit.

4. *Echinocactus Wislizeni*. (Engelm. in Wizlizenus's report.) "October 26th, 1846." In addition to the description in Dr. W.'s report, which I have drawn up from dried specimens, I observe in this figure that the species has 21 oblique ribs, is of an oval shape, and bluish green color; the ribs are acute, but not compressed, according to the representation of a section, and the groves corresponding.

5. *Echinocactus*, "October 25th, 1846, 18 inches in diameter." Height equal to the diameter; shape ventricose, contracted towards the vertex, therefore somewhat urceolate; with 21 straight sharp ribs; spines apparently 8, straight, brown, color of plant bright green; vertex whitish, (tomentose?) fruit 1 or $1\frac{1}{2}$ inches long, oval, yellowish or reddish. Seed obovate, obliquely truncated at base, full 1 line long, black, opaque, slightly roughened; embryo curved or hooked, cotyledons accumbent, partly buried in the large farinaceous albumen.

This species is distinct from all other New Mexican species examined by me, and is most probably undescribed. I propose to name it after its zealous discoverer, who has, surmounting numberless difficulties, though occupied by severe and arduous duties, found leisure to do so much for the advancement of our knowledge of the wild countries traversed by him, *echinocactus Emoryi*.

6. Cereus. "November 21st, 1846, 3 feet high."

There can be but little doubt but that we have here a species before us, which I have received from Dr. Wislizenus and from Dr. Gregg, from the neighborhood of Chihuahua, and which I have described in Dr. W's report by the name of *C. Greggii*, erect, branching, with 5 compressed ribs, dark green, with whitish areolæ, and about 8 short dusky spines.

The specimen figured here is very remarkable on account of the fruit, which was unknown to me. Provided the drawing is correct, we have here a smooth oval acuminate fruit crowned with the remains of the corolla, and supported by a distinct stipe of a bright crimson color. A stipe, as well as such an acumination, I have not seen in any other fruit of a cactus. Fruit, with the long acumination, $2\frac{1}{2}$ inches long, $\frac{3}{4}$ to 1 inch in diameter, stipe about $\frac{1}{2}$ inch long.

7. *Opuntia.* "Very abundant on the Del Norte and Gila." No date nor statement whether the figure represents the natural size or is smaller.

The species belongs to the section *ellipticæ* of Salm, it is ascending, older stems prostrate, branches and younger joints erect, 8—10 inches high; joints orbicular obovate, rounded, obtuse or sometimes acutish, of a bluish green color, $1\frac{1}{2}$ to $2\frac{1}{2}$ inches long, and little less wide; spines short and whitish; berries obovate, scarlet, only about 3 or 4 inches long. If the figure represents the natural size, this species ought to bear the name *O. microcarpa.*

8. *Opuntia.* "October 28th, 1846, common on the Gila." Much branched, sub-erect, joints obovate, often acutish, purplish, with two or three longer brown spines directed downwards; fruits obovate, red. In the figure, the joints are $1\frac{1}{2}$—2 inches long, and 1—$1\frac{1}{4}$ wide; fruit about 3 lines long.

There are several opuntiæ known with purple colored joints, but none in the least resembling this, and I must consider it as a distinct species to whichI would give the name of *O. violacea.*

9. *Opuntia?* "October 22d, 1846. Abundant on the Del Norte and Gila." A remarkable plant apparently more like a *mammilaria* than like an *opuntia.* The fruit is also represented without areolæ or tubercles, exactly like the smooth fruit of a *mammilaria*; but this may be an oversight in the artist. The habit of the plant suggests the belief that it is an opuntia of the section *cylindraceæ.*

Joints or branches ascending, cylindrical, tuberculated, 4—6 inches long. 1—$1\frac{1}{4}$ inches in diameter; tubercles very prominent, with about 8 long (1—$1\frac{1}{2}$ inches) straight spines; fruits obovate, umbilicate, scarlet, towards the top of the branches, about 9 lines long, and 6 in diameter.

It is a distinct species which I am gratified to dedicate to the skilful artist who has drawn all these figures, Mr. J. M. Stanly, I therefore propose for it the name *opuntia Stanlyi.*

10. *Opuntia.* "November 3d, 1846, 4 feet high." Stem erect, with verticillate horizontal, or somewhat pendulous branches; branches cylindrical, strongly tuberculated, about 8 lines in diameter, with short spines on the tubercles; fruit pale yellow, clavate, tuberculate, umbilicate, 1 to $1\frac{1}{2}$ inches long, 6—8 lines in diameter.

This is probably the *opuntia arborescens, Engelm.* in *Williz's report,* though the spines are represented as being shorter than in my specimens of *O. arborescens* from New Mexico and Chihuahua.

11. *Opuntia.* "November 2d, 1846. Somewhat resembling the

last, but forming 'low wide spreading bushes.'" Joints more slender, only about 4 or 5 lines in diameter, alternating (not opposite nor verticillate,) forming with the stem an acute angle, sub-erect, tubercles more prominent, ærolæ whitish at their lower edge, with 3 dusky deflexed spines; fruit clavate, tuberculate, pale yellow, 1 inch long, 4 lines in diameter.

I believe this to be an undescribed species, and would propose the name for it of O. Californica.

12. *Opuntia.* "October 10th, 1846, abundant," 3 feet high, with spreading branches, the same in circumference.

I can see no difference between this figure and a plant which I have received from El Passo, by Dr. Wislizenus, and which I have described in his report under the name of *O. vaginata.*

Nos. 13—15 are no cacti. In 13 I recognise the *Kœberlinia zuccarini*, a shrub common in the chaparals of northern Mexico, which has been collected in flower about Parras and Saltillo, by Drs. Wislizenus and Gregg. The fruit is unknown so far; the specimen figured is however in fruit; the berry (?) is globose, $\frac{3}{4}$—1 line in diameter, crowned with the rudiment of the style. It was collected October 23d, 1846, and is described as a shrub 3 feet high, with low spreading boughs.

14. Collected "November 15, 1846. 4 feet high, rare," is perhaps another species of the same genus, but the entire absence of flower or fruit make it impossible to decide.

Branches similar, straight, leafless, ending in robust dark spines; but much elongated and sub-erect, not horizontal, as in No. 13.

15. "October 22d. Very abundant, 3 feet high, fruit 5 inches long." It is entirely unknown to me, perhaps an agave? at least some amaryllidaceous plant, if the fruit is correctly represented, with large radical leaves, and a ribbed or angular inferior fruit crowned with the remains of the flower.

In your letter you figure and describe a cactus plant, of which you have before sent me the seeds, if I am correct about this from your notes, I would describe it in the following manner:

Stem tall, erect, simple, or with a few erect branches, below without spines; ribs about 20, oblique or spiral; fruit large, edible; seeds small (0.7 lines long,) obovate, obliquely truncate at base, black, smooth, shining, embryo hooked, no albumen; cotyledons foliaceous incumbent.

Stems 2—5 feet in circumference, and 25 to 60 feet high.

The only true *cereus* approaching this in size is *cereus* Peruvianus; but this is vastly different. The question then arises whether our species is not one of the few arranged now under the genus *pilocereus;* but if it is a constant fact that the cotyledons of *pilocereus* are thick and globose, our species cannot belong here; the cotyledons are absolutely those of a true *cereus.* It is called in California *pitahaya*, but it appears that the Mexicans call by that name all large columnar cacti, the fruit of which is edible. The plant which is commonly called *cereus variabilis*, is widely different from this California giant.

I propose for it the name *cereus gigantens.*

DALEA FORMOSA.

FALLUGIA PARADOXA.

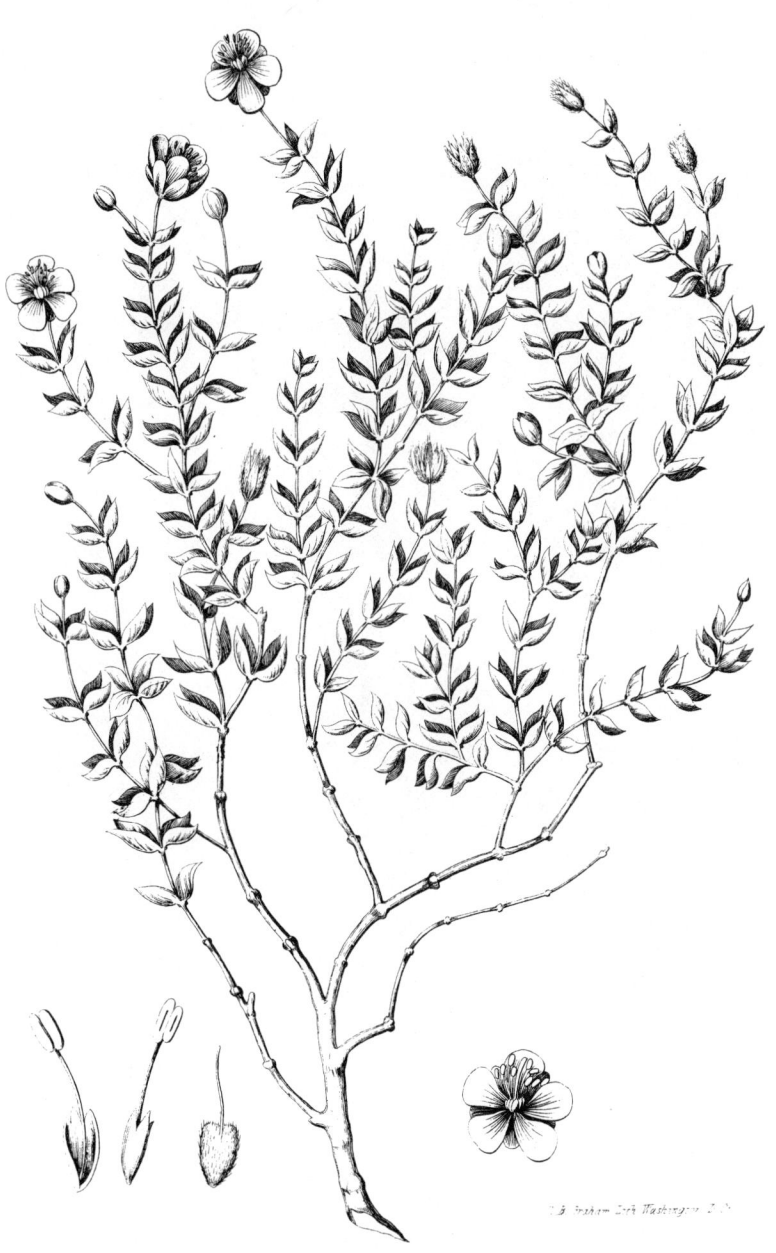

LARREA MEXICANA.

ZINNIA GRANDIFLORA.

RIDDELLIA TAGETINA.

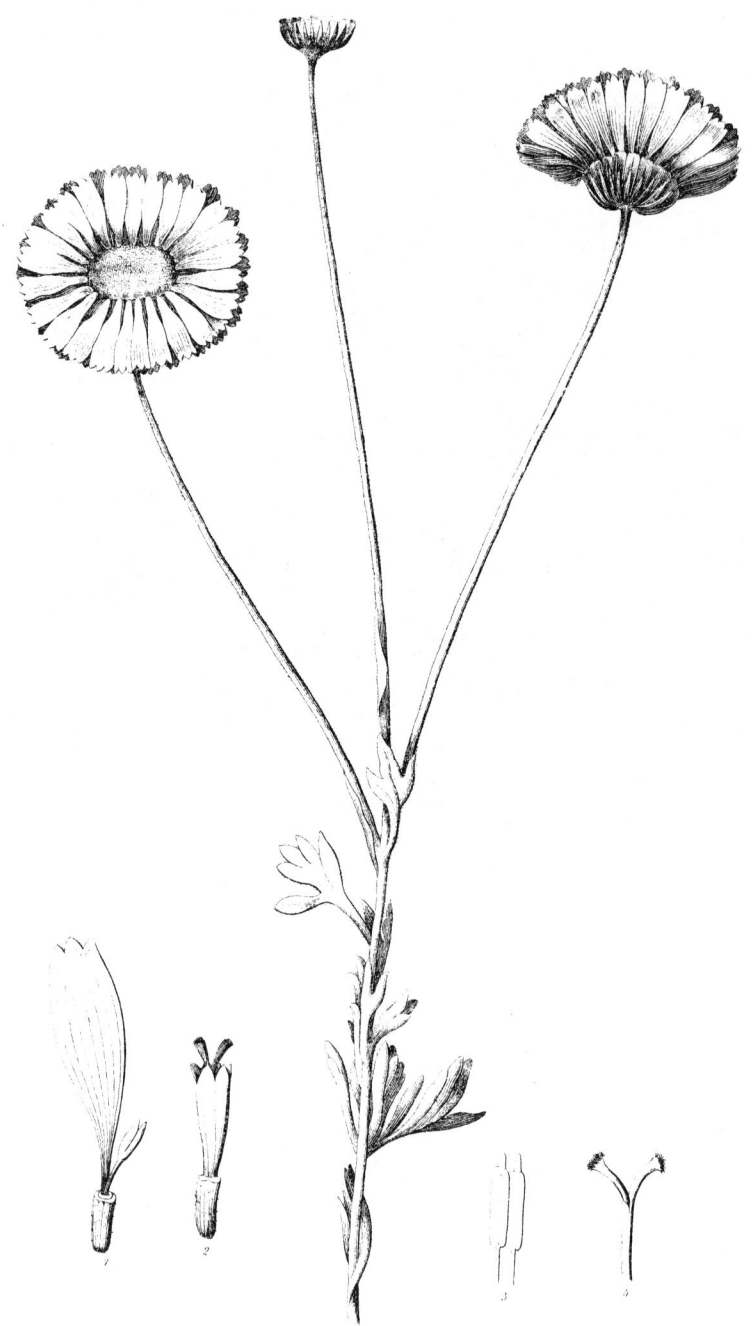

VI

ARCTOSTAPHYLOS PUNGENS.

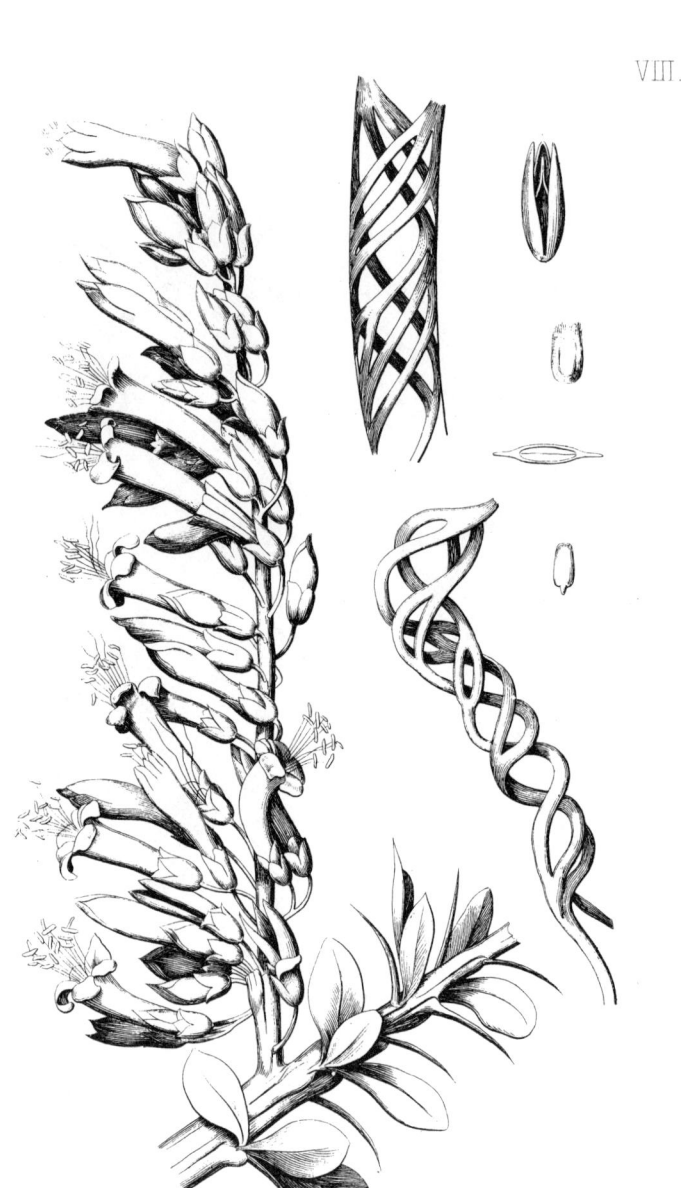

FOUQUIERA SPINOSA

QUERCUS EMORYI

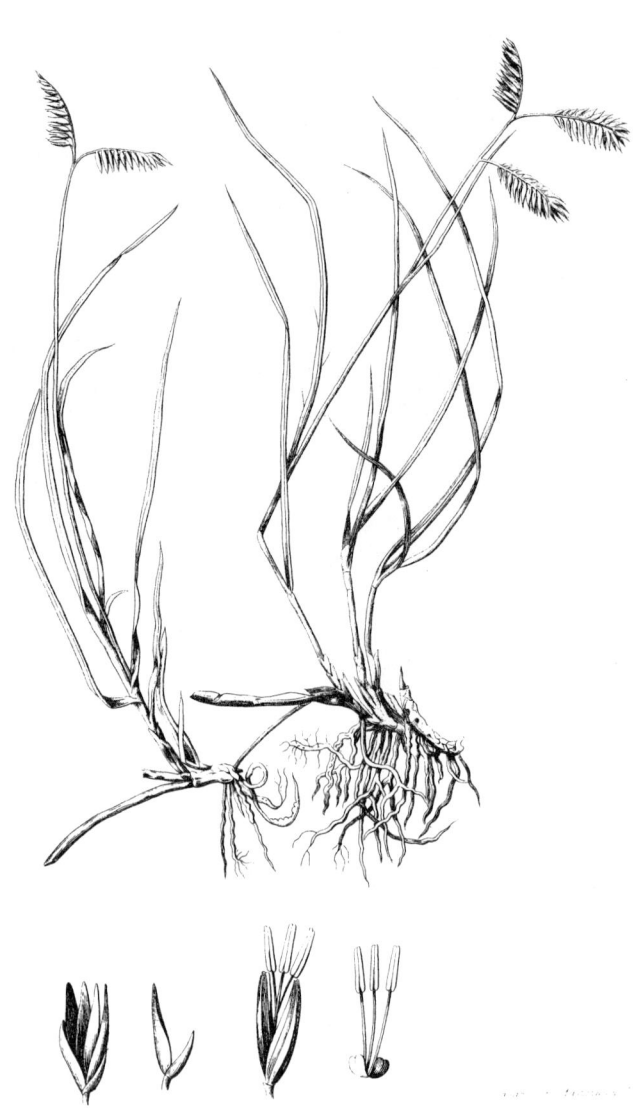

SESLERIA DACTYLOIDES.

IPOMŒA LEPTOPHYLLA.

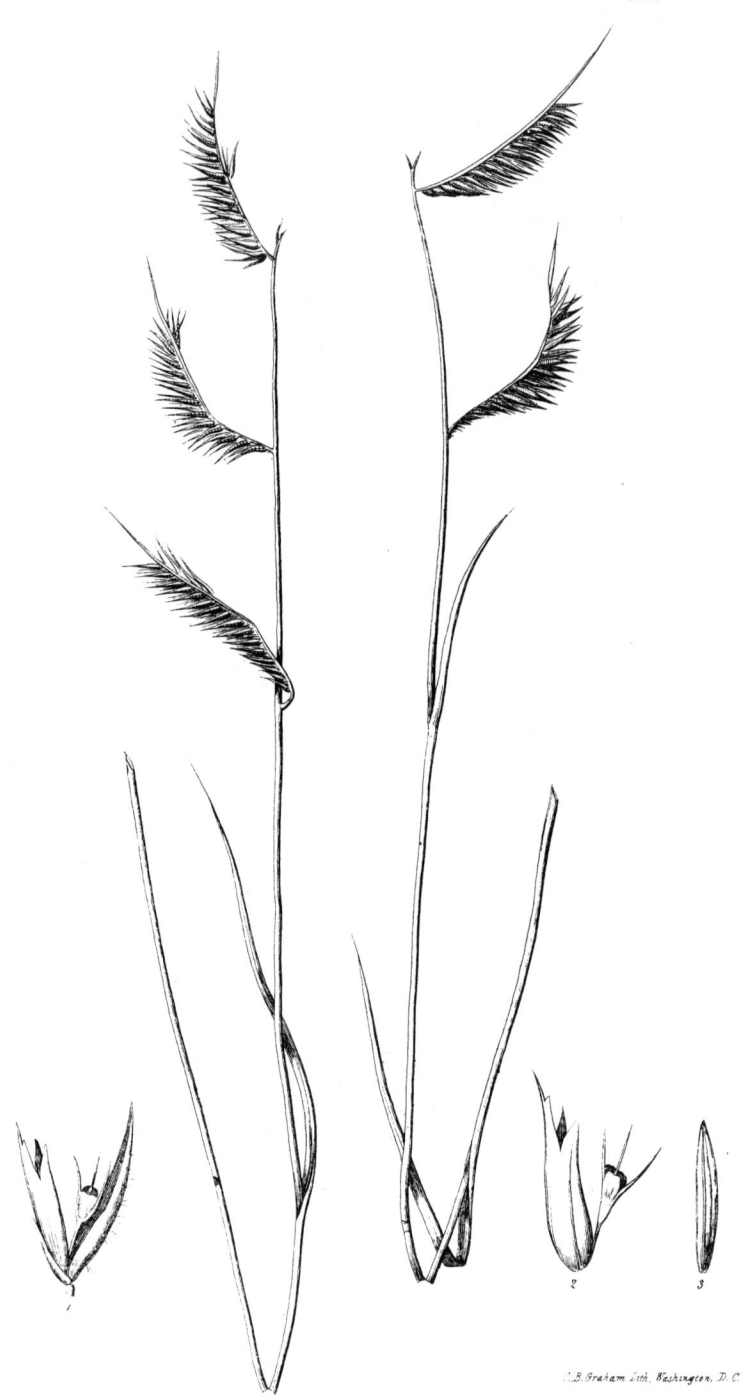

CHONDROSIUM FŒNEUM.

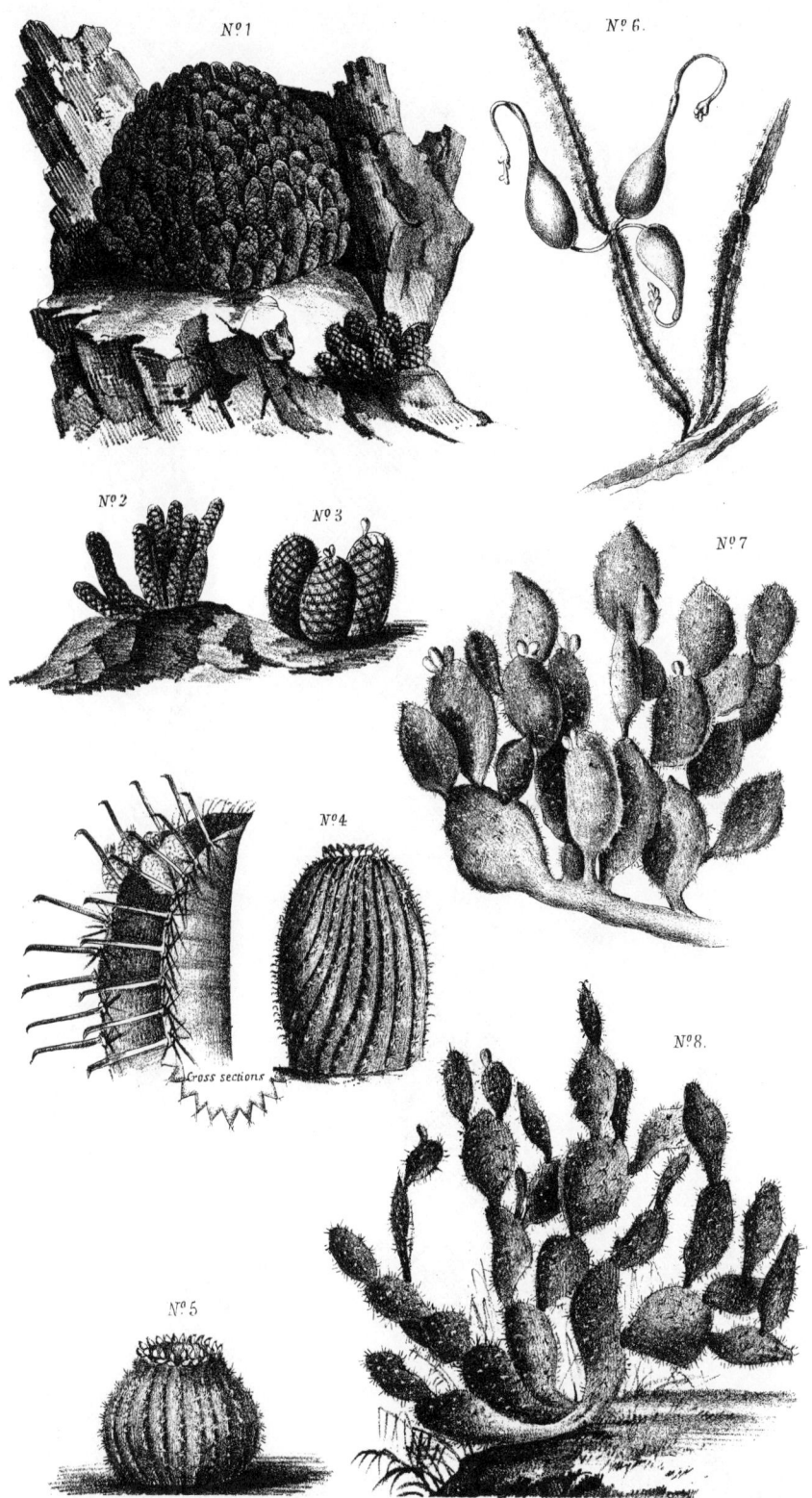

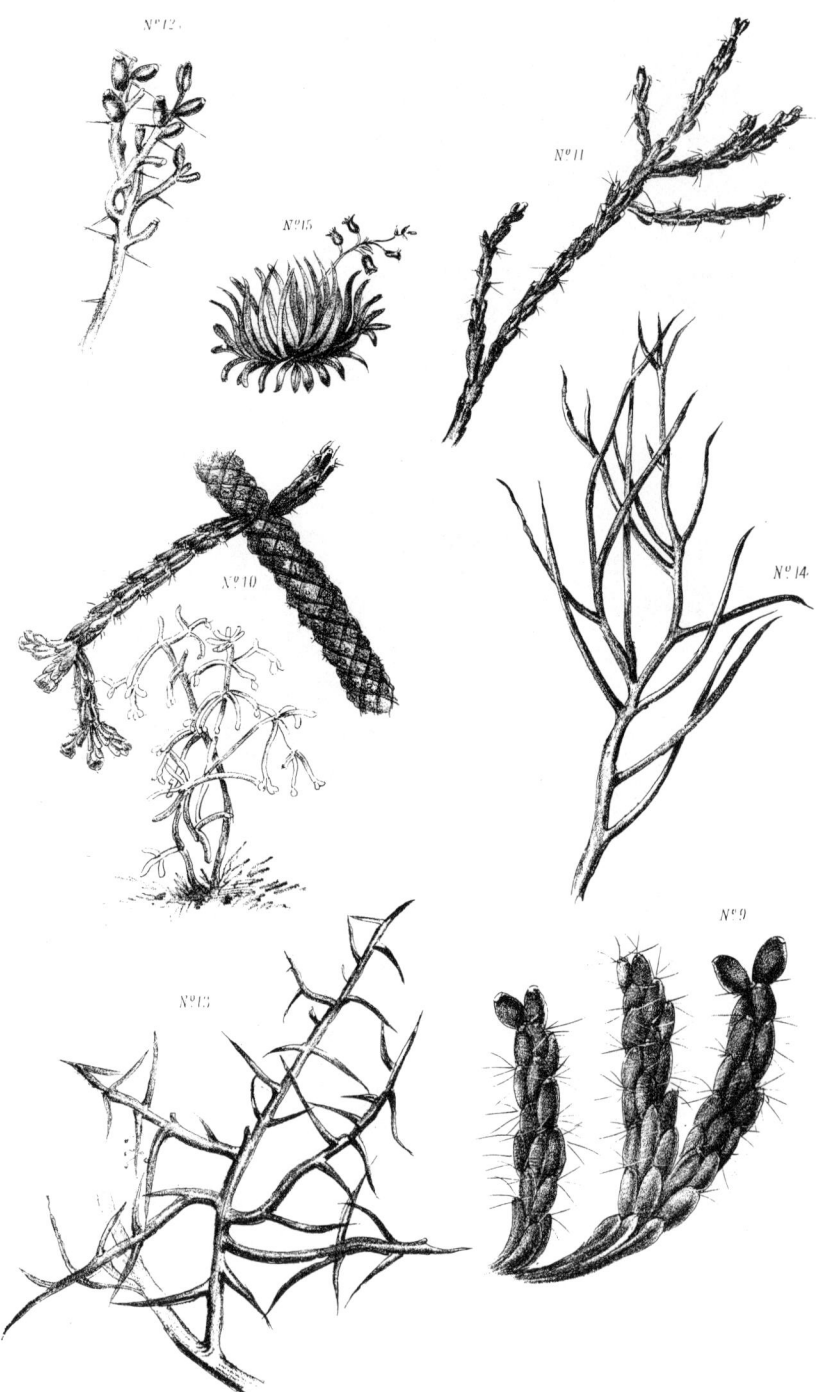

The large white seed is that of an *opuntia* of the section *cylendraceæ*, embryo circular, curved around a pretty large albumen, but not spiral.

Very truly, yours,

G. ENGELMANN.

APPENDIX No. 3.

Table of meteorological observations.

Places of observation.	Date.	Time.	Barometer.	Thermometer. Attached.	Thermometer. Free.	Thermometer. Wet bulb.	Approximate altitude.	Remarks.
Fort Leavenworth	June 23	3 p. m.	73.75	C. 18	F. 62¼	F.		Raining, NE.
Do	June 24	9 a. m.	74.24	16½	73			Wind NE.; cloudy.
Do	do	12 m.	74.11	19	71½			Wind NNE.; cloudy.
Do	do	3 p. m.	74.12	19	70			Cloudy, with occasional showers.
Do	June 25	9 a. m.	74.20	21.5	70			Cloudy.
Do	do	12 m.	74.04	24	77			Cloudy.
Do	do	3 p. m.	73.98	25½	77			Light clouds; wind SE.
Do	June 26	9 a. m.	73.92	22½	78			Few light clouds; wind west.
Do	do	12 m.	74.16	24.5	76			
Do	do	3 p. m.	73.90	26	78			Clear wind NW.; gentle breeze.
Do	June 27	3 p. m.	73.81	21	75			Clear.
Camp 2, Strangers' creek	June 28	6 a. m.	73.64	30	84	80	⎫	
Do	June 29	5 p. m.	73.68	21	70	68	⎬ 1044.	
Camp 3, Kansas river	June 30	5.30 a. m.	74.09	22	72	71.5	850.	Clear.
Camp 4, Oregon trail, on the Makurussi	June 31	6 p. m.	74.20	26	78	73.5	781.	Gentle breeze NE.; very fair.
Camp 4, Oregon trail, on the Makurussi	July 1	5.30 a. m.	74.40	20.5	71	69	⎫	Cloudy.
Camp 5, on the Santa Fé road	do	7 p. m.	73.58	27½	79	74½	⎬ 1060	Very fair; clear and beautiful sunset.
Do	July 2	5 a. m.	73.60	21	70	67	⎭	Heavy mist and dew.
Camp 6, on 110 creek	do	7 p. m.	73.28	29	82	75	⎱ 1179.	Brisk wind from SW.
Do	July 3	5 a. m.	73.28	21	72	69	⎰	Fresh breeze south.
Camp 7	do	7 p. m.	72.77	27	81	74	⎱ 1363.	Strong breeze; wind SSE.
Do	July 4	4.30 a. m.	72.86	22	70	69	⎰	Clear.

Camp 8, Big John spring......	July 4	7 p. m. ..	72.64	29	83	77	1456	Wind SE.
Do do	July 5	4.30 a. m.	72.54	23	73	70		Clear; temperature Big John spring 53° Fa.
Camp 9, Diamond spring	do	7 p. m. ..	72.33	24½	78	75	1511	Very fair; no wind.
Do do	July 6	4.30 a. m.	72.49	23	73	70		Cloudy: temperature of spring 54° Fa.
Camp 10, Cottonwood stream ..	do	7 p. m. ..	72.64	28	83	76	....	Clear.
Do do ..	July 7	6 a. m. ..	72.85	24	77	74	....	Clear; gentle breeze south.
Do do ..	do	6 p. m. ..	72.86	27	80	73½	1372	Gentle breeze SE.
Do do ..	July 8	4.30 a. m.	72.81	20	70	68	....	Hazy; very heavy dew.
Camp 11, Turkey creek........	do	7 p. m. ..	72.26	25	78	72½	....	Wind SE.
Do do	July 9	4 a. m. ..	72.17	21½	73	70½	....	Cloudy; drizzling rain.
Camp 12, Little Arkansas river	do	7 p. m. ..	71.89	25	77½	73		Wind E. by S.; raining during the day.
Do do	July 10	4 a. m. ..	72.	23½	75	72½	1695	Appearance of rain; lightning, with thunder; wind E. by S.
Camp 13, branch of Cow creek	do	7 p. m. ..	71.88	26½	78½	76	1703	Clear; has been raining most of the day.
Do do	July 11	4 a. m. ..	71.97	22	72	71		Cloudy; heavy rain during night.
Camp 14. Arkansas river, where the Santa Fé road first strikes it.	do	7 p. m. ..	71.94	27	79	75		Very fair and calm.
Camp 14, Arkansas river, where the Santa Fé road first strikes it.	July 12	4.30 a. m.	71.99	20	69	67	1642	Heavy mist and dew.
Camp 15, on the Arkansas.....	do	7 p. m. ..	71.59	28	77½	73	1840	Sun set fair; no wind.
Do do	July 13	4.30 a. m.	71.53	20	68½	67		Misty.
Camp 16, Pawnee fork	do	7 p. m. ..	71.07	28	79	74		Light breeze from east.
Do do	July 14	6 a. m. ..	71.26	22	73	71½		Very fair.
Do do	do	7 p. m. ..	71.29	30	81½	74		Wind E. by S.
Do do	July 15	5.30 a. m.	71.40	22	72½	70	1932	Fair.
Do do	do	7 p. m. ..	71.49	27	79	71		Wind E. by S.
Do do	July 16	5 a. m. ..	71.60	19½	67	64		Fair; light breeze E. by S.
Camp 17, on the prairies, out of sight of, and about two miles from, the river.	July 17	5 a. m. ..	71.44	13	55	53	1797	Clear; light easterly wind.
Camp 18, on the prairie........	do	7 p. m. ..	71.	23	70	58½	2013	Wind east.
Do do	July 18	5 a. m. ..	71.	17	61	57		Clear; strong breeze S. by E.
Camp 19, on the Arkansas	do	7 p. m. ..	70.85	26	76	67	2196	Clear; strong wind SE.
Do do	July 19	5.20 a. m.	70.44	16½	62	58½		Clear; strong wind south.
Camp 20, Jackson grove.......	do	7 p. m. ..	69.92	27	78	69½	2519	Wind E. by S.; clear.
Camp 21, on the Arkansas	July 20	7.30 p. m.	69.50	26	80	68	2652	
Do do	July 21	8 a. m. ..	69.48	20	69½	64½		Cloudy in the west.
Camp 22, on the Arkansas	do	7 p. m. ..	68.83	30	86	67	2940	Heavy clouds to the west, and furious wind about 8 p. m. from the same quarter.

APPENDIX No. 3.—METEOROLOGICAL OBSERVATIONS—Continued.

Places of observation.	Date.	Time.	Barometer.	Thermometer. Attached.	Thermometer. Free.	Thermometer. Wet bulb.	Approximate altitude.	Remarks.
				C.	F.	F.		
Camp 22, on the Arkansas	July 22	7 a. m.	68.94	22¼	74¼	64	2940	Clear; light breeze E. by N.
Camp 23, on the Arkansas	do	7 p. m.	68.67	30	86	66	2988	Sky overcast in the west.
Do	July 23	5 a. m.	68.79	19	67	65		Clear; light wind E. by S.
Camp 24, on the Arkansas	do	7 p. m.	68.10	26	81	70½	3268	Strong wind SE.; sky overcast to the west.
Do	July 24	5.30 a. m.	68.28	19	68	63		Clear; wind E. by S.
Camp 25, on the Arkansas	do	4.45 a. m.	67.94	29	83	74	3319	Clear; light breeze SE.
Do	July 25	7 p. m.	67.95	21½	72	64¼		Clear; wind light, SE.
Camp 26, on the Arkansas	do	5 a. m.	67.75	30	84	61	3396	Overcast in the west; wind south.
Do	July 26	7 p. m.	67.82	23	71½	62		Wind E. by S.; darkly overcast in the east.
Camp 27, on the Arkansas	do	7 p. m.	67.29	29½	84½	68	3594	Clear; wind E. by S.
Do	July 27	5 a. m.	67.26	21	70	64		After a severe hail storm, with thunder and lightning, dark clouds in the east; appearance of more rain; wind SE.
Camp 28, on the Arkansas	do	7 p. m.	66.69	25	74½	65	3779	Clouds in west; no wind.
Do	July 28	5 p. m.	66.80	20	66	62		Clear; no wind.
Camp 29, on the Arkansas	do	7 p. m.	66.51	29½	78	62		Clear.
Do	July 29	5 a. m.	66.60	16	58	54	3862	Sky overcast in the NW.; strong wind NE.
Camp 30, near Bent's fort	do	7 p. m.	66.51	25	76	62		Clear.
Do	July 30	6 p. m.	66.61	20	69	59½		Clear; wind E. by S.
Do	do	7 p. m.	66.42	29	84¼	67		Clear.
Do	July 31	6 a. m.	66.46	15	62	57		Clear.
Do	do	7 p. m.	66.43	33	87	67	3942	Clear; strong breeze E. by S.
Do	August 1	5 a. m.	66.38	18	64¼	55		Clear.
Do	do	7 p. m.	66.21	32	86	62		Wind E. by S.; clear.
Do	August 2	6 a. m.	66.18	21	70	58		Clear.
Camp 31, on the Timpa	do	7 p. m.	65.10	31	86	61	4523	Clear; high wind SE.
Do	August 3	5.30 a. m.	65.11	21	71	57		Wind south.
Camp 32, on the Timpa	do	7 p. m.	64.74	30½	87	61	4761	Slight haze; wind south.

Do do	August 4	5 a. m.	64.81	21	71½	55	4761	Wind south.
Camp 33, Hole in the Prairie	August 5	5.30 a. m.	62.57	19	68	55	5560	Clear; wind W. by S.
Camp 34, on the Purgatory	do	7 p. m.	61.79	25½	80	62	5896	Strong wind W. by S.
Do do	August 6	5.30 a. m.	61.91	15	60	52		Clear; wind SW.
Camp 35, valley of the Raton	do	7 p. m.	58.93	22	70	53	7169	Clear.
Do do	August 7	6 a. m.	59.04	14	59½	54½		Sky clear; sun just rising above the mountain.
Summit of the Raton	do	10.30 a. m.	58.01	25	74	......	7754	Fair.
Camp 36, on the Canadian	do	7 p. m.	61.28	23½	72	63	6112	Cloudy in the east after a slight chair.
Do do	August 8	6 a. m.	61.27	12	57	52		Clear; no wind.
Do do	do	7 p. m.	61.26	23½	72	62½		Dark clouds in the west; calm.
Do do	August 9	5.30 a. m.	61.30	11	53	51		Clear.
Camp, 37	do	7 p. m.	61.27	22¼	70½	66	6109	Sky overcast in the SW.; light shower on the March 4, p. m.
Do	August 10	5 a. m.	61.26	12½	56	52		Wind SW.; hazy towards south.
Camp 38, on Cummaron Citon	do	7 p. m.	61.46	24	69½	58½	6027	Sky overcast in the west.
Do do	August 11	5 a. m.	61.34	10	51	48½		Clear and calm.
Camp 39, on the Ocaté	do	7 p. m.	59.43	23	71	63	6946	Cloudy, and overcast in the west.
Do do	August 12	6 a. m.	59.56	16½	61½	53		Darkly overcast in the west; wind east.
Camp 40, at the Pools	do	7 p. m.	60.20	21	69	59	6670	Wind E. by N.; sky overcast in the west.
Do do	August 13	6 a. m.	59.82	11½	52	49		Clear.
Camp 41, on the Sapillo	do	6 p. m.	60.65	20½	68	64	6395	Just cleared off after a very heavy shower from the SW.
Do do	August 14	5.30 a. m.	60.60	14½	56½	54		Clear and calm.
Camp 42, at the village of the Vegas.	do	6 p. m.	60.69	24	72	69	6418	Clear and calm.
Camp 42, at the village of the Vegas.	August 15	6 a. m.	60.65	13	55	54		Clear and calm.
Camp 43, Vernal Springs	do	6 p. m.	60.87	28	75	65	6299	Clear and calm.
Do do	August 16	5.30 a. m.	60.98	14	57½	53		Clear and calm.
Camp 44, half mile south of the Pecos.	do	6 p. m.	60.76	25	75	63	6346	Sky overcast in the west.
Camp 44, half mile south of the Pecos.	August 17	5.30 a. m.	60.82	14	57	53		Clear and calm.
Camp 45, on the Pecos, near Peco's village.	do	6 p. m.	59.73	21½	69	65	6366	Light wind and rain from east.
Camp 45, on the Pecos, near Peco's village.	August 18	5.15 a. m.	59.72	15¼	61½	59		Heavy clouds and mist; rain throughout the night.
Santa Fé	August 19	6 a. m.	59.56	14	59	55½	6846	Sky clouded; looks like rain; calm.
Do	do	6 p. m.	59.52	20½	67	59		Sky clear; no wind.
Do	August 20	7 a. m.	59.61	18½	62¼	59		Clear.

APPENDIX No. 3.—METEOROLOGICAL OBSERVATIONS—Continued.

Places of observation.	Date.	Time.	Barometer.	Thermometer: Attached.	Thermometer: Free.	Thermometer: Wet bulb.	Approximate altitude.	Remarks.
Santa Fé	August 20	6 p. m.	59.50	C. 19	F. 64	F. 53		Clear; wind E. by N.
Do	August 21	6 a. m.	59.84	18	$53\frac{1}{2}$	56		Clear.
Do	do	6 p. m.	59.75	18	$58\frac{1}{2}$	55		Cloudy after rain.
Do	August 22	6 a. m.	60.03	17	57	53		Clear and calm.
Do	do	6 p. m.	59.80	19	60	$58\frac{1}{2}$		do
Do	August 23	7 a. m.	59.97	$17\frac{3}{4}$	64	55		do
Do	do	6 p. m.	59.71	21	64	60		do
Do	August 24	7 a. m.	59.83	19	61	56		Clear.
Do	do	6.30	59.53	22	$65\frac{1}{2}$	61		do
Do	August 25	8 a. m.	59.67	20	64	$56\frac{1}{2}$		Clear; gentle breeze N. by E.
Do	do	6 p. m.	59.78	19	62	58		Raining; wind NE.
Do	do	7.30 a. m.	60.04	19	62	57		Sky overcast; looks like rain; no wind.
Do	August 26	6 p. m.	59.92	20	$60\frac{1}{2}$	$56\frac{1}{2}$	6846	Clear.
Do	August 27	7 a. m.	60.01	17	$57\frac{1}{2}$	$52\frac{1}{2}$		do
Do	do	6 p. m.	59.82	$21\frac{1}{2}$	$63\frac{1}{2}$	57		Calm and clear.
Do	August 28	8 a. m.	59.87	19	60	56		do
Do	do	6 p. m.	59.74	22	71	58		do
Do	August 29	7 a. m.	59.88	20	62	$51\frac{1}{2}$		do
Do	do	8 p. m.	59.69	$22\frac{3}{4}$	74	$61\frac{1}{2}$		Clear and calm.
Do	August 30	8 a. m.	59.77	$19\frac{1}{2}$	$66\frac{1}{2}$	$54\frac{1}{2}$		do
Do	do	6 p. m.	59.47	$23\frac{1}{2}$	75	59		do
Do	August 31	6 p. m.	59.37	22	70	58		Clear.
Do	September 1	7 p. m.	59.50	18	61	54		Clear and calm.
Do	do	6 p. m.	59.35	$21\frac{1}{2}$	$69\frac{1}{2}$	60		do
Camp 47, Galisteo creek	September 2	6 p. m.	63.92	$27\frac{1}{2}$	$80\frac{1}{2}$	62		Clear; wind SW.
Galisteo creek	do	6 a. m.	62.58	$14\frac{1}{2}$	56	51	5158	Clear and fair.
Camp 48, two miles below San Felipe.	September 3	5.45	63.15	27	77	63		Clear and calm.

164   Ex. Doc. No. 41.

San Felipe	September 4	6 a. m.	63.45	18	61	......	5158	Gentle wind E. by S.
Camp 49, quarter of a mile south of the Alameda.	do	5.30 p. m.	64.08	24½	75	59	....	Fair; wind NW.
Camp 49, quarter of a mile south of the Alameda.	September 5	6 a. m.	63.63	13½	54	51	....	Fair and calm.
Camp 50, on the Rio del Norte, 8½ miles below Albuquerque	do	6 p. m.	63.61	24½	74½	58	....	Wind SW
	September 6	6.30 a. m.	63.85	10	51	49	....	Fair and calm.
Camp 51, near Pualta, almost 500 feet NW. of the Chavez church.	September 7	7.15 a. m.	64.06	17	63	55	4862	
Camp 52, about one mile north of Tomé.	do	6.30 p. m.	64.39	29½	74	62	....	Calm and clear.
Camp 52	September 8	6.30 a. m.	64.26	14	57	53	....	Fair and calm.
Camp 54, on the return, same as camp 49.	September 9	6 p. m.	63.17	21½	67	57	....	Clear and calm.
Camp 54, on the return, same as camp 49.	September 10	7 a. m.	63.53	8½	50	48	....	do
Camp 55, about one mile south of San Felipe.	do	6 p. m.	63.47	25	67	57	....	Calm and clear.
Camp 55, about one mile south of San Felipe.	September 11	7 a. m.	63.86	8½	46	......	....	do
Camp 56	do	6 p. m.	61.94	28½	73½	58	....	do
Do	September 12	6 a. m.	62.01	14	56	......	....	Clear; wind E. by S.
Santa Fé	September 13	8 a. m.	59.70	21	69	59	....	Clear and calm.
Do	do	6 p. m.	59.57	24¼	74	61½	....	Sky overcast in the south; wind E. by S. light refreshing shower at 4 p. m.
Do	September 14	6 p. m.	59.77	22	70½	63	....	Sky overcast immediately after a shower; no wind.
Do	September 15	7 a. m.	59.91	21	68	58	....	Calm and clear.
Do	do	6 p. m.	59.73	19½	65	......	....	Just clearing off after a shower; wind NE.
Do	September 16	8 a. m.	59.67	20	66½	59	....	Clear and calm.
Do	do	6 p. m.	59.54	22	70½	52	....	Calm and clear.
Do	September 17	8 a. m.	59.75	19	64	54	....	Clear and calm.
Do	do	6 p. m.	59.58	23	71	56	....	do
Do	September 18	6 p. m.	59.66	23	74½	62	....	Calm and clear.
Do	September 19	7 a. m.	59.80	20	65	54	....	do
Do	do	6 p. m.	59.65	22	71	54	....	Sky overcast in the south; faint thunder.
Do	September 20	8 a. m.	59.79	19¾	66	52		
Do	do	5.30 p. m.	59.75	22	71	53½	....	Clear and calm.
Do	September 21	7.30 a. m.	59.91	18	63	51	....	Clear; light wind E. by S.

APPENDIX No. 3.—METEOROLOGICAL OBSERVATIONS—Continued.

Place of observation.	Date.	Time.	Barometer.	Thermometer. Attached.	Thermometer. Free.	Thermometer. Wet bulb.	Approximate altitude.	Remarks.
Santa Fé	September 21	6 p. m.	59.66	C. 22	F. 72	F. 63		Light shower of rain; wind NE.
Do	September 22	6 p. m.	59.35	20	67½	57		Sky overcast; wind west.
Do	September 23	7 a. m.	59.41	17	58½	51		Clear.
Do	do	6 p. m.	59.28	21	66½	56		Calm and clear.
Do	September 24	7 a. m.	59.49	16	59	53		Fair; wind from NE.; a heavy shower during the night.
Camp 57	September 25	6 p. m.	62.13	20¼	63	50½	5820	Fair and calm.
Do	September 26	5.45 a. m.	62.08	3	36			During the night high wind E. by N.
Camp 58, where the road strikes the river Del Norte.	do	6 p. m.	63.88	24	65	53	4910	Calm and clear.
Camp 58, where the road strikes the river Del Norte.	September 27	6 a. m.	64.06	6¼	40			do
Camp 59, about one mile south of San Dia.	do	6 p. m.	64.08	23	68	53	4846	do
Camp 59, about one mile south of San Dia.	September 28	6 a. m.	64.12	5	40	37¼		do
Camp 60	do	6 p. m.	63.93	25	63	58	6904	do
Do	September 29	6 a. m.	64.07	5	38	37		do
Camp 61. First camp on the west side of the Rio del Norte, about 7 miles below Albuquerque.	do	6 p. m.	64.27	21¼	67	56		do
Camp 61. First camp on the west side of the Rio del Norte, about 7 miles below Albuquerque.	September 30	6 a. m.	64.32	3	36	37	4756	do
Camp 62, 7 miles below Isoletta	do	6 p. m.	64.53	26¼	70¼	58	4636	Clear and calm.
Do	October 1	6 a. m.	64.70	12¼	51	47		Calm and clear.

Camp 63, below Tomé 9 miles	do ..	6 p. m. ..	64.59	25½	69	54	4670	No wind; clear.
Do do	October 2 ..	6 a. m. ..	64.48	4¼	37	35		Clear and calm.
Camp 64....................	do ..	6 p. m. ..	64.65	30½	70¼	57		do
Do	October 3 ..	6 a. m. ..	64.70	4¼	38½	39	4615	do
Do	do ..	6 p. m. ..	64.66	29	72	55		do
Do	October 4 ..	6 a. m. ..	64.65	5	40	38		Calm and clear.
Camp 65....................	do ..	6 p. m. ..	64.79	26	7½	54	4556	Clear and calm.
Do	October 5 ..	6 a. m. ..	64.76	5½	41	37		do
Camp 66, near Socorro	do ..	5.30 p. m.	64.72	27	72¼	56	4563	Calm and clear; strong breeze from SE. during the afternoon.
Do do	October 6 ..	6 a. m. ..	64.83	11	51	45		Clear; light wind south.
Camp 67....................	do ..	6 p. m. ..	64.79	25	75	57	4595	Sky overcast in east, and a strong wind from south.
Do	October 7 ..	6 a. m. ..	64.56	10	50	46		Clear and calm.
Camp 68....................	do ..	6 p. m. ..	64.72	24	71	58	4576	Strong wind from south, which has been blowing all day.
Do	October 8 ..	6 a. m. ..	64.74	10½	48	42		Clear and calm.
Camp 69....................	October 9 ..	6 a. m. ..	65.16	1½	34½	33½	....	do
Camp 70, east side of the Del Norte.	do ..	5.30 p. m.	65.24	24½	71½	54		Fair; light wind from south, which has blown strong from the same quarter during the day.
Camp 70, east side of the Del Norte.	October 10 ..	6.30 p. m.	65.26	1½	35	......		Clear and calm.
Camp 70, east side of the Del Norte.	do ..	5.30 p. m.	65.37	20¼	62	48	4241	Clear; wind S. by W.
Camp 70....................	October 11 ..	6 a. m. ..	65.73	1	30	......		Clear and calm.
Do	October 12 ..	6.30 a. m.	65.99	1½	30	......		do
Do	do ..	5.30 p. m.	65.74	25	69	57		do
Do	October 13 ..	6 a. m. ..	65.85	1½	27	......		do
Camp 71....................	do ..	5.30 a. m.	65.73	20	66	50	4138	do
Do	October 4 ..	6 a. m. ..	65.76	2	34	......		do
Camp 72....................	do ..	5.30 p. m.	65.73	26	72	56	4164	Clear; light wind from the south.
Do	October 15 ..	6 a. m. ..	65.68	6	42	40		Clear and calm.
Camp 73. First after leaving the Del Norte.	do ..	5.30 p. m.	64.15	26	76	53	4810	Clear; light wind S. by W.
Camp 73....................	October 16 ..	6 a. m. ..	64.22	9	48½	......		Clear; light wind SW.
Camp 74....................	do ..	5.15 p. m.	63.99	22	70	51	5229	Light clouds; wind strong from SW.
Do	October 17 ..	6 a. m. ..	63.06	3	35½	......		Clear; no wind.
Camp 75, in the mountains, between the Del Norte and copper mine.	do ..	5 p. m. ..	62.73	16	61½	49	5426	Clear; light wind south.

APPENDIX No. 3.—METEOROLOGICAL OBSERVATIONS—Continued

Place of observation.	Date.	Time.	Barometer.	Thermometer. Attached.	Free.	Wet bulb.	Approximate altitude.	Remarks.
				C.	F.	F.		
Camp 75, in the mountains, between the Del Norte and copper mines.	October 18	6 a. m.	62.73	24	27½	....	5426	Calm and clear.
Top of hill No. 1, between camp 75 and 76.	do	11 a. m.	61.98	14	59	....	....	Clear; no wind.
Top of hill No. 2	do	11.40 a. m.	61.73	20	64	....	....	
Top of hill No. 3	do	1 p. m.	60.63	23	72	....	6387	Clear and calm.
Camp 76, near the copper mines	do	5 p. m.	61.30	16	58	49	6167	do
Top of hill	October 19	5.30 a. m.	61.28	3	35	....	....	Cloudy in the west; indications of rain from that quarter.
	do	1.22 p. m.	61.29	19½	66	....	....	Clear sunrise.
Camp 77	October 20	6.30 a. m.	64.77	2½	37	....	4587	Clear and calm.
Camp 78, on the Gila	do	5 p. m.	65.58	21	70	54	4347	Cloudy; no wind.
Do	October 21	6 a. m.	65.64	4½	40	....	....	Light breeze south; clear.
Camp 79, on the Gila	do	5 p. m.	66.22	23½	71	56	4096	Cloudy and calm.
Do	October 22	6 a. m.	66.38	7	44	43	....	Clear; wind east.
Do	do	5 p. m.	66.66	24	74	56	3989	Cloudy in the west; no wind.
Camp 80, on the Gila	October 23	6 a. m.	66.63	13	57	49	....	Clear; wind south.
Do	do	5 p. m.	67.08	24½	74	54	....	Clear and calm.
Camp 81, on the Gila	October 24	6 a. m.	66.94	4	27	....	....	Clear; light wind SW.
Do	do	5 p. m.	66.93	20½	69	53	3732	Clear and calm.
Do	October 25	6 a. m.	66.84	3	27½	....	....	Sky bright; no wind.
Camp 82, on the Gila	do	5.30 p. m.	67.22	20	66½	50	3615	Sky clouded in the west; light air from NE.
Do	October 26	6 a. m.	67.38	1½	34	....	....	Bright clouds; wind light E. by N.
Camp 83, on the Gila, about 50 feet above the river.	do	5 p. m.	68.17	23	70	50	3147	
Top of ridge between camp 82 and 83, on the road.	do	11.40 a. m.	63.58	20	63	51	....	Fair, with light wind from east.

Camp 83, on the Gila	October 27	6.30 a. m.	68.31	12	54½	46		Sky overcast; wind east; very light; rain during the night.
Do do	do	5 p. m.	68.33	17	62	52	3147	Very light rain at intervals during the day, and faint thunder; strong wind now from NE.
Do do	October 28	6 a. m.	68.35	12½	55½	50		Wind east; sky overcast; looks like rain.
Camp 84, on the Gila, about 20 feet above the river.	do	5 p. m.	68.87	20	65	55	2969	Sky bright, but clouds; calm.
Camp 84	October 29	6 a. m.	68.91	1	35	......		Calm; foggy in the west.
Camp 85, on the Gila, 20 feet above the river.	do	5 p. m.	69.40	20¼	66	52	2852	Calm and clear.
Camp 85, on the Gila, 20 feet above the river.	October 30	6 a. m.	69.03	4	39½	......		Brilliant clouds in the east immediately before sunrise; calm.
Camp 86, 10 feet above the river	do	5 p. m.	69.53	18¼	63	......	2674	Wind moderate south; sky overcast in the west.
Do do	October 31	6 a. m.	69.72	2¾	36	......		Calm; misty around horizon; light clouds overhead.
Camp 87, on the Rio San Francisco, about two miles from the mouth, at the Gila.	do	5 p. m.	69.82	19	64	52	2557	Clear and calm.
Camp 87, on the Rio San Francisco, about two miles from the mouth, at the Gila.	November 1	6 a. m.	69.90	3	25	......		Clear; no wind.
Ridge between 87 and 88	do	2.35 p. m.	64.82	21	62	......	4763	
Top of peak near camp 88, about 1½ miles west.	do	p. m.	62.58	19	61	......	5724	Wind light W. by S.; sky clear.
Camp 88, in the mountains, on the trail cutting off a bend of the Gila.	do	5 p. m.	64.66	14	54½	42	4748	Clear and calm.
Camp 88, in the mountains, on the trail cutting off a bend of the Gila.	November 2	6 a. m.	64.54	06	40½	......		Slightly overcast; calm.
Camp 89, Disappointment creek	do	5 p. m.	66.81	19	61	55		Clear; light air SE.
Do do do	November 3	6 a. m.	66.95	1½	32	......	3781	Clear and calm.
Do do do	do	5 p. m.	67	19½	63	55		do
Do do do	November 4	6 a. m.	66.91	06	44	40		Sky overcast; no wind.
Camp 90, on the Gila	November 5	6 a. m.	70.99	13½	57	47	2172	Cloudy and thick mist around the horizon; wind SE.
Camp 91, on the San Pedro	do	5 p. m.	71.30	21½	67	52		Clear and calm.
Do do	November 6	5 p. m.	71.22	24	68½	58	2115	do
Do do	November 7	6 a. m.	70.98	1	33	......		do

APPENDIX No. 3.—METEOROLOGICAL OBSERVATIONS—Continued.

Place of observation.	Date.	Time.	Barometer.	Thermometer. Attached.	Thermometer. Free.	Thermometer. Wet bulb.	Approximate altitude.	Remarks.
Camp 92, on the Gila...........	November 7	5 p. m.	70.79	C. 20	F. 69	F. 50¼	} 2122	Dark clouds in the west; wind south.
Do	November 8	6 a. m.	71.72	5	41	.....		Heavy rain during the night; morning foggy; no wind.
Camp 93, on the Gila...........	do	5 p. m.	71.98	14	53	48½	} 1751	Calm and clear.
Do do	do	6 a. m.	71.94	4	37	.....		Heavy frost this morning; sky clear.
Camp 94—Carson's Plains, on the Gila.	November 9	5 p. m.	72.27	15	55	50		Clear and calm.
Camp 94—Carson's Plains, on the Gila.	November 10	6 a. m.	72.35	3	27	.....	} 1596	Sun not risen; sky murky; no wind.
Camp 95—Carson's Plains, on the Gila.	do	5 p. m.	72.93	19	65	53		Clear and fair.
Camp 95—Carson's Plains, on the Gila.	November 11	6 a. m.	73.00	4	37	.....	} 1419	do.
Camp 96, in the Pijmos village, on the Gila.	do	5 p. m.	73.23	23¾	71	60		Calm and fair.
Camp 96, in the Pijmos village, on the Gila.	November 12	6 a. m.	73.25	5	40	.....	} 1308	Sky clear; bright clouds in the east as the sun is rising; no wind.
Camp 97, about 4 miles from the Gila, after passing the Pijmo village.	do	5 p. m.	73.69	20	64	51		Clear and calm.
Camp 97, about 4 miles from the Gila, after passing the Pijmo village.	November 13	6.30 a. m.	73.48	3	26	.....	} 1150	do.
Camp 98, on trail of the cut-off, — miles from the Gila.	do	7.30 p. m.	72.35	14	56	.....	1644	Calm; stars shining bright. Left camp 98 at 4 a. m. on the 14th; too early for morning observation.

Ex. Doc. No. 41.

Location	Date	Time						Remarks
Camp 99, on the Gila	November 14	5 p. m.	73.87	18	63	57½		Calm; clear.
Do	November 15	7.15 a. m.	74.22	7	44		845	Calm; clouds and mist around the horizon; we had rain in the night, which commenced about 12 o'clock, and lasted two hours.
Do	do	5 p. m.	74.64	15	58	48		Clear and calm.
Do	November 16	6.15 a. m.	74.83	4	24			Clear; no wind.
Camp 100, on the Gila	November 17	5 p. m.	75.13	14	52½	48	501	Brilliant sunset; clear and calm.
Do	do	6.45 a. m.	75.42	12	44			Sky clear; strong wind from the west.
Camp 101, on the Gila	November 18	5 p. m.	75.77	16	56	45	293	Clear and calm.
Do	do	6 a. m.	75.90	5	20½			Sky clear; no wind.
Camp 102, on the Gila	November 19	5 p. m.	76.5	13	50	42	231	Calm and clear.
Do	do	6 a. m.	75.92	5	21			Calm and clear; thermometer, noon, 72.
Camp 103, on an island of the Gila	do	5 p. m.	76.02	15	52	46		Calm and clear.
Camp 103, on an island of the Gila	November 20	6 a. m.	75.98	3	24¾		236	Sky clear; no wind. At noon, on the march, thermometer 74.
Camp 104, on the Gila	do	5 p. m.	76.12	20	56	48	248	Fair and calm.
Do	November 21	6 a. m.	75.85	5	19			Sun not risen; calm and clear.
Camp 105, on the Gila	do	5 p. m.	76.10	19	61	.53	253	Clear and fair.
Do	November 22	6 a. m.	75.94	2	33			Sky clear; star light; no wind.
Camp 106, near the mouth of the Gila	do	5 p. m.	75.67	23	69	51		Clear and calm.
Camp 106, near the mouth of the Gila	November 23	7.30 a. m.	75.57	9¼	49¼			Sun obscured by clouds.
Camp 106, near the mouth of the Gila	do	5 p. m.	76.17	16	60	43	254	Strong wind from the east, which has been blowing all day; has just subsided; sky clouded, and misty around the horizon.
Camp 106, near the mouth of the Gila	November 24	6 a. m.	76.88	7	40			Wind northeast; clear.
Camp 107, on the east bank of the Rio Colorado	do	5 p. m.	76.84½	13¾	59½	44		Clear sunset; calm.
Camp 107, on the east bank of the Rio Colorado	November 25	6 a. m.	76.54	3	27			Bright clouds in the east; before sunrise; no wind.
Camp 108, first camp on the Jornada	do	5 p. m.	76.28	16	57½	46		Camp on the Jornada; calm and fair.
Camp 108, first camp on the Jornada	November 26	5 a. m.	75.93	5	21		210	Before daylight; stars shining bright; calm.
Camp 109, at an old mill on the Jornada	do	5 p. m.	76.28	18	60		176	Clear and calm.

APPENDIX No. 3.—METEOROLOGICAL OBSERVATIONS—Continued.

Place of observation.	Date.	Time.	Barometer.	Thermometer. Attached.	Thermometer. Free.	Thermometer. Wet bulb.	Approximate altitude.	Remarks.
				C.	F.	F.		
Camp 109, at an old mill on the Jornada.	November 27	6.30 a. m.	76.14	1	32			
Camp 110—Salt Lake, on the Jornada.	do	9 p. m.	70.55	6¼	45½		176	Clear; bright moon, and star-light.
Camp 111, on the Jornada, Cariso creek.	November 28	5 p. m.	75.40	16	59½	52	52	Calm and clear.
Camp 111, on the Jornada, Cariso creek.	November 29	6.30 a. m.	75.56	3	36¼			Foggy around the western horizon; bright clouds in the east; just before sunrise; light wind from the west.
Camp 112	do	5 p. m.	72.71	17	60	51	445	Heavy clouds around the western horizon, and wind from the same quarter.
Do	November 30	7 a. m.	72.66	11	50½			Dark, heavy clouds hanging over the mountains in the west;- sky bright in the east.
Do	do	5 p. m.	72.39	11¾	53		1539	High wind from the west, and cloudy in the same quarter.
Camp 112, Valle Citron	December 1	6.30 a. m.	72.50	7	39			Sky clear of clouds, but misty around the western horizon; wind continues from west.
On the Divide	do	12.20 p. m.	69.64	11	49		2670	Clear; wind high from the west.
Camp 113	do	5 p. m.	70.37	8	42			High wind from the west, and heavy clouds in the same quarter.
Do	December 2	6.30 a. m.	70.41	5	38		2331	Night damp; heavy dew this morning; wind moderate from the west; sky bright in the east, but overcast in the opposite quarter.
Camp 114, at Warner's "Agua Caliente."	do	5 p. m.	68.75	8	47½	43	3013	Calm and clear.

Camp 114, at Warner's "Agua Caliente."	December	3	6.30 a. m.	68.66	$2\frac{1}{4}$	28	......		Heavy frost; sky overcast; no wind.
Camp 114, at Warner's "Agua Caliente."	do		5 p. m....	68.67	11	49	46	3013	Sky darkly overcast; light wind west.
Camp 114, at Warner's "Agua Caliente."	December	4	7 a. m....	68.50	5	$40\frac{1}{2}$	41		Cloudy; heavy mist; appearance of rain.
Camp 115, Santa Isabella, on Captain Storer's rancho.	December	5	do	68.50	4	38	......	3050	Wind west; raining, and heavy mist around the horizon.
Camp 117, San Pascual........	December	6	5 p. m....	75.38	$11\frac{1}{4}$	52	$47\frac{1}{2}$	716	Day fair throughout; clear sunset; wind moderate from SW.
Do do	December	7	7.45 a. m.	75.75	$5\frac{1}{2}$	36	......		Clear; wind moderate SE.
Camp 118....................	December	8	6.30 a. m.	75.39	$1\frac{1}{2}$	33	......		Heavy frost; no wind; sky overcast with dark clouds.
Do	do		5 p. m....	75.23	11	$50\frac{1}{2}$	......		Clear; wind NW.
Do	December	9	6.30 a. m.	....	......	35	......	477	Fair and calm.
Do	do		5 p. m....	75.54	$12\frac{1}{2}$	53	......		do
Do	December	10	6.30 a. m.	....	......	30	......		
Do	December	11	do	....	......	31	......		
San Diego....................	December	13	5 p. m....	76.41	14	57	......		Wind high SE. It rained during last night, and this morning until noon, with the wind from same quarter.
Do	December	14	Sunrise ...	....	......	55	......		Clear and calm.
Do	do		5 p. m....	76.80	16	61	58		Light clouds; calm.
Do	December	15	8 a. m....	77.03	14	59	$56\frac{1}{2}$		Thick mist around the horizon; light air from south.
Do	do		5 p. m....	76.94	14	59	56	30	Sky cloudy; calm; light rain at noon.
Do	December	16	8 a. m....	76.76	13	57	52		Sky clear; fair and calm.
Do	December	17	8.30 a. m.	76.55	12	$55\frac{1}{2}$	......		Sky overcast; calm.
Do	do		5 p. m....	76.37	15	$59\frac{1}{2}$	$55\frac{1}{2}$		Sky slightly overcast; no wind.
Do	December	18	8.30 a. m.	76.70	13	56	52		Clear and calm.
Do	do		5 p. m....	76.55	17	62	58		Sunset brilliant; no wind; fair.
Do	December	19	9.15 a. m.	76.81	14	59	54		Sky clouded; looking like rain; calm.
Do	do		5 p. m....	76.76	$15\frac{1}{4}$	$62\frac{1}{2}$	58	....	Brilliant sunset; clear and calm.
Do	December	20	8.30 a. m.	77.	14	$58\frac{1}{2}$	54	....	Cloudy; no wind.
Do	do		5 p. m....	76.82	15	61	58	....	Clear; brilliant sunset; calm.
Do	December	21	8.30 a. m.	76.97	$13\frac{1}{4}$	57	54	....	Quite fair and calm.
Do	do		5 p. m....	76.72	16	61	56	....	Clear and calm.
Do	December	22	8.30 a. m.	76.81	14	$58\frac{1}{2}$	54	....	Fair; no wind.
Do	do		5 p. m....	76.73	$15\frac{1}{2}$	$62\frac{1}{4}$	$59\frac{1}{2}$	....	Cloudy in the west; calm.
Do	December	23	8 a. m....	76.80	15	60	$56\frac{1}{2}$	....	Sky clouded and darkly overcast; looks like rain; no wind.

APPENDIX No. 3.—METEOROLOGICAL OBSERVATIONS—Continued.

Place of observation.	Date.	Time.	Barometer.	Thermometer.			Approximate altitude.	Remarks.
				Attached.	Free.	Wet bulb.		
				C.	F.	F.		
San Diego	December 23	5 p. m.	76.83	16	60½	57½		Brilliant sunset; just clearing off; no wind.
Do	December 24	8.43 a. m.	76.77	15	59	55		Cloudy; wind light NE.
Do	do	5 p. m.	76.58	17	60½	57½		Cloudy in the west; calm.
Do	December 25	8.30 a. m.	76.42	15	60	57		Clear and calm.
Do	do	5 p. m.	76.47	18	65	62		Wind east; brilliant sunset; fair.
Do	December 26	8.30 a. m.	76.66	17	63			Raining moderately, though steady; no wind.
Do	do	5 p. m.	76.52	17	64	59		Clear and calm.
Do	December 27	8.30 a. m.	76.72	16	60½	59		Wind NW; quite fair. We had a heavy shower during the night.
Do	do	5 p. m.	76.70	16	60	56		Clear and calm.
Do	December 28	do	76.75	16	60	55		Clear sunset; wind N. by W.
Do	December 29	8 a. m.	76.55	14	56	52		Cloudy; no wind.

APPENDIX No. 4.

TABLE

OF

GEOGRAPHICAL POSITIONS.

APPENDIX No. 4.

TABLE OF GEOGRAPHICAL POSITIONS.

Date.	Places of observation.	Distance from camp to camp.	Total distance from Fort Leavenworth.	North latitudes.	In time.	In arc.	Authorities.
				Deg. min. sec.	*H. min. sec.*	*Deg. min. sec.*	
1846: June 23	Fort Leavenworth, on the Missouri			39 21 14	6 18 56	94 44 00	Latitude of Fort Leavenworth by W. H. Emory. Longitude of Fort Leavenworth by J. N. Nicollet.
30	Camp 4, Oregon trail, about one mile from where it strikes the Wakarcissi creek	43	43				W. H. Emory.
July 4	Camp 8, Big John Spring	81	124	38 54 08	6 20 08		do
5	Camp 9, Diamond Spring	20	144	38 39 28	6 24 58		do
6	Camp 10, Cotton-wood creek	29	173		6 26 09		do
	Camp 13, Cow creek	58	231	38 29 30	6 28 07		do
11	Camp 14, bend of the Arkansas river, where the road strikes it	22	253	38 21 17	6 33 28		do
13	Camp 16, Pawnee Fork	35	288	38 10 10	6 35 41		do
19	Camp 20, Jackson Grove	64	352	37 41 38	6 38 22		do
22	Camp 23, Arkansas, on the river	66	418	37 57 39	6 42 29		do
25	Camp 26, Arkansas, on the river	64	482	38 01 08	6 46 44		do
30	Camp 30, Bent's Fort	82	564	38 02 53	6 52 04		do
Aug. 3	Camp 32, on the Timpa	34	598	37 44 56	6 54 16		do
5	Camp 34, on the Purgatory	53	651	37 11 59	6 56 47.9		do
6	Camp 35, on the Raton	17	663	37 00 21	6 57 01		do
7	Camp 36, on the Canadian	17	685	36 47 34	6 56 59	103 01 00	do

Ex. Doc. No. 41. 177

Sept.	10	Camp 38, on the Cimmaron Citron	30	715	36	27	50	6	58	39	104	39	45	do
	12	Camp 40, at the Pools, about one mile west of the road	50	765	35	54	21	6	59	49	104	57	15	do
	14	Camp 42, about one mile south of the Vegas	27	792	35	35	05	7	00	46	105	11	30	do
	15	Camp 43, Vernal Springs	19	811	35	23	19	7	01	23	105	20	45	do
		Camp Santa Fé	62	873	35	41	06	7	04	05.5	106	01	23	do
	10	Camp on the Rio del Norte, about one mile below San Felipe	33	911	35	25	30	7	06	16.2	106	34	04	do
	4	Camp on the Rio del Norte, near the Alameda			35	11	20	7	07	00	106	45	00	do
	6	Camp at Peralta, near Señora Chavis's private chapel			35	50	57	7	07	03.4	106	47	06	do
	30	Camp 62, a little south of, and about one mile west of Peralta	48	959	34	48	33	7	07	14.2	106	48	33	do
Oct.	4	Camp 65, west bank of Rio del Norte, about two miles below Limatar	52	1011	34	07	39	7	07	54	106	58	29	do
	7	Camp 68, west bank of Rio del Norte	37	1048	33	41	19	7	03	14	107	03	36	do
	9	Camp 70, east bank of Rio del Norte			33	20	02	7	08	57	107	04	17	do
	15	Camp 73, first camp after leaving Rio del Norte	68	1116	32	55	04	7	10	25	107	36	15	do
	17	Camp 75, in the mountains, between the Del Norte and Copper Mines	38	1154	32	42	11	7	12	90	108	00	00	do
	19	Camp 77, Night creek	47	1201	32	50	54	7	14	32	108	38	00	do
	20	Camp 78, first camp on the Rio Gila	8	1209	32	50	03	7	15	00	108	45	00	do
	22	Camp 80			32	33	13	7	16	30	109	07	30	do
	24	Camp 81, on the Gila	50	1259	32	44	52	7	17	23	109	22	34	do
	26	Camp 83, on the Gila	38	1297	32	53	16	7	18	06.3	109	31	34	do
	30	Camp 86, on the Gila	63	1360	33	12	10	7	21	23	110	20	46	do
	31	Camp 87, on the San Francisco, about two miles from its mouth	9	1369	33	14	29	7	22	01.6	110	30	24	do
Nov.	2	Camp 89, Disappointment creek	21	1390	33	14	54	7	23	00.4	110	45	06	do
	5	Camp 91, on the San Pedro, near its mouth	38	1423	32	57	43	7	23	19.5	110	49	53	do
	8	Camp 93, on the Gila	29	1457	33	05	40	7	24	52.6	111	13	10	do
	10	Camp 95, on the Gila	37	1494	33	04	21	7	27	03.8	111	45	53	do
	12	Camp 97, between Pijmos and Coco Maricopas villages	23	1517	33	09	28	7	28	28.8	112	07	13	do
	14	Camp 99, on the Gila	44	1561	32	59	22	7	31	20	112	50	01	do
	17	Camp 101, on the Gila	39	1600	32	55	52	7	33	41.6	113	25	25	do
	19	Camp 103, on an island in the Gila	39	1639	32	43	38	7	35	50.7	113	57	41	do

APPENDIX No. 4—GEOGRAPHICAL POSITIONS—Continued.

Date.	Places of observation.	Distances measured by the viameter.		North latitudes.	West of Greenwich.		Authorities.
		Distance from camp to camp.	Total distance from Fort Leavenworth.		In time.	In arc.	
				Deg. min. sec.	*h. min. sec.*	*Deg. min. sec.*	
1846.							
Nov. 21	Camp 105, on the Gila	26	1665	32 43 17	7 37 22.8	114 20 43	W. H. Emory.
22	Camp 106, about one and a half mile south of the junction of the Gila and Colorado of the west	22	1687	32 42 09	7 38 28.6	114 37 09	do
25	First camp after leaving the Rio Colorado	22	1709	32 40 22	7 39 45.8	114 56 28	do
28	Camp 111, Cariso creek	77	1786	32 52 33	7 44 24.6	116 06 09	do
29	Camp 112, Valle Citon	16	1802	32 58 15	7 45 22.7	116 20 40	do
Dec. 2	Camp 114, a few hundred yards south of Warner's rancheria	35	1837	33 16 57	7 46 34.8	116 38 43	do
7	Camp 118, battle ground of the 7th	50	1887	33 03 42	7 48 14	117 03 29	do
	San Diego, (public square)	29	1916	32 45 00	7 48 44	117 11 00	Latitude by W. H. Emory. Longitude by Sir Ed. Belcher.

APPENDIX No. 5.

TABLE

OF

ASTRONOMICAL OBSERVATIONS.

APPENDIX No. 5.

ASTRONOMICAL OBSERVATIONS.

NOTE.—The lunar distances were reduced by Professor Hubbard, by Bessel's method, which is presumed to be the most accurate method known. The important changes made in the longitude of one or two leading positions, must, therefore, depend for authentication upon the observations themselves.

These observations have not, in all cases, been multiplied to the extent desired, owing to the nature of the service on which the undersigned was employed; but there is no reason on the face of them for doubting the results deduced.

W. H. EMORY.

June 21, 1846.—*Fort Leavenworth.*

DETERMINATION OF TIME.

Time, p. m.			Double altitudes of *a* Lyræ in the east.			Chronometer fast.		
h.	*m.*	*s.*	*Deg.*	*min.*	*sec.*	*h.*	*m.*	*s.*
4	01	46.5	102	00	20	6	53	14.9
4	04	52	103	09	35	6	53	14.8
4	06	15.2	103	40	30	6	53	15.4
4	07	30.0	104	08	20	6	53	15.7
4	08	27.1	104	29	35	6	53	16.0
4	09	56.7	105	02	30	6	53	17.6
4	11	18.5	105	33	30	6	53	16.6
4	12	46.2	106	07	20	6	53	14.1
4	13	57.3	106	53	35	6	53	15.0
4	15	59	107	18	40	6	53	16.7

Thermometer 60°.

APPENDIX No. 5—Continued.

June 21, 1846.—Fort Leavenworth.

DETERMINATION OF TIME.

Time, p. m.	Double altitude of Arcturus in the west.	Chronometer fast.
h. m. s.	Deg. min. sec.	h. m. s.
4 27 39.8	126 57 50	6 53 19.2
4 29 18.0	126 08 10	6 53 17.4
4 30 32.0	125 46 50	6 53 20.2
4 32 30.2	125 10 20	6 53 18.5
4 33 59.1	124 44 00	6 53 20.2
4 35 31.5	124 14 40	6 53 17.0
4 37 14.7	123 43 00	6 53 18.1
4 38 52.8	123 12 05	6 53 17.2
4 40 35.3	122 41 15	6 53 21.9 rej.
4 42 17.0	122 08 00	6 53 18.7

Thermometer 60°.

	h. m. s.
Chronometer fast by 10 obs. of east star	6 55 15.68
Chronometer fast by 9 obs. of west star	18.50
Mean	6 53 17.09

DETERMINATION OF INDEX ERROR.

	m. s.
Off the arc	31 50
On the arc	31 10

Index error = + 20″.

Ex. Doc. No. 41.

APPENDIX No. 5—Continued.

June 21, 1846.—*Fort Leavenworth.*

DETERMINATION OF LATITUDE.

Time, p. m.			Double altitudes of Polaris.			Latitude.		
h.	m.	s.	Deg.	min.	sec.	Deg.	min.	sec.
4	59	03.0	76	36	40	39	21	29
5	01	02.2	76	37	55	39	21	34
5	03	28.6	76	38	55	39	21	22
5	05	13.5	76	40	50	39	21	24
5	06	50.3	76	41	05	39	21	28
5	08	22.5	76	41	45	39	21	23
5	09	50.8	76	42	30	39	21	10
5	11	12.2	76	43	50	39	21	27
5	12	29.6	76	44	35	39	21	36
5	13	55.0	76	45	20	39	21	33
5	15	18.8	76	46	20	39	21	39
5	16	44.7	76	47	10	39	21	36
5	18	15.0	76	48	20	39	21	45
5	19	41.8	76	48	40	39	21	28
5	21	23.5	76	49	50	39	21	32
5	23	06.0	76	51	10	39	21	41

Mean of 16 observations, 39° 21' 30".

Ex. Doc. No. 41.   183

APPENDIX No. 5—Continued.

June 21, 1846.—Fort Leavenworth.

DETERMINATION OF TIME.

Time, a. m.—June 22.	Double altitudes of sun's upper limb.	Time, p. m.—June 21.	Chronometer fast.
h. m. s.	Deg. min.	h. m. s.	h. m. s.
5 05 42.0	125 50	8 45 51.8	6 53 17.8
5 03 15.8	123 40	8 46 19.8	6 53 18.23
5 02 46.0	123 30	8 46 49.7	6 53 18.33
5 02 17.0	123 20	8 47 17.0	6 53 17.48
Lost.	123 10	8 47 46.0	
5 01 19.2	123 00	8 48 15.1	6 53 17.58
5 00 51.5	122 50	8 48 43.5	6 53 17.53
5 00 23.5	122 40	Lost.	
4 59 54.5	122 30	8 49 39.7	6 53 17.58
	122 20	8 50 08.5	
	122 10	8 50 36.2	
	122 00	8 51 06.0	

NEW SERIES.

3 47 37.5	95 40	10 01 57.5	6 53 17.96
3 47 11.5	95 30	10 02 24.0	6 53 18.21
3 46 44.2	95 20	10 02 50.2	6 53 17.66
3 46 18.5	95 10	10 03 15.5	6 53 17.46
3 45 52.5	95 00	10 03 41.5	6 53 17.46
3 45 26.8	94 50	10 04 08.3	6 53 18.01
3 45 11.0	94 40	10 04 34.1	6 53 18.01
3 44 34.0	94 30	10 05 00.0	6 53 17.46
3 44 08.5	94 20	10 05 26.2	6 53 17.81
3 41 57.5	93 30	10 07 38.2	6 53 18.31
3 41 32.5	93 20	10 08 03.0	6 53 18.21
3 41 15.3	93 10	10 08 28.0	6 53 17.11
3 40 39.5	93 00	10 08 55.2	6 53 17.81
3 40 14.2	92 50	10 09 21.0	6 53 18.06
Lost.	92 40	10 09 47.0	
3 39 21.5	92 30	10 10 11.9	6 53 17.06
Ther. 60°		Ther. 75°	

Mean of 22 observations, 6h. 53m. 17.76s.

APPENDIX No. 5—Continued.

June 22, 1846.—*Fort Leavenworth.*

DETERMINATION OF TIME.

Time, a. m.			Double altitudes of sun's upper limb.		Time, p. m.			Chronometer fast.		
h.	*m.*	*s.*	*Deg.*	*min.*	*h.*	*m.*	*s.*	*h.*	*m.*	*s.*
3	48	02.5	95	50	10	01	42.5	6	53	16.69
3	47	37.5	95	40	10	02	08.2	6	53	17.04
3	47	11.5	95	30	10	02	33.5	6	53	16.69
3	46	44.2	95	20	10	02	59.1	6	53	15.84
3	46	18.5	95	10	10	03	26.5	6	53	16.69
3	45	52.5	95	00	10	03	52.0	6	53	16.44
3	45	26.8	94	50	10	04	18.0	6	53	16.59
3	45	01.0	94	40	10	04	45.1	6	53	17.24
3	44	35.0	94	30	10	05	11.0	6	53	17.19
3	44	08.5	94	20	10	05	36.8	6	53	16.84
	Lost.		94	10	10	06	2.3			
	Lost.		94	00	10	06	28.5			
3	41	57.5	93	30	10	07	45.8	6	53	15.84
3	41	32.5	93	20	10	08	11.8	6	53	16.34
3	41	05.3	93	10	10	08	38.8	6	53	16.24
3	40	39.5	93	00	10	09	05.0	6	53	16.44
3	40	14.2	92	50	10	09	30.2	6	53	16.29
Ther. 68°					Ther. 74°					

Mean of 15 observations, 6*h.* 53*m.* 16.52*s.*

APPENDIX No. 5—Continued.

June 24, 1846.—Fort Leavenworth.

DETERMINATION OF TIME.

Time, p. m.	Double altitudes of Lyræ in the east.	Chronometer fast.
h. m. s.	Deg. min. sec.	h. m. s.
4 26 24.0	115 45 10	6 53 06.2
4 27 37.8	116 13 05	6 53 06.0
4 29 38.0	116 58 30	6 53 06.6
4 30 55.7	117 27 55	6 53 06.7
4 32 37.5	118 06 40	6 53 06.3
4 33 58.2	118 37 10	6 53 06.7
4 35 33.7	119 13 45	6 53 05.9
4 37 47.0	120 04 25	6 53 05.9
4 39 30.2	120 44 05	6 53 04.7

Thermometer 66°.

Time, p. m.	Double altitudes of Arcturus in the west.	Chronometer fast.
h. m. s.	Deg. min. sec.	h. m. s.
4 44 52.0	117 22 50	6 53 11.5
4 46 47.5	116 44 55	6 53 14.6 rej.
4 48 19.0	116 13 00	6 53 11.8
4 50 06.8	115 35 35	6 53 09.8
4 54 31.5	114 04 40	6 53 09.7
4 55 58.5	113 34 30	6 53 09.8
4 57 14.2	113 09 10	6 53 14.3 rej.
4 58 38.5	112 38 40	6 53 09.3
5 00 26.7	112 01 45	6 53 12.0
5 02 05.0	111 27 25	6 53 12.2

Barometer 39.52   Thermometer 64°.
           34.57

	h. m. s.
Chronometer fast by 9 obs. of east star	6 53 06.58
Chronometer fast by 8 obs. of west star	10.76
Mean	6 53 08.67

APPENDIX No. 5—Continued.

June 25, 1846.—Fort Leavenworth.

DETERMINATION OF TIME.

Time, p. m.			Double altitudes of sun's upper limb.		Time, a. m.—June 26.			Chronometer fast.		
h.	m.	s.	Deg.	min.	h.	m.	s.	h.	m.	s.
10	08	34.5	93	20	3	42	24.5	6	53	07.09
10	09	00.0	93	10	3	41	59.5	6	53	07.35
10	10	44.2	92	30	3	40	15.0	6	53	07.31
10	11	10.2	92	20	3	39	48.5	6	53	06.71
10	11	36.5	92	10						
10	12	02.8	92	00	3	38	58.0	6	53	08.02
10	14	38.0	91	00	3	36	20.5	6	53	06.88
10	17	14.2	90	00	3	33	44.0	6	53	06.73
10	17	40.0	89	50						
Ther. 78°					Ther. 74°					

Barometer, 39.50.
34.48.

Mean of 7 observations, 6h. 53m. 07.16s.

June 26, 1846.—Fort Leavenworth.

DETERMINATION OF TIME.

Time, a. m.			Double altitudes of sun's upper limb.		Time, p. m.			Chronometer fast.		
h.	m.	s.	Deg.	min.	h.	m.	s.	h.	m.	s.
3	38	58.0	92	00	10	12	07.0	6	53	05.97
	Lost.		92	10	10	11	41.2			
3	39	48.1	92	20	10	11	14.2	6	53	04.57
3	40	15.0	92	30	10	10	48.2	6	53	05.07
3	40	40.8	92	40	10	10	22.5	6	53	05.12
3	41	09.2	92	50	10	09	57.5	6	53	06.32
3	41	33.0	93	00	10	09	30.2	6	53	05.07
3	41	59.5	93	10	10	09	04.2	6	53	05.31
3	42	24.5	93	20	10	08	40.3	6	53	05.86
3	42	50.8	93	30	10	08	10.8	6	53	05.76
3	43	16.5	93	40		Lost.				
3	44	42.0	93	50	10	07	21.2	6	53	05.06
3	45	10.2	94	00	10	06	54.5	6	53	05.81
Ther. 74°					Ther. 80°					

Mean of 11 observations, 6h. 53m. 05.45s.

Ex. Doc. No. 41.

APPENDIX No. 5—Continued.

June 26, 1846.—*Fort Leavenworth, N. W. angle of square.*

DETERMINATION OF LATITUDE.

Time, p. m.	Double altitudes of a Ophiuchi, near the meridian.	Latitude.
h. m. s.	Deg. min. sec.	Deg. min. sec.
4 29 57.5	94 36 40	39 21 12
4 31 35.8	94 39 20	39 21 00
4 33 00.0	94 40 30	39 21 12
4 34 14.0	94 41 50	39 21 07
4 35 47.9	94 42 50	39 21 11
4 37 20.0	94 43 40	39 21 08
4 38 51.2	94 44 10	39 21 06
4 40 19.7	94 44 15	39 21 05
4 42 05.0	94 43 25	39 21 20
4 43 35.5	94 42 30	39 21 27
4 45 03.8	94 41 50	39 21 18
4 46 19.0	94 40 40	39 21 18
4 48 10.0	94 38 25	39 21 27
4 49 25.2	94 37 10	39 21 15
4 50 39.8	94 34 30	39 21 38
4 52 01.2	94 32 15	39 21 35
4 53 35.8	94 29 10	39 21 37

Thermometer 64°.

Mean of 17 observations, 39° 21' 17".

Ex. Doc. No. 41.

APPENDIX No. 5—Continued.

June 26, 1846.—*Fort Leavenworth.*

DETERMINATION OF LATITUDE.

Time. p. m.	Double altitude of Polaris.	Latitude.
h. m. s.	Deg. min. sec.	Deg. min. sec.
4 58 46.5	76 47 45	39 21 21
5 00 03.2	76 48 40	39 21 24
5 01 37.2	76 49 50	39 21 30
5 02 50.8	76 50 20	39 21 23
5 03 59.0	76 51 20	39 21 31
5 05 07.2	76 52 10	39 21 35
5 06 12.1	76 53 05	39 21 42
5 07 55.2	76 53 40	39 21 29
5 09 20.0	76 54 50	39 21 38
5 10 27.1	76 55 35	39 21 39
5 11 19.8	76 56 05	39 21 37

Barometer, 39.42 inches.
" 34.41 "

Thermometer 64°.

Mean of 11 observations, 39° 21′ 32″.

Ex. Doc. No. 41

APPENDIX No. 5—Continued.

[Without using horizon glass.]

June 26, 1846.—*Fort Leavenworth.*

DETERMINATION OF LATITUDE.

Time, p. m.	Double altitudes of *a* Ophi- uchi, near the meridian.	Latitude.
h. m. s.	Deg. min. sec.	Deg. min. sec.
5 49 39.8	126 23 20	39 20 01
5 51 37.8	126 28 40	39 20 00
5 52 20.2	126 32 55	39 20 19
5 54 26.0	126 35 05	39 20 00
5 56 40.7	126 38 20	39 20 48
5 58 38.6	126 38 40	39 21 06
6 00 57.0	126 40 50	39 20 44
6 02 39.2	126 39 55	39 21 05
6 04 05.4	126 38 15	39 21 36
6 06 34.0	126 36 45	39 21 16
6 07 55.1	126 34 20	39 21 55
6 09 18.7	126 33 05	39 21 15
6 10 21.2	126 29 50	39 19 45
6 11 43.5	126 27 20	39 19 32
6 13 23.2	126 23 45	39 20 16

Thermometer 63.

Barometer, 39.42.
    34.41.

Mean of 15 observations, 39° 20′ 37″.

		Latitude of Fort.		
		Deg.	m.	s.
Latitude by 16 observations of Polaris, June 21..		39	21	30
" 11 " Polaris, June 26..			21	32
" 17 " *a* Ophiuchi, June 26			21	17
" 15 " *a* Ophiuchi, June 26			20	37
Mean........................		39	21	14

APPENDIX No. 5—Continued.

June 26, 1846.—*Fort Leavenworth.*

DETERMINATION OF TIME.

Time, p. m.			Double altitudes of ——— in the east.		
h.	m.	s	Deg.	min.	sec.
6	21	08.0	117	18	45
6	22	49.0	117	55	10
6	25	23.5	118	42	15
6	27	06.0	119	25	50
6	28	20.0	119	52	10
6	31	13.2	120	53	50
6	32	11.0	121	13	00
6	33	17.5	121	38	25
6	34	41.0	122	08	05

Barometer, 39.42.
34.41.

Thermometer 60°.

So much noise from the barracks, that I have no confidence in these observations.

APPENDIX No. 5—Continued.

June 27, 1846.—*Fort Leavenworth.*

DETERMINATION OF TIME.

Time, a. m.—June 21.	Double altitudes of sun's upper limb.	Time, p. m.—June 26.	Chronometer fast.
h. m. s.	Deg. min.	h. m. s.	h. m. s.
3 39 19.0	92 00	10 12 07.0	6 52 06.09
3 39 40.0	92 10	10 11 41.2	6 52 06.63
3 40 04.8	92 20	10 11 14.2	6 52 05.63
3 40 32.0	92 30	10 10 48.2	6 52 06.13
3 40 57.2	92 40	10 10 22.5	6 52 05.88
3 41 22.8	92 50	10 09 57.5	6 52 06.18
3 41 47.7	93 00	10 09 30.2	6 52 04.98 rej.
3 42 16.0	93 10	10 09 04.2	6 52 06.15
3 42 41.0	93 20	10 08 40.3	6 52 06.68
3 43 07.8	93 30	10 08 13.8	6 52 06.83
3 43 32.6	93 40	lost.	
3 44 00.0	93 50	10 07 21.2	6 52 06.63
3 44 24.8	94 00	10 06 54.5	*6 52 05.68

Mean of 11 observations, $6h. 52m. 06.22s.$

Ex. Doc. No. 41.

APPENDIX No. 5—Continued.

June 30, 1846.—*Camp No.* 4.

DETERMINATION OF LATITUDE.

Time, p. m.			Double altitude of *a* Serpentis, near the meridian.			Latitude.		
h.	m.	s.	Deg.	min.	sec.	Deg.	min.	sec.
3	49	20.8	115	59	10	38	53	54
3	50	36.8	116	00	10	38	54	05
3	51	41.7	116	01	15	38	53	59
3	52	52.0	116	02	05	38	53	58
3	54	01.0	116	02	45	38	53	53
3	55	32.7	116	02	55	38	53	54
3	56	55.8	116	02	45	38	53	55
3	58	04.5	116	01	40	38	54	15
3	59	4.8	116	01	25	38	53	50
4	00	46.0	116	00	00	38	54	07
4	02	3.1	115	58	31	38	54	10
4	03	20.0	115	56	50	38	54	08
4	04	33.0	115	53	40	38	53	45

The four last observations rather doubtful; musquitos so very troublesome.

Mean of 13 observations, 38° 53' 59".

Ex. Doc No 41. 193

APPENDIX No. 5—Continued.

June 30, 1846.—*Camp No.* 4.

DETERMINATION OF LATITUDE.

Time. p. m.	Double altitudes of Polaris.	Latitude.
h. m. s.	Deg. min. sec.	Deg. min. sec.
4 13 42.0	75 35 50	38 54 00
4 15 19.8	75 37 30	38 54 23
4 16 36.0	75 38 30	38 54 33
4 17 58.2	75 39 05	38 54 27
4 19 27.7	75 39 50	38 54 27
4 20 50.0	75 40 00	38 54 09
4 22 2.8	75 40 40	38 54 08
4 23 0.0	75 41 25	38 54 13
4 24 34.2	75 42 20	38 54 16
4 26 28.5	75 43 15	38 54 14
4 27 48.7	75 43 55	38 54 10

Thermometer, 67°.

              Deg. min. sec.
Latitude by 13 observations of Polaris, 38 54 18
Latitude by 13 observations of *a* Serpentis,   53 59

 Mean .... 38 54 08 lat. of camp.

13

Ex. Doc. No. 41.

APPENDIX No. 5—Continued.

June 30, 1846.—Camp 4.

DETERMINATION OF TIME.

Time, p. m.	Double altitudes of α Lyræ in the east.	Chronometer fast.
h. m. s.	Deg. min. sec.	h. m. s.
3 30 19.1	102 54 10	6 54 05.5
3 32 16.0	103 37 55	6 54 05.3
3 33 51.0	104 13 30	6 54 00.3 rej.
3 34 54.2	104 38 05	6 54 03.3
3 36 21.5	105 09 55	6 54 06.0
3 37 29.8	105 35 50	6 54 05.0
3 38 49.0	106 05 15	6 54 06.4

Thermometer, 68°.

Time, p. m.	Double altitudes of Arcturus in the west.	Chronometer fast.
h. m. s.	Deg. min. sec.	h. m. s.
4 33 00.0	114 07 30	6 54 12.9
4 34 16.0	113 40 40	6 54 12.7
4 35 28.7	113 15 00	6 54 12.3
4 36 44.0	112 48 30	6 54 12.4
4 37 49.0	112 24 55	6 54 11.0
4 39 03.5	111 59 20	6 54 13.4
4 40 18.7	111 32 30	6 54 16.1 rej.
4 41 47.0	111 01 10	6 54 14.0
4 42 38.2	110 42 20	6 54 12.5
4 44 34.0	110 00 00	6 54 10.2
4 45 48.5	109 33 50	6 54 12.1

Thermometer, 66°.

	h. m. s.
Chronometer fast by 6 obs. of east star	6 54 05.30
Chronometer fast by 10 obs. of west star	12.55
Mean	6 54 8.82

APPENDIX No. 5—Continued.

July 4, 1846.—*Camp* 8, *Big John Spring.*

DETERMINATION OF TIME.

Time, p. m.			Double altitude of sun's upper limb:		Chronometer fast.		
h.	*m.*	*s.*	*Deg.*	*min.*	*h.*	*m.*	*s.*
10	33	24.2	86	10	6	58	49.7
10	33	50.8	86	00	6	58	50.6
10	34	17.0	85	50	6	58	51.0
10	34	41.8	85	40	6	58	50.3
10	35	08.2	85	30	6	58	51.1
10	35	33.7	85	20	6	58	50.9
10	35	59.0	85	10	6	58	50.6
10	36	25.8	85	00	6	58	51.7
10	36	49.2	84	50	6	58	49.4
10	37	17.0	84	40	6	58	51.6
10	37	42.0	84	30	6	58	51.0
10	38	08.5	84	20	6	58	51.8
10	38	35.2	84	10	6	58	52.9
10	38	58.7	84	00	6	58	50.7

Thermometer, 88°.

Mean of 14 observations, 6*h.* 58*m.* 50.96*s.*

Ex. Doc. No. 41.

APPENDIX No. 5—Continued.

July 5, 1846.—*Camp* 8, *Big John Spring.*

DETERMINATION OF TIME.

Time, a. m.			Double altitudes of *a* Aquilæ in the west.			Chronometer fast.			
h.	m.	s.	Deg.	min.	sec.	h.	m.	s.	
10	31	28.0	85	48	40	6	58	47.9	
10	32	30.8	85	28	30	6	58	50.8	
10	33	37.0	85	04	20	6	58	46.6	
10	34	57.9	84	36	05	6	58	47.4	
10	36	25.8	84	06	35	6	58	47.9	
10	38	06.2	83	31	25	6	58	46.8	
10	39	10.0	83	09	35	6	58	47.9	
10	40	09.7	82	48	30	6	58	47.0	
10	41	04.5	82	28	40	6	58	44.9	rej.
10	42	03.2	82	08	30	6	58	46.0	

Mean of 9 observations, 6*h.* 58*m.* 47.59*s.*

Ex. Doc. No. 41.   197

APPENDIX No. 5—Continued.

July 5, 1846.—Camp 8, Big John Spring.

DETERMINATION OF LATITUDE.

Time, a. m.	Double altitudes of Polaris.	Latitude.
h. m. s.	Deg. min. sec.	Deg. min. sec.
10 03 11.0	79 24 45	38 39 50
10 04 43.8	79 25 50	38 39 55
10 06 16.7	79 26 25	38 39 44
10 07 31.0	79 27 20	38 39 52
10 09 20.0	79 28 20	38 39 53
10 11 54.0	79 29 50	38 39 54

Time, a. m.	Double altitude of Saturn, near the meridian.	Latitude.
h. m. s.	Deg. min. sec.	Deg. min. sec.
10 16 59.0	77 13 20	38 38 43
10 18 39.9	77 12 55	38 38 59
10 19 46.2	77 12 15	38 39 16
10 21 37.3	77 11 55	38 39 10
10 22 52.0	77 11 30	38 39 05
10 24 01.8	77 10 35	38 39 11
10 25 29.2	77 09 00	38 39 10
10 26 49.0	77 08 05	38 39 11

Thermometer 75°.

Latitude of camp.

		Deg.	min.	sec.
Latitude by 6 observations of Polaris............		38	39	51
" 8 " " Saturn				06
Mean		38	39	28

Ex. Doc. No. 41.

APPENDIX No. 5—Continued.

July 5, 1846.—*Camp 9, Diamond Spring.*

DETERMINATION OF LATITUDE.

Time, p. m.	Double altitudes of Polaris.	Latitude.
h. m. s.	*Deg. min. sec.*	*Deg. min. sec.*
3 53 40.0	74 58 35	38 36 52
3 55 03.2	74 59 10	38 36 48
3 56 33.0	75 00 15	38 36 58
3 58 06.5	75 00 55	38 36 54
3 59 11.0	75 01 40	38 36 58
4 00 05.0	75 02 00	38 36 54
4 01 07.0	75 02 35	38 36 56
4 01 59.0	75 03 00	38 36 54
4 03 13.5	75 03 35	38 36 53
4 04 35.7	75 04 35	38 36 57
4 10 58.0	75 07 25	38 36 57
4 12 00.0	75 08 20	38 36 49
4 13 07.2	75 09 25	38 36 49
4 14 56.0	75 09 55	38 36 50
4 15 56.2	75 10 40	38 36 51

Thermometer 72°.

Mean of 16 observations, 38° 36′ 52″.

Ex. Doc. No. 41.   199

APPENDIX No. 5—Continued.

July 5, 1846.—Camp 9, Diamond Spring.

DETERMINATION OF TIME.

Time, p. m.	Double altitudes of *a* Lyræ in the east.	Chronometer fast.
h. m. s.	Deg. min. sec.	h. m. s.
3 26 57.2	106 40 45	6 59 54.8
3 28 49.8	107 21 55	6 59 58.4
3 29 55.7	107 47 20	6 59 57.0
3 30 45.0	108 07 25	6 59 53.2
3 32 32.0	108 47 10	6 59 54.9
3 33 39.7	109 11 55	6 59 57.2
3 34 38.2	109 32 50	6 59 60.4
3 35 34.0	109 55 40	6 59 56.0
3 36 31.5	110 17 40	6 59 55.4
3 37 24.7	110 37 40	6 59 55.8
3 38 47.5	111 9 00	6 59 55.9

Thermometer 72°.

Time, p. m.	Double altitudes of Arcturus in the west.	Chronometer fast.
h. m. s.	Deg. min. sec.	h. m. s.
4 20 57.0	113 44 20	6 59 60.8
4 22 02.0	113 21 15	6 59 60.9
4 23 07.8	112 52 35	6 59 60.2
4 24 16.0	112 33 15	6 59 60.2
4 25 20.8	112 10 00	6 59 60.0
4 26 09.7	111 52 35	6 59 60.4
4 27 10.7	111 30 25	6 59 59.5
4 28 11.0	111 08 30	6 59 58.9
4 29 33.8	110 38 55	6 59 59.8

Thermometer 71°.

			h.	m.	s.
Chronometer fast by 11 observations of east star			6	59	56.27
" " " 9 " we'st star					60.08
Mean			6	59	58.18

APPENDIX No. 5—Continued.

July 6, 1846.—*Camp* 10, *Cottonwood Grove.*

DETERMINATION OF TIME.

Time, p. m.	Double altitudes of *a* Lyræ, in the east.	Chronometer fast.
h. m. s.	Deg. min. sec.	h. m. s.
4 05 32.8	122 05 00	7 01 54.0
4 06 40.0	122 31 55	7 01 57.0
4 07 59.5	123 01 10	7 01 54.3
4 09 07.0	123 27 55	7 01 52.0
4 10 21.8	123 56 55	7 01 51.1
4 11 45.8	124 28 15	7 01 53.7
4 13 04.5	124 59 20	7 01 51.5
4 14 24.0	125 29 50	7 01 51.7

Time, p. m.	Double altitudes of Arcturus in the west.	Chronometer fast.
h. m. s.	Deg. min sec.	h. m. s.
4 19 30.0	113 37 55	7 01 56.5
4 20 52.8	113 07 50	7 01 54.9
4 22 43.2	112 28 15	7 01 54.8
4 24 04.3	111 59 15	7 01 55.2
4 25 25.2	111 30 35	7 01 56.6
4 27 26.5	110 45 50	7 01 54.1
4 29 40.0	109 57 55	7 01 55.8
4 32 42.8	108 51 10	7 01 55.5
4 34 54.0	108 13 40	7 01 57.1
4 35 46.2	107 44 15	7 01 56.6
4 38 05.8	106 52 55	7 01 55.8
4 39 14.0	106 26 55	7 01 54.6

Thermometer 72°.

	h. m. s.
Chronometer fast by 8 observations of east star	7 01 52.44
" " 12 " west star	55.62
Mean................................	7 01 54.03

APPENDIX No. 5—Continued.

July 6, 1846.—*Camp* 10, *Cottonwood Grove.*

DETERMINATION OF LATITUDE.

Time, p. m.	Double altitudes of Polaris.	Latitude.
h. m. s.	Deg. min. sec.	Deg. min. sec.
4 49 21.0	75 17 45	38 29 44
4 53 05.0	75 19 35	38 29 25
4 54 07.0	75 20 35	38 29 35
4 55 36.2	75 21 35	38 29 35
4 56 58.3	75 22 10	38 29 25
4 58 07.0	75 22 35	38 29 12
4 59 31.0	75 23 50	38 29 26
5 01 14.7	75 25 20	38 29 35
5 02 28.7	75 26 10	38 29 38
5 03 46.0	75 27 05	38 29 37

Thermometer, 71°.

July 7, 1846.—*Camp* 10.

Time, p. m.	Double altitudes of Polaris.	Latitude.
h. m. s.	Deg. min. sec.	Deg. min. sec.
4 16 45.0	74 59 45	38 29 31
4 19 27.5	75 01 05	38 29 22
4 20 16.0	75 01 40	38 29 27

Thermometer 68°.

	Deg. min. sec.
Latitude by 10 obs. of Polaris, July 6............	38 29 31
Latitude by 3 obs. of Polaris, July 7............	27
Mean of 13 observations	38 29 30

APPENDIX No. 5—Continued.

July 7, 1846.—*Camp* 10, *Cottonwood Grove.*

DETERMINATION OF TIME.

Time, a. m.	Double altitudes of sun's upper limb.	Chronometer fast.
h. m. s.	Deg. min.	h. m. s.
4 01 24.2	95 50	7 01 50.3
4 01 50.4	96 00	7 01 50.7
4 02 16.2	96 10	7 01 50.8
4 02 41.8	96 20	7 01 50.4
4 03 07.0	96 30	7 01 49.8
4 03 58.8	96 50	7 01 49.9
4 04 50.8	97 10	7 01 50.3
4 05 17.0	97 20	7 01 50.5
4 05 42.7	97 30	7 01 50.4
4 06 08.7	97 40	7 01 50.5
4 06 34.0	97 50	7 01 49.9
4 06 59.6	98 00	7 01 49.6

Thermometer, 88°.

Mean of 12 observations, 7*h.* 04*m.* 50.26*s.*

Ex. Doc. No. 41.

APPENDIX No. 5—Continued.

July 7, 1846.—*Camp* 10, *Cottonwood Grove.*

DETERMINATION OF TIME.

Time, p. m.	Double altitudes of sun's upper limb.	Chronometer fast.
h. m. s.	Deg. min.	h. m. s.
10 17 49.0	93 20	7 01 54.0
10 18 14.5	93 10	7 01 53.6
10 18 38.8	93 00	7 01 52.4
10 19 05.1	92 50	7 01 52.8
10 19 31.0	92 40	7 01 53.1
10 19 57.0	92 30	7 04 53.4
10 20 47.5	92 10	7 01 52.4
10 21 13.5	92 00	7 01 52.7
10 21 39.2	91 50	7 01 52.7
10 22 08.0	91 40	7 01 52.8
10 22 30.0	91 30	7 01 52.1
10 22 56.5	91 20	7 01 52.9
10 23 21.8	91 10	7 01 52.5
10 23 48.0	91 00	7 01 53.0

Thermometer, 90°.

Mean of 14 observations,   7h. 01m. 53.10s.

Time, p. m.	Double altitudes of Arcturus in the west.	Chronometer fast.
h. m. s.	Deg. min. sec.	h. m. s.
4 04 16.8	117 33 55	7 01 50.4
4 05 24.5	117 11 5	7 01 52.4
4 06 46.0	116 42 20	7 01 51.2
4 07 32.0	116 26 40	7 01 52.5
4 09 54.0	115 36 55	7 01 52.7

Mean of 5 observations,   7h. 01m. 51.84s.

204   Ex. Doc. No. 41.

APPENDIX No. 5—Continued.

July 11, 1846.—Camp 14, Bend of Arkansas.

Time, p. m.	Double altitudes of α Lyræ in the east.	Chronometer fast.
h. m. s.	Deg. min. sec.	h. m. s.
3 26 08.0	112 31 05	7 07 01.8
3 27 04.0	112 52 20	7 07 02.0
3 28 05.8	113 15 10	7 07 03.8
3 29 04.7	113 38 10	7 07 02.3
3 30 34.0	114 13 10	7 06 59.7 rej.
3 31 35.2	114 35 05	7 07 03.4
3 32 41.0	114 59 50	7 07 04.2
3 34 12.0	115 35 10	7 07 02.8
3 35 03.2	115 54 40	7 07 02.9
3 36 01.2	116 16 40	7 07 03.2
3 37 02.0	116 40 15	7 07 02.1
3 38 06.2	117 05 10	7 06 59.4 rej.

Time, p. m.	Double altitudes of Arcturus in the west.	Chronometer fast.
h. m. s.	Deg. min. sec.	h. m. s.
3 41 09.1	121 59 55	7 07 05.0
3 42 10.7	121 39 20	7 07 04.8
3 43 37.5	121 10 25	7 07 05.5
3 44 41.8	120 48 40	7 07 05.4
3 45 38.0	120 29 30	7 07 04.9
3 47 01.0	120 01 25	7 07 05.2
3 47 58.8	119 41 15	7 07 04.0
3 49 01.8	119 19 40	7 07 02.9
3 50 05.5	118 57 30	7 07 03.0
3 51 02.2	118 38 10	7 07 03.7
3 52 00.3	118 18 10	7 07 03.9
3 53 01.5	117 57 15	7 07 04.7

Thermometer, 71°.

	h. m. s.
Chronometer fast by 10 obs. of east star	7 07 02.85
Chronometer fast by 12 obs. of west star	04.42
Mean	7 07 03.64

Ex. Doc. No. 41.

APPENDIX No. 5—Continued.

July 11, 1846.—*Camp* 14, *Bend of Arkansas.*

DETERMINATION OF LATITUDE.

Time, p. m.	Double altitudes of Polaris.	Latitude.
h. m. s.	Deg. min. sec.	Deg. min. sec.
4 16 18.0	74 48 40	38 21 02
4 17 27.8	74 49 55	38 21 19
4 18 52.5	74 50 30	38 21 09
4 20 33.0	74 51 25	38 21 05
4 21 26.1	74 52 10	38 21 11
4 22 30.5	74 52 40	38 21 07
4 23 55.5	74 53 30	38 21 05
4 24 56.2	74 54 40	38 21 21
4 25 45.0	74 55 10	38 21 21
4 26 24.2	74 55 40	38 21 24
4 27 35.1	74 56 00	38 21 12
4 28 53.0	74 57 20	38 21 27
4 30 07.5	74 57 55	38 21 21
4 31 24.2	74 59 05	38 21 31
4 33 57.0	74 59 55	38 21 10
4 34 52.2	75 01 05	38 21 25
4 36 20.5	75 01 50	38 21 19
4 37 01.0	75 02 20	38 21 24
4 37 45.1	75 02 45	38 21 19
4 39 00.0	75 03 20	38 21 10

Thermometer 71°.

Mean of 20 observations, 38° 21' 16''.

Ex. Doc. No. 41.

APPENDIX No. 5—Continued.

July 11, 1846.—*Camp* 14, *Bend of Arkansas.*

DETERMINATION OF LATITUDE.

Time, p. m.	Double altitudes of α Ophiuchi, near the meridian.	Latitude.
h. m. s.	*Deg. min. sec.*	*Deg. min. sec.*
4 44 10.7	126 45 25	38 20 48
4 46 13.1	126 58 40	38 20 27
4 48 04.5	127 11 00	39 20 32
4 50 14.7	127 23 20	38 21 02
4 51 54.8	127 33 00	38 21 01
4 53 50.8	127 43 10	38 21 06
4 56 01.0	127 53 40	38 21 08
5 00 44.0	128 12 30	38 21 21
5 02 12.8	128 17 25	38 21 34
5 03 58.2	128 23 15	38 21 16
5 05 13.0	128 26 50	38 20 58
5 06 41.5	128 30 00	38 21 06
5 08 21.7	128 33 25	38 21 03
5 09 29.5	128 35 40	38 20 51
5 10 39.6	128 37 10	38 20 54
5 12 17.0	128 38 10	38 21 12
5 13 17.5	128 38 55	38 21 16
5 14 45.0	128 39 45	38 21 15
5 16 07.0	128 39 20	38 21 21
5 18 10.2	128 38 55	38 21 27
5 19 15.7	128 37 40	38 21 46
5 20 21.0	128 36 30	38 20 52
5 21 17.0	128 35 50	38 20 42
5 22 40.2	128 33 10	38 21 05
5 24 12.1	128 31 45	38 21 29
5 25 24.5	128 28 50	38 21 44
5 26 29.7	128 27 00	38 21 24
5 27 34.6	128 24 40	38 21 12

Thermometer 71°.

Latitude of camp.

Deg. min. sec.

Latitude by 28 observations of α Ophiuchi 38 21 18
" 20 " Polaris 16

Mean 38 21 17

Ex. Doc. No. 41.   207

APPENDIX No. 5—Continued.

July 13, 1846.—*Camp* 16, *Pawnee Fork.*

DETERMINATION OF TIME.

Time, p. m.	Double altitudes of *a* Lyræ, in the east.	Chronometer fast.
h. m. s.	Deg. min. sec.	h. m. s.
3 26 32.1	114 44 50	7 09 12.9
3 27 51.3	115 15 40	7 09 11.5
3 28 56.2	115 40 15	7 09 11.9
3 29 54.0	116 02 05	7 09 12.7
3 31 22.0	116 36 15	7 09 10.3
3 32 41.7	117 05 50	7 09 13.8
3 33 54.9	117 34 20	7 09 12.6
3 34 55.6	117 57 30	7 09 12.7
3 36 00.0	118 22 45	7 09 11.2

Thermometer 72°.

Time, p. m.	Double altitudes of Arcturus in the west.	Chronometer fast.
h. m. s.	Deg. min. sec.	h. m. s.
3 44 26.2	119 06 55	7 09 12.1
3 45 39.5	118 41 15	7 09 11.5
3 46 44.0	118 19 20	7 09 12.9
3 47 55.7	117 54 15	7 09 12.8
3 49 09.0	117 28 10	7 09 11.5
3 50 19.7	117 14 00	7 09 13.4
3 52 44.9	116 12 50	7 09 13.4
3 54 24.0	115 37 45	7 09 13.5
3 55 40.9	115 10 20	7 09 13.4

Thermometer 71°.

			h.	m.	s.
Chronometer	fast by	9 observations of east star	7	09	12.18
	"	9 " west star			12.74
		Mean....................	7	09	12.46

208   Ex. Doc. No. 41.

APPENDIX No. 5—Continued.

July 13, 1846.—Camp 16, Pàwnee Fork.

Time.	Double altitudes of Polaris.	Latitude.
h. m. s.	Deg. min. sec.	Deg. min. sec.
4 24 21.0	74 35 30	38 10 10
4 25 35.9	74 36 10	38 10 06
4 26 38.4	74 36 50	38 10 06
4 27 25.8	74 37 20	38 10 04
4 28 35.2	74 38 5	38 10 06
4 29 20.8	74 38 40	38 10 09
4 30 14.6	74 39 15	38 10 09
4 31 16.0	74 39 50	38 10 08
4 32 06.0	74 40 30	38 10 13
4 32 43.0	74 41 00	38 10 13
4 34 06.8	74 41 55	38 10 17
4 34 54.2	74 42 40	38 10 20
4 35 35.0	74 43 15	38 10 24

Thermometer 70°.

July 14, 1846.—Camp 16, Pawnee Fork.

Time.	Double altitudes of Polaris.	Latitude.
h. m. s.	Deg. min. sec.	Deg. min. sec.
4 39 43.5	74 47 55	38 10 05
4 41 00.0	74 48 55	38. 10 07
4 42 05.8	74 49 50	38 10 11
4 43 12.2	74 50 30	38 10 08
4 43 56.5	74 51 30	38 10 23

Latitude of camp.

Deg. min. sec.

Latitude, by 5 observations, July 14............ 38   10   10
   "   13   "   July 13............   16

Mean 38   10   11

APPENDIX No. 5—Continued.

July 14, 1846.—Camp 16, *Pawnee Fork*.

DETERMINATION OF TIME.

Time, p. m.	Double altitudes of α Lyræ in the east.	Chronometer fast.	
h. m. s.	Deg. min. sec.	h. m. s.	
3 32 15.8	118 28 15	7 09 08.5	
3 33 39.4	119 00 25	7 09 08.5	
3 34 34.0	119 21 50	7 09 07.0	
3 35 33.0	119 44 25	7 09 07.1	
3 36 28.8	120 04 20	7 09 11.0	rej.
3 37 37.0	120 32 40	7 09 05.4	rej.
3 38 49.3	120 59 28	7 09 08.0	
3 39 47.0	121 21 20	7 09 08.6	
3 41 07.2	121 52 05	7 09 08.8	

Time, p. m.	Double altitudes of Arcturus in the west.	Chronometer fast.	
h. m. s.	Deg. min. sec.	h. m. s.	
4 20 02.3	104 47 45	7 09 11.8	
4 21 03.8	104 23 55	7 09 09.8	
4 21 50.8	104 06 20	7 09 09.9	
4 22 31.6	103 50 55	7 09 09.7	
4 23 41.0	103 25 30	7 09 11.5	
4 24 55.0	102 57 15	7 09 07.6	rej.
4 25 58.7	102 33 30	7 09 11.2	
4 26 57.5	102 11 50	7 09 11.1	
4 28 05.0	101 45 20	7 09 10.1	

Thermometer 71°.

	h. m. s.
Chronometer fast by 7 obs. of east star	7 09 08.04
Chronometer fast by 8 obs. of west star	10.84
Mean	7 09 09.44

14

APPENDIX No. 5—Continued.

July 19, 1846.—Camp 20, Jackson Grove.

DETERMINATION OF TIME.

Time, p. m.	Double altitudes of Arcturus in the west.	Chronometer fast.
h. m. s.	Deg. min. sec.	h. m. s.
3 26 44.5	118 20 50	7 11 38.9
3 28 02.5	117 52 50	7 11 36.1
3 29 15.2	117 27 35	7 11 38.8
3 30 13.8	117 06 15	7 11 38.0
3 31 24.0	116 41 15	7 11 38.7
3 32 16.5	116 23 30	7 11 41.7
3 33 11.0	116 03 30	7 11 40.5
3 34 05.0	115 43 35	7 11 33.6 rej.
3 35 05.7	115 22 10	7 11 40.5
3 35 55.5	115 03 45	7 11 39.2
3 36 43.0	114 46 25	7 11 38.8
3 37 41.0	114 25 50	7 11 40.2

Thermometer 72°.

Time, p. m.	Double altitudes of *a* Lyræ in the east.	Chronometer fast.
h. m. s.	Deg. min. sec.	h. m. s.
3 13 28.8	117 37 30	7 11 38.2
3 14 37.0	118 13 10	7 11 39.6
3 15 26.0	118 22 10	7 11 36.3
3 16 30.8	118 37 40	7 11 37.5
3 17 45.0	119 15 40	7 11 39.0
3 18 44.9	119 38 55	7 11 38.4
3 19 54.5	120 06 00	7 11 37.7
3 21 00.0	120 30 20	7 11 38.1

Thermometer 72°.

	h. min. sec.
Chronometer fast by 11 obs. of west star	7 11 39.22
Chronometer fast by 8 obs. of east star	38.35
Mean	7 11 38.78

APPENDIX No. 5—Continued.

July 19, 1846.—Camp 20, Jackson Grove.

DETERMINATION OF LATITUDE.

Time, p. m.	Double altitudes of Polaris.	Latitude.
h. m. s.	Deg. min. sec.	Deg. min. sec.
3 43 52.0	73 26 30	37 41 53
3 45 01.3	73 27 10	37 41 52
3 46 12.5	73 27 55	37 41 35
3 47 05.5	73 29 00	37 41 51
3 48 06.3	73 29 40	37 41 56
3 49 00.0	73 30 00	37 41 46
3 50 04.0	73 30 30	37 41 41
3 50 43.8	73 31 00	37 41 45
3 52 01.0	73 31 35	37 41 39
3 53 05.0	73 32 00	37 41 33
3 54 00.0	73 32 40	37 41 33
3 56 12.8	73 33 40	37 41 23
3 56 52.5	73 34 20	37 41 30
3 57 31.7	73 35 00	37 41 38
3 58 16.8	73 35 40	37 41 44

Thermometer 72°.

Mean of 15 observations, 57° 41' 41".

APPENDIX No. 5—Continued.

July 19, 1846.—Camp 20, Jackson Grove.

DETERMINATION OF LATITUDE.

Time, p. m.			Double altitudes of α Herculis, near the meridian.			Latitude.		
h.	m.	s.	Deg.	min.	sec.	Deg.	min.	sec.
4	18	25.5	133	31	35	37	41	41
4	20	04.8	133	35	50	37	41	56
4	22	52.5	133	41	40	37	41	26
4	24	15.8	133	44	00	37	41	15
4	25	46.6	133	45	45	37	41	10
4	27	38.5	133	46	30	37	41	21
4	28	59.7	133	46	30	37	41	29
4	30	10.0	133	46	20	37	41	29
4	31	23.9	133	45	40	37	41	33
4	32	12.2	133	45	00	37	41	36
4	33	19.7	133	43	40	37	41	45
4	35	13.0	133	41	15	37	41	46
4	36	10.5	133	39	20	37	41	51
4	37	06.0	133	38	20	37	41	28
4	38	18.4	133	34	40	37	41	58

                                                      Deg. min. sec.

Latitude by 15 obs. of Polaris 37 41 41
Latitude by 15 obs. of α Herculis   35

Mean .... 37 41 38 lat. of camp.

APPENDIX No. 5—Continued.

July 19, 1846.—*Camp* 20, *Jackson Grove, Arkansas.*

DETERMINATION OF TIME.

Time.	Double altitude of the sun's upper limb.		Chronometer fast.		
h. m. s.	Deg.	min.	h.	m.	s.
10 34 23.6	89	30	7	11	38.2
10 34 50.2	89	20	7	11	39.3
10 35 15.8	89	10	7	11	39.4
10 35 42.0	89	00	7	11	40.1
10 36 07.0	88	50	7	11	39.7
10 36 32.3	88	40	7	11	39.5
10 36 57.0	88	30	7	11	39.7
10 37 23.8	88	20	7	11	40.1
10 37 48.0	88	10	7	11	38.7
10 38 14.2	88	00	7	11	39.4
10 38 39.7	87	50	7	11	39.5
10 39 04.8	87	40	7	11	39.2
10 39 30.3	87	30	7	11	39.3
10 39 54.7	87	20	7	11	38.3
10 40 21.8	87	10	7	11	39.8
10 40 47.8	87	00	7	11	40.5

Thermometer 88°.

Mean of 16 observations, 7*h*. 11*m*. 39.36*s*.

DETERMINATION OF INDEX ERROR.

	Min.	sec.
On the arc	31	20
Off the arc	31	40

Index error = + 10″.

APPENDIX No. 5—Continued.

July 22, 1846.—*Camp* 23, *Arkansas river.*

DETERMINATION OF TIME.

Time, p. m.	Double altitudes of a Aquilæ.	Chronometer fast.
h. m. s.	Deg. min. sec.	h. m. s.
4 27 17.2	90 30 10	7 15 38.9
4 28 39.6	90 57 40	7 15 39.1
4 29 36.5	91 17 30	7 15 37.2
4 30 35.3	91 37 10	7 15 37.3
4 31 32.2	91 54 15	7 15 43.0 rej.
4 32 34.8	92 15 55	7 15 40.3
4 33 46.7	92 40 20	7 15 38.7

Thermometer 68°.

Time, p. m.	Double altitudes of Arcturus, in the west.	Chronometer fast.
h. m. s.	Deg. min. sec.	h. m. s.
4 37 33.7	88 34 30	7 15 39.3
4 38 20.0	88 16 20	7 15 39.1
4 39 17.5	87 54 20	7 15 40.3
4 40 43.8	87 20 40	7 15 40.5
4 41 30.7	87 01 50	7 15 39.1
4 42 19.1	86 43 10	7 15 39.8
4 43 30.8	86 15 50	7 15 41.7

Thermometer 68°.

	h. m. s.
Chronometer fast by 6 observations east star....	7 15 38.58
Chronometer fast by 7 observations west star ...	39.97
Mean..................	7 15 39.28

APPENDIX No. 5—Continued.

July 22, 1846.—*Camp* 23.

DETERMINATION OF LATITUDE.

Time, p. m.	Double altitudes of Polaris.	Latitude.
h. m. s.	Deg. min. sec.	Deg. min. sec.
4 49 32.5	74 47 10	37 57 20
4 50 37.0	74 48 10	37 57 33
4 51 26.8	74 48 50	37 57 34
4 52 01.8	74 49 20	37 57 37
4 52 46.0	74 49 55	37 57 40
4 53 37.3	74 50 44	37 57 42
4 54 34.9	74 51 20	37 57 41
4 55 16.8	74 52 00	37 57 45
4 56 34.0	74 52 45	37 57 39
4 57 16.0	74 53 15	37 57 40
4 57 57.5	74 54 00	37 57 47

Thermometer 68°.

Mean of 11 observations, 37° 57' 39".

216   Ex. Doc. No. 41.

APPENDIX No. 5—Continued.

July 25, 1846.—*Camp 26, Arkansas river.*

DETERMINATION OF LATITUDE.

Time, p. m.	Double altitudes of Polaris.	Latitude.
h. m. s.	Deg. min. sec.	Deg. min. sec.
3 37 02.7	74 10 30	38 01 01
3 38 16.5	74 11 10	38 00 58
3 39 16.5	74 11 50	38 00 56
3 39 51.5	74 12 30	38 01 07
3 40 35.0	74 13 10	38 01 14
3 42 17.2	74 13 50	38 01 04
3 43 08.2	74 14 50	38 01 18
3 44 20.8	74 15 15	38 01 07
3 45 08.5	74 15 40	38 01 05
3 45 52.0	74 16 20	38 01 11
3 46 27.5	74 16 55	38 01 17
3 47 14.8	74 17 10	38 01 10
3 47 55.2	74 17 30	38 01 07
3 48 06.1	74 17 55	38 01 08
3 50 27.8	74 19 30	38 01 18

Thermometer 78°.

Mean of 15 observations, 38° 01' 08".

Ex. Doc. No. 41. 217

APPENDIX No. 5—Continued.

July 25, 1846.—Camp 26, on the Arkansas.

DETERMINATION OF TIME.

Time, p. m.	Double altitudes of Arcturus in the west.	Chronometer fast.
h. m. s.	Deg. min. sec.	h. m. s.
3 54 48.2	102 04 05	7 19 46.2
3 56 33.8	101 24 50	7 19 48.5
3 58 09.7	100 47 50	7 19 47.0
3 59 13.7	100 23 25	7 19 46.9
4 00 17.8	99 59 20	7 19 47.9
4 01 28.6	99 31 40	7 19 46.4
4 02 27.7	99 08 55	7 19 45.8
4 03 30.0	98 45 40	7 19 47.4
4 04 33.5	98 20 20	7 19 44.8 rej.

Thermometer 77°.

Time, p. m.	Double altitudes of a Aquilæ in the east.	Chronometer fast.
h. m. s.	Deg. min. sec.	h. m. s.
4 11 05.8	87 32 30	7 19 46.9
4 12 20.7	87 58 20	7 19 46.7
4 13 14.5	88 16 20	7 19 48.0
4 14 46.7	88 47 55	7 19 47.8
4 15 43.0	89 06 20	7 19 50.0
4 16 34.6	89 24 40	7 19 48.7
4 17 32.5	89 44 50	7 19 46.2
4 18 34.0	90 04 50	7 19 48.4
4 19 47.8	90 30 10	7 19 47.0
4 20 32.2	90 53 15	7 19 52.5 rej.

Thermometer 77°.

	h. min. sec.
Chronometer fast by 8 obs. of west star	7 19 47.01
Chronometer fast by 9 obs. of west star	47.78
Mean	7 19 47.40

APPENDIX No. 5—Continued.

July 29, 1846—*Camp 30, near Bent's Fort.*

DETERMINATION OF TIME.

Time, p. m.			Double altitudes of Arcturus in the west.			Chronometer fast.		
h.	m.	s.	Deg.	min.	sec.	h.	m.	s.
4	20	28.0	83	19	10	7	25	31.6
4	21	57.7	87	44	30	7	25	32.4
4	22	59.0	87	20	25	7	25	31.9
4	24	02.0	86	56	00	7	25	32.4
4	25	09.8	86	29	30	7	25	32.4
4	25	57.5	86	10	50	7	25	32.3
4	26	59.2	85	46	43	7	25	32.3
4	28	04.7	85	20	05	7	25	29.7
4	28	56.5	84	59	40	7	25	29.4
4	30	01.0	84	35	10	7	25	31.2
4	31	01.5	84	11	50	7	25	32.2

Time, p. m.			Double altitudes of *a* Aquilæ in the east.			Chronometer fast.		
h.	m.	s.	Deg.	min.	sec.	h.	m.	s.
4	34	06.8	98	20	30	7	25	32.3
4	35	39.8	98	48	50	7	25	33.6
4	36	50.1	99	10	20	7	25	33.8
4	37	48.6	99	28	30	7	25	33.9
4	39	17.0	99	55	30	7	25	33.2
4	40	44.0	100	21	20	7	25	35.0
4	41	58.0	100	44	20	7	25	32.6
4	43	28.8	101	12	10	7	25	30.0
4	44	24.5	101	26	55	7	25	35.9
4	45	35.0	101	48	40	7	25	32.6
4	46	57.7	102	13	20	7	25	31.4

Thermometer 66°

	h.	m.	s.
Chronometer fast by 11 observations of west star..	7	25	31.62
" 12 " east star...			32.12
Mean	7.	25	32.37

APPENDIX No. 5—Continued.

July 30, 1846.—*Camp 30, near Bent's Fort.*

DETERMINATION OF TIME.

Time, p. m.	Double altitudes of Arcturus in the west.	Chronometer fast.
h. m. s.	*Deg. min. sec.*	*h. m. s.*
3 33 05.8	104 59 30	7 25 32.1
3 34 37.0	104 24 50	7 25 30.1
3 35 32.5	104 04 05	7 25 31.6
3 37 00.8	103 30 55	7 25 31.9
3 38 00.0	103 08 30	7 25 31.8
3 39 08.5	102 42 30	7 25 31.4
3 40 06.2	102 20 50	7 25 31.9
3 41 00.0	102 00 20	7 25 31.6
3 42 12.5	101 32 30	7 25 29.7

Thermometer 74°.

Time, p. m.	Double altitudes of α Aquilæ in the east.	Chronometer fast.
h. m. s.	*Deg. min. sec.*	*h. m. s.*
3 46 06.8	83 40 25	7 25 29.4
3 47 23.0	84 07 00	7 25 30.1
3 49 03.5	84 41 50	7 25 31.3
3 50 02.5	85 03 20	7 25 29.0
3 50 56.0	85 21 10	7 25 31.3
3 51 48.1	85 40 00	7 25 29.2
3 52 46.5	86 00 10	7 25 33.5
3 53 35.7	86 16 30	7 25 32.1
3 54 46.0	86 42 10	7 25 28.2

Thermometer 74°.

	h. m. s.
Chronometer fast by 9 obs. of west star	7 25 31.46
Chronometer fast by 9 obs. of east star	30.44
Mean	7 25 30.95

APPENDIX No. 5,—Continued.

July 30, 1846.—*Camp* 30, *near Bent's Fort.*

DETERMINATION OF LATITUDE.

Time, p. m.	Double altitudes of Polaris.	Latitude.
h. m. s.	*Deg. min. sec.*	*Deg. min. sec.*
4 01 31.0	74 38 55	38 02 47
4 03 07.8	74 39 55	38 03 03
4 04 23.0	74 41 15	38 03 06
4 05 17.1	74 41 50	38 02 54
4 06 17.0	74 42 30	38 02 52
4 07 15.2	74 43 00	38 02 46
4 08 08.0	74 43 50	38 02 52
4 09 04.5	74 44 20	38 02 50
4 10 12.2	74 45 20	38 02 55
4 11 18.5	74 45 50	38 02 45
4 12 20.0	74 46 55	38 03 06
4 13 26.0	74 47 40	38 02 54
4 14 11.2	74 48 30	38 03 04

Thermometer 74°.

Mean of 16 observations, 38° 02' 55".

Ex. Doc. No. 41.   221

APPENDIX No. 5—Continued.

July 30, 1846.—*Camp* 30, *near Bent's Fort.*

DETERMINATION OF TIME.

Time, a. m.			Double altitudes of sun's upper limb.		Time, p. m.			Chronometer fast.		
h.	m.	s.	Deg.	min.	h.	m.	s.	h.	m.	s.
4	23	02.3	90	00	10	40	02.5	7	25	30.06
4	23	29.7	90	10	10	39	36.0	7	25	30.52
4	23	55.0	90	20	10	39	10.0	7	25	30.18
4	24	20.2	90	30	10	38	44.2	7	25	29.80
4	24	47.3	90	40	10	38	17.5	7	25	30.10
4	25	38.8	91	00	10	37	26.0	7	25	30.11
4	26	03.2	91	10	10	37	00.0	7	25	29.42
4	26	56.5	91	30	10	36	08.0	7	25	29.98
4	30	02.0	92	40	10	33	06.0	7	25	31.76
4	30	51.8	93	00	10	32	14.0	7	25	30.67
4	31	18.8	93	10	10	31	47.7	7	25	31.03
4	31	44.0	93	20	10	31	22.3	7	25	30.94
4	32	10.0	93	30	10	30	57.4	7	25	31.50
4	32	37.0	93	40	10	30	29.5	7	25	31.06
4	33	02.8	93	50	10	30	04.2	7	25	31.32
4	33	28.8	94	00	10	29	37.5	7	25	30.99

Thermometer 78°.

Mean of 16 observations, 7h. 25m. 30.59s.

DETERMINATION OF INDEX ERROR.

	Min.	sec.
On the arc..................................	31	30
Off the arc	31	30

Index error = 00″.

Ex. Doc. No. 41.

APPENDIX No. 5—Continued.

July 30, 1846.—*Camp* 30, *near Bent's Fort.*

DETERMINATION OF LATITUDE.

Time, p. m.			Double altitude of α Aquilæ, near the meridian.			Latitude.		
h.	*m.*	*s.*	*Deg.*	*min.*	*sec.*	*Deg.*	*min.*	*sec.*
6	24	18.8	120	40	40	38	02	37
6	25	30.0	120	42	30	38	02	44
6	26	47.5	120	46	10	38	02	14
6	27	58.0	120	47	10	38	02	37
6	29	05.5	120	48	50	38	02	33
6	30	07.6	120	50	10	38	02	28
6	31	16.5	120	50	50	38	02	36
6	32	37.0	120	51	50	38	02	31
6	33	37.0	120	52	10	38	02	32
6	35	02.8	120	52	30	38	02	27
6	36	26.0	120	53	00	38	02	04
6	37	48.8	120	52	25	38	02	01
6	38	57.1	120	51	00	38	02	21
6	39	56.5	120	49	50	38	02	28
6	41	04.6	120	48	55	38	32	15
6	42	06.5	120	47	10	38	02	25
6	44	38.0	120	42	50	38	02	22
6	47	08.8	120	37	20	38	02	16

Thermometer 68°.

Mean of 18 observations, 38° 32' 25".

Ex. Doc. No. 41.   223

APPENDIX No. 5—Continued.

July 31, 1846.—*Camp* 30, *near Bent's Fort.*

DETERMINATION OF LONGITUDE BY LUNAR DISTANCE.

Time, p. m.	a Aquilæ, and moon's west limb.	Double altitude of moon's upper limb.	Longitude.
h. m. s.	*Deg. min. sec.*	*Deg. min. sec.*	*h. m. s.*
3 12 39.6	75 42 10	64 09 50	6 50 05.1
3 16 04.0	75 41 30	63 34 10	6 48 45.1
3 18 55.8	75 40 30	63 01 30	6 48 57.5
3 21 04.0	75 39 30	62 41 40	6 49 55.9
3 26 06.8	75 37 40	61 48 20	6 50 29.8
3 28 11.8	75 37 00	61 23 50	6 50 29.8
3 30 23.3	75 36 25	60 56 40	6 50 02.1

Time, p. m.	Spica Virginis, and moon's west limb.	Moon's lower limb.	Longitude.
h. m. s.	*Deg. min. sec.*	*Deg. min. sec.*	*h. m. s.*
3 40 33.0	24 26 40	57 46 50	6 55 13.7
3 46 51.0	24 27 55	56 49 10	6 55 02.9
3 48 54.0	24 28 40	56 01 40	6 52 19.2
3 50 58.2	24 29 20	55 33 40	6 52 22.7

Thermometer 78°.

	h. m. s.
Longitude by 7 observations of *a* Aquilæ	6 49 49.33
" 4 " Spica	6 53 -44.12
Mean.......................	6 51 46.72

224   Ex. Doc. No. 41.

APPENDIX No. 5—Continued.

July 31, 1846.—*Camp* 30, *near Bent's Fort.*

DETERMINATION OF TIME.

Time, a. m.	Double altitudes of sun's upper limb.	Time, p. m.	Chronometer fast.
h. m. s.	Deg. min.	h. m. s.	h. m. s.
4 18 04.2	87 50	10 44 49.5	7 25 27.20
4 18 31.0	88 00	10 44 23.5	7 25 27.62
4 18 55.9	88 10	10 43 57.2	7 25 26.93
4 19 21.7	88 20	10 43 32.0	7 25 27.24
4 19 48.0	88 30	10 43 05.5	7 25 27.15
4 20 13.6	88 40	10 42 39.8	7 25 27.10
4 20 39.0	88 50	10 42 13.8	7 25 27.21
4 21 06.0	89 00	10 41 48.0	7 25 27.42
4 21 32.0	89 10	10 41 22.0	7 25 27.43
4 21 57.5	89 20	10 40 57.7	7 25 28.04
4 22 23.0	89 30	10 40 30.0	7 25 26.94

Thermometer 77°.

Mean of 11 observations, 7*h*. 25*m*. 27.50*s*.

Ex. Doc. No. 41. 225

APPENDIX No. 5—Continued.

July 31, 1846.—*Camp* 30, *near Bent's Fort.*

DETERMINATION OF TIME.

Time, p. m.	Double altitudes of Arcturus in the west.	Chronometer fast.
h. m. s.	Deg. min. sec.	h. m. s.
4 05 05.8	91 12 50	7 25 28.0
4 05 52.3	90 54 05	7 25 26.3
4 06 40.5	90 35 55	7 25 28.0
4 07 36.4	90 14 20	7 25 28.1
4 08 32.7	89 52 50	7 25 29.0
4 09 27.7	89 31 00	7 25 27.9
4 10 22.8	89 09 30	7 25 27.8

Time, p. m.	Double altitudes of a Aquilæ in the east.	Chronometer fast.
h. m. s.	Deg. min. sec.	h. m. s.
4 12 45.2	94 04 50	7 25 26.3
4 13 46.0	94 23 50	7 25 29.0
4 14 48.2	94 44 45	7 25 26.3
4 15 50.0	95 04 35	7 25 26.5
4 16 35.0	95 19 20	7 25 25.7
4 17 43.8	95 40 30	7 25 28.4
4 18 47.0	96 01 00	7 25 26.5

	h. m. s.
Chronometer fast by 7 obs. of west star	7 25 27.87
Chronometer fast by 7 obs. of east star	26.96
Mean	7 25 27.41

APPENDIX No. 5—Continued.

July 31, 1846.—*Camp* 30, *near Bent's Fort.*

DETERMINATION OF LATITUDE.

Time. p. m.			Double altitudes of Polaris.			Latitude.		
h.	*m.*	*s.*	*Deg.*	*min.*	*sec.*	*Deg*	*min.*	*sec.*
4	27	45.2	75	00	30	38	02	45
4	28	50.0	75	01	15	38	02	43
4	30	06.3	75	01	50	38	02	33
4	31	20.5	75	02	50	38	02	36
4	32	07.5	75	04	00	36	02	55
4	33	07.0	75	04	40	38	02	52
4	34	08.8	75	05	30	38	02	52
4	35	19.6	75	06	05	38	02	43
4	36	13.0	75	06	30	38	02	36
4	44	03.0	75	13	00	38	02	55
4	45	20.7	75	13	30	38	02	40
4	46	26.8	75	14	20	38	02	40
4	47	09.0	75	14	50	38	02	39
4	48	05.5	75	15	40	38	02	46
4	48	46.6	75	16	05	38	02	39
4	49	35.2	75	16	50	38	02	45

Thermometer 76°.

Mean of 16 observations, 38° 02′ 44″.

Ex. Doc. No. 41.

APPENDIX No. 5—Continued.

July 31, 1846.—*Camp 30, near Bent's Fort.*

DETERMINATION OF LATITUDE.

Time, p. m.			Double altitudes of *a* Aquilæ, near the meridian.			Latitude.		
h.	m.	s.	Deg.	min.	sec.	Deg.	min.	sec.
6	22	36.0	120	44	30	38	03	17
6	24	28.5	120	47	30	38	03	48
6	25	38.0	120	49	50	38	03	20
6	26	55.2	120	51	10	38	03	17
6	28	05.2	120	52	05	38	03	16
6	29	00.0	120	52	40	38	03	10
6	30	08.0	120	52	40	38	03	20
6	31	18.2	120	52	00	38	03	11
6	32	21.0	120	51	30	38	03	54
6	34	04.7	120	51	30	38	03	31
6	34	47.5	121	51	05	38	03	23
6	35	35.0	120	50	00	38	03	34
6	36	39.8	120	48	20	38	03	49
6	37	41.8	120	47	50	38	03	24
6	38	37.8	120	45	50	38	03	44
6	39	25.5	120	45	20	38	03	18
6	40	07.0	120	43	20	38	03	40

Thermometer 68°.

Mean of 17 observations, 38° 03' 28".

APPENDIX No. 5—Continued.

July 31, 1846.—Camp 30.

DETERMINATION OF LONGITUDE.

Time, p. m.	Distance of α Aquilæ from moon's west limb.	Longitude.
h. m. s.	Deg. min. sec.	h. m. s.
3 12 39.6	75 42 10	6 50 05.1
3 16 04.0	75 41 30	6 48 45.1
3 18 55.8	75 40 30	6 48 57.5
3 21 04.0	75 39 30	6 49 55.9
3 26 06.8	75 37 40	6 50 29.8
3 28 11.8	75 37 00	6 50 29.8
3 30 23.3	75 36 25	6 50 02.1

Time, p. m.	Distance of α Virginis from moon's west limb.	Longitude.
h. m. s.	Deg. min. sec.	h. m. s.
3 40 33.0	24 26 40	6 55 13.7
3 46 51.0	24 27 55	6 55 02.9
3 48 54.0	24 28 40	6 52 17.2
3 50 58.2	24 29 20	6 52 22.7

APPENDIX No. 5—Continued.

August 1, 1846.—Camp 30.

DETERMINATION OF LONGITUDE.

Time, p. m.	Distance of a Virginis from moon's west limb.	Longitude.
h. m. s.	Deg. min. sec.	h. m. s.
3 24 02.0	37 40 05	6 53 22.0
3 27 34.5	37 41 30	6 53 30.1
3 29 27.8	37 42 05	6 53 11.0
3 31 30.0	37 43 00	6 53 38.3
3 33 31.5	37 43 40	6 53 24.2
3 35 48.0	37 44 25	6 53 11.0

Time, p. m.	Distance of a Aquilæ from moon's west limb.	Longitude.
h. m. s.	Deg. min. sec.	h. m. s.
3 39 46.5	65 37 15	6 50 24.7
3 41 50.2	63 36 30	6 50 36.8
3 43 39.7	63 35 50	6 50 48.8
3 45 43.5	63 34 55	6 51 31.0
3 48 29.2	63 33 50	6 52 04.1
3 49 58.5	63 33 20	6 52 04.1
3 51 24.6	63 32 50	6 52 07.2

	h. m. s.
Longitude by 14 observations of a Aquilæ	6 50 35.86
Longitude by 10 observations of a Virginis	6 53 31.36
Mean	6 52 03.61

APPENDIX No. 5—Continued.

August 1, 1846.—*Camp* 30, *near Bent's Fort.*

DETERMINATION OF TIME.

Time, a. m.			Double altitudes of sun's upper limb.		Time, p. m.			Chronometer fast.		
h.	*m.*	*s.*	*Deg.*	*min.*	*h.*	*m.*	*s.*	*h.*	*m.*	*s.*
5	41	17.5	118	00	9	21	28.0	7	25	28.42
5	41	47.8	118	10	9	20	57.7	7	25	28.33
5	42	18.0	118	20	9	20	27.0	7	25	28.10
5	42	47.2	118	30	9	19	57.0	7	25	27.71
5	43	17.6	118	40	8	19	26.7	7	25	27.78
5	43	48.0	118	50	9	18	55.8	7	25	27.54
5	44	19.0	119	00	9	18	25.8	7	25	28.05
5	44	48.8	119	10	9	17	55.7	7	25	27.92
5	45	18.6	119	20	9	17	25.3	7	25	27.64
5	46	20.2	119	40	9	16	24.2	7	25	27.81
5	46	50.8	119	50	9	15	55.8	7	25	28.02
5	47	21.0	120	00	9	15	23.2	7	25	27.84

APPENDIX No. 5—Continued.

August 3, 1846.—Camp 32.

DETERMINATION OF TIME.

Time, p. m.	Double altitudes of Arcturus in the west.	Chronometer fast.
h. m. s.	Deg min. sec.	h. m. s.
3 42 40.2	96 04 00	7 27 03.3
3 45 35.7	94 55 50	7 27 03.0
3 47 24.0	94 14 05	7 27 03.7
3 48 17.8	93 52 30	7 27 01.9
3 49 02.7	93 35 30	7 27 03.0
3 49 52.5	93 16 10	7 27 03.1
3 50 31.6	93 01 00	7 27 03.1
3 51 18.8	92 41 50	7 27 01.2

Thermometer 76°.

Time, p. m.	Double altitudes of a Aquilæ in the east.	Chronometer fast.
h. m. s.	Deg. min. sec.	h. m. s.
3 54 06.0	91 36 40	7 27 02.3
3 54 46.8	91 49 50	7 27 04.0
3 55 38.5	92 07 30	7 27 02.9
3 56 40.0	92 27 25	7 27 04.9
3 57 36.1	92 46 00	7 27 05.1
3 58 25.2	93 02 40	7 27 04.1
3 59 13.1	93 17 40	7 27 06.9

Thermometer 76°.

	h. m. s.
Chronometer fast by 8 obs. of west star	7 27 02.79
Chronometer fast by 7 obs. of east star	04.31
Mean	7 27 03.55

232   Ex. Doc. No. 41.

APPENDIX No. 5—Continued.

August 3, 1846.—Camp 32.

DETERMINATION OF LATITUDE.

Time. p. m.	Double altitudes of Polaris.	Latitude.
h. m. s.	Deg. min. sec.	Deg. min. sec.
4 03 41.0	74 15 05	37 44 59
4 04 36.6	74 15 55	37 45 06
4 05 28.5	74 16 30	37 45 01
4 06 25.0	74 16 55	37 44 55
4 07 11.8	74 17 40	37 45 01
4 08 09.7	74 18 05	37 44 54
4 09 03.5	74 18 35	37 44 50
4 09 46.3	74 18 55	37 44 45
4 10 39.0	74 19 55	37 44 55

Thermometer 75°.

Mean of 9 observations, 37° 44′ 56″.

Ex. Doc. No. 41. 233

APPENDIX No. 5—Continued.

August 5, 1846.—*Camp* 34, *on the Purgatory.*

DETERMINATION OF LATITUDE.

Time, p. m.	Double altitudes of Polaris.	Latitude.
h. m. s.	Deg. min. sec.	Deg. min. sec.
4 06 29.5	73 15 05	·37 12 06
4 07 52.0	73 15 50	37 11 59
4 08 51.2	73 16 40	37 12 03
4 09 53.3	73 17 10	37 11 55
4 12 43.0	73 19 30	37 12 02
4 13 40.8	73 20 05	37 11 59
4 15 15.5	73 20 55	37 11 49
4 15 53.4	73 21 40	37 11 58
4 19 55.0	73 24 20	37 11 46
4 20 38.8	73 25 30	37 12 06
4 21 14.6	73 25 50	37 12 04
4 21 50.0	73 26 10	37 12 00
4 22 34.6	73 26 40	37 11 54

Thermometer 67°.

Wind very high; observations imperfect.

Mean of 13 observations, 37° 11′ 59″.

APPENDIX No. 5—Continued.

August 5, 1846.—*Camp* 34, *on the Purgatory.*

DETERMINATION OF TIME.

Time, p. m.	Double altitudes of *a* Aquilæ, in the east.	Chronometer fast.
h. m. s.	*Deg. min. sec.*	*h. m. s.*
4 28 01.5	104 44 20	7 29 24.7
4 29 21.3	105 06 55	7 29 26.9
4 30 16.6	105 22 50	7 29 27.2
4 31 24.0	105 41 50	7 29 28.6
4 32 12.7	105 55 50	7 29 28.4
4 33 14.5	106 13 30	7 29 28.2
4 34 28.0	106 35 00	7 29 25.6

Thermometer 67°.

Mean of 7 observations, 7*h.* 29*m.* 27.09*s.*

APPENDIX No. 5—Continued.

August 6, 1846.—*Camp* 35, *in the Raton.*

DETERMINATION OF LATITUDE.

Time, p. m.	Double altitudes of Polaris.	Latitude.
h. m. s.	Deg. min. sec.	Deg. min. sec.
3 46 15.5	72 40 50	37 00 36
3 47 57.8	72 41 40	37 00 25
3 49 20.7	72 42 40	37 00 26
3 50 48.8	72 43 40	37 00 22
3 51 52.7	72 44 20	37 00 20
3 53 05.5	72 45 20	37 00 24
3 54 07.5	72 45 50	37 00 15
3 55 28.0	72 46 30	37 00 06
3 56 21.6	72 47 30	37 00 17

Thermometer 64°.

Mean of 9 observations, 37° 00′ 21″.

APPENDIX No. 5—Continued.

August 6, 1846.—*Camp* 35, *in the Raton.*

DETERMINATION OF TIME.

Time, p. m.	Double altitudes of Arcturus in the west.	Chronometer fast.
h. m. s.	Deg. min. sec.	h. m. s.
4 00 00.8	85 48 55	7 29 28.4
4 01 09.0	85 22 15	7 29 29.6
4 02 09.0	84 58 20	7 29 29.4
4 03 06.6	84 35 45	7 29 30.2
4 04 19.7	84 08 05	7 29 33.8 rej.
4 05 12.5	83 45 50	7 29 30.7
4 06 18.8	83 19 55	7 29 31.9

Thermometer 64°.

Time, p. m.	Double altitudes of α Aquilæ in the east.	Chronometer fast.
h. m. s.	Deg. min. sec.	h. m. s.
4 11 33.4	101 09 55	7 29 31.9
4 13 42.8	101 50 00	7 29 32.3
4 14 54.7	102 11 50	7 29 33.5
4 15 50.5	102 28 40	7 29 34.4
4 16 43.6	102 45 10	7 29 33.5
4 17 42.5	103 03 10	7 29 33.2
4 18 52.0	103 24 10	7 29 33.4

Thermometer 63°.

	h. m. s.
Chronometer fast by 6 observations of west star..	7 29 30.03
Chronometer fast by 7 observations of east star..	33.17
Mean........................	7 29 31.60

APPENDIX No. 5—Continued.

August 7, 1846.—*Camp* 36, *on the Canadian, south side, about one and a half mile below the crossing.*

DETERMINATION OF TIME.

Time, p. m.	Double altitudes of Arcturus in the west.	Chronometer fast.
h. m. s.	Deg. min. sec.	h. m. s.
3 35 22.7	94 01 50	7 29 20.2
3 36 14.5	93 41 30	7 29 20.6
3 37 01.0	93 22 30	7 29 19.1
3 37 45.3	93 04 55	7 29 18.9
3 38 39.0	92 44 20	7 29 20.5
3 39 34.6	92 21 40	7 29 18.9
3 40 13.0	92 04 50	7 29 14.8 rej.
3 41 02.0	91 47 35	7 29 20.1

Thermometer 59°.

Time, p. m.	Double altitudes of *a* Aquilæ, in the east.	Chronometer fast.
h. m. s.	Deg. min. sec.	h. m. s.
3 43 56.5	93 43 00	7 29 22.7
3 45 13.3	94 09 30	7 29 21.6
3 46 15.8	94 30 20	7 29 22.6
3 47 01.0	94 46 00	7 29 21.0
3 47 53.8	95 03 05	7 29 24.5
3 48 43.0	95 19 50	7 29 22.8
3 49 36.2	95 37 40	7 29 23.2
3 50 34.0	95 57 15	7 29 22.5

Thermometer 59°.

	h. m. s.
Chronometer fast by 7 observations of west star ...	7 29 19.76
" 8 " east star ...	22.61
Mean..................	7 29 21.18

APPENDIX No. 5—Continued.

August 7, 1846.—*Camp* 36.

DETERMINATION OF LATITUDE.

Time, p. m.	Double altitudes of Polaris.	Latitude.
h. m. s.	*Deg. min. sec.*	*Deg. min. sec.*
3 55 48.0	72 23 45	36 47 11
3 56 59.3	72 24 55	36 47 25
3 57 59.3	72 25 40	36 47 25
3 59 09.0	72 27 00	36 47 37
4 00 32.6	72 28 10	36 47 52
4 01 39.0	72 28 50	36 47 38
4 02 25.3	72 29 55	36 47 54
4 03 31.0	72 30 25	36 47 44
4 04 15.0	72 31 00	36 47 45
4 05 24.2	72 31 10	36 47 25
4 06 15.5	72 31 40	36 47 21

Thermometer 59°.

Mean of 11 observations, 36° 47′ 34″.

Variation of the needle, determined by the eastern elongation of Polaris, = 12° east.

APPENDIX No. 5—Continued.

August 8, 1846.—*Camp* 36.

DETERMINATION OF TIME.

Time, p. m.	Double altitudes of *a* Aquilæ in the east.	Chronometer fast.
h. m. s.	Deg. min. sec.	h. m. s.
4 01 14.8	100 44 25	7 29 16.8
4 02 07.6	100 59 55	7 29 20.4
4 03 02.2	101 17 20	7 29 19.8
4 03 53.7	101 33 30	7 29 19.7
4 05 12.8	101 57 45	7 29 21.4
4 06 08.8	102 15 50	7 29 19.1
4 07 03.7	102 33 25	7 29. 17.2
4 08 03.5	102 52 30	7 29. 15.1 rej.

Time, p. m.	Double altitudes of Arcturus in the west.	Chronometer fast.
h. m. s.	Deg. min. sec.	h. m. s.
4 10 06.0	78 37 10	7 29 17.7
4 11 00.8	78 15 30	7 29 18.7
4 11 57.7	77 52 30	7 29 18.9
4 12 48.0	77 32 05	7 29 17.3
4 13 59.8	77 03 25	7 29 17.4
4 14 53.7	76 41 30	7 29 16.6
4 15 38.0	76 24 20	7 29 18.1
4 16 42.5	75 57 35	7 29 15.9
4 17 32.5	75 38 30	7 29 18.2
4 18 12.8	75 21 30	7 29 16.1

Thermometer 63°.

	h. m. s.
Chronometer fast by 7 obs. of east star..........	7 29 19.29
" 10 " west star..........	17.49
Mean	7 29 18.34

DETERMINATION OF INDEX ERROR.

	Min. sec.	Min. sec.
On the arc................	31 40	31 35
Off the arc	31 45	31 45

Index error = + 3.7.

240   Ex. Doc. No. 41.

APPENDIX No. 5—Continued.

August 10, 1846.—*Camp* 38, *on the Ciman Citon.*

DETERMINATION OF TIME.

Time, p. m.	Double altitudes of Arcturus in the west.	Chronometer fast.
h. m. s.	Deg. min. sec.	h. m. s.
3 10 58.7	99 36 40	7 30 32.9
3 11 49.0	99 17 25	7 30 34.3
3 12 40.2	98 56 45	7 30 33.1
3 13 43.5	98 31 40	7 30 32.7
3 14 31.0	98 13 00	7 30 32.9
3 15 17.0	97 54 45	7 30 32.6
3 16 10.0	97 34 10	7 30 33.5

Thermometer 59°

Time, p. m.	Double altitudes of α Aquilæ in the east.	Chronometer fast.
h. m. s.	Deg. min. sec.	h. m. s.
3 18 54.0	89 01 35	7 30 33.1
3 20 08.2	89 27 40	7 30 34.1
3 21 17.1	89 52 25	7 30 33.1
3 22 34.1	90 18 45	7 30 35.6
3 23 43.8	90 43 20	7 30 35.6
3 24 43.5	91 03 55	7 30 36.5
3 25 27.0	91 20 00	7 30 34.4

Thermometer 59°.

	h. m. s.
Chronometer fast by 7 obs. of east star............	7 30 34.63
Chronometer fast by 7 obs. of west star..........	33.14
Mean	7 30 33.88

Ex. Doc. No. 41. 241

APPENDIX Nσ. 5—Continued.

August 10, 1846.—*Camp* 38.

DETERMINATION OF LATITUDE.

Time, p. m.	Double altitudes of Polaris.	Latitude.
h. m. s.	Deg. min. sec.	Deg. min. sec.
3 29 03.5	71 33 25	36 27 43
3 29 58.0	71 34 00	36 27 44
3 31 09.0	71 35 10	36 27 52
3 32 20.0	71 35 50	36 27 47
3 33 25.0	71 36 50	36 27 54
3 34 36.5	71 37 30	36 27 50
3 35 27.2	71 38 20	36 27 59
3 36 14.5	71 38 50	36 27 55
3 37 03.8	71 39 10	36 27 47
3 37 45.4	71 39 55	36 27 52
3 38 44.0	71 40 30	36 27 51

Thermometer, 58°.

Mean of 11 observations, 36° 27′ 50″.

16

APPENDIX No. 5—Continued.

August 12, 1846.—*Camp* 40.

DETERMINATION OF TIME.

Time, p. m.	Double altitudes of a Lyræ, in the west.	Chronometer fast.
h. m. s.	Deg. min. sec.	h. m. s.
9 16 50.0	71 35 30	7 31 26.9
9 17 38.5	71 18 15	7 31 28.3
9 18 44.6	70 53 50	7 31 27.7
9 19 43.0	70 31 50	7 31 26.0
9 20 24.2	70 16 10	7 31 24.4
9 21 11.8	69 59 20	7 31 25.9
9 22 03.6	69 40 15	7 31 25.5

Time, a. m.—August 13.	Double altitudes of sun's upper limb.	Chronometer fast.
h. m. s.	Deg. min.	h. m. s.
4 05 34.3	77 50	7 31 25.0
4 06 00.5	78 00	7 31 26.1
4 06 26.2	78 10	7 31 26.7
4 06 51.7	78 20	7 31 27.1
4 07 16.2	78 30	7 31 26.5
4 07 41.0	78 40	7 31 26.2
4 08 05.0	78 50	7 31 25.1
4 08 29.2	79 00	7 31 24.1
4 08 54.2	79 10	7 31 24.0
4 09 20.0	79 20	7 31 24.6
4 09 44.6	79 30	7 31 24.1

Thermometer 66°.

	h. m. s.
Chronometer fast by 11 observations of sun in east	7 31 25.49
Rate for 7 hours....................................	88
Chronometer fast at 13h., August 12...............	7 31 26.37
Chronometer fast by *a* Lyræ, in the west	26.39
Mean..............................	7 31 26.38

Ex. Doc. No. 41.   243

APPENDIX No. 5—Continued.

August 12, 1846.—*Camp* 40.

DETERMINATION OF LATITUDE.

Time, p. m.	Double altitudes of Polaris.	Latitude.
h. m. s.	Deg. min. sec.	Deg. min. sec.
9 27 11.2	74 33 30	35 54 06
9 28 38.0	74 34 25	35 54 19
9 30 09.0	74 35 00	35 54 20
9 31 14.7	74 35 30	35 54 24
9 32 18.5	74 36 00	35 54 29
9 33 18.5	74 36 00	35 54 18
9 34 27.0	74 36 50	35 54 31
9 35 25.8	74 37 00	35 54 26
9 36 38.5	74 37 15	35 54 22
9 37 38.5	74 37 30	35 54 19

Thermometer 49°.

Mean of 10 observations, 35° 54′ 21″.

APPENDIX No. 5—Continued.

August 14, 1846.—*Camp* 42, *about one mile south of the Vegas.*

DETERMINATION OF TIME.

Time, p. m.	Double altitudes of Arcturus in the west.	Chronometer fast.
h. m. s.	Deg. min. sec.	h. m. s.
3 42 51.8	81 21 30	7 32 05.0
3 44 19.8	80 45 45	7 32 05.1
3 45 35.9	80 16 15	7 32 08.9
3 46 38.2	79 50 50	7 32 08.7
3 47 42.7	79 24 20	7 32 08.1
3 48 58.6	78 53 10	7 32 07.4
3 49 55.0	78 30 30	7 32 08.1

Thermometer 60°.

Time, p. m.	Double altitudes of α Aquilæ, in the east.	Chronometer fast.
h. m. s.	Deg. min. sec.	h. m. s.
3 52 21.4	105 59 30	7 32 06.3
3 53 39.0	106 23 45	7 32 05.5
3 54 51.7	106 47 25	7 32 01.5
3 56 02.5	107 08 20	7 32 03.8
3 57 12.0	107 29 35	7 32 03.1
3 58 18.8	107 49 50	7 32 02.9
3 59 19.0	108 07 30	7 32 04.4

Thermometer 60°.

```
                                                       h.  m.   s.
Chronometer fast by 7 observations of east star...    7  32  03.93
          "         7       "        west star...            07.36
                    Mean........................      7  32  05.64
```

Ex. Doc. No. 41. 245

APPENDIX No. 5—Continued.

August 14, 1846.—*Camp* 42, *one mile south of the Vegas.*

DETERMINATION OF LATITUDE.

Time, p. m.	Double altitudes of Polaris.	Latitude.
h. m. s.	Deg. min. sec.	Deg. min. sec.
4 03 54.2	70 23 25	35 34 50
4 05 06.0	70 24 10	35 34 46
4 05 51.0	70 25 30	35 35 08
4 06 52.5	70 25 50	35 34 55
4 08 09.0	70 26 50	35 34 56
4 09 09.0	70 28 10	35 35 13
4 10 11.5	70 29 10	35 35 21
4 11 12.0	70 29 50	35 35 15
4 11 59.0	70 30 35	35 35 20

Thermometer 60°.

Mean of 9 observations, 35° 35' 05".

Ex. Doc. No. 41.

APPENDIX No. 5—Continued.

August 15, 1846.—*Camp* 43, *Vernal Spring.*

DETERMINATION OF TIME.

Time, p. m.	Double altitudes of Arcturûs in the west.	Chronometer fast.
h. m. s.	Deg. min. sec.	h. m. s.
3 25 03.0	87 14 30	7 32 35.7
3 25 59.0	86 51 40	7 32 35.5
3 26 57.1	86 28 30	7 32 36.7
3 27 45.2	86 08 50	7 32 36.5
3 28 26.7	85 51 30	7 32 35.4
3 29 09.8	85 33 55	7 32 35.3
3 29 57.3	85 15 10	7 32 36.7

Thermometer 68°.

Time, p. m.	Double altitudes of *a* Aquilæ in the east.	Chronometer fast.
h. m. s.	Deg. min. sec.	h. m. s.
3 33 34.8	101 18 30	7 32 30.9
3 34 31.1	101 38 25	7 32 30.3
3 35 34.1	101 58 30	7 32 32.3
3 36 23.0	102 14 30	7 32 32.8
3 37 10.5	102 30 05	7 32 32.8
3 38 15.0	102 51 40	7 32 31.2
3 39 17.0	103 11 15	7 32 33.2

Thermometer 65°.

		h. m. s.
Chronometer fast by 7 observations of east star		7 32 31.93
" " " 7 " west star		35.97
Mean......................		7 32 33.95

Ex. Doc. No. 41.   247

APPENDIX No. 5—Continued.

August 15, 1846.—*Camp* 43.

DETERMINATION OF LATITUDE.

Time, p. m.	Double altitudes of Polaris.	Latitude.
h. m. s.	*Deg. min. sec.*	*Deg. min. sec.*
3 48 13.5	69 50 40	35 23 05
3 49 19.5	69 51 30	35 23 06
3 50 03.2	69 52 15	35 23 12
3 51 08.5	69 53 30	35 23 25
3 51 59.2	69 54 25	35 23 32
3 53 06.0	69 54 55	35 23 23
3 53 59.0	69 55 25	35 23 10
3 54 54.0	69 56 20	35 23 03
3 55 49.5	69 57 00	35 23 24

Thermometer 65°.

Mean of 9 observations, 35° 23′ 19″.

APPENDIX No. 5—Continued.

August 19, 1846.—*Santa Fé.*

DETERMINATION OF TIME.

Time, p. m.	Double altitudes of *a* Coronæ Borealis in the west.	Chronometer fast.
h. m. s.	*Deg. min. sec.*	*h. m. s.*
4 32 23.0	93 16 00	7 34 49.3 rej.
4 33 37.7	92 47 05	7 34 52.8
4 34 35.0	92 23 40	7 34 52.4
4 35 26.8	92 02 00	7 34 50.9
4 36 20.0	91 41 05	7 34 52.5
4 37 12.9	91 18 50	7 34 50.7
4 38 31.7	90 48 20	7 34 54.4 rej
4 39 26.0	90 24 35	7 34 50.1
4 40 23.0	90 01 40	7 34 50.6

Thermometer 60°.

Time, p. m.	Double altitudes of *a* Pegasi in the east.	Chronometer fast.
h. m. s.	*Deg. min. sec.*	*h. m. s.*
5 10 46.0	77 41 25	7 34 62.7 rej.
5 11 51.2	78 10 00	7 34 55.5
5 12 39.6	78 28 25	7 34 57.9
5 13 38.8	78 51 20	7 34 59.5 rej.
5 14 22.0	79 10 00	7 34 56.0
5 15 19.0	79 33 20	7 34 54.4
5 16 23.8	79 57 20	7 34 54.5
5 17 31.2	80 23 20	7 34 61 2 rej.
5 18 32.5	80 49 30	7 34 56.8

Thermometer 59°.

                                                                                                 h. m. s.
Chronometer fast by 6 observations of east star.... 7 34 55.82
Chronometer fast by 7 observations of west star...   51.43

               Mean....................... 7 34 53.62

APPENDIX No. 5—Continued.

August 19, 1846.—*Santa Fé.*

DETERMINATION OF LATITUDE.

Time, p. m.	Double altitudes of Polaris.	Latitude.
h. m. s.	Deg. min. sec.	Deg. min. sec.
5 24 20.0	71 51 10	35 40 47 rej.
5 25 34.0	71 52 40	35 41 03
5 26 51.0	71 53 50	35 41 09
5 27 52.5	71 54 40	35 41 11
5 28 47.0	71 55 40	35 41 18
5 30 07.5	71 56 30	35 41 12
5 30 55.2	71 57 10	35 41 13
5 31 28.0	71 57 55	35 41 23

Thermometer 59°.

Mean of 7 observations, 35° 41' 13''.

APPENDIX No. 5—Continued.

August 20, 1846.—Santa Fé.

DETERMINATION OF TIME.

Time, p. m.	Double altitudes of Coronæ Borealis.	Chronometer fast.
h. m. s.	Deg. min. sec.	
3 40 19.0	93 25 45	
3 41 49.5	92 47 10	
3 43 04.7	92 17 50	

Time, p. m.	Double altitudes of Arcturus in the west.	Chronometer fast.
h. m. s.	Deg. min sec.	
3 44 54.5	72 01 20	
3 45 46.2	71 40 30	
3 46 46.2	71 17 00	
3 47 36.2	70 56 10	
3 48 28.0	70 35 40	
3 49 26.9	70 11 00	
3 50 18.0	69 50 25	
3 51 09.8	69 29 50	
3 52 01.0	69 08 50	

Thermometer 62°.

Ex. Doc. No. 41. 251

APPENDIX No. 5—Continued.

August 20, 1846—*Santa Fé.*

DETERMINATION OF LATITUDE.

Time, p. m.	Double altitudes of Polaris.	Latitude.
h. m. s.	*Deg. min. sec.*	*Deg. min. sec.*
3 57 08.4	70 46 30	35 41 17
3 58 20.2	70 47 20	35 41 14
3 59 14.0	70 47 50	35 41 11
3 59 50.0	70 48 30	35 41 14
4 50 47.8	70 49 30	35 41 21
4 01 18.5	70 49 50	35 41 19
4 01 57.5	70 50 10	35 41 15
4 02 56.0	70 51 05	35 41 27
4 03 12.0	70 51 10	35 41 25

Thermometer 62°.

Mean of 9 observations, 35° 41′ 13″.

APPENDIX No. 5—Continued.

August 21, 1846.—*Santa Fé.*

Time, a. m.			Double altitudes of the sun's upper limb.	
h.	*m.*	*s.*	*Deg.*	*min.*
5	09	35.5	98	50
5	10	04.0	99	00
5	10	58.0	99	20
5	11	25.5	99	30
5	11	53.8	99	40
5	12	21.5	99	50
5	12	47.8	100	00
5	13	44.0	100	20
5	14	12.5	100	30
5	14	39.2	100	40

Thermometer 68°.

Ex. Doc. No. 41. 253

APPENDIX No. 5—Continued.

August 22, 1846.—*Santa Fé.*

DETERMINATION OF TIME.

Time, a. m.—August 23.	Double altitudes of sun's upper limb.	Time, p. m.—Aug. 22.	Chronometer fast.
h. m. s.	*Deg. min.*	*h. m. s.*	*h. m. s.*
4 57 26.0	93 40	10 18 08.2	7 34 46.44
4 56 58.0	93 30	10 18 36.8	7 34 46.82
4 56 31.3	93 20	10 19 02.8	7 34 46.55
4 56 05.0	93 10	10 19 28.7	7 34 46.42
4 55 38.5	93 00	10 19 55.6	7 34 46.70
4 55 11.2	92 50	10 20 22.5	7 34 46.50
4 54 44.5	92 40	10 20 50.0	7 34 47.03
4 54 17.5	92 30	10 21 15.0	7 34 46.10

Thermometer 64°.

Mean of 8 observations, 7*h.* 34*m.* 46.58*s.*

APPENDIX No.5—Continued.

August 22, 1846.—*Santa Fé*.

DETERMINATION OF TIME.

Time, a. m.			Double altitudes of sun's upper limb.	
h.	*m.*	*s.*	*Deg.*	*min.*
5	19	22.8	102	00
5	19	51.0	102	10
5	20	19.8	102	20
5	20	43.8	102	30
5	21	10.0	102	40
5	21	43.5	102	50
5	22	13.0	103	00
5	22	40.5	103	10
5	23	08.5	103	20
5	23	36.0	103	30
5	24	05.4	103	40
5	24	34.0	103	50
5	25	03.0	104	00

Thermometer 60°.

Ex. Doc. No. 41.   255

APPENDIX No. 5—Continued.

August 22, 1846.—*Santa Fé.*

Time, p. m.			Double altitude of Coronæ Borealis.		
h.	*m.*	*s.*	*Deg.*	*min.*	*sec.*
4	29	08.0	89	46	50
4	30	17.0	89	19	20
4	31	14.0	88	55	10
4	31	55.3	88	59	00
4	32	48.1	88	18	20
4	33	56.7	87	50	00
4	34	58.1	87	25	00
4	35	43.2	87	06	50
4	36	32.8	86	46	20

Thermometer 64°.

Time, p. m.			Double altitudes of *a* Pegasi.		
h.	*m.*	*s.*	*Deg.*	*min.*	*sec.*
5	43	19.5	95	12	35
5	44	20.5	95	35	40
5	45	24.9	96	01	05
5	46	02.0	96	14	15
5	46	48.0	96	32	30
5	47	30.0	96	48	50
5	48	18.0	97	07	00
5	49	06.8	97	26	00
5	49	57.5	97	45	25

Thermometer 64°.

Ex. Doc. No. 41.

APPENDIX No. 5—Continued.

August 22, 1846.—*Santa Fé*.

Time, p. m.			Double altitudes of *a* Aquilæ near the meridian.		
h.	*m.*	*s.*	*Deg.*	*min.*	*sec.*
5	00	33.0	125	16	05
5	01	29.5	125	18	05
5	02	32.0	125	21	00
5	03	39.3	125	23	55
5	04	54.0	125	27	20
5	06	20.8	125	30	15
5	07	18.0	125	31	30
5	08	21.5	125	33	10
5	09	17.5	125	33	50
5	10	04.8	125	34	20
5	11	10.6	125	35	40
5	14	10.0	125	38	40
5	16	12.0	125	37	40
5	17	28.4	125	36	55
5	18	15.5	125	35	00
5	21	14.2	125	32	20
5	22	39.5	125	29	00
5	23	50.0	125	23	40
5	25	16.5	125	21	05
5	26	37.0	125	17	00

Thermometer 64°.

APPENDIX No. 5—Continued.

August 23, 1846.—*Santa Fé.*

DETERMINATION OF TIME.

Time, a. m.	Double altitudes of sun's upper limb.	Time, p. m.	Chronometer fast.
h. m. s.	*Deg. min.*	*h. m. s.*	*h. m. s.*
4 54 17.5	92 30	10 19 46.5	7 34 44.54
4 54 44.5	92 40	10 19 19.8	7 34 44.69
4 55 11.2	92 50	10 18 54.0	7 34 45.13
4 55 38.5	93 00	10 18 26.6	7 34 45.07
4 56 05.0	93 10	10 17 50.5	7 34 45.26
4 56 31.3	93 20	10 17 34.0	7 34 45.15
4 56 58.0	93 30	10 17 05.8	7 34 44.39
4 57 26.0	93 40	10 16 39.4	7 34 45.10
4 57 52.0	93 50	10 16 13.5	7 34 45.22
4 58 20.1	94 00	10 15 47.1	7 34 46.02
4 58 45.8	94 10	10 15 19.7	7 34 45.21
4 59 15.5	94 20	10 14 52.5	7 34 45.45
4 59 39.8	94 30	10 14 24.0	7 34 44.35

Thermometer 69°.

Mean of 13 observations, 7*h.* 34*m.* 45.05*s.*

APPENDIX No. 5—Continued.

August 23, 1846.—*Santa Fé.*

DETERMINATION OF LATITUDE.

Time, p. m.	Double altitudes of α Aquilæ, near the meridian.	Latitude.
h. m. s.	Deg. min. sec.	Deg. min. sec.
4 59 37.0	125 24 40	35 40 22
5 00 47.0	125 26 00	35 41 00 rej.
5 01 38.8	125 28 55	35 40 23
5 02 57.8	125 30 40	35 40 39
5 03 50.7	125 32 00	35 40 38
5 04 51.5	125 33 20	35 40 37
5 06 17.0	125 34 30	35 40 44
5 07 22.5	125 35 25	35 40 39
5 09 24.5	125 36 00	35 40 41
5 10 42.0	125 36 10	35 40 34
5 11 41.0	125 36 10	35 40 25
5 12 31.5	125 36 00	35 40 17
5 13 47.5	125 34 50	35 40 22
5 15 35.6	125 33 00	35 40 17
5 16 42.3	125 30 10	35 40 54 rej.
5 17 58.5	125 27 50	35 40 58 rej.
5 19 12.5	125 26 05	35 40 36
5 20 10.0	125 23 40	35 40 43

Thermometer 69°.

Mean of 15 observations, 35° 40′ 32″.

APPENDIX No. 5—Continued.

August 24, 1846 —*Santa Fè*.

Time, a. m.			Double altitudes of sun's upper limb.	
h.	*m.*	*s.*	*Deg.*	*min.*
4	55	39.0	92	40
4	56	04.0	92	50
4	56	32.2	93	00
4	56	59.0	93	10
4	57	25.8	93	20
4	57	53.8	93	30
4	58	19.7	93	40
4	58	47.0	93	50
4	59	14.5	94	00
4	59	42.1	94	10
5	00	08.5	94	20

Thermometer 68°.

APPENDIX No. 5—Continued.

August 28, 1846—*Santa Fé.*

Time, p. m.			Double altitudes of sun's upper limb.		Time, a. m.—August 29.		
h.	m.	s.	Deg.	min.	h.	m.	s.
10	45	22.0	80	00	4	26	24.5
10	45	48.1	79	50	4	25	58.5
10	46	14.5	79	40	4	25	32.5
10	46	40.0	79	30	4	25	05.5
10	47	07.5	79	20	4	24	39.2
10	47	32.0	79	10	4	24	14.5
10	47	58.2	79	00	4	23	47.5
10	48	21.8	78	50	4	23	21.2
10	48	51.8	78	40	4	22	55.5
10	49	16.4	78	30	4	22	29.0
10	49	42.7	78	20	4	22	03.4
10	50	08.6	78	10	4	21	35.3
10	50	34.6	78	00	4	21	12.2
10	51	00.0	77	50	4	20	44.5
10	51	26.2	77	40	4	20	18.8
10	51	52.5	77	30	4	19	53.0

Thermometer 70°.   Thermometer 66°.

APPENDIX No. 5—Continued.

August 29, 1846.—Santa Fe.

DETERMINATION OF LONGITUDE.

Time, p. m.	Distance of a Aquilæ from moon's western limb.	Double altitudes of moon's lower limb.
h. m. s.	Deg. min. sec.	Deg. min. sec.
3 05 55.0	55 49 50	60 38 10
3 07 05.0	55 49 00	60 25 10
3 09 59.0	55 48 00	59 53 50
3 12 03.8	55 46 55	59 33 30
3 15 12.0	55 45 45	58 55 30
3 17 00.0	55 45 20	58 35 30
3 19 05.6	55 44 20	58 11 20
3 21 19.0	55 43 40	57 45 40

Thermometer 69°.

APPENDIX No. 5—Continued.

August 29, 1846.—*Santa Fé.*

DETERMINATION OF TIME.

Time, a. m.	Double altitudes of sun's upper limb.	Time, p. m.	Chronometer fast.
h. m. s.	Deg. min.	h. m. s.	h. m. s.
4 26 24.5	80 00	10 43 51.5	7 34 31.65
4 25 58.5	79 50	10 44 18.8	7 34 32.31
4 25 32.5	79 40	10 44 44.6	7 34 32.22
4 25 05.5	79 30	10 45 10.6	7 34 31.73
4 24 39.2	79 20	10 45 38.0	7 34 32.29
4 24 14.5	79 10	10 46 03.8	7 34 32.84
4 23 47.5	79 00	10 46 30.0	7 34 32.45
4 23 21.2	78 50	10 46 55.8	7 34 32.21
4 22 55.5	78 40	10 47 21.5	7 34 32.22
4 22 29.0	78 30	10 47 47.0	7 34 31.73
4 22 03.4	78 20	10 48 13.5	7 34 32.18
4 21 35.3	78 10	10 48 40.0	7 34 31.39
4 21 12.2	78 00	10 49 05.8	7 34 32.75
4 20 44.5	77 50	10 49 31.8	7 34 31.91
4 20 18.8	77 40	10 49 57.8	7 34 31.67
4 19 53.0	77 30	10 50 24.2	7 34 32.38
Thermom. 66°.		Thermom. 72°.	

Mean of 16 observations, 7*h*. 54*m*. 32.12*s*.

Ex. Doc. No. 41. 263

APPENDIX No. 5—Continued.

August 29, 1846.—*Santa Fe.*

DETERMINATION OF LATITUDE.

Time, p. m.	Double altitudes of Polaris.	Latitude.
h. m. s.	Deg. min. sec.	Deg. min. sec.
5 22 59.8	72 22 05	35 41 35
5 23 50.5	72 22 20	35 41 20
5 24 54.0	72 23 10	35 41 23
5 25 30.0	72 24 00	35 41 34
5 26 21.5	72 24 30	35 41 30
5 27 04.8	72 25 30	35 41 44
5 27 58.5	72 26 00	35 41 39
5 28 57.0	72 26 40	35 41 37
5 29 42.5	72 27 05	35 41 33

Thermometer 68°.

Mean of 9 observations, 35° 41′ 33″.

APPENDIX No. 5—Continued.

August 29, 1846.—*Santa Fe.*

DETERMINATION OF LATITUDE.

Time, p. m.	Double altitudes of *b* Aquarii, near the meridian.	Latitude.
h. m. s.	*Deg. min. sec.*	*Deg. min. sec.*
6 23 30.0	96 10 15	35 40 56
6 24 16.8	96 10 25	35 41 09
6 25 13.8	96 10 30	35 41 11
6 26 46.8	96 10 30	35 41 11
6 27 32.0	96 11 15	35 40 44
6 28 22.8	96 11 00	35 40 43
6 29 04.7	96 10 20	35 40 54
6 29 34.2	96 09 55	35 40 58
6 30 15.5	96 09 25	35 41 01
6 30 59.0	96 58 30	35 41 12
6 31 33.5	96 08 00	35 41 12

Thermometer 66°

Mean of 11 observations, 35° 41′ 01″.

Ex. Doc. No. 41.   265

APPENDIX No. 5—Continued.

August 29, 1846.—*Santa Fe.*

DETERMINATION OF LATITUDE.

Time, p. m.	Double altitudes of a Aquarii, near the meridian.	Latitude
h. m. s.	Deg. min. sec.	Deg. min. sec.
6 51 57.5	106 26 30	35 40 49
6 53 23.0	106 28 10	35 40 56
6 54 36.8	106 29 40	35 40 52
6 55 44.0	106 30 55	35 40 45
6 57 42.0	106 32 30	35 40 35
6 58 56.1	106 32 10	35 40 57
7 01 45.8	106 32 00	35 41 01
7 03 19.2	106 31 30	35 40 57
7 04 11.0	106 30 50	35 41 01
7 05 00.0	106 29 55	35 41 09
7 06 10.8	106 28 30	35 41 18
7 07 20.0	106 27 30	35 41 08
7 08 38.4	106 26 30	35 40 45
7 09 22.8	106 24 45	35 41 05

Thermometer 66°.

Mean of 14 observations, 35° 40′ 57″.

Ex. Doc. No. 41.

APPENDIX No. 5—Continued.

August 29, 1846.—Santa Fe.

DETERMINATION OF LONGITUDE.

Time, p. m.	Distance of α Aquilæ from moon's west limb.	Longitude.
h. m. s.	*Deg. min. sec.*	*h. m. s.*
3 05 55.0	55 49 50	7 05 52.5 rej.
3 07 05.0	55 49 00	7 04 25.1
3 09 59.0	55 48 00	7 04 41.8
3 12 03.8	55 46 55	7 03 48.4
3 15 12.0	55 45 45	7 03 51.1
3 17 00.0	55 45 20	7 04 33.8
3 19 05.6	55 44 20	7 03 59.1
3 21 19.0	55 43 40	7 04 25.8

August 30, 1846.—Santa Fe.

Time, p. m.	Distance of Antares from moon's west limb.	Longitude.
h. m. s.	*Deg. min. sec.*	*h. m. s.*
3 42 09.0	16 15 55	7 04 39.7
3 43 39.8	16 16 40	7 04 02.2
3 48 23.8	16 18 20	7 03 59.3
3 50 33.5	16 18 50	7 04 42.6
3 51 48.0	16 19 20	7 04 28.2
3 52 49.1	16 19 40	7 04 36.8
3 55 59.5	16 20 30	7 04 22.4
3 56 57.5	16 21 15	7 04 08.0

	h. m. s.
Longitude by 7 observations of α Aquilæ	7 04 14.73
" 8 " Antares	7 04 22.40
Mean.......................	7 04 18.56

APPENDIX No. 5—Continued.

September 1, 1846.—*Santa Fe.*

DETERMINATION OF TIME.

Time, p. m.	Double altitudes of *a* Coronæ Borealis.	Chronometer fast.
h. m. s.	Deg. min. sec.	
3 29 17.8	97 57 35	
3 30 52.0	97 20 00	
3 31 40.1	97 00 15	
3 32 32.5	96 39 10	
3 33 32.0	96 14 30	
3 34 26.0	95 53 10	
3 36 32.1	95 01 30	

Time, p. m.	Double altitudes of *a* Aquarii, in the east.	Chronometer fast.
h. m. s.	Deg. min. sec.	
3 53 23.8	92 10 30	
3 54 28.6	92 34 00	
3 55 16.5	92 51 40	
3 56 07.6	93 09 50	
3 57 08.8	93 31 20	
3 57 50.5	93 46 30	
3 58 34.3	94 02 15	

Thermometer 70°.

APPENDIX No. 5—Continued.

September 4, 1846.—*Camp* 49, *on the Rio del Norte, near the Alalavo.*

DETERMINATION OF TIME.

Time, p. m.	Double altitudes of *a* Aquilæ in the east.	Chronometer fast.
h. m. s.	*Deg. min. sec.*	*h. m. s.*
2 41 22.8	108 33 40	7 37 03.0
2 42 06.5	108 46 35	7 37 04.0
2 43 00.5	109 02 40	7 37 04.7
2 43 42.0	109 14 55	7 37 05.4

Thermometer 64°.

Time, p. m.	Double altitudes of Arcturus in the west.	Chronometer fast.
h. m. s.	*Deg. min. sec.*	*h. m. s.*
2 53 28.8	69 52 00	7 37 06.2
2 54 15.5	69 34 15	7 37 07.5
2 55 10.0	69 09 20	7 37 03.2 rej.
2 56 11.9	68 45 40	7 37 07.2
2 57 07.0	68 23 00	7 37 06.9
2 58 09.8	67 57 55	7 37 08.5
2 59 04.0	67 35 35	7 37 08.0
2 59 58.4	66 13 00	7 37 07.2
3 00 49.0	65 52 50	7 37 07.7

Thermometer 64°.

	h. m. s.
Chronometer fast by 4 obs. of east star............	7 37 04.28
Chronometer fast by 8 obs. of west star..........	07.40
Mean........................	7 37 05.84

APPENDIX No. 5—Continued.

September 4, 1846.—*Camp* 49, *on the Rio del Norte, near the Alalavo.*

DETERMINATION OF LATITUDE.

Time, p. m.	Double altitudes of Polaris.	Latitude.
h. m. s.	Deg. min. sec.	Deg. min. sec.
3 06 11.0	69 51 35	35 11 19
3 07 03.0	69 52 25	35 11 21
3 08 35.5	69 53 35	35 11 17
3 09 45.0	69 54 20	35 11 18
3 10 51.3	69 55 10	35 11 17
3 11 48.5	69 56 00	35 11 20
3 12 44.0	69 56 30	35 11 13
3 13 20.0	69 57 10	35 11 20
3 13 56.8	69 57 55	35 11 32
3 14 54.5	69 58 30	35 11 21
3 15 30.3	69 59 00	35 11 22
3 16 19.0	69 59 40	35 11 25
3 17 03.4	70 00 00	35 11 18

Thermometer 64°.

Mean of 13 observations, 35° 11′ 20″.

Ex. Doc. No. 41.

APPENDIX No. 5—Continued.

September 6, 1846.—*Peralta, about* 500 *feet north of the Charois chapel.*

DETERMINATION OF TIME.

Time, p. m.	Double altitudes of a Coronæ Borealis.	Chronometer fast.
h. m. s.	Deg. min. sec.	h. m. s.
5 36 42.2	87 58 00	7 37 15.9
3 37 43.6	87 31 55	7 37 13.6
3 38 44.0	87 07 45	7 37 14.9
3 39 37.1	86 46 15	7 37 15.4
3 40 42.5	86 19 45	7 37 15.8
3 41 46.0	85 53 10	7 37 14.4
3 43 09.0	85 19 00	7 37 13.7
3 44 14.3	84 51 50	7 37 12.5
3 45 01.2	84 33 20	7 37 14.0
3 46 12.8	84 03 50	7 37 13.4
3 47 12.3	83 39 40	7 37 13.6
3 48 03.8	83 18 50	7 37 14.1

Thermometer 60°.

Mean of 12 observations, 7h. 37m. 14.28s.

APPENDIX No. 5—Continued.

September 6, 1846.—*Peralta.*

DETERMINATION OF LATITUDE.

Time, p. m.	Double altitudes of Polaris.	Latitude.
h. m. s.	Deg. min. sec.	Deg. min. sec.
3 53 54.0	69 54 30	34 50 49
3 56 13.5	69 56 30	34 50 55
3 57 39.0	69 57 10	34 50 56
3 58 52.8	69 58 40	34 50 56
4 00 03.7	69 59 40	34 50 59
4 01 09.2	70 00 45	34 51 06
4 02 16.8	70 01 20	34 50 57
4 11 29.2	70 07 55	34 50 58
4 12 37.5	70 09 40	34 51 05
4 13 30.2	70 10 10	34 50 59
4 14 51.0	70 10 50	34 50 47
4 15 52.5	70 11 55	34 50 55
4 16 58.1	70 13 00	34 51 03

Thermometer 56°.

Mean of 13 observations, 34° 50′ 57″.

APPENDIX No. 5—Continued.

September 6, 1846.—*Peralta.*

DETERMINATION OF TIME.

Time, p. m.	Double altitudes of *a* Pegasi, in the east.	Chronometer fast.
h. m. s.	*Deg. min. sec.*	*h. m. s.*
4 36 53.8	91 52 10	7 37 15.2
4 37 44.5	92 12 10	7 37 15.1
4 38 31.5	92 31 00	7 37 14.3
4 39 14.0	92 47 50	7 37 14.0
4 40 03.9	93 07 30	7 37 13.8
4 41 16.3	93 35 30	7 37 14.9
4 42 16.5	93 59 40	7 37 13.5
4 43 30.8	94 29 10	7 37 12.5
4 44 29.7	94 51 40	7 37 13.9

	h. min. sec.
Chronometer fast by 9 obs. of east star..........	7 37 14.13
Chronometer fast by 12 obs. of west star..........	14.28
Mean	7 37 14.20

APPENDIX No. 5—Continued.

September 10, 1846.—*Camp* 55, *on the Rio del Norte, about one mile south of San Felippe.*

DETERMINATION OF LATITUDE.

Time, p. m.	Double altitudes of Polaris.	Latitude.
h. m. s.	Deg. min. sec.	Deg. min. sec.
3 01 13.1	70 34 10	35 24 47 rej.
3 02 04.2	70 36 10	35 25 37
3 02 56.2	70 36 50	35 25 37
3 03 42.8	70 37 30	35 25 35
3 04 25.5	70 37 30	35 25 32
3 05 25.5	70 38 40	35 25 33
3 06 11.1	70 39 15	35 25 33
3 07 35.2	70 40 05	35 25 23
3 08 48.0	70 40 40	35 25 15

Thermometer 52°.

Mean of 8 observations, 35° 25′ 30″.

Ex. Doc. No. 41.

APPENDIX No. 5—Continued.

September 10, 1846.—*Camp* 55.

DETERMINATION OF TIME.

Time, p. m.	Double altitudes of a Coronæ Borealis, in the west.	Chronometer fast.
h. m. s.	Deg. min. sec.	h. m. s.
3 13 37.8	89 47 05	7 36 06.6
3 16 43.0	89 20 50	7 36 07.3
3 17 34.9	88 59 40	7 36 07.1
3 18 28.7	88 37 45	7 36 06.7
3 19 30.7	88 12 50	7 36 08.6
3 20 37.4	87 44 45	7 36 05.3
3 21 27.0	87 24 15	7 36 04.6

Time, p. m.	Double altitudes of a Pegasi, in the east.	Chronometer fast.
h. m. s.	Deg. min. sec.	h. m. s.
3 47 10.1	78 32 10	7 36 03.4
3 48 00.0	78 51 30	7 36 05.2
3 48 37.5	79 14 20	7 36 05.7
3 50 07.5	79 42 10	7 36 06.3
3 51 04.2	80 05 50	7 36 05.8
3 51 44.5	80 21 20	7 36 05.4
3 52 48.5	80 46 50	7 36 05.4
3 53 49.8	81 11 05	7 36 05.4

Thermometer 52°.

	h. m. s.
Chronometer fast by 8 obs. of east star............	7 36 05.19
Chronometer fast by 7 obs. of west star	06.60
Mean...................	7 36 05.90

Ex. Doc. No. 41. 275

APPENDIX No. 5—Continued.

September 13, 1846.—*Santa Fe.*

DETERMINATION OF TIME.

Time, a. m.	Double altitudes of sun's upper limb.	Chronometer fast.
h. m. s.	Deg. min. sec.	h. m. s.
4 31 12.0	76 30 00	7 33 54.2
4 31 39.8	76 40 00	7 33 54.4
4 32 07.5	76 50 00	7 33 54.3
4 32 35.8	77 00 00	7 33 54.9
4 33 02.3	77 10 00	7 33 53.6
4 33 32.0	77 20 00	7 33 55.5
4 34 00.2	77 30 00	7 33 55.9
4 34 27.2	77 40 00	7 33 55.0
4 34 54.8	77 50 00	7 33 54.7
4 35 22.7	78 00 00	7 33 55.7
4 35 51.1	78 10 00	7 33 55.1
4 36 19.0	78 20 00	7 33 55.1
4 36 46.5	78 30 00	7 33 54.6

Thermometer 59°.

Mean of 13 observations, 7*h.* 33*m.* 54.78*s.*

DETERMINATION OF INDEX ERROR.

	Min. sec.	Min. sec.
On the arc..........................	31 20	31 40
Off the arc.........................	31 50	31 50

Index error = + 10″.

Ex. Doc. No. 41.

APPENDIX No. 5—Continued.

September 13, 1846.—*Santa Fe.*

DETERMINATION OF TIME.

Time, a. m.	Double altitudes of sun's upper limb.	Chronometer fast.
h. m. s.	*Deg. min. sec.*	*h. m. s.*
10 53 10.2	67 10 00	7 33 53.4
10 53 37.5	67 00 00	7 33 54.1
10 54 03.0	66 50 00	7 33 53.1
10 54 30.3	66 40 00	7 33 53.8
10 54 56.3	66 30 00	7 33 53.3
10 55 22.7	66 20 00	7 33 53.2
10 55 49.0	66 10 00	7 33 53.0
10 56 15.2	66 00 00	7 33 52.7
10 56 41.0	65 50 00	7 33 52.1
10 57 08.4	65 40 00	7 33 53.0
10 57 36.5	65 30 00	7 33 54.7
10 58 01.0	65 20 00	7 33 52.7
10 58 29.2	65 10 00	7 33 54.5

Thermometer 74°.

Mean of 13 observations, 7*h.* 33*m.* 53.50*s.*

APPENDIX No. 5—Continued.

September 17, 1846.—*Santa Fe.*

Time, a. m., Sept. 18.	Double altitudes of the sun's upper limb.	Time, p. m.
h. m. s.	Deg. min.	h. m. s.
4 48 02.0	80 20	10 09 13.0
4 47 32.8	80 10	10 09 42.6
4 47 02.0	80 00	10 10 11.0
4 46 34.0	79 50	10 10 42.0
4 46 04.2	79 40	10 11 10.2
4 45 36.0	79 30	10 11 39.5
4 45 06.8	79 20	10 12 09.4
	79 10	10 12 38.8
	79 00	10 13 07.5
Thermometer 68°.		Thermometer 72°.

Ex. Doc. No. 41.

APPENDIX No. 5—Continued.

September 17, 1846.—*Santa Fe.*

DETERMINATION OF LATITUDE.

Time, p. m.			Double altitudes of b Aquarii, near the meridian.			Latitude.		
h.	*m.*	*s.*	*Deg.*	*min.*	*sec.*	*Deg.*	*min.*	*sec.*
5	02	37.0	96	06	55	35	40	34
5	04	14.0	96	08	40	35	40	35
5	05	29.0	96	09	30	35	40	44
5	06	48.9	96	10	20	35	40	46
5	08	05.5	96	11	05	35	40	42
5	09	57.5	96	11	20	35	40	47
5	11	39.8	96	11	20	35	40	44
5	13	09.0	96	11	15	35	40	33
5	14	29.5	96	09	55	35	40	51
5	16	00.0	96	08	50	35	40	50
5	17	29.8	96	07	20	35	40	50
5	19	06.8	96	05	10	35	40	55

Thermometer 60°.

Mean of 12 observations, 35° 40' 44".

Ex. Doc. No. 41.

APPENDIX No. 5—Continued.

September 17, 1846.—Santa Fe.

DETERMINATION OF LATITUDE.

Time, p. m.	Double altitudes of Polaris.	Latitude.
h. m. s.	Deg. min. sec.	Deg. min. sec.
5 26 53.8	73 16 20	35 41 11
5 28 25.8	73 17 20	35 41 12
5 29 40.0	73 18 15	35 41 18
5 30 59.5	73 19 20	35 41 26
5 32 11.0	73 20 20	35 41 34
5 33 48.0	73 21 10	35 41 30
5 35 31.8	73 22 40	35 41 43
5 36 37.8	73 23 35	35 41 45
5 39 05.5	73 24 15	35 41 26
5 41 01.0	73 25 40	35 41 34

Thermometer 60°.

Mean of 9 observations, 35° 41′ 30″.

By North Star.				By South Star.			
	Deg. min. sec.				Deg. min. sec.		
Aug. 19..	35 41 13	7 obs.		Aug. 25..	35 40 32	15 obs.	
" 20..	35 41 18	9 "		" 29..	35 41 01	11 "	
" 29..	35 41 33	9 "		" 29..	35 40 57	14 "	
Sept. 17..	35 41 30	9 "		Sept. 17..	35 40 44	12 "	
Mean..	35 41 23.5			Mean..	35 40 48.5		

Mean of north, and south 35° 41′ 06″, latitude of Santa Fé.

APPENDIX No. 5—Continued.

September 18, 1846.—*Santa Fe.*

Time, a. m.			Double altitudes of sun's upper limb.	
h.	*m.*	*s.*	*Deg.*	*min.*
4	45	06.8	79	20
4	45	36.0	79	30
4	46	04.2	79	40
4	46	34.0	79	50
4	47	02.0	80	00
4	47	32.8	80	10
4	48	02.0	80	20
4	48	30.5	80	30
4	49	00.5	80	40
4	49	30.0	80	50
4	49	58.0	81	00

Thermometer 68°.

Ex. Doc. No. 41. 281

APPENDIX No. 5—Continued.

September 21, 1846.—Santa Fe.

DETERMINATION OF TIME.

Time, a. m.—Sept. 22.	Double altitudes of sun's upper limb.	Time, p. m.	Chronometer fast.
h. m. s.	Deg. min.	h. m. s.	h. m. s.
4 41 25.5	76 20	10 12 47.0	7 33 38.18
4 40 58.6	76 10	10 13 14.8	7 33 37.26
4 40 29.2	76 00	10 13 46.2	7 33 38.39
4 40 01.0	75 50	10 14 14.3	7 33 38.48
4 39 31.5	75 40	10 14 42.9	7 33 38.16
4 39 03.0	75 30	10 14 12.6	7 33 38.99
Thermom. 65.		Thermom. 74°.	

Mean of 6 observations, $7h.\ 33m.\ 38.24s.$

Ex. Doc. No. 41.

APPENDIX No. 5—Continued.

September 22, 1846.—*Santa Fe.*

Time, a. m.			Double altitudes of sun's upper limb.	
h.	*m.*	*s.*	*Deg.*	*min.*
4	38	38.8	75	20
4	39	03.0	75	30
4	39	31.5	75	40
4	40	01.0	75	50
4	40	29.2	76	00
4	40	58.6	76	10
4	41	28.5	76	20
4	41	59.5	76	30
4	42	27.5	76	40
4	42	57.0	76	50
Lost by clouds.			77	00

Thermometer 65°.

Ex. Doc. No. 41. 283

APPENDIX No. 5—Continued.

September 23, 1846.—*Santa Fe.*

DETERMINATION OF TIME.

Time, p. m.	Double altitudes of *a* Andromedæ, in the east.	Chronometer fast.
h. m. s.	Deg. min. sec.	h. m. s.
5 03 21.8	119 03 15	7 33 35.7
5 04 29.0	119 30 35	7 33 35.6
5 05 29.0	119 54 40	7 33 36.3
5 06 36.8	120 22 45	7 33 34.9
5 07 27.0	120 42 10	7 33 37.2
5 08 10.8	121 04 05	7 33 36.0
5 09 11.0	121 22 10	7 33 42.6 rej.
5 09 54.1	121 41 25	7 33 38.2
5 10 36.3	121 58 55	7 33 37.2
5 11 36.5	122 23 50	7 33 36.0

Thermometer 62°.

Time, p. m.	Double altitudes of *a* Lyræ, in the west.	Chronometer fast.
h. m. s.	Deg. min. sec.	h. m. s.
5 14 47.5	101 07 00	7 33 37.3
5 15 44.0	100 43 50	7 33 33.4 rej.
5 16 32.8	100 26 20	7 33 36.5
5 17 20.5	100 07 30	7 33 34.9
5 18 10.5	99 48 20	7 33 34.9
5 19 01.8	99 27 55	7 33 32.8 rej.
5 19 51.0	99 10 05	7 33 35.4
5 20 52.8	98 46 20	7 33 35.0
6 21 49.5	98 25 20	7 33 36.1

Thermometer 62°.

	h. m. s.
Chronometer fast by 9 obs. of east star..........	7 33 36.34
Chronometer fast by 7 obs. of west star..........	35.81
Mean...............................	7 33 36.08

APPENDIX No. 5—Continued.

September 30, 1846.—*Camp* 62, *seven miles below Isolett, west bank Rio del Norte.*

DETERMINATION OF LONGITUDE.

Time, p. m.	Distance of Antares from moon's western limb.	Longitude.
h. m. s.	*Deg. min. sec.*	*h. m. s.*
3 04 20.8	67 11 30	7 08 40.9
3 06 18.6	67 12 15	7 09 06.1
3 11 05.8	67 13 20	7 06 41.4
3 14 13.5	67 14 20	7 07 44.3
3 16 04.2	67 14 50	7 07 25.4
3 18 14.5	67 15 40	7 07 53.7
3 20 08.5	67 16 30	7 08 37.8
3 21 48.5	67 17 05	7 08 47.2

Thermometer 48°.

Time, p. m.	Distance of *a* Pegasi from moon's western limb.	Longitude.
h. m. s.	*Deg. min. sec.*	*h. m. s.*
3 36 07.5	38 56 10	7 04 55.2
3 38 19.2	38 55 00	7 05 44.7
3 39 58.8	38 54 30	7 05 21.3
3 43 32.0	38 53 20	7 04 52.6
3 44 47.5	38 52 30	7 05 44.7
3 49 21.8	38 50 55	7 05 21.3
3 50 53.0	38 50 25	7 05 05.6
3 53 04.0	38 49 40	7 04 50.0

Thermometer 48°.

	h. m. s.
Longitude by 8 observations of Antares	7 08 07.10
Longitude by 8 observations of *a* Pegasi........	05 14.42
Mean.......................	7 06 40.76

Ex. Doc. No. 41.   285

APPENDIX No. 5—Continued.

September 30, 1846.—Camp 62.

DETERMINATION OF TIME.

Time, p. m.	Double altitudes of *a* Andromedæ, in the east.	Chronometer fast.
h. m. s.	Deg. min. sec.	h. m. s.
4 06 17.5	105 51 05	7 36 24.0
4 07 04.8	106 10 45	7 36 23.5
4 07 54.0	106 31 35	7 36 22.0
4 08 47.6	106 54 05	7 36 20.8
4 09 30.0	107 10 30	7 36 23.4
4 10 23.8	107 33 05	7 36 21.3
4 11 21.9	107 56 25	7 36 25.6

Thermometer 48°.

Time, p. m.	Double altitudes of *a* Lyræ, in the west.	Chronometer fast.
h. m. s.	Deg. min. sec.	h. m. s.
4 25 41.8	109 55 15	7 36 25.7
4 26 44.0	109 31 25	7 36 25.2
4 27 28.8	109 13 50	7 36 24.7
4 28 12.0	108 57 00	7 36 24.5
4 28 55.8	108 40 10	7 36 22.9
4 29 45.0	108 20 50	7 36 24.2
4 30 39.0	107 59 55	7 36 23.4

Thermometer 48°.

	h. m. s.
Chronometer fast by 7 observations of east star..	7 36 22.66
Chronometer fast by 7 observations of west star..	24.37
Mean..................	7 36 23.52

Ex. Doc. No. 41.

APPENDIX No. 5—Continued.

September 30, 1846.—*Camp* 62.

DETERMINATION OF LATITUDE.

Time, p. m.	Double altitudes of Polaris.	Latitude.
h. m. s.	*Deg. min. sec.*	*Deg. min. sec.*
4 35 38.0	71 29 50	34 48 28
4 42 11.0	71 34 00	34 48 34
4 43 09.0	71 34 40	34 48 36
4 44 10.0	71 35 20	34 48 37
4 44 46.0	71 35 40	34 48 34
4 45 18.5	71 36 05	34 48 36
4 46 16.8	71 36 35	34 48 34
4 47 21.5	71 36 55	34 48 24

Thermometer 48°.

Mean of 8 observations, 34° 48′ 33″.

Ex. Doc. No. 41. 287

APPENDIX No. 5—Continued.

October 4, 1846.—*Lamp* 65, *west bank Rio del Norte, about two miles below Linitans.*

LUNAR DISTANCE.

Time, p. m.	Fomalhaut and moon's western limb.	Double altitude of moon's lower limb.
h. m. s.	Deg. min. sec.	Deg. min. sec.
4 04 09.8	47 15 50	66 37 10
4 06 01.8	47 15 50	67 20 40
4 07 09.2	47 16 35	67 46 20
4 08 53.8	47 17 10	68 27 00
4 11 57.5	47 18 45	69 38 40
4 13 40.0	47 19 10	70 18 50
4 15 32.0	47 20 05	71 01 30
4 17 08.0	47 20 35	71 38 30

Time, p. m.	Aldebaran and moon's western limb.	Double altitude of moon's lower limb.
h. m. s.	Deg. min. sec.	Deg. min. sec.
4 28 56.5	51 59 05	76 09 40
4 31 05.0	51 58 40	76 58 40
4 32 46.0	51 57 45	77 36 10
4 34 43.0	51 56 30	78 19 50
4 36 58.0	51 56 10	79 10 30
4 38 35.0	51 55 35	79 47 50
4 40 27.0	51 54 55	80 38 50
4 41 41.5	51 54 10	80 57 00
4 43 13.0	51 53 40	81 31 30

Thermometer 60°.

APPENDIX No. 5—Continued.

October 4, 1846.—*Camp 65, west bank of the Rio del Norte.*

DETERMINATION OF LATITUDE.

Time, p. m.	Double altitudes of Polaris.	Latitude.
h. m. s.	*Deg. min. sec.*	*Deg. min. sec.*
2 22 50.5	68 42 50	34 07 27
2 24 00.0	68 44 00	34 07 34
2 24 50.0	68 44 55	34 07 42
2 26 07.8	68 45 55	34 07 40
2 27 14.2	68 46 50	34 07 42
2 28 16.2	68 47 45	34 07 45
2 28 58.0	68 48 20	34 07 46
2 30 09.8	68 49 10	34 07 47
2 30 58.7	68 49 50	34 07 44
2 31 36.5	68 50 10	34 07 39
2 32 19.8	68 50 35	34 07 34
2 33 09.0	68 51 10	34 07 32

Thermometer 64°.

Mean of 12 observations, 34° 07′ 59″.

APPENDIX No. 5—Continued.

October 4, 1846.—*Camp* 65, *west bank of the Rio del Norte.*

DETERMINATION OF TIME.

Time, p. m.	Double altitudes of *a* Andromedæ, in the east.	Chronometer fast.
h. m. s.	*Deg. min. sec.*	*h. m. s.*
3 01 27.9	85 21 25	7 36 51.0
3 02 21.8	85 43 50	7 36 49.7
3 03 01.2	85 58 30	7 36 53.8 rej.
3 03 54.0	86 21 15	7 36 51.1
3 04 42.5	86 41 25	7 36 50.5
3 07 23.0	87 45 45	7 36 50.2
3 08 23.0	88 12 05	7 36 50.1
3 09 10.5	88 31 50	7 36 49.6
3 09 45.8	88 46 20	7 36 49.5
3 10 31.5	89 04 50	7 36 50.1

Thermometer 62°.

Time, p. m.	Double altitudes of *a* Lyræ, in the west.	Chronometer fast.
h. m. s.	*Deg. min. sec.*	*h. m. s.*
3 46 00.0	118 58 50	7 36 52.2
3 46 58.8	118 35 35	7 36 51.3
3 47 59.0	118 12 50	7 36 53.5
3 48 57.5	117 49 50	7 36 53.1
3 49 43.8	117 32 25	7 36 54.7
3 50 31.7	117 12 30	7 36 51.7
3 51 14.8	116 56 25	7 36 53.6
3 52 09.8	116 34 45	7 36 53.1

Thermometer 62°.

```
                                               h.   m.    s.
Chronometer fast by 9 obs. of east star......  7   36   50.20
      "              18   "     west star ...             52.90

      Mean ............................        7   36   51.56
```

APPENDIX No. 5—Continued.

October 5, 1846.—*Camp* 66, *near Socorro.*

Time, p. m.			Double altitudes of *a* Andromedæ.		
h.	*m.*	*s.*	*Deg.*	*min.*	*sec.*
3	36	56.2	101	37	30
3	38	15.8	102	10	10
3	38	58.7	102	28	25
3	39	47.5	102	38	25
3	40	46.8	103	13	10
3	41	30.0	103	31	05
3	42	05.5	103	46	50

Time, p. m.			Double altitudes of *a* Lyræ, in the west.		
h.	*m.*	*s.*	*Deg.*	*min.*	*sec.*
3	46	28.0	117	10	35
3	47	29.7	116	47	00
3	48	22.0	116	26	05
3	49	19.5	116	04	00
3	50	12.8	115	43	35
3	51	10.1	115	22	10
3	51	58.5	115	02	40

Thermometer 58°.

Ex. Doc. No. 41. 291

APPENDIX No. 5—Continued.

October 7, 1846.—*Camp* 68, *west bank of the Rio del Norte.*

DETERMINATION OF TIME.

Time, p. m.	Double altitudes of *a* Andromedæ, in the east.	Chronometer fast.
h. m. s.	Deg. min. sec.	h. m. s.
4 38 30.5	130 21 55	7 37 02.3
4 39 38.2	130 50 05	7 37 02.2
4 40 37.8	131 14 15	7 37 03.6
4 41 30.5	131 36 30	7 37 02.7
4 42 27.0	132 00 20	7 37 01.8
4 43 11.5	132 19 10	7 37 01.3
4 43 55.7	132 37 05	7 37 01.9

Thermometer 62°.

Time, p. m.	Double altitudes of *a* Lyræ, in the west.	Chronometer fast.
h. m. s.	Deg. min. sec.	h. m. s.
4 47 29.0	90 21 10	7 37 06.4
4 48 06.0	90 06 40	7 37 05.6
4 49 02.0	89 45 25	7 37 06.0
4 49 51.8	89 26 05	7 37 05.5
4 50 38.7	89 08 50	7 37 07.2
4 51 37.8	88 45 50	7 37 06.2
4 52 31.4	88 24 55	7 37 05.2
4 53 20.0	88 06 00	7 34 04.2
4 54 06.0	87 49 00	7 37 05.8

Thermometer 62°.

	h. m. s.
Chronometer fast by 7 obs. of east star............	7 37 02.26
Chronometer fast by 9 obs. of west star............	05.79
Mean	7 37 04.02

APPENDIX No. 5—Continued.

October 7, 1846.—*Camp* 68, *west bank of the Rio del Norte.*

DETERMINATION OF LATITUDE.

Time, p. m.	Double altitudes of Polaris.	Latitude.
h. m. s.	Deg. min. sec.	Deg. min. sec.
5 20 51.02	69 53 45	33 41 04 rej.
5 22 12.8	69 54 45	33 41 16
5 23 18.0	69 55 10	33 41 16
5 23 46.0	69 55 30	33 41 20
5 24 37.0	69 55 50	33 41 20
5 25 26.0	69 56 10	33 41 18
5 26 03.5	69 56 35	33 41 22
5 26 45.0	69 56 50	33 41 21
5 27 24.0	69 57 05	33 41 20
5 28 09.5	69 57 20	33 41 18

Mean of 9 observations, 33° 41′ 19″.

Ex. Doc. No. 41.   293

APPENDIX No. 5—Continued.

October 10, 1846.—Camp 70.

DETERMINATION OF LATITUDE.

Time, p. m.	Double altitudes of b Aquarii, near the meridian.	Latitude.
h. m. s.	Deg. min. sec.	Deg. min. sec.
3 34 46.0	100 46 50	35 19 19
3 35 56.5	100 48 00	33 19 45
3 37 15.5	100 49 55	33 19 36
3 38 38.2	100 51 10	33 19 41
3 39 49.0	100 51 30	33 19 50
3 40 57.05	100 53 10	33 19 28
3 41 57.5	100 54 10	33 19 10
3 43 12.8	100 54 35	33 19 05
3 45 12.5	100 53 50	33 19 24
3 46 15.0	100 53 05	33 19 36
3 47 02.0	100 52 20	33 19 47
3 47 51.2	100 51 50	33 19 45
3 48 58.8	100 51 10	33 19 41
3 50 19.0	100 49 40	33 19 45
3 51 55.2	100 47 40	33 19 45
3 52 54.5	100 46 20	33 19 42
3 54 32.8	100 42 40	33 19 68

Thermometer 48°.

Mean of 17 observations, 33° 19′ 38″.

Ex. Doc. No. 41.

APPENDIX No. 5—Continued.

Ooctober 10, 1846.—*Camp* 70.

DETERMINATION OF LATITUDE.

Time, p. m.	Double altitudes of Polaris.	Latitude.
h. m. s.	*Deg. min. sec.*	*Deg. min. sec.*
4 02 30.2	68 36 35	33 20 15
4 03 47.0	68 37 50	33 20 29
4 05 11.2	68 38 05	33 20 11
4 05 54.5	68 38 50	33 20 19
4 06 44.0	68 39 55	33 20 37
4 07 31.3	68 40 10	33 20 30
4 08 19.2	68 40 40	33 20 30
4 09 12.5	68 41 10	33 20 28
4 09 43.5	68 41 25	33 20 26
4 10 34.0	68 41 50	33 20 24
4 11 15.5	68 42 30	33 20 31
4 12 08.5	68 43 10	33 20 36
4 13 03.0	68 43 00	33 20 14
4 14 05.0	68 44 00	33 20 25
4 14 45.8	68 44 20	33 20 24
4 15 20.8	68 44 35	33 20 21
4 15 56.8	68 44 50	33 20 19

	Latitude of camp.
	Deg. min. sec.
Latitude by 17 observations of *b* Aquarii.......	33 19 38
" " " Polaris.........	33 20 25
Mean.....................	33 20 02

APPENDIX No. 5—Continued.

October 10, 1846.—*Camp* 70, *east side of the Rio del Norte.*

DETERMINATION OF TIME.

Time, p. m.	Double altitudes of sun's upper limb.	Chronometer fast.
h. m. s.	Deg. min.	h. m. s.
5 01 7.5	75 30	7 37 42.5
5 01 39.2	75 40	7 37 41.9
5 02 12.8	75 50	7 37 42.6
5 02 45.0	76 00	7 37 42.0
5 03 18.0	76 10	7 37 42.0
5 03 51.8	76 20	7 37 42.8
5 04 23.5	76 30	7 37 42.5
5 04 56.9	76 40	7 37 41.8
5 05 30.5	76 50	7 37 42.2
5 06 03.0	77 00	7 37 41.5

Thermometer 68°.

Mean of 10 observations, 7*h*. 37*m*. 42.18*s*.

296   Ex. Doc. No. 41.

APPENDIX No. 5—Continued.

October 10, 1846.—Camp 70.

DETERMINATION OF TIME.

Equal altitudes of sun.

Time, a. m.—Oct. 11.	Double altitudes of sun's upper limb.	Time, p. m.—Oct. 10.	Chronometer fast.
h. m. s.	Deg. min.	h. m. s.	h. m. s.
4 57 49.3	74 00	9 52 44.5	7 37 37.67
4 57 18.2	73 50	9 53 16.0	7 37 38.07
4 56 45.0	73 40	9 53 49.0	7 37 38.16
4 56 12.5	73 30	9 54 20.8	7 37 38.00
4 55 41.5	73 20	9 54 51.0	7 37 37.79
4 55 09.2	73 10	9 55 25.5	7 37 38.07
4 54 37.3	73 00	9 55 56.0	7 37 38.55
4 54 04.7	72 50	9 56 26.3	7 37 37.59
4 53 33.5	72 40	9 56 59.0	7 37 38.50
4 53 01.0	72 30	9 57 30.0	7 37 37.90
4 52 28.8	72 20	9 58 01.2	7 37 37.63
4 51 25.3	72 00	9 59 04.5	7 37 37.87

Mean of 12 observations, 7h. 37m. 37.99s.

DETERMINATION OF INDEX ERROR.

	Min. sec.
On the arc..........................	31 30
Off the arc..........................	31 50

Index error = + 10″.

Ex. Doc. No. 41. 297

APPENDIX No. 5—Continued.

October 11, 1846.—Camp 70.

DETERMINATION OF TIME.

Equal altitudes of the sun.

Time, a. m.	Double altitudes of sun's upper limb.	Time, p. m.	Chronometer fast.
h. m. s.	*Deg. min.*	*h. m. s.*	*h. m. s.*
4 51 25.3	72 00	9 56 54.5	7 37 35.60
4 51 57.0	72 10	9 56 21.7	7 37 35.05
4 52 28.8	72 20	9 55 50.3	7 37 35.25
4 53 01.0	72 30	9 55 19.0	7 37 35.70
4 53 33.5	72 40	9 54 46.0	7 37 35.45
4 54 04.7	72 50	9 54 18.8	7 37 37.45 rej.
4 54 37.3	73 00	9 53 43.0	7 37 35.85
4 55 09.2	73 10	9 53 09.0	7 37 24.80
4 55 41.5	73 20	9 52 38.5	7 37 35.70
4 56 12.5	73 30	9 52 05.8	7 37 34.85
4 56 45.0	73 40		
4 57 18.2	73 50		
4 57 49.3	74 00		
Ther. 60°.		Ther. 80°.	

Mean of 9 observations, 7*h*. 37*m*. 55.36*s*.

APPENDIX No. 5—Continued.

October 12, 1846.—Camp 70.

DETERMINATION OF TIME.

Time, p. m.	Double altitudes of a Andromedæ, in the east.	Chronometer fast.
h. m. s.	Deg. min. sec.	h. m. s.
3 07 55.0	100 34 25	7 37 29.1
3 09 03.8	101 01 50	7 37 32.1 rej.
3 10 07.5	101 30 10	7 37 27.8
3 11 07.8	101 55 40	7 37 27.0
3 12 08.2	102 19 25	7 37 30.4 rej.
3 13 31.2	102 55 30	7 37 26.9
3 14 29.8	103 20 10	7 37 26.4
3 15 43.8	103 50 05	7 37 28.7
3 16 40.5	104 14 00	7 37 28.2
3 17 27.2	104 33 10	7 37 28.9

Thermometer 42°.

Time, p. m.	Double altitudes of a Lyræ, in the west.	Chronometer fast.
h. m. s.	Deg. min. sec.	h. m. s.
3 21 45.0	115 52 10	7 37 31.9
3 22 26.8	115 35 40	7 37 31.5
3 23 06.0	115 20 30	7 37 31.9
3 23 49.8	115 03 20	7 37 31.7
3 24 40.2	114 43 30	7 37 31.3
3 25 27.8	114 24 50	7 37 31.2
3 26 15.8	114 06 10	7 37 32.5
3 27 02.0	113 48 20	7 37 31.9
3 28 05.5	113 22 50	7 37 30.2

Thermometer 42°.

	h. min. sec.
Chronometer fast by 8 obs. of east star............	7 37 27.88
Chronometer fast by 9 obs. of west star............	7 37 31.57
Mean....................	7 37 29.72

APPENDIX No. 5.—Continued.

October 13, 1846.—*Camp* 70.

Time, p. m.			Double altitudes of *a* Lyræ, in the west.		
h.	*m.*	*s.*	*Deg.*	*min.*	*sec.*
3	46	40.8	104	32	30
3	47	47.3	104	07	30
3	48	49.0	103	43	40
3	49	51.2	103	20	20
3	50	36.5	103	01	50
3	51	40.5	102	37	10

Thermometer 42°.

APPENDIX No. 5—Continued.

October 13, 1846 —*Camp 71, west side of the Rio del Norte.*

Time, p. m.			Double altitudes of *a* Andromedæ.		
h.	*m.*	*s.*	*Deg.*	*min.*	*sec.*
3	37	49.1	114	46	00
3	39	17.5	115	23	10
3	40	14.0	115	45	45
3	41	17.3	116	12	30
3	42	08.0	116	34	15
3	42	57.8	116	54	40

Thermometer 42°.

Ex. Doc. No. 41. 301

APPENDIX No. 5—Continued.

October 15, 1846.—*Camp* 73, *on a small stream—first camp after leaving the Del Norte.*

DETERMINATION OF TIME.

Time, p. m.	Double altitudes of *a* Andromedæ, in the east.	Chronometer fast.
h. m. s.	*Deg. min. sec.*	*h. m. s.*
3 57 13.2	108 39 15	8 19 06.7
3 58 20.8	109 08 15	8 19 05.2
3 59 04.2	109 27 10	8 19 03.6 rej.
3 59 45.7	109 44 00	8 19 05.0
4 00 32.5	110 03 30	8 19 05.4
4 01 20.7	110 23 05	8 19 07.8
4 01 58.5	110 38 40	8 19 07.7

Time, p. m.	Double altitudes of *a* Lyræ, in the west.	Chronometer fast.
h. m. s.	*Deg. min. sec.*	*h. m. s.*
4 22 34.5	103 28 35	8 19 10.6
4 23 35.0	103 04 40	8 19 09.6
4 24 41.2	102 38 40	8 19 08.9
4 25 24.5	102 22 20	8 19 10.2
4 26 19.5	102 01 20	8 19 11.2
4 26 57.1	101 47 05	8 19 12.1
4 27 47.6	101 27 45	8 19 12.3

Thermometer 66°.

	h. m. s.
Chronometer fast by 6 observations of east star...	8 19 06.30
" 7 " west star...	8 19 10.70
Mean.....................	8 19 08.50

Ex. Doc. No, 41.

APPENDIX No. 5—Continued.

October 15, 1846.—*Camp* 73.

DETERMINATION OF LATITUDE.

Time, p. m.	Double altitudes of Polaris.	Latitude.
h. m. s.	Deg. min. sec.	Deg. min. sec.
4 07 21.8	67 34 40	32 54 37 rej.
4 08 05.2	67 35 40	32 54 53
4 08 57.5	67 36 20	32 54 56
4 09 33.5	67 36 50	32 54 59
4 10 30.0	67 37 45	32 55 08
4 11 25.8	67 38 10	32 55 04
4 12 26.5	67 39 15	32 55 15
4 13 50.0	67 39 55	32 55 10
4 14 30.0	67 40 10	32 55 04

Mean of 8 observations, 32° 35′ 04″.

Ex. Doc. No. 41. 303

APPENDIX No. 5—Continued.

October 17, 1846.—Camp 75.

DETERMINATION OF TIME.

Time, p. m.	Double altitudes of *a* Andromedæ in the east.	Chronometer fast.
h. m. s.	*Deg. min. sec.*	*h. m. s.*
3 35 11.8	99 49 50	8 25 53.9
3 36 11.8	100 14 55	8 25 54.0
3 36 58.0	100 35 10	8 25 51.8
3 37 49.5	100 56 10	8 25 53.2
3 38 38.5	101 16 40	8 25 53.4
3 39 30.0	101 38 15	8 25 53.3
3 40 13.5	101 55 50	8 25 54.9

Thermometer 38°.

Time, p. m.	Double altitudes of *a* Lyræ in the west.	Chronometer fast.
h. m. s.	*Deg. min. sec.*	*h. m. s.*
3 45 10.2	117 29 55	8 25 57.8
3 46 15.2	117 03 30	8 25 55.3
3 47 06.8	116 43 50	8 25 56.6
3 47 56.2	116 24 20	8 25 56.2
3 48 56.2	116 00 25	8 25 54.9
3 49 47.8	115 40 25	8 25 55.4
3 51 16.0	115 06 25	8 25 56.8

	h. m. s.
Chronometer fast by 7 obs. of east star...........	8 25 53.50
Chronometer fast by 7 obs. of west star	8 25 56.14
Mean......................	8 25 54.82

APPENDIX No. 5—Continued.

October 17, 1846.—Camp 75.

DETERMINATION OF LATITUDE.

Time, p. m.	Double altitudes of b Aquarii, near the meridian.	Latitude.
h. m. s.	Deg. min. sec.	Deg. min. sec.
3 57 57.0	102 04 40	32 42 18
3 59 04.0	102 05 50	32 42 08
4 00 13.0	102 07 00	32 42 03
4 01 40.0	102 07 50	32 42 05
4 02 54.4	102 08 30	32 41 59
4 03 56.0	102 08 05	32 42 18
4 05 00.0	102 08 10	32 42 16
4 06 16.5	102 07 55	32 42 15
4 07 22.0	102 07 40	32 42 10
4 08 17.0	102 07 25	32 42 02
4 09 33.0	102 06 35	32 41 58
4 10 46.5	102 04 50	32 42 15
4 11 44.0	103 03 25	32 42 22

Thermometer 38°

Time, p. m.	Double altitudes of Polaris.	Latitude.
h. m. s.	Deg. min. sec.	Deg. min. sec.
4 16 53.8	67 16 30	32 42 09
4 18 04.0	67 16 50	32 41 58
4 18 47.2	67 17 50	32 42 15
4 19 45.0	67 18 30	32 42 17
4 20 57.8	67 18 50	32 42 03
4 21 50.0	67 19 25	32 42 05
4 22 36.0	67 20 20	32 42 18
4 23 10.5	67 20 40	32 42 17
4 23 42.0	67 21 15	32 42 26

Thermometer 38°.

Latitude of camp.

Deg. min. sec.

Latitude by 13 obs. of b Aquarii 32   42   10
Latitude by 9 obs. of Polaris..................... 32   42   12

Mean 32   42   11

Ex. Doc. No. 41. 305

APPENDIX No. 5—Continued.

October 19, 1846.—*Camp* 77.

DETERMINATION OF TIME.

Time, p. m.	Double altitudes of *a* Lyræ, in the west.	Chronometer fast.
h. m. s.	*Deg. min. sec.*	*h. m. s.*
5 10 51.3	82 39 10	8 28 01.6
5 11 42.0	81 50 00	8 28 02.0
5 12 29.9	81 32 10	8 28 03.0
5 13 20.8	81 13 10	8 28 04.1
5 14 03.0	80 56 40	8 28 02.9
5 15 06.8	80 32 40	8 28 03.7
5 16 16.0	80 05 55	8 28 02.6

Thermometer 50°.

Mean of 7 observations, 8*h.* 28*m.* 02.84*s.*

DETERMINATION OF LATITUDE.

Time, p. m.	Double altitudes of Polaris.	Latitude.
h. m. s.	*Deg. min. sec.*	*Deg. min. sec.*
5 20 51.8	68 11 20	32 50 31
5 21 48.0	68 12 20	32 50 46
5 22 49.5	68 12 40	32 50 40
5 23 34.2	68 13 30	32 50 55
5 24 12.0	68 14 00	32 50 61
5 25 43.8	68 14 40	32 50 59
5 26 27.5	68 15 20	32 50 70
5 27 15.0	68 15 30	32 50 66
5 28 51.0	68 15 40	32 50 55

Thermometer 50°.

Mean of 9 observations, 32° 50′ 54″.

20

APPENDIX No. 5—Continued.

October 20, 1846.—*Camp* 78, *on the Rio Gila*.

DETERMINATION OF LATITUDE.

Time, p. m.	Double altitudes of *b* Aquarii, near the meridian.	Latitude.
h. m. s.	*Deg. min. sec.*	*Deg. min. sec.*
3 50 18.0	101 48 50	32 49 48
3 51 05.8	101 49 40	32 49 50
3 52 01.0	101 50 30	32 49 53
3 52 49.7	101 50 45	32 50 07
3 53 41.0	101 51 50	32 49 52
3 54 28.0	101 51 55	32 50 02
3 55 19.8	101 52 20	32 50 01
3 56 23.0	101 52 50	32 49 54
3 57 25.8	101 52 55	32 49 53
3 58 02.8	101 52 40	32 50 00
3 59 20.8	101 51 50	32 50 16
4 00 15.5	101 51 20	32 50 19
4 01 22.0	101 50 50	32 50 14
4 02 28.2	101 50 20	32 50 03
4 03 06.5	101 49 50	32 50 00
4 04 19.2	101 48 10	32 50 09

Time, p. m.	Double altitudes of Polaris.	Latitude.
h. m. s.	*Deg. min. sec.*	*Deg. min. sec.*
4 28 08.0	67 43 20	32 50 01
4 29 05.5	67 44 10	32 50 05
4 29 38.0	67 44 50	32 50 15
4 30 16.8	67 45 20	32 50 21
4 31 07.0	67 45 40	32 50 16
4 31 52.1	67 46 15	32 50 21
4 32 34.0	67 46 30	32 50 15
4 33 12.8	67 46 55	32 50 16
4 33 47.0	67 47 20	32 50 18

Thermometer 50°.

Deg. min. sec.
Latitude by 16 observations of *b* Aquarii, 32 50 01
Latitude by 9 observations of Polaris, 32 50 14

Mean .... 32 50 08 lat. of camp.

APPENDIX No. 5—Continued.

October 20, 1846.—Camp 78.

DETERMINATION OF TIME.

Time, p. m.	Double altitudes of a Andromedæ in the east.	Chronometer fast.
h. m. s.	Deg. min. sec.	h. m. s.
4 10 38.3	117 46 30	8 30 29.2
4 11 39.0	118 11 55	8 30 29.6
4 12 25.7	118 31 35	8 30 29.6
4 13 15.0	118 52 35	8 30 29.0
4 14 11.2	119 15 55	8 30 29.8
4 15 04.0	119 39 00	8 30 27.8
4 15 53.0	119 59 40	8 30 27.7

Thermometer 50°.

Time, p. m.	Double altitudes of a Lyræ in the west.	Chronometer fast.
h. m. s.	Deg. min. sec.	h. m. s.
4 19 33.8	101 20 05	8 30 29.2
4 20 17.8	101 04 10	8 30 32.2
4 21 00.8	100 47 30	8 30 32.2
4 21 49.7	100 28 20	8 30 31.8
4 22 38.0	100 08 55	8 30 30.0
4 23 17.8	99 53 10	8 30 29.4
4 24 04.0	99 35 35	8 30 30.2

Thermometer 50°.

	h. min. sec.
Chronometer fast by 7 obs. of east star............	8 30 28.96
Chronometer fast by 7 obs. of west star	8 30 30.71
Mean	8 30 29.83

Ex. Doc. No. 41.

APPENDIX No. 5—Continued.

October 22, 1846.—Camp 80, on the Gila.

DETERMINATION OF LATITUDE.

Time, p. m.	Double altitudes of b Aquarii, near the meridian.	Latitude.
h. m. s.	Deg. min. sec.	Deg. min. sec.
3 46 12.0	102 10 50	32 38 29
3 47 08.8	112 12 20	32 38 19
3 48 07.5	103 13 30	32 38 15
3 49 02.8	102 14 50	32 37 59
3 49 47.8	102 15 30	32 37 56
3 50 40.7	102 16 25	32 37 56
3 51 24.9	102 16 30	32 37 42
3 52 14.0	102 16 10	32 38 10
3 53 15.8		
3 54 29.0	102 15 55	32 38 21
3 55 17.5	102 15 50	32 38 19
3 56 09.8	102 15 30	32 38 19
3 56 54.0	102 15 00	32 38 23
3 57 38.0	102 14 30	32 38 28
3 58 21.0	102 14 00	32 38 23
3 59 20.5	102 13 20	32 38 16
4 00 18.5	102 12 20	32 38 18
4 01 03.8	102 11 40	32 38 07

Thermometer 62°.

Mean of 17 observations, 32° 38′ 13″.

Ex. Doc. No. 41. 309

APPENDIX No. 5—Continued.

October 22, 1846.—*Camp* 80, *on the Gila.*

DETERMINATION OF TIME.

Time, p. m.	Double altitudes of *a* Andromedæ in the east.	Chronometer fast.
h. m. s.	*Deg. min. sec.*	*h. m. s.*
4 04 53.8	116 53 05	8 34 42.2
4 05 58.8	117 20 20	8 34 42.6
4 06 51.0	117 43 05	8 34 40.8
4 07 37.0	118 02 20	8 34 41.2
4 08 45.6	118 30 10	8 34 43.9
4 09 37.8	118 53 00	8 34 41.9
4 10 24.8	119 13 10	8 34 41.1

Thermometer 62°.

Time, p. m.	Double altitudes of *a* Lyræ in the west.	Chronometer fast.
h. m. s.	*Deg. min. sec.*	*h. m. s.*
4 13 45.0	102 01 25	8 34 42.1
4 14 34.8	101 43 10	8 34 43.2
4 15 25.8	101 23 30	8 34 43.7
4 16 13.2	101 04 30	8 34 44.3
4 16 55.0	100 48 40	8 34 45.4
4 17 43.2	100 29 10	8 34 43.6
4 18 28.0	100 12 00	8 34 44.1

				h. m. s.
Chronometer fast by	7 observations of east star	8 34 41.96
" "	7 " west star	8 34 43.77
Mean....................	8 34 42.86

Ex. Doc. No. 41.

APPENDIX No. 5—Continued.

October 24, 1846.—*Camp* 81, *on the Gila.*

DETERMINATION OF LONGITUDE.

Time, p. m.			Distance of Fomalhaut, from moon's western limb.		
h.	*m.*	*s.*	*Deg.*	*min.*	*sec.*
2	32	14.8			
2	34	03.6	67	42	20
2	35	16.8	67	42	15
2	37	04.5	67	41	45
2	38	39.0	67	40	55
2	39	57.8	67	40	30
2	41	12.5	67	40	05
2	42	38.5	67	39	55
2	44	02.0	67	39	10
2	46	01.0	67	38	20
2	47	17.0	67	37	40
2	48	35.8	67	37	10
2	50	04.0	67	36	50

Thermometer 68°.

Longitude by mean of observations, 7*h.* 12*m.* 17.4*s.*

Ex. Doc. No. 41. 311

APPENDIX No. 5—Continued.

October 24, 1846.—*Camp* 81, *on the Gila.*

DETERMINATION OF TIME.

Time, p. m.	Double altitudes of *a* Andromedæ in the east.	Chronometer fast.
h. m. s.	*Deg. min. sec.*	*h. m. s.*
3 13 24.8	98 23 55	8 35 05.6
3 14 25.2	98 50 00	8 35 05.8
3 15 15.5	99 10 50	8 35 04.3
3 16 04.7	99 31 30	8 35 04.1
3 16 50.6	99 51 30	8 35 02.2
3 17 41.0	100 11 50	8 35 04.1
3 18 38.0	100 36 15	8 35 03.6
3 19 33.0	100 58 10	8 35 04.3
3 20 17.5	101 17 35	8 35 03.7

Thermometer 54°.

Time, p. m.	Double altitudes of *a* Lyræ in the west.	Chronometer fast.
h. m. s.	*Deg. min. sec.*	*h. m. s.*
3 23 15.0	118 53 55	8 35 04.5
3 24 01.2	118 37 20	8 35 08.3 rej.
3 24 54.0	118 15 10	8 35 04.5
3 25 34.0	117 59 50	8 35 05.3
3 26 15.5	117 43 20	8 35 04.7
3 26 59.8	117 25 50	8 35 04.3
3 27 40.8	117 09 30	8 35 03.4
3 28 24.0	116 52 30	8 35 05.4
3 29 08.0	116 35 30	8 35 03.7

		h. m. s.
Chronometer fast by 9 observations of east star....		8 35 03.97
Chronometer fast by 8 observations of west star...		8 35 04.48
Mean..........................		8 35 04.22

APPENDIX No. 5—Continued.

October 24, 1846.—*Camp* 81, *on the Gila.*

DETERMINATION OF LATITUDE.

Time, p. m.	Double altitudes of *b* Aquarii, near the meridian.	Latitude.
h. m. s.	Deg. min. sec.	Deg. min. sec.
3 34 52.0	101 51 50	32 45 03
3 35 59.5	101 53 50	32 44 56
3 37 17.9	101 55 50	32 45 01
3 38 51.8	101 57 30	32 45 17 rej.
3 40 02.5	102 00 20	32 44 31
3 41 12.0	102 00 40	32 44 57
3 42 21.2	102 02 25	32 44 31
3 43 45.0	103 03 20	32 44 26
3 45 10.8	102 03 15	32 44 41
3 46 30.0	102 03 40	32 44 31
3 47 36.0	102 04 00	32 44 16
3 48 22.8	102 03 10	32 44 34
3 49 13.2	102 03 10	32 44 22
3 50 06.8	102 02 20	32 44 31
3 51 14.2	102 01 40	32 44 28
3 52 10.0	102 00 55	32 44 20
3 53 07.0	102 00 15	32 44 08 rej.
3 54 18.8	101 58 10	32 44 24
3 55 37.6	101 55 25	32 44 45
3 57 13.5	101 52 40	32 44 43

Mean of 18 observations, 32° 44' 37".

Latitude by 12 obs. of Polaris......... 32 45 06
Latitude by 18 obs. of *b* Aquarii....... 32 44 37

Mean of north and south stars... 32 44 52 lat. of camp.

Ex. Doc. No. 41. 313

APPENDIX No. 5—Continued.

October 24, 1846.—*Camp* 81, *on the Gila.*

DETERMINATION OF LATITUDE.

Time, p. m.	Double altitudes of Polaris.	Latitude.
h. m. s.	*Deg. min. sec.*	*Deg. min. sec.*
2 56 31.0	66 39 20	32 45 14
2 57 30.5	66 40 20	32 45 14
2 58 18.8	66 40 45	32 45 01
2 58 58.5	66 41 10	32 44 57
2 59 39.2	66 42 00	32 45 06
3 00 34.5	66 42 45	32 45 09
3 01 24.0	66 43 15	32 45 07
3 02 21.5	66 44 10	32 45 13
3 03 18.8	66 44 55	32 45 15
3 03 58.8	66 45 20	32 45 12
3 04 57.0	66 45 50	32 45 08
3 05 55.6	66 46 20	32 44 59

Thermometer 62°.

Mean of 12 observations, 32° 45′ 06″.

Ex. Doc. No, 41.

APPENDIX No. 5—Continued.

October 26, 1846.—Camp 83, on the Gila.

DETERMINATION OF LONGITUDE.

Time, p. m.	Distance of *a* Pegasi from moon's western limb.	Double altitudes of moon's lower limb.
h.　m.　　s.	Deg. min. sec.	Deg. min. sec.
4　14　49.0	56　00　10	63　59　20
4　16　28.2	55　59　10	63　14　40
4　18　20.8	55　58　30	62　47　00
4　19　43.5	55　58　10	62　26　10
4　22　33.0	55　57　30	61　43　55
4　24　11.8	55　57　10	61　19　20

Thermometer 66°.

DETERMINATION OF TIME.

Time, p. m.	Double altitudes of ―――― in the west.
h.　　m.　　　s.	Deg.　min.　sec.
5　　19　　35.8	96　　03　　40
5　　20　　24.0	95　　46　　20

Time, p m.	Double altitudes of *a* Lyræ in the west.
h.　　m.　　　s.	Deg.　min.　sec.
5　　25　　51.0	70　　07　　10

Ex. Doc. No. 41.   315

APPENDIX No. 5—Continued.

October 27, 1846.—*Camp* 83, *on the Gila.*

DETERMINATION OF LATITUDE.

Time, p. m.	Double altitudes of Polaris.	Latitude.
h. m. s.	Deg. min. sec.	Deg. min. sec.
2 40 42.0	66 50 10	32 55 11
2 41 27.8	66 50 50	32 55 15
2 42 29.2	66 51 35	32 53 15
2 44 02.0	66 52 50	32 53 18
2 45 15.3	66 53 40	32 53 12
2 46 10.8	66 54 30	32 53 17
2 46 58.5	66 55 10	32 53 20
2 47 46.7	66 55 45	32 53 19
2 48 28.8	66 56 10	32 53 16

Thermometer 51°.

Mean of 10 observations, 52° 55' 16''.

316   Ex. Doc. No. 41.

APPENDIX No. 5—Continued.

October 27, 1846.—*Camp* 83, *on the Gila.*

DETERMINATION OF TIME.

Time, p. m.	Double altitudes of *a* Andromedæ, in the east.	Chronometer fast.
h. m. s.	Deg. min. sec.	h. m. s.
2 54 45.6	94 11 05	8 38 24.3
2 55 30.5	94 29 00	8 38 26.3
2 56 16.7	94 48 05	8 38 26.8
2 57 08.5	95 09 05	8 38 28.1
2 57 50.4	95 27 10	8 38 26.8
2 58 36.8	95 47 25	8 38 24.8
2 59 57.8	96 11 45	8 38 26.4
3 00 22.0	96 30 10	8 38 27.6
3 01 08.2	96 49 55	9 38 26.5

Thermometer 51°.

Time, p. m.	Double altitudes of *a* Lyræ, in the west.	Chronometer fast.
h. m. s.	Deg. min. sec.	h. m. s.
3 28 13.0	113 46 20	8 38 28.4
3 29 20.2	113 20 05	8 38 28.6
3 30 12.0	112 59 55	8 38 28.8
3 31 21.0	112 33 05	8 38 29.2
3 32 22.0	112 09 05	8 38 28.8
3 33 11.0	111 48 40	8 38 25.0 rej.
3 33 55.8	111 32 10	8 38 28.0
3 34 45.0	111 13 05	8 38 28.4
3 35 33.0	110 54 10	8 38 28.0

Thermometer 51°.

Mean of 17 observations, 8*h.* 58*m.* 27.46*s.*

Ex. Doc. No. 41. 317

APPENDIX No. 5—Continued.

October 27, 1846.—Camp 83, on the Gila.

DETERMINATION OF LONGITUDE.

Time, p. m.	Distance of α Pegasi from moon's western limb.	Double altitude of moon's lower limb.
h. m. s.	Deg. min. sec.	Deg. min. sec.
4 46 05.5	42 43 40	74 31 50
4 47 41.0	42 42 50	74 10 10
4 49 05.5	42 42 30	73 51 40
4 50 53.0	42 42 00	73 27 40
4 54 56.0	42 40 30	72 31 10
4 56 52.5	42 39 35	72 04 40
4 58 31.8	42 38 50	71 40 00
5 00 28.3	42 38 20	71 13 10
5 02 42.0	42 37 20	70 41 00
5 04 09.2	42 37 10	70 19 20
5 05 59.5	42 36 35	69 52 15

Thermometer 50°.

Longitude, by mean of observations, 7h. 13m. 04.24s.

APPENDIX No. 5—Continued.

October 30, 1846.—*Camp* 86, *on the Gila.*

DETERMINATION OF TIME.

Time, p. m.			Double altitudes of ——— in the east.		
h.	*m.*	*s.*	*Deg.*	*min.*	*sec.*
8	26	01.0	98	19	05
8	26	50.0	98	38	10
8	28	23.0	99	14	50

DETERMINATION OF LATITUDE.

Time, p. m.			Double altitudes of Polaris.			Latitude.		
h.	*m.*	*s.*	*Deg.*	*min.*	*sec.*	*Deg.*	*min.*	*sec.*
8	34	30.5	69	14	50	33	12	05
8	35	46.0	69	14	30	33	12	05
8	36	51.2	69	14	30	33	12	14
8	37	37.8	69	14	10	33	12	11
8	39	01.8	69	15	50	33	12	13
8	40	03.5	69	13	20	33	12	16
8	41	19.0	69	13	05	33	12	11
8	42	55.0	69	12	35	33	12	13
8	44	29.0	69	11	40	33	12	01
8	45	40.5	69	11	20	33	12	04
8	46	27.0	69	11	15	33	12	10
8	47	26.8	69	11	05	33	12	15
8	48	22.7	69	10	45	33	12	17

Thermometer 55°.

Mean of 13 observations, 33° 12′ 10″.

Ex. Doc. No. 41. 319

APPENDIX No. 5—Continued.

October 30, 1846.—*Camp* 86, *on the Gila.*

DETERMINATION OF TIME.

Time, p. m.	Double altitudes of Aldebaran, in the east.	Chronometer fast.
h. m. s.	*Deg. min. sec.*	*h. m. s.*
8 55 13.8	124 55 50	8 41 02.9
8 56 14.5	125 16 35	8 41 04.9
8 57 24.0	125 41 05	8 41 04.9
8 58 26.8	126 03 30	8 41 03.7
Clouds.		
9 00 44.8	126 51 15	8 41 04.7
9 01 54.0	127 15 15	8 41 04.5
9 03 32.8	127 48 55	8 41 05.1
9 05 35.8	128 31 10	8 41 04.2
9 06 41 9	128 53 15	8 41 05.0

Thermometer 55°.

Mean of 9 observations, 8*h.* 41*m.* 04.43*s.*

APPENDIX No. 5—Continued.

October 30, 1846.—*Camp* 86, *on the Gila.*

DETERMINATION OF LONGITUDE.

Time, p. m.	Distance of Aldebaran from moon's western limb.	Double altitudes of moon's lower limb.
h. m. s.	*Deg. min. sec.*	*Deg. min. sec.*
9 23 27.0	72 07 35	58 47 40
9 25 06.0	72 06 50	58 10 50
9 27 55.8	72 05 35	57 06 30
9 30 03.5	72 04 25	56 18 00
9 31 55.8	72 03 25	55 36 10
9 33 36.0	72 02 40	54 58 20
9 35 27.8	72 01 40	54 15 30
9 37 40.8	72 00 25	53 24 50
9 39 28.8	71 59 30	52 43 20

Thermometer 50°.

Ex. Doc. No. 41.   321

APPENDIX No. 5—Continued.

October 31, 1846.—*Camp* 87, *on the San Francisco, about two miles from its mouth.*

DETERMINATION OF LATITUDE.

Time, p. m.			Double altitudes of *b* Aquarii, near the meridian.			Latitude.		
h.	*m.*	*s.*	*Deg.*	*min.*	*sec.*	*Deg.*	*min.*	*sec.*
3	17	31.8	100	58	50	33	14	29
3	18	33.7	101	01	00	33	14	04 rej.
3	19	28.5	101	01	20	33	14	19
3	20	33.5	101	02	05	33	14	25
3	21	45.0	101	02	50	33	14	26
3	22	50.9	101	03	30	33	14	22
3	24	00.7	101	03	45	33	14	25
3	25	54.2	101	04	10	33	14	13
3	27	13.7	101	04	30	33	13	53 rej.
3	28	28.0	101	03	10	33	14	15
3	29	51.5	101	02	10	33	14	16
3	31	00.0	101	01	00	33	14	20
3	32	14.2	100	59	45	33	14	16
3	33	31.5	100	57	40	33	14	27

Thermometer 50°.

Mean of 12 observations, 33° 14′ 21″.

APPENDIX No. 5—Continued.

October 31, 1846.—Camp 87.

DETERMINATION OF TIME.

Time, p. m.			Double altitudes of a Andromedæ in the east.			Chronometer fast.		
h.	m.	s.	Deg.	min.	sec.	h.	m.	s.
3	40	05.0	118	29	40	8	41	31.2
3	41	18.2	119	01	00	8	41	29.7
3	42	04.2	119	20	00	8	41	30.4
3	43	12.5	119	49	10	8	41	29.2
3	44	13.0	120	13	25	8	41	31.9
3	45	10.8	120	38	20	8	41	30.3
3	46	06.0	121	01	30	8	41	30.3
3	47	01.0	121	24	55	8	41	29.4
3	48	05.8	121	51	40	8	41	30.5

Thermometer 50°.

Time, p. m.			Double altitudes of a Lyræ, in the west.			Chronometer fast.		
h.	m.	s.	Deg.	min.	sec.	h.	m.	s.
3	57	51.0	97	34	30	8	41	32.8
3	58	41.8	97	14	50	8	41	32.8
3	59	29.0	96	56	35	8	41	32.9
4	00	12.8	96	39	50	8	41	33.2
4	01	10.7	96	17	25	8	41	33.1
4	02	24.0	95	49	30	8	41	34.2
4	03	13.3	95	30	05	8	41	33.2
4	03	52.0	95	15	10	8	41	33.2
4	04	46.9	94	54	10	8	41	33.7
4	05	25.5	94	39	10	8	41	33.4
4	06	18.0	94	18	30	8	41	32.4

Thermometer 50°.

Mean of 20 observations, 8h. 41m. 54.75s.

Ex. Doc. No. 41. 323

APPENDIX No. 5—Continued.

October 31, 1846.—Camp 87.

DETERMINATION OF LONGITUDE.

Time, p. m.	Distance of d Aquilæ from moon's western limb.	Double altitudes of the moon's upper limb.
h. m. s.	Deg. min. sec.	Deg. min. sec.
4 28 54.2	70 52 15	99 35 55
4 31 02.5	70 58 40	100 17 30
4 34 36.0	70 59 40	101 26 10
4 36 37.3	71 00 55	102 03 30
4 40 35.8	71 01 20	103 18 40
4 42 14.0	71 01 30	103 48 00
4 44 25.0	71 02 00	104 28 15
4 48 19.6	71 04 05	105 38 50
4 50 07.8	71 04 30	106 10 20
4 51 38.0	71 05 40	106 37 40
4 55 08.5	71 06 20	107 03 10
4 56 00.0	71 07 20	107 53 00
4 57 57.0	71 08 10	108 26 30

Thermometer 43°.

Time, p. m.	Distance of a Aldebaran from moon's western limb.	Double altitudes of the moon's upper limb.
h. m. s.	Deg. min. sec.	Deg. min. sec.
5 17 49.0	59 10 20	113 39 20
5 20 59.6	59 09 40	114 24 40
5 24 43.8	59 08 25	115 16 50
5 26 19.5	59 07 45	115 38 20
5 28 07.8	59 07 05	116 02 30
5 29 39.4	59 06 20	116 22 10
5 32 01.8	59 05 35	116 51 55
5 33 33.5	59 04 45	117 11 00
5 35 08.8	59 04 05	117 30 10

Thermometer 40°.

	h. m. s.
Longitude by west star	7 23 15.07
Longitude by east star......................	20 18.09
Mean..	7 21 47.30

APPENDIX No. 5—Continued.

October 31, 1846.—*Camp* 87.

DETERMINATION OF LATITUDE.

Time, p. m.	Double altitudes of Polaris.	Latitude.
h. m. s.	Deg. min. sec.	Deg. min. sec.
5 52 35.2	69 22 35	34 14 28
5 53 26.0	69 22 55	34 14 32
5 54 28.2	69 23 30	34 14 42
5 55 36.5	69 23 40	34 14 39
5 56 21.0	69 23 55	34 14 41
5 57 06.8	69 24 05	34 14 39
5 57 42.8	69 24 10	34 14 38
5 58 24.5	69 24 20	34 14 39
5 59 16.2	69 24 30	34 14 36
6 00 01.3	69 24 40	34 14 36
6 00 33.0	69 24 55	34 14 40

Thermometer 39°.

Mean of 11 observations, 33° 14′ 37″.

FOR INDEX ERROR.

	Min. sec.
On the arc	31 55
Off the arc	31 30

Ex. Doc. No. 41. 325

APPENDIX No. 5—Continued.

November 2, 1846.—*Camp* 89, *Disappointment creek.*

DETERMINATION OF TIME.

Time, p. m.	Double altitudes of *a* Andromedæ in the east.	Chronometer fast.
h. m. s.	*Deg. min. sec.*	*h. m. s.*
3 20 05.0	113 10 50	8 42 04.9
3 20 50.8	113 31 10	8 42 01.4 rej
3 21 40.3	113 51 05	8 42 05.3
3 22 45.0	114 17 20	8 42 05.5
3 23 44.0	114 43 10	8 42 02.7
3 24 29.5	115 01 30	8 42 04.4
3 25 13.0	115 20 05	8 42 03.5
3 26 03.8	115 41 15	8 42 03.8
3 26 52.0	116 01 55	8 42 02.7

Thermometer 40°.

Time, p. m.	Double altitudes of *a* Lyræ in the west.	Chronometer fast.
h. m. s.	*Deg. min. sec.*	*h. m. s.*
3 28 38.4	106 06 10	8 42 09.9 rej.
3 30 25.0	105 22 35	8 42 04.6
3 31 09.6	105 05 20	8 42 05.6
3 31 53.0	104 49 00	8 42 06.1
3 32 38.0	104 31 25	8 42 06.9
3 33 18.0	104 15 35	8 42 06.3
3 34 05.3	103 57 10	8 42 06.1
3 34 50.2	103 39 50	8 42 07.8
3 35 35.5	103 22 10	8 42 05.5

Thermometer 40°.

Mean of 16 observations, 8*h*. 42*m*. 04.96*s*.

APPENDIX No. 5—Continued.

November 2, 1846.—*Camp* 89.

DETERMINATION OF LATITUDE.

Time, p. m.	Double altitudes of Polaris.	Latitude.
h. m. s.	*Deg. min. sec.*	*Deg. min. sec.*
3 39 40.8	68 27 40	33 14 57
3 40 47.6	68 28 05	33 14 49
3 41 48.5	68 28 45	33 14 50
3 42 29.0	68 29 10	33 14 50
3 43 31.6	68 29 45	33 14 48
3 44 13.7	68 30 20	33 14 54
3 45 06.9	68 31 10	33 15 02
3 46 03.5	68 31 20	33 14 53
3 46 57.1	68 31 55	33 14 54
3 47 43.5	68 32 20	33 14 53
3 48 55.8	68 32 55	33 14 57
3 49 13.0	68 33 20	33 14 57

Thermometer 40°.

Mean of 12 observations, 33° 14′ 54″.

APPENDIX No. 5—Continued.

November 5, 1846.—*Camp* 91, *on the San Pedro.*

DETERMINATION OF LATITUDE.

Time, p. m.	Double altitudes of *b* Aquarii, near the meridian.	Latitude.
h. m. s.	*Deg. min. sec.*	*Deg. min. sec.*
2 58 31.0	101 33 45	32 57 15
2 59 48.8	101 34 55	32 57 28
3 01 16.1	101 35 50	32 57 35
3 02 57.5	101 36 50	32 57 31
3 04 17.6	101 37 40	32 57 25
3 05 24.8	101 38 00	32 57 19
3 07 06.4	101 37 30	32 57 29
3 07 51.5	101 36 55	32 57 39
3 10 02.8	101 36 30	32 57 14
3 10 42.8	101 35 45	32 57 19
3 11 30.7	101 35 20	32 57 11
3 12 34.0	101 34 10	32 57 11
3 13 30.6	101 32 30	32 57 26

Thermometer 52°.

Mean of 13 observations, 32° 57′ 23″.

APPENDIX No. 5—Continued.

November 5, 1846.—*Camp No.* 91, *on the San Pedro.*

DETERMINATION OF TIME.

Time, p. m.	Double altitudes of *a* Andromedæ, in the east.	Chronometer fast.
h. m. s.	*Deg. min. sec.*	*h. m. s.*
3 18 27.5	117 33 45	8 41 45.6
3 19 29.2	118 00 30	8 41 42.8
3 20 29.5	118 25 40	8 41 44.2
3 21 30.8	118 51 30	8 41 44.1
3 22 17.5	119 10 50	8 41 44.8
3 23 24.0	119 39 10	8 41 43.9
3 24 24.0	120 04 30	8 41 43.7
3 25 38.8	120 35 40	8 41 44.4
3 26 43.0	121 03 05	8 41 43.4

Thermometer 52°.

Time, p. m.	Double altitudes of *a* Lyræ, in the west.	Chronometer fast.
h. m. s.	*Deg. min. sec.*	*h. m. s.*
3 29 32.5	100 48 35	8 41 48.4
3 30 32.8	100 24 30	8 41 46.6
3 31 46.0	99 57 05	8 41 49.1
3 32 43.8	99 33 45	8 41 46.8
3 33 33.0	99 14 15	8 41 45.8
3 34 30.8	98 52 25	8 41 47.1
3 35 25.7	98 31 35	8 41 48.4
3 36 14.8	98 12 10	8 41 47.5
3 37 11.8	97 50 05	8 41 47.3

Thermometer 52°.

Mean of 18 observations, 8*h.* 41*m.* 45.76*s.*

APPENDIX No. 5—Continued.

November 5, 1846.—*Camp* 91, *on the San Pedro, about* ———
, from its mouth at the Gila.

DETERMINATION OF LATITUDE.

Time, p. m.	Double altitudes of Polaris.	Latitude.
h. m. s.	Deg. min. sec.	Deg. min. sec.
3 40 39.0	68 01 30	32 57 54
3 41 55.5	68 02 30	32 58 02
3 43 23.6	68 03 00	32 57 55
3 44 11.5	68 04 00	32 58 07
3 45 23.8	68 04 20	32 58 07
3 46 39.8	68 05 15	32 58 04
3 47 26.0	68 05 55	32 58 04
3 48 12.8	68 06 20	32 58 09
3 49 22.8	68 06 45	32 57 59
3 50 37.6	68 07 30	32 58 03
3 51 16.0	68 07 30	32 58 03
3 51 54.7	68 08 10	32 58 03

Thermometer 52°.

Mean of 12 observations, 32° 58' 03".

APPENDIX. No. 5—Continued.

November 5, 1846.—*Camp* 91, *on the San Pedro.*

DETERMINATION OF LONGITUDE.

Time, p. m.			Distance of α Arietis from moon's eastern limb.			Double altitudes of moon's upper limb.		
h.	*m.*	*s.*	*Deg.*	*min.*	*sec.*	*Deg.*	*min.*	*sec.*
12	29	20.0	48	22	30	134	00	30
12	31	01.5	48	22	40	133	26	20
12	32	40.8	48	22	55	132	50	10
12	34	14.2	48	23	40	132	17	35
12	36	29.0	48	23	40	131	30	30
12	38	25.5	48	23	55	130	48	30
12	40	22.6	48	25	40	130	05	30
12	42	09.5	48	26	30	129	27	00
12	43	37.8	48	26	50	128	54	10
12	44	51.5	48	27	10	128	28	10
12	47	31.2	48	27	40	127	29	30
12	49	26.8	48	28	15	126	45	50

Thermometer 32°.

Ex. Doc. No. 41. 331

APPENDIX. No. 5—Continued.

November 5, 1846.—Camp 91, on the San Pedro.

DETERMINATION OF LONGITUDE.

Time, p. m.	Distance of Regulus from moon's eastern limb.	Double altitudes of moon's upper limb.
h. m. s.	Deg. min. sec.	Deg. min. sec.
12 57 55.2	65 18 45	123 36 00
12 59 49.5	65 18 00	122 52 15
13 01 38.0	65 17 20	122 11 15
13 05 13.8	65 16 35	121 34 40
13 04 47.5	65 16 00	120 59 30
13 06 04.5	65 15 30	120 29 50
13 07 57.8	65 14 55	119 46 40
13 09 15.0	65 14 30	119 16 20
13 10 51.5	65 13 55	118 49 00

Thermometer 32°.

Longitude, by mean of observations, 7*h*. 23*m*. 46.9*s*.

APPENDIX No. 5—Continued.

November 6, 1846.—*Camp* 91, *on the San Pedro.*

DETERMINATION OF TIME.

Time, p. m.	Double altitudes of α Andromedæ in the east.	Chronometer fast.
h. m. s.	Deg. min. sec.	h. m. s.
3 12 38.0	116 51 40	8 41 32.2
3 13 45.8	117 20 15	8 41 32.0
3 14 31.0	117 40 00	8 41 30.5
3 15 26.0	118 02 45	8 41 31.1
3 16 19.7	118 24 50	8 41 32.3
3 17 17.6	118 50 05	8 41 30.1
3 18 12.8	119 12 25	8 41 32.2
3 18 59.8	119 33 15	8 41 29.6

Thermometer 64°.

Time, p. m.	Double altitudes of α Lyræ in the west.	Chronometer fast.
h. m. s.	Deg. min sec.	h. m. s.
3 22 56.5	101 45 35	8 41 35.1
3 23 53.8	101 21 55	8 41 31.5 rej.
3 24 44.8	101 03 15	8 41 34.4
3 25 22.5	100 49 05	8 41 35.6
3 26 11.2	100 29 50	8 41 34.6
3 27 07.5	100 08 15	8 41 35.3
3 28 00.5	99 47 45	8 41 35.6
3 28 55.8	99 25 50	8 41 34.3

Thermometer 64°.

APPENDIX No. 5—Continued.

November 6, 1846.—*Camp* 91, *on the San Pedro.*

DETERMINATION OF LONGITUDE.

Time.	Distance of Aldebaran from moon's western limb.	Double altitudes of moon's upper limb.
h. m. s.	*Deg. min. sec.*	*Deg. min. sec.*
7 43 11.0	25 53 55	65 27 10
7 44 45.2	25 54 25	66 06 20
7 47 03.8	25 55 35	67 03 10
7 49 18.0	25 56 15	67 58 10
7 51 03.0	25 57 15	68 40 50

Thermometer 42°.

Immersion of Jupiter's satellite, 6*h*. 42*m*. 40*s*.

APPENDIX No. 5—Continued.

November 8, 1846.—*Camp* 93, *on the Gila.*

DETERMINATION OF LATITUDE.

Time, p. m.	Double altitudes of *b* Aquarii, near the meridian.	Latitude.
h. m. s.	Deg. min. sec.	Deg. min. sec.
2 49 26.8	101 19 40	33 05 18
2 50 27.5	101 20 15	33 05 25
2 51 29.0	101 20 50	33 05 28
2 52 28.7	101 21 20	33 05 27
2 53 22.9	101 21 35	33 05 27
2 54 37.6	101 21 40	33 05 30
2 56 03.5	101 22 00	33 05 16
2 56 56.0	101 21 40	33 05 18
2 57 44.2	101 21 00	33 05 27
2 59 11.0	101 20 30	33 05 14
3 00 19.9	101 19 20	33 05 20

Thermometer 44°.

Mean of 12 observations, 33° 05′ 24″.

Time, p. m.	Double altitudes of Polaris.	Latitude.
h. m. s.	Deg. min. sec.	Deg. min. sec.
3 30 26.0	68 17 40	33 05 48
3 31 20.0	68 18 10	33 05 48
3 32 32.5	68 18 40	33 05 43
3 33 38.5	68 19 45	33 05 58
3 34 29.0	68 20 10	33 05 55
3 35 07.2	68 20 45	33 06 02
3 35 47.0	68 21 20	33 06 09
3 36 28.8	68 21 45	33 06 09
3 37 18.0	68 22 15	33 06 01

Thermometer 42°.

Mean of 9 observations, 33° 05′ 57″.

Ex. Doc. No. 41. 335

APPENDIX No. 5—Continued.

November 8, 1846.—*Camp* 93, *on the Gila.*

DETERMINATION OF TIME.

Time, p. m.	Double altitudes of *a* Andromedæ, in the east.	Chronometer fast.
h. m. s.	Deg. min. sec.	h. m. s.
3 05 32.0	116 43 10	8 42 39.2
3 06 26.8	117 05 45	8 42 40.3
3 07 27.6	117 32 40	8 42 37.0
3 08 33.5	117 59 15	8 42 39.5
3 09 30.0	118 23 40	8 42 37.9
3 10 22.3	118 45 20	8 42 39.5
3 11 13.8	119 06 55	8 42 38.6
3 12 24.6	119 36 50	8 42 38.2

Thermometer 42°.

Time, p. m.	Double altitudes of *a* Lyræ, in the west.	Chronometer fast.
h. m. s.	Deg. min. sec.	h. m. s.
3 15 31.0	102 07 10	8 42 41.6
3 16 29.5	101 44 40	8 42 42.2
3 17 19.0	101 25 55	8 42 43.5
3 18 21.5	101 01 35	8 42 43.2
3 19 10.8	100 42 55	8 42 44.4
3 20 02.8	100 21 40	8 42 41.6
3 20 46.8	100 01 45	8 42 42.0
3 21 42.2	99 43 15	8 42 41.9

Thermometer 42°.

Mean of 16 observations, 8*h*. 42*m*. 40.66*s*.

APPENDIX No. 5—Continued.

November 10, 1846.—*Camp* 95, *Caroon plain, on the Gila.*

DETERMINATION OF TIME.

Time, p. m.	Double altitudes of *a* Andromedæ, in the east.	Chronometer fast.
h. m. s.	*Deg. min. sec.*	*h. m. s.*
2 51 20.2	113 20 05	8 44 24.1
2 52 11.5	113 41 35	8 44 23.3
2 53 21.0	114 10 30	8 44 24.0
2 54 10.8	114 30 50	8 44 25.3
2 55 03.8	114 53 05	8 44 23.3
2 56 05.0	115 19 25	8 44 23.9
2 56 59.6	115 42 15	8 44 24.0
2 57 52.1	116 04 35	8 44 25.3

Thermometer 52°.

Time, p. m.	Double altitudes of *a* Lyræ, in the west.	Chronometer fast.
h. m. s.	*Deg. min. sec.*	*h. m. s.*
3 03 15.5	104 30 25	8 44 29.5
3 04 18.0	104 05 30	8 44 27.7
3 05 07.8	103 46 10	8 44 27.9
3 06 01.1	103 25 40	8 44 28.5
3 06 47.8	103 07 35	8 44 28.6
3 07 30.8	102 51 20	8 44 29.8
3 08 13.5	102 34 10	8 44 28.4
3 09 00.5	102 15 45	8 44 29.1
3 09 47.8	101 57 50	8 44 29.3

Thermometer 52°.

Mean of 18 observations, 8*h.* 44*m.* 26.52*s.*

Ex. Doc. No. 41.   337

APPENDIX No. 5—Continued.

November 10, 1846.—*Camp* 95.

DETERMINATION OF LATITUDE.

Time, p. m.	Double altitudes of Polaris.	Latitude.
h. m. s.	*Deg. min. sec.*	*Deg. min. sec.*
3 27 02.0	68 16 25	33 04 25
3 27 55.8	68 16 45	33 04 20
3 28 50.0	68 17 20	33 04 22
3 29 41.8	68 17 55	33 04 26
3 30 30.0	68 18 15	33 04 22
3 31 14.5	68 18 30	33 04 17
3 31 52.5	68 18 55	33 04 20
3 32 23.8	68 19 10	33 04 17
3 33 08.5	68 19 40	33 04 21
3 34 00.5	68 19 55	33 04 14
3 34 44.0	68 21 00	33 04 31 rej.
3 35 44.5	68 21 00	33 04 18
3 36 25.8	68 21 30	33 04 27

Thermometer 50°.

Mean of 12 observations, 33° 04' 21".

Ex. Doc. No. 41.

APPENDIX No. 5—Continued.

November 12, 1846.—*Camp* 97, *below Pimos village, about four miles from the Gila.*

DETERMINATION OF LATITUDE.

Time, p. m.			Double altitudes of *b* Aquarii, near the meridian.			Latitude.		
h.	*m.*	*s.*	*Deg*	*min.*	*sec.*	*Deg.*	*min.*	*sec.*
2	35	15.0	101	09	45	33	09	32
2	37	17.0	101	12	20	33	09	10
2	38	28.5	101	12	45	33	09	22
2	39	53.8	101	13	05	33	09	29
2	40	55.8	101	13	40	33	09	20
2	41	50.3	101	14	05	33	09	09
2	43	05.5	101	13	25	33	09	25
2	43	40.0	101	12	50	33	09	37 rej.
2	44	29.8	101	13	10	33	09	18
2	45	18.0	101	12	45	33	09	17
2	46	12.0	101	12	00	33	09	22
2	47	07.5	101	11	20	33	09	19
2	48	25.0	101	10	25	33	09	07
2	49	41.5	101	08	25	33	09	19

Thermometer 50°.

Mean of 13 observations, 33° 09′ 19″.

Ex. Doc. No. 41.   339

APPENDIX No. 5—Continued.

November 13, 1846.—*Camp* 97.

DETERMINATION OF LONGITUDE.

Time, a. m.	Distance between sun's and moon's nearest limbs.	Double altitude of moon's lower limb.
h. m. s.	*Deg. min. sec.*	*Deg. min. sec.*
4 16 46.8	60 36 45	
4 18 10.0	60 56 25	
4 20 59.5	60 56 05	
4 23 05.2	60 55 30	114 18 15
4 24 45.8	60 55 00	114 20 50
4 26 17.0	60 54 20	114 22 25
4 28 09.2	60 34 25	114 23 30
4 31 26.5	60 33 05	114 25 00
4 33 00.0	60 32 50	114 24 50
4 34 47.3	60 52 45	114 23 40
4 36 04.8	60 32 05	114 22 10
4 38 25.0	60 31 25	114 19 30
4 40 07.6	60 31 05	114 16 10
4 41 26.5	60 30 30	114 13 50

Thermometer 54°.

INDEX ERROR.

On the arc........................ 31.55″
Off the arc........................ 32.25.

APPENDIX No. 5—Continued.

November 12, 1846.—Camp 97.

DETERMINATION OF TIME.

Time, p. m.			Double altitudes of α Andromedæ, in the east.			Chronometer fast.		
h.	m.	s.	Deg.	min.	sec.	h.	m.	s.
2	55	19.8	117	53	15	8	45	23.8
2	56	27.2	118	21	15	8	45	25.2
2	57	31.0	118	48	20	8	45	24.5
2	58	17.0	119	07	10	8	45	25.7
2	59	04.7	119	27	40	8	45	22.5
2	59	48.5	119	46	15	8	45	23.9
3	00	32.8	120	04	55	8	45	23.8
3	01	29.2	120	29	15	8	45	22.1
3	02	16.8	120	48	25	8	45	24.1
3	03	05.0	121	08	38	8	45	24.2

Thermometer 50°.

Time, p. m.			Double altitudes of α Lyræ, in the west.			Chronometer fast.		
h.	m.	s.	Deg.	min.	sec.	h.	m.	s.
3	07	26.8	100	15	40	8	45	26.9
3	08	11.2	99	59	05	8	45	28.5
3	09	19.8	99	31	50	8	45	27.9
3	10	05.5	99	14	15	8	45	27.2
3	11	03.8	98	51	45	8	45	27.3
3	11	45.5	98	35	45	8	45	27.9
3	12	50.0	98	10	55	8	45	28.2
3	13	47.2	97	48	40	8	45	27.9
3	14	35.5	97	29	50	8	45	27.5
3	15	24.8	97	10	30	8	45	26.8
3	16	19.8	96	49	10	8	45	26.7
3	17	05.0	96	31	25	8	45	26.0

Thermometer 50°.

Mean of 22 observations, 8h. 45m. 25.79s.

APPENDIX No. 5—Continued.

November 12, 1846.—*Camp* 97.

DETERMINATION OF LATITUDE.

Time, p. m.	Double altitudes of Polaris.	Latitude.
h. m. s.	Deg. min. sec.	Deg. min. sec.
3 28 58.5	68 31 50	33 09 40
3 29 52.5	68 32 20	33 09 41
3 30 46.0	68 32 50	33 09 41
3 31 51.8	68 33 05	33 09 31
3 33 16.0	68 34 00	33 09 35
3 34 05.0	68 34 35	33 09 40
3 35 03.8	68 34 55	33 09 33
3 36 07.0	68 35 40	33 09 38
3 37 04.0	68 36 05	33 09 35
3 37 41.8	68 36 45	33 09 43
3 38 34.2	68 37 00	33 09 58
3 39 11.5	68 37 35	33 09 31

Thermometer 48°.

Mean of 12 observations, 33° 09' 37".

Ex. Doc. No 41.

APPENDIX No. 5—Continued.

November 13, 1846.—*Camp* 97.

DETERMINATION OF TIME.

Time, a. m.	Double altitudes of sun's upper limb.	Chronometer fast.
h. m. s.	*Deg. min. sec.*	*h. m. s.*
5 41 04.8	50 23 10	8 45 18.9
5 42 28.7	50 47 35	8 45 19.7
5 42 59.0	50 57 15	8 45 17.2
5 43 40.0	51 08 50	8 45 18.5
5 44 34.0	51 24 55	8 45 17.3
5 45 38.5	51 43 20	8 45 18.6
5 46 35.8	52 00 10	8 45 17.7
5 47 05.8	52 09 00	8 45 17.2
5 47 42.5	52 18 28	8 45 21.0 rej.
5 48 38.0	52 35 15	8 45 17.8
5 49 22.5	52 48 05	8 45 17.7
5 50 14.5	53 02 35	8 45 18.8

Thermometer 60°.

Mean of 11 observations, 8*h.* 45*m.* 18.13*s.*

Ex. Doc. No. 41. 343

APPENDIX No. 5—Continued.

November 14, 1846.—*Camp* 99, *on the Gila.*

DETERMINATION OF TIME.

Time, p. m.	Double altitudes of a Andromedæ, in the east.	Chronometer fast.
h. m. s.	Deg. min. sec.	h. m. s.
2 42 53.0	114 56 50	8 47 49.3
2 43 54.6	115 22 45	8 47 49.2
2 44 54.2	115 47 50	8 47 51.2
2 45 57.5	116 13 45	8 47 50.7
2 46 48.0	116 35 35	8 47 49.2
2 47 47.0	117 00 10	8 47 47.6
2 48 32.0	117 19 00	8 47 50.1
2 49 21.5	117 40 05	8 47 49.5

Thermometer 50°.

Time, p. m.	Double altitudes of a Lyræ, in the west.	Chronometer fast.
h. m. s.	Deg. min. sec.	h. m. s.
3 17 07.0	94 16 50	8 47 54.0
3 17 55.8	93 58 10	8 47 52.9
3 18 44.0	93 39 40	8 47 53.2
3 19 38.8	93 19 10	8 47 54.8
3 20 37.0	92 55 20	8 47 51.3
3 22 02.8	92 21 15	8 47 48.5 rej.
3 22 52.8	92 03 10	8 47 51.7
3 23 37.0	91 46 20	8 47 52.2

Thermometer 50°.

Mean of 15 observations, 8h. 47m. 51.23s.

APPENDIX No. 5—Continued.

November 14, 1846.—*Camp* 99, *on the Gila.*

DETERMINATION OF LATITUDE.

Time, p. m.	Double altitude of Saturn, near the meridian.	Latitude.
h. m. s.	Deg. min. sec.	Deg. min. sec.
2 52 36.2	84 14 10	32 59 17
2 53 33.0	84 15 40	32 59 07
2 54 23.5	84 16 30	32 59 10
2 55 06.8	84 17 05	32 59 13
2 56 52.5	84 18 30	32 59 14
2 58 08.2	84 19 55	32 58 53
2 59 15.5	84 20 05	32 59 03
3 00 25.8	84 20 50	32 58 50
3 01 51.5	84 20 30	32 59 03
3 02 48.0	84 20 10	32 59 10
3 03 50.0	84 19 55	32 59 10
3 04 54.8	84 19 15	32 59 17
3 06 04.8	84 18 35	32 59 21
3 07 19.2	84 17 45	32 59 16
3 08 26.8	84 17 10	32 59 04
3 09 22.8	84 15 40	32 59 20
3 10 10.8	84 14 40	32 59 22

Thermometer 50°.

Mean of 17 observations, 32° 59′ 10″.

APPENDIX No. 5—Continued.

November 14, 1846.—Camp 99, on the Gila.

DETERMINATION OF LATITUDE.

Time, p. m.	Double altitudes of Polaris.	Latitude.
h. m. s.	Deg. min. sec.	Deg. min. sec.
3 28 14.8	68 14 20	32 59 36
3 29 28 5	68 14 35	32 59 25
3 30 27.0	68 15 15	32 59 29
3 32 19.0	68 16 00	32 59 20
3 33 36.8	68 17 05	32 59 34
3 35 02.5	68 18 05	32 59 40
3 36 06.8	68 18 25	32 59 34
3 37 08.5	68 19 05	32 59 39
3 38 04.6	68 19 45	32 59 35

Thermometer 50°.

Mean of 9 observations, 32° 59' 34".

Ex. Doc. No. 41.

APPENDIX No. 5—Continued.

November 15, 1846.—*Camp* 99.

DETERMINATION OF TIME.

Time, p. m.	Double altitudes of *a* Andromedæ, in the east.	Chronometer fast.
h. m. s.	Deg. min. sec.	h. m. s.
2 41 43.6	116 12 05	8 47 36.7
2 42 41.7	116 35 50	8 47 38.3
2 43 22.5	116 53 20	8 47 37.5
2 43 59.8	117 08 20	8 47 38.8
2 44 35.0	117 23 45	8 47 37.6
2 45 28.0	117 46 20	8 47 36.9
2 46 14.8	118 05 40	8 47 37.6
2 46 56.0	118 23 10	8 47 37.2

Thermometer °.

Time, p. m.	Double altitudes of *a* Lyræ, in the west.	Chronometer fast
h. m. s.	Deg. min. sec.	h. m. s.
2 48 47.8	103 38 55	8 47 40.1
2 49 42.0	103 18 35	8 47 41.2
2 50 23.0	103 02 05	8 47 40.6
2 51 06.8	102 44 10	8 47 57.5 rej.
2 51 50.0	102 28 40	8 47 40.8
2 52 38.5	102 08 50	8 47 38.2
2 53 19.0	101 53 55	8 47 40.4
2 54 15.2	101 32 05	8 47 40.4

Mean of 15 observations, 8*h*. 47*m*. 38.91*s*.

Ex. Doc. No. 41.   347

APPENDIX No. 5—Continued.

November 14, 1846.—*Camp* 101, *on the Gila.*

DETERMINATION OF TIME.

Time, p. m.	Double altitudes of Algerib, in the east.	Chronometer fast.
h. m. s.	Deg. min. sec.	h. m. s.
3 14 02.8	116 17 50	8 49 33.0
3 15 00.0	116 38 55	8 49 32.9
3 16 12.5	117 05 45	8 49 32.3
3 17 12.5	117 26 55	8 49 34.2
3 18 08.0	117 47 30	8 49 33.2
3 19 02.5	118 07 35	8 49 32.4
3 19 55.3	118 26 45	8 49 32.4
3 20 42.2	118 43 25	8 49 33.1
3 21 52.8	119 09 15	8 49 31.9

Thermometer 40°.

Time, p. m.	Double altitudes of *a* Lyræ, in the west.	Chronometer fast.
h. m. s.	Deg. min. sec.	h. m. s.
3 24 29.8	87 31 20	8 49 37.1
3 25 16.8	87 13 20	8 49 37.2
3 26 03.5	86 55 10	8 49 36.6
3 26 57.8	86 34 10	8 49 36.0
3 28 02.0	86 08 45	8 49 33.9 rej.
3 28 52.6	85 49 55	8 49 35.4
3 29 54.3	85 26 20	8 49 38.3
3 30 35.5	85 10 50	8 49 36.1
3 31 14.0	84 56 20	8 49 37.1

Thermometer 40°.

Mean of 17 observations, 8*h*. 49*m*. 34.76*s*.

APPENDIX No. 5—Continued.

November 17, 1846.—*Camp* 101.

DETERMINATION OF LATITUDE.

Time, p. m.	Double altitudes of Polaris.	Latitude.
h. m. s.	*Deg. min. sec.*	*Deg. min. sec.*
3 51 28.5	68 22 55	32 55 40
3 52 32.8	68 23 20	32 55 38
3 53 52.3	68 24 05	32 55 43
3 54 46.0	68 25 10	32 56 05
3 56 07.0	68 25 00	32 55 41
3 57 42.8	68 25 50	32 55 46
3 58 50.5	68 26 25	32 55 48
3 59 35.0	68 27 00	32 55 58
4 00 13.5	68 27 25	32 56 00
4 00 52.8	68 27 45	32 56 02
4 01 28.0	68 28 05	32 56 04
4 02 20.0	68 28 20	32 56 00

Thermometer 38°.

Mean of 12 observations, 32° 55' 52".

APPENDIX No. 5—Continued.

November 19, 1846.—*Camp* 103, *on an island of the Gila.*

DETERMINATION OF TIME.

Time, p. m.	Double altitudes of *a* Lyræ, in the west.	Chronometer fast.
h. m. s.	Deg. min. sec.	h. m. s.
3 40 47.5	78 47 20	8 51 21.6
3 41 34.8	78 29 00	8 51 20.7
3 42 21.0	78 10 45	8 51 18.7
3 43 12.0	77 51 05	8 51 17.9
3 44 16.5	77 26 55	8 51 18.8
3 45 04.3	77 09 10	8 51 19.7
3 45 48.2	76 52 35	8 51 19.9
3 46 34.8	76 34 55	8 51 19.9
3 47 26.5	76 15 10	8 51 19.4

Thermometer 50°.

Time, p. m.	Double altitudes of *a* Arietis, in the east.	Chronometer fast.
h. m. s.	Deg. min. sec.	h. m. s.
3 53 19.0	97 50 55	8 51 17.1
3 54 11.2	98 13 10	8 51 16.5
3 54 57.8	98 32 00	8 51 18.4
3 55 39.8	98 50 05	8 51 17.4
3 56 32.0	99 12 20	8 51 16.8
3 57 21.0	99 33 10	8 51 16.3
3 58 40.0	100 05 45	8 51 18.0
3 59 30.8	100 27 45	8 51 16.4
4 00 11.0	100 44 45	8 51 16.4
4 00 51.2	101 01 35	8 51 16.5

Thermometer 50°.

Mean of 19 observations, 8*h*. 51*m*. 18.30*s*.

Ex. Doc. No. 41

APPENDIX No. 5—Continued.

November 19, 1846.—*Camp* 103.

DETERMINATION OF LATITUDE.

Time, p. m.	Double altitudes of Polaris.	Latitude.
h. m. s.	*Deg. min. sec.*	*Deg. min. sec.*
4 08 37.0	68 09 05	32 43 55
4 09 32.5	68 10 00	32 44 13
4 10 37.8	68 10 00	32 44 01
4 11 06.5	68 10 25	32 44 08
4 12 42.0	68 10 50	32 44 02
4 13 27.2	68 11 00	32 43 59
4 14 10.8	68 11 25	32 44 03
4 14 32.0	68 11 50	32 44 09
4 15 57.0	68 12 20	32 44 12
4 16 46.0	68 12 50	32 44 18
4 17 56.5	68 12 55	32 44 09
4 19 33.0	68 13 10	32 44 00
4 20 40.5	68 13 25	32 43 55

Thermometer 46°.

Mean of 13 observations, 32° 44' 05".

Ex. Doc. No. 41.   351

APPENDIX No. 5—Continued.

November 19, 1846.—*Camp* 103.

DETERMINATION OF LATITUDE.

Time, p. m.			Double altitudes of Procyon, near the meridian.			Latitude.		
h.	*m.*	*s.*	*Deg.*	*min.*	*sec.*	*Deg.*	*min.*	*sec.*
12	16	18.0	125	34	55	32	43	40
12	17	58.8	125	39	55	32	43	00
12	20	46.8	125	43	15	32	43	37
12	23	26.2	125	46	15	32	43	27
12	25	00.5	125	48	00	32	42	58
12	27	09.0	125	48	10	32	42	55
12	29	42.0	125	46	30	32	43	04
12	31	34.0	125	42	35	32	44	02
12	33	49.8	125	41	50	32	42	39
12	34	47.7	125	39	05	32	43	06
12	36	54.5	125	35	40	32	42	21

Thermometer 28°.

Mean of 11 observations, 32° 43′ 11″.

Ex. Doc. No. 41.

APPENDIX No. 5—Continued.

November 21, 1846.—*Camp* 105, *on the Gila*.

DETERMINATION OF TIME.

Time, p. m.	Double altitudes of α Lyræ, in the west.	Chronometer fast.
h. m. s.	*Deg. min. sec.*	*h. m. s.*
3 21 02.0	83 44 15	8 52 28.0
3 21 49.2	83 25 35	8 52 26.4
3 22 43.9	83 05 10	8 52 27.6
3 23 27.8	82 48 25	8 52 27.6
3 24 17.2	82 29 55	8 52 28.6
3 25 12.0	82 08 35	8 52 27.7
3 25 55.5	81 52 15	8 52 28.2
3 27 16.0	81 20 20	8 52 25.0 rej.
3 27 55.9	81 06 05	8 52 27.6

Thermometer 40°.

Time, p. m.	Double altitudes of α Arietis, in the east.	Chronometer fast.
h. m. s.	*Deg. min. sec.*	*h. m. s.*
3 32 43.3	92 00 30	8 52 25.9 rej.
3 33 36.0	92 24 00	8 52 21.9
3 34 32 0	92 47 10	8 52 22.8
3 35 40.8	93 16 10	8 52 23.0
3 36 27.6	93 35 45	8 52 23.3
3 37 16.8	93 57 15	8 52 21.4
3 38 19.5	94 23 45	8 52 21.3
3 39 15.5	94 47 30	8 52 20.9
3 40 15.0	95 12 40	8 52 21.8

Thermometer 40°.

Mean of 16 observations, 8*h*. 52*m*. 24.8*s*.

APPENDIX No. 5—Continued.

November 21, 1846.—*Camp* 105.

DETERMINATION OF LATITUDE.

Time. p. m.	Double altitudes of Polaris.	Latitude.
h. m. s.	*Deg. min. sec.*	*Deg min. sec.*
3 45 29.0	68 00 30	32 42 58 rej.
3 46 38.8	68 01 40	32 43 17
3 47 23.8	68 01 50	32 43 13
3 48 20.7	68 02 10	32 43 10
3 49 03.1	68 02 30	32 43 12
3 49 47.8	68 03 05	32 43 19
3 50 24.2	68 03 25	32 43 22
3 50 58.0	68 03 50	32 43 27
3 51 49.5	68 04 00	32 43 22
3 52 25.0	68 04 10	32 43 20
3 53 04.9	68 04 20	32 43 16
3 53 46.8	68 04 30	32 43 13
3 54 23.5	68 04 45	32 43 13

Thermometer 40°

Mean of 12 observations, 32° 43′ 17″.

APPENDIX No. 5—Continued.

November 22, 1846.—*Camp* 106, *near the mouth of the Gila*, 5, *p. m.*

DETERMINATION OF LONGITUDE.

Time, p. m.	Distance of Fomalhaut from moon's western limb.	Double altitudes of moon's lower limb.
h. m. s.	Deg. min sec.	Deg. min. sec.
2 41 39.0	46 52 15	58 40 50
2 44 10.8	46 51 40	58 01 20
2 46 53.8	46 50 20	57 18 30
2 49 15 0	46 49 45	56 41 10
2 52 36.2	46 48 45	55 46 20
2 56 17.5	46 47 30	54 46 10
3 02 06.0	46 45 35	53 (8 55
3 03 49.2	46 45 10	52 49 50
3 06 13.8	46 44 40	51 58 50

Thermometer 60°.

Longitude, by mean of observations, 7*h*. 40*m*. 50.00*s*.

Ex. Doc. No. 41.   355

APPENDIX No. 5—Continued.

November 22, 1846.—*Camp* 106, *near the mouth of the Gila.*

DETERMINATION OF TIME.

Time, p. m.	Double altitudes of *a* Lyræ, in the west.	Chronometer fast.
h. m. s.	Deg. min. sec.	h. m. s.
3 14 13.3	85 09 35	8 53 20.9
3 15 17.7	84 44 55	8 53 20.9
3 16 17.6	84 21 35	8 53 19.8
3 17 13.8	83 59 30	8 53 18.3
3 18 05.9	83 40 10	8 53 19.8
3 18 54.0	83 21 40	8 53 19.5
3 19 53.0	82 59 00	8 53 19.2
3 20 44.8	82 40 05	8 53 21.5
3 21 35.2	82 20 15	8 53 20.0

Thermometer 60°.

Time, p. m.	Double altitudes of *a* Arietis, in the east.	Chronometer fast.
h. m. s.	Deg. min. sec.	h. m. s.
3 28 17.5	91 26 10	8 53 16.7
3 29 06.0	91 47 40	8 53 14.2
3 29 58.8	92 09 40	8 53 16.0
3 30 49.8	92 30 20	8 53 16.8
3 31 33.5	92 49 30	8 53 15.0
3 32 28.0	93 11 25	8 53 18.6
3 33 33.8	93 40 10	8 53 15.2
3 34 55.0	94 14 15	8 53 15.5
3 35 54.8	94 39 15	8 53 18.0

Thermometer 60°.

Mean of 18 observations, 8*h*. 53*m*. 18.10*s*.

APPENDIX No. 5—Continued.

November 22, 1846.—Camp 106.

DETERMINATION OF LATITUDE.

Time, p. m.	Double altitudes of Polaris.	Latitude.
h. m. s.	Deg. min. sec.	Deg. min. sec.
3 48 19.5	68 01 50	32 42 21
3 49 26.0	68 02 15	32 42 19
3 59 18.0	68 02 30	32 42 18
3 59 59.8	68 02 25	32 42 08
3 52 56.0	68 03 30	32 42 15
3 54 08.0	68 04 10	32 42 15
3 55 12.8	68 04 20	32 42 14
3 56 07.8	68 05 05	32 42 25
3 57 10.9	68 05 20	32 42 22
3 58 23.2	68 05 35	32 42 14
3 59 26.8	68 05 45	32 42 08
4 00 35.2	68 06 05	32 42 05
4 01 51.8	68 06 45	32 42 11

Thermometer 60°.

Mean of 13 observations, 32° 42′ 15″.

APPENDIX No. 5—Continued.

November 23, 1846.—*Camp* 106.

DETERMINATION OF TIME.

Time, p. m.			Double altitudes of Saturn in the west.		
h.	m.	s.	Deg.	min.	sec.
2	39	36.5	85	06	00
2	40	38.5	85	04	50
2	41	37.0	85	03	20
2	42	42.8	85	02	50
2	43	20.0	85	01	10
2	44	01.0	85	00	00

Thermometer 56°.

DETERMINATION OF LONGITUDE.

Time, p. m.			Distance of α Arietis from moon's western limb.			Double altitudes of moon's lower limb.		
h.	m.	s.	Deg.	min.	sec.	Deg.	min.	sec.
3	15	51.0	88	30	55	68	50	20
3	20	08.8	88	28	10	67	47	20
3	22	08.5	88	27	20	67	17	45
3	28	06.0	88	24	45	65	46	50
3	30	41.5	88	23	50	65	06	55
3	34	08.5	88	22	30	64	11	50
3	35	54.8	88	21	40	63	44	00

Thermometer 56°.

	h.	m.	s.
Longitude by α Arietis	7	39	46.5
Longitude by Fomalhaut	7	40	50.0
Mean...........................	7	40	18.25

APPENDIX No. 5—Continued.

November 25, 1846.—Camp 106.

Time, p. m.	Double altitudes of a Arietis, in the east.	Chronometer fast.
h. m. s.	Deg. min sec.	h. m. s.
3 42 58.8	99 22 55	8 53 02.9
3 43 56.0	99 46 25	8 53 04.5
3 44 37.8	100 02 45	8 53 07.4 rej.
3 45 31.8	100 26 20	8 53 05.3
3 46 22.0	100 48 10	8 53 03.7
3 47 10.8	101 08 35	8 53 03.9
3 47 59.0	101 28 65	8 53 03.5
4 48 55.5	101 52 25	8 53 04.6
4 49 39.0	102 11 20	9 53 03.1

Thermometer 54°.

Time, p. m.	Double altitudes of a Lyræ, in the west.	Chronometer fast.
h. m. s.	Deg. min. sec.	h. m. s.
3 54 46.8	68 12 40	8 53 05.1
3 55 48.0	67 49 40	8 53 04.9
3 56 36.5	67 32 15	8 53 06.8
3 57 18.3	67 16 40	8 53 06.8
3 58 08.8	66 57 50	8 53 06.8
3 58 53.8	66 40 25	8 53 05.1
3 59 32.8	66 26 20	8 53 06.3
4 00 20.8	66 08 10	8 53 03.5
4 01 04.0	65 52 30	8 53 06.7

Thermometer 52°.

Mean of 17 observations, 8h. 53m. 04.86s.

APPENDIX No. 5—Continued.

November 23, 1846.—*Camp* 106.

Time, p. m.			Double altitudes of Sirius, near the meridian.			Latitude.		
h.	*m.*	*s.*	*Deg.*	*min.*	*sec.*	*Deg.*	*min.*	*sec.*
11	14	39.8	81	34	55	32	42	06
11	15	36.0	81	35	20	32	42	11
11	16	30.7	81	36	10	32	41	,59
11	17	33.6	81	36	20	32	42	05
11	18	36.8	81	36	40	32	42	01
11	19	33	0	81	36	30	32	42	23 rej.
11	21	17.5	81	36	20	32	42	06
11	22	17.0	81	36	20	32	41	57
11	23	06.0	81	35	45	32	42	04
11	23	54.8	81	35	10	32	42	07
11	24	40.0	81	34	45	32	42	05
11	25	41.6	81	34	05	32	42	01
11	27	00.0	81	33	10	32	41	51

Thermometer 46°.

Mean of 12 observations, 32° 42′ 03″.

APPENDIX No. 5—Continued.

November 25, 1846.—Camp 108—first camp after leaving the Rio Colorado.

DETERMINATION OF TIME.

Time, p. m.	Double altitudes of α Lyræ, in the west.	Chronometer fast.
h. m. s.	Deg. min. sec.	h. m. s.
3 05 57.5	84 02 20	8 53 63.1 rej.
3 06 40.8	83 44 15	8 53 59.2
3 07 27.9	83 26 35	8 54 01.1
3 08 16.5	83 07 45	8 53 59.5
3 09 10.9	82 46 50	8 53 59.2
3 09 59.8	82 28 35	8 53 60.4
3 10 48.0	82 09 30	8 53 58.7
3 11 34.8	81 51 35	8 53 58.6

Thermometer 46°.

Time, p. m.	Double altitudes of α Arietis, in the east.	Chronometer fast.
h. m. s.	Deg. min. sec.	h. m. s.
3 16 18.5	91 06 00	8 53 54.4
3 17 14.0	91 31 25	8 53 49.8 rej.
3 17 52.5	91 45 15	8 53 55.6
3 18 31.6	92 02 00	8 53 54.9
3 19 15.0	92 20 55	8 53 53.4
3 19 58.5	92 39 35	8 53 52.8
3 20 39.5	92 56 30	8 53 53.8
3 21 26.8	93 16 20	8 53 54.0

Thermometer 46°.

Mean of 14 observations, 8*h*. 53*m*. 56.82*s*.

APPENDIX No. 5—Continued.

November 25, 1846.—*Camp* 108.

DETERMINATION OF LATITUDE.

Time, p. m.	Double altitudes of Polaris.	Latitude.
h. m. s.	*Deg. min. sec.*	*Deg. min. sec.*
3 24 40.5	67 52 05	32 40 11
3 25 46.2	67 52 55	32 40 22
3 26 45.0	67 53 10	32 40 16
3 27 31.8	67 53 30	32 40 16
3 28 51.5	67 54 20	32 40 24
3 29 44.0	67 54 40	32 40 22
3 30 26.8	67 55 05	32 40 25
3 31 06.5	67 55 45	32 40 33
3 32 01.0	67 55 45	32 40 24
3 33 25.0	67 56 30	32 40 30

Thermometer 44°.

Mean of 10 observations, 32° 40′ 22″.

APPENDIX No. 5—Continued.

November 28, 1846.—*Camp* 111.

DETERMINATION OF LONGITUDE.

Time, p. m.	Distance of Aldebaran from moon's western limb.	Double altitude of moon's lower limb.
h. m. s.	*Deg. min. sec.*	*Deg. min. sec.*
5 27 34.0	49 25 25	129 01 40
5 29 22.8	49 24 45	129 05 50
5 31 16.0	49 23 55	129 08 25
5 33 17.5	49 23 05	129 11 10
5 05 15.8	49 22 35	129 12 20
5 37 22.8	49 21 50	129 13 00
5 39 25.8	49 21 15	129 12 40
5 41 25.8	49 20 25	129 11 10

Thermometer 44°.

Longitude, by mean of observations, 7*h*. 43*m*. 06.4*s*.

Ex. Doc. No. 41. 363

APPENDIX No. 5—Continued.

November, 28, 1846.—*Camp* 111.

DETERMINATION OF LONGITUDE.

Time, p. m.	Distance of Fomalhaut from moon's western limb.	Double altitudes of moon's lower limb.
h. m. s.	*Deg. min. sec.*	*Deg. min sec.*
5 48 54.0	50 32 50	128 57 30
5 51 03.8	50 33 30	128 50 20
5 53 43.7	50 34 10	128 40 30
5 58 03.5	50 35 35	128 22 15
6 01 58.0	50 36 10	128 00 00
6 05 24.1	50 37 50	127 38 30
6 08 12.5	50 39 00	127 19 20
6 10 19.2	50 39 00	127 03 20
6 15 10.0	50 40 30	126 40 10
6 16 02.7	50 41 20	126 15 30
6 19 19.0	50 42 40	125 45 50

Thermometer 44°.

	h.	*m.*	*s.*
Longitude by Fomalhaut.....................	7	43	43.01
Longitude by Aldebaran		54	06.04
Mean........................	7	43	24.75

APPENDIX No. 5—Continued.

November 28.—*Camp* 111, *Cariso creek, first after passing the Jornada.*

DETERMINATION OF TIME.

Time, p. m.	Double altitudes of α Lyræ, in the west.	Chronometer fast.
h. m. s.	Deg. min. sec.	h. m. s.
2 49 25.5	87 31 40	8 57 58.4
2 50 20.0	87 10 40	8 57 57.2
2 51 10.0	86 51 20	8 57 56.8
2 51 54.5	86 34 45	8 57 37.9
2 52 43.0	86 15 30	8 57 56.4
2 53 23.3	86 00 20	8 57 57.0
2 54 18.2	85 39 35	8 57 57.7
2 55 07.3	85 19 50	8 57 55.2
2 55 51.5	85 03 35	8 57 55.0

Thermometer 48°.

Time, p. m.	Double altitudes of α Arietis, in the east.	Chronometer fast.
h. m. s.	Deg. min. sec.	h. m. s.
3 02 01.8	88 21 15	8 57 56.7
3 03 06.2	88 47 45	8 57 58.2
3 03 59.8	89 10 05	8 57 58.8
3 04 55.5	89 33 45	8 57 58.2
3 05 55.8	89 59 45	8 57 56.7
3 06 47.8	90 21 10	8 57 57.8
3 07 47.5	90 46 30	8 57 57.3
3 08 32.8	91 05 25	8 57 57.7
3 09 21.5	91 27 35	8 57 53.7 rej.

Thermometer 48°.

Mean of 17 observations, 8*h.* 57*m.* 57.26*s.*

APPENDIX No. 5—Continued.

November 28, 1846.—*Camp* 111.

DETERMINATION OF LATITUDE.

Time, p. m.	Double altitudes of Polaris.	Latitude.
h. m. s.	Deg. min. sec.	Deg. min. sec.
3 23 15.0	68 19 25	32 52 31
3 24 09.0	68 19 40	32 52 28
3 25 04.5	68 20 00	32 52 25
3 26 06.5	68 19 30	32 51 56 rej.
3 26 50.0	68 21 20	32 52 43
3 27 35.0	68 21 35	32 52 40
3 28 22.5	68 21 40	32 52 33
3 29 34.5	68 21 50	32 52 24
3 30 52.0	68 22 20	32 52 24
3 32 11.8	68 23 20	32 52 37
3 33 20.0	68 23 40	32 52 34
3 34 02.5	68 23 55	32 52 33
3 35 20.0	68 24 25	32 52 39

Thermometer 46°.

Mean of 12 observations, 32° 52′ 33″.

APPENDIX No. 5—Continued.

November 29, 1846.—*Camp* 112, "*Valle Citon.*"

DETERMINATION OF TIME.

Time, p. m.			Double altitudes of *a* Lyræ, in the west.			Chronometer fast.		
h.	*m.*	*s.*	*Deg*	*min.*	*sec.*	*h.*	*m.*	*s.*
2	47	23.8	87	10	05	8	58	44.1
2	48	17.0	86	49	10	8	58	42.7
2	49	13.9	86	27	20	8	58	42.6
2	50	03.5	86	08	25	8	58	42.9
2	50	51.5	85	50	15	8	58	43.5
2	51	32.0	85	35	05	8	58	44.2
2	52	24.2	85	14	45	8	58	43.3
2	53	12.4	84	56	10	8	58	42.9

Thermometer 50°.

Time, p. m.			Double altitudes of *a* Arietis, in the east.			Chronometer fast.		
h.	*m.*	*s.*	*Deg.*	*min.*	*sec.*	*h.*	*m.*	*s.*
2	58	01.0	87	59	50	8	58	43.7
2	58	50.3	88	21	20	8	58	41.9
2	59	30.0	88	37	35	8	58	42.9
3	00	19.2	88	53	30	8	58	42.4
3	01	20.3	89	23	55	8	58	42.9
3	02	16.5	89	48	35	8	58	40.5
3	03	10.8	90	10	35	8	58	42.4
3	04	12.0	90	36	40	8	58	41.8
3	05	04.2	90	58	35	8	58	41.7

Thermometer 50°.

Mean of 17 observations, 8*h*. 58*m*. 42.78*s*.

Ex. Doc. No. 41. 367

APPENDIX No. 5—Continued.

November 30, 1846.—*Camp* 112.

DETERMINATION OF TIME.

Time, p. m.	Double altitudes of *a* Lyræ, in the west.	Chronometer fast.
h. m. s.	Deg. min. sec.	h. m. s.
2 47 58.8	85 21 15	8 58 31.2
2 48 46.6	85 02 55	8 58 31.2
2 49 38.8	84 42 55	8 58 30.7
2 50 27.5	84 24 15	8 58 30.5
2 51 11.0	84 07 45	8 58 30.7
2 51 55.2	83 50 40	8 58 30.3
2 52 45.0	83 31 20	8 58 29.3
2 53 29.9	83 14 25	8 58 29.9
2 54 21.7	82 55 05	8 58 31.1

Thermometer 48°.

Time, p. m.	Double altitudes of *a* Arietis, in the east.	Chronometer fast.
h. m. s.	Deg min. sec.	h. m. s.
3 14 21.0	96 37 20	8 58 28.1
3 16 50.8	97 40 10	8 58 27.6
3 17 25.0	97 54 10	8 58 29.1
3 19 40.6	98 50 50	8 58 29.9
3 22 24.8	99 59 55	8 58 29.5

Thermometer 48°.

Mean of 14 observations, 8*h*. 58*m*. 29.69*s*.

Boisterous and cloudy. The ground at this camp is spongy, and shaken by the lightest tread.

APPENDIX No. 5—Continued.

November 29, 1846.—*Camp* 112.

DETERMINATION OF LATITUDE.

Time, p. m.	Double altitudes of Polaris.	Latitude.
h. m. s.	*Deg. min. sec.*	*Deg. min. sec.*
3 08 45.0	68 26 20	32 58 24
3 09 51.8	68 26 40	32 58 24
3 10 47.5	68 27 30	32 58 32
3 12 02.0	68 27 45	32 58 20
3 13 02.5	68 27 55	32 58 13
3 13 52.5	68 28 15	32 58 10
3 14 33.5	68 28 35	32 58 12
3 15 26.0	68 28 55	32 58 10
3 16 04.0	68 29 10	32 58 09
3 16 40.8	68 29 20	32 58 02
3 17 27.0	68 29 55	32 58 14
3 18 06.2	68 30 00	32 58 8

Thermometer 50°.

Mean of 12 observations, 32° 58′ 15″

APPENDIX No. 5—Continued.

December 2, 1846.—*Camp* 114, "*Warner's.*"

DETERMINATION OF TIME.

Time, p. m.			Double altitudes of α Lyræ, in the west.			Chronometer fast.		
h.	m.	s.	Deg.	min.	sec.	h.	m.	s.
2	45	26.8	83	51	55	8	59	16.0
2	46	22.5	83	31	10	8	59	17.2
2	47	17.9	83	10	05	8	59	17.3
2	47	56.8	82	54	55	8	59	16.4
2	48	44.0	82	37	35	8	59	18 1
2	49	31.7	82	18	30	8	59	15.6
2	50	25.8	81	57	55	8	59	16.4
2	51	13.0	81	40	15	8	59	16.3
2	51	57.8	81	23	50	8	59	17.9

Thermometer 34°.

Time, p. m.			Double altitudes of α Arietis, in the east.			Chronometer fast.			
h.	m.	s.	Deg.	min.	sec.	h.	m.	s.	
2	58	40.8	92	59	40	8	59	15 6	
2	59	32.3	93	20	50	8	59	16.6	
3	00	24.0	93	42	35	8	59	16.4	
3	01	19.5	94	06	55	8	59	13.7	rej.
3	02	12.5	94	28	30	8	59	15.2	
3	03	31.2	95	00	55	8	59	16.6	
3	04	19.3	95	21	05	8	59	16.5	
3	05	16.8	95	44	50	8	59	17.2	
3	05	58.5	96	03	20	8	59	14.8	

Thermometer 36°.

Mean of 17 observations, $8h.$ $59m.$ $16.46s.$

APPENDIX No. 5—Continued.

December 2, 1846.—*Camp* 114, "*Warner's.*"

DETERMINATION OF LATITUDE.

Time, p. m.			Double altitudes of Polaris.			Latitude.		
h.	m.	s.	Deg.	min.	sec.	Deg.	min.	sec.
3	11	12.8	69	09	55	33	17	21
3	12	11.8	69	09	10	33	16	40
3	13	33.5	69	09	25	33	16	29
3	14	51.5	69	10	55	33	17	00
3	16	28.9	69	11	35	33	17	09
3	17	51.0	69	12	10	33	17	09
3	18	35.8	69	12	10	33	16	47
3	20	31.0	69	12	50	33	16	49
3	21	03.8	69	13	25	33	16	58
3	21	52.0	69	13	40	33	16	58
3	22	23.8	69	13	55	33	16	59
3	23	13.0	69	14	10	33	16	59

Thermometer 64°.

Mean of 12 observations, 33° 16' 57"

APPENDIX No. 5—Continued.

December 8, 1846.—*Camp* 118, *San Bernardo*.

DETERMINATION OF TIME.

Time, p. m.	Double altitudes of a Lyræ, in the west.	Chronometer fast.
h. m. s.	Deg. min. sec.	h. m. s.
3 19 03.0	62 19 00	8 59 41.2
3 20 28.8	61 49 25	8 59 40.8
3 21 20.2	61 30 20	8 59 40.4
3 22 17.9	61 09 30	8 59 41.6
3 22 59.5	60 53 55	8 59 40.7
3 23 46.2	60 36 35	8 59 40.4
3 24 34.7	60 19 25	8 59 39.3
3 25 28.8	59 59 20	8 59 41.5
3 26 06.8	59 44 60	8 59 40.5

Thermometer 40°.

Time, p. m.	Double altitudes of a Arietis, in the east.	Chronometer fast.
h. m. s.	Deg. min. sec.	h. m. s.
3 34 46.0	117 46 30	8 59 36.9
3 35 41.8	118 09 15	8 59 37.5
3 36 32.8	118 30 15	8 59 37.6
3 37 13.8	118 47 35	8 59 36.5
3 38 13.8	119 12 35	8 59 35.8
3 38 59.6	119 30 30	8 59 38.1
3 39 40.0	119 47 25	8 59 37.5
3 40 34.7	120 09 30	8 58 38.5

Thermometer 40°.

Mean of 17 observations, 8h. 59m. 38.95s.

Ex. Doc. No. 41.

APPENDIX No. 5—Continued.

December 8, 1846.—*Camp* 118, *San Bernardo.*

DETERMINATION OF LATITUDE.

Time, p. m.			Double altitudes of Polaris.			Latitude.		
h.	m.	s.	Deg.	min.	sec.	Deg.	min.	sec.
3	44	15.0	69	01	30	33	03	49
3	45	10.0	69	01	50	33	03	45
3	45	45.5	69	02	00	33	03	46
3	46	32.2	69	02	00	33	03	40
3	47	10.8	69	02	10	33	03	41
3	48	00.8	69	02	30	33	03	45
3	48	34.6	69	02	40	33	03	46
3	49	25.8	69	02	35	33	03	38
3	50	04.0	69	02	30	33	03	32

Thermometer 40°.

Mean of 9 observations, 33° 03′ 42″.

Ex. Doc. No. 41.

APPENDIX No. 5—Continued.

December 15, 1846.—Camp 120, San Diego.

DETERMINATION OF TIME.

Time, p. m.	Double altitudes of a Areitis, in the east.	Chronometer fast.
h. m. s.	Deg. min. sec.	h. m. s.
3 33 31.0	129 04 15	8 58 38.1
3 34 24.0	129 25 25	8 58 39.1
3 35 15.8	129 46 10	8 58 39.2
3 36 26.8	130 15 40	8 58 36.9
3 37 30.0	130 41 20	8 58 36.4
3 38 23.2	131 02 10	8 58 37.8
3 39 23.9	131 26 40	8 58 37.4
3 40 22.5	131 50 20	8 58 36.9

Thermometer 50°.

Time, p. m.	Double altitudes of a Pegasi, in the west.	Chronometer fast.
h. m. s.	Deg. min. sec.	h. m. s.
3 52 26.5	123 38 45	8 58 41.6
3 53 43.8	123 11 55	8 58 41.2
3 54 42.8	122 50 55	8 58 42.0
3 55 34.7	122 33 10	8 58 40.9
3 56 25.0	122 16 45	8 58 44.2 rej.
3 57 22.3	121 55 40	8 58 41.6
3 58 13.0	121 37 40	8 58 41.3
3 59 04.5	121 19 40	8 58 41.9
4 00 05.2	120 58 10	8 58 42.1

Thermometer 50°

Mean of 16 observations, 8h. 58m. 39.65s.

APPENDIX No. 5—Continued.

December 15. 1846.—*San Diego.*

DETERMINATION OF LATITUDE.

Time, p. m.	Double altitudes of Polaris.	Latitude.
h. m. s.	Deg. min. sec.	Deg. min. sec.
4 17 32.0	68 33 55	32 45 41
4 18 27.8	68 33 35	32 45 30
4 19 21.5	68 33 55	32 45 39
4 20 49.2	68 33 55	32 45 37
4 21 33.0	68 33 45	32 45 32
4 22 09.0	68 33 35	32 45 27
4 23 00.8	68 33 55	32 45 37
4 23 46.5	68 33 30	32 45 24
4 24 28.0	68 34 00	32 45 40
4 25 12.5	68 33 40	32 45 30
4 25 49.0	68 33 50	32 45 34
4 26 20.8	68 33 50	32 45 34

Thermometer 50°.

Mean of 12 observations, 32° 45′ 34″.

Ex. Doc. No. 41.   375

APPENDIX No. 5—Continued.

December 16, 1846.—*San Diego.*

DETERMINATION OF LATITUDE.

Time, p. m.	Double altitudes of Ceti, near the meridian.	Latitude.
h. m. s.	Deg. min. sec.	Deg. min. sec.
6 04 16.0	121 24 45	32 44 40
6 06 24.2	121 27 40	32 44 32
6 07 36.5	121 28 35	32 44 37
6 08 16.2	121 29 05	32 44 35
6 09 41.8	121 30 40	32 44 07
6 10 53.2	121 31 20	32 43 52
6 12 04.0	121 31 05	32 43 55
6 12 43.8	121 30 20	32 44 11
6 13 43.0	121 30 30	32 43 51
6 15 08.5	121 29 00	32 44 02
6 16 02.5	121 26 20	32 45 51

Thermometer 40°.

Mean of 11 observations, 32° 44′ 12″.

APPENDIX No. 5—Continued.

December 16, 1846.—*San Diego.*

DETERMINATION OF TIME

Time, p. m.			Double altitudes of Aldebaran, in the east.			Chronometer fast.		
h.	*m.*	*s.*	*Deg.*	*min.*	*sec.*	*h.*	*m.*	*s.*
4	40	14.0	90	52	50	8	58	24.7
4	41	04.8	91	13	30	8	58	25.6
4	41	41.2	91	29	35	8	58	23.1
4	42	30.5	91	49	25	8	58	24.7
4	43	19 8	92	10	00	8	58	24.1
4	44	17.5	92	33	15	8	58	25.6
4	45	25.5	93	01	35	8	58	25.1
4	46	29.5	93	29	15	8	58	22.1 rej.
4	47	27.2	93	52	15	8	58	21.7 rej.

Thermometer 50°.

Mean of 7 observations, 8*h*. 58*m*. 24.70*s*.

Time, p. m.			Double altitudes of ———— in the west.		
h.	*m.*	*s.*	*Deg.*	*min.*	*sec.*
5	27	32.5	104	32	40
5	28	15.2	104	14	45
5	29	03.8	103	55	10
5	29	43.5	103	37	55
5	30	29.6	103	18	15
5	31	11.0	103	01	15
5	32	10.5	102	36	50
5	33	40.3	101	58	20
4	35	21.6	101	16	10
5	36	09.8	100	56	10
5	37	06.5	100	32	30

Thermometer 50°.

APPENDIX No. 5—Continued.

December 19, 1846.—San Diego.

DETERMINATION OF TIME.

Time, p. m.			Double altitudes of sun's upper limb.	
h.	m.	s.	Deg.	min.
11	23	04.8	48	00
11	24	26.0	47	40
11	25	05.8	47	30
11	25	43.7	47	20
11	26	22.5	47	10
11	27	01.5	47	00
11	27	38.0	46	50
11	28	19.8	46	40
11	28	55.7	46	30
11	29	31.5	46	20

Thermometer 64°.

DETERMINATION OF INDEX ERROR.

	Min. sec.	Min. sec.
On the arc..................	32 15	31 55
Off the arc	32 25	32 40

APPENDIX No. 5—Continued.

December 19, 1846.—San Diego.

DETERMINATION OF TIME.

Time, p. m.	Double altitudes of ——— in the west.	Chronometer fast.
h. m. s.	Deg. min. sec.	h. m. s.
6 11 05.2	114 03 10	
6 12 09.0	113 36 25	
6 12 52.0	113 18 15	
6 13 35.8	112 59 35	
6 14 25.0	112 39 30	
6 15 17.5	112 19 50	
6 16 10.5	111 57 30	
6 17 24.0	111 25 30	
6 18 22.5	111 01 05	
6 19 54.0	110 23 00	

Thermometer 50°.

Time, p. m.	Double altitudes of *a* Orionis, in the east.	Chronometer fast.
h. m. s.	Deg. min. sec.	h. m. s.
6 29 36.8	97 07 30	8 57 49.5
6 30 36.6	97 29 05	8 57 50.3
6 31 21.2	97 45 15	8 57 50.5
6 32 10.0	98 04 05	8 57 47.4
6 32 56.5	98 19 50	8 57 51.5
6 33 39.8	98 35 05	8 57 51.6
6 34 28.5	98 53 15	8 57 50.0
6 35 15.8	99 08 55	8 57 53.7
6 36 00.8	99 25 30	8 57 52.8
6 36 39.8	99 40 25	8 57 50.2

Thermometer 50°.

Mean of 10 observations, 8h. 57m. 50.75s.

Ex. Doc. No. 41.

APPENDIX No. 5—Continued.

December 19, 1846.—*San Diego.*

DETERMINATION OF LATITUDE.

Time, p. m.			Double altitudes of α Ceti, near the meridian.			Latitude.		
h.	*m.*	*s.*	*Deg.*	*min.*	*sec.*	*Deg.*	*min.*	*sec.*
5	53	16.0	121	27	10	32	44	18
5	54	38.5	121	29	45	32	43	48
5	55	44.0	121	30	30	32	43	48
5	56	30.5	121	30	45	32	43	53
5	57	26.8	121	31	00	32	43	57
6	00	32.5	121	32	10	32	43	15
6	01	16.5	121	32	20	32	42	59
6	02	02.8	121	31	50	32	42	59
6	02	58.0	121	30	40	32	43	10
6	03	42.8	121	39	20	32	43	26
6	04	51.5	121	27	25	32	43	40

Thermometer 50°.

Mean of 11 observations, 32° 43' 34".

APPENDIX No. 5—Continued.

December 20, 1846.—San Diego.

DETERMINATION OF LATITUDE.

Time, p. m.	Double altitudes of Polaris.	Latitude.
h. m. s.	Deg. min. sec.	Deg. min. sec.
6 30 15.2	67 58 35	32 45 44
6 31 04.8	67 58 20	32 45 49
6 31 51.5	67 57 50	32 45 45
6 32 35.0	67 57 10	32 45 36
6 33 10.8	67 56 55	32 45 37
6 36 51.5	67 55 10	32 45 37
6 37 40.1	67 54 50	32 45 40
6 38 21.5	67 54 10	32 45 30
6 39 09.8	67 54 05	32 45 39
6 39 49.8	67 53 25	32 45 30
6 40 50.0	67 53 05	32 45 34
6 41 32.5	67 52 35	32 45 31

Thermometer 45°.

Mean of 12 observations, 32° 45' 38".

APPENDIX No. 5—Continued.

December 20, 1846.—San Diego.

DETERMINATION OF TIME.

Time, p. m.	Double altitudes of ——— in the west.	Chronometer fast.
h. m. s.	Deg. min. sec.	h. m. s.
6 03 15.5	115 36 20	
6 04 11.2	115 11 10	
6 04 51.5	114 55 45	
6 05 41.5	114 31 04	
6 06 26.5	114 15 50	
6 07 15.7	113 55 40	
6 08 13.2	113 31 50	
6 08 53.2	113 15 20	
6 09 32.8	112 53 18	

Thermometer 45°.

Time, p. m.	Double altitudes of a Orionis, in the east.	Chronometer fast.
h. m. s.	Deg. min. sec.	h. m. s.
6 15 16.8	93 18 55	8 57 43.0
6 16 18.3	93 41 25	8 57 44.5
6 17 02.0	93 58 40	8 57 42.0
6 17 51.5	94 16 30	8 57 43.5
6 18 40.0	94 35 50	8 57 42.8
6 19 30.0	94 53 40	8 57 42.1
6 20 23.8	95 13 50	8 57 41.3
6 21 17.8	95 33 45	8 57 41.6
6 22 05.5	95 51 10	8 57 42.0

Thermometer 45°.

Mean of 9 observations, 8h. 57m. 42.58s.

APPENDIX No. 5—Continued.

December 21, 1846.—*San Diego.*

DETERMINATION OF TIME.

Time, p. m.			Double altitudes of *a* Andromedæ, in the west.			Chronometer fast.		
h.	*m.*	*s.*	*Deg.*	*min.*	*sec.*	*h.*	*m.*	*s.*
6	03	19.2	99	40	55	8	57	28.3
6	04	14.5	99	18	10	8	57	29.3
6	05	00.5	98	58	25	8	57	28.1
6	05	52.8	98	37	05	8	57	29.5
6	06	45.8	98	14	05	8	57	27.4
6	07	31.0	97	54	40	8	57	26.4
6	08	20.0	97	35	25	8	57	29.3
6	09	09.2	97	14	50	8	57	29.3
6	09	52.5	96	56	20	8	57	28.6

Thermometer 45°.

Time, p. m.			Double altitudes of *a* Orion, in the east.			Chronometer fast.		
h.	*m.*	*s.*	*Deg.*	*min.*	*sec.*	*h.*	*m.*	*s.*
6	16	16.8	95	15	30	8	57	25.8
6	17	06.8	95	34	15	8	57	25.1
6	18	00.5	95	53	50	8	57	25.7
6	18	57.8	96	15	05	8	57	25.3
6	19	40.5	96	30	15	8	57	27.1
6	20	25.7	96	48	05	8	57	23.3
6	21	16.5	97	05	30	8	57	26.3
6	22	06.0	97	23	35	8	57	26.4
6	23	03.5	97	45	40	8	57	23.3

Thermometer 45°.

Mean of 18 observations, 8*h.* 57*m.* 26.90*s.*

APPENDIX No. 5—Continued.

December 21, 1846.—San Diego.

DETERMINATION OF LATITUDE.

Time, p. m.	Double altitudes of a Ceti, near the meridian.	Latitude.
h. m. s.	Deg. min. sec.	Deg. min. sec.
5 42 48.0	121 23 40	32 44 32
5 44 04.5	121 25 45	32 44 29
5 45 36.0	121 27 05	32 44 45
5 46 58.0	121 28 45	32 44 32
5 48 15.8	121 28 45	32 44 53
5 50 11.8	121 29 35	32 44 45
5 51 04.0	121 30 00	32 44 30
5 52 25.7	121 29 10	32 44 42
5 53 36.6	121 28 50	32 44 30
5 54 43.0	121 27 35	32 44 38
5 56 15.2	121 25 55	32 44 45
5 57 26.2	121 23 40	32 44 51

Thermometer 45°.

Mean of 12 observations, 32° 44′ 39″.

APPENDIX No. 5—Continued.

December 23, 1846.—San Diego.

DETERMINATION OF LATITUDE.

Time, p. m.	Double altitudes of a Ceti, near the meridian.	Latitude.
h m. s.	Deg. min. sec.	Deg. min. sec.
5 33 04.0	121 20 10	32 44 57
5 34 05.5	121 22 45	32 44 38
5 35 16.0	121 26 60	32 43 28 rej.
5 36 32.0	121 27 20	32 44 10
5 37 15.0	121 28 00	32 44 15
5 38 09.8	121 28 45	32 44 20
5 38 51.8	121 29 05	32 44 26
5 39 55.5	121 29 50	32 44 22
5 41 06.5	121 29 50	32 44 34
5 42 16.2	121 30 30	32 44 17
5 44 23.8	121 30 20	32 44 03
5 45 24.6	121 29 00	32 44 23
5 46 24.8	121 28 20	32 44 17
5 47 33.0	121 27 40	32 44 00
5 48 35 7	121 24 40	32 44 46
5 49 25.8	121 23 05	32 44 55
5 50 24.5	121 22 40	32 44 15
5 51 09.8	121 21 05	32 44 18

Index error + 17.5″.

Thermometer 54°.

Mean of 17 observations, 32° 44′ 24″.

Ex. Doc. No. 41.   385

APPENDIX No. 5—Continued.

December 23, 1846.—San Diego.

DETERMINATION OF TIME.

Time, p. m.	Double altitudes of α Andromedæ, in the west.	Chronometer fast.
h. m. s.	Deg. min. sec.	h. m. s.
5 54 56.5	99 41 10	8 56 58.0
5 55 33.0	99 26 10	8 56 58.7
5 56 16.8	99 07 25	8 56 57.7
5 57 08.5	98 46 15	8 56 58.9
5 57 58.2	98 26 10	8 56 60.4
5 58 54.6	98 01 50	8 56 58.9
5 59 52.8	97 37 20	8 56 58.5
6 01 23.8	96 59 15	8 56 58.5
6 02 10.0	96 39 40	8 56 57.8

Thermometer 54°.

Time, p. m.	Double altitudes of α Orion, in the east.	Chronometer fast.
h. m. s.	Deg. min. sec.	h. m. s.
6 06 25.5	94 42 45	8 56 54.8
6 07 17.5	95 01 45	8 56 54.3
6 08 02.5	95 18 35	8 56 55.1
6 08 57.6	95 38 35	8 56 55.9
6 09 47.8	95 56 10	8 56 58.6
6 10 25.2	96 10 35	8 56 56.9
6 11 02.0	96 23 25	8 56 58.7
6 11 55.6	96 43 45	8 56 56.59
6 12 43.5	97 01 20	8 56 56.7

Thermometer 54°.

Mean of 18 observations, 8h. 56m. 57.52s.

.25

APPENDIX No. 6.

WASHINGTON CITY, *October* 8, 1847.

SIR: I have the honor to submit, herewith, a report of such objects of natural history as came under my observation while I was attached to the topographical party, under your command, during the journey from Fort Leavenworth to Fent's Fort.

The plants which were collected were submitted to the inspection of Dr. Torrey, to whom I am indebted for their names.

With great respect, I am, sir, your most obedient servant,

J. W. ABERT.
Lieutenant U. S. Top. Engineers.

To. Lieut. W. H. EMORY,
U. S. Topographical Engineers.

Notes of Lieutenant J. W. Abert.

On the 27th of June, 1846, we set out from Fort Leavenworth. The day was clear and bright; the woods were rejoiced with the voice of the mocking bird, and of the many little warblers that would join in the chorus of his song; the bluebird was there with his sprightly notes, and the meadow lark, perched on some tall mullein weed, caroled forth his song of love. As we were heartily tired of remaining quiet, we were well prepared to enjoy the beautiful scenes that our progress gradually developed. The ground is what is called "rolling prairie," of gentle curves, one swell melting into another.

The soil around is extremely rich; the whole country is verdant with the rank growth of the "tall grass," as it is called by way of eminence, when compared with that which grows beyond the region of the walnut and the hickory.

Here are many varieties of useful timber: the hickory, the walnut, the linden, the ash, the hornbeam, the maple, the birch, and the beech, also the cotton wood; but, beyond the limits of the "tall grass," there is the cotton wood only.

Five miles from Fort Leavenworth we passed a large butte, called "Pilot Knob;" its top is flat, and unites with the vallies below in a curve like that of a rope slackly drawn; spreading over the valleys, and climbing almost to the top of the butte, we saw fine forests of timber, consisting chiefly of oak. Among the shrubs, we noticed the hazel, (corylus Americanus,) and the button bush, (cephalantus occidentalis;) among these the wild grape had twisted its tendrils and was growing so luxuriantly that it was with great difficulty one on horseback could force his way through.

On the hill sides, the wild rose was still in bloom, and mingled its pink flowers with the beautiful white clusters of the Jersey tea, (ceonothus Americanus.) The prairies were covered with tall stalks of the rattlesnake weed, (rudebeckia purpurea.)

Some of our mules proved very refractory, but we soon conquered them with the aid of the "lazo," or cabriesto, as it is often called—a rope of hair, or plaited hide, 50 to 60 feet long, in which a noose is formed that, by a skilful hand, is easily thrown over the mule's head, the noose being gradually tightened, the animal soon falls to all appearance lifeless. Now, the bridle, the saddle, and packs are fixed, the noose loosened, and the mule rises ready for the journey.

After a march of twelve miles, we encamped near a log house, close to a fine spring of cold clear water. Here we noticed the white hickory, or downy hickory, (juglans pubescens,) the chestnut oak, (quercus primus acuminata,) the spicewood, (laurus benzoin,) and, deep in the woods, the modest May apple, (podophyllum peltatum,) and bloodroot, (sanguinaria canadensis.)

As we retired to rest, the sky became cloudy, and in a little time a plentiful shower of rain fell, which annoyed us greatly as it drove through our tents.

28*th*.—During the early portion of the morning, the rain continued with some abatement, and, as the sky showed signs of clearing off, we commenced making our arrangements for the march. I went down to a log house close by, and, whilst examining it, was attracted by the chirping of birds, and, on searching, found that the sound proceeded from the chimney, and I there discovered a beautiful nest, in the shape of a half basket, firmly attached to the chimney walls with clay, lined internally with horse hair and soft grass, and covered externally with moss; within were five unfledged birds, their eyes scarcely open, and at every sound they heard they would open their mouths and scream for food. The anxious parent several times darted down near my head. I wished much to ascertain its species, but, although it lit on the trees near the house, I could not get near enough to make any decision, and, as I did not desire to kill a bird with young, I had to content myself with the name some of our people gave it, to whom I pointed it out, and who called it the "grey bird."

After some little trouble with the mules, we got off about 7 o'clock; the rain had made the roads slippery, and the wheels cut into the soft mould so that the mules labored hard; at length we reached a sudden rise, where, in spite of our efforts, we were obliged to remain until one of the volunteer teamsters, seeing our difficulty, kindly brought us three yoke of oxen, and soon drew us up the slope. Passing on over gently rising and falling swells and vallies, with the delightful breeze that one almost always meets on the prairies, we felt our spirits rising with the clearing away of the clouds, and when the sun broke forth in splendor the sensation was truly exhilirating. Whenever we rode to one side of the road, we noticed that our horses would frequently sink to the fetlock, and saw on the ground little piles of loose earth, like small ant hills, being about 5 inches high and 10 or 12 inches in diameter at the base, and without any opening; they are formed by the sand rats or gophers, (pseudostoma bursarius,) and although their habitations cover the prairies, there are few persons I have met with who have ever seen them.

On our route we started several prairie chickens, (tetrao cupida.) After a march of 11 miles we reached Stranger creek, a romantic little stream of water, clear as crystal, that ripples over a pebbly bottom. The banks are high and composed of rich loam that nourishes immense oaks and sycamores, (platanus occidentalis.) The banks were now so slippery from the rain, and so steep withal, that we were necessitated to unload our wagons before we could achieve the ascent. We were soon encamped, and had our bedding exposed to the sun to dry. We noticed a great quantity of the orange colored asclepias, (asclepias tuberosa,) around which gaudy butterflies were flitting. The low grounds near us were covered with a prickly button-head rush, (eryingium aquaticum,) the roots of which, when candied over, formed the kissing comfits of Falstaff.

The woods were skirted by a dense growth of hazel, plum trees, and tangled grape vines. Here, too, we found the little quail, (ortix virginiana,) suddenly rising up from under our feet, and startling us with the whizzing sound of its wings. This evening the mosquitoes were very numerous, and we lay down to be tormented by these provoking pests; but few of us were able to sleep, although none of us slept very comfortably last night.

29th.—Yesterday evening, we found that the hind axletree of our wagon had been split in crossing the creek; and, being fearful lest we should break down at some place where good timber could not be obtained, we sent out two men to procure a piece of timber, and they soon brought in a fine piece of hickory, dragging it into camp by the means of a "lazo" that they had affixed to it and had then passed round the neck of a mule. Luckily for us, there was a good carpenter in the volunteer camp, and although his tools consisted only of a saw, an axe, a drawing knife, and an auger, he, nevertheless, managed to fashion a very good axletree. This work detained us until 1 o'clock, when we started for the Kansas river, having, through the kindness of Colonel Ruff, obtained a new teamster in place of the one who deserted last night.

The prairie was yet what is called rolling; the flat bottoms were covered with the rosin weed or polas plant, (silplicum laciniatum,) whose pennate-parted leaves have their lobes extending like fingers on each side of the mid rib. It is said that the planes of the leaves of this plant are coincident with the plane of the meridian; but those I have noticed must have been influenced by some local attraction that deranged their polarity.

The orange colored asclepias, (A. tuberosa,) and the melanthium virginicum, a white-flowering bush, were also abundant.

The timber on the ravines consisted of the white oak, (Q. alba,) black jack oak, (Q. ferruginea,) mulberry, (morus rubra,) walnut, (F. nigra,) the hickory, the red bud, (ericis canadensis.) The nettles (urtica canadensis) had grown to the height of 7 or 8 feet, all of which show the prodigal fertility of the soil.

As we approached the Kansas river its tributaries seemed to multiply rapidly, and the rolls in the prairie became more abrupt.

At 3 o'clock, we ascended a high ridge that gave us a fine view of the whole surrounding country. Presently reaching a little stream, whose banks were excessively steep and slippery, the wagons attempted to ascend; but one of the wagon wheels sank deep in the mud, and completely stopped all progress; we were therefore obliged to unload everything, and then clap all hands to the wheel, when we rose the hill amid the cheers of the men. A Frenchman, mounted on a wild mule, had already crossed and was standing on the western bank, which is 10 or 12 feet in height, when the mule suddenly sprung off the bank into the creek, just grazing with its feet the head of one of the men over whom it passed in its desperate leap. No one was hurt, and the Frenchman still sat as firm as ever.

As we neared the Kaw or Kansas river, some of us went in advance and soon reached an Indian house; the occupants said they were Shawnees. They appeared to be very comfortably fixed; had plenty of fine looking cattle, pigs, and chickens; within a few yards of the house, a clear stream of good water spouted forth from the side of a hill. We learned of the Indians that the distance to the Kaw river was 1½ miles.

Crossing a high ridge, we enter the Kanzas bottom; it was overgrown with a tall grass (arundo phragmites) from 5 to 6 feet high, and mingled with this was the long-leafed willow and the cotton wood. A quarter of a mile from the river bank, we entered the timber, consisting of the varieties already mentioned; the ground on which it grew was a deep loose sand difficult to get through.

In the river we found two large flat boats or scows manned by Shawnee Indians, dressed in bright-colored shirts, with shawls around their heads. The current of the river was very rapid, so that it required the greatest exertions on the part of our ferrymen to prevent the boats from being swept far down the stream. We landed just at the mouth of the Wakaroosa creek. Here there is no perceptible current; the creek is 14 feet deep, while the river does not average more than 5 feet, and in several places is quite shoal.

It was nearly 10 o'clock before all our company had crossed, and was so dark that we could scarcely see to arrange camp; so we lay down on the river bank and sent our horses out on the prairie to graze. We finished our suppers at 12 o'clock and lay down again to sleep; but, worn out as we were, the mosquitoes showed us no compassion, and large hooting owls, (bubo virginianus,) as if to condole with us, commenced a serenade.

The pure cold water of the Wakaroosa looked so inviting that some of us could not refrain from plunging beneath its crystal surface; one of the flat boats formed a convenient place from which to spring. The sun was rising, surrounded by golden clouds; in one of the flat boats, three of the Indians who had assisted in ferrying us over were soundly sleeping, and far away stretched the gradually diminishing trees that overhung the Kanzas water; the kingfisher (alcedo alcyon) was darting along, uttering his shrill rattling scream; flocks of paroquets (centurus Carolinensis) were circling over head, screaming and darting amid the tall walnut and sycamore trees.

We now made ready for our march, having engaged a fine looking Indian lad to go with the party. Our horses had not had much time to eat last night, and seemed disinclined to pass through the luxuriant grass that lay on each side of our road, and were constantly trying to snatch a mouthful of the delicious herbage.

At $8\frac{1}{4}$ o'clock we had a glimpse of the Wakaroosa buttes; on our right there was a large corn field, of about 30 acres, then a line of timber stretching as far as the eye could reach; on our left lay the broad rolling prairie, and directly in front we could see the road crossing the swells of the prairie, until it could be no longer distinguished. As we continued to advance we found that our road lead us directly between the two buttes.

We soon reached them, and then saw the "divide" that separates the waters of the "Wakaroosa" from those of the "Alaris des cygnes," or Osage; (as it is called near its mouth;) upon this divide the Santa Fé road is laid out.

We soon saw the Oregon trail, which here unites with that to Santa Fé; shortly after passing the junction of these trails we reached a steep declivity that forms the bank of a small stream, and noticed that the Indians had been working here for coal; in the superincumbent shale we found traces of fossils resembling the broad flat leaves of the iris (fridæ.) While we were examining this formation, my horse, that had been driven almost mad by the flies, (tabani,) broke from his fastenings and rushed into the creek, in order to roll in the water, and thus free himself from his tormentors; what a misfortune! for my saddle and pistols were on his back; some of the party dashed towards him, and, springing up, he galloped off, scattering all my accoutrements on the road; but I recovered every thing, even my pistols.

We continued on over a broad flat-bottom of marshy land, but found, before we had proceeded far, that our course bore too much to the north. We, however, continued to follow on in hopes it would take a turn, but were disappointed. As it was now late, we encamped on the Wakaroosa river, having marched nine miles. During the day, our animals suffered greatly from the horse-fly, (tabani;) these flies completely covered the necks and shoulders of the horses and mules, tormenting them excessively.

Amongst the birds observed this day, were the dove, (ectopistes Caroliniensis;) the flicker, (gieus auratus;) the blue bird, (sialia Wilsonnii;) the bunting, (pipilo erythrossthalmus;) and the crow, (corvus Americanus.) The last mentioned birds were lounging near a large cornfield, and were, doubtless, watching with interest the ripening of the grain.

Those friends of the prairie voyageur, the cow-bird, (molothrus pecoris,) made their appearance, and no sooner had we picketed our animals than those birds installed them on their backs.

The elder (sambucus pubescens) was still in bloom, and the orange asclepias still displaying its gaudy flowers, much to the delight of the brilliant butterflies that sported around it, and are so constantly found near it, that it is often called the butterfly plant.

Our camp is on a high point which separates the branches of a little stream; the grass around is good, and our situation high, and must bid defiance to the mosquitoes. Along the margin of the creek I found a beautiful lily, (lilium tigrinum,) of a bright orange color, and beautifully dotted.

On *July* 1 we arose early and made our way back to the trail we had left. After a march of three miles we reached the route sought for; we then rose to the top of the " divide," which unites with the Wakaroosa valley by a series of slopes that resemble the exterior slopes of parapets, their crests changing direction suddenly, so as to form sharp angles like those of a bastion; we ascended 15 feet, and on taking a bearing back, found that the Wakaroosa buttes were north 40° east.

After travelling three miles further, we reached the broad trail of the traders from Independence, Missouri, to Santa Fé.

As our horses moved through the grass, the horse-flies seemed to be shaken from the spikelets, as the farina from the stamens of corn, when shaken by the wind; then rising up, they covered the heads and necks of the poor animals, making them frantic with pain; they would rub against each other, and stamp their hoofs; and some would place their heads so as to get the benefit of the switchings of another's tail; and even the riders were annoyed by their desperate efforts to get rid of these persecutors.

Before we had proceeded far, we met a man driving an ox team; he had accompanied some of the volunteer companies to carry provisons; and, having emptied his wagon, he was now on his return. He told us that it was twenty miles from the next pool to water, so we determined to camp soon; and, having made a march of eleven miles, we pitched our tents on the very same spot on which we had encamped one year previous. Here we collected some beautiful flowers, amongst which were the rudbeckia hirta, and the delicate bed straw, (galium tinctorum.)

The stream upon which we were was then merely a line of unconnected pools. The only trees to be seen were some tall elms, (ulmus Amer.,) in whose tops several turkey vultures (cathartes aura) were preparing to go to roost, while below, amongst the willow brush that bordered the stream, some cat birds (orpheus carol.) kept up a low conversation as they plunged into the inmost recesses of the undergrowth.

July 2.—As we had the twenty mile stretch to make to-day without water, we arose early. The dew last night had been very heavy, and we found little pools of water standing on the tops of our mosquito bars, for we had been obliged to desert the tent where our bars could not be fixed conveniently.

The mounds made by the gophers or sand rats were more abundant than heretofore, and in several places a number of these mounds had been made so close together that the distinctness of each was completely lost in the mass, covering an area of five or six feet.

Our road was full of plovers, (charadicus marmoratus;) they would run along before us with great rapidity; then stop until we approached quite close, when they would run off again. Thus they kept travelling before us all day. We shot several of them, and I preserved some of their skins, more as a memento of the prairies than as a curiosity, for these birds are very abundant in the United States, from Canada to the gulf of Mexico.

As we proceeded on our journey, we heard the confused hum of thousands of grasshoppers, now and then broken by the chirping of the cricket. These insects are found in great abundance, and obtain greater size than any I have seen elsewhere. I got a cricket this morning that measured $1\frac{1}{2}$ inches in length of its body.

We now entered on the level prairie, where nothing was to be seen but a wide expanse of green grass, and the sky above filled with cumulus clouds, the shadows of which, as they fell upon us, added to the refreshing effects of the delightful breeze one generally meets upon the the prairie. After travelling a long distance over a country, the irregularities of which were so imperceptible that one almost doubted their existence, we reached that position which I took to be the top of the divide. Here lay the half devoured carcass of an ox that had, doubtless, succumbed to the fatigues of the journey and deprivation of water; for these animals suffer much more from want of water than the mule. Some turkey vultures, sailing above our heads, showed that they were not ignorant of the locality of the carrion.

In a little while after passing the ox's carcass, we reached 110 mile creek, which is 22 miles distant from our last night's camp. At this creek there is a fine grove of timber, containing all the varieties found in the vicinity of Kansas river.

About 12 o'clock we reached this creek, and we here found the robin, (turdus migratorius,) the cat bird and the blue bird; and, high above us, the swallow-tailed hawk (nauclerus fuscatus) was sweeping round in graceful circles, its white head glancing in the sunlight. I asked the Indian lad to shoot it for me with his rifle; but he gazed upwards at the bird, and seemed so struck with the beauty of its movements that he uttered not a word, but shook his head to signify that the bird was too fair for him to kill it. I should think it impossible for smaller birds ever to escape this hawk, which unites the form and swiftness of the swallow with the boldness and strength of wing of the falcon.

Nigh the banks of the stream there was a low piece of ground covered with the purple monarda, (monarda allophylla.) The gaudy butterflies that I have spoken of before, as flitting around the asclepias, were now sucking the sweets of these flowers.

Before we had fairly pitched our tents, young Mr. Nourse, of Washington city, entered our camp. He had, alone, boldly set off from Fort Leavenworth the day after we had left, determined to overtake us. We were delighted at his safe arrival; nor were we less pleased when we found that he had brought letters from the friends and relatives whom we had left behind.

July 3.—We arose early this morning to gain as much of the cool portion of the day as possible, determined to push on and see if we could not get rid of the flies that are so troublesome to our horses. The poor brutes seem to have no time to graze; and, when picketed out, they employ their feeding time in rolling in the grass and kicking frantically, so that the ground resounds with the stamping of their hoofs; and, in taking observations with the aid of the artificial horizon, one is obliged to select a spot at some distance from the horses, to prevent the jar which they produce from disturbing the surface of the mercury. The season appears to be unusually dry; 110 mile creek, which at this time last year was full of water, now has only a few scattered pools in its bed.

All day we had a brisk breeze from the southwest, making the travelling very pleasant. The plover and cow birds were playing along the road in front of us, and catching the grasshoppers that were scattered around in unlimited profusion.

At 10 o'clock, having marched 15 miles, we reached Independence creek, so called by Colonel Frémont, in consequence of our encamping here on the 4th of July, one year previous. This creek contains the only running water we have seen since leaving our camp by the Wakaroosa river. Along the road side, I gathered a plant called lamb's quarter, (chenopodium album,) the plaintain weed, (plantago major,) and a beautiful sensitive plant, with a yellow flower, slightly resembling the violet, (cassia chamaecrista.)

We encamped seven miles beyond Independence creek, in a ravine timbered with the elm, the cotton wood, the hickory and the oak. Some of our hunters went out and killed several wild turkeys, (meleagris gallopaoo.) We saw a flock of curlew, (numenius longirostris,) and some teal, (anas carol.)

Saturday, July 4.—At $5\frac{1}{2}$ o'clock, this morning, we crossed the creek upon which we had encamped, and soon reached an elevated piece of ground, from whence we could see our road crossing a high ridge in a direction S. 60° W. Whilst prosecuting our march we noticed two distant spots in the horizon; and, as we neared them, we judged, from the white light that one of the objects reflected, that they might be mounted men. Before long we met them, and found our conjectures correct. They said they were traders, and had been as far as Council grove.

At 7 o'clock, we crossed a stream of running water; at 8 o'clock, we reached one composed of pools, its banks heavily timbered with walnut, and we also noticed the buckeye, (pavia lutea,) and, skirting the stream, gooseberry bushes, (ribes triflorum,) and elder. At 12 o'clock, we reached Rock creek. This stream is very appropriately named, as its banks chiefly consist of rock. Near where the road crosses there is a large pool from four to five feet in depth, forming a fine bathing place; but we did not stop here, as we were anxious to reach some eminent place in honor of the day. We pushed forward for "Big John spring," which we reached at 5 o'clock. Here we luxuriated on the delightful cool water of this celebrated spring, reclining under the shade of a tall oak "sub tegmine querci," at whose base this spring originates; the temperature of the water being only 53°, while that of the air ranges above 80°.

We saw to-day two beautiful varieties of the evening primrose, (œnothera biennis,) the white and the yellow. We noticed amongst the birds the brown thrush, (orpheus rufus,) the king bird, (muscicapa tyrannus,) the grouse (tetrao cupido,) and the little quail.

Sunday, July 5th.—We wished, as we started this morning, that we could have taken this spring along with us, the water was so beautifully clear and so cold, and the spring shaded from distance around by a grove of the walnut, the sycamore, and the oak, around the trunks of which the ivy (rhus radicans) clambered, and at the roots of which grew beautiful lychnis.

Two miles from our point of departure is Council grove, where there is a fine stream of running water, and great quantities of quartz and highly fossiliferous limestone.

Shortly before Council grove, we passed the grave of a white man, who had been murdered by an Osage Indian; a circular pile of stones marks his resting place; from the crevices between the stones the ivy has shot forth; over the grave a long pole leans mournfully. When I viewed this simple grave, my mind turned to the proud monuments which are built up by the wealthy in our great cities, and which are daily leveled with the ground to give place to some improvement. Here, on the wild prairie, the Indian and the rude hunter pass by this spot, and not for worlds would they remove one stone.

Continuing our march, we travelled over a distance of 20 miles, when we reached "Diamond spring." This is a fine large spring, of three or four feet across, the water extremely cold; the temperature of the spring is 54°, while that of the air, the thermometer in the shade, is 87°

I procured at this place a beautiful white thistle, (cnicus acarna,) of delicious fragrance. We saw a great many night hawks (chordeiles virgins) and plovers, as well as several herds of deer, (cervus virginianus.) I also collected some of the great grasshoppers of the prairies.

Monday, July 6th.—As we set out on our march, the wagon mules took a freak in their heads and endeavored to run off with the provision wagon, but the driver turned them into the wide prairie, and soon succeeded in quieting them for a time, but he had several trials for the mastery before the day's march was over. After travelling 15 miles, we arrived at "Lost spring," but did not stop as its appearance was not inviting.

We noticed near the road numerous large puff balls or fungi, that resembled, both in size and appearance, human skulls of most beautiful whiteness; the under side is puckered as if a napkin had been thrown over a round body and drawn with a string; the interior resembles flour, except that it coheres.

Continuing our journey, we pressed forward rapidly, in order to reach Cottonwood fork, which is nearly thirty miles from the place where we were encamped this morning. We had a tedious march and did not reach the creek until 3 o'clock.

Our animals were very much jaded, and add to this that, the moment we reached our goal, myriads of horse flies attacked our cavalcade furiously. In the efforts of the beasts to rid themselves of the flies, they often became entangled in the "cabrestoés;" we were obliged to protect some of them by loose clothing; the mosquitoes, too, were troublesome to horses and riders.

Cottonwood fork is a tributary of the Neosha, as well as Council grove creek and the waters intermediate. This stream is timbered with large cotton wood trees that keep a continued rustling of their leaves, for the slightest breeze makes them tremble.

We noticed here thickets of the elder (S. canadensis) in full bloom. The beautiful monarda (M. allophyla) covered the low portions of the banks of this stream, while on the little sand bars, and close to the water's edge, a dense growth of the long leaved willows overhung the clear water, in which sported the black bass, the cat fish, and the sun fish. Just where the road crosses, there is a fine pool of water, from five to six feet deep and twelve feet wide.

Tuesday, July 7.—We concluded that it would be best to remain here for the day, as our animals looked much harrassed by what they have already undergone. We employed ourselves in getting all our affairs arranged in complete order; for we expect that this is the last stop that we shall make for some time to come. Everything was overhauled, our clothes were all washed, and all those arrangements, such as a journey of this kind suggest, but which our continued movement did not permit us to accomplish, were this day executed.

Around our camp the ground looked golden with the different varities of the golden rod, (solidago,) and along the stream we saw box elder, (acer negundo,) and extended thickets of plum bushes.

Not far from the camp we saw some antelope, (dicranocerus furcifer,) so we sent out an old voyageur with the Indian hunter in pursuit of them; but they returned unsuccessful, and reported that the antelope were extremely shy.

About 4 o'clock several companies of volunteers made their appearance, and until it was quite late we heard the tramp of horses, the clashing of sabres, and jingling of spurs; at last they all arrived, and the camp was quiet, save the howl of the sentinel wolf.

Wednesday, July 8.—At 5 o'clock this morning we were on the route for the Turkey creeks; they are three in number, and unite a few miles below the points where our road crosses them; the day was pleasant, for the sky was overcast.

We had now reached the short grass, that is not more than four or five inches in length, and we saw little patches of the true buffalo grass, (sesleria dactyloides,) a short and curly grass, so unique in its general character that it at once catches the eye of the traveller.

On either side of us we observed little circular spots marking the places where the buffalo once wallowed; for these huge animals have a habit of throwing themselves on their sides upon the ground; they then commence walking, as it were, with their feet on the circumference of a circle; this causes their bodies to revolve, and thus result circular depressions in the prairies; these, after a rain, are for a long time filled with water, with which the traveller is often fain to slake his thirst.

These old wallows are now overgrown with plants that grow more luxuriantly than on other portions of the prairie. There is the splendid coreopsis (coreopsis tinctoria) and the silver margined euphorbia; (euphorbia marginata;) these at once arrest the attention.

It is seldom, now, that the buffalo range this far; no signs of old excrements are to be seen, and the bleached bones left upon the plains by the hunter have long since mouldered away. Towards the close of the day we found the frontal bone of a buffalo's skull, the only sign, in addition to the wallows, of this animal having been once abundant.

Along the road were numbers of the beetle, laying in their winter stores, "haud nonignari aut incauta futuri." We stopped to noon, at 11½ o'clock. After a halt of half an hour, we started again, and at 12½ o'clock, formed our camp on Turkey creek. Here not a stick of timber is to be seen, but we found some beautiful plants with brilliant scarlet flowers (malva pedata) and roots which are eatable. We also obtained specimens of the pomme blanche, (psoralea esculenta,) and in the waters of Turkey creek we caught some sun perch and catfish.

The men killed several rattlesnakes near our camp, and one a grey snake, marked with a row of blackish spots along the back; it is said never to exceed two feet in length, and is called the grey rattlesnake. Before dark, the sky became black with clouds, whose appearance was soon followed by a heavy shower of rain.

This day, 9th, at daylight, we struck our tents and commenced our march; heavy clouds were at intervals passing over us and completely deluging us with rain. When the rain would cease, we would stop a few moments and let our animals rest. We noticed some buffalo skulls near the road; they must have lain here many years, as they were crumbling to pieces. At 3 o'clock we reached the Little Arkansas, a tributary of the great river the name of which it bears. This stream is from five to eight feet in width, and averages five inches in depth; on its banks were some large elms and box elder; we also saw the common elder, (sambucus,) narrow leafed willow, and the grape, (vitis aestivalis,) the sorel (oxalis stricta) and lamb's quarter, (chenopodium album,) grew near the stream.

The rain had ceased as we entered camp, and as the antelope appeared abundant and at no great distance, Menard was sent to shoot some of them, but his gun had got so wet during the day it would not fire.

We noticed to-day the pink sensitive plant (schrankia uncinata) of most delicious fragrance, so that my hat, into which I had thrust some specimens, was pleasantly perfumed. With this plant, we also found a white variety, (darlingtonia brachypoda,) the flowers and leaves are smaller than the plant first mentioned, and has no odor.

Late in the evening several of the volunteer companies came up; they said they were suffering for want of provisions; as the commissary waggons had got on too far in advance, they sent forward to have some of them return. But we were all suffering from a cause that produced in some of us feelings more unpleasant than hunger; the blowfly had peopled our blankets with living masses of corruption; it is said that these insects were never before seen so far out in the prairies.

Friday, 10th.—It is still raining, the clouds are chasing each other rapidly across the sky, and now and then the rain pours heavily down. We remained in camp some time waiting for the rain to stop. We thus lost several hours, but we found travelling in the prairies rather increased the chafing of our animals. We noticed to-day some swallows, (hirundo bicolor,) also the turtle dove, the little quail, the blue jay, (garulus cristatus,) and the king fisher (alcedo alcyon.)

We collected some lamb's quarter and had it cooked, and noticed along the road side the purslane, (portulaca oleracea;) this also would answer for the table of the prairie voyageur. Our day's journey was 16 miles.

Saturday 11th.—We were up this morning at $3\frac{1}{2}$ o'clock, and ready for the start. Our arrangement of mosquito bars was broken in upon last night by a heavy shower of rain that forced us to retreat to our tents.

After marching three miles, we reached Cow creek; it was very difficult to cross on account of the miry bottom, but we got safely over without great delay. Before we had proceeded far, we caught sight of the "plum buttes," bearing N. 20° W. We passed through a large village of prairie dogs, (Arctomys Ludoviciana;) although now deserted, there were fresh signs of the dogs having thrown out some earth from their excavations. Last night's rain had, doubtless, forced them to leave their houses. In the ponds that had settled on the plain, we saw several craw fish, and the crickets were gathered around some ant hills. As our wagons moved along the road, the lizards (lacerta lineatus) were darting rapidly along the ruts in front of it, anxious to escape being crushed. The common land turtle (testudo clausa) were also very abundant. As we got quite near the Plum buttes, we caught sight of the buffaloes, (bos americanus,) and some five or six of our party immediately gave chase. The buffaloes ran around in a circle of three-fourths of a mile in diameter; so those who were near the centre of this circle had an excellent view of the chase. Holster pistols were the only arms used, and we soon had the pleasure of seeing one of the animals fall; the other then turned off into the wide prairie.

Near the buttes we collected some beautiful Gaillardias of different species. Gaillardia amblyodon and G. pinnatifida we found abundant over the remainder of our day's route. After a march of eight miles more we reached the banks of the Arkansas river, where we encamped. Here we found a large train of wagons, belonging to Messrs. Hoffman, of Baltimore.

Sunday, July 12.—We left the Arkansas and marched to Walnut creek, where we found Mr. Hoffman's party, they having started before daybreak. We here noticed the prairie gourd (cucumis perennis) and the cactus, (cactus opunta;) also the "pinette de prairie," or liatris pychnostachia, with a great abundance of the common sunflower, (helianthus annuus;) the bright scarlet malva (malva pedata) and the silver edged euphorbia, (E. marginata;) also the purslane, the convolvulus (ipomen leptophylla) rudbeckia hirta, and a species of cockle burr; and on all sides the little mounds of loose earth thrown up by the gopher, (psedostoma *brissarius*.)

We left Walnut creek at 3 o'clock, and entered upon vast plains of the buffalo grass, (sesleria dactyloides.) After a march of 11 miles we camped within five miles of the famed Pawnee rock. Our camp was a mile from the river; but we drove our horses to water and got our buckets filled. As there was no wood, we used the "bois de vache," and lay down near the smoke of the fires to avoid the mosquitoes. We had no sticks to support our mosquito bars. When we first arrived, the country around was covered with buffalo, but it was too late in the day to hunt; we therefore lay down quietly with the intention of having a fierce chase in the morning.

July 13*th*.—Last night we had a terrible serenade from a large drove of prairie wolves, (canis latrans.) These animals always hang on the heels of the buffalo, to pick up the infirm and those the hunters have wounded, as well as to prey on what is left of the slaughtered.

We got off in good time, and Lieutenant Emory, in company of one of our hunters, started for the buffalo. We saw the chase; as the herd would divide, and let the horsemen pass through, we heard the rumbling sound of their many feet; but at last they crossed the bluff that extends towards the north from Pawnee rock, and were lost to our view. Lieutenant Emory killed one of the herd; but our hunter came into camp empty handed. We halted a short time to pack the buffalo meat, and then proceeded to Ash creek. This creek was dry, so we continued our route among herds of buffalo that were continually dashing across our road, and at length reached Pawnee fork after a march of 18 miles.

The waters of this creek were so high that we could not cross; the trees along the sides of the banks were half hidden; the whirling eddies were rushing along with great velocity; the willows that grew on the banks were waving under the strong pressure of the water, and brush and large logs were hurriedly borne along on the turbid bosom of the stream. We therefore camped by the side of the creek to await the subsiding of its waters. The country around was covered with the (cucumis perennis) prairie gourd, and we found it to be infested with those little striped insects that so much annoy the farmer in the United States, by the ravages they commit amongst the young vines.

This creek is timbered with the elm, (ulmus Americana,) and the box elder, (aceo negundo.) We frequently, during the day, noticed the purslane and the "pinette de prairie;" in the low grounds the splendid coreopsis and the euphorbia were displaying their beauties; and on the uplands the prickly pear was seen in great abundance, but it had passed its bloom.

During the afternoon a man by the name of Hughes was drowned in attempting to cross the stream; there were two men with him at the time, but the current was so violent that it soon swept him out of reach. His friends brought his clothes to our camp, where they left them until they could recover the body.

We saw to-day large flocks of the tropical or yellow-headed blackbird, (agelajus xantocephalus,) also the common blackbird, (quis calus versicolor,) and the Baltimore oriole, (icterus Baltimore.)

July 14*th*.—We were obliged to remain here all day, still waiting the pleasures of the waters. In the meanwhile I set one of the men to work to dig up a root of the beautiful prairie convolvulus, (ipomea leptophylla.) This man worked for several hours, for the ground was extremely hard, so that he was at last obliged to tear it up, leaving much of the top root behind. This root extended for about one foot and of not more than one-half inches in diameter, then it suddenly enlarged, forming a great tuber, 2 feet in length and 21 inches in circumference. The Cheyenne Indians told me that they eat it, that it has a sweet taste, and is good to cure the fever. They called it badger's food, and sometimes the man root, on account of its great size, for they say some of them are as large as a man. We also procured here the Mexican poppy, (argemone Mexicana;) noticed quantities of a willow brush, and several specimens of the tooth-ache tree, (near zanthoxylum fraxinum.) This morning Laing brought me a very large toad, (rana musica,) far exceeding any I ever before have seen. During the day I made a sketch of the country around our camp; the most recognisable feature is the bluff just on the west side of the stream, close to the ford.

In the evening some of us went over to visit Mr. Hoffman's camp; one of the gentlemen attached to the party had just returned from his first hunt, having killed four fat cows and brought in their tongues. Thus far we have noticed several plants that have been so common that I have neglected to mention them. One is the lead plant, or tea plant, (amorpha canescens,) and is in some places so abundant as to displace almost every other herb; the other is what our men call prairie indigo, (baptisia leucantha,) it bears a large black cylindrical pod, filled with kidney-shaped seed.

July 15*th*.—This morning we commenced making a raft, determined to wait no longer, and by sundown had completed a raft of dry wood, capable of bearing 1,000 pounds without being overloaded. The men worked with great energy, and it was truly exciting to see them straddle the huge logs and float down in the rapid current whose waters were rushing along with such a fierce rapidity, dimpling the surface of the stream with miniature whirlpools, and making the willows, now covered midway by the inundating waters, bend and spring as if moved by a hurricane. Sometimes rafts of brush and loose logs came rushing along, but the men stuck fast to the logs they bestrode, screaming out in wild excitement, as if to drown the gurgling sound of the wild waters.

To-day we saw several large white cranes with black-tipped wings; (grus Americanus,) and Laing killed me some rattlesnakes, (crotalus horridus) and several prairie snakes. Along the creek we found an abundance of plums (prunus virgins) and cherries.

Thursday, 16th.—As our raft was now completed we commenced crossing all our camp equipage, and by 11 o'clock everything was safely transferred to the south side of the stream. We were obliged to carry over much less at a time than we had hoped to have done, for our raft, built of the dryest wood that we could find, became water logged. The elm and box elder were the only trees we could get, and when green their specific gravity is but little less than that of water. The wagon body was placed upon the raft to distribute the weight that might be placed in it equably. A rope was stretched across on which a noose could slide, and this noose, by a long rope, was attached to our raft to prevent its being swept away in case the stretched rope should break. This precaution proved most wise, as the rope did break, but the knots upon it prevented the noose from sliding off, and our craft swung round into an eddy where it was comparatively calm.

We now proceeded to cross our cavalcade; some of the horses were first driven and went bravely over; others were very troublesome, but at length, seeing their companions enjoying the luxuriant grass, they all plunged in and arrived safe on the opposite side. Some had to struggle hard to get up the banks, that, in addition to their steepness, were covered with a thick coating of mud, deposited by the waters. It was a beautiful sight to see some of the finest of our horses spring from the high banks of the stream, to see the splash of spray as it showered around when the horse disappeared, and again to see the noble animal rise above the wave, snorting and dashing the waters from his mane, as he swam for the opposite shore. Our Indian lad seemed to enter into the spirit of the scene; he seized the cabresto of one of the wildest horses and dragged him down into the water; running out upon the raft, he stood for a moment, and then plunged into the stream, throwing his arms alternately as he dashed across. It is in such scenes as this that the Indians excel; their fine limbs, dark hair, and flashing eye lend all the imagination could desire to perfect the wild grace of motion, the picturesque of attitude that such occasions develope.

The water had fallen nearly 3 feet during the past night, and as it still continued to fall, the troops commenced crossing at the regular ford, which is one-fourth of a mile above us; but lost several of their horses. To-day, the man who was drowned yesterday was buried, his body having been found by our men engaged in rafting. His friends sent to us for his clothes in which to bury him; and, before the sun went down, he was deposited in his long resting place: "requiescat in pace."

At 11 o'clock, Colonel Doniphan came to our camp and informed us that General Kearny wished to see us. We afterwards learned that the general had some inquiries to make in regard to the route by the Smoky Hill fork; a route that Lieutenant Peck and myself had travelled when we were attached to the command of Colonel Frémont; but the roughness of that country, the absence of all roads, and the scarcity of water and wood, and the poverty of the pasturage, render the Arkansas river route much to be preferred.

At 3 o'clock we commenced our march, and soon struck a road that we pursued until near 10 o'clock at night, when we encamped near some pools of water, having been made aware of our approach to them some time before they were in sight, by the cry of the killdeer plovers, (charadrius vociferous.) We soon kindled our fires of "bois de vache," and then found we had camped in a prairie dog village; a bad place for picketing horses, as the neighborhood is generally destitute of grass. On our march we obtained a singular species of cactus, resembling roundish bodies covered with long protuberances, whose tips were crowned with stars of white spines, (near mammilarea sulcata.)

We saw during the day many skylarks; (alanda alpertris;) they allowed us to approach quite close before they took wing and as they flew through the air sang sweetly.

Friday, 17th.—We have now entered that portion of the prairie that well deserves to be considered part of the great desert. The short, curly buffalo grass (sesleria dactyloides) is seen in all directions; the plain is dotted with cacti and thistle, (carduus lanceolatus,) while only in buffalo wallows one meets the silver margined euphorbia; and in the prairie dog villages, a species of asclepias, with truncated leaves.

We saw several wild horses; in one group there were three, and with our spy glasses we had a fine opportunity for examining them. There was a bay, a roan, and a black; they stood for some time gazing at us as if completely absorbed in looking at the strange sight, when, as we approached, they raised their long flowing tails and dashed off with their long manes waving round their necks, and with a speed that soon carried them out of view. Unlike the mustangs, these looked to be large and beautifully proportioned.

Buffaloes seemed as if trying to surround us. We saw scarcely anything else far or near. The whole horizon was lined with them, and their figures would sometimes shoot up to an immense height, as their change of position caused the visual rays to pass through mediums of different refracting power, while seeming lakes would spring into existence, whose farthest shore seemed widely separated from us by the broad volume of water that intervened.

There were many dusky wolves (canis nubilus) prowling around the buffalo; the latter paid no regard to them, but let the wolves approach without showing the least repugnance, although the wolves devour the young calves and attack the cows at certain periods when they are least able to defend themselves. This species of wolf does not congregate in large packs like the prairie wolf, but roams solitary.

This evening five Pawnee Indians came into our camp. They were on foot, naked, and had their faces painted. As our party was very small, and we knew from the behavior of these fellows that there were plenty of Indians near us, we changed our position for one more defensible. All our horses were picketed close to the camp; the cabrestoes were shortened; wagons and tents arranged, so as to form a compact ring; the arms examined and the guard doubled; the whole camp was in a state of watchfulness, momentarily expecting an attack. I lay for the greater part of the night by the side of a wagon, with my rifle across the tongue, constantly expecting to see some redskins crawling amongst our horses; but the night was undisturbed, save with the howling of wolves and the bellowing of buffalo.

Saturday, 18*th*.—This morning, as soon as it was light, we saw a large band of buffalo, not more than 300 yards from us, walking slowly to the ponds close by; they were to the west of us, and as the wind did not blow towards them they paid but little regard to our proximity.

Some of the patriarchs of the band were on the lead; they were all moving with slow and measured tread, as if attending a funeral. Now and then some of them would cast a sinister glance towards us, but still continued to move on with the same slow pace. I got my spy-glass in order to examine them with great minuteness, and thence commenced making sketches. Soon there was a general commotion amongst the buffalo; they raised their tails, tossed their heads into the air; now and then the bulls would dash at each other, when suddenly the whole band separated into small dense groups that scampered off to the four winds of heaven. We instinctively grasped our guns, not knowing whether friend or foe might appear, and soon saw a number of horsemen urging their jaded steeds under the pricky spur. At every touch the impatient riders gave, the tails of the wearied horses were thrown into the air, and the slow gait at which they moved showed that they had been riding fast and far. They were pursuing a buffalo of immense size, apparently wounded; the buffalo now turned, but his intended victim shyed, and as the horsemen passed by, we saw the smoke of several shots burst forth; the horsemen now turned, and ere long the buffalo lay extended upon the ground. We saw them all dismount, and in a little while after Captain Karsons rode into our camp. We inquired the position of the main body, which we were anxious to rejoin, for ourselves were suffering from the harrassing night we had passed, and our horses were suffering from our being necessitated to picket them so closely for fear of Indians; and both ourselves and our horses daily suffered from want of water. As we were moving along, a band of buffaloes ran towards us; but as they passed, kept off some distance, running parallel with the road. Our Indian friend noticed them, and as they passed, dismounted, stooped down, and drew up his rifle; as the smoke burst forth from the muzzle of his piece, we saw a fine buffalo cow lash her heels high in the air, and then continued to jump and kick for a quarter of a mile or more, when she fell and all the rest of the herd gathered around her. We already had the meat of two fat cows, and as the wagons were so far from the place where the cow had fallen, she was left to feed the wolves.

The ruts of the road were full of little lizards, sunning themselves; as we approached they would dart briskly away, manifestly disinclined to play the part of devotees to Juggernaut.

In crossing to the river we found the ground in many places covered with beautiful gallardias (g. amblyodon) and the eupatorium, while in the moist grounds we saw the curious dodder twining in its golden tendrils all the plants that grew around it, forming an inextricable entanglement.

Among the birds, we saw many of the sky-larks and several avosets (recuroirostra ames.) The tail and its coverts white, wings black and white, legs blue, and bill recurved.

When we first struck the river, we met with Major Clark's battalion of artillery, a fine body of troops, well uniformed and of soldierly bearing.

Having marched a few miles along the river bank, we formed our camp, after travelling this day a distance of 19 miles.

Sunday, July 19th.—Marching along the Arkansas bottom one is struck with the variety of swamp grasses. Here we find the triangular grass, (scirpus triguctio,) and mingled with it in great abundance the scouring rush (equisetum hyemale) and the beautiful liatris (liatris spicata.)

After we had started, I went back three miles to meet Gen. Kearny in order to get some one to go with us and show us the exact location of the capture of the party of Texans by Capt. Cooke, 2d dragoons, in 1843. General Kearny detailed Lieutenant Love, who showed us the spot that we sought. On the south side of the river, there is a large grove of cotton wood trees that extends some distance along the river bank, and is the first grove of any size that the travelle west meets after passing Pawnee fork, which, by the route we came, is 64 miles distant.

In the evening we went to General Kearny's camp to get some of the horses shod. We had expected to have gone not more than three or four miles, but only reached them after a ride of eight miles, so deceived were we with regard to the distance by the purity of the atmosphere. As it was quite late, we concluded to remain here until the camp should overtake us in the morning.

Monday, 20th.—This morning we had not marched far when we saw General Kearny's guard stop and encamp. Soon Lieutenant Emory, who had crossed the river, rode over and informed us that General Kearny was very ill, and ordered one of our wagons to remain for the purpose of conveying the general on by easy stages; for our wagon was light and had good springs, while all the other wagons with the army were without springs and roughly built, like common Santa Fé trade wagons.

This day we made a march of 31½ miles, passing along the top of a barren ridge, between one and two miles from the river. Nothing was to be seen but the curly buffalo grass, now parched by the summer's heat. The sun poured down his rays most lavishly; the men all dismounted and walked, in order to rest and to relieve themselves from the singular sensation produced by the heat. First one and then another of the party became ill, and several were seized with a severe vomiting.

In the evening I went over to Major Clarke's camp, in order to have an axletree made. There I saw many who appeared to be ill; amongst them were Captain Weightman and Lieutenant Dorn.

I returned to our camp and passed a sleepless time, listening to the footsteps of the guard; and, now and then, the conversation of the French boys broke upon the stillness of the night; they, too, were not able to sleep soundly. We were all extremely anxious with regard to General Kearny's health.

Tuesday, July 21*st.*—This morning we presented quite a sorry looking array of human faces. At day-break I was seized with a vomiting, which lasted some time; I was obliged to send for the doctor. I however determined to push forward in compliance with the order of Lieutenant Emory, who was with General Kearny, and committed myself to the wagoner's care, while Lieutenant Peck took command of the camp. Lying here, my eye roved over but a confined prospect; under me were bundles of bedding, with blankets, red, blue and white; near me, a sick man, languidly gazing upward; above me, the bended bows of the wagon that supported a large white cover, through which the sun beat with intense heat; and, in front, through a little hole, one caught sight of the landscape dancing to and fro as the wagon jolted along.

We formed our camp, after a march of 11 miles, at the Santa Fé crossing, and in the vicinity of Major Clarke's battalion of artillery, so that we could have an opportunity of completing our axletree that we began yesterday. We soon saw our wagon, and learned that General Kearny had perfectly recovered.

At this place we obtained some beautiful purple lilies, (eustoma russeliana,) and Mr. Nourse brought me a psoralia, with a monosepalous calyx. On the opposite side of the river there are several Indian bodies, wrapped in blankets and skins, exposed on platforms of lodge poles, high up in cottonwood trees, where they are safe from wolves and the sacrilegious touch of men. The air of the prairie produces rapid desiccation, and, in this respect, resembles that of Egypt and the islands of the ancient Guanches.

From the 21st of July until our arrival at Bent's fort, on the 29th, being all the time sick, I have no recollection of anything that transpired, excepting a drawing that I made of the sand rat, (pseudostoma brissarius.) The body and legs are covered with yellowish brown hair, plumbeous at the base; belly, white; anterior claws, strong and large; posterior claws, short; iris, black; ear, projecting slightly. On each side of the upper jaw are two exterior pouches,

1 4-5 inches in depth; tail covered with short hair, a little less in length than one half the length of the body; body about 6 inches in length. The pouch is covered with short white hair, and capable of being turned inside out. This, I think, was a young one; hence the slight differences in the size and the color of its legs, and the tail being covered with hair.

Captain Turner, of the 1st dragoons, brought me a (ortygometra carolinus;) these birds are in plenty along the Arkansas bottom; this one was caught after a short chase, for it flew a short distance only, when it appeared to be too much fatigued, or too much bewildered to rise again.

Of the plants that occur between the Arkansas crossing and Bent's fort, I cannot do better than refer to the list appended to this report, in which they are arranged in the family to which they belong, and the locality mentioned in which they were obtained.

As one approaches Bent's fort, he meets with many varieties of artemisia, with the obione canescens, and a plant which is extremely useful to the Mexicans as a substitute for soap, by them called the palmillo, by us Adams needle, or Spanish bayonet; its botanical name is the yucca angustifolia. We also have the prairie gourd, (cucumis perennis;) that is abundant also from Bent's fort to Santa Fé. We have the bartonia, several varieties of solanas, several varieties of œnothera, the martynia, the cleome, the salicornia, ipomea, and erigonums. Amongst the trees, several varieties of populus; amongst which are the populus canadensis and p. monolifera; several varieties of salix, and the plum and cherry.

Amongst the animals, we have the panther, (felis concolor;) the wild cat, (felis rufa;) the white wolf, (canis nubilus;) the prairie wolf, (canis latrans;) the silver-grey fox, (canis cinerea argentus;) and the prairie fox, (canis velox;) prairie dog, (arctomys ludoviciana;) the gopher, (pseudostoma brissarius;) the antelope, (dicranocerus furcifer;) the grey bear, (ursus ferox;) also a species of vespertitia and species of ground-squirrel; it is said that there are three different varieties. Along the Arkansas, where there is sufficient cover, one finds the red deer, (cevus virgin.,) one also finds the badger, (taxus labradoricus;) and the polecat, (mephitis Amer.) The Indians at the fort showed me a racoon (procyon lotor) skin, they said had been obtained in the neighborhood.

Amongst the birds, the turkey vulture, (cathartes atra;) wild turkey, (meleagris gallipavo;) quail, (ortix virgina;) red-headed woodpecker, (picus erythrocephalus;) meadow lark, (sturnella ludoviciana;) night hawk, (chordeiles virgins;) cow-birds, (molothrus pecoris;) dove, (ectopistes carolin;) flickers, (picus auratus;) raven, (corvus corone;) and the railtailed buzzard, (batco borealis.) There has also been found on the Arkansas, within eight miles of Bent's fort, a singular and but little known bird, called the pasana, (geococyx viaticus.)

RANUNCULACEÆ.

Clematis Virginiana. Raton pass and the mountain passes near Santa Fé.
Delphinium azureum. Raton pass.
Podophyllum peltatum. Woods near Kanzas river, and at Council grove.
Ranunculus acris. Near the Wakaroosa buttes.
Thalicterum cornuté. Near Pawnee fork.
Anemone Pennsylvaniana. Between "El Rio Cañadian" and "El Rio Moro."
Ranunculus aquatalis. Found in the "Raton creek" and head waters of the Purgatory creek.

MENISPERMACEÆ.

Menispermum Canadense. Near "Big John spring."

PAPAVERACEÆ.

Argemone Mexicana. First seen at "Pawnee fork," thence on to the Moro.
Sanguinaria Canads. Woods near the Missouri and Kaw rivers.

CAPPARIDACEÆ.

Polenisia graveolens. Near "Bent's Fort," and in the valley of the Timpas.
Cleone intequifolia. At "Big Sandy creek," "Bent's Fort," and Cañadian.

VIOLACEÆ.

Viola cucullata. Banks of "Pawnee fork."

CARYOPHYLLACEÆ.

Lyclinis. Woods of Council grove.

HYPERICEÆ.

Hypericum ellipticum. August 11.

PORTULACEÆ.

Portulacca oleracea. By the road side from "Pawnee fork" to the crossing of the Arkansas.

LINACEÆ.

Linum regidum. From "Pawnee fork" to "Arkansas crossing."

GERANICEÆ.

Geranium Frémontia. Occurs throughout the "Raton pass."

OXALIDACEÆ.

Oxalis violacea. Near Council grove.
——— stricta. From Kaw river to Council grove.

ANACARDIACEÆ.

Rhus glabrum. Bank "Kaw river" and Wakaroosa river.
    radicans. Woods at "Big John spring."
    near R. aromatica. August 13.

MALVACEÆ.

Sphæralcae stellata, *Torr. and Gr.* "Raton pass" and "Rio Cañadian."
Sida coccinea. Arkansas river and El Rio Cañadian.
Malva pedata. Cottonwood fork and bottoms of Arkansas river.
Sida, (new species.) August 17.

VITACEÆ.

Vitis æstivalis. Along the Arkansas river and Purgatory creek.
    riparia. Stranger creek.
    vulpina. 110 Mile creek.

RHAMNACEÆ.

Ceanothus ovalis, *var. intermedia*, (*Torr. and Gr.*) Kaw river and Council Grove.
    Americanus. Fort Leavenworth.

ACERACEÆ.

Acer negundo. Banks of Pawnee fork.

LEGUMINOSEÆ.

Astragalus. Bent's fort and Ocaté creek.
Glycyrrhiza glabra. Arkansas river.
Gymnocladus Canads. Kaw river.
Petalostemum, (new species.) At "Ojo Vernal."
Psoralea esculenta. "110 Mile creek" and along the Arkansas river.

Robinia pseudo acacia. Purgatory creek, near the Raton pass.
Baptisia lencantha. As far as Pawnee fork.
Cassia chamæcrista. First seen July 3, thence to the Arkansas crossing.
Petalostemum candidum. High prairies, as far as Bent's Fort.
    violaceum. With the preceding.
Psoralea floribunda. Pawnee fork.
Dalea laxifolia. With the preceding.
Lathyrus linearis. August 9.
Amorpha canescens. Fort Leavenworth to Pawnee fork.
Schrankia uncinata. Stranger creek to Arkansas crossing.
Darlingtonia brachy-loba. Pawnee fork and 110 Mile creek.
Glycyrrhiza lepidota. August 13.
Cereis Canads. Kanzas river.

ROSACEÆ.

Cerasus Virginiana. Kanzas river, Arkansas river, and Purgatory creek.
Fragaria Virginiana. Kaw river.
Rubus occidentalis. Missouri river and Kaw river.
    villosus. With the preceding.
Prunus Amer. Pawnee fork, Arkansas river, and Cañadian river.
Cralœgus coccineus. Stranger creek.
Rosa lucida. Kaw river.

ONAGRACEÆ.

Œnothera. Several species occur from Kaw river to Bent's Fort.
Gaura coccinea. August 13.

LOASEÆ.

Mentzelia nuda. Bent's Fort and valley of the Timpas.

GROSSULARIACEÆ.

Ribes accreum. Purgatory creek and Timpas, near its head.
    triflorum. Diamond spring.

CACTACEÆ.

Opuntia Missouriana. Pawnee fork, Purgatory creek, and Cañadian river.
Mammillaria sulcata. Near Pawnee fork.

CORNACEÆ.

Cornus paniculata. Big John spring.
    stolonifera. Stranger creek.
    Florida. Kaw river.

CAPRIFOLIÆ.

Symphoncarpus glomeratis. Purgatory creek.
    occidentalis. With the preceding.
Symphora racemosa. Big John spring.

UMBELLIFERÆ.

Sium latifolium. Diamond spring.
Angelica. Head water, Purgatory creek.
Eryngium aquaticum. Near Wakaroosa creek.

RUBIACEÆ.

Galium tinctorum. Ponds near Lost spring.
Cephalanthus occidentalis. Stranger creek.

COMPOSITÆ.

Senecio (near) palustris. Raton.
   filifolius. Bent's fort to Santa Fé.
Rudbeckia. Fort Leavenworth to Arkansas crossing.
   hirta. Lost spring to Jackson's grove·
Erigeron strigonium. Pawnee fork.
Eupatorium purpureum. Turkey creek, Arkansas crossing, and Bent's fort.
Eurotia lanata. Rio Cañadian to Santa Fé and south.
Frémontia vermiculs. Valley of the Timpas.
Grindelia squarrosa. Arkansas river, near the crossing.
Solidago altissima. Bent's fort.
Solidago. Cotton-wood fork.
Liatris spicata. Crossing of the Arkansas river.
   squarrosa. Plum buttes.
Silphium lacenatum. From Fort Leavenworth to Cottonwood.
Coreopsis tinctorea. Turkey creek to Bent's fort.
Asters. With the preceding.
Gaillardia amblyodon. Plum buttes, and on the Moro.
       With the preceding. (Leaves lanceolate.)
   piumatifida.
Helianthus. Abundant from Coro creek to Santa Fé.
   dentatus. At San Miguel.

ERICACEÆ.

Arctostaphylos uranasi. Council grove.

LOBELIACEÆ.

Lobelia leptostacliza. Cottonwood fork.
  cardinalis. Bent's fort.

CAMPANULACEÆ.

Campanula rotundifolia. Raton pass.

OLEACEÆ.

Fraxinus Americanus. Ash creek.

APOCYNACEÆ.

Apocinum androsacmifolium. Lost spring.

ASCLEPIADACEÆ.

Asclepias verticillata. Stranger creek and Pawnee fork.
    tuberosa. Fort Leavenworth to Cottonwood fork.

CONVOLVULACEÆ.

Ipomea leptophylla. Walnut creek to the Canadian river.
Cuscuta Americana. In the bottoms near the "caches."
Convolvulus. (Near sepium.) August 14.
Euploca convolvulaceæ. Raton pass.

BORAGINACEÆ.

Myosotis glomerata. Arkansas river, near caches.

POLEMONIACEÆ.

Gilia (cautua) longiflora. Raton pass.

LABIATÆ.

Hedeoma leptophylla. Near crossing of Arkansas
Monarda fistulosa. Near caches.
    allophylla. 110 creek; Cottonwood fork.
Mentha peperita. Bent's fort.
Salvia azurea. Arkansas bottoms and New Mexico.
Teucrium Virginicum. Pawnee fork.

SOLANACEÆ.

Solanum nigrum. Bent's fort.
    triflorum. Arkansas river, near crossing.
Nycterum lobatum. From the caches to Bent's fort.
Physalis. August 4.
    lobatum. Near Bent's fort.

SCROPHULARIACEÆ.

Pedicularis canads.   Near Pawnee fork.

CHENOPODIACEÆ.

Chenopodium album.   From Fort Leavenworth to crossing.
Frémontia vermicularis.   Purgatory creek and Timpas.
Artemisia.   Purgatory creek.
Obione canescens.   Valley of the Timpas.
Salicornia herbacea.   Arkansas river crossing.

VERBENACEÆ.

Verbena pinnatifida.   Rio Canadian and Rio Rayado.
       angustifolia.   Little Arkansas river.
Lippia cuneifolia.   From Pawnee fork to Santa Fé.

CUCURBITACEÆ.

Cucumis perennis.   From Walnut creek to Santa Fé.

NICTAGINEE.

Oxybaphus, (new to me.)   *Torr.*   Slender branching spears. "Rio los Animas."
       nictaginea.   Raton and "Rio Canadian."

POLYGONACEÆ.

Erigonum.   Walnut creek.
       tomentosum.   Council grove.
Polygonum, (long lacerated sheath, no flowers.)   Walnut creek.
       amphibium.   Turkey creek.

LAURACEÆ.

Laurus benzoin.   Kaw river and Council grove.

EUPHORBIACEÆ.

Euphorbia marginata.   Pawnee fork to Bent's fort.
       hypericifolia.   Turkey creek.
       ?   By the road side, near the "caches," and in the buffalo wallows.
Croton capitatum.   Crossing of the Arkansas river.

URTICACEÆ.

Humulus lupulus. Raton pass and Canadian river.
Morus rubra. Council grove and Kaw river.
Urtica canadensis. Kaw river and Stranger creek.

ULMACEÆ.

Ulmus Americana. Pawnee fork.
Celtis crassifolia. Woods at Council grove.

AMENTACEÆ.

Salix longifolia. Council grove, 110 Mile creek.
    (no flowers or fruit.) Arkansas river.
Populus monolifera. Timpas, at head of Purgatory creek.
    canadensis. From Kaw river to Santa Fé.
    (new to me..) *Torr*. Rio Canadian.
Salix augustifolia. Arkansas river.

CONIFERÆ.

Juniperus Virginica. Timpas, and from Purgatory creek to Santa Fé.
    (different from Virginica.) *Torrey*. Near Santa Fé.
Pinus monophyllus. Raton pass to Santa Fé.
    rigida. As above.

MONOCOTYLEDONOUS OR ENDOGENOUS PLANTS.

ALISMACEÆ.

Sagittaria sagittifolia. Head of Timpas.

MELANTHACEÆ.

Melanthuim Virginicum. Stranger creek and Wakaroosa river.

LILACEÆ.

Yucca angustifolia. From Bent's fort to "Fra Cristobal."
Lilium tigrinum. Wakaroosa river.
Enstoma Ruseliana. Bottom of Arkansas and Cañadian.
Alluim vienale? Raton pass.

JUNEACEÆ.

Juncus tenuis. Raton pass.

COMMELINACEÆ.

Tradescantia Virginica. Fort Leavenworth to "110 Mile creek."
    rosea. With the preceding.
Commelina angustifolia. Pawnee rock and Raton pass.
    (long accuminated spatha.) Raton.

SMILACEÆ.

Smilax rotundifolia. Kaw river, Council grove, and 110 Mile creek.

CYPERACEÆ.

Scispus triqueter. Low grounds near Arkansas crossing.
    atrovirens. Pawnee fork.
Cyperus filiculmis. Little Arkansas.
Carex festuca. Wakaroosa river.

GRAMINEÆ.

Arundo phragmites. Arkansas, Timpas, and Cañadian rivers.
Sesleria dactyloides. Pawnee fort to Bent's fort.

Agropyrum. Stranger creek.
Atheropogon olygostachium. Canadian river.
Koeleria nitida. Pawnee fork.

EQUISETACEÆ.

Equisetum hyemale. Near crossing of the Arkansas.

APPENDIX No. 7.

WASHINGTON, *December* 6, 1847.

SIR: I have the honor, at your request, to address you a brief memoir on the subject of the district of country in Sonora, Mexico, which I passed over in November and December last, with a wagon train, when I deviated, in search of a practicable route, from the mule trail of Brigadier General S. W. Kearny, on his march from New Mexico to California.

When he turned off from the Rio Grande, opposite the copper mines and the heads of the Gila river, I kept the river for thirty miles to the south, and making a southern bend, turned again towards the north, and struck his route (as surveyed by Mr. Emory of your corps) just above the village of the Pimo and Maracopa Indians, an estimated distance of 444 miles.

Immediately below the point of deviation, on the Rio Grande, the country bordering the river became sensibly flatter and less broken. I left the river when in view of a point marked on the common maps as "San Diego," and the distant view towards "El Paso" proved the country to be unbroken and comparatively level.

From the high valley of the river I ascended to the *table land* of Mexico, by an almost insensible slope over *smooth* prairie. For 150 miles on this smooth level table land, which is studded with isolated hills or mountains, I journeyed without any difficulty, passing over but three hills, in two cases, I know, in the third, I believe, unnecessarily. I then, unexpectedly and suddenly, arrived at a great break off to a lower level of country, the descent to which was very broken and rough mountains for fifteen miles. I found, however, that I had at that moment fallen into an old wagon trail, which led, I was told, from Yanos. I was able to get my wagons through, following a stream all the way, and descending in the 15 miles possibly a thousand feet. This was the head of the Huaqui river, which empties into the California gulf. I was told that this was called the Pass of Guadaloupe.

I then passed an unbroken country, about 80 miles, when I fell upon the José Pedro river, which empties into the Gila. I descended this without difficulty of ground about 80 miles. In turning off there is an ascent to nearly level country of, perhaps, above an hundred feet, but it could be made very gradual. It is then about 48 miles to Tueson, a town of about 500 inhabitants with a fort and garrison. This distance is over much smooth ground, maintaining the same general level. Tueson is in a rich and well cultivated valley, where there is also a dense forest of *maguey*. From Tueson it is some 75 miles to the Gila. It is a level plain, generally of clay, where my wagons and footmen (water being very scarce) passed at the rate of about 30 miles a day.

On the map which I made, and which is in your bureau, is marked a route considerably to the north of Guadaloupe pass, which, some of my guides believed, would avoid that broken descent, and be fouud to be nearly level throughout to San Pedro, at the point where I turned off from that beautiful little river. The most sensible and experienced of these men, Laroux, who lives in Taos, New Mexico, and who had trapped on the Gila and passed in a different direction over that country, was decidedly of this opinion, but his knowledge, on the other hand, was sufficient to forbid to explore it, in my situation, on account of scarcity of water.

The Rio Grande bottoms for a hundred miles above, and at the point where I left, are well timbered; there is no timber on the table land, save upon the small mountains which are everywhere to be seen; this is cedar and pine, but of small growth. Rock is everywhere to be had, secondary rocks of almost every kind; but by this wonderfully level route, the continent may be passed with scarcely a view of granite. As far as Tueson the gramma grass is abundant; it will fatten cattle while working, and in winter. The route from Tueson passes through a country abounding in exceedingly rich gold mines.

I am, very respectfully, sir, your obedient servant,
P. ST. GEO. COOKE,
Major 2d Dragoons.

To Col. J. J. ABERT,
Topographical Engineers.

A Doctor Comes to California

JOHN STROTHER GRIFFIN, M.D.
From a photograph in the possession of Mrs. John Griffin Johnston

A Doctor Comes to California

The Diary of John S. Griffin,
Assistant Surgeon with Kearny's Dragoons,
1846-1847

WITH AN INTRODUCTION AND NOTES
BY GEORGE WALCOTT AMES, JR.
AND A FOREWORD
BY GEORGE D. LYMAN, M. D.

SAN FRANCISCO
CALIFORNIA HISTORICAL SOCIETY
MCMXLIII

Reprinted from the

CALIFORNIA HISTORICAL SOCIETY QUARTERLY

Volume XXI, Numbers 3 and 4, and

Volume XXII, No. 1

Copyright 1943 by California Historical Society

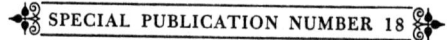
SPECIAL PUBLICATION NUMBER 18

Lawton R. Kennedy, Printer

San Francisco

✥ Foreword ✥

By George D. Lyman, M. D.

THERE ARE hundreds of diaries that were written on overland journeys to California. The majority were produced on Northern trails: on the old Oregon trail, by way of Independence, the Platte River and South Pass, and on the Humboldt River trail, branching off from Fort Hall. Comparatively few were set down by those using the trails of the Southwest. Although many followed the Southern overland tracks, very few detailed narratives of their treks have reached printer's ink.

That is one reason why "A Doctor Comes to California," John Strother Griffin's diary of his experiences on the old Santa Fe-Gila River-trail is significant. It is one of the few descriptive narratives extant of a journey over a Southwest trail.

Another reason why Griffin's Journal is important is that it is historic; it is first hand information on the "Army of the West" and the conquest of California in 1846-47. Bancroft, in writing that part of the history of California, depended on a transcription of Griffin's diaries. "His Journal of '46-47," writes Bancroft, "is one of the best authorities extant." Unfortunately he did not have the original as here presented.

There are only two complete diaries of Kearny's march from Santa Fé to San Diego in existence: one of these is Griffin's and the other is Emory's *Notes of a Military Reconnoissance, from Fort Leavenworth, in Missouri, to San Diego, in California.* There were two other diarists in the "Army of the West": Colonel Philip St. George Cooke and Kearny's aide-de-camp, Captain Abraham R. Johnston. On October 2, when confirmation of the death of Colonel James Allen of the Mormon Volunteers reached "The Army of the West," General Kearny selected Colonel Cooke to succeed him. Thus the Cooke Journal is first hand information only as far as the Rio Grande, and the Johnston Journal terminated tragically on December

4, almost on the eve of San Pascual. Thus Griffin's Journal remains one of two complete authorities on Kearny's historic march to California.

Again "A Doctor Comes to California" is important from a medical and surgical standpoint. For the greater part of Kearny's march to San Diego, Dr. Griffin was the only surgeon with the column. As the care of the wounded and sick played a conspicuous role in the progress of "the Army of the West" and hence in the Conquest, it is well to examine the diary from that angle.

Finally the Journal is important because Griffin became one of California's outstanding medical men. He was one of the three pioneer physicians in the pueblo of Los Angeles. By only two other medicos was he preceded. Dr. John Marsh received a license to practice there in 1836, and Dr. Richard S. Den, an Irishman, was licensed in 1844.

Dr. Griffin was born in Fincastle, Virginia, in 1816, the scion of two outstanding Southern families: the Hancocks and the Griffins. Left an orphan at an early age, he was reared by his maternal uncle, George Hancock, of Louisville, Kentucky. There he received the benefits of a classical education and then went to Philadelphia. In 1837 he was graduated with the degree of M.D. from the Medical Department of the University of Pennsylvania. After graduation he returned to Louisville, where he practiced his profession until 1840. That year he entered the United States Army as assistant surgeon. The next six years he served as such under General Worth in Florida and on the southwest frontier at Fort Gibson.

At the commencement of the Mexican War in 1846, Griffin was attached to the "Army of the West" commanded by Colonel (later General) Kearny, as assistant surgeon of the First Dragoons, with the rank of captain. With Dr. Simpson, he was with the triumphant "Army of the West" when Kearny entered Santa Fé in August 1846 and took possession of New Mexico without firing a hostile gun or spilling a drop of blood. Circumstances which led the General to believe that he could conquer the fiery Californians in the same way.

On September 25, Drs. Simpson and Griffin were with the "Army of the West" when General Kearny left Santa Fé with three hundred of the 1st Dragoons mounted on mules. Kearny's object was the conquest of California. His papers, dated Washington, June 3, ordered him to take possession of California, co-operate with the naval forces which would probably be found in possession of the ports. Having secured the country, he was to organize a temporary civil government in California. Down the valley of the Rio Grande Kearny led his column in patched and ragged uniforms. Before these men lay a march of over one thousand miles and almost a desert from beginning to end. On account of scarcity of water, grass, and game, the dragoons were warned of the severity of the trip. Some said the "Army of the West" would never get through to California. Previously, several

FOREWORD

small parties had made this trip, notably Dr. John Marsh and the Patties, but never had it been negotiated by a large detachment of troops. But Kearny's column felt they were able to go wherever Mexicans or Indians could. They were able to endure as much fatigue, cold, hunger, and thirst. They were hardy fellows, these dragoons, brave, staunch, and loyal in adversity, as you will see. They thought nothing of laying down their lives for one another. On the first day out the mules began to fag, but not the dragoons. They had a duty to perform. They intended to "annex a Pacific Empire"; for that purpose they were lusting for a fight with the Californians.

Near Socorro, on the sixth of October, the dragoons were surprised to see charging upon them a party of men, yelling like Indians. They could see that the leader was small in person and stoop shouldered, with reddish hair, a freckled face, and soft blue eyes It proved to be Kit Carson with fifteen men. He had important dispatches to deliver in Washington, California had been subjugated by Stockton and Frémont. There was no opposition to American rule. The Stars and Stripes floated in every port. Commodore Stockton was organizing a civil government. Frémont was to be made governor. On hearing this news, Kearny was chagrined. Frémont and Stockton had accomplished his mission; they had stolen his thunder. Even Griffin was disappointed. Like the rest of the dragoons he had been anticipating "a little kick up with the Californians." Kit Carson's news blasted all their hopes. Their expedition was reduced to mere escort duty. They were bitterly disappointed. They wanted to fight for California.

General Kearny determined to take Carson to guide him to California. Carson resisted bitterly. He had pledged himself to deliver these important dispatches to Washington, to the President himself. To no avail. Kearny insisted.

On the strength of these dispatches General Kearny decided to take only two Companies—C and K of the 1st Dragoons—with him to California. Three companies of about two hundred men he would send back to New Mexico—a move he would eventually bitterly regret. Now Dr. Simpson and Dr. Griffin drew straws to see which surgeon should go to California with the "Army of the West." Thus Griffin's career depended on the grain stalk he drew on the Rio Grande. Griffin won, and he soliloquized: Was it a gain to have such a march going? If he got there, was it a gain to have just such another march returning?

Reduced to slightly over a hundred men, the "Army of the West" got under way with merry hearts and light packs. Every dragoon felt renewed confidence in having Carson as a guide. Every one of them was aching for a bout with the Californians. But Carson was contemptuous of the latter as warriors. They had no courage, he claimed. They would never fight.

Long before the "Army of the West" reached the Colorado River both men and animals were exhausted. Lack of water, fodder, and roads had exacted a heavy toll. Many of the animals had died, and the column still had a terrible desert to pass. While resting here, Kearny and his men learned some disturbing news from passing cattle drovers and a captured Mexican dispatch bearer. There had been a counter revolution in California. The tricolor of Mexico floated from every port. Kearny was amazed, and well he might be; all over again California had to be conquered and he had only a personal escort to accomplish the reconquest. Alarming reports were read in the intercepted dispatches. "We may expect," Griffin wrote in summing up his reactions in his Journal, "a small chunk of hell when we get over there."

A captured Mexican was well plied with brandy. It was thought that, when liquor loosened his tongue, he would divulge something of importance to Kearny's column. But even in his cups he succeeded only in increasing apprehension; the dragoons should not consider entering California with such a small force.

Nevertheless, on November 25 Kearny's column forded the Colorado. Before them lay the terrible *jornada del muerto*, the ninety-mile desert without water. After three days, the desert delivered the dragoons, half starved and famished, into a desolate country of cacti and yucca. Here sharp thorns tore at the bare legs of the dismounted. Animals gave way by the score. While dragoons starved, the wolves feasted. In packs they followed in the wake of the column. Let a mule even stagger and the pack was at his throat and the air became hideous with the fight for the carcass. On military inspection on the 30th, the column was found well-nigh naked. Some of the dragoons were barefooted and weather-beaten, but in the swarthy, sunburnt faces was no sign of quailing.

Now it was wintery December, frost was in the air, wind was blowing, snow falling in near-by mountains. Overcoats were in order; the dragoons shivered in their ragged uniforms. On December 2 Aqua Caliente, Warner's Rancho, on the extreme frontier of California, came into view. Sixty miles westward lay San Diego. Here was stirring news for them, their fears about California were confirmed. Again the Californians were in the saddle, well armed, well mounted, and furious at the approaching invaders. On hearing these reports Kearny sent a messenger to Stockton at San Diego. He wanted the Commodore to send reinforcements and guides as quickly as possible. This Stockton did.

On December 5 the reinforcements arrived, with Captain Gillespie, Lieutenant Edward F. Beale and his Delaware Indian, and Midshipman James M. Duncan with thirty-five men and a four-pounder. Further, Stockton warned that directly ahead, in the path of Kearny's advance, was posted a hostile force of Californians. Stockton suggested that Kearny make a surprise attack upon these forces.

FOREWORD

More or less fully, Gillespie's forces confirmed Kit Carson's opinion of the Californians. They were cowards and would not fight.

Although rain was falling, the news that a hostile force lay directly ahead was welcome news to the dragoons. Tired and exhausted and wet, as they were, they wanted to be brought face to face with the Californians. When Griffin heard about that hostile force ahead, he wrote in his Journal, "I should suppose we would try and capture these gentlemen." Kearny, too, lusted for fight. And so, on the rainy night of December 5, at an officers' meeting in Kearny's tent, an attack was decided upon. Captain Moore, one of the ablest of the column's officers, too, wanted a surprise attack. His logic was good. Surprise the Californians, drive off their horses, and the dragoons would win. Everyone knew that a Californian without a horse was helpless and hopeless. Moore was overruled. Kearny wanted a reconnaissance. The Californians were at San Pascual, nine miles distant. That night in the fog, Lieutenant Hammond and three men were sent to reconnoitre. About 2:00 A.M., Hammond was back. He had found the hostile camp. He had been discovered by the Californians but not pursued. "Viva California" they had yelled as he rode up the mountain.

Kearny's horses were stiff and worn out. His men were almost naked, wet to the skin and benumbed by cold, yet they burned for action. Though they had been in the rain all night, Griffin claims their arms were not reloaded. Bancroft adds that their swords were rusted in their scabbards. Although he was unaware of the size of the opposing force, Kearny did know that the surprise element was impossible. Nevertheless he decided on a night attack. "Off we put," wrote Griffin, "in search of adventure."

Boots and saddles was sounded. By three o'clock Kearny's column was drawn up in battle array, with Captain Johnston in the lead with fifteen dragoons, including Kit Carson. Then came the General with Captain Emory and Captain Warner; following them came Captain Moore with forty or fifty dragoons, and so on down the column to the two howitzers and Major Swords. It was just dawn as the column, on their stiff and unruly animals, descended the mountain to the plain of San Pascual. Ahead they could see the camp fires of the Californians burning brightly. While it was still too dark to distinguish friend from foe, a charge was sounded. With battle cries, Captain Johnston and his dragoons bounded across the plain. The rest of the column, as best they could on their fagged animals, followed. As they advanced through the gray light the dragoons could see the Californians, mounted on magnificent horses, with muskets ready and lances set. The Californians discharged their muskets and pistols. At the first shot, with a musket-ball through his forehead, Captain Johnston fell dead and a dragoon toppled over badly wounded. Kit Carson was unhorsed but rolled to safety. In confusion the Americans fell upon the lances. Just at this moment, the Californians retreated. Pell-mell, the gallant Captain Moore, mounted on a white horse, and his dragoons followed and fell afoul the ambush. The dragoons' mounts were too stiff, too fagged and too unmanageable for a cavalry charge. There was lack of precision and of massed attack. Seeing what was happening in the ranks of his adversary, Pico, the Californian leader, suddenly wheeled his column and swept galloping back, with long lances tossing obliquely across the gray sky. The hand to hand struggle that raged was brief and horrible. Rusty sabres and clubbed guns, in the benumbed hands of exhausted dragoons mounted on stiff and unmanageable mounts, against nine-foot lances in the deft grasp of the world's most skillful horsemen mounted on mustangs, as agile as wasps. Griffin claims that not more than fifty Americans ever saw the Californians. Off their mounts the dragoons were brushed like so many flies. On the ground they were lanced like buffalo. In ten minutes one-third of the "Army of the West" was wiped out. Seventeen were killed. Eighteen were badly wounded. (No two reports agree.) As the howitzers came into action the Californians again retreated. In the thick of the melée was the General himself. He was wounded in two or three places, one wound a severe one in the loin. He would have been killed had it not been for the quick action of Captain Emory. The gallant Captain Moore, broken sword in hand, put up a desperate resistance, was lanced to death. His brother-in-law, Lieutenant Hammond, in coming to his rescue received lance wounds between the ribs, which proved fatal that day.

Griffin, too, was in the thick of the battle. At one time with an unloaded pistol in hand, he was surrounded by hostile "devils." Perhaps the runaway howitzer saved "his flint." Lieutenant Hammond was the first wounded man that the Doctor encountered. Instructing him to go to the rear where he would attend him, the Doctor was caught in the ensuing confusion, and they were separated. General Kearny needed immediate assistance. He was bleeding profusely, and so was Captain Gillespie from three wounds, one over the heart. With thirty-five and more killed and wounded, the doctor had his hands full.

San Pascual was the bloodiest battle ever fought on California soil. A disaster of magnitude to American arms. In his official dispatches, because he had been left in possession of the battlefield, Kearny spoke of the conflict as a victory—but the only thing victorious about the two skirmishes was the way the dragoons fought. Those engaged virtually fought to the death. With valor and distinction they fell. In the face of overwhelming odds, they held their ground and died gallantly with their faces to the foe.

Before dawn the ten minute battle of San Pascual was over. Stunned by the catastrophe, the survivors camped on the field of disaster. All were in a deplorable condition. No water, no provisions, and harassed all day by the victorious Californians, who lay in waiting for the final kill. General Kearny's wounds were so severe that he was forced to give up the command. In his place Captain H. S. Turner took over. The first thing the Captain did was to dispatch Alexis Godey, Frémont's old scout, to San Diego for help and ambulances to transport the badly wounded. As the battleground was surrounded by Californians, Turner doubted that Godey could get through to San Diego.

That day, from dawn to dusk, Griffin worked with skill and diligence. Some of his patients had from one to ten lance wounds. Arms had been run through as many as three times. Several would never mount a horse again. As they had to be transported, ambulances had to be built.

Early that morning Dr. Griffin came to General Kearny, where he sat bleeding from his wounds. He offered to dress his injuries. "First," replied Kearny, "go and dress the wounds of the soldiers who require attention more than I do, and when you have done that come to me." Griffin proceeded to execute that order. While busily engaged elsewhere, he happened to glance around just at the moment the General keeled over backward, exhausted by loss of blood. Immediately Griffin ran to his assistance. He propped him up, restored him to consciousness, stopped the haemorrhaging and dressed his wounds.

Not satisfied with caring for all the dragoons, Griffin dispatched a message to the camp of the Californians that he would come to them and dress their wounded. But General Pico sent back word that his services were not needed, that none of the Californians required medical attention.

As soon as he had revived and his men had rallied, General Kearny decided to move on to San Diego The dead were collected: the bodies of Captain Johnston, Captain Moore, Lieutenant Hammond, and fourteen other officers and privates were lashed to the backs of as many mules. It was a sad and melancholy picture. For two hours the pack animals waited for the column to move. Then Dr. Griffin decided that the wounded were in no condition for transport. Under cover of darkness the dead were buried in a willow copse, while a pack of howling wolves supplied a requiem.

That night was cold and damp, the ground so littered with rock and cacti that Dr. Griffin could not find smooth places enough to lay his wounded. Sleep was impossible. Notwithstanding the fatigue of the previous day and night, not a dragoon could slumber. All night the wolves and the Californians kept up a patrol. Not an American could escape, bragged General Pico to his superior.

Day dawned on December 7 on the most tattered and ill-fed detachment of men that ever the United States mustered under the colors. Ahead on the road to San Diego could be seen the California pickets; a portion of their forces disputed the way. The sick and wounded, through the indefatigable exertions of Dr. Griffin, were doing well. Although weak from loss of blood, General Kearny was able to mount his horse and resume command. Spies could be seen on every hilltop. Momentarily the column expected an attack, keeping the men in a continuous state of excitement. Arranging the wounded in six travois in the middle of his column, Kearny moved off in close order toward San Diego in the direction of the rancheria San Bernardo. Kit Carson was now in command of the advance guard of fifteen men. Although Dr. Griffin and the mountain men had made the wounded as comfortable as possible in their trailing ambulances, nevertheless as the travois bobbed and grated over the rocky ground their suffering was intense. Just at sunset as the column reached the foot of a detached hill, the Californians, in a cloud of dust and with lances swinging, debouched from the hills and came charging down the valley. Over the possession of this hill the third skirmish of the Battle of San Pascual took place. Kearny ordered his men to take possession of the butte. In the action several of the dragoons were badly wounded, but none was killed. Ultimately Kearny found himself in possession of the hillcrest. His wounded were safe, but his sustenance, his cattle, were driven away. Griffin, to say nothing of the General, was now convinced that if they attempted to fight their way to San Diego with the ambulances they must sacrifice their wounded as well as their supplies. It was therefore decided to stay on the hill all night and have Dr. Griffin dress the wounds of the invalided.

As they gained the crest of the hill they found that they were surrounded by patrols of mounted Californians. Escape was impossible. They would have to fight their way out. There was no water; no fodder for the animals but mesquite and manzanita.

On the morrow, ambulances or no ambulances, Kearny was determined to cut his way to San Diego. That night they dug a hole for water and obtained a modicum for man but none for the poor beasts. And they killed the fattest of their mules for meat. After that the butte, where they were beleaguered, became known as Mule Hill. Here among the rocks, Dr. Griffin dressed the wounds of his patients. But on the morning of the eighth he found that the invalided were in no condition to be moved. To have attempted to take them down that hill and sally out on the plain below, where they could see the Californians' lances awaiting, would have been suicide. One-half the fighting force would have been required to take care of the sick, the other half never could fight off the Californians. Therefore it was decided to wait until the men could be transported on horseback. Momentarily help was expected from Godey's mission to San Diego.

That morning, on the plain below them, Dr. Griffin spied a commotion in the camp of the Californians. Shortly after he learned the cause. The scout Godey, who had gone to San Diego for reinforcements, had been captured. Also he learned that Commodore Stockton had refused to send assistance. Hopes on Mule Hill were dashed. On discovering these facts, Kearny determined, at all hazards, to march for San Diego. Every hour on the hill was making his position worse. Be the consequences what they would, he was resolved to move. A council of officers was held. Backed by Kit Carson, the officers virtually forced Kearny to remain on Mule Hill. Their only hope lay in sending word to Stockton and getting help from San Diego. At this juncture, Lieutenant Beale, his Delaware Indian boy, and Kit Carson, volunteered to make the attempt. It was a hazardous journey through the vigilant lines of the Californians. But when Kit volunteered, Kearny agreed to wait. Godey and the others had failed, maybe Carson could make it.

Carson was already a worry in the camp of the Californians. They knew he was among the beleaguered on Mule Hill. The Americans were at their mercy; they intended to keep Carson there. He was as sly as a wolf. He was the logical one to go to San Diego for help but the Californians did not intend that he should ever escape. Further they knew that Kearny had no food and no water. In the end the invaders must die or capitulate. To be sure that no one was sent from Mule Hill to get help, Pico threw three cordons of Californian lancers covering a distance of two or three miles about the base of the butte. Between them he kept a patrol moving. In significant Spanish the patrol warned, *Se escarpa el lobo*, "the wolf will escape."

As soon as dusk fell, out of Kearny's camp, Carson, Beale and the Indian crept. They dared not stand erect less they be silhouetted against the sky. Down the hill they went on hands and knees. All around them they could see mounted Mexican sentries with their long lances. "Those lances swinging against the sky were full of menace." Those same sharp blades that had stabbed the life out of Hammond, Moore, and a dozen more of their comrades would stab the life out of them if they were discovered. They took off their shoes and tied the strings around their belts. They discarded their canteens, when they rattled against the rocks. Down on their bellies the scouts crawled. All night they wormed their way below. In the darkness cactus could not be avoided, thorns entered their flesh. Stones cut their feet. Down they crept, inch by inch. Through the second cordon. Through the third. At last they reached some trees where they could stand erect. They were barefooted. They had lost their shoes. They had thirty miles to go for help—barefoot, over rocks, gravel, cactus, in the dark. (It was one of the great heroic exploits of the winning of the West. The deed is commemorated by a bronze plaque in the Smithsonian Institution at Washington.)

On Mule Hill they burned all their baggage so as to be rid of encumbrances, dismounted the men and determined to perform the rest of the march on foot. Around the mountain the Californians were constantly parading. They were careful not to come within gunshot range. The dragoons were reduced to mule meat. It was poor fare for the wounded. Griffin noted that for the sick it was so coarse that "it does not go." "After all," adds Griffin, "some of my poor fellows have as many as eight wounds on a side.

Three are run through the arm." On the tenth the brave Sergeant Cox died. Griffin had one less man for his ambulances.

All day of the tenth the beleaguered waited for reinforcements. When they did not come, Doctor Griffin gave the welcome information that all the sick but two were able to get into the saddle. Orders were then given that the column should march the next morning. There was little expectation that Carson, Beale or the Indian could get through the Californian lines and reach San Diego. When no help came it was assumed that they had been captured or killed.

That night, with heavy spirits the dragoons threw themselves down on their hard beds. They were firmly convinced that come the morrow they would have to fight their way to San Diego. Again there was no sleeping, but the men rested quietly. They were waiting for the break of day when they would go down the hill and give the enemy a trouncing.

Suddenly, around 2:00 A.M., a voice speaking in English cut the stillness of the night. In a few minutes listeners could hear the tramp of a column of men. Following the hail of the sentinel came a detachment from San Diego. They mustered two hundred strong, eighty marines and one hundred and twenty sailors under the command of Commodore Stockton's aide-de-camp, Lieutenant Gray. From them the dragoons learned that Beale, Carson, and the unsung hero, the Delaware Indian, had arrived safely in San Diego only to find that the marines were already on the March for the relief of Mule Hill. Gladly Griffin and the rest of the dragoons vacated their beds, while the tired marines tumbled in. When they later awoke, savory mule soup was simmering. The jack tars were highly delighted to play soldier. About one thing only were they discontented, the Californians. On their way to Mule Hill the enemy had not had the decency to give them a fight.

The junction of these forces came as a complete surprise to the Californians. Now all chances of a successful attack upon the Americans was removed. Leaving most of their cattle behind them they vacated the premises. "Incredible," wrote Emory in his diary.

On December 11, down the mountain in close order marched the dragoons. The road toward San Diego led through a waterless rolling country devoid of trees. All of Griffin's patients were now mounted save two. Those two in their litters suffered the agonies of the damned from the roughness of the road.

Kearny's column had covered about twelve miles when, on ascending a slight elevation, the Pacific Ocean in all its majesty lay spread out to their view. The sight produced strange emotions in one mountain man. Never before had he seen an ocean. "Lord," he exclaimed as he opened his arms. "There is a great prairie without a tree."

On the twelfth, about 4:00 P.M., in torrents of rain the bedragged dragoons marched into San Diego. Griffin was grateful when he found that

FOREWORD

the post surgeons had prepared everything in their power for his wounded men and every attention that warm and generous hearts could extend to the poor fellows. But the Doctor was worried about his two ambulance cases. One David Streeter had eight lance wounds on one side of the neck, five in the chest, and one on each hip. As for the other, Kennedy, Griffin feared that his spine was fractured and that meningitis had set in.

Kearny had no more than arrived than the question of rank began to fester in his soul. Who should have precedence in California — the Commodore or the General? This futile discussion would worry politicians for the next decade.

On January 1, when the commands of Commodore Stockton and General Kearny were united, John Griffin became the ranking medical officer.

It was then decided that the combined force at San Diego should move northward to co-operate with Frémont's advance from Monterey against Los Angeles.

On December 29, Griffin with some six hundred men marched out of San Diego and headed toward Los Angeles by way of San Luis Rey and San Juan Capistrano. No opposition was encountered until the willow-lined banks of the San Gabriel River were reached. Here the Californians, five to six hundred strong under General Flores, were encountered. Here on December 8 the Battle of San Gabriel was fought, and on the ninth the contending forces engaged in the Battle of La Mesa, the last engagement on California soil. Realizing the hopelessness of further resistance, the Californians withdrew before the battle was really begun. The following day Los Angeles surrendered.

Following the "Cahuenga Capitulation" General Kearny was transferred to San Diego and Dr. Griffin was placed in charge of the General Hospital. From May 1847 until May 1849 he was in Los Angeles under Colonel Jonathan D. Stevenson. On that date he was transferred to the staff of General Persifor F. Smith, as medical officer. From 1850 to 1853, Dr. Griffin remained at Benicia. Then he was ordered back to San Diego to accompany Major Samuel P. Heintzelman on an expedition against the Yuma Indians on the Colorado River. In 1853 he was ordered to report for duty at Washington, D. C.

Iu 1854 he resigned his commission and returned to Los Angeles. There he opened offices for the practice of medicine and surgery. In addition he developed into one of the outstanding citizens of Los Angeles. Such was his medical reputation throughout the state that when James King of William was critically injured in San Francisco, Griffin was summoned from Los Angeles to give his opinion in that famous case.

Not all of Dr. Griffin's time was devoted to medicine. In 1857 when Los Angeles was terrorized by organized banditti and the sheriff and his party were killed, Los Angeles was placed under martial law. By general consent,

Dr. Griffin was placed at the head of the semi-military defense organization by the citizens.

In addition he was an original incorporator and stockholder of the Los Angeles City Water Company and The Farmers and Merchants Bank.

At the organization of the Los Angeles County Medical Association Griffin was chosen to be first president. On June 7, 1856, Dr. Griffin was elected superintendent of the Los Angeles Public Schools. The same year he married Miss Louisa Hayes, first woman public school teacher in Los Angeles.

In 1858 Dr. Griffin became owner of the San Pascual Rancho. In a sense he may be called the father of one of Los Angeles' most beautiful suburbs. Parts of this rancho became the property of his sister, Eliza, widow of Albert Sidney Johnston, Confederate hero, who died at the battle of Shiloh.

On August 23, 1898, Dr. Griffin died in Los Angeles. He was eighty-two years old, the ideal of an intrepid, fearless, genial, capable medical man. For almost fifty years he had carried on his profession. His skill as a surgeon and physician was statewide. His expert understanding endeared him both to native Californians and Americans. He died with the respect and affection of his fellow men.

Such was John Strother Griffin, master medical man, master of medical principles, master of its art. When circumstances were possible, he cured —when impossible, he comforted.

⁂ Introduction ⁂

By *George Walcott Ames, Jr.*

UNITED STATES strategy in the Mexican War contemplated offensive operations in several theatres. There was to be a land thrust from the northeast frontier at the principal towns in north central Mexico, another drive farther to the west at Chihuahua, the capture of Santa Fé, and the invasion of California by an "army of the west." A landing on the east coast and a march against Mexico City itself were later projected, while a vigorous naval blockade of both coast lines was instituted from the very outbreak of hostilities.

It was to the "Army of the West" that John Strother Griffin, assistant surgeon, United States Army, was attached in 1846. Under the command of Colonel–later General–Stephen Watts Kearny, First Dragoons, the "army" was to go overland to New Mexico; after capturing and pacifying the territory, march was to be resumed to California. Upon arrival, the cooperation of any naval forces found along the coast was to be invited, and complete possession was to be taken of the area.

To support the original force, consisting principally of dragoons and mounted Missouri volunteers, which marched from Fort Leavenworth, reinforcements were despatched from the East by the United States Government as soon as they could be assembled and outfitted. Colonel Sterling Price took a regiment of Missouri volunteers to Santa Fé; the Mormons, who had planned to settle in the Far West, were induced to contribute a battalion which marched overland to San Diego but by a more southerly route than Kearny's; a regiment of New York volunteers under Jonathan D. Stevenson sailed around the Horn to San Francisco; and a battery of regulars from the Third Artillery, with all needful materials for building harbor defenses, also arrived by way of the Horn.

When Kearny arrived in California he found Commodore Robert Field

Stockton commanding the naval forces on the coast. Stockton had succeeded Commodore John Drake Sloat, who had taken all of the important northern towns by July 17, 1846. Under Stockton the southern part of the territory was as easily occupied as the north. The naval forces met their first important opposition when they were compelled to evacuate Los Angeles in late September and early October. Troops were being concentrated at San Diego for movement once more against the Pueblo, when the army arrived. With the battles of San Gabriel and La Mesa in January 1847, all organized hostility was finally crushed. Stockton refused to recognize Kearny's orders as civil governor and supported Colonel John Charles Frémont, whom he, Stockton, had appointed to the office. Frémont, contending that he held a commission from Stockton, also refused, at first, to obey Kearny's orders. Kearny, with less than a hundred men to enforce his commands, bided his time until Commodore William Branford Shubrick arrived to replace Stockton. The general's unwillingness to force the issue, particularly in regard to Frémont, was deeply resented by most of the army officers, who felt that a politician's son-in-law should not be given special consideration.

Several accounts have been written of the army's departure from Fort Leavenworth in the summer of 1846, the rendezvous at Bent's Fort, and the occupation of Santa Fé. Lieutenant James William Abert, who did not journey farther west than New Mexico, and Lieutenant William Hemsley Emory wrote official reports which give probably the best descriptions; these were printed in government documents which have made them easily accessible to the interested reader. Lieutenant Emory continued the journey to the Pacific Coast and reported on events through the final cessation of hostilities. Captain Abraham Robinson Johnston, who was killed in the battle of San Pascual, also wrote an interesting account of the hardships passed through on the journey between Santa Fé and the California settlements.[1] Another journal written on that march, one which carried on the tale much farther in point of time and events after arrival in California, is that of assistant surgeon John S. Griffin. Of this, however, only a portion has been published: two or three pages were printed in a local history of Los Angeles,[2] and a few paragraphs in *Pioneer Notes from the Diaries of Judge Benjamin Hayes*.[3] A longer version, a supposedly complete copy in the handwriting of one of Hubert Howe Bancroft's numerous secretaries, lies in the Bancroft Library at the University of California, in Berkeley. In his *History of California* Bancroft gives no indication that only a section of the whole, albeit a large section, was copied; nor does he use any portion after January 10, 1847, although he or his copyist must have known of the remainder. The fact that his copyist and the present editor find the same words illegible would indicate that what he did have was taken from the original. That journal remained in the possession of the family until 1941, when,

INTRODUCTION 15

through the generosity of Mrs. John Griffin Johnston, widow of Dr. Griffin's grandnephew, it was presented to the California Historical Society.

The journal which Griffin[4] kept is valuable in that it reveals the character of an interesting "Yanqui" of early American Los Angeles and that it gives new shades of meaning to certain not too well understood episodes of California history. Particularly worthy of note was Griffin's attitude toward his work and profession, the antithesis of that of Dr. Cadwallader Cuticle, the navy surgeon, whom Herman Melville caricatures in *White Jacket*. Griffin well knew his own limitation. He was always seeking new treatments and discarding old methods; yet his concern for his patient was always present.

The good doctor's writing, while fairly legible in the main, at times is a trial to the editor. This and his use of anatomical terms and pharmaceutical abbreviations and a fanciful method of spelling proper names and Spanish words make certain passages difficult to understand. In the text of the Journal, therefore, well known anatomical names or those which appear in the ordinary dictionary are not explained, although spelling has been corrected where necessary. Pharmaceutical phrases have been more fully interpreted. Misspelled proper names and Spanish words are corrected only on their first appearance. In tracing full names of persons to whom Griffin refers, Hubert Howe Bancroft's "Pioneer Register and Index," in Volumes II to V of his *History of California*, is indispensable, as is Francis B. Heitman's *Historical Register and Dictionary of the United States Army*.

For anyone who is interested in delving deeper into the background, the most convenient place for finding additional facts as well as the best source for authorities is again Bancroft, *History of California*, V. As has been mentioned, Emory's *Notes of a Military Reconnoissance* is excellent and makes a fine complement, while the accompanying map of the route from Santa Fé to San Diego is a most valuable adjunct when reading Dr. Griffin's diary.[5]

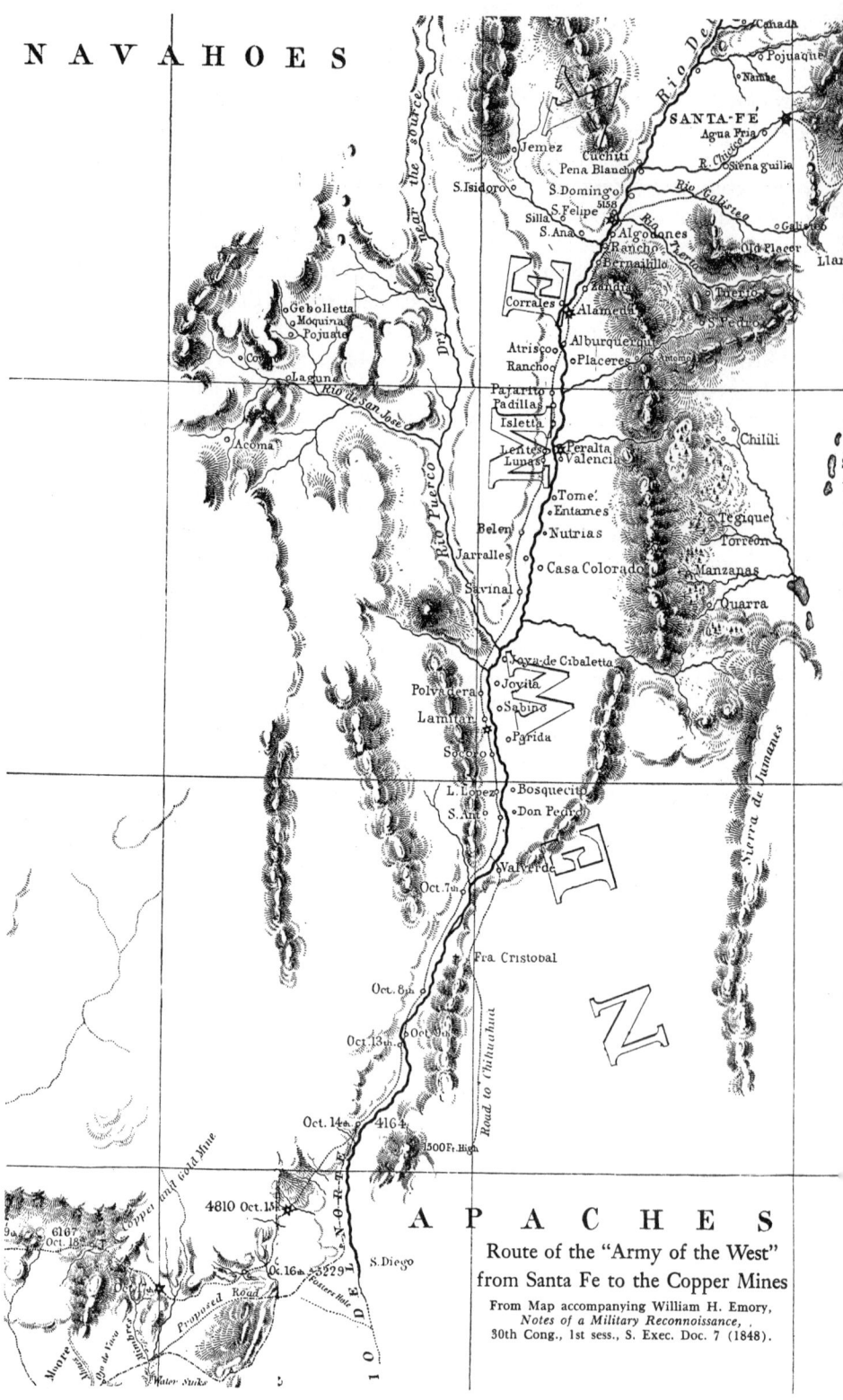

Part I

Over the Southern Route to California

From Santa Fe to the Gila River · Along the Gila to the Colorado
From the Colorado River to Warner's Ranch

From Santa Fe to the Gila River

Camp near St Philippe,
Sept 26th 1846.

WE left Santa Fe yesterday—that is to say, Genl. Kearny, Staff, & myself and joined the Dragoons at their camp near Del Gordo's Ranch[6]—found all hands in great spirits at the prospect of the trip —not as volunteers but as men who had a duty to do & intended to do it.

26. Left camp early & had a hard days march through a perfectly barren country, one that would not feed a single goose to the acre. All the men are mounted on mules—some of them devlish poor at that. One or two gave out to day. This is a bad prospect for California to have the animals giving out the first day. It is said that there is gold in the sands, and that a man can make a living washing dirt, it is well this can be done for I am damned if any one could make a living ploughing. St Philippe is an Indian Village near the Rio Grande [del Norte]. I have not seen it yet, but several of the people have been in camp selling corn, mellons &c.

27. Left camp early, passed St. Philippe—a good looking town, and two other villages—the last called Barnardeo,[7] this country on the Rio Grande is better than that about Santa Fe—fine vineyards, Peaches, Mellons and other fruits the best grapes I have ever seen—by calculation of my own we are fifty six miles from Santa Fe to night The mules purchased by the Qr master are extremely weak many of them are nearly given out, the officers are becoming great jockeys, trading horses for mules, and we do get bit like the devil, to-morrow it is said we cross the Rio Grande.

28, 29, 30th Sept. For the last three days I have been engaged in riding about through the country, trading horses for mules this has been the occupation of most of the officers, and we have all succeeded pretty much alike that is to say, a fine horse for a most indifferent mule, the Mexicans, we have all come to the conclusion, are great rascals, and are not burthened with any great amount of the article called conscience.[8] They are entirely too sharp for us, and for a conquered people are treated with a damn sight more courtesy than they deserve. This may appear a strange remark but our general has a regular Board every morning to assess damages, comitted by our poor half starved mules on their corn fields, and the result is that the amount of damages assessed is generally about twice as much as has really been sustained by the owner of the field. All of which is duly charged to the unlucky wight whose horse or mule may have been caught, thus doing two things, paying the Mexican more money than he ever dreamed his field would produce, and feeding Uncle Sams cattle at the expense of the officers and soldiers of the said good old Uncle—now I do not think this is all quite fair, for if a man does not earn his pay marching over these sands in New Mexico, he would not earn it mauling rails in Missouri, besides this is a most expensive country—it takes every red cent a poor devil can rake together to keep body and soul together and then to be made to pay for feeding Uncle Sams mules is rather too strong a pull—Since the 27th we have been marching slowly along the banks of the Rio Grande—and devlish poor banks they are—nothing but sand, and sand hills and barren Mountains with occasionally a Mexican settlement. We passed through an indian village to day.[9] these people live quite as well as the Mexicans, in the same sort of houses, the only difference is that they enter from the roof. they are a better looking people than the Mexicans, and seem to be their equal in every way—the great majority speak Spanish, though it is said a Mexican cannot acquire their language. At St Philippe some 40 miles back it was said that we had decended 1300 feet from Santa fe. We have been going down hill ever since. There is a perceptible change in the climate, the days being very warm and the nights not so cold—though ice formed last night. We are encamped to night in the neighborhood of Tomé, a Mexican Village on the East side of the Rio Grande.[10] We crossed the River yesterday at Al[b]uquerque, the Residence of the former governor Armejo [Manuel Armijo]. I took dinner at Al[b]uquerque, in regular Mexican style—one dish at a time with *tortillias* and lots of red pepper. We ended with grapes. This is decidedly the best thing in all Mexico. Our sick report is small, though we will be obliged to send back one poor fellow, in consequence of a dislocation of the clavicle. Paid for mutton this evening on account of the mess 75 cts

Oct. 1st—This morning, we found one of the mess minus. Stauntons'[11] servant a Mexican concluded to leave the camp last night & did so with his (Staunton's) best horse and up to this time we have heard nothing of him, this only confirms me in my belief that they are certainly the damndest rascals that can be found any where. The country marched through to day better than yesterday, country on the River well populated, passed through several villages, marched some 16 miles.[12] I am at present sick and am fearful that I shall be obliged to return to Santa Fe. I hope however this will not be the case. I will ride in the wagon tomorrow & hope that will stop the further development of the infernal disease.

Oct. 2d–We made an early start this morning. The country not much settled, and but little grass, the country being sandy. We are encamped opposite a small Mexican village on the opposite side of the Rio Grande—[13] the Alcalde sent us word that we had better keep a bright look out on our animals, as some Navahoe Indians were seen about yesterday. These Indians whip the Mexicans, and drive off cattle, whenever it pleases them to do so and the Mexicans make little resistance. This is a very poor grazing country, & up to this time I have not seen three thousand head of cattle since I left Santa Fe, nor is there grass or grain sufficient in this country to feed more than a regiment of Dragoons. We marched today about 15 or 17 miles— no timber in the country except cotton wood, and that hard to find, I gave 25 cts yesterday for one little stick to cook my breakfast by.

Oct. 3d. Last night an express arrived from Santa Fe—announcing the arrival of Col. Price with a part of his regiment,[14] at that time we received no mail, letters or papers, and not one word of news, at this we all swore like troopers, at friends, post masters & commanding officers, however it is all the same to me, as it will all be news when we hear it, & I do reckon we shall find out something when we arrive at Monterey. The news of Captain Allens death was confirmed poor fellow—he is gone.[15] I wonder how many more of us will go, before we return to the United States for I am damned if I do call this Uncle Sam, whatever Mr Polk may say. We have remained quiet in camp all day waiting for the ox-teams to come. One Company C–Capt Moore was sent off to trounce the Navahoes who were said to be giving the Spaniards the devil [with]in some 11 miles of us.[16] Capt Cook left camp to day to return to Santa Fe to take command of the Mormons.[17]

Oct. 4. This morning we had an increase in the number of animals in the command. Major Sumners[18] Lady of the Lake was delivered safely of a small colt, which was abandoned shortly after its birth. We marched over some ten miles of deep sand—it fatigued our animals very much to get through it. This I suppose is only a beginning of what we are to have from here to Monterey. We passed several poor Mexican villages. Capt Moor could not catch the Navahoes. I heard to day the Gen¹. directed the commanding officer at Santa Fe to make fierce war on the red rascals. The banks & bottoms of the Rio Grande has presented a much better appearance to day than I have yet seen—more grass, and timber, some beautiful groves of cotton wood—and grazing enough for thousands of animals—yet we have seen scarcely any stock to day—the Indians have plundered the poor devil[s] of Mexicans out of every thing. We marched some 16 miles to day.[19] The day has been warm, the atmosphere presenting very much the same appearance as our Indian summer in the States nor has it rained since we left Santa Fe.

Oct. 5. We made an early start this morning, but marched a short distance, and encamped near Secora [Socorro], a small Mexican village. Tomorrow we leave the Rio Grande & strike west across the mountains for the Rio Gila. As we look at them from the valley of the Rio Grande they present rather a forbidding front, nothing in the world but sand, lava and trap rock. They are not very high and that is a comfort, and it is said after we get to the top of the mountain it is a prairie from there to the Gila—good grass—but water hard to find, and devlish little of it when found. The valley of the Rio Grande has appeared decidedly prettier to day than I have yet seen it. in one place it looked a little like the Missouri Bottom, the river here is a rapid stream, about 120 or 200 feet wide, dividing off, so as to make many islands, the water is Muddy & Reddish, nearly the color of the Red River. There seems to be plenty of soft shell turtles & Cat fish in the river & lots of Wild geese and Sand Hill cranes—the only game I have seen in New Mexico—

6 & 7—On the 6th I was not able to write up my journal to day, in consequence of being busily engaged till bed time, about ten oclock while marching along, some 8 or 9 men came charging up to us with an Indian yell. These turned out to be [Kit] Carson, the celebrated mountain man and his party on his way to Washington with an express from Capt [Robert F.] Stockton of the Navy & Col [John C.] Fremont announcing that they had taken California & that the latter was to be governor of the same. This created considerable sensation in our party, but the general feeling [was] one of disappointment and regret—most of us hoped when leaving Santa Fe —that we might have a little kick up with the good people of California but this totally blasted all our hopes, and reduced our expedition to one of mere escort duty the Genl taking the same view of the matter took only two Companies C & K, 1st Drags, and left the remaining three in New Mexico under command of Major Sumner.[20] We parted with our friends with regret. Dr Simpson[21] & myself drew straws to see who should go to California, and I won, if it be said to be a gain to have such a march going and if we get there to have just such another returning. Mr. Fitzpatrick took Carson's mail, and left for Washington.[22]

7th—After duly turning over our property, which I did all to one fifth chains, for which I must get Ingalls[23] receipt upon my return from California, and taking leave of the fellows left behind, we put out, with merry hearts & light packs on our long march—Carson as guide, every man feeling renewed confidence in consequence of having such a guide. The county we passed through to day, the valley of the Rio Grande was decidedly the most desireable portion I have yet seen of New Mexico, The Towns being scattered about in beautiful clumps, fine grass and every thing looking as fresh as in spring. The hills are as bleak and sterile as ever—this country is not occupied. The Mexicans cant stay in it for the Indians. I forgot to mention that several Apachee indians came into camp yesterday, and that four are now with us. The Gen¹. I suppose intends collecting the tribe for a council as we pass through the country. We did not leave the Rio Grande yesterday as I supposed we would, but continued on it & will do so for some time. We left the trail to Chihuahua to day. I think we are encamped to night opposite or below Fra Cristobal. From the way the Gen¹. marched to day, I should say he was on his way in Earnest. We have come some 23 miles. The day has been clear with a strong south wind blowing the dust in our faces. This has annoyed us much & made my eyes quite sore.

8th Oct. The Gen¹. pushed out early this morning, had us all astir in tolerably quick time after revallie. We travelled well for some two or three miles, and then struck the most infernal route prehaps that has been seen, with the exception of the country ahead. it was one succession of reedy bottoms, sand hills and occasionally a sprinkling of tolerable thick cotton wood—but what was most annoying, was the chapparal this has long thorns on it, and we found it pretty thick in the high lands, this annoyed our mules in the team greatly, and if there be much of it ahead it will be impossible to pass through it. The leaf of the plant looks like the honey locust. We saw some bear tracks to day—a flock of turkeys and a deer was killed by Mr. Stanley.[24] It is reported that several coveys of black patridges have been seen. The country passed over to day was not so pretty as we saw yesterday. Yet from the size of the trees, I should say the bottoms were better and would produce well.

Oct. 9th We have not made more than 7 or 8 miles to day. it has been decidedly the hardest days journey we have yet had, it was with the greatest difficulty that the wagons could be brought up at all. The guide Carson declares that he believes it impossible to get wagons through and I think the Gen¹. is becoming of the same opinion, five of the team mules utterly caved and the remainder were so near to it, that the difference could scarcely be told, it was one succession of hills and what is called in this country cañons (pronounced canyons). The sides of the hills being nothing but beds of Lava, when on top of the hills chapparal, prickly pear & sand, so withall the poor mules had a devil of a time, this is the poorest country I have yet seen in New Mexico, though the River bottoms are good The Genl is now consulting with the guides & Mr Martin about taking on the wagons. The general opinion is to abandon them. To day we have seen several flocks of what we call black patridges, their plumage is very beautiful with a long top knot on the head—They fly, run and call very much like our quail, they are a longer bird than the quail, but not heavier I think. I have not eaten any of them yet, four or five were killed, but only two found in consequence of the thick brush and undergrowth that they were among. One man saw some 10 or 12 deer after coming into camp. I was out saw great sign both of deer & bear but could not find any of the animals. I think when we leave this camp we shall go on packs—There is no sickness in camp. The day was slightly cloudy, with a breeze blowing from the south as there has been for the last three days—there is distant lightning in the East, but no rain has fallen near us yet.

An express came up to us about 12 oclock to day—from some alcalde, announcing that the Navahoes were about to attack the mexican settlements and wipe them out—there was said to be a Mexican by name Sandone who was said to have joined these Indians, the Gen[l]. sent back word that the troops in the country should look after the Navahoes, and directed Major Sumner to take a hand.

Oct. 10th. Last night the council determined that wagons could not be taken any farther—it was therefore determined to leave them—an express[25] was immediately sent to Major Sumner for a party to take back the wagons, and to send us the pack saddles. We have remained in camp all day, reducing our baggage so that it might be packed—it had already been cut down to the lowest point, at the camp & Santa Fe. I suppose by the time we arrive at Monterey if we have the Georgia uniform on it will be as much as we can reasonably expect. Some Mexicans brought mules into camp to trade the Gen[l]. finding they had been trading with the Apachees without a license confiscated the whole of them.

11 & 12th Oct remaining quiet in camp, nothing going on. All impatient except the mules who—(if the personal pronoun can be applied to them) seem to be very well contented. We have good grass on the other side of the River, and the poor things seem to enjoy the rest very much, particularly the team mules. We have all been engaged in weighing flour[,] pork &c. so as to adjust our packs equally. We are inexperienced in this mode of progression, and I expect nothing else but that we will ruin the backs of most of our animals. last night we amused ourselves having an illumination in camp, and Burning up the Qr Masters Tar, against which the Major strenuously protested, and gave us all a lecture on economy—which was all perfectly natural & proper for a quarter master.[26]

Oct. 13th—We crossed the river and moved our camp some mile[s] to better grass. Shortly after getting into camp Lt Ingalls came up with the mail, and notice that the pack saddles would be up in an hour or two. So tomorrow we are off for California in earnest. The mail brought us up but little news only an order, and an old N. Y. Herald—which had little or nothing in it. I received a letter from Philadelphia, from some unknown friend, who signs himself R. K. P. The Lord only knows who he is, I don't. he speaks of meeting with some cousin of mine in philadelphia Who she is the

Lord knows for I dont I can swear—the rest of his letter I cant read, so I will use it for gun wadding—there is nothing going on in camp. Carson the guide says it will take us fifty days to go to St Diego. this is the 13—by that calculation it should take some time about the 1 or 3ᵈ of Dec. *Whew* [?] but it is a long time to live on the prairies or rather desert and maybe on half rations at that, with not a very brilliant prospect of enjoyment or ease even when we get to Monterey. N. B. [*Nota bene*] Moor says I owe hime $5.00, borrowed in my name by Chorbano.[27]

Oct. 14ᵗʰ—This morning we were all up early, adjusting packs, and our spaniards were in great requisition. This was a perfectly new mode of doing business to us, the consequence was we expected to see some little fun by the mules raising the devil generally only two or three of them got into a muss and caused their packs to be thrown off. My own kit got somewhat damaged, but upon the whole I think we shall get along swimmingly. The country passed over most miserable, though the River bottoms looked well at a distance but *perhaps* it was only distance that lent enchantment to the view. The River here is some fifty or seventy five yards wide rapid and muddy. Mountains in all directions, the country extremely rugged, and no game. So endeth the chapter. We marched nearly 18 miles to day.

15ᵗʰ & 16ᵗʰ Oct. On the 15ᵗʰ after leaving our camp on the Rio Grande, and following down the River some four miles, we struck off to the S. W. the mountains appearing as a barrier on our front. One pass appeared and for that we struck, we crossed two enormous cañons, and camped in the third. We found fine water in the two last. A new growth of trees The oak—a peculiar species, leaf small and serrated, acorn small, and sweet, a walnut, in appearance like the white walnut, the country rugged. We marched this day 24 or 25 miles. On the 16ᵗʰ left camp early, and had a devil of a hill to climb at the start, it was a breather after we got to the top of it—found a beautiful country—the finest stock country I have yet seen in New Mexico —the whole earth covered with grammer [grama] grass—a most nutritious food for Cattle and horses—stock water in abundance, in the small streams and I think a good deal of land might be cultivated by irrigation. We marched to day 18 or 20 miles, it is a little cloudy this evening—this is the first cloudy day we have had since leaving Santa Fe.

17ᵗʰ & 18ᵗʰ. Oct. Last night I did not write my journal in consequence of getting into camp late, and it being excessively cold. We travelled principally through mountain passes, along beds of the small streams, which seem to be dry at this season of the year—the road excessively rough. We were ascending mountains nearly all day—they were covered to their very tops with the finest species of grass—in the evening we crossed the Rio Mimbres, a small clear mountain stream, out of which Capt Turner[28] had caught about a dozen of the finest Brook trout. Capt T had been sent forward by the Genl to find the Apachees, but did not succed in doing so. We saw many Apachee lodges scattered about through the prairie, the bottoms and side of the mountains, covered with a species of dwarf oak, very much like the live oak—it is evidently the evergreen—and several species of cedar that I have not seen before. The Bottom of the Mimbres was quite a fine piece of land, with pretty good timber, no game—from some cause unknown to myself, my Mule Manuel saw fit to throw me over his head which he did in less time than any four foot animal, has ever done before. On the 18th we started early,—the morning being very cold, continued to travel through pretty much the same sort of passes as yesterday, with occasionally a beautiful mountain vally. About 12 miles from our Camp, we came to the copper mines. We found here quite an extensive town, which had been deserted, the mine seems to have been worked to a considerable extent, as there were shafts running in every direction, it is said an American named McKnight worked them and obtained a fine profit—in fact made a fortune, that there was a large per centage of gold found in the copper—in fact so much as to pay the transportation of the copper from hence to the City of Mexico.[29] There is said to be a pretty good wagon road running here from the passo Del Norte. I was in several of the shafts—the copper ore seemed to be plenty and very rich—as I cut out a piece of metal nearly pure—it is in veins in the rock, which seems to be a sand stone. We passed on beyond the Mines and encamped on a beautiful creek—about two miles from the mines—I saw a Black tail deer near the mines the first I have yet seen. After we had encamped Red Sleeve the principal chief of the Apachees,[30] with one of his men came into camp he was quite friendly, and the Genl gave him some presents. We move on tomorrow about 15 miles where the chief says he will meet us with his people. it is quite warm to-night and a little cloudy.

19th & 20th. Oct. On the 19th the Genl promised us a short march, the Apachees had promised to meet us at a certain point, sixteen miles distant, so we started out in fine spirits, expecting to have a pleasant evening in camp the Indians disappointed us, and when we arrived at the point designated we found that the grass had been all eaten up. Carson our guide had gone back with a party of officers to the copper mines. The old Mexican, who was acting as guide for the day reported water nine miles ahead so off we put, marched till dark, no water, continued the march, and it was 10 oclock before our poor mules got into camp. Many of them gave out, and one got drowned, it had a heavy pack and rushed into the water, and perished—fine grass, mountains &c. After we had been in camp a short time the Apachees came up.

20th. This morning presents were made to the Indians, and then an attempt to trade for mules We found them sharp traders, and only succeeded in getting two or three. They were armed—some with guns, bows and arrows and all with lances, they are said to be very formidable with these weapons, they are finely mounted, expressed the greatest friendship, and lasting hos-

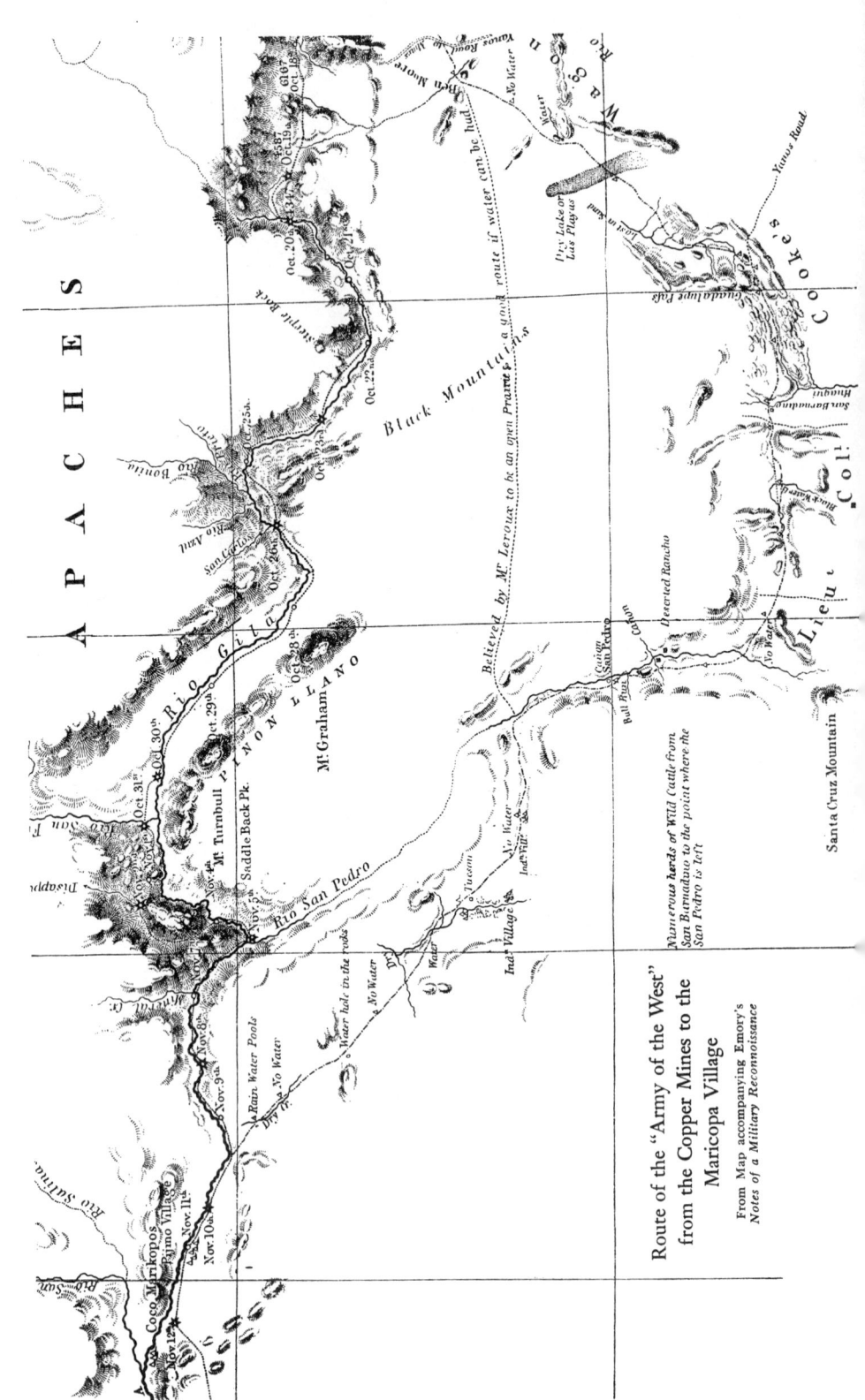

tility against the Mexicans, they seem to think that the Mexicans are great rascals and that they have a right to kill them whenever they can. Many of them had Mexican saddles, cartridge boxes, and different parts of the Mexican dress, all of which had no doubt been plundered from some poor devil who they had killed. We followed down a branch of the Gila [Night Creek] to day, and about 3 oclock came to that stream, it is a fine bold, beautiful mountain stream but with no land about it that can be cultivated, cotton wood timber, fine fish, plenty caught this evening. No game, though I found plenty of deer sign. We have marched in the last two days forty five miles.

Along the Gila to the Colorado

Oct. 21st This has been a long and fatiguing days journey. When we left camp this morning we had two difficulties presented to us—the one a most steep and rugged mountain, the other a cañon of the river, we took the latter as the lesser evil, followed down the Gila some five or six miles and finally turned the steepest point of the mountain, in following the course of the river, we were obliged to cross it every half mile or so, the mountain jutting down to the very edge of the stream, making a very picturesque affair of it— but damn bad roads—the fact is we have so much of the grand, & sublime scenery that I am tired of it. After turning the flank of the mountain we ascended it, and found it bad enough even at that. Carson said this was a turnpike road in comparison to the other route. We struck the river about 3 or 4 oclock in the evening and found the country quite open. More fish have been caught this evening   I tried my hand but could not get even a nibble—plenty of deer & turkey sign to day—none seen. I had to take a *pleasant* ride of some miles on the back trail to see a sick man—this made me late in getting into camp   Our march to day some 18 miles by my computation. The Howitzers have not come up yet, and it is now 8 P M—poor Davidson[31] he has a sweet time of it—these are the only wheeled vehicles we have along, and they are about as much trouble as all the packs put together   Our pack animals begin to suffer dreadfully from sore backs, and the beef cattle are becoming so tender footed that the[y] are driven along with the greatest difficulty. Some Indians came up shortly after we started this morning—We have seen nothing of them since, the rascals are loafing along after us to steal some mules, I suppose.

Oct. 22d. We arrived late in camp this evening as usual having marched 18 or 20 miles—the country is better than that passed over yesterday. Kept the river bottom for a few miles, but was again headed off by another cañon —we then had a rough country, the Howitzers broke down another set of mules yesterday   these devlish things cost us more in the shape of mules than a Company of Dragoons. Captain Johnston lost one of his mules[32]—

with the pack—he has gone back after it. We are to march ten miles a day till he overtakes us—

Oct. 23ᵈ. This morning we left camp about 9 oclock, crossed the River, and marched down the bottom on the north side of the stream, the road was quite level, but ye gods the dust. I never suffered or saw men suffer more from any trifling annoyance in my life. The grass & weeds indicated quite strong soil, and might be cultivated by proper irrigation. We saw one or two wild geese & two or three flocks of ducks—the advanced guard saw the black quail & the common quail of the United States No other game was seen, the fact is Carson says he never knew a party on the Gila, that did not leave it starving, this I am fearful will be our case before we leave—Marched about 16 or 17 miles.

Oct. 24 The Genˡ determined to remain quiet to day. We have been fishing & caught nothing. Capt Johnston got up about 12 M. he caught his mule and found most of his pack. ruins of ancient buildings seen yesterday and broken crockery.[33] No fish caught, and only one wild goose killed.

25ᵗʰ. We left camp early this morning continued to travel along the River Gila, had a hard and rugged days march. Encamped on a high hill or rather mountain, near the river, had to pack wood & water up the hill for more than ¼ of a mile, good grass.

27. On the 26ᵗʰ we left camp early revallie having been sounded at 4 A.M. Orders were issued the night before that we should have every thing prepared to start so soon as there was light sufficient to see this was represented as being a hard day—and it was not belied, it was one succession of mountains so covered with sharp stones that I do not believe our mules touched the ground once in five miles. A mule without shoes stood no chance, many could not be driven, and many from exhaustion fell by the wayside, and no effort on the part of the men could get them any farther. Some ten or twelve utterly give up—the men were coming in last night till one oclock, and five or six had to lay out in the mountains, one poor fellow lost the way and following a ravine our camp fires being in sight, tumbled over a bluff thirty feet high—but fortunately did not get hurt much. There is a mule now on the mountain opposite to us that can be driven neither up or down. The Howitzers did not get in Water had to be sent back to the men—the River from our last camp to this runs through a cañon, the water is inaccessible for any thing but a bird—therefore we were obliged to do without it all day —the men and animals suffered very much.

There was some rain last night, and it is now raining. A few days wet weather will use up the remainder of our animals, and we shall be obliged to foot it from here to California. The Genˡ. determined to stay still this morning until 12 M, when we start to look for grass. Our animals had but little last night.

28ᵗʰ—After 12 M yesterday, the Genˡ. concluded to remain in camp the balance of the day. Men were coming in camp all day with broken down mules, and cattle. The Howitzers got in about 1 P M—plenty of fish caught, and two turkeys killed by Mr. Stanly, the artist. This morning we are all up bright and early preparing for a start. When my cavalry were driven up I found one of them my poor old pony so used up that I was obliged to abandon him—he will I think do well and perhaps be the sire of a new race of horses in the mountains. Several mules were left also. After travelling a few miles over rough broken country, we got into the river bottom, and have come on finely all day. No hills or stone, but deep sand and plenty of dust. The River tolerably well wooded with cotton wood—some thickets of a species of wood that I do not know—the bottom was better to day than I have yet seen it on the Gila, and might be cultivated by irrigation—passed the ruins of several buildings in some places the cedar posts were standing. The buildings were evidently quite large—and pieces of crockery were scattered about in great profusion—we have found these ever since we got on the Gila. Some pieces are plane, some painted black & white, & red & black.[34] Who could have done this—there is no record nor tradition that I have heard of, of the Mexicans having lived in this country, and the present race of Indians evidently never either built so extensively or made the crockery—that they may have smashed it is quite likely as they seem to have a genius that way, in common with all the red skin rascals I have ever seen yet. The River at this point is some 60 yds broad and very rapid and quite deep it is cloudy, and has been raining in the mountains to our left all day— No game seen—yet every day we see plenty of deer & turky tracks. great numbers of the patridge of the country must rise along the river as we constantly see their tracks and occasionally a covey of birds very few water fowl.

29 Oct. This morning it had cleared off beautifully—but a few drops of rain fell last night. This evening however it has clouded up again. We have made a fine march to day, had good roads, we struck the main Indian trace used by the red rascals for going into Sonora, where they plunder the Mexicans to their hearts content, of mules, Horses, women & children[35]—This latter two articles they make slaves of. We are now in the Quietero (I believe so they are called—though I do not know how to spell the word) country.[36] They are represented by our guide as being great rascals and thieves—they will steal our mules if possible—therefore we keep pretty good guard for them—none have been seen to day, though some were seen at a distance yesterday. Saw plenty of broken crockery, but no ruins of buildings. Some of our party maintain that the buildings were erected by the Aztecs, but I do think if it were so we would hardly find cedar posts standing—though it is a wood that lasts a long time. It is said that on the Salt River a branch of the Gila, that large villages are found, & dikes &c. showing that the earth had been cultivated—the bottom of the river quite large &

might be cultivated by irrigation—the river seems to be high at times overflowing the country to a considerable extent. The Engineer party I believe named a large mountain to the west of us, Mount Dallas, after the Vice president.[87] This grass is not good—long but tough and wiry.

30th Oct. To day has been pretty much the same as yesterday, only the road a little rougher—hills, &c—no game except patridges, centipedes, tarantulas & rattlesnakes, musquite bushes & cotton wood. Two Indians seen and caught to day—could not make them understand any thing, they were most infernally frightened—a few presents made to them—

31st Oct. Cloudy this morning, a few drops of rain last night. considerable rain fell near us yesterday but we caught none of it—this evening clear. Left camp ¼ to 8 oclock—marched down the River—pretty much the same as yesterday—except the country rougher and more broken. After marching some ten miles encamped, on a branch of the Gila—called I believe the San Francisco. We came thus early to a halt—about 12 M—because the great Cañon of this River commences here, and we will in all probability not be able to get water again for two days. Some Indians came and hailed us—a white flag sent out and a talk held with them, but I believe they could not be induced to come into camp. The mules are breaking down fast and our beef cattle are giving out fast. We usually kill the most foot sore, and it often happens that the poor beast cannot be made to get up—so as to be killed decently—and it is devlish poor & tough beef at that. The trail that we are now travelling is strewn with the carcasses of cattle these have been driven from Sonora by the Indians—they steal constantly from the Mexicans. This is muster day, & the rolls have been made out.

1st Nov. The guide warned us this morning that we would march but six or seven miles before we should leave the River—we would be headed off by a cañon—and it might be three days before we should see water again—this was rather a gloomy prospect—We therefore filled everything that was portable and would hold water—with that fluid—coffee pots, gourds, canteens, and some had their gum elastic cloaks made up in the shape of bags, and filled with water. We started out on an Indian trail, up the mountain. Carson had never travelled this trail, and did not know any thing of country on it but from its course he thought it best for us to follow it. We followed on up the trail & up the mountain—sometimes a very good road, then again rough. Saw many of the most beautiful amygdaloid stones—The mountains covered with fine grass, and the most enormous cactus. They were fully thirty feet high—and from 18 inches to 2½ feet in diameter. We found a nut also of very agreeable flavour. About 4 P M—we saw cotton wood to our great surprise and joy in a ravine. We at once made search, and found water, not in any great quantity yet sufficient to keep us from suffering—I had walked nearly all day—as we were constantly ascending—had but one drink of water all day. A man may easily imagine our joy when the water was discovered, as we had made up our minds to do on about a quart each for three days—and all this time our poor mules were to have none. We have made about 17 miles to day—9 of which was up the mountain.

2ᵈ Nov.—Revellie sounded this morning at 4 oclock and by day light we had breakfasted and all prepared for an early start, when we saw Indians on the top of the mountain, being extremely anxious to establish friendly relations with them, Carson was sent up to try and get them into camp, but they would not come, nor allow more than one person to approach them, and he must be unarmed—finally by leaving a hostage, one was induced to come in —he of course was received kindly, & presents made to him—then another came, when the first went back, and finally a third, who could speak a little spanish. With the last our interpreter and Carson talked—made him understand where we were going, and that we were at war with the Mexicans, and did not wish to injure the Indians, that we wanted to trade for mules and horses—All of this he seemed well satisfied with—but could not understand what the devil we wanted with the artillery. They however went off seemingly well contented, furnishd us a guide to conduct us to water, and promised to bring mules to-morrow. It is said that an American from Sonora killed their chief and several others of the tribe a few years since in the most treacherous manner, and what was the worst of it, there were sixteen other Americans in the neighborhood trapping who had received no notice of this fellows intentions and knew nothing of the murder. The Indians attacked them and killed the whole number.[38] We traveled down the mountain to day —rough road—and camped on a little stream about 2 P M. The stream is well wooded—with cottonwood, sycamore—the first I have seen in New Mexico —and ash—

3ᵈ. Nov.—It being understood that we would not move camp to day, We were quite fashionable in our breakfast hour and took matters and things in the most quiet manner, every one hoping to be the possessor of a good fat mule or horse before night. About 8 oclock a few Indians made their appearance—when the quarter master—Major Swords—pitched his tents and opened shop—about twenty Indians came in fine formed, active healthy looking fellows, but most scantily provided with any thing like clothing. The red & blue cloth, with the blankets & knives were shown in the most tempting manner. After some time, a trade was made—one blanket a piece of scarlet, 4 yds of domestic—a paper of paint, two butcher knives and some rings & glasses for a mule. for this price we succeeded in getting seven mules—not fat or remarkable for sound backs either. The chief then arrived—a good looking man of some thirty five years dressed in beaver skin. This fellow first embraced the General, made a long speech to him, and as usual among Indians commenced beging. We found him the greatest beggar in the crowd —he found this unprofitable, When he wished to sell a mule for more than any one else—this the Major would not give—when the chief mounted his horse and put off since when we have not seen any thing of the red rascals—not one half came in that promised, and so ended our fond anticipations of a remount, and getting rid of a bale of Indian goods. There was one old squaw—a perfect old beggar—from the tone of her voice, dressed in fine muslin & Brussels lace—this had evidently been the ball dress of some Mexican belle[39]—in fact most of the Indians had Spanish saddles—or some part of the clothing of the Mexicans—evidently plundered. Many of their horses & mules were branded. They told us that there were now two parties on a plundering expedition into the Mexican country. We saw one boy some 15 years old, very handsome—and intelligent in his looks—who told us he was a Mexican. We wished to make up a purse to buy him—but so soon as the proposition was made his master bundled him up and put off with him—the boy did not seem to be discontented—nor did he express any wish to quit the Indians[40]—he was from a place in Sonora called St Ana—we are now within 80 miles of the settlements of Sonora. The Indians brought in the muscal [mescal]—the whole plant I think recently gathered and roasted—the heart of it was extremely pleasant—much in taste like a sweet potatoe only sweeter and more juicy they had it preserved also—as we saw it among the Apachees. They proffered us acorns—and the chief had money—plundered from the Mexicans no doubt—An old squaw showed us some metal—which some of us thought to be ammoniate of silver. She would not part with it—at any reasonable price.

4th & 5th. Nov. On the 4th we left camp early, nothing having been seen of our friends the Pelomaroes[41]—(so the Indians are called) Our road laid over the tops of—and along the sides of the most steep and rugged mountains, occasionally we would come to a little vally—where the oak, walnut, cotton wood and ash were found—No water however—though it might be had no doubt by digging a little in the sand—towards evening we got into a little valley and reached our camp at 5½ or 6 P M having marched some 25 miles—The men were coming up until 10 oclock at night. Hammond[42] with the rear guard and Howitzers did not get up. We saw in the valley—a large trail of cattle & Indians—no doubt these were just out of Sonora.

On the 5th we left camp about 9 A.M. travelled down the river, through a cañon—still continued on the cattle trail—found a little steer left by the Indians—and encamped about 3 P M—some ¾ or 1 mile on the St Pedro—above its mouth this little stream is also called the Hog river by the Americans—from the number of wild Hogs found on it—the country passed over barren mountains, and utterly worthless—

6th. This has been a most weary day, the Howitzers being left in the mountains and the great difficulty of getting any thing along with wheels, caused the loss of another day—they have not got up yet—and the lord knows when they will arrive—though I have no doubt that Hammond and his party—have worked like devils to get the cursed things ahead. There has been no excitement—or nothing else in camp the only consolation a man has, is that his mule is feeding and may be able to carry him another day farther on the journey—our pack animals are getting in a most pitiable condition—their backs cut all to pieces—and so poor and weak that they can hardly be goaded along. Then the beef—poor and tender footed—When they get into camp, and one of them has to be butchered—he meets his death—lying down, nor can the poor devil be made to stand up long enough to be decently disposed of—every bush in the country is full of thorns—and every piece of grass so soon as it is broken becomes a thorn at both ends—every rock you turn over has a tarantula or centipede under it, and Carson says in the summer—the most beautiful specimens of rattle snakes are scattered around in the greatest profusion. The fact is take the country all together, and I defy any man who has not seen it—or one as utterly worthless—even to imagine any so barren—The cactus is the only thing that does grow, and we saw some of them yesterday—I should say 50 feet high—one was measured and found to be 45 feet high. Yesterday our rear met a party of Indians—The red rascals would have nothing to do with the soldiers but wished to trade with a Mexican who was with the party—& desired the Mexican to bring his wares to the bushes at some distance from the party—but the Mexican could not be prevailed upon to leave the company—They (the Indians) no doubt wished to murder the poor devil. I have been asleep nearly all day—waked up in a horrible humour—hope to feel better tomorrow. We are now within some fifty miles of a Mexican post in Sonora—lord if they only knew our condition I do think they might trade our Genl off for La Vega[43]—The Howitzers have got in so we leave in the morning bright and early.

7th. Started from camp about 8 oclock—followed the River bottom all day. The road very good—except the dust, and if you did happen to ride off of the beaten trace you stood a reasonable chance of having your mules leg broken The ground seems hollow beneath—& your animal is constantly stumbling or falling with you by sliping through up to the fetlock & sometimes nearly to the knee—The whole face of the country is perfectly barren —the only thing growing being a little cotton wood—the cactus in the lord knows how many varieties—the Artemisia & musquite. We are encamped to night among the mountains again—no game seen to day little grass in our camp—Three Indians have come in two Quiriteroes & one Navajoe[44]—our march to day has been about 18 miles. The frost has not touched the leaves of the cotton wood much—not more than it would in Missouri by the middle of Sept.—it has clouded up this evening and looks like it might rain—the wind being from the S west. The command is remarkably healthy not a man on the sick report whose disease could in any manner be attributed to the country—

8. & 9th Nov. On the night of the 7th it clouded up and threatened a great storm of wind and rain, after blustering till about 11 oclock P M—it rained

very hard, for about half an hour and then cleared off. This is the first rain of consequence that we have had since leaving Sante Fe. It was quite cool all day. We travelled through a cañon all day crossed the river very frequently which made it disagreeable, in consequence of the depth of the stream our feet and legs got wet—Our Indians staid in camp all night, promised to bring in horses, mules, & cattle, to trade, but failed to do so—this however did not disappoint us any as we have learned not to put much faith in their promises. After getting in camp tried my hand fishing, as usual failed to catch any thing—then tried it hunting, being incited thereto by seeing several geese— Killed a hawk & one patridge. little or no grass for animals, and very little seen all day—

9th Last night we had a white frost—the first I have seen on the march— and in fact the first appearance I have seen of moisture in the air—as we have had no dew—The morning quite chilly. Our course continued through the cañon for some two or three miles. This part of the cañon presented the grandest scene I have yet seen in the Rocky Mountains. The cliffs were some hundred and fifty feet & perfectly precipitous. They are basaltic I believe After leaving the cañon, we came suddenly on a large plain with mountains in the distance. One piece of good news the guide told us and that was—that we were through the mountains. No man can imagine our relief, who has not toiled through them for the last forty days on tired and damn contrary mules—The bottom almost destitute of grass and covered with musquite wood. The soil is not sandy, but is more like that found in an extremely dusty road in the States—and beaten down a little with rain— There is some sort of animal that burrows under it in every direction, which makes it disagreeable as well as unsafe to leave the beaten trail. We found more ruins, and broken crockery, and our antiquaries will persist in saying that it is remains of ancient Aztec houses. After marching some 20 miles we found a patch of coarse grass—where we encamped, our mules however seem to enjoy it very much—and well they may, for they have been on devlish short rations for the last two nights and likely to be so for some time to come—if report speaks true.

10th & 11th Nov. Our course to day still continued through the bottom of the Gila, the same powder baked for soil—but we were agreeably disappointed in finding an occasional patch of grass—the advance of our party saw what is known in this country as the Casa Montazuma, this is a house of considerable extent, and apparently fine finish, built of cement and sand, and the inside of a very fine finish. The rafters I was told by a person who inspected it, had evidently been hewn off with a stone axe or hatchet. They were of cedar. The house occupied a most commanding position—there is no tradition either among the Mexicans or Indians as to what time it was built.[45] About 6 oclock we encamped in a grassy bottom some six miles above the Pimas village, here it seems we were first discovered by the Indians

—and the Genl received a message from the chief to know who we were, where we were going and with what intention we were coming into their country all of which being answered in a satisfactory manner—and being informed that we would trade for provisions, they at once hurried off and by nine o clock our camp was crowded with them with various articles to trade, such as corn, beans in great abundance—water mellons mollasses made from the prickly pair—which has very much the taste of preserved quinces —white beads and red cloth were the articles most in in demand—they came in to trade with us with the greatest confidence, showing not the slightest fear as the mountain Indians did[46]—They were most eager to trade—and kept Major S. at it till ten o clock.

11th. Our camp still full of the Indians they encamped with us last night, and accompanied us this morning to their village—which we found to be some six miles from our camping place These are an agricultural people their fields are well fenced, and the land well irrigated—they are well mounted on fine horses and mules, their houses mud hovels, thatched They raise cotton, corn & beans in great abundance, and the best mellons I have yet seen in this country. Many of them speak spanish, and alltogether, I think they live better and have more than the people of New Mexico—they are extremely honest—last night, we left every thing we had laying about as usual, nothing was missing, and to day while trading with them, theyhad free access to the tent—and not an article was missing, although they might have been stolen with the greatest ease. They are armed with the bow, bludgeon & shield, and are considered formidable by the neighbouring tribes. their bow is much larger than I have observed among any other Indian tribe—they cultivate cotton to a considerable extent—they seem to pull the plant up, about the time the pod opens, dry it & pick the wool at their leisure. They manufacture their own blankets from cotton, shirts &c. Their cloth though coarse is of beautiful texture the threads being perfectly even, and in fact it looks as well as the article commonly used for summer clothing called I believe everlasting We purchased from them for a few pounds of beads, over an hundred pounds of corn meal & flour. They place great value on the beads and white domestic is also a cash article. The men I think are below the ordinary hight, though they are muscular—and appear healthy. They wear their hair very long, many of them I think had it over two feet, they could sit upon it easily. Their women are ugly and coarse looking, have merely a petticoat girted around the loins—all the upper part of the person being perfectly naked.[47] We have succeeded in getting one beef.

12th. Nov. The trading commenced this morning most briskly again—for flour & meal and the supply was fully equal to the demand—besides the traders in meal and flour there were many others who went off sadly disappointed that they could not sell their wares—these consisted as yesterday of beans, sweet corn, shelled corn, water mellons, red pepper, & the molasses spoken of before. About ½ past 8 we left camp and marched some sixteen miles, at least ten of the number through well cultivated fields, that had been planted in cotton, Wheat Corn and mellons. They have the greatest abundance of food, and take care of it well, as we saw many of their storehouses full of pumpkins, mellons, corn &c.—their village is scattered at intervals on the river for some twenty five miles—there are two distinct bands—the Pimas, & Mericopas—each having their seperate chief—and seperate village.[48] We left some ten broken down mules with them to be turned over to Capt Cook—also one or two bales of goods—this I think will test their honesty— if they turn the goods over to Cook they certainly deserve half for their honor[49]—from the number I saw to day, and the extent of the village below where we left it—I should suppose there were fully two thousand persons. We are now trading for cattle—they value them at $10 a head. I saw them spinning cotton. This is done entirely by hand—the cotton has a very fine and silky appearance. The trade still continues These people seem to enjoy fine health. We have seen no place of burial, though we have travelled half through their village nor have I seen a man, woman or child who presented the appearance of ill health. One man seemed to have some cutaneous affection that did not affect his general health—and one or two had but one eye. There were no cases of deformity, or idiocy so commonly met with about our Indian Villages. They all seemed sprightly good tempered fellows—and there were as many or more children than a person would meet with in one of our new States among the same number of people—they wear their hair very long the men much longer than the women. We have had no reason up to this time to alter our opinion as regards their honesty. They have had the free range of the camp, access to any place that pleased them, allowed to handle and examine every thing, and not one article that I have heard of has been missing

13th & 14th Nov. On the 13th we had a repetition of the same scene of trading—Indians wandering about camp in all directions. The chief of the Mericopas paid us a visit, and received presents—all of which he divided out among the attendants, reserving nothing for himself. These are a much finer looking set of Indians than the Pimas, the men are larger and more muscular —on an average much taller—the women are ugly—large and fat They are people of the same habits all agriculturalists—fond of drink—offered us any price—or to trade—any thing they had for liquor. We succeeded in obtaining here two beeves—for a blanket and some 14 yds of white domestic—and one yard of red cloth. At 12 o clock we left camp—marched through a perfectly barren country. We [at] 8 oclock at night, encamped no water or grass for our animals.

14. We had revellie sounded so soon as the moon rose this morning and in half an hour was under way. The mules were nearly mad for water and something to eat—but we were obliged to drive them out though this was

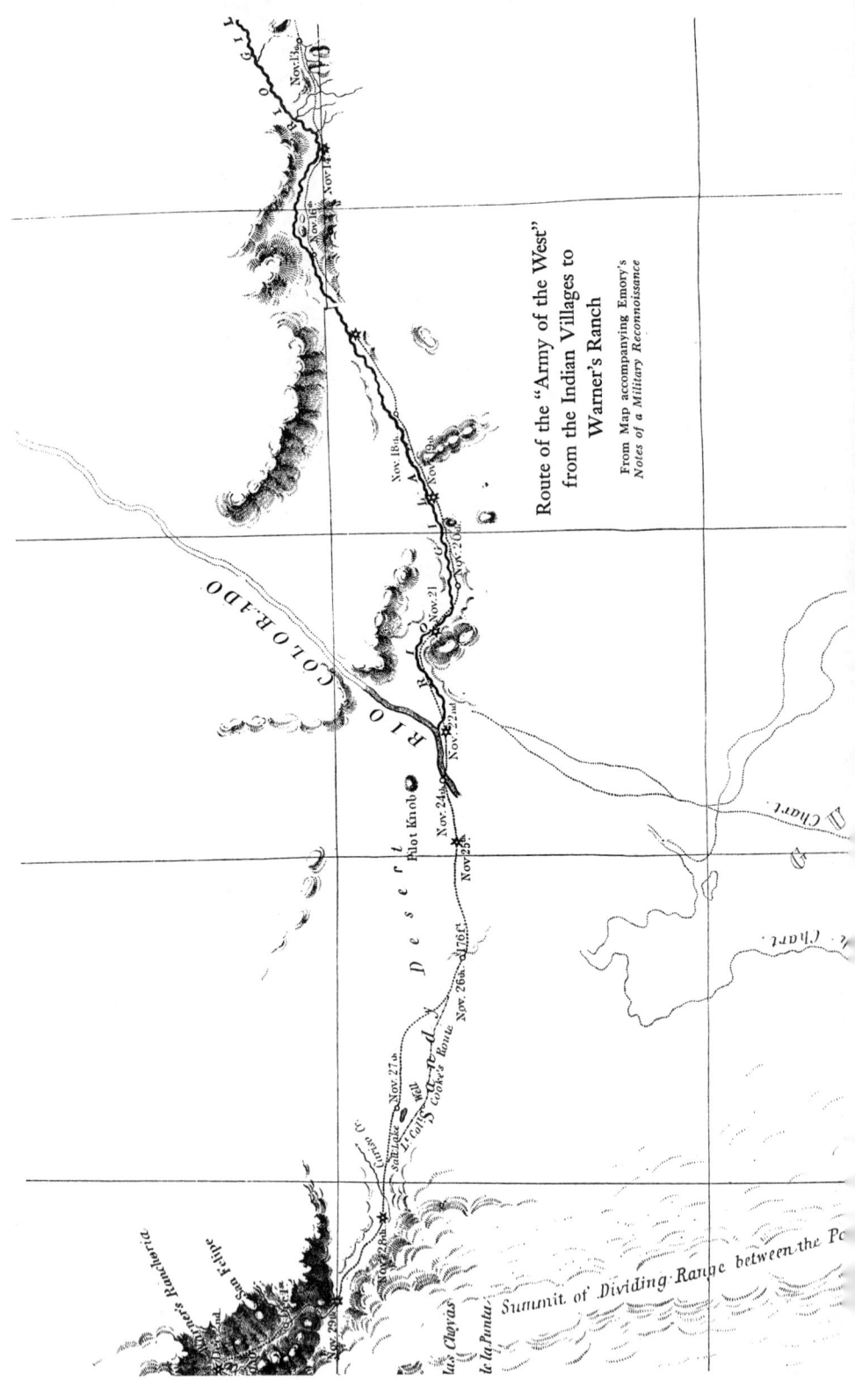

attended with great difficulty, for soon as their ropes were untied every one was for taking the back track, and if your eyes were off them for a minute, you found the mule gone—and probably making the best of his way to yesterdays camp. About day break we passed through a gorge of mountains —from this place to the river—it is a gentle descent we went ahead finely— and at 11½ A.M. struck the river The country is destitute of every thing save the musquite—and other kindred bushes. The cactus is from 1 inch to 40 feet—covered with thorns. After striking the river we marched down some 4 or 5 miles—and found a camp of dry grass and weeds. The river here is considerably larger than where we last saw it, as the Salt River comes in just below the Pimas—it is also a little brackish. We have marched since 12 yesterday I think about 45 miles.

15th. This being sunday and the mules still showing great fatigue from their hard march and starvation, the Genl. concluded to remain quiet for the day. The loss in mule flesh in crossing the jornado [*jornada*], 6 and a great many that could just be driven in camp.

16th.—We left camp this morning at 7½ A.M. Every thing in the way of mule flesh looking bright considering the state they were in. Marched down the River—or in its course. The bottom extends out on each side on the north to some mountains say ten miles off on the south to a greater distance—The mountains are not so high as those we have passed through—but are if any thing more rough—and jagged and forbiding in their appearance—they look black from the volcanic stone on them—this is Basalt—and we passed over a bed of it to day more than three miles—it looked like it had hardly time to get cold—since the fire left it—the country nothing but dust, sand musquite and cactus—not a bird seen except some ravens—and scarsely a spear of grass to ten feet square from this time to the mouth of the Gila. Carson says we must depend on seeds and willows immediately on the River banks for food for our mules—in spots—though they are few and far between a little patch of grass may be found, ten feet wide. This is immediately on the banks of the River and the Animal most frequently will have to stand in the water to pick the grass. We have marched 18 or 20 miles to day.

17th & 18th—One days march on the River is so much like unto another that one description will do for all that is to say—sand, dust, & a black stone, so blistered from the effects of heat that they look like they had hardly got cool—no grass, nothing but weeds & cactus. The River here is some 60 or 80 yards wide—on an average 3 feet deep and rapid. We have seen more water fowel in the last two days, than we have yet met with on the River—ducks, brant geese & swan. The cotton wood shows the effect of frost very little— not more than the same tree did when we left the Rio Grande a month since —On the night of the 17th we had considerable frost.—The mountains still continue on our right and left, and if any thing more jagged and forbiding in appearance than any we have yet passed. Some of them have the most fantastic forms. Our march for the last two days has been some 35 or 37 miles—I neglected to note a stone we passed on the 16th or rather a hill of stone—all carved up with Indian hieroglyphics—the sun moon & stars—horned frogs—Attempts at the human form divine, were the most frequent forms—they seemed to be of recent date—whether cut in sport or to commemorate some great event we could not tell—We also camped opposite to a stone last night with the names of Carsons party ca[r]ved on it as they passed from California to New Mexico last summer.[50]

19. 20. 21st 22 & part of 23 Nov. On the 19th I had to return to see a sick man left back by the rear guard, & this together with our days march cost me a ride of forty odd miles—20 of which I rode by night. Carson saw several mountain sheep and killed one. I found the command encamped on a pond—some miles from the river. On the 21st we started again made another long days march and encamped on a little slough with some poor salt grass. We found the greatest difficulty in obtaining water here as we were some two miles from the river and the thickest brush between that a man ever dreamed of, considering the thorns it was as bad as a Florida hammock. The 22d—We found this morning to our surprise and great joy that we were nearer by some days marches to the mouth of the Gila than we supposed. We started and found a tolerable patch of grass some nine miles from our last camp. here we passed the rest of the day—suffered again for water, as it was a half days journey to the river through the chapparal—I suppose the Army of occupation would call it and if they had to pass through much of it, I think they were more to be pitied than from any danger of the enemy here. We killed a deer and two geese.

22d. Started again early. Made a long days march—passed through some very rugged sand hills, imagined all day we could discover the course of the Colorado—in the evening as we approached the river, discovered the trail of a large body of horse—supposed this to be a Mexican force sent out from Sonora to intercept us, as we rode into camp—the Genl sent Carson ahead to find the whereabouts of the enemy, and said "find them Carson and we will fight them to night." All preparations were made to guard against a night attack the Howitzers were late in getting in—every man was directed to lay by his arms loaded, and prepared for instant action. thirty men were put on guard and distributed as pickets around the camp—spies sent out. Capt Johnston and Carson went out, and returned in an hour or so, but could discover nothing. They captured some horses, and a mare and colt. This latter circumstance lead us to believe that it was traders we had to deal with, besides Carson saw the tracks of women on the sand. We thought the Mexicans would hardly bring the fair creatures out to witness a blow up with us. Lt Emory went out with a party of twenty men—and brought in 3 or 4 Mexicans—about 12½ A.M. Then we learned that they were a party of traders on their way, or rather refugees from California to Sonora,[51] that they had some five hundred horses and mules—that they had been six days crossing from the settlements in California to the Colorado—that there was but one place on the route where water could be found—that they had been lost and suffered much—that a revolution had taken place, and that a Mexican by the name Flores was at the Pueblo governor,[52] in the name of the Mexican government—that he had some eight hundred men. they did not know where Frémont was—that there was another party in the country in favour of the Americans. They numbered some two hundred and were on the road fortifyed—between St Diago [San Diego] and the puebla—that they expected assistance from the American squadron. That the Mexicans had killed several Americans—and had Robedoux prisoner.[53] We were advised not to lose time as our presence would be of great benefit to our countrymen, and I rather think not many minutes will be lost. They told us they thought the Mexicans had two pieces of artillery—and that our people had either three or five. We have sent down to examine the drove of horses so as to pick out the best for our service. They look badly, and many of them are unbroken, never having had either bridle or saddle on them. Our men are nearly naked and barefooted Their feet are sore and leg weary—They have been marching many of them for the last four or five hundred miles. Our mules are all so that they can scarcely get along with a pack or a man on their backs, only the sick have been allowed to ride lately. This is rather a bad picture for men who have a hard campaign before them, but then our powder is dry, and guns in good order and if they dont pile an unreasonable number up before us—we will be able to give them a good sound thrashing, though Moor said two weeks since that we all deserved a good trouncing for coming into such a God forsaken country, however a couple of weeks or such a matter will show every thing. We are encamped just above the mouth of the Gila about one mile and a half. The Mexicans forded the Colerado so that saves us some trouble.

Part of 23ᵈ and 24ᵗʰ Nov. In the Evening Lts Emory and Warner were out making observations when they came across a Mexican in the bottom— something attracted their attention to the fellow, they searched him and found that he had a mail several letters addressed to Genˡ. Castro the former Mexican commander in California, were found.[54] All the reports we had heard from the horse drovers were confirmed. The Mexicans were bragging like the devil of having whipped some 450 sailors with 80 Mexican Dragoons they said they took a piece of artillery from the Navy called the Teazer, that the Web footed Yankies ran like the Devil[55]—that the young men of the country are perfectly furious, that they are fiends incarnate—so I suppose we may expect a small chunk of hell when we get over there. We obtained from the drovers some 20 animals wild and broken—On the 24ᵗʰ I went to the camp of the drovers and witnessed one of the finest scenes I ever beheld. The Mexicans were driving about in all directions lassoing the wild horses—

and our Dragoons so soon as they were caught mounted them. Some got thrown some kicked but they hung on to their animals—and finally succeeded in riding all except one fine bay mare. She was perfectly untamable—she kicked—plunged—struck—laid down—sulked & plaid the devil so completely in general—that we were obliged, to let her go. 12 dolls ahead was the price of horses and mules—or one broken down animal and two dollars to boot The drovers seemed surprised when they received pay for their animals, as they full well knew had we been a party of their own troops in a similar situation that devil a cent would they have got. They were well contented with their trade. They had a child born in their camp on the night of the 23^d. We all contributed tea sugar & coffee to the mother. They had nothing to eat but penolas[56] & corn mush—no shelter. We left camp at 2 P M. & encamped on the Colorado about dark—Marched ten miles—We cross the river & take the desert in the morning—if it be a worse one than that we leave it will be desolate indeed.

From the Colorado River to Warner's Ranch

25. 26. 27. & 28th Nov. We forded the Colorado on the morning of the 25th, the River nearly swiming the mules in places. We however crossed with little difficulty—our course laid through the bottom—in the evening we struck on the edge of the sand hills We passed in the bottom an old Sakiea [*acequia*] and encamped at an old well which we dug out, and obtained sufficient very bad water for drinking and cooking. Marched some 14 or 15 miles. We had been warned by Carson that we would have nothing for our animals to live on going across the desert Every man in consequence gathered all the grass he could on the river and packed on his mule. We also found a bean on the musquite that the mules seemed very fond of—we devoted the whole evening to gather it. The bean is sweet and very pleasant to the taste. We also found another product of the musquite that the animals are fond of—this is a small spiral pod—something in form like a cork screw—several of them being on the same stalk. it contains a great quantity of saccharine matter—and the Pimas grind it up with their pinola—to use instead of sugar—Our animals got no water to night. On the 26th made an early start and marched to a place knowen as the Alamo—or cotton wood tree—here we were engaged in cleaning out an old well and diging a new one. Water was obtained late at night—the very worst it was ever my misfortune to drink. We were engaged all night in watering the animals—two buckets full each was all that was allowed—and an officer stood by to see division fairly made. Some of our mules being wild and unused to such attention refused to have anything to do with the water. When such a subject was found, the bucket had to be buried in the sand or covered with grass. My riding mule was the most refractory of all. I however succeeded at last in

making him drink, by covering the water with the musquite bean. Many of the new purchased horses gave out to day—they failed even quicker than our weary and broken down animals—

27. We left camp early at 6½ A M marched till 9 P M—distance 32 miles —road heavy. The sand is much worse to go through than snow. We pushed to get to a lake—called the Lagoona by the Mexicans. When we arrived here we found it so salt that it was utterly impossible for man or beast to touch it—here the men suffered from want of water—we had nothing for our animals to pick except a little musquite brush. About 11 A M in the day, we had allowed our animals to pick a little dried up grass that we found on the plain—We found a little the day before. This probably was the only thing that enabled us to get through—& the pack forage together.

28—We left camp at 4 A M Marched hard and encamped on runing water —the Carisa or Clousa [Carrizo] Creek (I do not know how to spell it) it means the Cane creek in plain English—distance some 22 miles, here we found a little cane for our animals to brouse on and some water, the first they have had for thirty six hours. We are now over the desert. I have seen the Elephant and I hope I shall never be compelled to cross it again—The water we obtained the second night imparted such an infernal smell to my canteen that I fear I shall never be able to purify it again. The head spring of the creek near which we are encamped is warm—above blood heat it is in some hundred yards of camp—No living animal seems to make his abode on this bleak and desolate waste I do not recollect of seeing a single living thing except a crow, near our camp on the 26th two or three ants, and some half dozen large tarantulas near the creek as We came in on the evening of the 28th At the Lagoona we heard several wolves howling—but nothing that is useful to man could possibly exist in such a place. The mountains were on our left the whole way—some twenty miles distant, in front of us, and as we approached, another range seemed to commence on our right. This latter I believe is the commencement of the Sierra Navada, spoken of by Fremont. The range on our left is the coast range. On the morning of the 27 we had a fog, on the 28th a very dense one, so moist that our hair and the manes of the mules became quite wet. This I think is fog from the Californian gulph —as the wind was from the South west—and we could see it driven up before it—After getting in camp we all felt quite comfortable, and as we had had nothing like cooking for several days every man turned out the best he had —a canister of potted meat and a cup of tea—with a brandy toddy were the greatest luxuries that could be found—and we went at them with a will. We supped out. I took one supper at home—drank penola with Carson[57]—& wound up in the evening by eating again with Captain Moore—it seemed to me that there was no such thing as quenching my thirst I drank tea and water until I could stand no more, and yet I was thirsty and every one complained of the same. Many of the Messes had nothing but a pure vegetable diet—that is to say, bread—made of salt & flour & water or a little boiled corn, or beans, with not even meat enough to grease it—among the number in this situation was the general. The Engineer camp were even worse off it was reported that they had nothing at all for the men employed in the department, a Mexican who they had to herd their mules had stolen from them, and sold the provisions to another Mexican a trader who was allowed to travel with the troops. The fellow was caught in the fact—yet nothing was done with him except to put him under guard—this only goes to confirm me in my opinion formed in New Mexico—that these low Mexicans are the greatest scoundrels that are to be found any place—the question was seriously mooted whether a mule should be killed or not It was not done—but I suppose will be at the next camp—as we are fully seventy miles from any settlements.

29th.—The command left this morning about 9 A.M. Major Swords. and myself live together—Upon search being made it was found two of our mules are missing—so we will have to wait until they are found, or till those who have gone out to search for the lost ones return. it is now past 1 oclock, so I think there is little hopes of our catching the command to-night—and if they dont lay by tomorrow the lord knows when we shall see them—not before they get to settlements I suppose. About half past 3 P M. our Mexicans returned from the hunt after the lost mules, without finding them, from all he could see he believed that they had been stolen by Indians, this was rendered possible as he found one of the company mules dead, and it had been butchered, the fleece being taken out as if to eat.[58] We therefore put off for our next camp with the animals we had, first one gave out, then another until we were obliged to abandon four—to pack everything in the party—both public & private animals—About 11½ oclock, we discovered a camp but as we had understood the next camp was to be at least 20 miles from our last we feared that the fire we saw, was either straglers or Indians. We therefore prepared our arms and rode forward, but to our great joy, we discovered it to be our own people—encamped at a place called the Vayeaw Chitoes—little prairies—(the two Spanish words above I think is near the sound but I cant vouch for the orthography.)[59]

30th. Our mules all standing in need of rest—and something to eat. We have remained in camp—there are several old cornfields about, cultivated by the Indians—and the advanced guard found a bale of grass from which the Indians make rope laying by the side of the stream—some of it twisted into strings on sticks—this no doubt had just been left by the owners, who fled when they discovered us—the grass is of a fine beautiful fibre—white—and I would think—as good ropes might be made from it, as the Manilla rope. They seem also to use the grass for sewing—as we found with the bale of grass—several of their needles made of hard sticks painted—& with an eye drilled through them—the grass at this place is salt, the ground being incrusted with salt, it looks very much as if a slight fall of snow had just covered the ground—the salt is even incrusted on the grass—this purges the animals and also acts as a diuretic—the fact is it seems to weaken them more, than it does good. The water is bitter and salt—and this has been the character of every drop of water that I have tasted since leaving the Gila—this land we passed over yesterday perfectly unproductive—in one place the palmetto is found—Where we are encamped is perfectly destitute of timber. The wind has been from the N.W. all the day, and rain seems to be falling in the mountains—We have had a slight mist—it is extremely cold and disagreeable—We were reduced to day to kill a horse, for provisions. Some of the men had been for several days past on one fourth of one ration per Diem.

1st Dec. This is the first day of winter, and it feels like it. The wind is from N. & W. there is a slight fall of snow on the mountains. We feel the cold sensibly, and overcoats are in demand. We met an Indian to day, he could give us little or no information as to what was going on. he told us that there were many Americans at St Diego. The country passed through to day is perfectly barren—sand and gravel in the vallies—& mica sand stone & I believe granite in the mountains. We passed through a cañon to day, so narrow that an ordinary sized wagon could not have passed. About sun down we came to an Indian village—deserted.[60] There were the remains of corn fields and pea patches. The country is in a great measure destitute of timber & we were obliged to destroy their lodges for fire wood.

2d Dec. Still cold and bleak. Passed down the vally we were encamped in last night—or rather passed up the vally—as I believe the water ran to the East. Passed over a hill, in a kind of vally—here the live oak commenced, As we passed on we found them of magnificent dimensions. We saw to our left at a distance a most beautiful vally, with timber thrown about it in clumps, in the most picturesque manner. Some of this was live oak—the other I could not tell what species of timber it was. We saw several shrubs in bloom, & yesterday I forgot to mention I saw the bloom of what I was told was the century plant. This is the muscal from which the Indians make a very pleasant preserve. About 4 P M. we arrived at Warners,[61] the extreme frontier settlement of California, this man is living very comfortably—he seems to have plenty of stock, cattle, Horses & Sheep and certainly has a fine range for them. Warner is at present at St Diego I believe a prisoner, although he is an American from Connecticut. Yet I believe he is suspected of favouring the Mexicans rather more than his own countrymen. We found an American occupying Warner's premises by name Marshall—he was from New Hampshire—he was the only white man about when we rode up.[62] There was one fellow however upon seeing us approach, an Irishman I should judge from his brogue put off—but he was soon brought back by some Indians, who were about the Ranch. A Mexican was also brought in with the Irishman—from these we learned that the Mexicans were in arms and had possession of the Puebla de los Angelos—that the Americans were in force at St Diego, some five or six ships of war being there that Fremont was advancing on the Puebla with some four hundred Mexicans [*sic*] and about one hundred Indians—that the Mexicans were well armed—and exhibited vastly more courage than they did at the commencement of difficulties in the country—We also learned that there were several detached parties of the enemy between us and St Diego. They also expected the arrival of a Mexican force escorting prisoners out of the country to Mexico. This force they thought probable would arrive in our neighbourhood to night. They also told us of a parcel of mules belonging to Flores, the leader of the Mexicans in a vally some fifteen miles from where we now are, a command is now being organized and put in motion to capture the mules if possible.[63] We have obtained a supply of beef & mutton, so let what will happen we wont starve, the Irishman spoken of above is to act as guide. I forgot to mention that we met an old fellow with all of his family & horses fleeing from the country to Sonora, from what we can learn there are a great many making preperations for the same trip. There seems to be perfect anarchy in the Enemy's camp. My Hospital mule ran off this evening & broke my panniers all to the devil

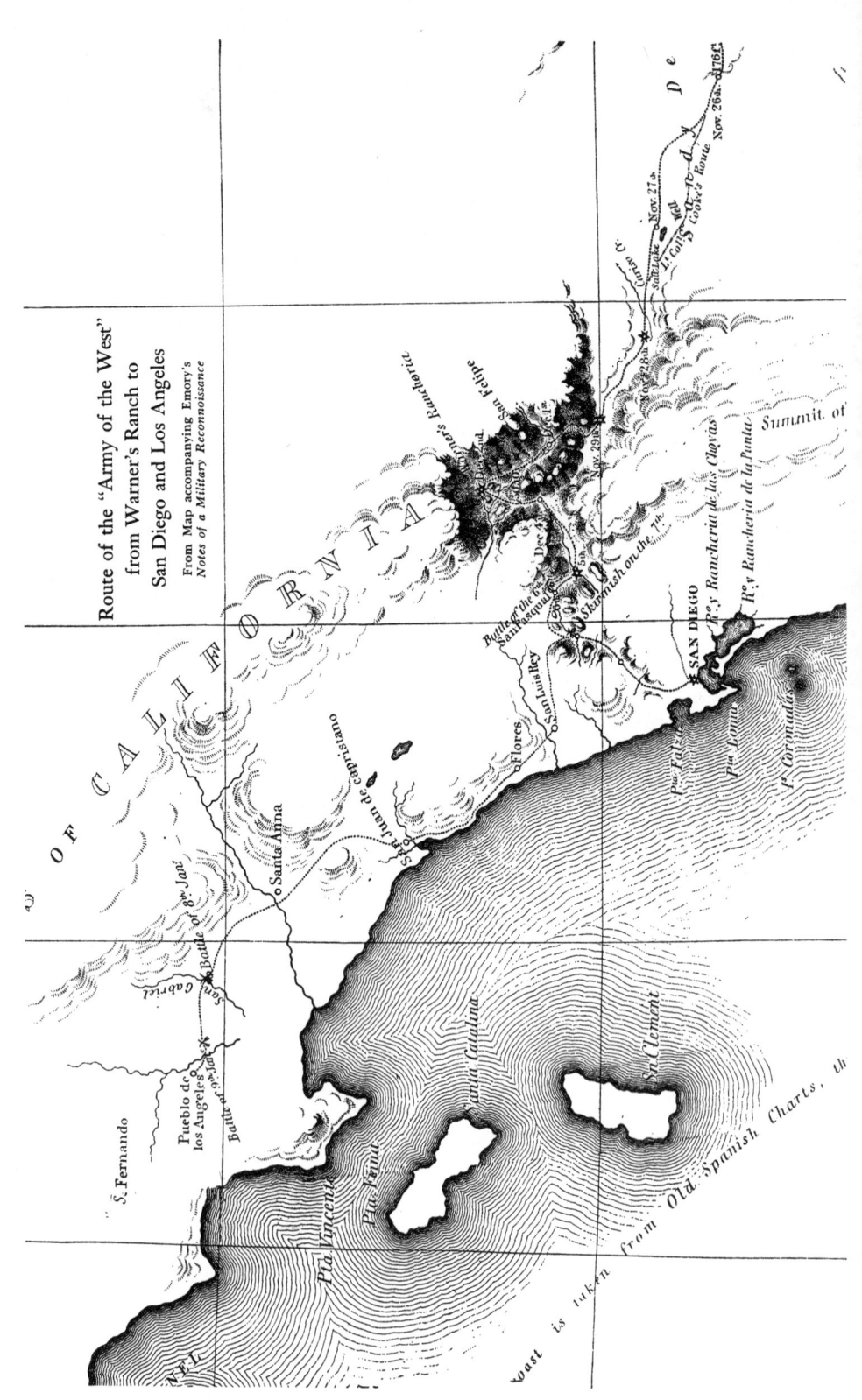

❧ Part II ❧

California: Conquest, Casualties and Cures

Warner's Ranch · Stokes' Ranch · Battle of San Pascual · San Diego · Treatment of Wounded · From San Diego to Santa Ana River · Battles of San Gabriel and La Mesa · Los Angeles. Treatment of Wounded · Kearny, Stockton, and Frémont · To San Diego Again · Hospital and Other Affairs at San Diego · Los Angeles under Colonel Stevenson · Treatment of the Sick

Warner's Ranch and Stokes' Ranch

3^d Dec. 9 o clock. This place of Warners is called the Aqua Calliente, there is a boiling spring heads just above Warner's house—it is a bold stream, there is a strong smell of sulphureted hydrogen, and where we are encamped there is a fine spring of cool, sweet water—this furnishes sufficient for stock & I suppose for irrigating the soil—The Ranch is some three miles distant from Warners house: about the house there is some ten or fifteen acres under cultivation, about one acre and a half which is a vineyard. We obtained some of the grapes dried—they were nearly as sweet as raisins & of fine flavour, & size—it is said wine in considerable quantities is made in this country. Warner has a small band of Indians about him, he uses these people for herdsmen and I suppose as servants generally; they are fine large, healthy looking fellows—and speak well for the salubrity of the climate. We also obtained some water mellons from the Indians—they are of good size— as to the flavour I cant speak, as I have not eaten of them yet. Last night we had a visit from an Englishman, by name Stokes,[64] who owns a Ranch some fifteen miles distant, he has remained neutral during the difficulties taking side with neither party. I believe he was a sailor—took a fancy for farming, at which he seems to have succeeded very well as he is represented as owning several Ranches, and some thousand head of cattle, he did not give much more information so far as I could learn than we had already obtained—he however consented to carry a letter to Com^d Stockton at St Diego. This morning the Genl is sending back a party of our Mexicans to Capt Cook to pilot him across the Desert.[65] Lt Davidson has not yet returned with his party.

3^d & 4th Dec. Lt Davidson returned about 1 P M. with some hundred young mules and horses, some of them had been broken and were fine animals, but the majority were perfectly worthless to us. We had them driven along however, as they can be made useful and they belonged to Flores, the rebel governor, Davidson also captured several guns, & lances, one very fine rifle. Upon the whole it was a very successful foray. The warm spring spoken of above was found to be of the temperature of 137° F—I saw some of the wheat produced on this Ranch—it was large grained, white and the bald headed, or beardless wheat We were told the produce was very great. The man who had charge of the farm said he would sow 35 bushels, and expected to reap 1000—rather a large product I should suppose—Their mode of thrashing is rather primitive. We wanted some flouer. The man in charge therefore put all hands to work thrashing out. They rub the heads of wheat between the palms of their hands and winow it by letting it fall and blowing the chaff away with their breath and the wind—they grind between two stones, by hand. The quality of the ground is quite good—black but rather sandy. We marched about half past 8 A.M. continued down the vally, which we found to be beautiful—some of the most lovely scenes presented themselves that I have ever looked at—the live oak scattered about in the most beautiful clumps—stones of large size—and luxuriant grass— the day was most disagreeable, cloudy, and a drizzling beating rain all day—with a cold wind—in the evening we encamped at Stokes ranch—called St Isabelle. I believe this was an old mission or rather the Ranch of a mission called St Isabelle. We found the buildings here much better than at Warners—everything presenting a much neater appearance, the work no doubt of the priests—as usual the Indian village was near the house—these Rancheroes seem to live in fuedal style—each man has his band of Indian dependents—who are completely subject to his authority. Warners Major Domo told us he could raise 300 fighting men in a few hours. These Indians are peacible in their nature— their chief made a speech to the Genl last evening—in which he declared his wish not to engage in the war in any manner, but that he was perfectly willing to go to work. Of course this was what the Genl advised them to do, to keep at peace and work hard—and they would be well treated. They are certainly in a most miserable condition, worse by far than worst treated slaves in the United States. They seem to live on the offal of the ranches principally. Stokes seems to have a large stock, and his Major Domo—Seignor Bill—and old sailor promised to find us carts to transport our baggage to St Diego— this Seignor Bill treated us with the most distinguished hospitality giving a

CALIFORNIA: CONQUEST, CASUALTIES, CURES   45

supper to the officers—turning out his mutton, grapes, and tortillas in great profusion. This was good, but his wine was abominable.[66] Seignor Bill gave the Genl some information of a party of Mexicans at some mission on our road with some 500 animals. I should suppose we would try and capture these gentlemen The only game I have seen yet has been wild pigeons, hares, & Ducks—no great number of the first and last.

Battle of San Pascual

5th-6th, 7th, 8th, 9th, 10th, 11th On the morning of the 5th we marched from Stokes Ranch with Seignor Bill for guide, but bill having drank the night previous rather freely of his own or rather Stokes Liquor found himself very much in the humor for chasing wild horses the next morning, and a Band of mares presenting themselves Bill took after them got thrown and declared he would not go any further with [us]. At this the General demured, and mounted the Seignor with a couple of the guard by his side. Bill took us on the wrong rode once but soon corrected the mistake, in marching a few miles further. We met Capt Gallespies party,[67] from St Diago consisting of 35 men, and one small 4 lb Gallespie encamped his party soon after we met, and we passed on to a ranch [Santa María] some eight miles distant, there we found wood and water, but no grass. We had therefore to march two miles farther on where we encamped, in a grove of live oak but no water except that which was falling from the heavens—and the rain did come down most severely. A party of the enemy being reported in our vicinity—it was first determined that Capt Moore should take sixty men and make a night attack but for some reason the Genl altered his mind, and sent Lieut Hammond with three men to reconnoiter. Hammond found the enemy at some 10 miles distant, but was discovered—and as he ran off with his party the Mexicans gave three cheers—

6th—We were all afoot about 2 A.M. and expected to surprise the party of Mexicans, though we had been in the rain all night our arms were not reloaded, but boots and saddles was the word, and off we put in search of adventure, in two miles from our camp we met Gallespie with his company, which fell in[68]—in our rear— Major Swords was left back with the baggage, and thirty men. Another party some 10 or 15 men were left back with Gallespies four pounder. This reduced our fighting men to about 85 all told— with these and two howitzers we marched forward. The morning was excessively cold, and we felt it more as the most of us were wet to the skin. After passing over a mountain and travelling as near as I can judge some ten or eleven miles we came in sight of the enemys fires. We marched down the mountain so soon as we arrived on the plain the shout and charge was commenced from the advance. After runing our jaded and broken down mules and horses some ¾ or a mile, the Enemy fired on us. The balls whistled about most infernally for a while but the light was not sufficient, for me to distinguish any thing like a line of the Enemy, on my left however from the flashing of the guns I could see that there was a considerable row, and in a few moments the Enemy broke and, we found they had made a stand in front of a Ranchereo. This was called St Pasqual. At this time a fellow came dashing by, and I saw he was a Mexican several shots were fired at him when he fell I think as well as I could judge by the light, day was just breaking—it was Lt Beal[69] of the Navy who fired the shot. At this time another fellow came dashing by presenting with his hat &c a most Mexican look—when bang went a dragoon pistol—but missed another dragoon who happened to be near—drew his sabre and was about cutting the man down when I yelled out to him to stop as the man was one of Gallespies party—by this time we were very much disordered—our men some being mounted on fresh horses, and others on poor and broken down mules could not come. Capt Moor however ordered the charge to be continued and it was in the most hurly burly manner—not more than ten or fifteen men being in line and not over forty all together on they went however—the Enemy continued to retreat for about ½ mile further when they rallied and came at us like devils with their lances—being mounted on swift horses—and most of our fire arms having been discharged or missed fire from the rain of the night previous, our advance was perfectly at their mercy. The men wheeled, and by this time a howitzer being near rallied on the gun, and drove the enemy off—Hammond was the first wounded man I saw, he had been in the advance with Moore—and got a lance wound on the left side between the 8th and 9th ribs—I told him to go a little farther to the rear and I would attend to him. At this time I was sepperated from him—when the Gen¹ saw me and told me he was wounded and wished my services, shortly after the devils got around me, and like to have fixed my flint—but I got off by dropping my gun which I snapped at a fellow and drawing an empty pistol—this answered the purposes of a loaded one—I then met Capt Galespie who told me he was wounded he was bleeding most profusely, the wound being in front directly over the heart. Capt Gibson next called on me and in a few moments I found I had my hands full. Capt Johnston who led the first charge was killed by a gun shot wound in the head. I was told this was the only man of ours who—received any injury from gun shot—Moor was killed far in the advance leading the second charge and Hammond I was told received his wound in attempting to rescue Moor—a man by name of [Frank] Menard, of Capt Emorys party was killed, one of Gallespies men, 2 Sergts—1 Cop¹ and 11 privates of Dragoons and one missing—supposed to be killed—we lost one of our Howitzers in this action, the mules in it ran wild and ran off with the piece. There [were] but three men with it and one was killed and the other two desperately wounded—upon the whole we suffered most terribly in this action 4 officers wounded one Sergt. one Cop¹ and 10 privates, and

Mr Robedeaux our interpreter—in all 35 men killed and wounded and I should think there was not to exceed fifty men who saw the enemy[70]—We took two prisoners. The Enemy I think must have suffered as much as we did. This was an action where decidedly more courage than conduct was showed The first charge was a mistake on the part of Capt Johnston, the 2^d on the part of Capt Moor. After the Genl was wounded and the men were rallied he was anxious for another charge but was persuaded not to risk it. We drove the enemy from the field and encamped. All that day was engaged in dressing the wounded. On the 7th we left again on our march. Small parties of the Enemy hanging about in sight all day. in the evening we passed the Ranch of St Bernard, and killed some chickens for our wounded and drove some cattle off with us. When we had marched some miles from the Ranch the enemy again appeared and made another rush, to occupy a hill, where they could annoy us. They got to the top of the hill about the time we got half way up when the fight commenced and after two or three minutes the rascals ran, leaving three of their spears on the field. We occupied these heights as a camp for that night on the 8th we saw some commotion on the plain—in a short time a flag of truce was sent to us by Picot the commander of the Mexicans,[71] with some sugar & tea—a change of clothing for Capt Gallespie—which had been sent to Gallespie from St Diago, and he had taken them with the prisoners The capture of these three men we now found out caused the commotion on the plain in the morning We exchanged our prisoner for one of the men taken, and learned from him that Commodore Stockton refused to send us a reinforcement.[72] The Genl then determined to march out at all hazzards but in a council of officers, the Navy officers pledged themselves so strongly that Stockton would send relief, and on account of the wounded, the Genl consented to remain— in the evening Lt Beal of the Navy with Carson started again as an express to Stockton.[73] We burnt all of our baggage so as to have as little encumbrance as possible, dismounted the men and determined to perform the rest of the march on foot. We left our camp on the battle field of the 6th with 6 ambulances with wounded. The enemy are constantly hanging around us but are very careful not to come within gun shot— 9th We remained in camp, nothing going on the Enemy perading about on the mountains and the other side of the vally—We are reduced to mule meat— it does not go so coarse—after all some of my poor fellows have as many as 8 wounds on a side 3 are run through the arm—generally—they seem to aim with their lances so as to strike a man near the kidneys.

10th Sergt [John] Cox died this morning his wound on the left side, just above the crista of the Illeum [ilium]—he had singultus [hiccups] for several hours before death and vomited bloody water. We remain in camp to day waiting in case reinforcements be sent, if they are not sent we march in the morning at all hazzards. On the evening of the 10th we were grazing our animals at the foot of the hill near our camp—when we saw the Mexicans driving a band of wild horses towards us. Capt Gilispie who has been in this country during the war, immediately told us what they were up to. Their plan was to run them full speed among our animals, and in that way to take off all we had— in half an hour we saw them coming full speed—the wild devils with sheep skins & other things of that sort tied to their tails, it certainly presented one of the most beautiful sights we had ever beheld—but as we were warned of their intentions, we were prepared. We waited a few moments so as to entice some of the rascals in gun shot if possible, and then quietly drove our animals out of the way throwing out a strong body of men to meet the rascals if they should come within reach of our guns.—by a shout the drove of wild horses were turned One mule however with a sheep skin tied to his tail was so imprudent as to come within gun shot, forty balls I was told struck him, yet he did not fall, and was finally driven on the hill where we were encamped and butchered. This was a god send to us as the mule was fat, and that which we had been eating was not equal by any means to stall fed beef. The Genl ordered all things to be in readiness for marching in the morning. We all went to bed firmly convinced that we should be obliged to fight our way to St. Diago. About 2 A. M. of the 11th our sentinels heard a body of armed men approaching they were hailed, and to our great joy found to be friends sent to our relief from St Diego. They mustered two hundred strong, 80 marines & 120 sailors.[74] We of course were delighted to meet our friends. We immediately vacated our beds and surrendered them up to our tired comrades they turned in and took a comfortable snooze, waked up and found some mule soup prepared for their breakfast. They turned out the contents of their haversacks which consisted of jerked beef & bread & we all made a first rate breakfast—The Jack tars seemed highly delighted playing soldier, they turned out their tobacco & provisions most liberally to our men, and did not seem to be discontented with any thing but the enemy, and with him they were decidedly in the humor for growling with because, he did not have the decency to give them a fight before reaching our camp. Early on the morning of the 11th we left camp and marched to the Ranch called *poneascitoes* [Peñasquitas]—little stones—the country was quite barren, that is to say, the soil would not have been called rich—yet it produced a wild oat in great profusion. The hill sides were well set, so well that they looked as green as a wheat field. The oat was just sprouting, and was some two or three inches above the surface. I examined the grain and it was nearly as large as our own oats, the straw very similar. We collected to day some hundred head of cattle in fine condition, and at the Ranch, picked up about one hundred sheep—We also found plenty of chickens, pigs & a barrel of wine. As this ranch belonged to a man who was notorious as an enemy, we made free quarters, and took everything we wished to eat, and the barrel of wine for our sick & wounded.[75] We had a plentiful supper, &

laid down an took a good nights rest. Our two poor fellows who were in the litters suffered terribly from the roughness of the road.

San Diego—Treatment of Wounded

12th—We all arose freshened with the idea of reaching St Diego to day, and thus finishing this long weary march. We left and marched in to St Diego about 4 PM, where we received the warmest welcome and kindest attention from our naval friends. I found every thing so far as it was in the power of the surgeons post prepared for my wounded men, and every attention that a warm and generous heart extended to the poor fellows. The Congress & Portsmouth were laying at anchor in the bay, & the town of St Diego garrisoned by the crew & marines from these two ships.[76]

13th—The hospitality of our naval friends has enabled us to get along very comfortably. We have no vegetables however and but little bread. A party has gone south to capture horses, so as to enable the force now at this town to move out and take the field. They have no means of transporting provisions or even hauling their artillery—no cavallry—and our broken down stock has added nothing to our forces. As soon as animals can be obtained it is understood that we take the field. My wounded are all doing well with the exception of [David] Streeter & [Joseph] Kennedy. The first has 8 wounds on one side one in the neck, five in the chest and one on each hip. The second is pierced through the arm, and has some five stabs with the lance on the left side of the head. I fear the skull is fractured, and inflammation of the brain developed from the symptoms. We had an alarm last night. scouts of the enemy seem to be in our vicinity all the time— in the evening two Mexicans came in, and reported that there was a party of some forty, who were anxious to deliver themselves up, that Picot & his party who were opposed to us in the fight had gone to the puebla de los Angelos—The ship Stoneington has taken a party to the South in lower California to drive up mules and cattle.

14th—Another alarm last night. 3 Mexicans seen by our outpost. fired at them, but did not hit. My wounded are all yet alive—but two Streeter & Kennedy, continue in the most precarious condition. Mortification has taken place near the wound on the left hip, & looks as if it were about to be developed on the right side of the spine—about the 6 rib—near one of the stabs in the chest suppuration is most profuse and the man is delerious. he suffered greatly until about 12 last night, since that time he has been at ease. Kennedy, is perfectly sensible when spoken to nothing like stupor, or delirium when spoken to—but if left alone he sleeps never speaks or complains, and mutters incoherently. He has had his head shaved, cold constantly applied to the scalp, low diet, & cool drinks & cup to the temples & nucha. This morning a blister was applied to the back of the neck. I had bled him twice, previous to our arrival at St Diego, purged him freely. in all my cases of wounded, my treatment has been to deplete as far as I thought it safe under the circumstances all bled profusely after they were wounded. The two Mexicans who came in yesterday reported, that St Barbara was taken by the Americans, and that the only place left the Mexicans in the country was the puebla.⁷⁷—This report was not believed—as the only party who could have taken this place would be Fremont, and it is thought here that it will be two weeks yet before he reaches that town. I forgot to mention that some of our men, Capt Gelispie I think was told by a Mexican who brought the flag of truce the day after we encamped at St Bernardo, that Flores and all the principal leaders of the Californians were held by their party as prisoners, the people having no faith in their leaders. The two Mexicans who came in yesterday reported that Flores was marching with a force to attack this point —this I look upon as absurd.

20th Dec—Since I last wrote anything I have been constantly engaged with my wounded, and other duties. One poor fellow, Kennedy died last night. Upon an examination of the brain, there was found to be four punctured wounds penetrating through the bone, into the brain—driving the spicula of bone in front and wounding the meninges & brain— he has been comatose— for the last week—passing for the last few days his faeces & urine involuntarily—he did not seem to be sensible of any thing going on, and suffered but very little. We made free incissions, and exposed two of the largest wounds in the skull—extracted many spicula of bone. The other wounds had healed by the first intention, and it was not thought advisable to disturb them. The Trephine was proposed by myself to evacuate any purulent matter that might have formed on the brain and to extract spicula, but was objected to by the other gentlemen, on the grounds that all the indications were answered by exposing the wound, and extracting the spicula. There was no depression of the external table of the skull—and no spicula, could be discovered either with the finger or probe. Some days previous to death there was a discharge of purulent matter from the wounds of the skull which was promoted by poultices & warm fermentations. When we examined his brain today—we found nearly the whole left side softened—purulent matter formed almost down to the ventricles—and the meninges reddened and infected. Streeter is now improving slowly though he has suffered terribly. The abscess in the back was evacuated by a counter opening near the spine. The wound on the right hip near the sacrum mortified for a space two inches and a half in diameter, with excoriations runing down in the raphe near the anus, the slough begins to come away—and the abscess in the back to discharge much less—though even now he is bathed in the purulent discharge— he has colliquetive [colliquative] perspirations—but his appetite is good, the granulations under the mortified parts healthy—the other wounds in his body healing—and upon the whole I think he is improving—and if the sacrum does not become carious I have strong hopes of his recovery— he has had 10 grs. sul Quinine [sulfate of Quinine] 3 times per Diem. Brandy toddy, or sherry wine ad lib—nourishing diet, Beef steak &c and his bowels kept open with an enema his wound on the sacrum, has been dressed with lint soaked in a weak solution of the Chlorid Soda—with light dressings of Emplast adhesive & cerat simp[78]—The other wounds dressed merely with Emplast adhesive & cerat simp—

All of my other cases are doing well—light dressings & cleanliness being all that was required, the majority of the wounds, have suppurated, but are healing kindly by granulation—I think the hard marching we were obliged to make after leaving the St Bernard injured the great majority of them, and I made another mistake in taking out my sutures too soon. I shall in case of having similar cases to treat let the sutures remain, as they have done no injury in any case where I have left them. The Gen[ls] wound has almost entirely cicatrized—the punctured wounds through the arm have become better under the use of pressure judiciously applied—There is one punctured wound through the nates that is not improving so fast as I could desire.

As to the affairs going on generally I have not paid much attention to them. We have had many flags of truce and Mexicans coming in and delivering themselves up some of the very rascals who were in the fight at St Pasqual. They are well received and well treated. I fear from the way things are conducted that we are to have a second Florida business of it—We do not own at this present time more of California than we occupy with our forces, the enemy have the country and we have no communication with our friends in the north. The Sonoranians are runing off all the cattle and horses, and the fact is the country will have nothing in it after the war is over. Our General has no force at his command, and he seems low spirited. The Commodore speaks of marching on the Puebla, the head quarters of the Mexican force. This expedition is to leave the last of next week—it was first understood that we would go on the 22[d] but I suppose if we are off in five days thereafter we will do well. The party sent to the South for mules and cattle—under Capt Hensly [Samuel J. Hensley] of the California battalion returned this evening after making a very successful foray. I did not learn what number of animals he obtained—but all his men seemed pretty well mounted—

A few nights since some five hundred cattle were brought in, and a large herd of sheep— so far as beef and mutton go—we are in no fear of starving, though the animals may have that terror before their eyes—as there is little or no grass about—I visited the frigate Congress, a few days ago—a most elegant affair I found her to be. Was kindly and hospitably treated by the officers. Our Navy friends in fact wear well upon acquaintance. They are as kind and hospitable as it is possible for any persons to be, turn out any thing they have in the most liberal manner. Major Swords leaves in the morning to obtain supplies[79]—for the troops, we are much in need of Bread

Stuffs, Sugar, Coffee, clothing, and in fact every thing, and our friends of the Navy are not greatly better off than ourselves. 4 oz of Bread is the present allowance of bread per Diem per man—no vegetables—Some of the dragoons begin to report sick with dysentery & fever. This is no doubt brought on in a great measure from eating too much & exercising too little—The water at this place is miserable—being brackish and it is said urinary calculus is common at this point—

A report reached our camp the other day that the Indians had killed eleven Mexicans,—that these fellows had first attacked the Indians taken their cattle, & horses, & killed some five or six Indians—that at night the Indians had surrounded their camp taken the party prisoners—then took them off to some distance and shot them to death with arrows. All tell the same story as regards the number killed but vary as to the manner. Those best versed in California affairs believe these men were killed in the action of the 6th and that the Mexicans complain of the red skins to conceal their own loss. They acknowledge 1 killed and 14 desperately wounded—After the action of St Bernard, I sent word to Picot that I would be most happy to attend to his wounded—he replied that he had none—it is now said that his men are in the greatest state of excitement against him for not accepting my services.[80] We have a report in Camp—said to be brought in by Indians that there are many Americans with covered wagons near Warners Ranch if this should be so, it must be Cook with his Mormons, though I do not believe it possible for him to have arrived there yet.[81]

23d.—The wounded have continued to improve. [Jeremiah] Crabb & [John] Brown, punctured wounds through the arm, had slight suppuration— poultices applied & the pressure of the Bandages taken off, has caused it to improve. Streeter is better. The discharge from the back is less or almost reduced to nothing no fluctuation to be discovered, and the wounds begin to close. The wound on the sacrum presents a healthy appearance, the slough is perfectly defined, and the granulations are full and healthy—The wound of the sacrum is dressed every day by filling the cavity with dry lint and placing over it lint spread with simp cerate and the Dressings secured with adhesive straps—The nourishing diet—& Quinine continued. With all he begins to Emaciate—& the night sweats continue—I forgot to mention that a portion of Kennedys brain—a piece near as large as a dollar—was in a gangrenous state—the temporal bone also blackened. One case of dysenteria and a severe case of fever. This is of a low character—with no well defined remissions, the pulse not hard or full—the stomach irritable and bowels torpid. We have but little bread only four ounces per Diem, no vegetables—but plenty of fresh beef & mutton. I fear dysentery with this diet—the garrison is in a wretched state of police—the quarters like all Mexican houses are ill ventilated, cold and damp. As to military affairs we had what I suppose was intended for a grand review yesterday—20 dragoons on horses that would not have been used for any thing else in the United States, but for wolf bait —some 80 or one hundred marines—some 40 volunteer riflemen, and some 40 Jacktars—all mounted on horses & mules. This presented certainly the most grotesque cavalry parade I have ever witnessed—All hands however got along remarkably well with their horses—except the marines They either had the luck of getting the worst animals, or were the worst horsemen— A horse occasionally would become a little restive and give a slight kick— and off would roll the marine, bayonet—& musket—then another would give a shake—and off would go another marine—then some poor fellow had been made to believe that he could ride—and in an evil hour had put on the long California spur, when by some awkward movement or other he would get the spur in the horses flank—The consequence was, the horse would commence going ahead—the marine would check him but continue to spur, then would commence a short scene of plunging and kicking—the Marine abandoning all holts, except the pummel and the spurs in the flank. The affair terminated as a matter of course by the marine being rolled in the dust—but they exhibited the best of game, for so soon as they touched the ground they commenced grabing in all directions for the creatures and one fellow caught his horses tail. They remounted again—and some got a second fall. After this exhibition I believe it was decided that the marines & Jack tars would be more effective troops afoot, and it was left to their choice which they would take—foot or horse service—and to their honor they preferred the foot. The Marines are a fine body of Infantry as good I should suppose as could be raised in the United States. They are well drilled, active, healthy young men —and the Jack tars are not to be classed as Infantry but as Artillery. Jack has no superior as to fighting—he dont know what back out means. They are in first rate discipline, and if they only had shoes, there is certainly no reason why they should not make first rate soldiers.[82] All are out drilling today. The big guns were fired yesterday—and every thing portends important events. It is said a Mexican arrived in camp this morning with the news that Fremont was at some Ranch near Santa Barbara. The ranch is called the Tejon—he is represented as having four hundred men & two hundred Indians —the Mexicans mustering some seven hundred. Before this time I suppose the matter has been decided one way or the other I hope that this will quicken our movements.

26th Several cases of fever have occurred within the last few days. One case Hmbkey [Conrad Hembkey] of C. Company 1st Dragoons, died on the morning of the 25th after an illness of only 4 days—he complained of great pain in the head—soreness in the chest, and bowels—the bowels costive, tympanetic[,] tongue foul, & coated, stomach irritable The pulse was never very full or hard, nor was there great heat of surface I thought I could discover a paroxysm towards evening, like an intermittent On the evening of the 24th his brain became affected and he died in a state of delirium early the next morning, his hands & feet were cold and covered with a clammy perspiration, the head & body of natural temperature. I commenced the treatment with an emetic—this caused the discharge of great quantities of bilious matter—but I think did harm by increasing the irritability of the stomach & tenderness of the abdomen. Mercury in form of blue mass—oil & sul mag. None of them seem to have a proper purgative effect. Enemas were no better —cups applied over the abdomen gave no relief. On the evening of the 23rd he took an anodyne and seemed better in the morning—When I saw him about 8 PM, on the evening of the 24, he was Delirious with cold extremities &c as has been described—Sinepisms—Terebinthenatic frictions—blisters to Temples—cups—Turpentine internally & in Enemas—external warmth &c were used to call the blood to the extremeties without effect.—There are two cases of the same fever now in Hospital—in both cases I have given mercurial purgatives followed up with Ol Ricini, V.S. and one suferer[?] being clear of fever I have ordered him Quinine Sul V grs, 3 times per Diem, commencing at 12 M. he thought he had a chill last night about 12 oclock, and complained of great head ache—but that passed off about ten. he now complains of the greatest pain in the chest. The other case Sergt [Richard] Williams still having fever this morning, V.S. cups to temples ℞, Cal [Calomel] v grs Ipecac v gr m[?] 3 times per Diem[83]

Streeter poor fellow still continues to suffer dreadfully, but upon the whole he is improving—the abscess in the back has ceased discharging and the wounds are nearly all closed—The mortified spot on the sacrum begins to fill with healthy granulations. The bone is exposed but up to this time no exfoliation   he suffers most from an ulcer forming from pressure on the left hip— Every effort has been used to shield the part, and I hope we have succeeded by a dressing of lint confined by a broad split bandage. The other wounded are all doing well with the exception of Brown, who was punctured through the arm. This inflamed last night, the granulations becoming fungous-pitted all around the wound   an incission was made with a lancet, pressure with a bandage & warm solut acet plumb constantly applied.[84] We have not much news, as to public affairs. We are drilling constantly, preparing for our march on the Puebla. Genl Kearny it is now said will take the command at which the naval gentlemen seem much pleased. On the night of the 24th the Commodore sent an express to Co^l Fremont, informing him of our intended movements— it is now said—the Commodore informed me of it—that we would have one hundred Indians to accompany us in our march. —A ship of War is now coming in, so we will probably have some news this evening[85]—we had a fine ball last night, quite a turn out of good looking women.

From San Diego to Santa Ana River

30th. Dec. On the 29th we left St Diego on our march against the Puebla de los Angeles, the head quarters of the Enemy—All told the army numbers some six hundred—consisting of the crews of the Congress, Frigate, Portsmouth & Cyane sloops of war, Dragoons, Volunteers and Californians.[86] The Quarter Masters department is rather in a dilapidated state, some ten carts drawn by oxen, of the poorest sort, the artillery six pieces drawn by very poor mules—our Commissary department consists mostly in fresh beef—and whatever else we can pick up along the route. Commodore Stockton is the commander in chief and, Gen¹ Kearney has the immediate command of the troops. We had a late start and marched to the Soledad, it was nearly ten oclock when we got into camp— it rained like the devil, and we had wet jackets when we arrived in camp—On the 30th we started at 9 A.M., marched as hard as our poor devlish broken down animals could carry us— We passed by the Ranch called the Panischitoes, and camped on a creek the name of which I did not learn at some 3 miles distant from this Ranch— arrived late, consequently an uncomfortable camp—We heard from the Puebla today— it is said that Fremont is at Santa Barbara, with his force, that the Mexicans are in the greatest confusion, frequent assassinations &c— all of which is no doubt true, my sick men were left back at San Diego, the sailors stand the march very well, and will soon be good infantry it is said that we will have a fresh supply of horses and cattle tomorrow.

31st Dec 1846—This has been a beautiful day though the night was very cold, water freezing near the fire. The mountains at a distance covered with snow, the grass and wild oats springing up most luxuriently, and in a short time we will have fine pasturage, to night we encamped at the foot of the hill,—where we had the fight as we passed here, (I mean St Bernard [Bernardo Mountain]) I visited the place where we passed three very anxious days, every thing just as we left it, except poor Sergt Coxs grave the wolves had scratched down to the body, and eaten off part of his feet. The Californians I do not think had had any hand in it. We received report today that the Mexicans & a party of Indians had attacked the Indians about Warner's Ranch and killed some thirty of them.[87] These Indians are our friends, and have most certainly been encouraged to take up arms in our favour and I should think ought to be supported. The Commodore with his staff went up to the Ranch of St Bernard to spend the night, he took with him the marine guard, and one piece of artillery— it is said that there are now in our neighborhood some seventy Californians and 300 Indians in arms— This does not look much like Fremont was very near the puebla— Some little dysentery among the men, but generally they are healthy—

1st Jany 1847, This has been a most beautiful clear day—last night very cold—We passed over our old Battle ground near the Ranch of St Bernard— and at the Ranch found the marine guard drawn up. The commodore with his staff passed the night at the Ranch—and report says had a fine supper. The Commodore has the most enlarged view of the hardships of a soldiers life—he has a fine large tent well supplied with table furniture and bedstead, I am told—while our old Gen¹ has nothing in the world but his blankets & bear skin—and a common tent—one pack mule for himself, Capt Turner & servant   As for my mess it is a first rate one, Capt Gellespie being at the head of it, Emory, Capt Zeilin, Lt Renshaw,[88] of the Navy & myself. This is considered rather the crack concern in camp next to the Commodore's—   We passed by a small Ranch called the buena vista & encamped near an Indian village called buena ventura.[89] The distance marched to day variously estimated from fourteen to sixteen miles. We received another message from Jose Antonio Picot (the brother of Andreas, the man who fought us at San Pascual) that he had horses for us at his Ranch but it is said that he has ten men at the same place waiting our arrival, so as to despatch them to the Puebla, that notice may be given of our approach—   We saw a great many wild geese and a herd of antelope, one of which Carson killed. We have not much amusement on the march, but Jack tar, makes rather a queer Infantry soldier. The sailors begin to suffer much from sore feet. The most exciting scene we have is the lassoing of horses by the Californians. This we have frequent opportunities of seeing, as every horse we find that will be serviceable is at once seized upon, at night when we get into camp butchering comes on   then the californians lasso the cattle throw them and in fact manage them with the greatest ease

2d Jany. Today we have marched some six miles only—and arrived at the Mission of San Luis Rey—this mission is situated in an extensive vally, with beautiful grounds, it is a most extensive building—the front being five hundred feet including the church, which is said to be beautifully ornamented, it was locked up and we did not see the inside of it—though some of the sailors did break in at the back window, and I am sorry to say removed articles, fortunately of little value,   every effort was made to discover the sacriligious scamp but without avail—   The rooms in the Mission are very comfortable, and many of them ornamented with rude paintings, some of saints, and others of birds, marvelously favouring a goose,   the chairs are of the most capacious dimensions covered with dressed skins, the sofas also made of oak, and of like capacity with the chairs,   the finest and most extensive vineyard olive garden, and pear orchard   A great deal of land enclosed for gardens, the fences made of adobes covered with tyles, the lands well irrigated, and beautiful reservoirs for water. The internal face of the building is a square, about 300 feet on a side, with the corals—and what I took to be the quarters for the laborers on the right flank. There are collonades extending all around the four sides of the square.—The whole front from the church to the right, is a long row of collonades. The whole building presents a most grand appearance. it is built entirely of brick about eight inches broad and long, and some two inches thick—it is roofed first with reeds, then with some composition over that brick and earth, and covering all tyles, presenting very much the appearance of a flower pot split vertically and the bottom broken out, it is said that no less than 12,000 Indians were attached to this mission, they owned many Ranches, and the Padres clothed, fed and educated the Indians well, that all were happy. The missions were broken up in 1834, and their property seized and confiscated, the Indians driven to the mountains, or made slaves of. They have been constantly harrassing the Californians since. The Padres were said to have lived a most luxurious life, and were remarkable for their love to the most beautiful young Indian girls— A Mister Foster came in camp this evening and gave us some reports[90]—he says that Andreas Picot is at present the general of the Californians, that Fremont is reported to have left Santa Barbara last Sunday—and that Picot left the Puebla this morning for the purpose of giving Fremont battle, that the mexicans had some six hundred men—and they believed Fremont could not muster over two hundred— a party under Capt Hensley went over to Pieo Picot Ranch Santa Margarita, to obtain cattle and mules & if possible to surprise a small party of Californians, said to be there.[91]

4th [3d] Jany—Last night we were threatened with rain, this to us would be a serious misfortune, as we are badly provided with tents, not one half of the men could get under cover, the rains at this season of the year are extremely cold and disagreeable.[92] The men are generally in very fine health, a little dysentery being the only complaint— We made an early start from the Mission this morning, but in consequence of the broken country and bad state of the quarter masters department our progress was slow, and extremely laborious. Capt Hensly returned last night with some indifferent horses, and some forty fine [five?] oxen. Today we have been enabled to get two or three carts, which will aid us much in going ahead. We passed by an Indian village, some five miles from the Mission at I believe the lower end of the Ranch of San Margaritta—and encamped on a plain near the Ranch of Flores, belonging to one of the Picot family. Foster the Englishman, who brought us the reports yesterday of the movements of Fremont & the intentions of the Californians to march out and give him battle—is a Brotherinlaw of Picot. Andreas Picot by taking up arms has twice broken his parole, once given to Commodore Stockton and once to Capt Gilispie— he was told by doing so that he was risking all of his property and at the same time runing a reasonable chance of being shot or hung if taken. Foster says Picot believes the American government, will neither confiscate property—or shoot a man, though he may have violated the most sacred pledge— this I think is a misfortune, that our government has the reputation of exercising too much leniency. These fellows suppose that they can make war as long as it is convenient—and when they get tired of it—come in and be paid high wages for little or no services— This was too much the case in Florida and up to this time I have no doubt has been too much the case here.—The country begins to look beautiful, the young grass springing in all directions—the hills green with the wild oats—and some most beautiful flowers in bloom—among the rest I saw a beautiful variety of the pea, the bloom being red—and extremly rich— There is no timber except on the small streams, and then only a few sycamores.— the plains are covered with wild geese—white brant—& ducks. About 2 PM we had a view of the Pacific—and saw many whales spouting the water in the air—We are encamped within three quarters of a mile of the ocean. This evening a Californian who left San Diego with us by name Orsoona[93] came in camp. he reported that he had been taken prisoner by the enemy, had made his escape—and been pursued by them from the Mission of St John's to within a few miles of our present camp. It is believed by many persons in camp that these fellows make it convenient to be taken, and escape as it may suit their fancy. marched ten miles and a half—by measurement—

4th Jany—Some how or other I have missed a day in my reckoning, and lost a day, but it does not make much odds.[94] We left our camp early this morning, and would have been off at an earlier hour had not many of our artillery mules and oxen been absent, some 15 or 17 animals were lost.—We passed by the Ranch of Flores—quite an extensive concern, with a monument standing in front. This I suppose is a grave—and probably a bishop by the size of the cross— After leaving the Ranch, we had quite a rough road until we got near San Matteo [Mateo]—another Ranch of the Picot family—after leaving San Matteo we struck the Sea Shore—through a pass that an army could have been cut to pieces—without the loss of a man, on the part of those who attacked. The bluffs were from fifty to a hundred feet in height, and nothing but a bird could have got from the Sea Shore to the hills—We had a party of Riflemen on the hills as scouts, but if they had been attacked by a large force, we could have afforded them no support— The sand in many places heavy and hard to pace through— We arrived in camp near the Mission of San Juan—at 7 PM— About 11 A.M. we received a flag of truce, borne by a German, an Englishman—named Workman—and a californian.[95] They bore a letter from Flores to the Commodore. Flores signed himself Governor, and Commander in Chief in California. They wished to open negociations for peace. The assumption of these titles seemed to enrage the Commodore who claimed the titles himself— he sent word back that he would have nothing to do with Flores—that he Flores, was a rebel, and that he would shoot him, if the Commodore could only lay his hands on him— The envoys plead for the country— the Commodore said that if the people would come, and deliver up their arms that he might take into consideration any propositions they might make for peace—that he was not blood thirsty, but if he did not give up, that we had come to do our best and please God we would. Marched to day—19 miles.

5th We have marched 11½ miles to day, and encamped at the Ranch of los Alisos, or the Sycamores.—About two miles and a half from our camp of this morning, we passed the Mission of St John's *Clopestrano* [Capistrano], this Mission is situated in a most beautiful vally—with a fine runing stream near it, it is in rather a dilapidated condition, it is not so extensive as San Luis Rey—the church however must have been quite a handsome building— it is large two story high and well finished with cut stone arches over the doors windows &c—The cornice of the building was of fine cut stone—& the corners of the building the same. The rest of the building was of stone—and covered with cement & stucco work, the church is said to have been thrown down in 1822 by an earthquake—it is now used or has been for a stable. The building and Ranch all belongs to Foster the Englishman spoken of before. Foster told us that after the battle of San Pascual that the californians came to St Johns—that each man—told how many of our men they had killed individually—that upon computation taking of each man—they killed some 300 of our people. Of course the bragging must have been rare— We found here four Californians—who had been wounded in the action Foster also told us that these rascals after they had concluded to run—found some of our dead & wounded in the bushes, and actually stuck their lances in them, so that they might show blood on their lances. This is called fighting a civilized enemy, and we are not allowed even to take wood enough to make a fire, although our poor fellows suffer every night from the cold. We found many familys at the Mission—collected there since the war as a place of refuge. Foster treated the Commodore very nice—had wine—apples, pears &c The apples I tasted—they wanted flavour and were extremely tough. There are extensive dams now standing used in irrigation and the vally seems to have been in a high State of cultivation by the Padres—but everything is now going to decay— This morning Mr. Workman the envoy from the Puebla again made his appearance in camp— after some talk with the Commodore —Commodore Stockton sent a proclamation to the Californians offering them peace—on the condition that they would give up Flores and disperse to their Ranches. This I am fearful they will do—come in with some cock & bull story of Flores having escaped—they will be believed—& the Californians will disperse—we will withdraw our forces—leave a small garrison— and the first time they catch us off of our guard, they will pitch into us again —and every thing will have to be done over again. The country passed over destitute of trees—plenty of wild geese—ducks &c— Snow on the mountains in our front—every thing green and Spring like around us, except the nights & they are devlish cold—

6th We have had a long tiresome march today—over a dead level—little or no Grass—but immense numbers of cattle in all directions, About 12 [?] M we passed the ranch of *Supelvera* [Sepúlveda]—to whom I believe all the cattle belonged— We have had a strong wind from the snow capped peaks in our neighborhood—cold and disagreeable. Our tents can hardly stand now, We have had many reports in camp—one that the forces at the Puebla would meet us tomorrow or the next day—the other that they had all left for the north to fight Fremont. We encamped at the town or Ranch of St Anna— Just before leaving camp this morning McNealy [John McNeilly] of Company C 1st Dragoons shot himself by the accidental discharge of his pistol—the ball cut the phalangial bones—near the 3^d joint of the middle & ring finger of the right hand. Entered on the inner side of the little finger and passed out near the carpus on the out side of the little finger— The middle finger was amputated just below the joint & the ring finger at the joint— little or no hemorrhage—

7th We had a very disagreeable night of it the wind blew a perfect gale all night & kept it up until ten o clock to day. The dust was most distressing to weak eyes. We got corn for our animals.—The enemy made his appearance today for the first time—the rascals are much better mounted than anything we can muster, and they know it—the consequence is they are extremely impudent. to day they captured two of our vaccaroes [vaqueros] who were sent ahead, and also took Mr Foster our English *friend* prisoner. They however let him go again—as he made his appearance just before we got into camp. We had a report this morning that the enemy had eight hundred Indians in his employ—with which he intended to attack us— then again we heard that we should have a grand battle just before we arrived at the Ranch of los coyotes— This evening however the report is—that the forces 435—have left the Puebla to fight Fremont—that Flores with a small party—some forty strong has gone to lord knows where—that Andreas Picot is still in the Puebla—and that Ramon Corelea [Carrillo] is now in our neighbourhood, and that he is anxious to give up—if he can obtain forgiveness for his past sins—One of them—is only breaking his parole— this offense of a Mexican breaking his parole, does not seem to be looked upon as any great sin—Most of the leaders now in California are in the same predicament.— The rascals caught another of our vaccaroes out and struck him with the but of the pistol over the eye—knocked him down & I fear have fractured the poor fellows skull—The country passed over an extensive plain Just after leaving our camp this morning we crossed the Rio Santa Ana—a small stream sandy bottom & poor land—We encamped at the Ranch of los Coyotes—about 3 P M—

Battles of San Gabriel and La Mesa—Treatment of Wounded

8th Jany. We left our camp this morning early. it was reported to us that the enemy would certainly give us a brush that they had crossed the San Gabriel in force with 3 pieces of artillery. We saw their scouts hovering about all day—About 2½ P M we arrived at an Indian village near the San Gabriel—here we saw more scouts— Our line of battle was formed—the Volunteer riflemen leading as scouts—then the Dragoons & Cyane's Musketeers—4 pieces of Artillery, Marines & sailors—baggage in the centre. Cattle & rear guard with two pieces of Artillery—As we approached the river the Enemy appeared in great force. Some hundred or so crossed the river & threatened our advance. These however, soon retired and took post on the opposite side of the river— As we approached they let fly grape at us—but it fell short— We advanced steadily—the Dragoons and Cyane's Marines supporting the two guns which were in the advance— two large guns followed supported by the Marines and Congress crew—in this shape we took the river ran the enemy off & made a lodgement under the first bank —We exchanged shots here with the enemy—and dismounted one or two of their guns— One of the guns that dismounted a gun of the enemy—was fired & armed by Commodore Stockton.—After firing a few shots from the first bank we made a rush at the second. The plain between the points must have been two hundred and fifty yards broad—Across this we charged under the full fire from the Enemy. When we got about half way across—we were threatened with a charge—but the Jacktars threw themselves in square, and drove them off with the greatest ease. We continued to charge at the hill, topped it & ran our friends the Mexicans clearly out of the field. Many of our men did not fire a gun. We lost one man killed—8 wounded—and one I fear mortally wounded by the accidental discharge of a musket, We lost 21 horses. These were lost by the volunteers, tieing them as they went in action and forgot all about them—until it was too late. [Jacob] Hait an Artillery driver was shot in the chest, and I think [it] is rather a serious wound, another man of the Savannah crew received several flesh wounds—the remainder are merely slight wounds from spent balls—with the exception of the poor fellow who was accidentally wounded—

9th Jany All lights were put out early in the evening—about 11½ we had an alarm and all hands turned out under arms. This morning a Mexican came galloping up with a white flag—this man we found to be [Lorenzo] Soto—a californian who had been sent out by the commodore some days before—he reported that Fremont was at San Fernando within eight leagues of the Puebla—that two American ships had arrived at Santa Barbara— all hands supposed as a matter of course that Fremont would press forward and that we would meet at the Puebla or near it in the evening. When we first left camp we saw but few of the enemy in sight—although he had encamped within a mile of us in the evening—As we proceeded—we saw him—in considerable force on our right flank—we exchanged shots with our artillery—What damage we did to him we know not. The only hurt we sustained, was one mule—one ox wounded one of our men, a sailor shot himself in the foot. [Mark A.] Childs a dragoon was shot in the heel of the left foot, the ball ranged up, and I think is lodged in his ankle joint, a sailor was shot through the fleshy part of the thigh. Capt Gilispie & Capt Rowan[96] were hit by spent balls—We advanced across a plain for two miles under fire from the artillery. We were obliged to march slow in consequence of the broken down condition of our ox teams—nor could we leave our baggage to charge their guns—which we could have captured with the greatest ease—as one—the heaviest—a nine pounder was drawn by oxen. The enemy drew up at some distance—out of gun shot—at open order—threatening our right rear—& left front—finally they made the rush, and got most terribly peppered. I saw several fall and several horses were killed after the charge. They seemed to be perfectly convinced that they could do nothing with us. They withdrew and marched for the town. We encamped—on the stream some two miles below the town— it is said yesterday as they were marching their forces to meet us at the crossing of the San Gabriel—they thought it impossible for us to cross the river in their face—They therefore argued the question whether they would cut us to pieces or allow us to surrender. Last night the poor fellow one of the Cyanes men, who was accidentally shot by one of the marines died.[97] Hait one of the volunteers, died just after we got into camp. This poor fellow crossed the mountains with us and—was an old dragoon. Our party who came from New Mexico, has been terribly cut to pieces—nearly one half of our number either killed or wounded.[98]

Los Angeles—Treatment of Wounded

10th Jany. Last night we had an alarm in camp and all hands were up and in arms in a few moments—We encamped on the river about two miles below the town—there was no noise in the town everything as quiet as possible—occasionally a light was seen passing about, but no demonstration made on us—during the night a Mexican came in who had been sent in to observe what was going on, he however brought nothing in that I could hear of. About 9 A.m. a flag of truce was sent to us, by the enemy, informing us that they would not oppose our entering the town—as they did not wish us to destroy the place.[99] We however marched up in battle array, every thing prepared for action, as we entered the town the music struck up—The hights immediately over the town was lined by the drunken rascals, who were threatening us with their guns. Of these however we took no notice, but marched on steadily, although I felt the greatest inclination to shoot a rascal who had a dragoon coat on, and took particular delight in showing it—Another rode in front of us, cursing & swearing at us, shaking his gun, and occasionally taking aim at us—but he would not fire— just before we arrived in the square, we saw one of the rascals strike a californian knock him from his horse run at the man, and attempt to lance him—it was the impression that the man who was getting the worst of it was one of our vaccaroes—instantly a man cried out shoot the damned rascal no quicker said than done. Out rushed several of the Cyane's crew and blazed away—two or three dragoons followed their example—a rifle shot or two followed, and upon the whole I think the fellow got well peppered. So soon as the man who was down got released, he jumped up and ran off with the rest—and so ended the row, except the old Genl pitched into the men for their bad conduct in fireing without orders, and for shooting so cursedly bad,—in not killing the scoundrel instantly— Two guns with some two hundred men were ordered to occupy the hill—immediately over the town—and the rest were quartered about the town—every thing went on quietly till towards dark, when it was found many of the men were becoming drunk, the assembly was immediately blown—the guard increased and every precaution used to preserve order. I got a very comfortable house for my wounded—but no furniture. All are doing well, except the poor fellow Childs who suffers dreadfully from his wound. The ball is clearly lodged I think in the tibea [tibia]—the hemorrhage was considerable after the wound—and a substance that I took to be synovia—one of the other medical gentlemen thought so likewise oozed from the wound with the blood—the inflammation or swelling is not very great—nor is there much fever up to this time— the man McNealy who shot himself in the hand is doing well. I dressed his wound this evening— It is reported in camp, that Picot will come in tomorrow—and that the enemy have gone to attack Fremont. They said that it was no use to attack us any more, that we could not be broken. They rode around our square looking for a weak point but it could not be found. They had signals to designate the point when found—but it was not given I suppose— They were utterly surprised at our crossing the San Gabriel in their face in the way it was done—and said that men who were capable of such actions ought not to be shot— They had five hundred horsemen to oppose us the first day and upwards of four hundred the second— their loss is variously estimated from 68, to some ten or twelve. All of our accounts are very vague and not to be relied on—but I should think they must have lost many men. I saw them reel in their saddles from our discharge of musketry, and the rifles poured in the shot most beautifully on our right flank and rear which they attacked at the same time. They used musketry & grape

11th I have been engaged all day arranging my Hospital. I have not heard any thing that is going on, everything seems quiet, the citizens of the place do not so far as I can discover manifest very friendly feelings— Nothing heard from Fremont, last night there was a devil of a row among the men, liquor the cause of it all—although every precaution had been taken. An Indian was found dead this morning—how killed I do not know.

12th We still remain quiet. I have not been over the town yet, being so much engaged in arranging my Hospital. The wounded are not doing as well as I could wish. The bed clothing is scant—and they have nothing to lay on but the hard boards, and a blanket— Childs suffers considerably—his ankle swollen—and some fever— I gave him last night x grs massa ex Hyd, & ½ gr Tart Ant— during the night, I was obliged to Give him an opiate—this morning I dressed the foot applied a fresh poultice—and gave Sul mag ʒi. Tart ant i gr—m—[100] this evening the salts had not operated and an Enema was ordered— [William] Cope's arm very much swollen and inflamed, he took blue mass & Tart Ant last night—had incisions made in the arm— he suffered much—till towards morning—When I dressed the wound this morning suppuration had been established—and the appearance of the arm decidedly better— he took salts & Tart Ant this morning—& was quiet this evening.—Yesterday a Sailor was prowling about, when he met a californian some place in the suberbs—the Sailor claimed the californian as a prisoner, and the Californian claimed the sailor as both were armed— the friends of either party who happened to be within hail—would have decided the matter— the Californian seeing a couple of his friends called upon them to take the sailor—When Jack up and put a musket ball through the gentleman— and that ended the business. We have many reports as to the movements of Fremont and the enemy.—Fremont is said by some to have turned back—by others to be at this time within 8 miles of this place some say that Flores has gone out to give Fremont battle, others that he is at the mission of San Gabriel—We see scouts on the hills near the town every day— A fort is about to be constructed on the hill immediately commanding the place. We had a report that American troops had arrived at Warners pass—if this be so it must be Captain Cook with his Mormons— A large quantity of Wine and Brandy of the country has been seized and placed in store—so as to keep it out of the sailors way— this is the chief point in California where all wine is made, and great quantities is made—it is of fine flavour, as good I think as I ever tasted. The white wine is particularly fine—The grapes are said to be delicious—and all fruits abound. I ate of a very fine orange—grown near this place—the climate is very healthy, and taking every thing into consideration, I think this is decidedly one of the most desirable places I [have] ever been at.

13th This has been a day of excitement, this morning a Californian presented himself with a despatch from Picot—signed by Fremont, the contents of this I learned, was on Fremonts part granting Picot permission to take his Picots wounded men in San Fernando— The inference on our part was that Picot and Fremont had had a battle, also a cessation of hostillities until this evening, and commissioners were to be appointed to arrange affairs between the hostile parties in the country— The bearer of the despatch was questioned as to whether there had been a battle between Picot & the Forces under Fremont—but he declared there had been no meeting— The whole affair was inexplicable—but it was believed by many that a fight had taken place and Picot, was anxious to keep us from knowing any thing about the matter—so that no forces would be marched out from this place. This evening Col. Russell & Mr. Talbot arrived in town from Fremonts camp[101]— They informed us that Fremont had had no fight, and was within a days march of the Puebla—that Picot would be in tomorrow to deliver up his arms—that a treaty had actually been entered in—between the parties, Picot agreeing on his part to deliver up all arms—with the exception of his officers —and immediately upon the reception of this news it was announced that despatches would be sent tonight for the U.S. Flores it is said has fled for Sonora—some say with forty, others with a hundred men— it is certain however that he will run off all the horses in the country, while he is about it—[102]

My wounded were much better this morning. The swelling and discoloration had in a great measure left Child's foot, the Poultice continued & Low Diet, tonight the poultice renewed, he however complains of intollerable itching about the wound—

On the day of the battle of the 8th I have understood from Lieut Emory, that Commodore Stockton was anxious to encamp on the opposite side of the San Gabriel, from that which we occupied after the action of the 8th— I was standing near the Genl—after we took the first bank of the river. Commodore Stockton I think had just fired a piece of artillery, which was supposed to have dismounted one of the Enemy's, when I distinctly heard the Genl say (he had a pistol in each hand at the time) now Commodore "I am ready for the charge"— in a few moments the column did charge—and took the second hight— I have understood since that Mr Southwick paced off the distance from the 1st to the 2d bank, and found it to be 900 paces & upwards —these I should say were extremely short paces—though a man is not a very good judge of distance when under fire—it did not look to me to exceed 300 yards—[103]

14th — This has been a most disagreeable day, raining constantly. About 12 M. Frémont with his forces made their appearance, some mounted on sorry looking animals, and some on fine fat horses — The men all armed with the Rifle, and a fine looking set of fellows they were — stout and healthy, they had several pieces of Artillery, and among the rest, we saw the howitzer we lost at San Pascual— the only regret I had in seeing this was that the Enemy should have delivered it up, before we had an opportunity of taking it, or some other piece from the Mexicans; a treaty or state of truce no doubt now exists between the enemy and our forces. We took the wind out of Fremonts sails by capturing the Puebla—and whipping the enemy on the 8th & 9th, but he has shown himself the better politician by negociating first with the enemy— What the terms of the treaty may be—has not yet been divulged—but report says, that the stipulations are 1st that the Californians shall lay down their arms and retire to their occupations, and that all passed offences will be forgiven, and they will enjoy all the rights of American citizens[104] This is certainly most favourable terms for the Californians, considering the great force we now have against them—at the lowest estimate some 1100 men —and they cannot raise over five hundred, with their Artillery in such a state that it could be captured the very first time we got in action with them, Lt McLean of the Navy, commanding Fremonts artillery, Major Redding Paymaster,[105] & Col Russell were the negociators on our side. Picot was the head of the California Commissioners. This treaty, truce or whatever it may be is as I understand negociated without the knowledge of Commodore Stockton or Genl Kearny. The fact is, it is said that the Californians would not have negociated with Stockton on any terms, in consequence of the proclamation he sent them from the Mission of St. John's[106]—[Here the paper is torn.] he sent by, the commissioners to Flores who met us below the Mission— The junior officers have opinions of their own, and like all Americans will express them. They are decidedly opposed to the treaty and the terms granted to the Californians as not a man among them believes it will be observed on the part of the Californians with good faith, the only thing that can be said to justify their superiors, is that they are anxious to send a despatch home, to inform our government that California is now ours, so soon as the Forces are withdrawn, which they must be from the nature of things in a short time, being composed chiefly of sailors & Volunteers for 3 & six months—there being only one company of regular troops in the concern— The people will rise again, and we will have the same scenes enacted over again, it is reported however that Cook is at Warners pass— here we have some six hundred men who can be kept in service a short time then the New york regiment may arrive in the mean time. Two of our vaccaroes got into a fight today—one attempted to run the other through. he with the lance, got a pistol shot in the breast, right side, between the 7th & 8th ribs, the ball ranging downwards and backwards & came out about 3½ inches to the right of the spine— When the fellow came in [the] hospital his pulse was extremely feeble—& perspiration on his forehead, he was in a very depressed state, simple dressing applied to the wound with a roller & a little Brandy & Tinct opii[107] given, about 4 P M he had a passage from his bowels and passed about a quart of blood— at ten P.M, I examined him his pulse was good—breathing easy, and his surface [Paper torn.] the rest of the wounded are doing well, suppuration in most of the wounds has been established and in one or two the sloughs begin to come away and granulations to form.

As our fighting is all over it is well as one thinks of the scenes previous to the fight and during the action to note them down. On the morning of the 8th I accompanied the old Genl around to every division of the force on the field. The old fellow I believe had been informed that we would certainly have a fight that day. He appeared in fine spirits, and was particularly gay— he made a short speech to each corps as he passed, he did not fail to remind the men of the day, that it was the 8th of Jany—and that we had a right on that day to flog any thing that we might come in contact with—that after the fight that the Jack tars would have a good long yarn to spin to each other on the subject—and that then we would have a good fat bullock for our supper. Jack got the fight, as promised, licked the enemy—had an opportunity of spining a short yarn by the camp fire—but swore that the beef was not what had been promised—our Commissary seemed to have a desire to reserve the fat ones for some special purpose— We heard today that Genl. [Zachary] Taylor was at [blank] & that Santa Anna was at San Luis Potosi determined to give battle, that the Americans had taken Tampico, and that a large reinforcement was marching by that place to join Genl Taylor—that our army was exclusive of the reinforcement some 25,000 or 30,000 men; and that the Mexican force was about the same. The Californians had hung out in hopes of obtaining aid from Mexico, but when they were told of what had taken place they gave up all ideas of assistance— They declared that they had but two men killed—& 12 wounded, and 18 horses killed in the two actions, and what is singular, all of their wounded are officers. This report is not believed by us, they treat their soldiery with great brutallity—and hide them away when wounded—this we know, as we found six wounded men at the Mission of San John's, badly hurt, who had been shot in the action of San Pascual and Picot—declared he had no wounded. We heard when we arrived here—that they brought to this place 12 wounded, & 2 dead, these were probably persons of some property.

15 Jany. Everything in town going on, in the most quiet, and orderly manner, one would not suppose that there was in town more than the ordinary staid and quiet citizens, instead of over 1000 devil may care Jack tars and back woodsmen with thousands of gallons of liquor, to be had for the searching—not an outrage of any magnitude has been committed, nor half the disorder that would have been on any public day in the states— the terms of the treaty still remain enveloped in mystery and what will be our future course no one knows, nor do they seem to know, whether peace or war actually exists, such an uncertain state of affairs to say the least is very disagreeable to the uninitiated— Picot and several of the Mexican leaders have been in town nearly all day. Many believe that Picot is an honorable man and can be trusted, many believe that all of them are a pack of scoundrels, that fear alone can controle and that now they are only brought [to] terms by abject fear, and that the very first chance they get will turn against us. I heard that the

leaders were in conference with the commodore. It is reported outside, that Flores has run off for Sonora, with one hundred men, 21 [?] pieces of artillery, and four hundred horses—Others say that he has burnt the gun carriages and cashed the guns. None of these stories are believed by us outside barbarians, except that Flores may have run off, and stolen 400 horses. I have not seen Picot yet—but any way a despatch goes to the U.S. tomorrow— I understood that Col Fremont had told the Californians to disperse, and then deliver up their arms I wonder why they could not have been made to march in and deliver up their arms in a body, it would seem that it was a much more convenient way of obtaining them—and much more certain also. —My wounded still continue [to] improve—nothing like violent inflammation in any of the cases—Childs I look upon as being in the most critical situation, and at this present time I cannot discover a single bad symptom, the Indian who was shot yesterday, is in a very bad condition, his breathing is laborious—& quick, his pulse weak, and as far as I can comprehend him, he labours from excessive pain over the chest and abdomen. The man who shot himself, McNealy of C Company, 1st Drags, at the camp of the Alcytos is rapidly recovering. Two deserters have been found in Fremonts ranks, these men ran off from their companies G & F 1st Dragoons—at Fort Leavenworth last spring, one stole a fine horse belonging to Uncle Sam, the other stole nothing,— I forgot to mention that Dr. Henderson[108] thinks he discovered bilious matter oosing out of the wound on the Indians back—when the ball came out, judges that it was bile by the color & taste—It was discharged in considerable quantities—It is said in town that the Californians are in arms to the north, in Fremonts rear, that they threaten to attack Monterey. This of course will continue to be the case, until a sufficient military force is sent to occupy the country—and harsh measures are taken by our commanding officers.

Some artist among the Californians, drew a picture of the action of the 9th—which represented us in square, three deep, and our cattle & baggage in the centre. Under it was written "The infernal Yankee Coral"— They came into town after the fight, and said they would have broken our square when they charged, but that we stretched ropes or chains around us, using the Jack tars, as posts. This of course was an absurd story—but at the same time, I think is a great compliment to Jack—as it shows how steadily he met the charge. It is reported today that they acknowledge 70 killed & wounded in the two actions.[109]

16th Quietness and peace still reigns over the city of the angels, except a little drunkenness, nothing going on, the Jack tars begin to talk about their ships again, and going home. I understand from the officers that the time for which, many of them shipped has long since expired, yet they remain doing duty—and that too of a sort, that they are unaccustomed to, and moreover it is hard service for they have to dig and labour, at the fort on the hill—and yet

Jack does not grumble very much— some of the volunteers absolutely refused to work at the fort. I wonder who the patriots are in this case— Many of the Men who came with Fremont only enlisted for 3 months, their time has expired and in some instances I understand for several weeks. They have done their duty cheerfully, I understand—yet from all accounts there was some discont[ent] shown to day. This I think goes to show the policy of making the treaty we did with the Californians, so long as the men had an enemy before them they thought of nothing but whipping him—now he has disappeared. No one as yet knows exactly how. All hands begin to get impatient—and in a short time our forces must be scattered, and then the enemy will have the country again—for what confidence can be placed in men—who have broken their honor, and their commander Picot has twice done so.— The terms of the treaty have not been made public—but the delivery of arms it is understood was a sine qua non—yet they come in slowly—another cannon given up to day, they yet have two with them. Picot and his chief men have been in town all day, in close conference with Col Fremont, and consultations seems going on among all of our big guns—what may be in the wind I know not— I understand that the Genl. had sent or was sending an express, to see if there was any truth in the report of the arrival of Capt Cook at Warners Pass.

A ship of war is said to be at San Pedro. Mr. Thompson U.S.N. was despatched this evening to communicate with her.[110] Lt Gray, of the Navy, started as bearer of despatches for the U.S. this morning. One of Capt Fremonts captains, Jacob, accompanyed Mr Gray.[111]

Child complained of more pain this evening than usual, I discovered a little fluctuation this morning just below the internal Maleolus [Malleolus]—the discharge from the wound is bloody and extremely foetid. The Sloughs from Copes wound has come away, and the surface is clean and filling up with fine healthy granulations— The Indian who was shot a few days since died this morning—I was sent for and went immediately to the hospital ward. There I found a priest—who I suppose had come to give the poor fellow a safe conduct to the next world. The padre had a little silver vessel around his neck— the contents of which he seemed anxious to put upon the dying man. The virtues of the remedy seemed to depend entirely, upon there being a spark of life remaining—if the vital spark were extinct—the powers of the fluid seemed to be nul—he therefore wished my opinion as [to] whether there was not a spark remaining; I did not at first understand what the padre wished. I therefore examined the man and told him it was no use—the man was dead. This seemed to give great distress to those around—who I judged were relations, as they seemed to be firmly convinced that the padre could have absolved the poor fellow from all sins, by the miraculous virtues of the fluid. The man who committed the murder was placed in double irons and under guard— A heavy snow fell last night on the mountains, yet in the day it is pleasant down here in the valley—everything is green, and presents the appearance of Spring—the contrast between winter and spring is very great—and quite agreeable—the nights are rather cool—and none or very few of the houses have fire places in them.

Kearny, Stockton and Fremont

17th Jany: This has been a most beautiful clear day. I wish I could say it was the same in our political affairs, but they seem to be in the greatest state of confusion. This morning report says, that Commodore Stockton commenced organizing a civil government, his first act was to appoint Col Fremont governor, to this Gen¹ Kearny is said to have objected, as the President had sent him to this country as governor, and with powers to organize a government for the country, the General did not object to the man, as I have frequently heard officers say that Gen¹ K had said if Col. Fremont, would accept the appointment he should have it— to the General's communication the only reply the Commodore gave was an order suspending Kearny from all command.[112] Previous to this the General had given Fremont orders to make a report of the State of his command, and several other orders, the nature of which I do not recollect, all of which the Col utterly refused to obey, or disregarded. In the opinion of some Fremont's conduct has laid him liable to the charge of mutiny—at all events I think no other Lt Col. in the service would have paid so little attention to the orders of his commanding officer— As I predicted the whole force now assembled here will vanish, and we will have another revolution in the country in less than two months, tomorrow Gen¹. Kearny marches to San Diego, with what is left of his Dragoons, all told I do not believe we can muster over fifty men. On Wednesday it is said the Commodore marches with all of the naval force for San Pedro, leaving Fremont, with what will remain of his battalion. They are to be reorganized, and Gillespie [is] to act as Major. Mr McLean is to act as Major of Artillery—

I think our march on San Diego, in the present state of affairs is a mere fact of so many persons thrown out to be murdered, for our enemy is not conquered—They have not complied with the treaty entered in with Fremont, their arms have not been delivered up—we found by accident the remainder of their cannon, loaded and mounted, and I have no doubt unless the military force expected here from the U.S. quickly arrives that a revolution will take place in a few months—and if it does every bit of it is to be attributed to Fremonts thirst for glory, and Stockton's—I wont say what—but I only wish I could marry a Senators daughter; I might then set at defiance the orders of my superiors and do as I pleased. Of course as affairs are now Kearny has no forces at his command, and must submit— I do not like the march—for setting all danger aside, and I regard the chance of attack as being at least two to one in favour of it—I have had enough of march without any particular object— When we arrive at San Diego, I do not see that we have bettered our condition, and what is to become of us I know not. The vessel seen at San Pedro proved to be the Stonington, from San Diego—with provisions &c. She brought no news, nothing had been heard of Cooks arrival, so I suppose the report was false. The forces of the Enemy seems to have vanished no one knows, where or how, nor is there apparently any great attention paid to it—Arms I understand have not been given up in any numbers, and no one seems to care a damned. This [thus] it is to have men of doubtful positions—and command in camp— Genl Kearny has been most outragiously used both by Fremont and Stockton, they are both men of political influence, and of course they will go scot free and in all probability throw the whole blame on Kearny—and succeed in doing it too—[113]

To San Diego Again

Jany- 18th We left the puebla this morning, that is to say the General, Capts Turner, Emory, Lt. Davidson, myself and some forty five or fifty non commissioned officers and privates—of C. Company, 1st Dragoons. Our hearts were heavy and forebodings of misfortune not wanting, I believe that all of us are opposed to the movement except the General and Turner— As to myself I fully confess that it is nothing but my sense of duty as an officer that compels me to take the trip—A great majority of the men have as good as no shoes—some none atal—already they begin to complain of sore feet— a falling house it is said, will be deserted by the rats—so with us— Some of the servants refused to accompany the officers—upon whom they had been in attendance. Commodore Stockton said that he did not consider that peace was made with these people until they complyed with the terms of their treaty—that it had rendered up their arms. this they have not done— nor do they evince any disposition so far as I have heard—of doing so. They do not carry themselves as a people conquered or even overpowered—On the contrary they boast of having compelled us to make terms, and there is not an American who had been a resident in the country but expects another revolution—and yet we are exposed with this small force to be cut off—when a few days since it was not considered safe for a man to move without an army at his heels— I never in all my life undertook an expedition with so much reluctance, I feel as if misfortune was before me. I hope my forebodings may be without foundation—and when we arrive at San Diego, I do not see that we have bettered our condition. We have encamped on a tributary of the San Gabriel—below the point where the battle took place some four or five miles.

Jany 19th We left camp early. Considering that we are new hands at infantry the men march well. We crossed the Santa Anna river some miles below the town, and encamped on a Ranch near the bank of the stream— On the plain some distance from the river we met a couple of young Californians. They approached us with great caution, and showed any thing but confidence in our friendship They professed utter ignorance of any treaty; and were by no means certain in their own minds that peace did actually exist— We asked them if they would sell us horses—and a beef— to this they replied that they did not know that they were at liberty to do so —When we arrived at the camp—near the ranch—the owner was badly frightened—and from his maner I have now [no] doubt expected to be plundered. In this he was agreeably disappointed, as the officers assured him nothing should be touched that was not paid for—and now I think he begins to believe it—We got a bullock—and now seem on quite friendly terms—the hospitallity however is evidently forced—the country passed over, was an extensive plain in a great measure I think untillable from the want of water— No timber except on the stream and that Sycamore— The puebla is the best built town I have seen in the Mexican country—Many of the houses are good —but belong principally to foreigners—and the most of them Americans— the population is about 1000— the vineyards in the vicinity are extensive— and the grounds are beautiful—extensive orchards of pears & peaches—and taking it all in all it must be a very pleasant place— we found it so lived well & had the best of wine—

Jany 20th We are improving in our gait—we travel well and fast, but the men are decidedly tender footed. We heard to day of the arrival of Capt Cooks party, or rather the advance of it—at Warners Ranch. It is said that there are 8 men, with a member of Congress[114] come ahead—and are now at San Diego— It is reported that the Commodore is some eight miles in our rear, and sent an express ahead for us to wait for him— The country seems quiet

21st We camped last night near the Mission of San Johns— About Dark the Commodore and staff came up, and staid all night at the Mission— We left camp early, and after passing San Matteo the Commodore passed us— We went ahead—and did nothing more than a passing salute. Mr Hall & Le Roux[115] joined us—they were sent ahead by Capt Cook—who they left at the Pimas villages, he had got along finely—and took a town in Sonoro[116]—he had fifteen wagons with him, when he was left at the Pimas— The men get along with difficulty—their feet being very sore—We have encamped this evening at Los [Las] Flores—in sight of the ocean—whose roar we can hear—

22^{d} Jany—We left camp early; marched hard—passed the Mission of San Louis Rey, when we saw the Commodores party at a distance—and encamped at a place called bitter water—this is well named— We marched some 18 or 20 miles to day—

23ᵈ Jany to 3ᵈ Febry. On the 23ᵈ we left our camp at the bitter water, and marched out hoping to get to San Diego— it threatened rain—and as we had no tents pushed out accordingly. We arrived late in the evening at San Diego in a heavy storm of rain— We found everything had gone on quietly during our absence. No enemy appeared.—I found Streeter still alive—but extremely emaciated. The abcess on the back & side had returned, and discharged greatly. At first the discharge was extremely foetid, and mixed with air—his respiration much affected—When I returned, he was evidently improving—the discharge continuing, but of a more healthy appearance—his appetite good, night sweats, and hectic—The wound on the Sacrum had improved vastly—it had assumed a healthy appearance—granulations having filled up the cavity, with the exception of a small point on the right side—Carious pieces of bone had been discharged—and still continues to be—small pieces presenting themselves at every dressing—This discharge is not very great and is healthy—at present the Dressings to the sacrum are Solut nit argent, & Ung Resens. With a bandage—to the abscess nothing but cleanliness—No medicine given except Sul morphia & Acid Sul aromat[117]—at night and Wine or Brandy ad lib—with nourishing diet— his appetite now is good, little or no hectic—and very little night sweat—until yesterday he had no passage from his bowels for two weeks, an enema had been given but produced no effect—yesterday it was repeated and produced a slight effect. the retention of the faeces had produced no ill effects—his appetite is good, digestion good and respiration easy—no inconvenience in breathing from lying on back or either side. Child is about the same as when I left him at the Puebla—he was brought from that place on a ship—and came into Hospital on the 27ᵗʰ of Jany— the discharge is not healthy from the wound—being thin and rather foetid, there is a slight swelling of the ankle, and some pain and swelling, about each Malleolus—I think a slight fluctuation upon careful examination—he can move the Ankle joint and complains of little or no pain—With the probe hard substances can be detected which I think, are pieces of bone—he felt something move yesterday as if it were a piece of bone on the ball—his general health is good—appetite good, bowels regular—poultices & cold to the ankle has been the only dressing up to this time, McNealy—has nearly recovered—

Brown has anchylosis of the left arm, at the Elbow joint—and Crabb of the right Elbow and loss of power of movement, and numbness of the index finger of the right hand—the wounds have all healed—Osbornes [James A. Osbourne's] neck has got straight—and [John? or Amasa?] Palmer—has numbness and some pain about the right hip from his wound—

Col Cook arrived with his battalion of Mormons at the Mission of San Diego—Jany 29—1847— Genˡ Kearny, with Capt Turner and Lt Warner sailed for the north—on the Sloop Cyane on the 31st of Jany— We are all getting along here very agreeably. Cook has marched with his men to the Mission of San Luis Rey—where he will remain— I am now in charge of Hospital with our wounded it not being considered safe to remove Streeter— The Sloop Portsmouth sails to day for the coast of Mexico— Emory went as bearer of despatches from General Kearny—to the US—via Panama—in the brig *Maleckadel* [Malek Adhel][118]

Hospital and Other Affairs at San Diego

27th Febry. I still remain at San Diego—in charge of the Hospital—having only two sick dragoons Streeter and Child— Streeter has continued to improve—not rapidly however—his strength is much increased—appetite good —and not so much emaciated— the wound on the sacrum presents a healthy aspect—but does not heal fast in consequence of his being obliged to lay on his back— occasionelly—particularly when he has a passage—after being constipated for several days—he suffers greatly from twitchings in and around the wound—for the last few days the surface of the sore has been smooth, and no speculae of bone presented— The abcess in the side and back continues to discharge freely—an old cicatrix—near the spine—opened—and discharged freely—a few days since— his breathing is not affected—in whatever position he may assume, there are two or three little gatherings under the arm in the axilla—presenting much the appearance of bladders—these do not pain but have to be carefully washed, as they are apt to excoriate—the Sacrum & hip both excoriated—curing under the effects of Emplast Saponis[119]— to procure sleep it is still necessary to continue the Morphine and Acid Aromat— his diet is of the most nourishing quality & he has brandy, wine, & milk punch ad lib, Dressings to sacrum slightly stimulating—band[a]ge—cleanliness alone to abscess— Child upon the whole is better— The wound has closed—it discharged several pieces of bone from the heel— and some small pieces could be felt when the wound closed—The inflamed part is entirely confined around the internal Malleolus—two small abcesses have burst just below this point—and two days since I made free incisions near this point—but nothing of the ball could be discovered—the pain and inflammation is entirely confined to a small place around the internal Malleolus No appearance of swelling or pain at any other point— he cant move his ankle without causing pain—and hobbles about on his crutch— A man by name [Eugene] Russell—a Volunteer has been in hospital for two weeks— with Typhoid Fever—he had been sick for some time previous to being admitted. When he was admitted his pulse slow—skin cool—tongue dry and glossy—Mind much affected—not being able to fix his attention at any time upon any subject. When questioned answered slowly and frequently not to the purpose—deaf—picking at bed clothes &c— his treatment Cal[omel]—

purgatives—Wine—Quinine—blistering &c&c—cups to Spine—& abdomen & shaving head, his gums touched with mercury— on the 24th he had low muttering delirium passing urine & faeces unconsciously in which state he is at present—his gums have been touched with mercury but I do not see that it has done any good. This fever I should judge was common to the country as it is the fourth case I have seen of it.

As to public affairs we know little or nothing— The Sloop Dale passed by here some time since—on her way to Panama, by this vessel we learned of the arrival of Commodore Shubrick in the Independance—at Monterey— and also of the arrival of the Lexington, with the artillery from the U.S. That Commodore Biddle in the line of battle Ship Columbus would soon be here[120]— We have also had a visit from the Secretary of State, Co^l Russell[121] —who arrived at this place from the Puebla—on the 22^d of February—he was received on the Congress with a salute of five guns— from this gentleman we learned that all was peace and quietness about the puebla—that the Californians were well contented— The Co^l had with him a Californian—named *Boneea* (I believe) [José Mariano Bonilla?] this man was appointed a Captain by Fremont—he is said to be a fellow of notorious bad character—a gambler and the very first man who entered into the last revolution— two Californian gentlemen, who have been our friends since we landed here— who have contributed as much as any men in the country to the success of our flag—and had been appointed captains by Commodore Stockton, offered their resignations upon hearing of the appointment of this fellow Boneea, one of the above mentioned persons Don San Iego, offered to resign.[122] Don Miguel Pedreorano[123]—did not offer to resign, but informed me that he would do so if thrown in contact with Boneea. The Secretary of State [Colonel Russell] entered into conversations with the different officers freely and seemed to me to be very anxious to get their opinions as regards Fremonts controversy with Genl Kearny— The Co^l & myself had quite a hot discussion entering unpremeditated on my part but the whole tenor of his conversation seemed to invite argument and discussion— from this discussion I learned that Fremonts commission as Governor had been dated back to November 1846— Now I know from having heard Commodore Stockton so style himself—particularly on the occasion when the Flag of truce was received from Flores, near San Matteo—that he (Stockton) regarded himself as the Governor and Commander in chief of California—and I believe every officer so understood it—and moreover he was so regarded up to the day previous to Genl K's leaving the puebla.

About the 20th of this month Beale & Carson left for the U.S. via the Gila route and Santa Fe—they carryd despatches and a minister extraordinary from Fremont— from this place Russell sent a courrier to Carson, who had orders to remain at Warners pass until he received further instructions from

Fremont, Engineering is a great trade—all of our big guns are by the ears—and how the war [?] will terminate we shall see— Major Swords arrived from the Islands (Sandwich) on Feby [19]—he brought some provisions, but no money, for this article we are all suffering much— When we shall get away the lord knows—as neither the paymaster or Quarter master have one cent— On the 22^d the Commodore gave an elegant blow out on board of the Congress. The decorations were the flags of different nations, and the deck of the ship made decidedly the finest ball room I ever saw. We had all the ladies from San Diego, and everything went off in fine style—We have a little dance every evening at Señor [Juan] Bandini's, and upon the whole our time passes off agreeably— Last night I dreamed that there was another revolution, in my sleep I distinctly saw the Mexican flag—This dream has made a Strong impression on my mind—I do not put faith in dreams—but I thought I would note this—

10th March—The man Russell died of the fever—the Wounded men, Streeter & Child have continued to improve, Journalizing is rather dull work in these piping times of peace— The other day—the Julia arrived from the Puebla, bringing the report of the arrival of the Sloop Erie—at Monterey with a Co^l Mason on board[124]—this is supposed to be Co^l Mason of the 1s^t Drags who comes out here it is said to take the command of Stevensons Regiment—Stevenson to be Governor— several papers called the Californian published in Monterey by a chaplain of the navy called [Walter] Colton—were received[125]—These papers contain, what I think will be the commencement of a violent paper war between Kearny and Stockton—the piece referred to is a letter from the Angeles, giving an account of the march on that place and its being taken, by the forces under Commodore Stockton, Kearny is left out of the question entirely—and dirt thrown on his and Mervine's head for the Action of San Pascual & Domingos [Dominguez] Ranch[126]— A report from Gillespie was received, stating that he had been informed in the Puebla by a Californian who was in both actions—that they lost 27—killed and wounded at Pascual and 85 killed & wounded—(55 of whom have since died) at San Gabriel & the Mesa—

The weather has been excessively cold of late. The mountains to the south are covered with snow—and it hailed quite hard—a few days ago.

The influenza prevails at present as an Epidemic— It is attended with considerable fever—it seems to be from accounts very severe about San Luis & the puebla— Up to this time none of the Dragoons have had the disease—though they are nearly naked—and quite barefooted— The disease seems to be confined almost entirely to natives of the country— I believe I have not recorded here as I intended the honesty of my friends the Pimas Indians—the goods & mules that were left with them by General Kearny for Cooks command were untouched—although they had been advised to take them by the Mexicans—

CALIFORNIA: CONQUEST, CASUALTIES, CURES 77

14th March—We have had two arrivals from the Puebla in the last two days—the first the little French doctor[127]—who had been an assistant Surgeon in the California Battalion— he did not bring much news except that the Governor was extremely polite to all the natives—attended balls of all descriptions and that he was very popular, he said that there had been drank at a ball at that place—a health to the Independance of California—this however was denied by the second arrival— these were Mr. Dent [?], clerk to Paymaster Cloud[128] and Paymaster Redding [Reading] of the California battalion. The news brought by these gentlemen was very important— first it seems that Fremont has heard that there is a force marching from Sonora—some two thousand strong under the Command of General Castro and Pio Pico— This seems to have some foundation—as Fremont has sent a force to Warners pass of one hundred and seventy five men, and four pieces of Artillery. There seems also to be apprehensions of another rising in the country—the movements of persons who would likely be leaders seems to have attracted attention— The disappearance of large numbers of the best horses in the country—would seem to give farther confirmation to the reports—Major Redding says that a large band of horses have been discovered in the mountains—"cashed"— At this time our men are certainly not in a fit situation to take the field—no blankets—clothing or shoes—it is rather a bad showing for a march— Fremont sent an express to the north—so we will certainly have an arrival in a few days— he spoke of the suffering of an Emigrant party in the mountains—18 of whom attempted to come in—12 men and 6 women—The men all perished—all of the women were brought in on the backs of Indians—they were forced to eat of the bodies of those who were dead—in one case a woman eat part of her brother.[129] The weather has become warmer—but is still disagreeably cold in the shade—the cattarrhal fever that prevailed so extensively begins to abate—this epidemic seems confined to natives of the country or persons who have resided here a long time.

17th March—On the 15th, Lt Halleck of the Engineers arrived from Monterey[130]—he came around Cape Horn with the Artillery— he brought orders from the General—it seems that the Government stood up to the General—and Fremont give up. The troops at San Luis Rey are to garrison that point—the Puebla—and this place One Company—B—of the Mormon Battalion got in to day. Major Swords, Cloud & Lt Halleck left for the north this morning—Lt Stoneman[131] with his detachment of Dragoons also left for the puebla de los Angeles—where the dragoons are to be stationed— Halleck informed us of the arrival of Commodore Biddle in the Columbus—It seems the report of the invasion of the Sonoranians, was all as I thought it would turn out—for Buncombe Fremont I suppose did not wish to go to Monterey, so the report originated and the men were not sent to Warners pass

I believe that the fruit trees about here are in bloom. There are precious few of them, however. I mean of the trees not of the bloom— The wild oats are heading out, but are not more than 6 or 8 inches high— The animals are getting quite fat, but a horse is a most useless animal to a man situated as I am here—if he is kept up for riding he will starve to death—and if he is allowed to run out you will lose him—so I think they are most useless— My sick men continue to improve—Streeter's wounds are healing—but he has a bad cough —which I am fearful will ultimately carry him off—Child is nearly well so far at least as appearances go—

27th Yesterday the Frigate Savanah left this port for the U.S. she had been laying off this harbour for two or three days—last from Monterey—does not bring much news— However a portion of Stevenson's regiment has arrived[132]—and the rest may be expected shortly. Many reports reach here but no great faith should be placed in them. The dispute for the governorship seems to have ceased, although efforts are being made yet to retain Fremont in power. He Fremont seems to have become immensely popular with the Californians, at least one would be led to believe so— A petition, remonstrance or something of the sort was received here—brought by Don San Jego [Santiago Argüello], on the bark Julia from the Puebla. I did not see this paper, but so far as I could learn the purport of it was, a remonstrance against Kearnys taking upon himself the office of governor. This has been circulated at all the towns. This paper created much excitement here— An order was also received by Don San Jeago—directing not to turn over horses —Guns &c to any officer or Corps unless by special order from Fremont or, to an agent of his— Commodore Stockton did not go home on the Savanah—

The health of the place has improved since I last wrote in my journal. The weather has become warm and pleasant—and the influenza has passed off— Among the Mormons I have two cases—one of Dysenteria the other Febris —quite severe Streeter has suffered very much of late—his wounds continue to heal—but his appetite is bad, bowels irregular—Colliquetive sweats —and about the same hour every day suffers greatly from pain. This seems to be over the whole back— Morphia relieves him when he remains comparatively easy for the next twenty-four hours— Child continues about the same—not much improvement—

20th [30th?] March. Journalizing continues to be a most dull and profitless employment. Nothing of private or public interest going on, and take it all in all I am heartily tired of life in San Diego. A mail route from hence to San Francisco, to be carried by soldiers has been established to arrive every 15 days—This goes to show that there has been some improvement. The establisment of the Capital at Monterey seems to give great dissatisfaction to the Californians— We have had many rumors of combats with the Indians, about the Puebla—according to these reports the dragoons have been thrashed, killed &c without doing much injury— We have heard since that all reports are false, with the exception that the Dragoons killed four Indians & took two or 3 prisoners—and one or two Dragoons slightly injured— These reports seem to be originated about the Puebla by some malicious persons for the purpose of annoying—There seems to have been quite an excitement at the puebla, upon the arrival of Cook with his battalion at that place. Capt Owens then in command of the California Battalion refused to deliver up artillery &c as he had reecived orders from Fremont[133]—orders not to give up until he Fremont returned from Monterey— The Captain held out, and quite a sparring match took place—so far as wit and badinage was concerned —and from all I hear the Captain in this contest, got rather the better of Cook. Col Mason arrived and put all things to rights— What has become of the California Battalion—we have not learned—or what course will be taken by Fremont—or what will be done with him seems to be uncertain. We have had a little official correspondence here between Santiego E Arguello, and our Mormon Captain [Jesse D.] Hunter, Fremont had given to Santiego as a Captain in the California Battalion an order, not to deliver up horses, artillery &c &c at this point. This order he signed—not as Lt Co^l or Governor, but with his name alone— When called upon by Mason to know whether he had ever given such an order—he denied it— Dr. Sanderson wrote to me by Col Masons request to obtain this order if possible or a copy of it—Cook at the same time ordered Hunter to obtain it—Of course I merely gave my assistance to Hunter—Santiego would not give the order or copy—

The prejudice against the Mormons here seems to be wearing off—it is yet among the Californians a great term of reproach to be called Mormon—yet as they are a quiet, industrious, sober, inoffensive people—they seem to be gradually working their way up— they are extremely industrious—they have been engaged while here in digging wells, plastering houses, and seem anxious and ready to work— The Californians have no great idea of their soldier like quallities and in action would not dread them much—this arises in a great measure from their dress—carriage &c—which is as unlike any soldier—as any thing could possibly be—Yet I think if brought into action they would prove themselves good men—as I am told they are generally fine shots—and they drill—tolerably well— They are barefooted and almost naked—several of them are sick—with Intermittent fever— The day before yesterday a merchantman named the Moscow, arrived in port from the north—no news— She is in a leaky condition—and with difficulty was brought into port—she applied to Commodore Stockton for assistance, and it was at once given— The Commodore had appointed this day for leaving the port—but in consequence of the necessity of giving the Ship assistance it is said he will not go for several days. A Vessel came into port from the North this morning—believed to be the Julia—though not certainly known yet— Streeter has improved rapidly since I last noticed his case—his cough has ceased in a great measure little or no pain on the back—abscess healed up & I believe solid & well Wound on sacrum nearly healed Child has also improved—

23ᵈ April—Last night an express arrived from the Puebla de los Angeles—and went aboard the Congress immediately— Report says there is a duel on the tapis between Col Mason & Fremont—the latter challenged Mason—who accepted. The affair was to have come off at the Puebla but for some cause, was postponed until the arrival of the parties at Monterey; the weapons chosen double barrell shot guns;[134] no other news—

25 April—This evening another express arrived from the Puebla—and went immediately aboard, what the contents of the despatches were I have not learned— a report reached here from the Puebla that 1500 Mexicans were marching on us—and the commanding officer directed to be vigilant—and also that munitions of war had been landed some place or other— from all I can learn from the Puebla there seems to be some doubt whether Fremont ever gave Santiago Arguello the orders—spoken of by me in a letter to Dr Sanderson. S wrote me that when called on by Mason to know whether or not he had issued orders to Santiago, that Fremont denied having done so, as Commander of the California Battalion— The following is a true copy—word for word of the order. Lt Maddox[135] of the Marine Corps has a certified copy—

Cuidad de los Angeles—
18 March 1847.

Sir,

You are hereby ordered to take especial care of all the public arms, & munitions of war including artillery &c &c for which I am liable & turn them over to no Corps without my especial order, or the order of some authorized acting under me.—

Very Respectfully
Yr Obdt Servt
(Signed)   J. C. FREMONT.

To Capt Don
   Santiago Arguello
     Calif. Battln.

Cuidad de los Angeles.
18 March 1847.

Sir

You are hereby ordered at your most convenient opportunity and with as little delay as possible to collect all the horses belonging to government—between this point and San Diego, and keep them subject to my order, or the order emenating from some officer under my orders—

Very Respectfully
Your Obdt Servt—
(Signed)   J. C. FREMONT.

To Capt D
   Santiago Arguillo
     Calif Battln.

If the above be not orders then I have never seen one. They are not signed officially, but they are directed so—and it would seem that the whole tenor of the order was that a superior, the commander, was giving the most positive instructions to an inferior— It is said the Congress leaves here tomorrow—

27 April. Last night the wife of Captain Hunter died of Typhoid fever—or rather I think a malignant form of Quotidian fever. The attack was issued [ushered] in with severe rigors, some six days ago—with great difficulty of breathing and oppression, followed by high fever. About 11 A M each day the same attack came—with cramps & irregular nervous twitchings—serous diarrhoea—mind affected—purgative of Calomel, Massa ex Hyd &c given until slight ptyalism produced—her breasts became inflamed, and before death suppurated. The nervous twitchings were stopped by the use of small doses of morphia & Assafoetida. The chill checked by Quinine—her brain became very much excited Delirium for two days previous to death—and deafness— She finally died last night about 10 P M in great pain— This was the first American woman who ever bore a child in San Diego—

The Frigate Congress got out of the harbor yesterday. She sails today for the South, if there be any truth in the report of the arrival of a Mexican force to the South. Commodore Stockton proclaimed his intention of fighting them, if there was any chance of success—his object is also to ascertain if there be any truth in the report as to arms having been landed— San Vincente [Vicente] & San Tomassa [Santo Tomás] are said to be the points where they were landed—it is said a French brig brought them there from Acapulco. Stockton made a speech to his men before sailing yesterday—it seems from what he says that if pushed to the last, he will make the pass of San Vincente as renowned as Termopylae [Thermopylae]. Ye Gods what gass—

6th May—So little happens at San Diego, that journalizing is a most dull business, one naturally takes notice of all the reports—and considering the communication we have a plenty of them, on the 28th the Merchant Ship Vandalia, arrived from the north. She created quite an excitement as she is so large and fine a vessel, that she was taken for a Man of War. On the 2d of May, paymaster Cloud arrived and payed the Troops—on the 4th this has created some excitement— and then the Captain of the Mormon Company, arrested a fellow—an Englishman named Johnson, servant to the priest at San Tomassa, as a spy— This man professed to have been aboard of the ship, said to have brought arms— he reported that the Captain had told him there were arms aboard—but he has told so many stories that one does not know what to credit— I think there is little doubt however that arms have been landed—but whether they will be used or not is another question— A man arrived from lower California a few days since—who reported all things were quiet there— he says the Commodore, with Santiago Arguello, Don Miguel [Pedrorena] & twenty men had gone from Santa Vincente to San Tomassa to look for the arms—that no Mexican troops had been heard of— On the 4th a man named Walker arrived from the Aqua Calliente—who reports that the Indians from the Corasita, had come in—reporting that a large body of people were coming in by that route. What they were the Indians did not know— The reports of Mexican troops coming caused the greatest alarm and uneasiness among the residents of this place—they have been extremely friendly to the American cause—in fact the only place in California where natives are really friendly, and if the Mexicans should come and gain only a temporary advantage—they would suffer very much— from the movements of the Californians some faith seems to have been placed, in the reports, and it was believed that mischief of some sort was intended— On the 5th Mr. Norris[136] Secretary to Commodore Stockton arrived via Monterey—from the United States—he came on the Sloop of War Preble from Monterey or Callao— he brings little or no news— The determination on the part of the President [James K. Polk] to prosecute the War with great vigour—and the ready compliance of Congress with his views, seems to be the best— flying reports are said to have reached Monterey that the Castle of San Juan De Ulloa has been taken—and that Taylor has had another fight, in which he was victorious—That Santa Anna has been deposed—and General [Gabriel] Valencia takes his place— Mr. Norris arrived here from San Pedro in the schooner Julia— If an enemy be coming we are not making very extensive preparations to meet him— The Mormons after their payment took a little spree—some few men drunk and two or three black eyes—or small fights occurred—but much less drinking gambling &c occurred among them than I have ever witnessed among any troops after a payment— They are extremely industrious—and avaricious. They get all the pelf they can—and keep all they get. They are constantly employed by the citizens, and one is engaged in constructing a horse mill—This is looked upon in San Diego—as the greatest feat that has been ever undertaken in these parts. We have an Alcalde named Fitch[137]—an old sea Captain—who knows about as much of law as he does of religion— two Yankees got into a law suit the other day—one accused the other of stealing mules, horses &c— The party accused was defended by a Mormon lawyer— The fellow acknowledged several of the charges brought against him—but the Lawyer so confused the judge that he not only found the man guiltless, but ordered the accuser to pay all costs— Therefore the Mormon lawyer and the accused party determined to bring suit against the accuser so that damages might be obtained for slander. When they notified the judge that they wished to bring the suit—he asked who would try the case— You—answered the Mormon lawyer—I'll see you damned first replied the Judge—and what is more if you bother me any more with your damned suits I'll put the whole gang of you to work—

and this ended the matter. My patients are all doing well. Streeter begins to walk about—his wounds having healed. The weather is damp and cold and he complains of some pain in consequence. Child is doing well—

11th May. Yesterday the Congress and Julia came in sight About 1 AM this morning several of the officers came up to town—diligent search had been made for the arms &c said to be deposited at San Vincente and San Tomassa—but nothing could be discovered. The Ship had been in the port as had been reported, but no arms seems to have been landed. The Commodore despatched Indians to the Rio Colorado, who brought back word that there was no sign of a Mexican force but that the Indians were taken [waging] a small private war out there on their own account. Lt Rowan U S N & Mr Norris, Commodore Stockton's secretary started from here this morning for Monterey by land—The Congress did not enter the port, but will sail directly for Monterey—where it is said the Commodore will take another ship and sail directly for the U.S. The Thos. H. Perkins a transport ship touched us on the 7th of May—on her way to Manilla— Last night I was so unfortunate as to have a man of the Mormon Battalion to die—Private Albert Dunham of B Company died about 3 A.M. this morning— On the 7th of May after playing ball—and exercising rather freely—he was suddenly seized with violent pains in the back of the neck & head (he had been subject to Rheumatic Attacks) he was brought in Hospital May 8th—The pains were extremely severe in the neck and back of the head, bowels costive, pulse full but not quicker or harder than natural skin natural—was sullen and evinced little disposition to answer question when addressed, ℞ Massa ex Hyd. Ext Colocynth Comp aa x Grs—and apply a stimulating liniment on warm flannel cloths to neck— on the morning of the 9th was some better The medicine had operated freely, and the Liniment and external warmth seemed to give some relief—although the pain was still severe. The pulse and skin seemed little affected, ℞ Sul Mag℥j Tart Ant i Gr. Aqua of M [Several illegible words follow, possibly in shorthand.] wine glass full every half hour till free operations are produced—Continue warm applications— in the evening some salts had operated very freely— The pain still continuing cups no 6 applied to back of neck—At bed time warm applications— ℞ Massa ex Hyd x Grs—Ipecac i Gr, Opii i Gr—& repeat often & Ipecac if he cant sleep—he has not slept any for two nights— 10—in morning was found to be much worse—had rested but little during the night— Inflammation and some discoloration around the right eye—Delirium—tongue not coated nor has it been— ℞ ol Ricini ℥j[138]—Apply blister to back of neck— The inflammation of Eye continued to increase rapidly—and the discoloration spread over the temple and part of the forehead, The swelling of the Eye about 2 PM— was enormous and looked as if it would burst—The Tunics much injected, and the pupil apparently perfectly insensible—at least it did not contract or dilate At first an Emolient poultice applied—but could not be retained in consequence of his picking at it—as in fact he was constantly doing at the bed clothing Stimulating Enemas given blisters to Extremities &c—without the slightest effect   (when the Inflammation of Eye was first noticed cups applied to the Temple)—At bed time X Grs Calomel given— he rapidly got worse About 3 PM—his Extremities commenced getting cold, his pulse being much depressed—Delirium—breathing with difficulty—and he finally expired about 3 A M this morning— he was comatose several hours before death—and could not be roused sufficiently at any time during the day, so as to give a rational answer to any question. Post Mortem, The Brain was carefuly examined about 10 hours after death The veins of the Dura Mater much distended with blood, the ventricles full of a Bloody serum, and a deposite on the arachnoid resembling coagulable lymph—This could not be removed with a sponge and water—

Los Angeles Under Colonel Stevenson
Treatment of the Sick

June 5th 1847. I left San Diego May 13 1847, by order of Lt Col. Cooke—and arrived in the Puebla de los Angeles, in two days and a half. The next day went to duty. Genl Kearny left the day before I arrived—for San Pedro where he would embark on one of the U.S. Vessels for Monterey—from thence he would go to the United States as soon as practicable— I was informed of the *pleasant* news that I might expect to make California my home for some time to come—That is to say if the Californians will allow us to do so—and I think they are great fools if they do—for in a short time our force will be much reduced by the Mormon Battalion being disbanded—and then we leave some points where there is plenty of cannon, San Diego for instance so guarded —that it only invites attack. I found much sickness in the command, and a great disposition on the part of the men of Col Stevensons Regiment to shirk work. They are all engaged in building a fort on the hill and this digging goes decidedly against the Stomachs of these valiant volunteers of the 7th N. Y. R. V. The fact is they are the poorest material for Soldiers I have ever seen—broken down gentlemen, infirm tradesmen &c &c at least it is so with the two Companies E. & G. stationed here.

On the Morning of the 4th of June I was requested to see an old Man at the House of Mr Prior [Nathaniel Miguel Pryor], near this place. The old man had been bitten in several places by a dog on the 23 of March last— All the wounds—(which were very severe) had healed up with the exception of one through the right hand—this had continued to discharge but slightly—occasionally showing disposition to mortification—a little stimulating ointment had been used which generally caused the hand to assume a healthy appearance— The man had been much reduced by the long confinement—though he was still quite corpulent— he had been improving very fast up to the night of the 3rd of June—only complaining of wandering pains—over his body and in the abdomen— This he attributed to Rheumatism—which he had been subject to— during the night he was seized with a desire to drink water—which he found it imposible for him to do in consequence as he described it, of a ball rising in his throat— When I saw him which was about 5½ A M he was sane, but seemed to be in great distress suffering from the want of sleep—he was extremely sleepy, and thirsty—it seemed to produce violent agitation through out his whole system to even look upon water— I urged him to take some water—he attempted it several times—it seemed a violent effort for him to take the cup—when he brought it to his mouth, it seemed to produce the most violent convulsive movements of the muscles of his throat—abdomen and chest—He did take with a great effort a little thin corn meal gruel—This aversion to fluids increased until he could not bear to hear the word water mentioned—The mention of it causing him the most terrible fright and convulsions—he vomited and strained constantly in efforts to vomit—until he ruptured some small blood vessel— his mind about 12 M became flighty but upon speaking he gave a rational answer—his pulse was at each examination gradually weaker and more rapid. The saliva viscid and hard to expectorate— The hand looked as if mortification had taken place to a considerable extent— his eyes blood shot—he gradually grew worse, his mind wandering and confused— A short time before death he became sane—At this time he took a little *attole* [atole]—mixed with 3 V of Tinct opii—it produced no effect— he died about 8 A.M. on the morning of the 5th—

There was no news in the country everything seems quiet—though so far as I can see no particular good feeling among the men—the women seem better contented—

9 July. Since I last wrote, nothing of public importance in the vicinity has taken place, rumors of revolution are constantly afloat, a flagstaff has been erected on the hill, within the Fort. The flag was first hoisted on the 4th July, salutes fired, and the work christened Fort Moor. This ceremony seems to have given our friends the Californians great offence—during the time the staff was being erected various threats were made that it would be burned or cut down and supplanted by a better looking one with the Mexican colors—from the tone of feeling throughout the country, I have no doubt the slightest cause, would light up another revolution, The arrival of a single hundred men from Sonora would produce this effect—particularly at this time as the Mormon Battalion will be discharged in a few days—and Colonel [Henry S.] Burton of the 7th N.Y.R.V. and his companies leave for the South, to occupy La Paz—a port in lower California; our Company is at Santa Barbara—and our garrisons seem to be scattered about over the country in like force— San Diego an important point will be left entirely without a garrison and the

only force in this section of the country will be one Company of Dragoons dismounted, and two companies of N.Y. Volunteers— We have threats made constantly against us—and yet our governors and Commandants by their acts would seem to invite a revolution—by keeping all their force in the north, both army and Navy—On the morning of the 5th of July a most barbarous assassination was committed on a frenchman [Julien Bertalot] by whom the act was committed is not known but suspicion attaches to one of our Dragoons by name [Samuel E.] Cooper—also a Store was Robbed the same night of a large amount of money—This Robbery was no doubt committed by Soldiers of the Volunteer Regiment, and one Dragoon— On the night of the 4th we had a ball given by the officers in honor of the day,[139] and also one by the non commissioned officers—everything went off very pleasantly except one little circumstance. Don Jose Antonio Carrillo thought proper to express his decided disapprobation of the mode of dancing of the American officers—and said they were like all the rest of their nation beasts. The officers hearing of this determined to kick up a small fuss— the Colonel Stevenson hearing of the affair determined to call all hands to his quarters next morning and at supper accordingly invited every body— we assembled the next morning had a speech from the Coronel defining our position &c— One remark he made was not exactly agreed to by the Juniors, that was that an officer receiving an insult from a Californian the affair should be taken notice of by the Authorities—& Vice Versa— This was objected to, as the officers claimed the right of looking out for their own private quarrels— One of the Mormon officers who was more particularly alluded to than the rest had determined to castigate the Don, but the public manner in which the Colonel had noticed it seemed to preclude any course of the kind, and particularly as the persons then and there did take a drink to the said Don José Antonio— Jose Antonio acknowledged the soft impeachment of having called us a parcel of beasts but declared he had no intention of making it public a great deal of gass was expended on the occasion—but the affair was settled—and without some farther provocation, I suppose there will hardly be a fight. Col Burton brought us the news of Genl Scotts two victories of Vera Cruz and Puenta Nacional, a salute was fired in consequence— and notices stuck up at the alcalde's office which were duly cut to pieces and destroyed during the night. Our friends here have no good will toward us, and would if they only dared cut our throats with great pleasure.

There has been considerable sickness of late among the troops stationed here—an Epidemic Catarrh, very obstinate and attended with fever. On the morning of the 4th of July about 2½ A M Hammerly [John Hemerle] of Co C 1st Dragoons died—of Typhoid Fever—He had been a prisoner, and tried by a general court marshal—this seemed to have a great effect on him.

14th of August. As to public affairs we have absolutely nothing going on; our friends the Californians, received via Sonora the Mexican papers—detailing Scott & Taylors movements in Mexico—the taking of Vera Cruz the levying of taxes by old Taylor for the destruction of his baggage train, and the battle of *puente nacional*, seems to have acted as a soporific on their warlike feelings— talk of revolt now is not even heard of—every thing in that way is as quiet as possible—rumors of Indian hostilities seems even to have been forgotten—although I think the Californians have done their best to embroil us with a tribe called the St Luis Indians.—These fellows are however our warm friends. An Agent has been recently appointed, Capt Hunter late of the Mormon Battalion, this I hope will have the effect of quieting all reports— The Colonel leaves here to day for the purpose of holding council with all the Indians at San Luis Rey— Occasionally a rumor gets here from the North of disturbance between the Governors and the American settlers in the North— The ground of the difficulty seems to be the Mission lands, upon which our western men, following their true instinct and old habit have squatted—and are rather inclined to appropriate the lands &c to their own use— this the Governor objects to as the lands are private property, and as usual in such cases much talk—but no blood as yet—

The Company at Santa Barbara seems to have got in rather a disorganized State—and caused a court martial, the result of which was to send four of the number to Monterey in irons This seems to have quieted every thing— At this place every thing is quiet. Our military guard mounting is quite a show. Robbery has become very common of late—Stores, houses, persons riding & picking pockets. No less than five Robberys have taken place lately to considerable amounts—and the murder that occurred about the 4 of July— The worst of it is—there seems to be no means of finding out who are the authors of the crimes—So long as the Alcaldes supposed that it was a Dragoon who committed the murder they were excessively energetic—but the evidence being clear that the man was not guilty—no further prosecution was had in the case—

Sickness has prevailed to great extent both among the troops and the population here among the men—[William] Hopper of Co E died July [blank]. [Thomas] Bosquet Co. E. on 8 of August—[Charles A.] Webster Co E—on the 17th of August—all died—with the same fever:[140] The attack of this disease is not violent—but gradual—preceeded for some time—(in the two last cases it was so) by Diarrhoea, thin yellow, watery discharges—tongue coated, pulse not exhibiting much signs of disease or febrile action— in a few days the symptoms became worse—the tongue becoming black—chapped—and border around the teeth—slight delirium—nervous twitchings kicking at the bed clothes—position on back—and falling down in bed towards the foot— The Diarrhoea usually continues through the disease When checked, it becomes worse in other cases the tongue has been smooth the edges red—the centre dry & chapped, Post Mortem of two cases has shown that inflammation was present in mucous membrane of Small intestines Stomach—& large intestines—that ulcers had formed in the Duodenum, illieum, and in the Colon, in Webster there were many points of the intestines infected and inflamed as if ulceration were about to commence, The ulcers were large—ragged—and containing in their center a yellow spot— When this yellow substance was removed, the whole mucous and muscular tunics of the intestine seemed to be removed with it—The bowels in both cases contained little but discolored matter— in Webster the gall Bladder full of yellow bile—the liver I do not think was diseased—except it might have been larger than usual—I did not observe that the Spleen was diseased— The pancreas was extremely hard and indurated—the urinary bladder empty and much contracted—Heart and lungs healthy—

The fever seems to take to the remittent form—and keeps to this type through the whole course of the disease—There are many other men who have had the fever—but are now either convalescing or have recovered— I have not remarked that any course of treatment was particularly successful—Sul Quinine does not seem to have as good an effect here as I have observed in the fevers of the U.S—Mercury seems to be the best remedy— The people of the country are not exempt from the fever—among them however so far as I have seen Quinine answers every expectation. The cause of this difference I cannot account for—except it be that the unacclimated Americans—from the change of climate are more subject to Gastric enteric affections—from the heat of the climate, and possibly the dryness—as there has not been rain here since May—diseases of the Bowels such as colic—Diarrhoea, Dysenteria are very common, This I think is no doubt to be attributed to eating fruit—unripe.—The Diet of the Country is almost exclusively fresh meat, Beef—and a coarse Bread—tortillias, &c—made of corn meal or Wheat badly ground— The Diet of the soldiers is 4 times a week Beef— 3 times pork—and Bread of fine American flour— The Bread so far as I have seen is well baked, The men who have died—and had the disease worst— were generally temperate, Stout young men, two of the fatal cases—Hammerly—the Dragoon—and Webster were taken while in the guard House— the first under sentence of general Court Martial for mutinous conduct— the latter arrested for disobedience of orders— Their situation seems [to] have exercised a bad effect on their minds in both cases—and I have no doubt contributed considerably to the fatal termination of their disease— Some time since I extracted a large tumor (in July) from the shoulder of a Californian This tumor must have weighed fifteen pounds— he has recovered rapidly.

Notes

[References to "this *Quarterly*" in the following notes are to the *California Historical Society Quarterly*.]

1. William Hemsley Emory, *Notes of a Military Reconnoissance, from Fort Leavenworth, in Missouri, to San Diego, in California, Including Part of the Arkansas, Del Norte, and Gila Rivers* (Washington, 1848), 30th Cong., 1st sess., S. Exec. Doc. 7; also printed as 30th Cong., 1st sess., H. Exec. Doc. 41. The latter includes Abert's notes and report and Johnston's journal and will be cited in these notes as Emory, *op. cit.* Johnston's diary is also quoted in James Madison Cutts, *The Conquest of California and New Mexico, by the Forces of the United States, in the Years 1846 & 1847* (Philadelphia, 1847).

2. [Juan José Warner, Benjamin Hayes, and Joseph P. Widney], *An Historical Sketch of Los Angeles County, California*... (Los Angeles, 1876).

3. *Pioneer Notes from the Diaries of Judge Benjamin Hayes, 1849-1875* (Los Angeles: Privately printed, 1929).

4. Information concerning the life of Dr. Griffin will be found in Henry Dwight Barrows, "Memorial Sketch of Dr. John S. Griffin," *Historical Society of Southern California Annual Publication*, IV (1898), 183-85. Harris Newmark, *Sixty Years in Southern California, 1853-1913* (Boston and N. Y.: Houghton Mifflin Company, 1930) contains many scattered references to Dr. Griffin, and the story of San Pascual rancho will be found in W. W. Robinson, *Ranchos Become Cities* (Pasadena: San Pasqual Press, 1939), pp. 173-85.

5. The map is entitled "Military Reconnaissance of the Arkansas Rio del Norte and Rio Gila by W. H. Emory, Lieut., Top. Engrs. Assisted from Fort Leavenworth to Santa Fé by Lieuts. J. W. Abert and W. G. Peck, and from Santa Fé to San Diego on the Pacific by Lieut. W. H. Warner and Mr. Norman Bestor, Made in 1846-7, with the advance guard of the 'Army of the West,' under command of Brig. Gen. Stephen W. Kearny, Constructed under the Orders of Col. J. J. Abert, Ch. Corps Top. Engrs., 1847." It was drawn by Joseph Welch and engraved on stone by E. Weber & Co., Baltimore.

6. The dragoon camp was thirteen miles from Santa Fé. General Stephen Watts Kearny's staff consisted of Captain Henry Smith Turner, acting assistant adjutant general; Captain Abraham Robinson Johnston, aide-de-camp; Major Thomas Swords, quartermaster; Lieutenants William Hemsley Emory and William H. Warner, topographical engineers; and John Strother Griffin, assistant surgeon.

7. The first village was Algodones. Barnardeo is in reality Bernalillo. Johnston mentions a third town, Sandia. Emory, *op. cit.*, pp. 567, 568.

8. Lieutenant Emory and Captain Johnston also felt that the Americans came out second best in the horse-mule trading. Emory, *op. cit.*, pp. 46 and 568.

9. Probably Isleta. Emory says that the alcalde of Isleta was an Indian. *Op. cit.*, p. 47. Other settlements passed through on the 30th, according to Johnston, were Paharito, Padillo, and Los Lentes. *Op. cit.*, p. 569.

10. The party encamped at Los Lunas, according to Johnston. *Loc. cit.*

11. Henry Whiting Stanton, second lieutenant of First Dragoons.

12. Emory on this date mentions by name only one village, Belen, in his report, but he says that there were several well cultivated Indian rancherias near it. The camp site is not shown on his map. Emory, *op. cit.*, p. 48. Johnston mentions camping below Puebletors. *Op. cit.*, p. 570.

13. Emory calls it La Lloya and later, La Joya. On that day they passed through the village of Sabinal. Emory, *op. cit.*, pp. 48-49. Johnston states that the camp was opposite La Jozin. *Op. cit.*, p. 570.

14. Sterling Price, colonel of the Second Missouri Infantry, became governor of New Mexico upon his arrival in Santa Fé. He later served the Confederate States in the Civil War.

15. James Allen, captain of First Dragoons, had been sent by Kearny to recruit the Mormon Volunteers. News of Allen's death was received from Colonel Price. Stephen Watts Kearny to Roger Jones, Rio del Norte, October 3, 1846, Kearny Letter Book (original MS in Missouri Historical Society, St. Louis, Missouri).

16. Benjamin D. Moore, captain of First Dragoons. The town eleven or twelve miles away was the town of Polvadera. Emory and Johnston call it "Pulvidera." Emory. *op. cit.*, pp. 49, 57.

17. Philip St. George Cooke, captain of First Dragoons. The Mormon Battalion, consisting of about five hundred men, was recruited in about two weeks and mustered in at Council Bluffs, after the Mormons had begun their migration from Nauvoo, Illinois. The men were to be discharged in California at the end of their service. After Captain Allen's death at Fort Leavenworth, the Mormons marched to Santa Fé under the command of Lt. A. J. Smith, whom they heartily disliked. Cooke was ordered to open a wagon route between Santa Fé and California.

18. Edward V. Sumner, major of Second Dragoons.

19. Johnston says they camped five miles below Polvadera. Emory, *op. cit.*, p. 571. This would be a mile south of present day Lemitar.

20. Companies B, G, and I remained in New Mexico under Major Sumner. Emory, *op. cit.*, p. 572.

21. There are two Doctor Simpsons listed in Heitman's *Register*, Josiah and Richard French. Both served in the Mexican War. Unfortunately the organization in which each served is not given.

22. Thomas Fitzpatrick, the famous mountain man, who had served Kearny as guide on the campaign into New Mexico, was retained to direct the Army of the West to California. When the meeting with Carson took place, Kearny ordered Carson, who was more familiar with the California route, to act as guide, while Fitzpatrick took Carson's mail to Washington. Both men were undoubtedly disappointed at the order. Leroy R. Hafen and William James Ghent, *Broken Hand, the Life Story of Thomas Fitzpatrick, Chief of the Mountain Men* (Denver: The Old West Publishing Company, 1931), pp. 185-87.

23. Rufus Ingalls, second lieutenant of First Dragoons.

24. John Mix Stanley, draughtsman for Emory's party of topographical engineers.

25. According to Johnston, the express consisted of Corporal Joseph Clapin and a Mexican by the name of Tones. They were ordered to ride straight to Major Sumner without stopping—a distance of sixty miles. Emory, *op. cit.*, p. 574.

26. Thomas Swords, major of the Quartermaster Corps.

27. Chorbano is probably Jean B. Charbonneau, who was sent back on October 15 to act as a guide for Captain Cooke and the Mormons.

28. Henry Smith Turner, captain of First Dragoons and acting assistant adjutant general.

29. Robert McKnight had spent nine years in a Chihuahua prison before making his fortune in the copper mine, Santa Rita del Cobre. In 1828 Kit Carson had worked for him on the copper mine road as a teamster. The hostility of the Apaches had been a decided handicap. Edwin L. Sabin, *Kit Carson Days* (New York: The Press of the Pioneers, Inc., 1914), pp. 35-37. See also Emory, *op. cit.*, pp. 58-59 and 577-78.

30. Red Sleeve, Black Knife and Lasady, according to Johnston, were the three principal chiefs of the Apaches on the west of the Del Norte. Emory, *op. cit.*, p. 579.

31. John Wynn Davidson, second lieutenant of First Dragoons.

NOTES

32. Abraham R. Johnston, captain of First Dragoons and aide-de-camp to General Kearny.

33. Cf. Emory, *op. cit.,* pp. 64 and 581-82.

34. Cf. *op. cit.,* pp. 65-69 and 584-86.

35. "About five miles from camp, we fell upon the great stealing road of the Apaches; it was hard beaten, and in places many yards wide, filled with horses' mules' and cattle tracks, the latter all going one way—from Sonora. . . ." Johnston, in Emory, *op. cit.,* p. 586. According to Johnston the army used the "Kiataro" (Coyotero) trail for several days, still being on it November 5. *Op. cit.,* p. 591. Ruxton notes the incursions of the Apaches and Comanches and the resulting devastation in parts of northern Mexico. George Frederick Ruxton, *Adventures in Mexico and the Rocky Mountains* (London, 1847), pp. 100-2.

36. "Quietero" is Griffin's version of Coyoteros, a division of the Apaches. The Spanish meaning is wolf-men, so-called, supposedly because they ate wolves and coyotes but more probably because of their roving habits. Frederick Webb Hodge, ed., *Handbook of American Indians North of Mexico* (Washington, D. C., 1907-10), (Smithsonian Institution, Bureau of American Ethnology, Bull. 30) I, 356.

37. Mt. Dallas was named for George Mifflin Dallas. It does not appear on Emory's map.

38. Chief Juan José was killed by James Johnston and a man named Glisson. The party attacked by the Apaches was the Charles Kent party of twenty-two, trappers on the Gila. Bancroft gives reference to Benjamin D. Wilson, "Observations" (MS), whose party was also captured on the Gila. Wilson, however, managed to escape. Hubert Howe Bancroft, *History of Arizona and New Mexico* (San Francisco, 1886-90), p. 407. Johnson acted to gain a reward offered by the then Governor of Sonora, who allowed $100 for a scalp and $25 for a captive. After luring the Indians into camp, Johnson fired a six-pounder among them, killing a large number. Emory, *op. cit.,* p. 71.

39. Cf. Emory, *op. cit.,* pp. 73 and 590.

40. Cf. *op. cit.,* pp. 73 and 74.

41. Pinaleños, a division of the Apache, noted for their warlike character and hostility toward the United States. They carried on extensive raids on Sonora and Chihuahua. Hodge, *op. cit.,* II, 254.

42. Thomas C. Hammond, second lieutenant of First Dragoons.

43. General R. Díaz de la Vega, who was captured by the Americans at Resaca de la Palma in May 1846.

44. Emory says these Indians were of the Piñon Lano (piñon wood) tribe. Johnston calls them Apaches. Emory, *op. cit.,* pp. 78 and 594.

45. Casa Montezuma was also called Casa Blanca. Hodge points out that it should not be confused with Casa Grande. Hodge, *op. cit.,* I, 210. For a detailed description of the ruins see Johnston, in Emory, *op. cit.,* pp. 596-99.

46. The Pima, a division of the Piman family living in the Gila and Salt River valleys. They were a peaceable yet courageous people. Hodge, *op. cit.,* II, 252.

47. See also Emory's and Johnston's description of the Indians in Emory, *op. cit.,* pp. 82-85 and 599-602.

48. The Maricopas, an important Yuman tribe living with and below the Pima. Maricopa is their Piman name. Although each has a separate language, not understood by the other, the Maricopa and Pima joined for mutual protection against the Yuma and have lived together ever since. Hodge, *op. cit.,* p. 806.

49. For honesty of the Pima see Griffin's entry of March 10, 1847.

50. "This point Carson calls Independence Rock." Johnston, in Emory, *op. cit.,* p. 605.

51. Cf. *op. cit.,* pp. 95-96 and 608-9.

52. José María Flores had been elected governor of California by a decree of the assembly, October 26, 1846.

53. Louis Robidoux, brother of Antoine Robidoux, the guide, was captured at the battle fought at Chino ranch on September 26 and 27. Hubert Howe Bancroft, *History of California* (San Francisco, 1886-90), V, 311-12. There are many versions of the spelling of the name Robidoux.

54. General José Castro fled from California August 10, 1846, when Commodore Robert F. Stockton marched into Los Angeles.

55. This is the Mexican version of the battle of Dominguez Rancho, October 8, 1846, and is, on the whole, fairly accurate. Captain William Mervine landed his sailors from the *Savannah* at San Pedro and attempted to march to Los Angeles, in an effort to retake the city after the surrender of Lt. Archibald H. Gillespie and his garrison. Because of the lack of artillery, Mervine was forced to retreat to his ship. The number of Americans engaged has been variously reported. Bancroft says 350; Mervine, 288; Gillespie, 310; however, the adjutant's report for October 7-8, 1846, gives the detailed account and a total of 299, which must be accepted as correct. Henry W. Queen, Adjutant's Report, Dominguez, October 7-8, 1846 (original MS in Office of Naval Records and Library, Washington, D. C.). Bancroft gives the Mexican force as 110, which may be considered accurate. Bancroft, *History of California*, V, 318-19. The piece of artillery used by the Mexicans was not taken from the Americans but was the "Old Woman's gun."

56. Pinole is a meal of parched maize, mixed with sugar and spice.

57. "... a handful [of pinole] in a pint of water makes a most cooling and agreeable drink, ..." Ruxton, *op. cit.*, p. 197.

58. The "fleece" is the flesh covering the ribs. Mountain men considered the fleece of the buffalo particularly choice. Ruxton mentions it many times.

59. Vayeaw Chitoes is probably Vallecito. Johnston calls the place "Bayou Cita." Emory, *op. cit.*, p. 612.

60. San Felipe.

61. Jonathan Trumbull Warner, known in California as Juan José Warner, had come west for his health. After residing in California for several years he had applied to the Mexican Government for a land grant, which was approved in 1844. An additional acreage was granted to him in 1846. Joseph J. Hill, *The History of Warner's Ranch and Its Environs* (Los Angeles: Privately printed, 1927), pp. 101-11.

62. William Marshall, a deserter from the *Hopewell* at San Diego, in 1845. In 1851 he was hanged for having instigated the Pauma massacre. Bancroft, *op. cit.*, V, 567.

63. "Lieutenant Davidson, with 25 men, was dispatched with Carson and Sanders, to see if we could get a remount..." Johnston, in Emory, *op. cit.*, p. 614.

64. Edward Stokes came on the *Fly* from Honolulu and settled in California in 1840. With José Joaquin Ortega he was grantee of the Santa Ysabel and Valle de Pamo or Santa Maria ranchos. Emory gives the following description of Stokes's dress: "... he appeared in our camp, presenting a very singular and striking appearance. His dress was a black velvet English hunting coat, a pair of black velvet trowsers, cut off at the knee and open on the outside of the hip, beneath which were drawers of spotless white; his leggins were of black buck-skin, and his heels armed with spurs six inches long. Above the whole bloomed the broad merry face of Mr. Stokes, the Englishman." William H. Emory, *Notes of a Military Reconnoissance, from Fort Leavenworth, in Missouri, to San Diego, in California* (Washington, 1848), 30th Cong., 1st sess., H. Exec. Doc. 41, p. 106.

65. Francisco, sent by Kearny from Warner's Ranch, reached Captain Cooke while the latter was with the Pima Indians.

66. C[harles] E[dward] P[ickett] says that this wine was the cause of the defeat at San Pascual. *Daily Alta Californian*, November 13, 1868. Archibald H. Gillespie makes a fervent denial of this charge. *Ibid.*, November 14, 1868.

67. Archibald H. Gillespie, of the Marine Corps, who had been sent to California by the Government as a special agent. His letters to the Secretary of the Navy make an interesting story of events in California. George W. Ames, Jr., ed., "Gillespie and the Conquest of California," this QUARTERLY, XVII (June to December 1938), 123-40, 271-84, 325-50. Gillespie had been sent by Stockton to meet Kearny and advise him to attack the enemy.

68. Gillespie and his command had received permission to encamp two miles from the Dragoons, where there was a stand of grass for their animals.

69. Edward F. Beale, lieutenant United States Navy, a member of the Gillespie party from San Diego.

70. Bancroft cites the different opinions given as to the number of killed and wounded at San Pascual. He, himself, follows Griffin's Journal and notes. Bancroft, *History of California*, V, 346.

71. Andrés Pico, brother of Governor Pio Pico, was left in command by the flight of José Castro. When revolt broke out in the south in September of 1846, he was third in command under José María Flores. Upon the flight of Flores, after the battles in January 1847, Pico was again in command and surrendered to Frémont.

72. The three captured by the enemy were the Alexis Godey party which had been sent to San Diego after the battle to report and request reinforcements. The prisoner exchanged was Thomas H. Burgess. There seems to be some question concerning the letter from Stockton carried by Godey. According to Emory, Burgess reported hiding the letter under a tree, but a later search revealed that the message had been removed. Emory, *op. cit.*, p. 110. There is among the Abel Stearns papers in the Huntington Library, a letter purported to have been written by Stockton, saying that he has no mounts for his men and therefore cannot send a relief expedition. However, the signature is not in Stockton's handwriting. A note, added later, says in part: ". . . the letter was found by an Indian and given to Don Juan Bandini." At any rate, Burgess must have reported that assistance was not forthcoming or the officers would not have considered it necessary to despatch a second party to San Diego.

73. Carson and Beale were accompanied by Beale's Indian servant. Descriptions of their hazardous journey are given in several places. For an accurate account see Edwin L. Sabin, *Kit Carson Days* (New York, 1914), pp. 536-39.

74. This force under the command of Lt. Andrew F. V. Gray left San Diego on December 9, 1846.

75. This was the ranch of Francisco María Alvarado, who the United States troops considered had forfeited all rights by breaking his parole.

76. The *Congress* had arrived on October 31, 1846, and the *Portsmouth*, on December 9.

77. A rumor. Frémont did not arrive in Santa Barbara with his battalion until the 27th. John Charles Frémont, *Memoirs of My Life* (Chicago and New York, 1887), pp. 599-600. This is a good example of the constant rumors which were flying around and which kept the United States troops at nervous tension.

78. *Chlorid soda* is common salt. *Cerat simp* is simple cerate—a salve, or ointment.

79. Major Swords was dispatched on December 21, 1846, in the trading ship *Stonington* to the Sandwich Islands.

80. The Californian loss is still a matter of speculation. The Americans tended greatly to exaggerate the number of the enemy killed and wounded. Kearny's statement that there were six dead and wounded left on the field is unsupported by any evidence.

94 A DOCTOR COMES TO CALIFORNIA

Stephen Watts Kearny to Roger Jones, San Diego, December 13, 1846, 30th Cong., 1st sess., H. Ex. Doc. 1 (1848), 514-16. Griffin, on January 5, mentions finding four wounded Californians at San Juan Capistrano, supposedly victims of the battle of San Pascual. On the 14th he makes the number six. In any case it is reasonable to surmise that the Californians escaped very lightly.

81. Captain Cooke arrived at Warner's Ranch on January 21, 1847.

82. The lack of shoes was a problem when the sailors were forced to make long marches. Stockton remarks, "Our men were badly clothed and their shoes generally made by themselves out of canvas. . . ." Robert Field Stockton to George Bancroft, San Diego, February 5, 1847, Pacific Squadron Letters, Commodore Stockton's Cruise, June 1846-February 1847 (original MSS in Office of Naval Records and Library, Washington, D. C.).

83. A *sinapism* is a mustard poultice. *Terebinthenatic frictions*—turpentine rub. *Ol Ricini* is *Oleum Ricini* or castor oil. *V.S.* probably stands for V.S. cups (or cup) which are applied without previous scarification. *Quinine sul.* is quinine sulphate. *Gr.* is the abbreviation for grains.

84. *Acet plumb* is acetate of lead.

85. The *Cyane* came into San Diego harbor on the 26th.

86. Bancroft gives in detail the composition of the force and states that the total number was 607 men, of whom 44 were officers. Bancroft, *History of California*, V, 385-86.

87. The Pauma massacre in which eleven men were killed by Garra's band of Cahuillas and fugitive ex-neophytes of San Luis Rey. William Marshall, who was said to have instigated the affair, was afterward hanged for the offense. *Ibid.*, p. 567.

88. Jacob Zeilin, lieutenant of Marines on the *Congress* and acting captain in Stockton's battalion. William B. Renshaw, lieutenant in the Navy and acting captain in Stockton's battalion.

89. The camp was at Buena Vista.

90. John Forster, an Englishman, who had married into the Pico family.

91. Santa Margarita belonged to former governor Pio Pico. Hensley's mission was at least partially successful, as he returned next day with some horses and forty or forty-five oxen.

92. In this regard it is interesting to note William H. Meyers' sketch of the camp at San Gabriel. He depicts most of the tents as being of the A type. The camp is generously posted with sentries. William H. Myers, *Naval Sketches of the War in California* (New York: Random House, 1939), Plate X.

93. Probably Juan María Osuña.

94. The good doctor really did not lose a day but merely misdated January 3, calling it the 4th.

95. The messengers were Charles Flügge, William Workman, and Domingo Olivas.

96. Stephen C. Rowan, lieutenant in the Navy and acting major in Stockton's battalion.

97. Thomas Smith, ordinary seaman, Co. D. He was shot through the hip by accident.

98. The authorities do not agree on the number of casualties for the battles of the 8th and 9th, but Griffin was in a position to know. An easily obtainable list is given in Edwin Bryant, *What I Saw in California* (Santa Ana: Fine Arts Press, 1936), pp. 385-86.

99. The flag of truce was borne by William Workman, Eulogio Célis and Juan Avila.

100. *Massa ex Hyd* [*hydrargyrum*]—a pill of mercury. *Tart. Ant.* is antimony tartrate; *Sul. mag.* is magnesium sulphate or Epsom salts; ℥i—the doctor's symbol indicating two tablespoonfuls. The small letter "m" possibly indicates that the dose was given in the morning.

101. William H. Russell, who served as ordnance officer with the rank of major in the California Battalion, and Theodore Talbot, one of Frémont's original party, who served as lieutenant and adjutant of the California Battalion.

102. Flores resigned his command to Andrés Pico on January 11 and started that same night for Sonora. Bancroft gives the text of the Flores resignation as well as details of the flight. The number of men accompanying him was approximately thirty-six. Bancroft, *op. cit.*, V, 403-4, 407-8.

103. John Southwick was carpenter of the *Congress* and served as captain and chief engineer in Stockton's battalion. Griffin's point here is hazy. He is undoubtedly answering some current question but has failed to give the reader the entire context. It may refer to the controversy over leadership which occurred between Stockton and Kearny, or possibly to the question of Stockton's marksmanship.

104. The Articles of Capitulation, signed at the rancho of Cahuenga on January 13, 1847, by José Antonio Carrillo, squadron commander; Agustin Olvera, deputy; P. B. Reading, major California Battalion; Louis McLane, commanding Artillery California Battalion; W. H. Russell, staff captain California Battalion; and approved by Andrés Pico, squadron commander and chief of the National forces in California; and J. C. Frémont, lieutenant-colonel U. S. Army and "military commandant of California," were printed in this QUARTERLY, XIII (June 1934), 135-36. They are also to be found in 30th Cong., 2d sess., S. Exec. Doc. No. 31 (1849), and elsewhere.

105. Louis McLane came to California as a midshipman on the *Savannah*. After helping recruit and organize the California Battalion, he became captain of an artillery company, later ranking as major. Pierson B. Reading served as paymaster of the California Battalion with the rank of major.

106. On January 5, at Mission San Juan Capistrano, Commodore Stockton, at the instigation of William Workman, issued a proclamation offering a general amnesty to all Californians except Flores, on condition that he be given up as a prisoner. Bancroft, *History of California*, V, 387.

107. Tincture of Opium.

108. Andrew J. Henderson, assistant surgeon of the *Portsmouth*.

109. A consensus of Californian opinion seems to be that three were killed and not many more than fifteen wounded. Bancroft, *op. cit.*, V, 396.

110. William H. Thompson, midshipman on the *Congress* and acting lieutenant of Stockton's battalion.

111. Lieutenant Andrew F. V. Gray was appointed by Stockton, and Lieutenant Emory by Kearny, to carry dispatches to Washington. Gray was accompanied by Richard Taylor Jacob, a captain in the California Battalion. After some delay they sailed in the *Malek Adhel* on January 25, 1847. For the *Malek Adhel* see Note 118.

112. ". . . you will consider yourself suspended from the command of the United States forces in this place." Robert Field Stockton to Stephen Watts Kearny, January 16, 1847, quoted in Thomas C. Lancey's "Cruise of the Dale," San Jose *Pioneer*, January 1, 1881. This order is well known and is printed in many places. It is a good indication of Stockton's attitude toward Kearny throughout the whole controversy. Stockton clearly stepped beyond his authority.

113. This is a clear exposition of the opinion held by most army officers on the coast, of the controversy between Kearny on one side and Stockton and Frémont on the other. There seems to have been no doubt in their minds of the importance of political pull, and their only complaint, as Griffin states above, was that Kearny was too lenient in his treatment of Frémont. As an example of opinion which duplicates Griffin's sentiments, see Captain Turner's letters to his wife. Henry Smith Turner, "Letters about the Mexican War," *Glimpses of the Past*, Missouri Historical Society, II (December 1934-January

1935), 14 *et seq.* For further details of the difficulties between Kearny, Stockton, and Frémont, see Thomas Kearny, "The Mexican War and the Conquest of California," in this QUARTERLY, VIII (September 1929), 251 ff.; also *A Sketch of the Life of Com. Robert F. Stockton* (New York, 1856), pp. 146, 149-56; Appendix, pp. 26-48; *Defence of Lieut. Col. J. C. Frémont before the Military Court Martial* (Washington, 1848); and Bancroft, *op. cit.*, V, 414-32.

114. The Hon. Willard P. Hall, congressman from Missouri.

115. Leroux, one of the guides for the Mormons.

116. The town mentioned as taken by Cooke was Tucson.

117. *Nit argent* is silver nitrate. *Ungs Resens* is resin ointment. *Sul. morphia* and *Acid sul aromat.* are sulphate of morphia and aromatic sulphuric acid.

118. *Malek Adhel*, a Mexican brig cut out at Mazatlan by the boats of the *Warren*, on September 7, 1846. She was used by the United States Navy as a transport and dispatch boat on the Pacific Coast during the conquest. Log of the U.S.S. *Warren* (original MS in National Archives, Washington, D. C.).

119. Soap plaster.

120. Commodores William Branford Shubrick and James Biddle had been sent to increase the naval forces on the Pacific Coast. Shubrick arriving first, on January 22, 1847, superseded Stockton as commander of the fleet, and was in turn replaced by Biddle, on March 2, 1847. With the coming of Shubrick, the lack of cooperation between the Army and Navy forces on the Coast came to an end. Shubrick recognized Kearny as civil governor. The Lexington arrived on January 28, 1847, carrying a company of the 3rd Artillery under Captain Christopher Q. Tompkins, with materiel for building and maintaining fortifications.

121. William H. Russell had been appointed secretary of state to Governor Frémont, by Commodore Stockton.

122. Santiago Argüello held an honorary command as captain in the California Battalion.

123. Miguel Pedrorena acted as Stockton's aide and held the rank of captain in the California Battalion.

124. The U. S. storeship *Erie* arrived at Monterey on February 13, 1847. Colonel Richard Barnes Mason, 1st United States Dragoons, was on board, sent out to replace Kearny as civil governor when the latter should return home.

125. The first copy of the paper is dated August 15, 1846, and, according to Colton, appeared on that date. Walter Colton, *Three Years in California* (Cincinnati, 1850), p. 32. At least some of the copies were in circulation as early as the 13th. George W. Ames, Jr., "Horse Marines, 1846," this QUARTERLY, XVIII (March 1939), 79. Commodore Stockton is said to have provided the money, out of his own pocket, for establishing the newspaper. *A Sketch of the Life of Com. Robert F. Stockton*, pp. 156-57.

126. For the "paper war" see *ibid.*, Appendix, pp. 43-48.

127. It is difficult to determine the person to whom Griffin refers.

128. James H. Cloud was paymaster for the Mormon Battalion.

129. This, of course, has reference to the ill-fated Donner party. For the best all-around work on this tragedy see George Rippey Stewart, *Ordeal by Hunger, the Story of the Donner Party* (New York: Henry Holt and Co., 1936).

130. Henry Wager Halleck, lieutenant of Engineers, came with Company F, 3rd U. S. Artillery, to inspect the fortifications on the Pacific Coast.

131. George Stoneman, lieutenant of 1st Dragoons, came with the Mormon Battalion. He earned an enviable reputation in the Civil War as a cavalry leader and in the eighties was governor of California. Camp Stoneman, near Pittsburg, California, was recently named for him.

NOTES 97

132. The regiment was sent out in four ships, three of which left New York on September 26, 1846, and the fourth on November 13. The first three arrived in San Francisco during March of 1847; the *Thomas Perkins* on the 6th; the *Susan Drew* on the 19th; and the *Loo Choo* on the 25th. The fourth ship, the *Brutus*, arrived on April 18.

133. Richard Owens, one of Frémont's original party and captain of Company A, California Battalion. Owens River, Owens Valley, and Owens Lake were named for him.

134. Frémont challenged Mason because he considered himself insulted by the latter's manner in issuing orders. Mason requested that the affair be postponed until he had completed his duties at Los Angeles. The meeting never occurred because Kearny, on learning of the proposed duel, prevented it by official order.

135. William A. T. Maddox, lieutenant of Marines on the *Cyane* and *Congress*.

136. J. Parker Norris had been sent east by Stockton with dispatches in September 1846.

137. Henry Delano Fitch, one of the earliest and most popular of the foreign settlers in California.

138. ℞ the doctor's instruction to the pharmacist, an abbreviation from the Latin meaning "take thou," or "take thou of." *Massa ex Hyd. Ext Colocynth* is mercury with extract of bitter apple; the remainder of the prescription is unintelligible. *Ol Ricini* ℥j— two tablespoonfuls of castor oil.

139. For a description of this ball see *The Journal of John McHenry Hollingsworth of the First New York Volunteers* (San Francisco: California Historical Society, 1923), p. 30.

140. Bancroft lists these men as belonging to Company G, New York Volunteers.

THE CHICANO HERITAGE

An Arno Press Collection

Adams, Emma H. **To and Fro in Southern California.** 1887

Anderson, Henry P. **The Bracero Program in California.** 1961

Aviña, Rose Hollenbaugh. **Spanish and Mexican Land Grants in California.** 1976

Barker, Ruth Laughlin. **Caballeros.** 1932

Bell, Horace. **On the Old West Coast.** 1930

Biberman, Herbert. **Salt of the Earth.** 1965

Casteñeda, Carlos E., trans. **The Mexican Side of the Texas Revolution (1836).** 1928

Casteñeda, Carlos E. **Our Catholic Heritage in Texas, 1519-1936.** Seven volumes. 1936-1958

Colton, Walter. **Three Years in California.** 1850

Cooke, Philip St. George. **The Conquest of New Mexico and California.** 1878

Cue Canovas, Agustin. **Los Estados Unidos Y El Mexico Olvidado.** 1970

Curtin, L. S. M. **Healing Herbs of the Upper Rio Grande.** 1947

Fergusson, Harvey. **The Blood of the Conquerors.** 1921

Fernandez, Jose. **Cuarenta Años de Legislador:** Biografia del Senador Casimiro Barela. 1911

Francis, Jessie Davies. **An Economic and Social History of Mexican California** (1822-1846). Volume I: Chiefly Economic. Two vols. in one. 1976

Getty, Harry T. **Interethnic Relationships in the Community of Tucson.** 1976

Guzman, Ralph C. **The Political Socialization of the Mexican American People.** 1976

Harding, George L. **Don Agustin V. Zamorano.** 1934

Hayes, Benjamin. **Pioneer Notes from the Diaries of Judge Benjamin Hayes, 1849-1875.** 1929

Herrick, Robert. **Waste.** 1924

Jamieson, Stuart. **Labor Unionism in American Agriculture.** 1945

Landolt, Robert Garland. **The Mexican-American Workers of San Antonio, Texas.** 1976

Lane, Jr., John Hart. **Voluntary Associations Among Mexican Americans in San Antonio, Texas.** 1976

Livermore, Abiel Abbot. **The War with Mexico Reviewed.** 1850

Loyola, Mary. **The American Occupation of New Mexico, 1821-1852.** 1939

Macklin, Barbara June. **Structural Stability and Culture Change in a Mexican-American Community.** 1976

McWilliams, Carey. **Ill Fares the Land:** Migrants and Migratory Labor in the United States. 1942

Murray, Winifred. **A Socio-Cultural Study of 118 Mexican Families Living in a Low-Rent Public Housing Project in San Antonio, Texas.** 1954

Niggli, Josephina. **Mexican Folk Plays.** 1938

Parigi, Sam Frank. **A Case Study of Latin American Unionization in Austin, Texas.** 1976

Poldervaart, Arie W. **Black-Robed Justice.** 1948

Rayburn, John C. and Virginia Kemp Rayburn, eds. **Century of Conflict, 1821-1913.** Incidents in the Lives of William Neale and William A. Neale, Early Settlers in South Texas. 1966

Read, Benjamin. **Illustrated History of New Mexico.** 1912

Rodriguez, Jr., Eugene. **Henry B. Gonzalez.** 1976

Sanchez, Nellie Van de Grift. **Spanish and Indian Place Names of California.** 1930

Sanchez, Nellie Van de Grift. **Spanish Arcadia.** 1929

Shulman, Irving. **The Square Trap.** 1953

Tireman, L. S. **Teaching Spanish-Speaking Children.** 1948

Tireman, L. S. and Mary Watson. **A Community School in a Spanish-Speaking Village.** 1948

Twitchell, Ralph Emerson. **The History of the Military Occupation of the Territory of New Mexico.** 1909

Twitchell, Ralph Emerson. **The Spanish Archives of New Mexico.** Two vols. 1914

U. S. House of Representatives. **California and New Mexico:** Message from the President of the United States, January 21, 1850. 1850

Valdes y Tapia, Daniel. **Hispanos and American Politics.** 1976

West, Stanley A. **The Mexican Aztec Society.** 1976

Woods, Frances Jerome. **Mexican Ethnic Leadership in San Antonio, Texas.** 1949

Aspects of the Mexican American Experience. 1976
Mexicans in California After the U. S. Conquest. 1976
Hispanic Folklore Studies of Arthur L. Campa. 1976
Hispano Culture of New Mexico. 1976
Mexican California. 1976
The Mexican Experience in Arizona. 1976
The Mexican Experience in Texas. 1976
Mexican Migration to the United States. 1976
The United States Conquest of California. 1976
Northern Mexico On the Eve of the United States Invasion:
    Rare Imprints Concerning California, Arizona, New Mexico,
    and Texas, 1821-1846. Edited by David J. Weber. 1976